Catie,

With all
your ongoing research —

Alex Walham

Charitable hatred

MANCHESTER
1824

Manchester University Press

Politics, culture and society in early modern Britain

General editors

PROFESSOR ANN HUGHES
DR ANTHONY MILTON
PROFESSOR PETER LAKE

This important series publishes monographs that take a fresh and challenging look at the interactions between politics, culture and society in Britain between 1500 and the mid-eighteenth century. It counteracts the fragmentation of current historiography through encouraging a variety of approaches which attempt to redefine the political, social and cultural worlds, and to explore their interconnection in a flexible and creative fashion. All the volumes in the series question and transcend traditional interdisciplinary boundaries, such as those between political history and literary studies, social history and divinity, urban history and anthropology. They contribute to a broader understanding of crucial developments in early modern Britain.

Charitable hatred

Tolerance and intolerance in England, 1500–1700

ALEXANDRA WALSHAM

Manchester
University Press

Manchester and New York

distributed exclusively in the USA by Palgrave

Published by Manchester University Press
Oxford Road, Manchester M13 9NR, UK
and Room 400, 175 Fifth Avenue, New York, NY 10010, USA
www.manchesteruniversitypress.co.uk

Distributed exclusively in the USA by
Palgrave, 175 Fifth Avenue, New York, NY 10010, USA

Distributed exclusively in Canada by
UBC Press, University of British Columbia, 2029 West Mall,
Vancouver, BC, Canada V6T 1Z2

British Library Cataloguing-in-Publication Data
A catalogue record for this book is available from the British Library

Library of Congress Cataloging-in-Publication Data applied for

ISBN 0 7190 5239 4 *hardback*
EAN 978 0 7190 5239 2

First published 2006

15 14 13 12 11 10 09 08 07 06   10 9 8 7 6 5 4 3 2 1

Typeset in Scala with Pastonchi display
by Koinonia Ltd, Manchester

Printed in Great Britain
by CPI, Bath

... Charitie hath two offices, the one contrary to the other, and yet both necessary to bee used upon men of contrary sort and disposition. The one office of charitie is, to cherish good and harmlesse men, not to oppresse them with false accusations, but to encourage them with rewards to doe well, and to continue in well doing, defending them with the sword from their adversaries ... The other office of charity is, to rebuke, correct, and punish vice, without regard of persons, and is to be used against them onely that be evill men, and malefactours or evill doers ... it is aswell the office of charitie to rebuke, punish, and correct them that bee evill, as it is to cherish and reward them that bee good and harmelesse ... Therefore bear well away this one short lesson, that by true Christian charitie, God ought to be loved, good, and evill, friend, and foe, and to all such, wee ought (as we may) to doe good: those that be good, of love to encourage and cherish, because they be good: and those that be evill, of love to procure and seeke their correction and due punishment ... ('The second part of the sermon of charitie', in *Certaine sermons or homilies appointed to be read in churches*, London, 1623 edn; first publ. 1563)

For Patrick Collinson

Contents

Contents

Acknowledgements

T his book has taken a great deal longer to complete than envisaged at the outset. It has also altered its shape and expanded its scope significantly, uncomfortably outgrowing the mould of a student survey and developing into what I hope will be regarded as an original synthesis. Writing it has been challenging, stressful and (eventually) rewarding in equal measure and I have learnt much from the process. The decision to structure the book thematically rather than chronologically was a deliberate attempt to avoid the distortions associated with the linear models that have dominated the historiography of this subject. The inevitable consequence is an emphasis on continuity over discontinuity, though I have tried to demonstrate due recognition of intellectual shifts and social changes. Works of this kind are necessarily parasitic upon the research of other scholars and I should like to express my gratitude to all those whose hard labour at the coalface has made my own endeavours possible.

A number of other debts must be recorded. Firstly, I must thank Mark Greengrass, for whose New Frontiers in History textbook series this was initially commissioned, and without whose support and encouragement at critical points it would not have been finished. His most gracious act was to relinquish the book into the hands of the editors of another MUP series: Politics, Culture and Society in Early Modern Britain. I owe much to Ann Hughes, Peter Lake and especially Anthony Milton for responding to this overture with unexpected enthusiasm and for finding the work a home in their series. A number of colleagues and friends were kind enough to read and comment upon drafts of particular chapters and of the book as a whole (an act of supererogation!): Jeremy Black, Anne Dillon, Peter Marshall, Anthony Milton, Andrew Spicer and Susan Wabuda. They and others have saved me from many blunders: responsibility for any remaining errors of fact and judgement is my own. I am particularly grateful to Patrick Collinson for urging me to continue with this project when I most despaired of bringing it to completion and for his generous reassurance at every juncture. John Morrill must also be thanked for carving out time in his busy schedule to look at the book and offer wise and immensely helpful advice. Early versions of the argument were tried out in front of seminar audiences at the Universities of Sussex and Swansea, whose questions set me thinking in various directions. Successive cohorts of students at Exeter have also helped to crystallise and sharpen my ideas and

Acknowledgements

forced me to confront and interrogate early modern assumptions. Their interest and enthusiasm has been invigorating.

I am grateful to the University of Exeter for two periods of study leave which facilitated the writing of the book and to my colleagues in History for assisting me with particular lines of enquiry, keeping my spirits up, and bearing with the curious mixture of hyperactivity and despondency I have exhibited as it has edged towards completion.

Finally I would like to thank Manchester University Press for its tremendous patience and forbearance and for efficiently seeing the book through to publication.

Alexandra Walsham

List of figures

List of figures

Abbreviations

EETS	*Early English Text Society* (e.s. — extra series)
BL	British Library
CRS	Catholic Record Society
CSP Dom	*Calendar of State Papers Domestic*
EHR	*English Historical Review*
HJ	*Historical Journal*
JBS	*Journal of British Studies*
JEH	*Journal of Ecclesiastical History*
ODNB	*Oxford Dictionary of National Biography*
OED	*Oxford English Dictionary*
P&P	*Past and Present*
PS	Parker Society
RH	*Recusant History*
SCH	Studies in Church History
SCJ	*Sixteenth Century Journal*
SP	State Papers
TRHS	*Transactions of the Royal Historical Society*

All biblical references are to the King James version, unless otherwise stated.

Following house style and for the sake of clarity, the names of a number of religious groups have been capitalised. This should not, however, be taken to imply that they had a formal institutional existence or were recognised as distinct denominations in the period under discussion.

Chapter 1

Introduction

'Persecution' and 'toleration' are words that many readers of this book will instinctively position in polar opposition. Like other classic pairings, they carry connotations of mutual exclusivity and incompatibility. The antithesis between them is always tacitly assumed where it is not explicitly stated. Simultaneously, these terms are laden with emotive overtones. 'Persecution' is an act that modern society abhors. Its current dictionary definition is the infliction of death, torture or penalties for adherence to beliefs deemed heretical or injurious. By common consent, it involves unwarrantable harassment for one's opinions, infringement of the basic human entitlement to freedom of conscience written into constitutions and bills of rights. Often interchanged with tyranny, oppression and cruelty, persecution is an affront to Western liberal values – an evil which Amnesty International and other organisations are dedicated to uprooting and eradicating. 'Toleration', by contrast, is praised and applauded. Tolerance is idealised as a virtue and toleration implies institutional recognition of a set of ideas or a body of believers. Instinctively inked with equality, liberty and democracy, it lies at the heart of the modern Western world's flattering and complacent conception of itself as a 'civilised' society. Lauded as a benevolent legacy of the Enlightenment, it has come to symbolise the upward march of progress away from the barbarity and bigotry of the Dark Ages.

In late medieval and early modern England, however, persecution and toleration, intolerance and tolerance, were concepts and terms underpinned by very different presuppositions and assumptions. In a context in which truth was held to be single and indivisible, the persecution of dissident minorities was logical, rational and legitimate. Ecclesiastical and secular authorities were believed to have a solemn responsibility to punish those who departed from orthodoxy, to use any means necessary to uphold the true religion and reclaim those who strayed from the straight and narrow way. To take steps to correct religious deviance was a moral duty and a divinely ordained obligation, an act of compassion inspired by the conviction that heresy was, quite literally, soul-destroying.[1] To allow men and women to persist in heterodox opinions was in effect to condemn them to eternal torment in hell. Cruelty was thus a form of kindness. As St Augustine, the patriarch of persecutors, wrote in the early fifth century: 'What death is worse for the soul than the freedom to err?' 'It is better to love with severity than to deceive with indulgence'. Glossing the parable in St Luke's Gospel in which Jesus tells how a rich man whose guests had declined his invitation to a great feast commanded his servants to 'Go out into the highways and hedges, and compel them to come in, that my house may be filled' (*compelle intrare*) (Luke 14: 23), Augustine insisted that it was incumbent upon Christian rulers and magistrates to force the wayward to join the congregation of the faithful.[2] Coercion was a bitter but efficacious medicine; its purpose was to cure and educate, to liberate individuals from bondage to falsehood, rather than to erase and exterminate. To persecute was to display a charitable hatred: a charity towards the sinner that was inextricable from a fervent hatred of the sin that endangered his or her salvation. It was to mimic the loving discipline and fatherly chastisement of the Lord, who tried and tested the faithful in the fire of tribulation and who would divide the sheep and the goats, the wheat and the tares, with his sword and sickle at the Last Judgement.

In this sense, persecution was not merely a type of holy violence but 'an arm of pastoral theology'.[3] It was also a mechanism for deflecting the devastating providential judgements that God visited upon communities which neglected to carry out their responsibility to be their brothers' keepers and to expunge the wicked from within their midst. These convictions promoted the view that religious uniformity was crucial to the political stability and social order of a state as well as to its spiritual welfare. Unity of faith was supposed to be the best antidote to sedition and subversion and a preservative against internal dissolution, both being indirect manifestations of the wrath of the Almighty against iniquitous nations. Accordingly, toleration was anathema, a recipe for chaos and anarchy, if not an invitation to apocalyptic destruction. Any country that permitted religious pluralism was thus committing an act of corporate suicide. As we shall see in the course of this book, the influence of these inherited Augustinian assumptions in early modern England was both pervasive and tenacious.

Consequently, historians need to be sensitive to the contexts and circumstances in which the terms 'persecution' and 'toleration' were used in the sixteenth and seventeenth centuries. Then, as now, the former was invariably employed by those on the receiving end of policies of marginalisation and repression. Echoing Matthew 5: 11 ('Blessed are they which are persecuted for righteousness' sake: for theirs is the kingdom of heaven'), minority groups utilised this potent element of the lexicon to rally the faithful and to proclaim their integrity against the forces of evil and the devil. However, it is important to emphasise that many of those who used the word to denounce the unjust and unwarrantable severity of their enemies did not regard it as inconsistent for them to deal out the same savage treatment to their adversaries when they assumed a position of dominance and power themselves. When the tables were turned, the persecuted became persecutors, who vigorously defended their right to restrain their erstwhile oppressors. This apparent double standard was not rank hypocrisy. It grew out of an environment hostile to the modern idea that individuals are entitled to hold beliefs at odds with those espoused by the established Church and state. It made sense in a climate of opinion characterised by the conviction that there could only be one institutional embodiment of divine truth.

Christianity itself underwent precisely this kind of transformation in the fourth century, as it made the transition from a minority sect to an imperially sanctioned and supported religion. Coinciding with the conversion of the Emperor Constantine, it turned against pagans and heretics like the Gnostics, Novatians, Arians and Donatists, destroying their temples and unleashing a body of punitive edicts against the exponents of heterodox doctrine. It was in the context of this metamorphosis of molested 'lambs' into raging 'lions' that Augustine formulated his classic defence of persecution as a humanitarian duty.[4]

Protestantism followed a similar pattern of evolution. In the 1520s, reacting against a Church which had angrily excommunicated him and confident that exposure to the vernacular Bible would lead to sweeping evangelical revolution, Martin Luther had repudiated the use of force in matters of faith, arguing that under no circumstances should lay authorities seek to fight religious deviance with the secular sword, and insisting that God alone could re-educate the consciences of individual believers. Heretics were to be converted by Scripture not fire. Such propositions were condemned by Pope Leo X as pestilent, scandalous and contrary to Christian charity. Under the pressure of events, however, Luther soon changed his views. As the Reformation allied itself with magisterial power and confronted the dual challenge of institutionalisation and fragmentation, Luther modified his theology to justify civil intervention to suppress Anabaptists and other 'false brethren' and to protect and promote the hegemony of the fledgling Protestant Church to which his defiant writings had given rise.[5]

In early modern Europe, as Andrew Pettegree has remarked, toleration was usually 'a loser's creed', 'the party cry of the disappointed, the dispossessed, or the seriously confused', a slogan readily abandoned when events fell out in their favour.[6] It was a strategy to ensure survival and to facilitate restoration to exclusive rule rather than an end in and of itself. When the mantle of authority settled on religious dissidents and rebels, they all too often set aside the rousing rhetoric of liberty they had hitherto employed. Only a few isolated voices elevated respect for conscience into a universally applicable principle. Alternatively, toleration might be a tactical step towards reunification, an interim solution to the problem of religious disunity, an instrument for re-establishing communal peace and political concord.[7] Generally born of impotence and exhaustion, it was rarely a state of affairs that governments took proactive or positive measures to achieve in the course of this period. To quote Herbert Butterfield it was 'a *pis aller*' or stop-gap, 'a retreat to the next best thing, a last resort for those who often still hated one another, but found it impossible to go on fighting any more'.[8] On the whole it was a legislative condition of omission, of immunity and exemption from the requirement of conformity to the state religion.

'Toleration', then, emphatically did not mean religious freedom. Nor did it proceed from indifference or neutrality. To tolerate was not to recognise or to grant equal rights to a rival system of belief; it was to permit or license something of which one emphatically disapproved, to make a magnanimous concession to the adherents of an inherently false religion. Contingent and provisional, it was to confer a special privilege that could be withdrawn with-out warning. It was an act of forbearance, long-suffering and also indulgence, a conscious decision to refrain from persecuting something one knew to be wicked and wrong. Deriving from the Latin verb, *tolerare*, to bear or endure, the essence of 'toleration' was stoicism and self-restraint. To extend it to a person or group was to imitate the grace and mercy that the Almighty habi-tually exercised towards frail human beings. Indeed, the translators of the Douai-Rheims New Testament of 1582 explicitly described the remission of sins wrought by Christ's sacrifice on the cross as 'the toleration of God' (Romans 3: 26).[9] Often interchanged with *patientia*, in classical and early Christian writings *tolerantia* referred to a virtuous capacity to bear onerous physical and psychological burdens; in the course of the Middle Ages the term acquired a social and judicial dimension and came to denote a policy of passive non-interference by the authorities with attitudes and practices that they nevertheless unequivocally considered to be despicable.[10] In short, it too was a kind of charitable hatred.

To this extent, toleration was a paradoxical policy, a casuistical stance involving a deliberate suspension of righteous hostility and, consequently, a considerable degree of moral discomfort. From the outside looking in, it might look very much like apathy, cowardice and a contemptibly lax and lukewarm commitment to upholding the true religion. Throughout the period covered by this book, it was mainly used pejoratively. Its fiercest opponents denounced it with vituperative fervour, calling it a diabolical device, the hallmark of the Beast, 'the last and most desperate design of Antichrist', 'the whore of Babylon's backdoor'.[11] Together with other terms which implied a willingness to condone diversity and a conciliatory attitude towards doctrinal heterodoxy, it was a weapon in polemical controversy, a word used to wound, hurt, brand, stigmatise and slur. In the sixteenth century few wished to be tarred with this brush and regimes found it necessary to insist vociferously on their 'innocence from such [an] imagination'.[12] Some went so far as to boast of their intolerance. At the end of the seventeenth century, the Calvinist synod of Leiden firmly condemned it as a heresy and in 1691 the French bishop Jacques-Bénigne Bossuet proudly described Catholicism as the least tolerant of all faiths and creeds.[13]

Only gradually did 'toleration' cease to be a derogatory epithet and begin to be used in a more complimentary and flattering sense, to celebrate a catholicity of spirit and a commendable freedom from bigotry. Not until the late eighteenth and early nineteenth century did it lose its negative and critical overtones. As late as 1832, Pope Gregory XVI declared 'liberty of conscience' an 'absurd and erroneous opinion, or rather delirium', which sprang from 'the most foul well of indifferentism', and in 1864 it was listed in the Syllabus of Errors – a fact that no doubt helped to confirm the Catholic Church's back-wardness in the eyes of Victorian Protestant Englishmen who congratulated themselves that their own religion had discarded such outdated and illiberal views.[14]

In short, toleration is itself a form of intolerance. Goethe later commented that 'to tolerate is to insult', and in *The Rights of Man* (1791–92), Thomas Paine had declared it not the opposite of intolerance, but its counterfeit. 'Both are despotisms. The one assumes to itself the right of withholding Liberty of Conscience and the other of granting it.'[15] As the poet Samuel Taylor Coleridge wrote in 1809-10, 'The only true spirit of tolerance consists in our conscientious toleration of each other's intolerance.'[16] A century earlier the great Huguenot theorist of toleration, Pierre Bayle, recognised that there were circumstances in which a tolerant society had to protect itself by persecuting those who rejected pluralism and sought to subvert the conditions for peaceful coexistence.[17] These insights underline the point that the continuing tendency to situate 'persecution' and 'toleration' at opposite ends of the intellectual and political spectrum is deeply misleading. The idea that the two are inversely related, that one waxed as the other waned, seriously hampers our understanding of the religious culture of early modern England. One of the principal aims of this book is to suggest, on the contrary, that tolerance and intolerance are better seen as dialectically and symbiotically linked.

APPROACHES TO THE HISTORY OF TOLERANCE AND INTOLERANCE

And yet these polarities, and the problematic assumptions that underpin them, have long sustained and distorted the historiography of this subject. The history of 'the rise of toleration', as written by Lord Macaulay, W. E. H. Lecky, Samuel Rawlinson Gardiner and other nineteenth-century Whig writers,[18] was the story of the crowning triumph of liberalism and 'civilised' behaviour over blind prejudice and barbarous persecution. It occupied a central place in a teleological narrative that chronicled the development of modern society, heralding the Act of Toleration of 1689 as a major landmark and according John Locke pride of place in a pantheon of progressive thinkers. The Reformation was regarded as a watershed in the emergence of individualism and the apotheosis of private judgement and eirenic humanists like Desiderius Erasmus were revered as distinguished forerunners of later champions of religious liberty. To a greater or lesser extent, these works were also infected with the myths of English exceptionalism and Anglo-Saxon moderation. Free from the hideous activities of the Inquisition and mercifully immune to the ghastly atrocities of the Continental Wars of Religion, England, along with the Netherlands, was held up as a precocious example of a tolerant nation. Its Church derived its equilibrium from its unique *via media* between extremes, and its civic polity rested on an exemplary balance between monarchy and representative government.

Carried forward into the twentieth century by scholars such as William Haller, A. S. P. Woodhouse and W. K. Jordan, this inspiring story acquired fresh relevance in the shadow of the perceived Fascist threat to these cherished ideals. It was both an allegory and an emblem of the contemporary struggle to secure 'the fragile vessel of freedom' from destruction by 'totalitarian philosophy', as well as an exhortation to the present generation to protect 'its richest heritage' from being sacrificed 'on the altars of a new and brutal barbarism'. These books invested the 'Puritan Revolution' of the 1640s and 1650s with particular importance as a seedbed for enlightened ideas and continued the tradition of anointing a kind of apostolic succession of outstanding individuals who anticipated modern political as well as religious liberalism. By 1660, Jordan declared in his monumental four-volume study that 'the mass of responsible opinion' was convinced of the necessity if not the desirability of toleration; the task that remained was to make the requisite institutional adaptations which would translate this intellectual consensus into practice.'[19] The regressive steps taken by the Restoration Church were overshadowed by the immortal travails of nonconformity and the fresh wave of rousing calls for liberty of conscience that emanated from dissenters in the decades preceding the Glorious Revolution. In highlighting radical Protestantism's role in this legendary saga, these historians strongly reinforced its sectarian character. They also fed and fostered the pious legend that the Pilgrim Fathers laid the foundations for America's greatness as a model of democratic and egalitarian values. Simultaneously, such work was infused with the notion that the rise of toleration was a symptom of secularisation and a by-product of the growth of scepticism. These two positions were not incompatible in so far as Protestantism was widely seen as an agent of what the German sociologist Max Weber called 'the disenchantment of the world', a process of desacralisation that swept away vulgar superstition and irrational enthusiasm.[20]

Although it rejected any simple dichotomy between the two denominations, the Jesuit Joseph Lecler's *Toleration and the Reformation*, first published in French in 1955, may be seen as both a critique and a partial inversion of this confessional model. For Lecler too the old certainties that justified the suppression of heretics were called into question 'more or less everywhere during the religious and intellectual restiveness' of the sixteenth and seventeenth centuries. But, combating the triumphalist Protestant reading, he traced a different theoretical trajectory, locating the roots of these momentous developments in late medieval scholastic debate, underlining the intolerance of the magisterial reformers, and emphasising the gulf between early modern apologetics for toleration and 'later panegyrics of irreligion'. Moving beyond the usual 'prize-giving ceremony' in honour of pioneering tolerationist writers, it sought to situate these humanists, politicians and clergymen in their social milieu and it stressed the very real limits of the practical achievement of tolerance before 1700. In Lecler's analysis, Protestant England came not first but last in the league table of states that had extended liberty of conscience to religious minorities.[21]

Henry Kamen's briefer survey *The Rise of Toleration* (1967) offered a more independent and nuanced perspective which recognised the cyclical and reversible nature of the process and drew attention to the 'piecemeal application' of the principles whose evolution it endeavoured to trace. Conscious of both the advancing and ebbing tide of institutional arrangements for toleration, it concluded that religious liberty arose 'not so much because of the fundamental tenets of the Reformation', but because of the steady erosion of dogmatic belief by rationalist philosophies and 'the acceptance by bourgeois societies of free religion as a concomitant of free trade'. In large part, Kamen argued, it was a corollary of the policy of economic *laissez-faire*.[22]

In such works, toleration is on the whole firmly fixed within the domain of the history of ideas. Many are essentially narratives of the victory of the progressive thought of learned elites over a relentless and ingrained popular instinct to persecute. They rest on enduring assumptions about the innate intolerance of the Church and society in the central and late Middle Ages, the era of the great military drives against the Albigensians, of the crusades against the infidels, and of the notorious exploits of the Holy Office. This view has been both buttressed and complicated by the stimulating and controversial work of R. I. Moore. In *The Formation of a Persecuting Society* (1987) he argued that around 1100 Europe was seized with a zeal against deviance. Subject to increasingly insidious and systematic processes of classification, stigmatisation and marginalisation, heretics, lepers, Jews, and later homosexuals and prostitutes became the target of a 'deliberate and socially sanctioned violence' which consolidated their assimilation with pre-existing stereotypes and thereby provided the incentive and momentum for further acts of repression and exclusion. For Moore, this impulse did not swell up from the masses below but was generated instead from within the ranks of the burgeoning bureaucracies of contemporary monarchies. It was a function of the administrative centralisation of the Church and embryonic nation states, a side effect of the emergence of the proliferating apparatus of government and a weapon in the competition of the *literati* (literate elite) who serviced these institutions for social and political influence.[23]

Following in the footsteps of Herbert Butterfield,[24] recent publications, however, have done much to undercut the idea that the Reformation was a critical juncture in the demise of this persecuting society. On the contrary, it has been suggested that the period saw a continuation or even an intensification of intolerance. Here three books stand out as particular landmarks.

The first is the set of essays edited by Ole Grell, Jonathan Israel and Nicholas Tyacke arising from a conference held to mark the tercentenary of the Glorious Revolution and the Act of Toleration of 1689. Despite the model of linearity implied by its title, *From Persecution to Toleration* (1991) places considerable emphasis on the limits and the ambivalence of this process. While recognising William III's statute as a milestone, it stresses the extent to which it was the outcome of a political impasse and a 'peculiar concatenation of circumstances' rather than the ascendancy of principles of liberty and warns against underestimating the vigour and vitality of arguments for religious uniformity and coercion in Restoration England. Government policies were often guided by financial considerations and the direct impact of celebrated theorists like Locke on events was relatively small. Advocacy of toleration did become more widespread, but at the end of the seventeenth century 'the balance of mainstream political and religious opinion' still, on the whole, ran in the other direction.[25]

The second book is Ole Grell and Bob Scribner's *Tolerance and Intolerance in the European Reformation* (1996), which even more emphatically challenges the Whiggish paradigm. Rejecting models of 'organic growth', collectively the contributors to this volume play down the power of ideas and underline the contingency of moves towards toleration. Situating these initiatives in the specific and varied social and political contexts in which they evolved, they present toleration less as a considered policy of choice than a pragmatic, *ad hoc* manoeuvre to contain 'the centrifugal forces of chaos' and restore concord. The significance of the Reformation, it is suggested, lies less in its insistence on the right of individuals to exercise their consciences freely than in its questioning of authority and blind obedience. Out of the ensuing friction and conflict grew precarious and often impermanent arrangements for peace.[26]

The third landmark is *Toleration in Enlightenment Europe*, assembled by Ole Grell and Roy Porter in 2000, which sets about knocking the Enlightenment from its pedestal as the triumphant culmination of the struggle for freedom of conscience inaugurated by the Reformation, a 'predestined stage' in the emergence of a liberal society. The partial, ephemeral, and contested character of institutional advances in this area is a key theme of the book, as is the resurgent confessionalism of the late seventeenth century, particularly in France and Poland-Lithuania. Setting the tone for the essays that follow, the editors speak of the 'fluctuations' and 'equivocations' of toleration across this period. Other common threads are the ambiguities and the theological under-pinnings of Enlightenment thinking: the movement is depicted as lacking any 'clear' or 'distinct metaphysics' and Sylvana Tomaselli even questions how far towering figures like Voltaire and Rousseau conceived of toleration as a supreme moral virtue. Most contributors also resist the suggestion that abstract theories paved the way for its practical realisation. As Joachim Whaley writes of the Holy Roman Empire, socio-political necessities rather than the ratiocinations of philosophers brought about the licensed religious pluralism and denominational parity enshrined in the Peace of Westphalia in 1648. Despite clear strides forward intellectually, Europe never uniformly or comprehensively embraced toleration in the eighteenth century.[27]

The Edict of Nantes of 1589 has likewise been swept up in the historio-graphical shift that these three collections represent. New studies stimulated by the 400th anniversary of Henry IV's proclamation establishing the basis for Catholic-Huguenot coexistence have stressed the dangers of reading back into the past concepts at odd with its original intentions. They have highlighted the 'laboratories of memory' in which this document has been successively reinvented by later commentators intent upon discovering precedents for the cherished values of 'liberty' and 'conscience', words which were notably absent from the text.[28] Nor has that renowned haven of tolerance the Dutch Republic escaped the effects of the relentless march of revisionism. The myth of an indigenous Netherlandish spirit of freedom that not merely fired the revolt against Spain but then facilitated the most successful example of a multi-confessional society in early modern Europe has been replaced by a picture of pragmatic 'containment' and 'ambivalent semi-tolerance ... seething with tension'. Recent studies focus on the delicate, fluid and unsystematic arrange-ments that comprised it and the anomaly of a hegemonic Calvinist state that nevertheless created space for religious minorities in many civic environments.[29]

The hallowed narrative of the 'rise of toleration' has also been assaulted from the other end of the chronological spectrum. In a series of essay collections, notably *Beyond the Persecuting Society* (1998), John Laursen and Cary Nederman have argued that toleration was both theorised and exercised in medieval and early modern Europe on a scale hitherto unappreciated by historians. Casting aside the idea of 'a unilinear progression from darkness to light', detaching toleration from its Lockean and Enlightenment roots, and stressing the extent to which it could spring from the soil of religious dogmatism as well as from scepticism, they and their contributors stress the sheer diversity of discussion about, and practical manifestations of, tolerance before 1700. Detecting defences of it in a variety of unexpected quarters, they insist that these voices were not 'lonely souls' crying in the wind but symptomatic of a surprisingly eclectic intellectual climate. However, their book does suffer from a frustrating lack of precision about what constitutes the 'toleration' it claims to uncover, not least because the editors eschew tendentious definitions of the term in favour of allowing 'nuances of meaning' to evolve by themselves.[30] Nevertheless, Laursen and Nederman have helped to reconceptualise the relationship between persecution and toleration less in terms of a stark, black and white polarity than of an infinite range of shades of grey. They have helped us to see toleration as 'a troubling and tense paradox', 'a fickle two-way valve' between rejection and celebration of beliefs rather than 'a simple movement from isolation towards acceptance'.[31]

Within the last five years, however, there have been signs of a spirited post-revisionist backlash. In *How the Idea of Religious Toleration Came to the West* (2003), Perez Zagorin has reinjected fresh life into the fading historical model that charts the path from persecution to toleration. Proceeding from the premise that 'in a certain sense ideas rule the world', he emphatically rejects claims made for the decisive part played by political expediency and economic rationalism, stressing the potency of the arguments formulated by a familiar coalition of humanist and Protestant thinkers – from Erasmus and Castellio to Bayle – in precipitating its realisation in practice. Convinced of the interconnection between 'toleration' and 'religious freedom' as concepts, Zagorin's book has the not entirely unintended effect of resurrecting the Whig quest to locate the origins of Western liberalism in the sixteenth and seventeenth centuries.[32]

John Coffey's *Persecution and Toleration in Protestant England, 1558–1689* (2000), which appeared three years earlier, also makes a renewed case for the seventeenth century as a watershed and accords radical puritanism a key role in this process. Though he is at pains to stress the religious foundations of tolerationist ideas, Coffey contests claims about the severe limitations of puritan conceptions of 'liberty of conscience' and lends support to the older

suggestion that the godly Protestant writers of the 1640s and 1650s anticipated many of the key tenets of modern discourses of equality and freedom.
He accepts that religious intolerance still exerted enormous influence over
post-Reformation society, but argues that the reigns of the later Tudors and
Stuarts nonetheless witnessed 'a dramatic movement from persecution to
toleration and from religious uniformity to pluralism' as the monopoly of the
national Church progressively crumbled. 1644 is identified as a critical turning point: 'in that year the Augustinian consensus concerning persecution
was irreparably fractured'. By 1689, he writes, 'many', 'a substantial minority',
no longer believed that the Christian magistrate had a solemn duty to punish
heresy and schism. The chronological approach of the second half of this book
almost inevitably replicates the impression of teleological development and it
remains largely a political and intellectual history of the topic which makes
relatively few gestures towards exploring its social dimension. Above all, while
Coffey acknowledges that there was no 'absolute gulf fixed between persecution and toleration', his survey still rests implicitly on the presupposition that
they are adversarially related. Like earlier studies, it also works outward from
the idea that intolerance was the normal state of affairs in English parishes
throughout this period.[33]

In this regard, Coffey's overview contrasts quite markedly with the insights
that have emerged from a series of meticulously detailed investigations of
religious minorities in specific rural and urban contexts in recent years.
Reversing the angle of vision from the centre to the localities, and setting aside
public documents for parochial and regional archives, a growing number of
scholars are assembling a compelling body of evidence questioning, if not
contradicting, our instinctive assumption that 'religious beliefs of great
personal depth almost inevitably drove a wedge between those who held them
and those who did not' and invariably threatened and disrupted the existence
of harmonious social relations. The research of Derek Plumb, Christopher
Marsh and Bill Stevenson, among others, is highlighting the extent to which
dissenting groups were assimilated and integrated into wider society in this
period, and the capacity that people exhibited to absorb difference and tolerate
heterodoxy within their midst. Perhaps sometimes at the risk of fostering a
rosy vision of the village England we have now lost, these scholars have underlined the generally benign and conciliatory character of inter-confessional
relations and drawn attention to a persistent gulf between the rhetoric of
intolerance and the grassroots reality of what the late Bob Scribner termed 'the
tolerance of practical rationality'.[34]

In stressing equilibrium over enmity, and in replacing the accent on spontaneous hatred of and habitual hostility towards nonconformists with greater
sensitivity to the reluctance of officials and lay people to present religious
deviants to the Church and civil courts, such work concurs with the findings

of some recent studies of Catholic-Protestant relations on the European mainland. Close examination of communities in sixteenth- and seventeenth-century France, the Netherlands and the Holy Roman Empire has likewise led to a new appreciation of the degree to which members of competing faiths could live alongside each other without coming to blows, and of the role that initiatives for denominational bridge-building played in calming and pacifying violence in the wake, and even in the midst, of the Wars of Religion. Coexistence and inter-confessional co-operation are eclipsing ubiquitous conflict and fratricidal strife as the key agendas of historiographical discussion. Gregory Hanlon, for instance, explains the relative absence of confessional conflict in the town of Layrac-en-Brulhois in Aquitaine as a consequence of 'an intense sociability englobing most inhabitants in a cocoon of mutual relations'.[35] In the United Provinces, Willem Frijhoff emphasises, 'everyday ecumenism' and 'interconfessional conviviliality' coexisted with and counter-balanced 'a tenacious mentality of socio-religious exclusivism'.[36]

The very fact that historians have found it necessary to stress the considerable reserves of tolerance embedded in early modern society reveals just how deep-seated is the belief that the impulse to persecute was its most salient characteristic. The same presuppositions, which have long afflicted assessments of the period between 1000 and 1500, are coming under increasingly critical scrutiny by medieval historians. Alongside growing awareness of the ability of the pre-Reformation Church to accommodate a plurality of opinions and practices and find room for dissonant voices, the conventional portrait of the lay populace as an irrational mob is being discarded as a crude caricature that distorts our understanding of the complex dynamics of communal interaction. What is emerging in the place of 'simple models of conspiracy or opposition' is a more 'highly variegated social and intellectual landscape', the topography of which was shaped by interlinked processes of inclusion and exclusion. Deviant insiders like heretics and schismatics were perhaps treated more harshly than non-Christian outsiders such as Muslims and Jews but it is a mistake to draw too sharp a distinction in this regard. As well as illuminating the mechanisms and patterns of medieval repression, Scott Waugh, Peter Diehl and others stress the constant interchange between different cultures and the reluctance rather than the propensity of governments and their subjects to prosecute heresy. In a sophisticated analysis of 'communities of violence' in fourteenth-century France and Aragon, David Nirenberg has likewise sought to explode the dichotomies that posit hostility and conflict as 'the antithesis of associative action' and feeling, highlighting instead their 'fundamental interdependence'.[37]

These are insights that apply equally well to early modern Europe. As in the medieval period, a powerful potential for antagonism and hatred remained. Although an instinct for peaceful coexistence seems to have usually counter-balanced the forces tending towards animosity and militancy, the virus of intolerance, if often latent and in abeyance, was nevertheless always present, ready to flare up and wreak havoc when the conditions were right.[38] Rather than situate persecution and toleration, confrontation and co-operation, in stark opposition, this book explores their interconnections, probing the tensions at the heart of 'an almost schizophrenic religious culture, in which contradictory instincts jostled for supremacy'. Working from the assumption that social relations are 'not fundamentally harmonious, conflictive, consensual or repressive, but all of these' at the same time, it seeks to investigate them in relation to an ever-changing political, ecclesiastical and ideological atmosphere.[39]

THE LONG REFORMATION

It is important to stress that throughout this period the status of religious minorities in England was in a constant state of flux. Against the backdrop of a volatile domestic and international political context, no religious regime could be certain of retaining power and maintaining control of the mechanisms for defining and enforcing orthodoxy. Events at every level – parochial, civic and national – repeatedly proved that the governing elite could easily be toppled from their position of dominance. The pillars of the ecclesiastical establishment all too frequently became hunted dissidents forced to hide in corners and scurry to safety abroad – victims of the intolerance of those whom they had previously persecuted.[40]

Here the contingency of England's protracted and erratic Reformation deserves special emphasis. During the reign of Henry VIII (1509–47), religious policy tilted in different directions in accordance with the changing whims of the king, the exigencies of foreign and dynastic politics, and the rise and fall of the conservative and evangelical factions that competed for power at court. The momentous changes of the mid-1530s – the constitutional break with the papacy, the dissolution of the monasteries, the destruction of images, and the assault on traditional doctrine in the Ten Articles of 1536 – faltered in the following decade as Lutheran influence was tempered and clouded by a partial resurgence of traditional theology and practice. The passage of an Act banning the ordinary laity from reading the Bible in 1543 and the execution of the gentlewoman Anne Askew for denying transubstantiation in 1546 may be seen as emblems of the more limited and low-key reformism pursued by the Henrician regime in this period, though they also reflect an anxious reaction to the alarming spread of Anabaptism on the Continent.[41] Amidst such mixed signals, it must have been difficult for the laity to keep up to speed with what exactly constituted religious deviance in the eyes of the authorities. Many, nonetheless, collaborated with the government in the dismantling of traditional religion, forging 'new consciences to navigate the unprecedented circumstances in which they found themselves'.[42]

The accession of Edward VI to the throne in 1547 inaugurated a new phase of zeal against Catholic idolatry overseen by the Protector Somerset and the Duke of Northumberland, during which chantries, guilds and other trappings of popery fell under the iconoclasts' hammers and an English liturgy was introduced with the publication of the first Book of Common Prayer in 1549, to be replaced three years later with a revised version bearing even more clearly the marks of Reformed Protestant thinking. This was also apparent in the Forty-two Articles of 1552, which endorsed a memorialist interpretation of the Eucharist and discussed salvation in terms of the Calvinist dogma of predestination.[43] The populace hardly had time to digest and adapt to these developments before the sickly young king was replaced by his ardently Catholic half-sister, Mary, the daughter of Catherine of Aragon. After a short period of amnesty, Mary and her advisers ushered in a determined Counter-Reformation, repealing the reforming statutes of her father and brother, initiating a campaign of re-education, and reinvigorating the ancient heresy laws as a weapon against those who wilfully persisted in preaching and practising the Protestant Gospel in the face of official determination to extinguish it.[44] Thrice within the space of a single generation the boundary between orthodoxy and heterodoxy had been decisively relocated.

Mary's earnest, but in some respects, counter-productive attempt to restore England to papal allegiance was brought to an abrupt end five years later when the succession passed to Elizabeth, the last Tudor monarch. The Elizabethan settlement, as approved by Parliament in 1559, reinstated Protestantism as the established religion, though without the transparency or clarity for which many returning exiles fervently wished. The Acts of Supremacy and Uniformity and Royal Injunctions declared the Queen Supreme Governor, replaced the Latin mass with a vernacular service at which attendance was made compulsory, and ordered the swift removal of the physical paraphernalia of Catholic worship. However, too many ceremonial relics and remnants of Antichrist remained in the Book of Common Prayer to secure it the wholehearted endorsement of groups at the more intensely red and radical end of the Protestant spectrum. The curious ecclesiastical hybrid engendered by the settlement thus ended up fostering discontent and dissent on both its left and right wings. And while the Thirty-nine Articles of 1563 set the theology of the Church on firmly Calvinist foundations, they too contained areas of ambiguity that sowed the seeds for future dispute. Sharper polarities were slowly emerging, but many remained unclear about where exactly the perimeter fence between acceptable and unacceptable belief and behaviour stood.[45]

The middle decades of the sixteenth century provide particularly fertile ground for counter-factual speculation. The history of tolerance and intolerance in England might have looked very different if Edward VI had lived into adulthood and carried his godly convictions through to their final conclusions, if Mary had produced a healthy heir, or if Elizabeth had died of smallpox in 1562 or married a French Catholic prince. Conservatives who secreted illegal liturgical equipment 'waiting for the day', and eagerly anticipated the imminent demise or overthrow of the Elizabethan regime should not be dismissed as mere dreamers who built castles in the air. It was at least possible that plots and conspiracies to depose Elizabeth and set up Mary Queen of Scots in her place might have borne fruit and the providential myth of the divine wind that scattered the Spanish Armada in 1588 testifies indirectly to a well-grounded fear that Philip II's fleet had the capacity to crush and vanquish the English ships. The assassinations of the Dutch leader William of Orange in 1584 and the French monarch Henry IV in 1610 remind us that contemporary rulers were by no means invulnerable to fatal attack by their dissident subjects, as does the timely discovery of the Gunpowder Treason in 1605. Had any of these terrorist acts and military campaigns achieved their revolutionary aims it is not entirely inconceivable that England could have been engulfed in a religious war, like that which ravaged France in the second half of the sixteenth century and the Holy Roman Empire after 1618. It might just have become an arena for devastating outbreaks of internecine conflict that culminated in bloody massacre and led eventually to an uneasy negotiated truce broadly comparable to that enshrined in the Edict of Nantes of 1598.

English Catholics who nurtured hopes of the conversion of James Stuart to the faith of his murdered mother when he succeeded Elizabeth in 1603 clearly looked to the precedent of the pragmatic Huguenot king of Navarre, who is famously supposed to have declared that 'Paris was worth a mass'. That a formal toleration of Catholics might have been proclaimed cannot be ruled out: to many adherents of Rome the precedent set by his lenient treatment of their co-religionists in Scotland seemed a good omen. It was arguably the rash plot concocted by Robert Catesby, Guy Fawkes and their collaborators that turned James I against implementing a limited policy of licensed coexistence. It is also worth wondering what might have happened had Charles's proposed match with the Infanta Maria culminated in a lasting dynastic alliance with the house of Habsburg.

The onset of the Thirty Years War, the conquest of the Palatinate, and the flight of the Elector Frederick and Princess Elizabeth to The Hague in the early 1620s aroused fresh apprehension about the dangers of forcible re-Catholicisation by militant rulers backed by the resurgent Tridentine Church – especially in an environment sensitised to the presence of crypto-popery by the creeping rise of Arminianism and the drive for the 'beauty of holiness' endorsed by Charles I and implemented by Archbishop William Laud and the like-minded prelates whom he promoted up the ladder of the established Church.[46] As Jonathan Scott has recently argued, these developments in England must be integrated into their wider European milieu and recognised as a 'domestic attempt at counter-reformation confessional state-building'. While Caroline religious policy did not literally seek to reintroduce Roman Catholicism, it did represent a very serious threat to one potent vision of the Elizabethan and Jacobean Protestant heritage. In a very real sense, he suggests, England's 'long Reformation' was not merely incomplete but also insecure. Preachers and pamphleteers repeatedly warned that their own nation would soon taste the cup of divine wrath that had been poured out on Bohemia and it is clear that many of those who subsequently engaged in the British Civil Wars of 1638–51 saw themselves as fighting for the very survival of Protestantism itself. Historians may have been guilty of complacently predating the point at which the prolonged and haphazard process that was the English Reformation became irreversible.[47]

Similar observations might be made with regard to the decades after the Restoration, when events across the Channel inspired renewed anxiety about the threat that international Catholicism presented to Protestant nations. The Revocation of the Edict of Nantes in 1685 and the expulsion of many Huguenots by Louis XIV was a sharp reminder that at least one contemporary king still regarded the establishment of religious uniformity as his God-given mission. The efforts of Charles II, but more especially James II, to offer indulgence to Catholics in 1672 and 1688 were widely interpreted as attempts to reimpose the monopoly of the Church of Rome. They too need to be seen in relation to wider European trends, of which the Catholic absolutism of the Bourbon monarchy was the most eloquent and alarming expression. By the late seventeenth century, Protestantism may have been too deeply entrenched and too closely interwoven with patriotism to have allowed any such scheme to succeed, but the swirling instability of the European context should alert us to the faint possibility of alternative outcomes. The furore surrounding the fictitious Popish Plot of 1678 and the periodic repolishing of the legends of the Marian martyrs suggests that the spectre of persecution by an uncompromising Catholic regime remained close to the forefront of many contemporary minds. So too does the publication in 1690 of the Elizabethan Jesuit Robert Persons' *Memoriall for the intended reformation of England*, a blueprint for the forcible reclamation of England to the popish fold printed to emphasise the horrors that might have awaited the country had James II remained on the throne. The mixed benefits of hindsight have perhaps led historians to assume that Catholicism's fate as a minority sect was sealed much earlier than was in fact the case.

Returning to the Elizabethan origins of Protestant dissent, we must likewise avoid jumping to the conclusion that puritan attempts to prune away objectionable ceremonies and vestments and to remodel the Church of England along Presbyterian lines were destined to fail. The narrow defeat of proposals for further reform of ecclesiastical ritual at the Convocation of 1563 reveals that episcopal opinion on the subject was diverse and divided. Similarly, agitation in Parliament for radical revisions to the Prayer Book and even for abolition of the hierarchy of bishops found support in high quarters, despite the queen's implacable opposition to all such initiatives. Puritanism had powerful patrons within the Privy Council and at court, including William Cecil, Lord Burghley and Robert Dudley, the Earl of Leicester, and the complete marginalisation of the Presbyterian movement spearheaded by Thomas Cartwright and John Field was by no means inevitable in the first half of the reign. Many confidently expected that the Elizabethan settlement would be not 'a terminus' but 'a temporary stopping place'[48] and looked forward to celebrating the day that England came into conformity with the example set by that 'most perfect School of Christ', the Church of Geneva. The eclipse of Edmund Grindal and his replacement in 1583 by the disciplinarian John Whitgift did cast a significant shadow over these hopes and the damaging fall-out from the Marprelate Controversy of 1588–89, together with the trial of Cartwright and eight other ministers for seditious activity in Star Chamber in 1591, were further serious blows to the anti-episcopal cause. Despite Richard Bancroft's determination to round up and root out Presbyterian dissidents and the willingness of a growing number of moderates to work towards pastoral regeneration within the structures of an imperfect Church, we should underestimate neither the tenacity nor the radicalism of the late Elizabethan and Jacobean puritan underground. Simultaneously, the proliferation of household conventicles and other forms of voluntary religion was entrenching dissent at the parochial heart of the ecclesiastical establishment, in a manner that richly supplemented but also subtly subverted it.[49]

As the Millenary Petition of 1603 and the discussions among delegates at the Hampton Court Conference in 1604 revealed, there were many who optimistically supposed that the accession of the Scottish king would see significant concessions to godly scruples and a shifting of the goalposts by which ecclesiastical orthodoxy was defined. James and his bishops thwarted these aspirations by a vigorous campaign against liturgical nonconformity but the appointment of George Abbot as Archbishop of Canterbury in 1611 inclined some to feel more sanguine about the possibility of further reform in the future. As the assault on Calvinist predestinarian theology gathered pace in the 1610s and 1620s, puritanism acquired an increasingly aggressive and confrontational edge. The 'popish' innovations of Charles and Laud and their persecution of those who stood up to resist and condemn them served to galvanise the hotter sort of Protestants, water the semi-dormant seed of Presbyterianism, and propel many out of the national Church into the wilderness of exile and separatism.

The collapse of the Personal Rule and the summoning of the Long Parliament unleashed much pent-up feeling against the evil and antichristian institution of episcopacy, as attested by the passionate call for its abolition contained in the Root and Branch Petition presented to the House of Commons in December 1640. The outbreak of conflict in 1642 coincided with a concerted and ferocious attack on Laudianism and it initially looked as if the erection of a Presbyterian Church would follow swiftly on its heels. However, internal disagreement soon ensued, paralysing the progress of the West-minster Assembly set up in 1643 to erect a lasting settlement. The spread of sectarian radicalism added a further destablising element to the debates within the ranks of the godly about the nature of the confessional state that was to replace Charles I's. So too did the triangular and concatenating conflicts in Ireland and especially Calvinist Scotland, with whom Parliament sealed an alliance by the Solemn League and Covenant of 1643. These disputes festered on until 1646, when the office of bishop was formally abolished, eighteen months after Parliament had officially banned the Book of Common Prayer and substituted the Directory of Worship.

Toleration of dissent was not contemplated by these divines and politicians; only belatedly did it emerge as a possible solution to the rampant pluralism and win the support of those in a position to confer it. Events thereafter developed rapidly and in an unruly direction, culminating in the execution of the king in January 1649 for betraying his divine office and staining the land with the blood of his subjects.[50] The regicide deprived Royalists of their commander-in-chief but it provided Anglicans with a powerful mascot in the guise of a royal martyr. At least nominally, the Church that Charles had defended to the end was now a beleaguered minority. Those labouring to come to terms with the experience of defeat could not have predicted that only a decade later they would find themselves once more on top and in control; on the contrary, they had to face the possibility that they might remain permanently out in the cold.

The revolutionary experiment that was the English Republic saw the repeal of statutes enforcing church attendance in 1650 and a wave of millennial speculation about the imminent Second Coming of Christ and the free reign of the 'saints'. These fervent utopian dreams lost some of their lustre under the Cromwellian Protectorate, and several attempts were made to restrict the provisions of the Instrument of Government of 1653, which guaranteed a broad liberty of conscience, notably against the backdrop of the disturbing success of the Quaker movement. The blasphemous entry of James Nayler into Bristol in 1656 in a deliberate re-enactment of Christ's arrival in Jerusalem shook the puritan Parliament to its roots and spurred on initiatives to strengthen the sinews of official persecution. The main casualties of this reaction were anti-Trinitarian heretics and socially disruptive sectaries. The backward slide towards the safe havens of monarchy and religious uniformity was underway well before the end of the Interregnum.[51]

Even so, to many the Restoration seemed to have come out of the blue. 1660 was proclaimed an *annus mirabilis* and the re-establishment of the Church of England was heralded as a miracle of resurrection by the Anglican clergy. At the same time, the character of the ecclesiastical settlement embodied in statute in 1662 was by no means predetermined. Charles II's Declaration of Breda of April 1660 not only gave the godly grounds for anticipating that they might be accommodated within the mainstream, but promised toleration to those who were prepared to live peaceably. The passage of the Act of Uniformity disguises the two-year period of serious and nearly successful negotiation for the comprehension of Presbyterians and some other dissenters which preceded it, the peak of which was the Worcester House Declaration which announced that the Church of England would henceforth be governed by a combination of bishops and presbyters. The panic that followed the Fifth Monarchist uprising in January 1661 was one of the factors which enabled the hardliners to tighten their grip and shut the door on an unprecedented opportunity to alter the ecclesiological shape of this institution. Had the moderates been able to prevail, the scope and significance of nonconformity in Restoration England would have been greatly attenuated. As it was, under the baleful influence of the so-called 'Clarendon Code', persecution became the keynote of the 1660s and 1670s for Protestant Dissent. Along with the Roman Catholics, these groups benefited from the benign provisions of the short-lived Declarations of Indulgence issued by the later Stuart kings, but only at the cost of acknowledging their marginality and crossing the line into outright schism. These royal initiatives led to an intense wave of anti-popery, the chief consequence of which was the ousting of James II and the Glorious Revolution.[52]

The Act of Toleration of 1689 forms a convenient endpoint to the period tackled by this book but here too it is important to emphasise that the pressure of events was by no means inexorable and to extricate these developments from the encrusted layers of legend that have accumulated around them. William III's invasion rode pragmatically on the back of violent aversion to the idea of tolerating a committed Catholic monarch on the throne and the Dutch *stadholder* had to walk a tightrope between conciliating foreign powers on the Continent and appeasing public opinion in England. On the question of legal concessions to the Protestant sectarians, once again we need to consider the possibility of a rather different result. For a second time, the chance to revise and relax the criteria for full membership of the Church of England was passed up, on this occasion in favour of simply exempting dissenters from the rigour of penal laws, which still remained in force. Even then, it was not clear that the immunity from official intolerance was assured: Parliament considered limiting the life of the statute to seven years and the Occasional Conformity and Schism Acts of 1711 and 1714 represented significant regressions from the principle established twenty years earlier.[53]

What needs to be stressed, then, is the enduring fluidity of the ecclesiastical landscape in England during this period, and the continuing vulnerability of religious minorities to dramatic reversals of fortune that could transform them virtually overnight from victims into victors. One's status as a member of an inferior and unorthodox sect was rarely immutable or fixed. With these caveats and qualifications in mind, the rest of this book adopts a thematic rather than narrative structure. It offers a comparative analysis of contemporary attitudes to and treatment of a wide range of individuals and communities who found themselves at odds with the religio-political establishment in the course of this era.

RELIGIOUS MINORITIES IN ENGLAND 1500–1700

Much of the older historiography of persecution and toleration fell into the trap of reading back into the early modern period the denominational divisions that were not the cause but rather one of the long-term consequences of the successive upheavals which it experienced. It was the tumultuous events of the English Reformation and Revolution which crystallised confessional identities, not vice versa. The insular character and sectarian bias of much of the secondary literature on religious minorities has compounded the tendency to draw rigid boundaries between heresy and orthodoxy, dissent and conformity, in the sixteenth and seventeenth centuries, while the flexibility and imprecision of the derogatory labels contemporaries used to classify attitudes and stances – 'Lollard', 'papist', 'puritan', 'quaker' – only compounds our difficulties. To assume that early modern people were as aware of theological distinctions as modern scholars who spend hours studying, dissecting and categorising them in books is to do violence to the unstable and amorphous nature of religious affiliation at this time. It is to accord too little importance to the genuine confusion of individuals entangled in a bewildering series of institutional and intellectual adjustments and it runs the risk of investing groups on the outer fringes, but nevertheless within the broad embrace of the established Church, with an artificial coherence. It may even retrospectively construct and invent deviant movements from sets of tendencies that were actually far more diffuse and elusive, mistaking an agglomeration of idiosyncratic opinions for a unified creed.[54] Many individuals must have felt permanently stranded in a 'shifting no man's land', lingering in a prolonged state of limbo.[55] The dramatic public statements and recantations made by converts and apostates probably represent merely the tip of the iceberg of religious vacillation in this period.[56]

On the other hand, historians are also prone to prioritise belief over practice in a manner that may be deeply anachronistic. The absence of a formal canon of doctrine should not lead automatically to scepticism about the very existence of a sect or dissident group. Common patterns of observance, gesture and language and networks of social interaction, contact and solidarity could be as important as precisely specified precepts in defining a movement. Dissent was as much a cultural as a mental phenomenon; sometimes it was as much about who one knew as what one knew.[57] In other words, although there are grounds for thinking that the early modern era was critical in reconceptualising 'religion' less as 'a ritual system of living' than as a body of internalised dogma, the speed, impact and significance of this shift should not be overstated.[58] The Reformation did fossilise beliefs and foster increased self-consciousness via the dissemination of catechisms and the compilation of lists of definitive articles of faith, but it did not supersede outward conduct as a means of demarcating and binding the members of competing churches and religious communities and brotherhoods.

A related problem is the widespread reluctance to distinguish between hostility to individuals and hostility to the ideologies they espouse. We need to build into our analysis the insight that abstract hatred of a false religion as a system of thought was by no means incompatible with cordial relations with its human adherents. People might exhibit a profound opposition and aversion to a rival faith without translating this into a practical distaste of or destructive action against those who professed it. At the same time, it was arguably only in the course, and more especially towards the end of the two centuries covered by this book that the suffix 'ism' came into common usage, indicating a sentient awareness of Catholicism, Protestantism, Puritanism, Quakerism, and other denominational groupings as organised, institutionalised and clearly differentiated forms of the Christian religion. The growing use of this suffix to indicate a clinical or pathological condition is not without relevance.[59]

Nevertheless, it is necessary to identify the religious minorities whose experiences are the subject of this book.[60] The list begins with the later Lollards, followers of the Oxford academic John Wyclif (c.1330–84), posthumously excommunicated by the Council of Constance for his corrosive attacks on the clergy and theology of the late medieval Church. Following the debacle of Sir John Oldcastle's rising against Henry V in 1414, the movement shed its original academic and aristocratic character, surviving throughout much of the fifteenth century primarily in the circles of the middling and artisanal ranks of English society. Scholars continue to quarrel about how far these scattered pockets of heterodoxy underwent expansion or revival in the decades prior to England's secession from the Church of Rome. But it is clear that on the eve of the Reformation, the term was applied loosely and imprecisely to men and women who boldly criticised Catholic doctrines and ceremonies, including transubstantiation, images, purgatory, pilgrimage and the cult of saints, and who revered Scripture as the source of all spiritual authority and sustenance.[61]

In the 1520s, these heretics were joined by England's earliest Protestants, evangelicals inspired by Lutheran ideas imported largely via books from abroad, notably the notion of justification by faith alone. Passionately attached to the vernacular Bible, especially the New Testament in William Tyndale's translation, it was not always easy for the authorities to distinguish these new religious dissidents from their native Lollard forbears. Indeed, at the local level, initially the two tendencies often intermingled and merged. Exposure to Swiss Reformed theology gradually altered the complexion of English Protestantism, but also led to its diversification and fragmentation.[62] By the middle decades of the sixteenth century, a developing bias towards Calvinist predestinarianism was being challenged by the Freewillers headed by Henry Hart, whose contempt for the double doctrine of election and reprobation threatened the unity of the Marian Protestant reaction.

Equally disruptive was the presence of Anabaptism, which may be more accurately characterised as an unruly cluster of individuals holding disparate opinions rather than a cohesive and close-knit sect. Apart from their common rejection of the practice of infant baptism, there was relatively little linking those stigmatised by this emotive label, except in the eyes of officials convinced by the millenarian kingdom established by the Anabaptists in Münster in 1534–35 that they were all agents of social subversion and political sedition. Some espoused the Arian heresy, repudiating Trinitarian doctrine and denying the divinity of Christ; others were antinomians who insisted that the moral law did not bind the elect; and several spurned the precept that Jesus, through Mary, had assumed human flesh, including Joan Bocher, who was sent to the stake in May 1550 for stubbornly affirming this outrageous opinion.[63] Some of these exotic currents fed into the mystical movement known as the Family of Love, a brotherhood of believers founded by the mysterious Dutchman Hendrick Niclaes, whose ultimate aspiration was to attain a state of perfect spiritual union with God. The 1570s and 1580s were probably the heyday of this tiny and extremely reclusive minority movement and throughout the period it remained beyond the Protestant pale.[64]

As a result of the Reformation, Roman Catholics also became classified as deviants, though technically as traitors rather than heretics. The Henrician regime declared defence of papal supremacy a treason and several were executed for upholding this fundamental tenet, most famously Bishop John Fisher and Sir Thomas More. While Mary's reign provided some respite for committed Romanists, under Elizabeth and her Stuart successors, Catholicism was once more prosecuted by the civil and ecclesiastical authorities, mainly when it manifested itself in lay nonconformity and conspiratorial activity. The 1560s were a period of confusion but the energetic efforts of missionary priests trained in the Low Countries and Rome and sent back from 1574 onwards to redeem the souls of their countrymen from schism and heresy bore fruit in the growth of recusancy. Despite these clerical efforts, many church papists continued to conform and attend Protestant services. The English Catholic community may eventually have largely contracted into gentry households but we cannot afford to ignore the less socially exalted followers of this prohibited faith. Nor should the capacity of Jesuit and seminarian evangelists to win new converts from Protestantism be underestimated. This was not merely a religion of conservative recidivists who yearned for a return to the Mother Church of their medieval forbears. It was also infused with the invigorating spirit of Tridentine renewal.[65]

Protestant separatists who defiantly detached themselves from the national Church became another dissenting force to be reckoned with. Supplied with a compelling ideology by the writings of Robert Browne, Robert Harrison, John Greenwood and Henry Barrow, these groups declared the Church of England a limb of Antichrist, established the principle of voluntary covenantal membership, and laid the foundations for congregational self-governance. Their refusal 'to tarry for the magistrate' and their radical ecclesiology differentiated them from Presbyterians and puritans,[66] with whom they otherwise had many moral and intellectual priorities in common. The conscientious objections of these uncompromising Protestants made them the target of much government hostility and in the first half of the seventeenth century the boundary between puritans and those later identified as Independents or Congregationalists became increasingly blurred. A proliferation of gathered churches developed in the safety of exile in the Netherlands, under the leadership of John Smyth, John Robinson, William Ames and others; some, notably Henry Jacob, returned to London to set up semi-separatist congregations which maintained an element of intercommunion with the parochial Church of England as a point of principle.[67] Another group, directed by Thomas Helwys, formed the first General (or Arminian) Baptist church at Spitalfields in 1611. By the mid-1620s, there were offshoots in Coventry, Lincoln, Salisbury and Tiverton. A decade or so later, the more theologically conservative Particular (or Calvinist) Baptists emerged from the shade: like the General Baptists they believed in the complete separation of Church and state and practised adult baptism, but rejected their convictions about the universal redemption of mankind for the precept of predestination. The precise connections between these groups and the various branches of Dutch Mennonites are still in the process of being unravelled and clarified.[68] Equally, we must take care to avoid perpetuating the misleading impression that mainstream puritanism was hermetically sealed from and antipathetic to an underground sectarian tradition and radical antinomian fringe.[69]

During the Civil War, puritanism moved from the outer wings to the centre stage, but the collapse of the machinery for enforcing conformity and the breakdown of political control created a vacuum in which a variety of extreme religious movements were able to flourish, against which the orthodox godly turned in due course – the Seekers, Ranters, Adamites, Quakers, Muggletonians and Fifth Monarchists. Many of these groups rejected set forms of worship and traditional ecclesiastical structures and found their guiding light in the charismatic inner workings of the Holy Spirit rather than the 'dead letter' of the biblical text. Some of their adherents practised provocative methods of proselytising (such as running through the streets naked) and eschewed conventional ethics, engaging in activities which their enemies condemned as monstrous depravity and licentiousness.[70] The impact of separatism and sectarianism, however, appears to have been severely limited: it has been estimated that no more than 5 per cent of the populace attended religious assemblies other than those associated with their parish churches between 1643 and 1654. Episcopalian Anglicans were numerically a far more significant 'minority' during the Interregnum. Loyal defenders of the abolished Prayer Book and the hierarchy of bishops, they continued to practice their faith in the face of Cromwellian harassment in the 1650s and their 'passive strength' ensured the smooth reassumption of power by the Church of England in 1660.[71]

After the Restoration, puritanism in its multiple forms once more found itself on the wrong side of the law and until 1689 the various denominations of dissenters were obliged to operate illegally outside the established Church. Presbyterians, Baptists and Quakers were reduced to meeting in chambers and conventicles, though many of the first group clung to the hope that they might be able to rejoin the Anglican communion and did their best to maintain links with local ministers and lay people. The end of the seventeenth century also saw growing numbers of Socinians and deists. The former, also known as Unitarians, were rationalists in the mould of the sixteenth-century theologians Lelio and Faustus Socinus who dismissed the Trinity and did not recognise the divine status of Christ. They had been a source of concern since the 1630s. The deists denied the authority of the Bible and the need for revelation, and advocated a simple 'natural religion' shorn of the numinous aspects of traditional Christianity. Many of them, including the outspoken John Toland, were also advocates of toleration. The spread of these intellectual tendencies, designed to shake the pillars of priestcraft in the 1690s, greatly tested and troubled the Anglican establishment.[72]

The experience of three other religious communities also finds a place in this book. The first consists of the congregations of Calvinist immigrants from France and the Netherlands who settled in England in the course of these two centuries, beginning with the establishment by royal charter of the first 'stranger' churches in London under the superintendency of the Polish reformer John à Lasco in 1550. Others were established in southern and East Anglian ports such as Sandwich, Southampton and Norwich. With Elizabeth's accession, these groups came under the jurisdiction of diocesan bishops, providing a shining miniature example of Reformed church government to those who sought to remodel England's episcopal polity and set up rigorous synodal structures of discipline. In the latter half of the sixteenth century, against the backdrop of the persecutions that accompanied the Dutch Revolt and French Wars of Religion, more Walloon and Huguenot exiles flocked across the Channel, augmenting the ranks of existing foreign Protestant congregations and establishing new ones. These survived the unwelcome assaults on their autonomy by Archbishop Laud in the 1630s and Restoration attempts to bring them into liturgical conformity with the Church of England. The 1680s saw a new tidal wave of refugees fleeing the intolerance of the French state in the wake of Louis XIV's policy of forcing Huguenot families to quarter his troops (the *dragonnades*) and the revocation of the Edict of Nantes.[73]

Finally, attention will occasionally be paid to two non-Christian minorities – to the Muslims and Jews. Expelled from England by Edward I in 1290, in the Tudor and early Stuart period there were only a handful of Sephardim (semites of Iberian descent) living in this country, most of them recent immigrants from Spain and Portugal, where systematic purges were carried out in 1492 and 1497 respectively, supported by a campaign to root out dissemblers spearheaded by the Inquisition. Ostensibly *conversos*, beneath the outward veneer of Catholic practice, some of these continued to engage secretly in outlawed Jewish rites associated with the Sabbath and festivals like Passover. A number acquired positions of influence in the universities, at court, and within the rising medical and mercantile professions. In the 1650s, pressure for formal readmission of the Jews came from abroad, the chief spokesman for the cause being the Amsterdam Rabbi Menasseh ben Israel. Thereafter, the Jewish community gradually emerged out of the shadows into the daylight, growing in size due to wealthy Jewish settlers from Holland and particularly with the influx of Ashkenazi Jews from Germany and Poland in the early eighteenth century.[74] Muslims were an even more ephemeral presence, encountered largely by sailors, fishermen, traders and travellers in the course of journeys to the Mediterranean and North Africa, and interactions with the Moors and Ottoman Turks. Nevertheless, the enforced conversion of captured Englishmen by the Barbary pirates did bring the populace into closer contact with the world of Islam when these renegades returned home.[75]

Examination of official policy and popular treatment of social and moral deviants such as witches, criminals, sinners, homosexuals and prostitutes falls outside the parameters of this study, except in so far as these categories have an uncanny habit of overlapping and converging. As we shall see, religious dissidence was widely conflated with sexual aberration and ethical digression. Heretics were compared and confused with witches; Anabaptists were attacked as schismatics and papists; Catholics were assimilated with traitors and the papacy was denounced as the Whore of Babylon. In addition, as the period progressed, polemical labels became not merely increasingly unstable but also interchangeable. The compass of terms like Lollard and puritan stretched to a point where they ceased to be meaningful and groups at opposite ends of the intellectual spectrum found themselves being branded with nicknames originally coined to identify their professed enemies: hence the proliferation of such wild claims as the widespread allegation that the Quakers were actually Jesuits in disguise. To this extent, taxonomic analysis of sects and minorities is always a perilous exercise.

SILENCES, DISTORTIONS AND OPTICAL ILLUSIONS: THE PROBLEM OF THE SOURCES

The final task of this introduction is to examine the range of sources available for the history of tolerance and intolerance and to consider some of the methodological challenges posed by the topic. The first observation to be made is that, like beauty, religious deviance lies in the eye of the beholder. 'Heresy' and 'unorthodoxy' are subjective constructs, which arguably tell us more about those levelling such charges than they do about those against whom they are directed. They throw into sharp relief the preoccupations and priorities of the societies and cultures that engender them. The making of a 'heretic' or 'heretical' community is thus a twin-stranded process: it requires individuals or groups who criticise or oppose the status quo and officials willing and able to take active steps to isolate, restrain, repress and punish them.

Religious minorities are, therefore, difficult to study: we see them largely through a veil of prejudice, through the distorting lenses and tinted spectacles of hostile observers. Even more pertinent is the related point that our sources are intrinsically biased towards persecution. Like historical records in general, they tend to privilege conflict, violence and rupture. Official records document the legal discrimination of the heterodox, drawing attention to the points at which individuals failed to carry out their ecclesiastical and civil obligations, or infringed statutes and ordinances and so found themselves hauled before the church and secular courts. The problem with the statistics that scholars derive from the tabulation of these infractions is that they may bear witness not to an actual rise in deviant behaviour or belief but to growing contemporary anxiety about its incidence. They may reflect the hazards of uneven archival survival or more rigorous efforts at investigation, or an unpredictable mixture of both. Such sources frequently have the side effect of creating a second optical illusion: they exaggerate the importance of heroic resistance and stalwart separatism and render many manifestations of partial and occasional con-formity almost invisible. Dissimulation and equivocation are equally hard to detect and no less treacherous to assess.

The propaganda that persecuting authorities directed against dissenters may be similarly deceptive. Designed to discredit them as alien 'others', it was heavily conditioned by generic convention and strongly reliant upon pre-existing stereotypes of deviance. As mentioned above, in some cases the media of speech, script and print may even have been responsible for creating mirages of dissident movements which did not in fact exist. The fourteenth-century Heresy of the Free Spirit and the phenomenon of Ranterism have been the subject of controversial analyses along these lines by Robert Lerner and J. C. Davis respectively.[76] Richard Rex's recent survey of Lollardy insists that its significance has been exaggerated by the systematic preservation of Wycliffite texts by reformers determined to find legitimating historical precedents for the 'new religion'.[77] As Peter Lake argued in a seminal essay, anti-popery performed a similar function, providing Protestants with a means of labelling and expelling tendencies that seemed to jeopardise their integrity. The structure of this prejudice was such that it tended to inflate Catholicism to menacing proportions, creating a composite image in which superstition, ignorance and tyranny fused into an inversion or alter ego of the true religion.[78] Chris Marsh suggests that the drives against Familists in the 1570s owed something to the fact that they became 'a symbolic culprit', a 'punchbag' against which puritans 'sought to release their hostile anxieties'. In turn, in the 1630s, Laudian writers elevated Presbyterianism into an insidious spectre of subversion.[79] Catherine Davies has applied these insights to the Edwardian Anabaptists, comparing the campaign against them with 'using a sledgehammer to crack a nut' and concluding that 'if such radicals had not existed, it would have necessary to invent them'.[80] As Ann Hughes has argued in her recent monograph on Thomas Edwards's great anatomy of Civil War sects, *Gangraena*, there is, however, a danger in trying to unravel 'representations' from rhetorically neutral pictures of 'reality' too precisely. The labels, categories, stereotypes and texts through which people demonised their enemies influence how the world is expressed and understood: they often 'interact in a complex way with stigmatized groups' self-images in processes of identity formation'.[81]

As for the writings of oppressed sects themselves, these are inherently martyrological in character, memorials of their triumph over adversity and survival in spite of concerted efforts to suppress and extinguish them, texts which frequently portray government agents and ordinary lay people as furious fanatics and bloodthirsty sadists. Volumes celebrating the heroic afflictions of religious minorities invariably betray the influence of ancient prototypes like the accounts of the early Christian martyrs produced by Eusebius, while the ultimate model for the death of the Lord's faithful servants was the sacrifice of Christ on the cross as described in the Gospels. These patterns are apparent in works ranging from Foxe's *Actes and monuments* (1563) and the various published relations of the 'late' and 'sad sufferings of the people called Quakers' to

Richard Challoner's *Memoirs* of the Catholic missionary priests (1741–42). They are no less typical of Edmund Calamy's account of nonconformist ministers ejected from the Church of England in 1662, than of John Walker's narrative of the troubles of the episcopalian parish clergy at the hands of the Civil War puritans (1714). Petitions and pleas for clemency to persecuting regimes likewise emphasise and embroider the hardships of those on whose behalf they are presented and the letters written by ministers and priests to console and fortify their disheartened followers contain many echoes of the epistles of St Paul to the Corinthians, Ephesians, and other embattled biblical congregations. All such texts must be seen as subtle exercises in collective self-fashioning.

Both sets of sources are inclined to depict dissenting groups as 'catacomb cultures'[82] subject to constant harassment – in other words more marginalised, segregated and ghettoised than they may actually have been. While statutes and court records focus upon nonconformist infringements of the law, internal writings stress the resolute separatism and splendid isolation of their members and edit out embarrassing evidence of apostasy, collaboration and compromise. Intent on projecting a public image of indomitable resistance and moral rectitude, the latter were often carefully revised to remove material regarding intrasectarian squabbles and the extreme and scandalous conduct in which dissident groups like the Quakers had engaged in their earlier rebellious and unruly phases.[83]

We also face the problem that the processes by which members of religious minorities were detected may overstate both their intellectual character and their affinity with preconceived notions of what constitutes deviance. The checklists of erroneous opinions that late medieval bishops and ecclesiastical officials used to identify the heterodox and the leading questions they put to prisoners and suspects had the consequence of enhancing the unity of the assortment of individuals who were interrogated, thereby providing the incentive for even more systematic efforts to eradicate heresy[84] – in much the same way as the manuals employed by inquisitors on the Continent confirmed their impression of a diabolical plot to overturn Christendom and justified the drive to rid society of Satan's accomplices: witches. The many confessional histories to which the era of the long Reformation gave rise also overstated the antiquity of the religious traditions they chronicled. Anxious to avoid the charge of innovation, Protestant writers proudly traced their lineage back to a motley crew of medieval heretics. In celebrating such sects as their brothers and forerunners, they ironically embraced the allegations made by their enemies, further cementing the counter-legends that were mechanisms for disseminating intolerance against them.[85]

Later historiography has reproduced many of the distortions inherent in contemporary memoirs, annals and martyrologies. The works of denominational writers of the nineteenth and early twentieth centuries were equally sectarian and apologetic in nature, implicitly or explicitly intended to celebrate the sanctified origins and continuing solidarity of the separate churches of which they were members, to expose the evils of bigotry and persecution, and even to boost morale in the context of new drives against them. As Patrick Collinson has commented, preoccupied with questions of genealogy and descent, they exhibit a kind of tunnel vision that perpetuates the impression of mutual hostility between religious minorities and the political and ecclesiastical establishment. They adopt a vertical approach to the history of dissent that ignores its horizontal and lateral connections with the official Church from which it was theoretically separate and distinct.[86] Structured in terms of a rigid polarity between victims and tyrants, villains and heroes, they too have contributed significantly to creating an enduring image of late medieval and early modern England as a 'persecuting society'.

The history of tolerance, by contrast, is much harder to write. Traditional accounts which used the seminal texts of scholars and philosophers and the formal edicts and decrees officially licensing pluralism to index the rise of 'toleration' presented an overly simplified picture which eclipsed more casual, spontaneous and unspectacular acts of benevolence and forbearance, and lacked sensitivity to the mundane transactions that mitigated and ameliorated the harsh penalties laid down on paper. The vigour and vehemence of the heated polemics of the period can mislead us into thinking that the people who wrote and read them were equally intolerant in practice. In a period in which toleration was widely regarded as a morally reprehensible and foolhardy practice, contemporaries generally recorded it in a negative sense, chiefly in order to deplore and condemn it. Otherwise restraint and patience with heretics and deviants rarely impinge directly upon the historical record; they are all too often overshadowed by graphic and harrowing examples of vicious behaviour. To detect charity, harmony and peaceful coexistence, historians have to attune their ears to the telling silences in their sources and pay as much attention to what people omitted to do as what they actually did – to the gaps between theory and practice, between learned, articulate discourse and ordinary, everyday conduct. Since tolerance often manifests itself in actions rather than words, it is always at risk of being ignored by historians who regard verbal expression as supremely important. It requires us to engage in the hazardous and treacherous enterprise of reading between the lines and even against the grain of our documents, of inferring and interpolating on the basis of vague hints and thin slivers of evidence. The researchers who have caught glimpses of this shy and elusive creature in the villages, towns and cities of early modern England have done so only after months and years of painstaking detective work, reconstituting local communities in minute and microscopic detail, and matching scattered records concerning the interactions of otherwise anonymous individuals.

Drawing on recent scholarship on the religious minorities outlined above, as well as broader studies of ecclesiastical and political developments in the sixteenth and seventeenth centuries, the remainder of this book addresses the history of tolerance and intolerance under five main headings. Chapter 2 explores the establishment and enforcement of religious orthodoxy. It examines commonly articulated assumptions and justifications for pursuing this policy and looks at the institutions and methods employed by Church and state to compel and persuade dissenters to conform. In chapter 3, we assess how the populace at large responded to the presence of heretics and deviants in the communities in which they lived, and consider various manifestations of sectarian violence and popular prejudice. Chapter 4 turns to the range of ways in which religious minorities responded to official and local intolerance, to the dilemmas of conscience posed by the experience of proscription and oppression, and to how this affected the making of sectarian identities. Theories of toleration and the practical realities of tolerance form the subject of chapter 5, together with their somewhat contradictory and paradoxical by-products. Attention is devoted both to active initiatives on the part of the authorities and the charitable concessions which local people made to their heterodox neighbours. Finally, chapter 6 investigates the longer-term consequences of coexisting with difference; it reviews evidence of the processes of integration and assimilation taking place against the background of de facto pluralism and examines key features and symptoms of the confessionalisation of English society. It draws comparisons with some other European contexts and considers the value of suggestions that the eighteenth century witnessed the transformation of sects into denominations. This thematic structure may help us to evade some of the pitfalls of older approaches to the emotive topics of persecution and toleration and to avoid the teleologies and polarities which have hampered understanding of the interconnections between these two instincts and cultures – both in early modern England and in other periods and regions.

NOTES

1 To echo Blair Worden, 'Toleration and the Cromwellian Protectorate', in W. J. Sheils (ed.), *Persecution and Toleration*, SCH 21 (Oxford, 1984), p. 201.

2 Joseph Lecler, *Toleration and the Reformation*, trans. T. L. Westow, 2 vols (New York, 1960), i. 59; Mark Goldie, 'The theory of religious intolerance in Restoration England', in Ole Peter Grell, Jonathan I. Israel and Nicholas Tyacke (eds), *From Persecution to Toleration: The Glorious Revolution and Religion in England* (Oxford, 1991), pp. 337–8. See also P. R. L. Brown, 'St Augustine's attitude to religious coercion', *Journal of Roman Studies*, 54 (1964), 107–16.

3 Goldie, 'Theory', p. 337 and pp. 331–68 *passim*.

4 H. A. Drake, 'Lambs into lions: explaining early Christian intolerance', *P&P*, 153 (1997), 3–36.

5 See Martin Luther, *Temporal Authority* (1523), in David George Mullan (ed.), *Religious Pluralism in the West: An Anthology* (Oxford, 1998), pp. 85–94; Ole Peter Grell, 'Introduction', in Ole Peter Grell and Bob Scribner (eds), *Tolerance and Intolerance in the European Reformation* (Cambridge, 1996), pp. 4–6; John E. E. Dalberg-Acton, 'The Protestant theory of persecution', in *The History of Freedom and other Essays* (London, 1919 edn), pp. 150–87, at p. 154.

6 Andrew Pettegree, 'The politics of toleration in the Free Netherlands, 1572–1620', in Grell and Scribner (eds), *Tolerance and Intolerance*, p. 198. It may, however, be an exaggeration to say that it was 'only ever a loser's creed'.

7 See Mario Turchetti, 'Religious concord and political tolerance in sixteenth- and seventeenth-century France', *SCJ*, 22 (1991), 15–25.

8 Herbert Butterfield, 'Toleration in early modern times', *Journal of the History of Ideas*, 38 (1977), 573–84, at 573.

9 *The New Testament of Jesus Christ* (Rheims, 1582), Romans 3: 26. Wyclif translated the Greek word in question as 'sustenacion or bering up'; the King James version as 'forbearance': *OED*, s.v. 'toleration' 1582.

10 For helpful conceptual discussions, see T. M. Scanlon, 'The difficulty of tolerance', in David Heyd (ed.), *Toleration: An Elusive Virtue* (Princeton, NJ, 1996); Mary Warnock, 'The limits of toleration', in Susan Mendus and David Edwards (eds), *On Toleration* (Oxford, 1987), pp. 123–39; Susan Mendus, 'Introduction', in Susan Mendus (ed.), *Justifying Toleration: Conceptual and Historical Perspectives* (Cambridge, 1988), pp. 1–19, esp. pp. 3–6; István Bejczy, '*Tolerantia*: a medieval concept', *Journal of the History of Ideas*, 58 (1997), 365–84, esp. 368–70; John Christian Laursen, 'Orientation: clarifying the conceptual issues', in John Christian Laursen (ed.), *Religious Toleration: 'The Variety of Rites' from Cyrus to Defoe* (New York, 1999), pp. 1–11.

11 Phrases used by Daniel Cawdrey and Christopher Fowler in 1657 and 1655 respectively: Worden, 'Toleration and the Cromwellian Protectorate', p. 200.

12 As protested in a proclamation issued by Elizabeth I in 1602: Paul L. Hughes and James F. Larkin (eds), *Tudor Royal Proclamations*, 3 vols (New Haven, 1964–9), iii. 253.

13 Butterfield, 'Toleration', 573.

14 Henry Kamen, *The Rise of Toleration* (London, 1967), pp. 21, 241.

15 Quoted by Joachim Whaley, 'A tolerant society? Religious toleration in the Holy Roman Empire, 1648–1806' and Martin Fitzpatrick, 'Toleration and the Enlightenment movement', in Ole Peter Grell and Roy Porter (eds), *Toleration in Enlightenment Europe* (Cambridge, 2000), pp. 190, 46, respectively.

16 *OED*, s.v. 'tolerance'.

17 See John Christian Laursen, 'Baylean liberalism: tolerance requires nontolerance', in John Christian Laursen and Cary J. Nederman (eds), *Beyond the Persecuting Society: Religion Toleration before the Enlightenment* (Philadelphia, 1998), pp. 197–215.

18 Lord Macaulay, *The History of England from the Accession of James II*, 4 vols (London, 1967 edn; first publ. 1864); W. E. H. Lecky, *History of the Rise and Influence of the Spirit of Rationalism in Europe*, 2 vols (London, 1865); Samuel Rawlinson Gardiner, *The First Two Stuarts and the Puritan Revolution* (New York, 1970 edn; first publ. 1876). See also A. A.

Charitable hatred

Seaton, *The Theory of Toleration under the Later Stuarts* (Cambridge, 1911). In an essay of 1862 (see n. 5 above) Lord Acton did, however, underline the fundamental intolerance of the Protestant reformers.

19 William Haller (ed.), *Tracts on Liberty in the Puritan Revolution, 1638–1647* (New York, 1933–34); William Haller, *The Rise of Puritanism* (New York, 1938); William Haller, *Liberty and Reformation in the Puritan Revolution* (New York, 1955); A. S. P. Woodhouse (ed.) *Puritanism and Liberty* (London, 1938); W. K. Jordan, *The Development of Religious Toleration in England*, 4 vols (London, 1932–40), iii. 9–10; iv. 9–10, 468–9. Another work in the same spirit is Roland H. Bainton, *The Travail of Religious Liberty: Nine Biographical Studies* (Philadelphia, 1951).

20 Sometimes also translated as 'the elimination of magic from the world': Max Weber, *The Protestant Ethic and the Spirit of Capitalism*, trans. Talcott Parsons (London, 1930 edn), p. 105.

21 Lecler, *Toleration and the Reformation*, vol. i, pp. vii–viii; ii. 475, 493, and *passim*.

22 Kamen, *Rise of Toleration*, p. 240.

23 R. I. Moore, *The Formation of a Persecuting Society: Power and Deviance in Western Europe 950–1250* (Oxford, 1987), p. 5 and *passim*. See also Jeffrey Richards, *Sex, Dissidence and Damnation: Minority Groups in the Middle Ages* (London, 1991), p. 14 and *passim*, which emphasises the desire of towns, monarchies and an authoritarian papacy to deal with dissidents and deviants, and sees sexual aberrance as a common motive for their persecution. The emergence of an intolerant society and the evolution of an intellectual order that demonised and dehumanised non-Christians is also discussed in Dominique Iogna-Prat, *Order and Exclusion: Cluny and Christendom Face Heresy, Judaism and Islam (1100–1150)*, trans. Graham Robert Edwards (Ithaca, NY, 2002; first publ. 1998). I owe this reference to Sarah Hamilton.

24 Butterfield, 'Toleration'.

25 Ole Peter Grell, Jonathan I. Israel and Nicholas Tyacke (eds), *From Persecution to Toleration: The Glorious Revolution and Religion in England* (Oxford, 1991), esp. 'Introduction', pp. 12, 14–15, and ch. 13. Some of the early modern contributions to W. J. Sheils (ed.), *Persecution and Toleration*, SCH 21 (Oxford, 1984), anticipate this challenge, especially the essays by N. M. Sutherland, G. R. Elton and Blair Worden.

26 Grell and Scribner (eds), *Tolerance and Intolerance*. Quotations from Grell, 'Introduction', pp. 1, 12, and Heiko A. Oberman, 'The travail of tolerance: containing chaos in early modern Europe', p. 31.

27 Grell and Porter (ed.), *Toleration in Enlightenment Europe*. Quotations and citations: the editors' introduction, 'Toleration in Enlightenment Europe', pp. 1–22, at pp. 1, 13, 19; Sylvana Tomaselli, 'Intolerance, the virtue of princes and radicals', pp. 86–101; Whaley, 'A tolerant society?', p. 182. See also Henry Kamen, 'Inquisition, tolerance and liberty in eighteenth-century Spain', p. 255. The one dissenting voice in a volume otherwise marked by vigorous revisionism is Robert Wokler, 'Multiculturalism and ethnic cleansing in the Enlightenment', pp. 69–85.

28 Ruth Whelan and Carol Baxter (eds), *Toleration and Religious Identity: The Edict of Nantes and its Implications in France, Britain and Ireland* (Dublin, 2003), quotation from Ruth Whelan, 'The other '98', pp. 21–37, at p. 25. See also Nicholas Piqué and Ghislain Waterlot (eds), *Tolérance et Réforme: Elements pour une généalogie du concept de tolérance* (Paris, 1999), which focuses on the troubled evolution of the concept of tolerance in sixteenth- and seventeenth-century France.

29 R. Po-Chia Hsia and Henk van Nierop (eds), *Calvinism and Religious Toleration in the Dutch Golden Age* (Cambridge, 2002). Quotation from Benjamin J. Kaplan, '"Dutch" religious tolerance: celebration and revision', pp. 8–26, at p. 23, quoting Jonathan Israel. See also Christiane Berkvens-Stevelinck, Jonathan I. Israel and G. H. M. Posthumus Meyjes (eds), *The Emergence of Tolerance in the Dutch Republic* (Leiden, 1997), esp. Willem Frijhoff, 'Dimensions de la coexistence confessionelle', pp. 213–37; Richard Bonney and David Trim (eds), *Persecution and Pluralism: Calvinists and Religious Minorities in Early Modern Europe* (Berne, forthcoming 2005).

30 Laursen and Nederman (eds), *Beyond the Persecuting Society*. Quotations from the editors' 'General introduction: political and historical myths in the toleration literature', pp. 8, 1, 5 respectively. Cary J. Nederman and John Christian Laursen (eds), *Difference and Dissent: Theories of Toleration in Medieval and Early Modern Europe* (Lanham, MD, 1996); Laursen (ed.), *Religious Toleration*; Cary J. Nederman, *Worlds of Difference: European Discourses of Toleration, c.1100–c.1550* (University Park, PA, 2000), in which Nederman uses 'toleration' and 'tolerance' interchangeably. For another essay detecting the precedents of Lockean ideas, see Takashi Shogimen, 'From disobedience to toleration: William of Ockham and the medieval discourse of fraternal correction', *JEH*, 52 (2001), 599–622.

31 Quoting from T. J. Hochstrasser's review of Laursen (ed.), *Religious Toleration*, in *EHR*, 115 (2000), 909.

32 Perez Zagorin, *How the Idea of Religious Toleration Came to the West* (Princeton, 2003), pp. 12–13, and see pp. 5–7, 311, and *passim*.

33 John Coffey, *Persecution and Toleration in Protestant England, 1558–1689* (Harlow, 2000), pp. 5, 49, 206, 53 respectively and see pp. 159–60. Andrew R. Murphy's *Conscience and Community: Revisiting Toleration and Religious Dissent in Early Modern Europe and America* (University Park, PA, 2001) also stresses the intensely religious nature of early modern toleration debates, but offers a more cautious assessment of their intellectual and practical impact. This work of 'historically informed political theory' reasserts the limitations of tolerationist theory and practice in early modern England and America. The structure of social attitudes towards dissenters is not part of its remit (see p. xiii).

34 See Chapters 4 and 5, pp. 207–10 and 274–9, for discussion of this evidence and its significance. Margaret Spufford (ed.), *The World of Rural Dissenters 1520–1725* (Cambridge, 1995) contains essays by Plumb, Marsh and Stevenson which pursue this line of argument. The quotations are from Christopher W. Marsh, *The Family of Love in English Society, 1550–1630* (Cambridge, 1994), p. 176, and see pp. 14–15, 249–50; Christopher Marsh, *Popular Religion in Sixteenth-Century England: Holding their Peace* (Basingstoke, 1998), pp. 184–92. Bob Scribner, 'Preconditions of tolerance and intolerance in sixteenth-century Germany', in Grell and Scribner (eds), *Tolerance and Intolerance*, p. 38.

35 Gregory Hanlon, *Confession and Community in Seventeenth-Century France: Catholic and Protestant Coexistence in Aquitaine* (Philadelphia, 1993), p. 12. See also Philip Benedict, '*Un roi, une lois, deux fois:* parameters for the history of Catholic–Reformed coexistence in France, 1555–1685', in Grell and Scribner (ed.), *Tolerance and Intolerance*, pp. 65–93. Benjamin Kaplan is completing a book entitled *Divided by Faith: Religious Conflict and the Practice of Toleration in Early Modern Europe* (Cambridge, MA, forthcoming).

36 Willem Frijhoff, 'The threshold of toleration: interconfessional conviviality in Holland during the early modern period', in his *Embodied Belief: Ten Essays on Religious Culture in Dutch History* (Hilversum, 2002), pp. 39–65, at p. 44. See also his 'Dimensions de la coexistence confessionnelle', in Berkvens-Stevelinck, Israel and Posthumus Meyjes (eds), *Emergence of Toleration*, pp. 213–37.

37 Scott L. Waugh and Peter D. Diehl, *Christendom and its Discontents: Exclusion, Persecution, and Rebellion, 1000–1500* (Cambridge, 1996), quotations from the editors' 'Introduction', p. 5 and *passim*. David Nirenberg, *Communities of Violence: Persecution of Minorities in the Middle Ages* (Princeton, 1996), pp. 7, 9–10. See also R. N. Swanson, *Religion and Devotion in Europe c.1215–c.1515* (Cambridge, 1995), ch. 8.

38 Scribner, 'Preconditions', p. 47.

39 Marsh, *Popular Religion*, p. 191; Hanlon, *Confession and Community*, p. 6.

40 The footnotes to this section highlight only some notable and recent contributions to the historiography of each period. For the concept of the 'long Reformation', see Nicholas Tyacke (ed.), *England's Long Reformation 1500–1800* (London, 1998).

41 A. G. Dickens, *The English Reformation* (London, 1964; 2nd edn, 1989); Christopher Haigh (ed.), *The English Reformation Revised* (Cambridge, 1987); Eamon Duffy, *The Stripping of the Altars: Traditional Religion in England 1400–1580* (New Haven, 1992); Christopher Haigh, *English Reformations: Religion, Politics, and Society under the Tudors* (Oxford, 1993); Richard Rex, *Henry VIII and the English Reformation* (London, 1993); Diarmaid MacCulloch (ed.), *The Reign of Henry VIII: Politics, Policy and Piety* (Basingstoke, 1995); Peter Marshall and Alec Ryrie (eds), *The Beginnings of English Protestantism* (Cambridge, 2002); Alec Ryrie, *The Gospel and Henry VIII: Evangelicals in the Early English Reformation* (Cambridge, 2003).

42 Ethan H. Shagan, *Popular Politics and the English Reformation* (Cambridge, 2003), p. 309 and *passim*.

43 Diarmaid MacCulloch, *Thomas Cranmer: A Life* (New Haven, 1996); Diarmaid MacCulloch, *Tudor Church Militant: Edward VI and the Protestant Reformation* (London, 1999); Catharine Davies, *A Religion of the Word: The Defence of the Reformation in the Reign of Edward VI* (Manchester, 2002).

44 D. M. Loades, *The Reign of Mary Tudor: Politics, Government and Religion in England, 1553–1558* (London, 1979); Lucy Wooding, *Rethinking Catholicism in Reformation England* (Oxford, 2000); Eamon Duffy and David Loades (eds), *The Church of Mary Tudor* (Aldershot, 2005).

45 Norman Jones, *Faith by Statute: Parliament and the Settlement of Religion, 1559* (London, 1982); Diarmaid MacCulloch, *The Later Reformation in England 1547–1603* (Basingstoke, 1990; London, 2001).

46 Caroline Hibbard, *Charles I and the Popish Plot* (Chapel Hill, NC, 1983); Nicholas Tyacke, *Anti-Calvinists: The Rise of English Arminianism c.1590–1640* (Oxford, 1987); Kevin Sharpe, *The Personal Rule of Charles I* (New Haven, 1992); Julian Davies, *The Caroline Captivity of the Church: Charles I and the Remoulding of Anglicanism 1625–1641* (Oxford, 1992); Peter White, *Predestination, Policy and Polemic: Conflict and Consensus in the English Church from the Reformation to the Civil War* (Cambridge, 1992); Kenneth Fincham (ed.), *The Early Stuart Church, 1603–1642* (Basingstoke, 1993); Anthony Milton, *Catholic and Reformed: The Roman and Protestant Churches in English Protestant Thought 1600–1640* (Cambridge, 1995).

47 Jonathan Scott, *England's Troubles: Seventeenth-Century English Political Instability in European Context* (Cambridge, 2000), esp. ch. 5, p. 133.

48 To quote Wallace MacCaffrey, *Elizabeth I* (London, 1993), p. 51.

49 Patrick Collinson, *The Elizabethan Puritan Movement* (Oxford, 1990 edn; first publ. 1967); Patrick Collinson, *The Religion of Protestants: The Church in English Society 1559–*

1625 (Oxford, 1982); Peter Lake, *Moderate Puritans and the Elizabethan Church* (Cambridge, 1982); Peter Lake, *The Boxmaker's Revenge: 'Orthodoxy', 'Heterodoxy' and the Politics of the Parish in Early Stuart London* (Manchester, 2001); Nicholas Tyacke, *The Fortunes of English Puritanism, 1603–1640*, Dr Williams's Library, 44th lecture (London, 1990); Tom Webster, *Godly Clergy in Early Stuart England: The Caroline Puritan Movement, c.1620–1643* (Cambridge, 1997); Peter Lake and Michael Questier (eds), *Conformity and Orthodoxy in the English Church, c. 1560–1660* (Woodbridge, 2000).

50 Anthony Fletcher, *The Outbreak of the English Civil War* (London, 1981); George Yule, *The Independents in the English Civil War* (Cambridge, 1958); George Yule, *Puritans and Politics: The Religious Legislation of the Long Parliament* (Abingdon, 1981); Conrad Russell, *The Causes of the English Civil War* (Oxford, 1990); Conrad Russell, *The Fall of the British Monarchies 1637–1642* (Oxford, 1991); John Morrill, *The Nature of the English Revolution* (Harlow, 1993); Patricia Crawford, 'Charles Stuart, that man of blood', *JBS*, 16 (1977), 41–61.

51 Ivan Roots, *Commonwealth and Protectorate: The English Civil War and its Aftermath* (New York, 1966); William Lamont, *Godly Rule: Politics and Religion 1603–1660* (London, 1969); Claire Cross, 'The Church of England 1646–1660', in G. E. Aylmer (ed.), *The Interregnum: The Quest for Settlement 1646–1660* (London, 1972), pp. 99–120; Worden, 'Toleration and the Cromwellian Protectorate'; John Morrill (ed.), *Oliver Cromwell and the English Revolution* (Harlow, 1990); Jeffrey R. Collins, 'The Church Settlement of Oliver Cromwell', *History*, 87 (2002), 18–40.

52 I. M. Green, *The Re-establishment of the Church of England, 1660–1663* (Oxford, 1978); Ronald Hutton, *The Restoration: A Political and Religious History of England and Wales, 1658–1667* (Oxford, 1985); Paul Seaward, *The Cavalier Parliament and the Reconstruction of the Old Regime, 1661–1667* (Cambridge, 1988); Tim Harris, Paul Seaward and Mark Goldie (eds), *The Politics of Religion in Restoration England* (Oxford, 1990); John Spurr, *The Restoration Church of England, 1646–1689* (New Haven, 1991); N. H. Keeble, *The Restoration: England in the 1660s* (Oxford, 2002), esp. chs 5–6; John Miller, *Popery and Politics in England, 1660–1688* (Cambridge, 1973). A major new contribution is Gary S. De Krey, *London and the Restoration 1659–1683* (Cambridge, 2005) which appeared after this book went to press.

53 W. A. Speck, *Reluctant Revolutionaries: Englishmen and the Revolution of 1688* (Oxford, 1988); Grell, Israel and Tyacke (eds), *From Persecution to Toleration*; Lois Schwoerer (ed.), *The Revolution of 1688–1689* (Cambridge, 1992); J. R. Jones (ed.), *Liberty Secured? Britain Before and After 1688* (Stanford, CA, 1992); Dale Hoak and Mordechai Feingold (eds), *The World of William and Mary: Anglo–Dutch Perspectives on the Revolution of 1688–1689* (Stanford, CA, 1996); Tony Claydon, *William III and the Glorious Revolution* (Cambridge, 1996); Craig Rose, *England in the 1690s: Revolution, Religion and War* (Oxford, 1999), esp. ch. 5.

54 See the comments of R. N. Swanson, *Church and Society in Late Medieval England* (Oxford, 1989), pp. 323, 335, with regard to Lollardy.

55 A phrase borrowed from Andrew D. Brown, *Popular Piety in Late Medieval England: The Diocese of Salisbury 1250–1550* (Oxford, 1995), p. 206 and see p. 335.

56 On this phenomenon, see Michael Questier, *Conversion, Religion and Politics in England 1580–1625* (Cambridge, 1996).

57 As remarked by Richard G. Davies, 'Lollardy and locality', *TRHS*, 6th series, 1 (1991), 191–212, at 212.

58 Keith Thomas, *Religion and the Decline of Magic* (Harmondsworth, 1973 edn), p. 88. See also John Bossy, *Christianity in the West, 1400–1700* (Oxford, 1985), pp. 170–1.

59 See *OED*, s.v. 'ism'.

60 Again only a selection of key works are indicated in the footnotes to this section.

61 K. B. MacFarlane, *Wycliffe and the Beginnings of English Nonconformity* (London, 1952); J. A. F. Thomson, *The Later Lollards 1414–1520* (Oxford, 1965); Margaret Aston, *Lollards and Reformers: Images and Literacy in Late Medieval Religion* (London, 1984); Andrew Hope, 'Lollardy: the stone the builders rejected', in Peter Lake and Maria Dowling (eds), *Protestantism and the National Church in Sixteenth-Century England* (London, 1987), pp. 1–35; Anne Hudson, *The Premature Reformation: Wycliffite Texts and Lollard History* (Oxford, 1988); Shannon McSheffrey, *Gender and Heresy: Women and Men in Lollard Communities 1420–1530* (Philadelphia, 1995) and 'Heresy, orthodoxy and English verracular relgion 1480–1525', *P&P*, 186 (2005), 47–80; Margaret Aston and Colin Richmond (eds), *Lollardy and the Gentry in the Later Middle Ages* (Stroud, 1997); Richard Rex, *The Lollards* (Basingstoke, 2002).

62 A. G. Dickens, *Lollards and Protestants in the Diocese of York 1509–1558* (London, 1982 edn; first publ. Oxford, 1959); William A. Clebsch, *England's Earliest Protestants 1520–1535* (New Haven, 1964); John F. Davis, 'Lollardy and the Reformation in England', *Archiv für Reformationsgeschichte*, 73 (1982), 217–36; John F. Davis, *Heresy and Reformation in the South-East of England, 1520–1559* (London, 1983); Andrew Pettegree, *Marian Protestantism: Six Studies* (Aldershot, 1996); Patrick Collinson, 'Night schools, conventicles and churches: continuities and discontinuities in early Protestant ecclesiology', in Marshall and Ryrie (eds), *Beginnings of English Protestantism*, pp. 209–35; Ryrie, *Gospel and Henry VIII*.

63 Irvin Buckwater Horst, *The Radical Brethren: Anabaptism and the English Reformation to 1558* (Niewuwkoop, 1972); David Loades, 'Anabaptism and English sectarianism in the mid-sixteenth century', in Derek Baker (ed.), *Reform and Reformation: England and the Continent c.1500–c.1750*, SCH Subsidia 2 (Oxford, 1979), pp. 59–70; J. W. Martin, *Religious Radicals in Tudor England* (London, 1989); C. J. Clement, *Religious Radicalism in England 1535–1565* (Carlisle, 1997); Thomas S. Freeman, 'Dissenters from a dissenting Church: the challenge of the Freewillers, 1550–1558', in Marshall and Ryrie (eds), *Beginnings of English Protestantism*, pp. 129–56.

64 Alastair Hamilton, *The Family of Love* (Cambridge, 1981), esp. ch. 6; Marsh, *The Family of Love*.

65 John Bossy, *The English Catholic Community 1570–1850* (London, 1975); J. C. H. Aveling, *The Handle and the Axe: The Catholic Recusants in England from Reformation to Emancipation* (London, 1976); Caroline Hibbard, 'Early Stuart Catholicism: revisions and re-revisions', *Journal of Modern History*, 52 (1980), 1–34; Christopher Haigh, 'From monopoly to minority: Catholicism in early modern England', *TRHS*, 5th series, 31 (1981), 129–47; Alan Dures, *English Catholicism 1558–1642* (Harlow, 1983); Alexandra Walsham, *Church Papists: Catholicism, Conformity and Confessional Polemic in Early Modern England* (Woodbridge, 1993; 2nd edn 1999); Michael Mullett, *Catholics in Britain and Ireland 1558–1829* (Basingstoke, 1998); Marie B. Rowlands (ed.), *Catholics of Parish and Town 1558–1778*, CRS Monograph Series 5 (London, 1999); Ethan H. Shagan (ed.), *Catholics and the 'Protestant Nation': Religious Politics and Identity in Early Modern England* (Manchester, 2005).

66 Collinson, *Elizabethan Puritan Movement*; Patrick Collinson, *Godly People: Essays on English Protestantism and Puritanism* (London, 1983); Lake, *Moderate Puritans*; Christopher Durston and Jacqueline Eales (eds), *The Culture of English Puritanism, 1560–1700* (Basingstoke,

1996); Webster, *Godly Clergy*; John Spurr, *English Puritanism 1603–1689* (Basingstoke, 1998).

67 R. J. Acheson, *Radical Puritans in England 1550–1660* (London, 1990); Murray Tolmie, *The Triumph of the Saints: The Separate Churches of London 1616–1649* (Cambridge, 1977); B. R. White, *The English Separatist Tradition from the Marian Martyrs to the Pilgrim Fathers* (Oxford, 1971); Michael R. Watts, *The Dissenters: From the Reformation to the French Revolution* (Oxford, 1978), pt I. For the mid-seventeenth century, see Geoffrey F. Nuttall, *Visible Saints: The Congregational Way 1640–1660* (Oxford, 1957); Yule, *Independents*.

68 B. R. White, *The English Baptists of the Seventeenth Century* (London, 1983); Stephen Wright, 'The British Baptists and politics, 1603–49', unpubl. PhD dissertation (King's College, London, 2002).

69 Lake, *Boxmaker's Revenge*, passim, esp. pp. 397–403, 407, 413. See also David R. Como, *Blown by the Spirit: Puritanism and the Emergence of an Antinomian Underground in Pre-Civil-War England* (Stanford, CA, 2004).

70 A. L. Morton, *The World of the Ranters: Religious Radicalism in the English Revolution* (London, 1970); B. S. Capp, *The Fifth Monarchy Men: A Study in Seventeenth-Century English Millenarianism* (London, 1972); Christopher Hill, *The World Turned Upside Down: Radical Ideas during the English Revolution* (Harmondsworth, 1975 edn; first publ. 1972); Christopher Hill, Barry Reay and William Lamont (eds), *The World of the Muggletonians* (London, 1983); J. F. MacGregor and Barry Reay (eds), *Radical Religion in the English Revolution* (Oxford, 1984); J. C. Davis, *Fear, Myth and History: The Ranters and the Historians* (Cambridge, 1986). On the Quakers, see William C. Braithwaite, *The Beginnings of Quakerism* (Cambridge, 1970 edn; first publ. 1912) and *The Second Period of Quakerism* (Cambridge, 1961 edn; first publ. 1919); Barry Reay, *The Quakers and the English Revolution* (London, 1985); Adrian Davies, *The Quakers in English Society 1655–1725* (Oxford, 2000); Rosemary Moore, *The Light in their Consciences: The Early Quakers in Britain 1646–1666* (University Park, PA, 2000); Kate Peters, *Print Culture and the Early Quakers* (Cambridge, 2005).

71 John Morrill, 'The Church in England, 1642–9', in John Morrill (ed.), *Reactions to the English Civil War 1642–1649* (London, 1982), pp. 89–114, at p. 90; Spurr, *Restoration Church*, ch. 1. For Anglicanism, see Judith Maltby *Prayer Book and People in Elizabethan and Early Stuart England* (Cambridge, 1998) and '"The good old way": prayer book Protestantism in the 1640s and 1650s', in R. N. Swanson (ed.), *The Church and the Book*, SCH 38 (Woodbridge, 2004), pp. 233–56.

72 H. J. McLachlan, *Socinianism in Seventeenth-Century England* (Oxford, 1951); Richard H. Popkin, 'The deist challenge', in Grell, Israel and Tyacke (eds), *From Persecution to Toleration*, pp. 195–215; Justin Champion, *The Pillars of Priestcraft Shaken: The Church of England and its Enemies, 1660–1730* (Cambridge, 1992).

73 Andrew Pettegree, *Foreign Protestant Communities in Sixteenth-Century London* (Oxford, 1986); Ole Peter Grell, *Dutch Calvinists in Early Stuart London: The Dutch Church in Austin Friars 1603–1642* (Leiden, 1989); Ole Peter Grell, *Calvinist Exiles in Tudor and Stuart England* (Aldershot, 1996); Bernard Cottret, *The Huguenots in England: Immigration and Settlement c.1550–1700* (Cambridge and Paris, 1991); Marcel Backhouse, *The Flemish and Walloon Communities at Sandwich during the Reign of Elizabeth I (1561–1603)* (Brussels, 1995); Andrew Spicer, *The French-Speaking Reformed Community and their Church in Southampton 1567–c.1620*, Southampton Records Series 39 (Southampton, 1997); Robin D. Gwynn, *Huguenot Heritage: The History and Contribution of the*

Huguenots in Britain (Brighton, 2001 edn; first publ. 1985).

74 Cecil Roth, *A History of the Jews in England* (Oxford, 1978 edn; first publ. 1941); David S. Katz, *The Jews in the History of England 1485–1850* (Oxford, 1994); Todd Endelman, *The Jews of Georgian England 1714–1830: Tradition and Change in a Liberal Society* (Philadelphia, 1979); Todd Endelman, *The Jews of Britain, 1656 to 2002* (Berkeley, CA, 2002).

75 Nabil Matar, *Islam in Britain 1558–1685* (Cambridge, 1998); Nabil Matar, *Turks, Moors and Englishmen in the Age of Discovery* (New York, 1999).

76 Robert E. Lerner, *The Heresy of the Free Spirit in the Later Middle Ages* (Berkeley, CA, 1972); Davis, *Fear, Myth and History*.

77 Rex, *Lollards*, esp. ch. 6.

78 Peter Lake, 'Anti-popery: the structure of a prejudice', in Richard Cust and Ann Hughes (eds), *Conflict in Early Stuart England: Studies in Religion and Politics 1603–1642* (Harlow, 1989), pp. 72–106. See also Carol Z. Wiener, 'The beleaguered isle: a study of Elizabethan and early Jacobean anti-Catholicism', *P&P*, 51 (1971), 27–62.

79 Marsh, *Family of Love*, p. 126; Jason Peacey, 'The paranoid prelate: Archbishop Laud and the puritan plot', in Barry Coward and Julian Swann (eds), *Conspiracies and Conspiracy Theory in Early Modern Europe: From the Waldensians to the French Revolution* (Aldershot, 2004), pp. 113–34.

80 Davies, *Religion of the Word*, ch. 2, esp. pp. 68, 110.

81 Ann Hughes, *Gangraena and the Struggle for the English Revolution* (Oxford, 2004), p. 11.

82 To borrow a phrase from Alison Shell, *Catholicism, Controversy and the English Literary Imagination, 1558–1660* (Cambridge, 1990), p. 16.

83 For some examples of this process, see Susan Wabuda, 'Henry Bull, Miles Coverdale, and the making of Foxe's Book of Martyrs', in Diana Wood (ed.), *Martyrs and Martyrologies*, SCH 30 (Oxford, 1993), pp. 245–58; Susan Wabuda, 'Equivocation and recantation during the English Reformation: the "subtle shadows" of Dr Edward Crome', *JEH*, 44 (1993), 224–42; Freeman, 'Dissenters'; Walsham, *Church Papists*. For the editing of the Quaker George Fox's journal by Thomas Ellwood, see Nigel Smith (ed.), *George Fox: The Journal* (Harmondsworth, 1998), pp. xxii, xxx.

84 See Swanson, *Church and Society*, p. 335; Norman P. Tanner (ed.), *Heresy Trials in the Diocese of Norwich, 1428–31*, Camden Society, 4th series, 20 (1977), pp. 19–20; Anne Hudson, 'The examination of Lollards', repr. in Anne Hudson, *Lollards and their Books* (London, 1985), pp. 125–40.

85 Margaret Aston, 'Lollardy and the Reformation: survival or revival?', *History*, 49 (1964), 149–70; Patrick Collinson, 'Truth and legend: the veracity of John Foxe's Book of Martyrs', in A. C. Duke and C. A. Tamse (eds), *Clio's Mirror: Historiography in Britain and the Netherlands* (Zutphen, 1985), pp. 31–54; Euan Cameron, 'Medieval heretics as Protestant martyrs', in Diana Wood (ed.), *Martyrs and Martyrologies*, SCH 30 (Oxford, 1993), pp. 185–207.

86 Patrick Collinson, 'Towards a broader understanding of the early dissenting tradition', in his *Godly People*, pp. 527–62.

Chapter 2

Fraternal correction and holy violence: the pursuit of uniformity and the enforcement of religious orthodoxy

In sixteenth- and seventeenth-century England it was widely believed that persecution of a false religion and its adherents was not merely permissible but, moreover, a laudable and virtuous act of devotion and piety. The convictions that underpinned Bishop Richard Fox's decision to found Corpus Christi College, Oxford, in 1516 for 'the extirpation of heresy and error, and the augmentation of the orthodox faith' continued to find expression in sermons, tracts, pamphlets, proclamations and speeches throughout the Tudor and Stuart period.[1] Nowhere is the notion that religious heterogeneity was inherently noxious and evil more clearly articulated than in the various Acts of Uniformity issued by Henry VIII and his successors. In 1539, Parliament passed a statute 'abolishing diversity in opinions', the preamble to which underlined 'the great and quiet assurance, prosperous increase and other innumerable commodities which have ever ensued, come and followed of concord, agreement and unity ... as also the manifold perils, dangers and inconveniences which have heretofore in many places and regions grown, sprung and arisen' from discord and dissension in 'matters of Christian religion'. This act of six articles declared the eradication of alternative tenets a 'most godly enterprise' that would contribute to the glory and honour of the Lord and the comfort and welfare of the English people.[2] Such sentiments were echoed in the reign of Mary I by Cardinal Reginald Pole, who averred that there was 'no greater work of cruelty' to a nation or community than 'to nourish or favour' heretics within it.[3] Preaching at Westminster Abbey in 1571, Edwin Sandys, Bishop of London, issued an equally impassioned plea to assembled MPs for a concerted campaign of religious coercion. Calling for the 'compelling [of] all subjects to hear God's word and receive His sacraments', he warned his audience that pluralism was the bane of a Christian state: 'This liberty, that men may openly profess diversity of religion, must needs be dangerous ... One God, one king, one faith, one profession, is fit for one monarchy and commonwealth. Division weakeneth: concord strengtheneth ... Let conformity and unity in religion be provided for; and it shall be as a wall of defence unto this realm.'[4] In 1645, the puritan divine Edmund Calamy discoursed no less feelingly on the subject of his country's 'self-murdering divisions', while the statute restoring the Church of England and reinstating the Book of Common Prayer in 1662 insisted that 'nothing conduceth more to the settling of the peace of this nation', the propagation of the Protestant religion, and the allaying of 'the present distempers which the indisposition of the time hath contracted [...] than a universal agreement in the public worship of Almighty God'.[5] Two decades later, Bishop John Fell of Oxford would similarly denounce proposals for the comprehension and toleration of dissenters as utterly inimical to and 'certainly destructive of our reformed religion'.[6] Such writers were in no doubt that liturgical and theological disunity was the devil's work, a satanic stratagem to subvert the Church of Christ and seduce man and womankind to commit grievous sins.

A number of interrelated assumptions underlay this commitment to religious uniformity and provided a charter for persecution. The task of the first part of this chapter is to unravel this logic and delineate its various intellectual elements. The second part explores how the fusion of ecclesiastical and secular authority that predated, but was strongly cemented by, the Reformation led to the politicisation of religious deviance in the course of the period. It also examines the tensions engendered by differing conceptions of the relationship between the Church and the nation, and between the visible community of the faithful and the vast mass of the unregenerate. From there we turn to the questions and debates that arose around the aims, objectives and mechanisms of civil and ecclesiastical intolerance. The last section explores the institutions charged with enforcing uniformity and the full range of techniques they employed to repress theological dissent and liturgical nonconformity.

THE THEOLOGY OF RELIGIOUS INTOLERANCE

It must be stressed at the outset that in discussing the theme of correcting and punishing deviance Tudor and Stuart writers were heavily indebted to the work of St Augustine. In the early fifth century, in response to the threat presented by the North African sect of the Donatists, the bishop of Hippo had provided a blueprint for the doctrine of religious compulsion. Turning away from his earlier conviction that no one should be forced to embrace the faith of Christ against his or her will, he began to argue that coercion could be employed to induce the recalcitrant to accept the truth. In a series of famous letters, he not only justified the responsibility of the Church to discipline erring members but also upheld the right, and indeed duty, of civil authorities to utilise the law to give these spiritual sanctions weight and force. The state was under an obligation to supplement the work of the ecclesiastical hierarchy in rousing the wayward from their 'lethargic sleep' in schism and false belief and awakening them to the salvation which could only be found in the unity of the Catholic Church. Invoking the parable of the banquet and applying the lesson of *'compelle intrare'* to his own times, Augustine laid down principles legitimating the use of physical penalties against those who rejected or schismatically divided themselves from the doctrine and communion of Christ. Like the shepherd who brought his wandering sheep back to the flock by using his crook, the Christian magistrate could and should apply pressure to rescue individuals who strayed from the path of righteousness. Just as God used the 'sharp medicine of tribulation' as well as 'sweet instruction' to educate and reclaim sinners, so too were governors to chastise lovingly their deviant subjects.[7] The threat of punishment might effect a change of heart and secure their conversion.

The 'pedagogy of fear' that lay at the heart of Augustine's vision of just and loving persecution did not, however, extend to killing false believers. With St Jerome, he believed that room should always be left for the possibility of repentance: no brother should be suppressed prematurely. But other patristic writers like Optatus, Bishop of Milevis, adopted a more stringent attitude, asking 'Why should it be wrong to vindicate God by the death of those that are guilty?'[8] By the late thirteenth century this argument had become axiomatic. According to Thomas Aquinas's *Summa Theologica*, obstinate heretics deserved to be shut off from the Church and worldly society not merely symbolically by means of excommunication but also literally in the shape of bodily extermination. Those who wilfully defied and departed from the faith in which they had been baptised not only committed a heinous personal crime: they also presented a serious risk to the society in which they resided. Like decaying flesh, they had to be amputated to preserve the health of the community at large.[9]

This was the philosophical tradition within which the Catholic clergy and laity of pre- and post-Reformation England instinctively worked. The compelling claims of Augustine and Aquinas regarding the obligation of Church and state to use coercion to bring the heterodox back into the fold continued to be invoked by fifteenth- and early sixteenth-century prelates and politicians who battled to contain and extinguish Lollardy and later Lutheranism. Preaching at Paul's Cross in 1526 on the occasion of the recantation of the evangelical Robert Barnes and a public bonfire of prohibited books, John Fisher declared heresy 'a perilous weed', 'the seed of the devil' sowed to corrupt human hearts, blind their sight, quench their piety, and finally murder their souls. To permit such 'spiritual serial killers' to roam free was to expose the innocent to certain slaughter.[10] As Thomas More wrote in his famous *Dialogue* against William Tyndale, the 'carbuncle' of heresy had to be chopped out lest it infect the 'remanaunt' of the commonwealth. Capital punishment was like the surgical removal of a cancerous lump.[11]

The same points were powerfully restated by such figures as the Observant friar Alfonso de Castro, Bishop of Cuenca, one of the foremost Spanish authorities on the theory and practice of punishing heretics, who accompanied Philip II to England and published a book on the subject in 1556, urging him to carry on the godly work he had begun back in Spain.[12] In a sermon delivered the following year, Edmund Bonner preached that 'those that be evil, of love, we ought to procure unto them theyr correction' and exhorted governors to imitate the 'good surgeon [who] cutteth away a putryfied and festred member, for the love he hath to the hole body'. When Dr John Story, chancellor of Oxford and London, expressed his ardent hope that 'discreet severity' might restore 'universal unity in religion' he too was echoing the Augustinian dictum of charitable zeal.[13] At the turn of the seventeenth century, in his massive *Treatise of three conversions*, the Jesuit Robert Persons defended the Marian burnings of the 1550s in similar terms: it was the duty of Catholic authorities to punish 'not only spiritually by Ecclesiastical censures, but corporally also with the sword when need requireth' in order to prevent the ravenous wolf from devouring Christ's flock of lambs.[14] Such statements were predicated on a key distinction between just and unjust persecution most clearly articulated by the seminary priest Thomas Hide in a treatise of 1581. While the latter was afflicted with malicious and 'tyrannicall affection to oppress them', the former was applied with kindness and compassion to amend them.[15]

Despite their fierce denunciation of the barbarous cruelty of Marian Catholicism and the legendary brutality of the Inquisition, Protestants did not discard the heritage of the great Latin father. Augustine remained a revered source of authority for post-Reformation writers who sought to justify the enforcement of religious uniformity.[16] Like the author of the Lollard tract *The lanterne of lyghte* republished as evangelical propaganda in the 1530s, they too regarded coercion as a legitimate weapon in the quest to persuade the misguided to see the light of the Gospel: 'as juste wrath is no wrath, but a fervent diligence, so is rightwyse smytynge no smytynge'.[17] The Church of England homily 'on charity' composed before 1547 also stressed the responsibility of Christian governors to take steps to discipline erring subjects, even 'as every loving father correcteth his naturall son when he doeth amisse', and if necessary to sever such 'evill persons' from society permanently.[18] The exile George Joye likewise reprimanded the 'fond, foolish pity' of sparing a murderer or adulterer who 'hurteth the whole commonalty' and it is clear from the abortive Edwardian revision of canon law, the *Reformatio Legum*, that this precept was regarded as applying to religious deviants as well as moral offenders. Arians, Anabaptists and other arrogant radicals and 'fireballs' who spread perverse and pestilential opinions were to be treated as 'gangrenous members': to show clemency to those who peddled false doctrine was a misplaced mercy that put others in terrible peril.[19] Elizabethan writers from John Jewel to Richard Hooker agreed that rulers were duty-bound to pressure their people into hearing the message of freely given grace embedded in the Gospels. As Bishop Thomas Bilson reminded readers of his *True difference between Christian subjection and unchristian rebellion* (1585), St Paul himself had been 'compelled to Christianitie by corporeal violence'.[20]

These themes continued to be rehearsed during the Civil War, Interregnum and Restoration. The Presbyterian Thomas Edwards reiterated the claim that physical punishment could bring a heretic to his senses, as well as help to preserve the Church from the danger of fatal infection: 'there is in coercive power a naturalnesse and sutablenesse to work upon the outward man for the furtherance of spirituall good'.[21] In the 1660s, Bishop Gilbert Sheldon of London wrote that 'only a resolute execution of the law' could cure the great wounds inflicted by sectarianism and nonconformity: 'they who will not be governed as men by reason and persuasions should be governed as beasts by power and force'.[22] Alluding to Proverbs 23: 13–14 ('Withhold not correction from the child ... Thou shalt beat him with the rod, and shalt deliver his soul from hell'), others too subscribed to the view that rigorous discipline was nothing less than an act of benevolence and a branch of education. 'Punishments', declared the late seventeenth-century rector of Bath, Joseph Glanvill, were 'instruments of real reformation'; the 'soft and gentle remedies' of statutory penalties, said the Northamptonshire minister Thomas Ashenden in 1682, were applied in the hope that 'a little smart might make the scales peel off from men's eyes'. 'Exterior compulsion', observed the lay theologian Henry Dodwell, could be 'a probable occasion' to correct an erroneous conscience: fear had often 'proved the beginning of wisdom'.[23] The notion that suffering and pain could be therapeutic and regenerative was still alive and well after the Glorious Revolution, as revealed by several tracts published by John Locke's most eloquent opponent, the Oxford divine Jonas Proast. Writing against the Act of Toleration of 1689, Proast followed in the footsteps of earlier commentators in insisting that force could indeed be efficacious in the struggle to enlighten false believers and in condemning those who would allow men liberty to commit spiritual suicide. He too defended the Anglican penal laws against dissenters as a form of schoolmasterly chastisement, a set of gentle pricks to assist the pastoral process of catechesis.[24]

The Old Testament was a source of particular inspiration for Protestant theorists of intolerance. In setting forth the duties of the episcopate, Edwin Sandys cited Ezekiel 3: 8 ('if though speakest not to warn from his wicked way, his soul will I require at thine hand')[25] and it was a clerical commonplace that civil officials who allowed the sword to grow rusty in the scabbard would be held guilty as accomplices to the death of each and every heretic. To tolerate stubborn papists, urged a delegation of Irish bishops in November 1626, was to make one an 'accessory' not just to 'all their abominations of popery, but also ... to the perdition of the seduced people which perish in the deluge of Catholick apostasy'.[26] The Pentateuch provided an emphatic mandate for taking draconian action against misbelievers: Deuteronomy 13: 6–11 insisted that no mercy could be shown to those who enticed their brethren to worship other gods and ordered that idolaters be ruthlessly stoned to death. These convictions acquired special resonance in the context of the renewed emphasis on Hebrew models of kingship that accompanied the spread and entrench-ment of the Reformation and the growing belief that ancient Israel was the perfect pattern and prototype of the kind of godly nation which the Lord expected England to become. Just as biblical rulers like Josiah, Asa and Hezekiah had zealously purged their kingdoms of idolatry, so too were Tudor and Stuart sovereigns expected to endeavour to extirpate all traces of it from their realms, emulating Constantine, Justinian, Theodosius and other godly emperors of old.[27]

Throughout the period, royal proclamations, the preambles of parlia-mentary statutes and other forms of official propaganda were saturated with solemn claims about the weighty spiritual responsibilities of the Christian prince. Henry VIII consciously fashioned himself in the image of Hebrew kings like David and Solomon, not least on the illustrated title-page of the Great Bible and in his majestic performance, clad in the white of theological purity, at the trial of the sacramentarian John Lambert in 1538, when he disputed with the defendant and offered him one last chance to repent before sentencing him to death on the stake.[28] Propagation of the myth of the precocious young Protestant Edward VI as the reincarnation of Josiah was accompanied by much emphasis on his exemplary determination to remove all impediments to religious purity.[29] Philip and Mary declared themselves 'most entirely and earnestly' dedicated to 'the preservation and safety, as well of the souls as of the bodies' of 'all their good and loving subjects' and to the discovering and eradicating of all false doctrine, while an edict of Elizabeth insisted that it was 'a thing appertaining chiefly' to Christian monarchs 'to have a special care' to train up their people in the true religion and restrain those who sought to subvert it. James I, who likewise modelled himself on Moses and Solomon, acknowledged that 'our duetie towards God requireth ... that what untractable men doe not performe upon admonition they must be compelled unto by Authoritie'; it was incumbent upon 'a Religious and wise King ... [to] plant good seed with one hand' and 'to roote out with the other as farre as he can, the Cockle and Tares of Heresie that doe ordinarily grow up amongst the Lords Wheat'.[30]

The notion that early modern sovereigns were no less bound than their ancient forebears to uphold theological orthodoxy with the aid of physical might was integrally linked with the conviction that they had a divine commission to resurrect the severe sanctions against sin enshrined in the Mosaic law. Such assumptions were partly responsible for the Henrician act of 1533 making sodomy (homosexuality) a felony.[31] They permeated the body of legislation repressing drunkenness, swearing and sabbath-breaking placed on the statute book in the seventeenth century and they peaked with the Rump Parliament's notorious Adultery Act of 1650, which imposed the death penalty on those who broke the holy bond of matrimony and inflicted a three-month prison sentence on convicted fornicators.[32] This high conception of regal office survived the republican experiment of the 1650s and exerted influence for the rest of the century. As Tony Claydon has shown, the notion that the prince had a sacred duty to repress gross immorality and idolatry also lay at the heart of William III's 'godly revolution'. The politique architect of the Act of Toleration still found it vital to project himself as a pious enemy and avenger of popery and vice, a providential instrument exalted to the throne to defend the true Church and restore its original purity, a 'second Hezekiah'. It is a mistake to dismiss this empowering rhetoric as 'a conventional gift-wrapping for a case whose substance was other principles'. Queen Anne too would adopt it to unite the English nation behind her after 1702.[33]

Preachers invoked the same language to persuade monarchs and their advisers to grasp the nettle and deal out strict forms of discipline to religious deviants. Thus Cardinal Pole informed Mary: 'God hath given the sceptre and the sword into her Majesty's hands for no other reason than that ribaldry and disobedience to the holy laws may be punished'.[34] In a letter to the Lord Protector written in 1550, Jean Calvin admonished him not to flinch from executing seditious Anabaptists and obstinate Catholics as befitted the chosen deputy of the Almighty, 'seeyng that they quarell not onely agaynst the king, but also against God'.[35] Thomas Cranmer used similar arguments to urge Edward to sign the warrant condemning the Kentish heretic Joan Bocher, who had stubbornly refused to retract her belief that Christ had not taken flesh of the Virgin Mary. Invoking the harsh precedent in Exodus decreeing that blasphemers should be stoned to death, he reminded the young king that it was his obligation as the Lord's lieutenant to stamp out heinous error and impiety.[36] In 1572 Elizabeth I was exhorted by her bishops to set aside 'foolish pitie' and consent to the execution of her Catholic cousin, Mary Queen of Scots,[37] and in a sermon preached later that decade Edwin Sandys insisted that the magistrate must not recoil from shedding the blood of idolaters since the Almighty had commanded that false prophets should be judicially executed.

If kings and queens shirked this unsavoury task, they stood in danger of being convicted of soul-murder at the Last Judgement, not to mention running the risk of having their crowns knocked from their heads. The fate of the Old Testament ruler Saul, who had been dispossessed of his kingdom for negligently sparing wicked Agag, was held up as a stark example of how the Lord dealt with monarchs who were lax and lukewarm in upholding His cause.[38] In 1627, James Ussher, Archbishop of Armagh, would warn Charles I of the consequences of neglecting to compel recusants to attend the state Church in a hardly less menacing vein: this was 'to make way for the Lord to be angry with you, and consume you and your house'.[39] Nearly fifty years on, in 1675, the Peterhouse divine Miles Barne could be found lecturing Charles II at Whitehall on his responsibility to act as a 'nursing father' to his subjects and 'enforce spiritual censures by corporal penalties'.[40]

The heavy burden and mantle of religious persecution and coercion did not, however, fall solely upon anointed monarchs. It extended down the social ladder to lesser magistrates as well. They too were God's agents of wrath, as laid down in Romans 13. As the Ipswich preacher Samuel Ward declared in a sermon of 1618, they too had a duty to work in tandem with the ministry as a terror to evil doers, to be 'guardians and tutors' to those over whom they exercised jurisdiction – to exhibit what Richard Sibbes called 'holy violence' in the performance of their duties, which included restraining the false believers who lived within their midst.[41] These convictions reached a high point of intensity during the 'Puritan Revolution', acquiring particular urgency in the context of the widespread belief that the age was witnessing the final phase of a vast cosmic struggle against Antichrist and the devil and that persecution of the ungodly would hasten the advent of the long-awaited millennium. More generally, it was believed that every man was bound to act as his brother's keeper, sternly to rebuke his faults and forcibly to prevent him from falling into the abyss of damnation. In the course of a vehement polemical attack upon the Family of Love published in 1579, John Knewstub insisted that ordinary Christians had a responsibility 'to be the chief doers in the death and execution' of all heretics, even if they were their own friends and relatives.[42]

Underlying all the statements quoted above lay the assumption that failure to implement justice against religious and moral deviants was a recipe for divine retribution, if not complete destruction. As a speaker in the House of Commons declared in 1601, God would not allow such sins to go unpunished 'neither in the offenders themselves, nor in us that tolerate the same, but will lay his heavy hand of wrath and indignation upon this land'.[43] Intolerance of one's confessional enemies, no less than heinous sinners, was necessary to appease the rage of the Almighty and deflect devastating temporal judgements. It was taken for granted that to condone wicked doctrine and worship was to expose the nation at large to the threat of annihilation. The Edwardian bishop of Gloucester John Hooper used the episode of Jonah being thrown overboard to demonstrate that unless sinners were sharply disciplined the entire community would suffer.[44]

Two other biblical topoi were critical here: the case of Achan (Joshua 7), for whose treacherous theft of the forbidden spoil of Jericho God had punished Israel with military defeat until Joshua detected it and stoned him to death, and Phineas (Numbers 25: 1–8), who had stayed the plague inflicted as punishment for the unholy whoredom the Israelites had committed with the daughters of Moab by thrusting a javelin through the belly and loins of one copulating couple. Alluding to the former story, Sir Nathaniel Rich reminded the House of Commons in 1624 that no country could flourish 'so long as the execrable thing was among them' and a year later MPs called for due execution of the laws against Jesuits and papists as the 'best preservative' and 'cure' of the current epidemic ravaging the country.[45] The same fears underpinned the Solemn League and Covenant of 1643, which pledged to 'endeavour the extirpation of popery, prelacy, superstition, heresy' and 'schism', 'lest we partake in other men's sins and thereby be in danger to receive their plagues', as well as the days of public humiliation held later that decade to seek God's assistance for the suppression of sectarian error and blasphemy. The tale of Achan and the 'accursed thing' also played a considerable part in shaping the outlook and policies of Oliver Cromwell in the last years of his life.[46] In a tract of 1653, Alexander Ross insisted that 'the heavy judgements of God' would inevitably be poured down upon 'that State or Kingdom where contrary Religions are allowed'.[47] At root, the argument for persecution was an argument for sheer survival.[48]

Countries that turned a blind eye to error and heresy could also be punished more indirectly and subtly, in the form of sedition and anarchy, which would dissolve the internal sinews of society and in turn provoke the righteous anger of God. Thus William Laud warned in a sermon preached at Whitehall in 1625 that 'great and multiplied sin' would lead a nation to 'inwardly melt' and Roger L'Estrange wrote in his tract *Toleration discuss'd* (1663) that religious uniformity was 'the Ciment of both Christian, and Civil Societies: Take That away, and the Parts drop from the Body'.[49] Dissenters quite literally divided, rent and tore communities in pieces; their beliefs and practices presented an affront to conventional ethics and were corrosive of the structures of deference which were fundamental to its harmonious working. The refusal of Lollards to swear oaths threatened the established judicial order, as did the Jesuit doctrine of equivocation. The antinomian behaviour of Ranters and Quakers who ignored the deuteronomic taboos against sex outside marriage and 'went naked for a sign' offended traditional morality and the spectre of the polygamous kingdom of the Anabaptists in Münster was never far from the minds of contemporaries after it toppled in 1534–35, as an emblem of the chaos and evil to which unbridled heresy gave rise. Quaker pacifism was equally disturbing in a context in which the state lacked a standing army and relied on its citizens to defend it from foreign attacks. The

same sect's rejection of tithes undermined the operation of the national
Church and its disdain of symbolic gestures such as the doffing of one's hat to
a superior was regarded as a pernicious overturning of the established social
order. John Locke himself thought that it was 'properly the magistrate's
business' to suppress 'corrupt manners, and the debaucheries of life'. Where
doctrinal dissent was conjoined with 'lasciviousness, and all sorts of
debauchery', the state was within its rights to act to contain it.[50]

Heretics and papists were considered traitors to the state in a double sense:
their mere presence within a country provoked divine ire and their opposition
to the religion sanctioned by the dominant regime led them to perturb the
common peace and engage in desperate terrorist enterprises to overthrow the
status quo. It was only prudent for the authorities to restrain and expel
potential rebels using the weapon of penal legislation. Subversion was pre-
sumed to be second nature to dissenters and deviants and experience
repeatedly appeared to prove this premise to be correct. Lollardy quickly
became synonymous with rebellion in the fifteenth century, against the
backdrop of allegations that it had played a key role in stirring up the Peasants'
Revolt (1381) and the insurrections of 1414 and 1431.[51]

Pius V's papal bull of 1570 excommunicating the queen and absolving her
subjects of allegiance to her confirmed the connection between popery and
treachery, as did the long list of conspiracies in which Catholics were
implicated from the Elizabethan period onwards – starting with the Northern
Rising (1569), stretching through the various coups and assassination
schemes linked with Mary Queen of Scots to the Spanish Armada (1588), the
Gunpowder Treason (1605), and the Irish Massacre (1641), and culminating
in 1678 with the fantastic fiction that was Titus Oates' Popish Plot. The
Glorious Revolution itself bears witness to the fear that James II was intent
upon ruining the state by returning the nation to Roman thraldom. Puritans
also earned an enduring reputation for civil disobedience from the writings of
Calvinist resistance theorists like John Knox and Theodore Beza, the exploits
of fringe figures like the self-proclaimed messiah William Hacket, and above
all their involvement in the constitutional revolution which Restoration
historians would relabel the 'Great Rebellion'.[52] In the later part of the seventeenth century, the idea that dissenting conventicles were seedbeds of sedition
was lent credibility by nonconformist involvement in the Rye House Plot
(1683) and the Monmouth Rebellion (1685), while the link between radical
millenarianism and political insubordination was cemented by the Fifth
Monarchist rising led by Thomas Venner in 1661.

Such episodes provided grist to the mill of the Restoration divine Samuel
Parker whose *Discourse of ecclesiastical politie* (1669) powerfully defended the
case that 'supreme authority' and 'severe government over men's consciences
and Religious perswasions' was 'absolutely necessary to the Peace and

Happiness of ... Kingdoms'.[53] As Conrad Russell commented, as long as governments subscribed to the view that it was their duty to enforce adherence to the true religion, so the notion that subjects who espoused rival faiths were disloyal had the quality of a self-fulfilling prophecy.[54] And no one doubted that rulers were justified in intervening against individuals whose heterodox beliefs led them to commit outrageous criminal acts: Thomas Hobbes may have condemned official interference in people's private opinions in the *Leviathan* but he energetically upheld it where spiritual dissent precipitated public disorder.[55] By the 1670s and 1680s, a more secular rhetoric of reason of state was beginning to take root more widely within English society. Roger L'Estrange and others would accept that matters of 'meere religion' and personal faith were essentially outside the jurisdiction of the civil authorities but they justified persecution as a necessary remedy of the chaos and anarchy that typically resulted from untrammelled consciences. Mark Knights sees this subtle transmutation in the philosophy of religious coercion in the reign of James II as a significant turning point.[56]

The early modern ideology of religious intolerance thus comprised various strands and threads. Inspired by the thinking of the great patriarch St Augustine, grounded in the Hebrew and Christian scriptures, and supplemented by arguments drawn from past history and recent experience, it was a discourse that exerted enormous influence at the end of the seventeenth century, no less than at the beginning of the sixteenth. The chorus of voices vehemently defending the necessity, if not the virtue, of persecution vastly outnumbered the small minority who cried passionately and on principle for toleration.

THE RISE OF THE ERASTIAN STATE AND THE IDEAL OF A NATIONAL CHURCH

Before we proceed to examine the practical measures by which the early modern English state and Church sought to enforce uniformity and to persuade religious minorities to return to the fold, we must examine the legal and political context from which they grew. The idea that the ecclesiastical and civil authorities were joint partners in the pursuit and punishment of dissent had a long history in Europe and England: the forging of an alliance between them to defend and uphold orthodoxy predated the Reformation. The formalisation of this link may be traced to the late twelfth and thirteenth centuries, when the rise of the Cathars, Humiliati and Waldensians led to the establishment of the Inquisition and prompted the papacy to centralise procedures of investigation and prosecution. Lucius III's decree *Ad abolendam* (1184) ordered the handing over of obdurate heretics to the secular power for punishment and a bull of 1199 promulgated by Innocent III, *Vergentis in senium*, assimilated heresy with the Roman law crime of *lèse-majesté*. Endorsed by the Fourth Lateran Council in 1215, these conventions were integrated into the imperial legislation issued by Frederick II (Barbarossa) and in turn codified by a pontifical constitution issued by Gregory IX in 1231, *Excommunicamus et anathematisamus*. In 1298 Boniface VIII recommended that this be adopted as a model in all states.[57]

It was not until the emergence of Wycliffism in the fourteenth century that the question of applying these judicial procedures and reconciling them with the evolving principles of the Common Law really arose in relation to England. In the absence of an Inquisition, the responsibility for dealing with religious dissidence fell to the episcopal ordinaries. The duty of civil magistrates to co-operate with the bishops in the suppression of doctrinal heterodoxy was laid out in legislation passed in the reigns of Richard II and his successors. Statutes of 1382 and 1388 strengthened and streamlined the cumbersome process of invoking the writ *de excommunicatio capiendo*, giving lay officials a more prominent role in the discovery, arrest and punishment of heretics. The conflation of heresy with treason was already implicit in these acts but the convergence of spiritual dissent with political disobedience was further cemented under Henry IV and Henry V. Closely linked with the Lancastrian king's attempts to bolster the fragile legitimacy of his regime, the statute of 1401, *De heretico comburendo*, provided for the surrender of relapsed and contumacious heretics to the authorities for burning and ordered sheriffs and municipal officers to assist the episcopal hierarchy at each stage of the proceedings. Prompted by the insurrection led by Sir John Oldcastle, a further act of 1414 empowered a wide range of justices to initiate enquiries into the spread of seditious forms of religious deviance.[58] Such legislation was symptomatic of the extent to which the subordination of ecclesiastical to secular power preceded the formal breach with Rome in the 1530s and the theories of the Swiss theologian Thomas Erastus (1524–83), whose name has since become synonymous with it. A century before the Reformation the Crown had already encroached substantially on the autonomy of the English Church.[59]

These tendencies were, of course, greatly augmented and reinforced under the Tudors. Provoked by the papacy's refusal to sanction his divorce from Catherine of Aragon, in 1534 Parliament declared Henry VIII Supreme Head of the Church of England and invested him with the power to reform and redress all errors, heresies and ecclesiastical abuses. This was followed two years later by an act 'extinguishing the authority of the Bishop of Rome' and subjecting all who upheld and extolled it to the penalties, pains and forfeitures of the statute and writ *praemunire*. Although it was claimed that Royal Supremacy over *Anglicana Ecclesia* represented simply the restoration of an ancient right 'annexed and united to the imperial Crown of the realm', which had been wickedly usurped by the medieval popes, this legislation did mark a dramatic and revolutionary break with the past. It effectively established the English Church as an adjunct or department of the state, transformed the monarchy into a quasi-theocratic institution, and completed the politicisation of ecclesiastical deviance.[60] It embodied an audacious appropriation and redeployment of the title of 'Defender of the Faith' bestowed upon Henry by the Pope in 1521 for writing a humanist tract against the upstart Wittenberg monk, Martin Luther. The appointment of Thomas Cromwell as vicar-general and vicegerent of spirituals in 1535 was a further index of this process. At the same time, the independent authority of clerical ordinaries in cases of heresy was systematically whittled away and control of the definition and enforcement of religious orthodoxy was increasingly transferred to the laity.[61] This coincided with the elaboration and expansion of the treason laws as a mechanism for safeguarding the king's new pretensions as a kind of lay bishop: under 26 Henry VIII c. 13 (1534) anyone who slanderously and maliciously published or pronounced him a heretic, schismatic, tyrant or infidel was to be tried and convicted as a traitor.[62] In one unique and remarkable case, denial of the Royal Supremacy and conservative adherence to the papacy was itself defined as heresy. In 1538, the Observant Franciscan friar John Forrest went to the stake for upholding the jurisdictional claims of the vicar of Rome – the only man to be burnt for this offence by any Tudor regime.[63]

The Supremacy provided the legal framework for the Edwardian Reformation, though the personal, caesaro-papalist character it had under Henry VIII was attenuated by a new emphasis on Parliament. In 1554 the legislation was repealed, England restored to obedience to the Apostolic See, and the Lancastrian heresy statutes reinstated. Ironically, working in concert with the Houses of Commons and Lords, the new queen could achieve this only by exercising the very powers that had been invested in the Tudor monarchy by her father. The Marian Counter-Reformation was in effect, if not in name, an Erastian act. Under Mary, moreover, the responsibility for prosecuting religious dissidents remained largely in lay hands. When the Supremacy was formally renewed in 1559 as part of the Protestant settlement the less contentious title of 'Governor' was substituted for Head (which carried rather priestly overtones) in consideration of Elizabeth's inferior gender. Authority rested with the queen in Parliament rather than with the queen in and of herself. This was the legacy Elizabeth bequeathed to the Stuarts, and one that ultimately helped to ignite the constitutional crisis of 1640–42. Yet it would be wrong to imply that the Church meekly relinquished its role in the making of ecclesiastical policy: between 1550 and 1640 Parliament and Convocation recurrently tussled about the determination of the latter to initiate and formulate religious legislation.

The inexorable interweaving of spiritual deviance with political sedition also continued apace throughout the later Tudor period, as disloyalty to the monarchy was systematically conflated with rejection of the Church over which it presided. During the reigns of Elizabeth, James and their successors this resulted in the legislative coalescence of Protestantism with patriotism and an emotional and imaginative elision between Catholicism and treacherous support for foreign powers. The statute of 1585 against Jesuits and seminary priests made their very presence in England an act of high treason.[64] An implicit nexus between allegiance to the English state and allegiance to the Reformed religion persisted during the Commonwealth and Cromwellian Protectorate, despite the rhetoric of liberty of conscience and the elasticity of the parameters inside which Protestant 'orthodoxy' now resided. As Jeffrey Collins has recently stressed, despite repeated attempts to squeeze it into the 'interpretative corset' of the rise of toleration, the Church settlement of 1654 represented a continuation of a tradition of puritan imperialism intent upon asserting institutional hegemony over ecclesiastical affairs. It operated within and not outside the framework of Erastian ecclesiology and Cromwell himself constantly employed a language of monarchical supremacy over the clerical estate.[65] During the Restoration the right, indeed duty, of the civil magistrate to take steps to define and discipline moral and spiritual dissidence remained unquestioned by most members of the parliamentary and governing establishment. Even after the Act of Toleration, England remained a self-consciously confessional state.

One manifestation of these developments was the increasing tendency to punish religious deviants as felons and traitors rather than heretics. Under Henry VIII and Mary I individuals were notoriously burnt for their heterodox beliefs: around fifty suffered before 1547 and between 1555 and 1558 some 290 went to the stake. Edward VI exterminated only two extreme dissidents, Joan Bocher and George van Parris, and another eight Anabaptists and Arians would die by the flames during the reigns of Elizabeth and James.[66] But the general trend was to discipline members of rival churches and sects not for holding erroneous doctrinal opinions but rather for the subversive political consequences of doing so. The 'peculiar genius' of the Henrician Reformation, and the key to its success in minimising conservative opposition, argues Ethan Shagan, was to focus questions about its legitimacy on loyalty rather than theology.[67] The claim that Catholic missionaries were convicted not for their faith but rather for refusing to deny the right of the papacy to depose heretical monarchs would likewise become a mainstay of official propaganda after 1559, most notably William Cecil's famous *The execution of justice* (1584).[68] This embodied the desire of the regime to distance itself from the brutality of the Marian persecution and to avoid becoming the target of damaging allegations like those which had coagulated around the ardently Catholic daughter of Catherine of Aragon. As a strategy, it also reflected an awareness of England's vulnerability as a Protestant nation and a careful assessment of the risks involved in aggravating the phalanx of Catholic powers by which she was surrounded. But we should not accord exaggerated importance to this shift in the vocabulary of official intolerance. Arguably, the distinction between treason and heresy, crime and sin, was more technical and rhetorical than real in an Erastian context. Nor did it mean that persecution was any less fervent or intense: indeed, if anything, the politicisation of religious dissent strengthened it by fusing Protestantism with national feeling and fidelity to the monarchy and state.[69]

These tendencies mirrored trends in Europe as a whole. In the Holy Roman Empire the threat posed by the Anabaptists had prompted two important imperial mandates in 1528 and 1529, which charged these religious radicals with sedition as well as heresy and sanctioned their execution without prior ecclesiastical inquisition. Together these edicts amounted to a decisive step towards secularising the prosecution of religious deviance in this region. Enshrined in the Peace of Augsburg in 1555 and reaffirmed in the treaty sealed at Westphalia in 1648, the principle of *cuius regio, eius religio*, by which German princes were licensed to choose the faith to be espoused by their subjects, further consolidated the foundations for the civil discrimination and criminalisation of those who refused to conform with the official religion. It created the conditions for the coexistence of Protestant and Catholic rulers but it also reinforced their right to restrain and eradicate spiritual dissent within their own territories. In Gallican France, the trial and punishment of religious heterodoxy had likewise passed into the hands of secular judges and courts in the 1530s. Royal attempts to reach a peaceful rapprochement resulted in a cessation of burnings before the outbreak of the Wars of Religion in 1562. Henceforth, Huguenots were put to death for sedition and conspiracy rather than heresy, a shift reflected in the fact that they were no longer incinerated but hung, drawn and quartered. The progress of the Counter-Reformation in Catholic countries like Spain was marked by a parallel process of confessionalisation, by which Protestant heretics were progressively assimilated with disobedient citizens and perfidious rebels, though here, significantly, the Inquisition retained its primary jurisdiction over their trials.[70]

Such developments must also be viewed against the backdrop of the early modern sacralisation of monarchy. Solemnly anointed and crowned as the Lord's lieutenants on earth, medieval sovereigns had long been accorded quasi-sacerdotal status, but the sixteenth and seventeenth centuries saw the evolution of increasingly sophisticated theories of the divine right of kings.[71] This nurtured a culture of incipient absolutism which proved conducive to the pursuit of uniformity and the practice of religious persecution, as the reign of Louis XIV in France and particularly the revocation of the Edict of Nantes in 1685 were to show. In England these trends found early expression in Henry

VII's campaign to hedge the Tudor dynasty with the aura of divinity, and in official iconography, which sought to depict Henry VIII, Edward VI, Mary, Elizabeth and James as sacred bearers of the Lord's authority on earth – reincarnations of the most godly of the Old Testament kings. They became increasingly contentious during the Caroline period, particularly the Personal Rule, when the ecclesiastical policies sponsored by Charles I were popularly perceived to be subverting rather than buttressing the true Reformed religion. Ironically, however, the execution of the king in 1649 gave rise to a cult of royal martyrdom that served to enhance the hallowed character of the English monarchy and pave the way for the Restoration in 1660. The Exclusion Crisis and Glorious Revolution did not embody a rejection of the belief that princes were the images and anointed lieutenants of God so much as a conviction that a commitment to upholding the Protestant faith was intrinsic to their office. The 400 non-juring ministers who refused to swear allegiance to William and Mary on the grounds that their tenure of the throne breached the divine right of kings and the strength of the Jacobite cause after 1689 are themselves further testimonies to the enduring appeal of this ideology. In 1700 the legal, political and intellectual structures and preconditions for royal and state intolerance remained firmly in place.

It is no less important to emphasise the powerful influence which the ideal of an inclusive national Church exerted throughout the sixteenth and seventeenth centuries. Even at the end of the period only a minority advocated a policy of ecclesiastical disestablishment. The severing of links between Church and state that was a hallmark of Anabaptist ideology explains the horror with which these heretics were regarded by both Catholics and Protestants throughout Reformation Europe, as well as the hostility directed against those separatists and sectarians who held similar views. The Elizabethan and early Stuart puritans remained firmly committed to the concept of an official Church responsible for preaching the Gospel to the whole English populace, and even during the 1640s and 1650s it did not lose its appeal. The initial aim of the Parliamentarians was to create a system of rigid uniformity and to erect a Presbyterian (rather than episcopalian) institution with monopoly rights. They did not disagree with Laudians and Prayer Book Protestants on the need for an established – and consequently intolerant – Church of which all Englishmen and women were automatically members by virtue of their birth. It was more the pressure of events than carefully enunciated principles that brought about the experiment with pluralism of the 1650s and provided an environment within which alternative ecclesiologies began to crystallise. Strongly reasserted at the Restoration, it rode out the upheavals of the later Stuart period. The extent of continuing support for the notion of a national Church is attested by the repeated calls of both Anglicans and Presbyterians for comprehension and the genuine dismay they displayed at the prospect of a descent into legalised schism. The Toleration Act of 1689 did not dispense with or dismantle it but rather carved out a conditional niche for Protestant dissenters within what was an increasingly anomalous and anachronistic framework. And, of course, the Church of England still nominally retains its privileged status as the state religion to the present day.

What underpinned this institutional arrangement throughout the period under consideration was the charitable assumption that the entire nation, however lacking in knowledge and faith, was the people of God. It rested on a willingness to allow the distinction between the public visible Church and the invisible company of the Lord's predestined flock subsumed within it to remain ambiguous, to conflate the great corporation established by law with the tiny brotherhood of true believers upon whom the Almighty had bestowed the gift of grace and inwardly 'called'. The mystery that surrounded God's double decree meant that it was impossible to differentiate between the saved and the damned. Many who lingered within the official Church might actually be the children of Satan but it was unwarrantable for mere human beings to presume to eject them. 'Many things exclude from the kingdom of God', wrote Richard Hooker, 'although from the Church they separate not': this institution had a duty to embrace not merely the sincere but also 'hypocrites and dissemblers, whose profession at the first was but only from the teeth outward'.[72] As the separatist Henry Barrow commented, this was a belief that many puritans shared with apologists for the Protestant mainstream: 'these men still would have the whole land to be the Church, and everie parrish a particular congregation of the same'.[73]

However, the idea of the Church as an all-embracing institution was always in tension with those tendencies within Reformed Protestantism which fostered the rival precept that it should be a voluntary gathering of the elect alone. This inspired the secession of the followers of Barrow, Browne, Harrison and Greenwood from the Church of England, who felt themselves bound to withdraw from a body which compelled the visibly unworthy to receive communion and so pollute the holy sacraments, as well as engendering the separatism of the groups of Particular (or Calvinist) Baptists and Congregationalists that emerged in the early seventeenth century.[74] It also led some puritans committed to remaining within the promiscuous national Church as a kind of leaven in an otherwise unregenerate lump to develop ad hoc mechanisms for excluding the profane from access to the Eucharist and filtering out the remnant of the godly from the reprobate multitude. In parishes across the country, in imitation of Genevan standards of consistorial discipline, ministers expelled the ignorant and sinful from communion and administered it solely to select groups of 'saints' and 'scripture men'. At East Hanningfield in Essex in the 1580s, for instance, the rector William Seridge exercised his discretionary power to repel a substantial proportion of the laity, whom he adjudged morally unfit and doctrinally insufficient, and such practices would continue to be a source of grievance and tension in many local communities in the seventeenth century.[75] Simmering just beneath the surface of the established Protestant religion, these conflicting impulses and inclinations complicated the politics of tolerance and intolerance in Tudor and Stuart England and invested it with it a further dynamic and dimension.

THE PARAMETERS AND POLITICS OF PERSECUTION

While most contemporaries agreed that religious diversity was dangerous and that uniformity was the key to political and social stability, there was debate and disagreement about precisely what this meant in practice and about which measures could be employed to enforce and achieve it. Could ecclesiastical and civil officials be content with securing merely external conformity, or should they settle for nothing less than complete doctrinal compliance and inward evangelical conversion? Were monarchs bound to search not simply the 'outward shewe' but 'the very secrettes of the harte in God's cause', as the MP Thomas Norton asserted in the Commons in 1571, or was it unwarrantable for them to make 'windows into the souls' of their subjects?[76] Was it the duty of the Christian magistrate to punish individuals for holding heterodox opinions alone or was persecution permissible only when such beliefs spilled out of the silent chamber of the mind and manifested themselves in verbal sedition, physical disorder, or overt plots and conspiracies? Could one allow the Catholic mass or dissenting conventicles to take place behind closed doors and in private homes or was it obligatory to remove all occasions for idolatry and uproot every potential nest of heresy in the realm? Was it necessary that the liturgical rubrics laid down by the Book of Common Prayer were followed to the letter or could room be left for manoeuvre with regard to rituals and ceremonies that fell within the sphere of *adiaphora* or 'things indifferent' – topics on which Scripture was conspicuously silent? Such questions arose in relation to a variety of minority groups and sowed the seeds of internal division and friction between princes and politicians, clergy and laity, from the Henrician period onwards.

We may begin with the question of whether or not individuals could be executed simply for believing in a false religion. Declaring that there was 'no faute that more offendeth god', Sir Thomas More emphatically championed the right, indeed duty, of Christian princes to impose the death penalty for heresy in 1529.[77] The same conviction would supply Catholic writers with the ideological justification for Mary I's cycle of fires at Smithfield and elsewhere in the 1550s. Many sixteenth-century Protestants also vocally defended the view that those guilty of crimes of the mind should suffer the ultimate sanction. This was upheld by Martin Bucer in his *De regno christi* (1550) and by

Jean Calvin, under whose supervision the Genevan authorities executed the anti-Trinitarian heretic Michael Servetus in 1553.[78] Under the provisions of the Edwardian *Reformatio legum*, incorrigible Catholics as well as Anabaptists would have been exposed to the severest of temporal penalties.[79] Few evangelicals felt much discomfort about sending these false believers to the stake, and it is particularly striking to find the proto-martyr of the Marian Protestants, John Rogers, upholding the fire as the most merciful form of eliminating such offenders – a remark that provoked his friend John Foxe to riposte that he might find himself 'full of this same gentle burning'. Even under interrogation himself, John Philpot would maintain that Joan Bocher was 'well worthy to be burnt' for denying the divinity of Christ.[80]

The celebrated case of Servetus continued to be cited as a precedent for the harsh treatment of people who held extreme religious opinions, not least by James I, on whose express orders the obdurate Arians Bartholomew Legate and Edward Wightman were cut off from the Church of Christ as 'rotten members' and burnt at the stake in 1612 in front of many spectators – the last Englishmen to die by the flames.[81] Some Elizabethan clergy wanted the same sentence to be applied to the seduced disciples of the papal Antichrist. Alexander Nowell, Dean of St Paul's, told Parliament in 1563 that maintainers of a wicked religion should die by the sword – a view echoed by Bishop Edwin Sandys in more than one sermon.[82] In his *Doome warning all men to the judgemente* (1581), Stephen Batman, former chaplain to Archbishop Matthew Parker, likewise called for the institution of a law permitting Catholics to be killed for their religion alone. Without this, he declared, the 'Gospels Reformation' was incomplete and the realm would never find 'peacable tranquillitie' but rather lie in danger of 'a grievouser tyrannie'.[83]

Similar opinions were articulated during the parliamentary session of 1614, when zealous puritan MPs moved that anyone professing Catholicism deserved to die on the scaffold.[84] Behind such initiatives lay the assumption that the penalties laid down for idolatry and blasphemy in the Old Testament were still enforceable. This also animated those who demanded that the Quaker James Nayler be executed for his sacrilegious entry into Bristol in 1656, riding on a donkey in imitation of Christ's arrival in Jerusalem on Palm Sunday. Major General William Boteler argued that the false messiah should be stoned to death on the grounds that the law in Leviticus against blasphemers was no less binding than that against murderers. In the event, Nayler escaped capital punishment by just fourteen votes.[85] In England the statute of 1401 enabling acts of 'holy violence' against unrepentant heretics was not repealed until 1678.[86] North of the border in Scotland the Edinburgh medical student Thomas Aikenhead was executed for mocking the Incarnation and Trinity in January 1697.[87]

The fact that *De heretico comburendo* had fallen into desuetude more than half a century earlier should, however, alert us to presence of some dissenting voices. John Foxe, for instance, was deeply opposed to consigning the living bodies of men to the pyre, even where they held insupportable tenets, thinking this far too reminiscent of Roman barbarity. Embarrassed by the Edwardian regime's execution of religious radicals, he censored passages about these episodes from later editions of the *Actes and monuments*. He also protested eloquently against the burning of two Dutch Anabaptists in 1575 and pleaded for mercy for the Jesuit Edmund Campion in 1581.[88] The same year, a bill that would have made Familism a felony on the third offence prompted much controversy among members of Parliament about 'whether paines of death might be inflicted to an heretique'.[89] A number of early Stuart writers shared this unease about what Francis Bacon called 'sanguinary persecutions to force consciences', including Oliver Cromwell.[90] After the Restoration this view was articulated by Richard Perrinchief and Henry Thorndike, for whom the discipline of fire and faggot was at odds with the spirit of Christ and St Augustine.[91] In the 1690s Jonas Proast 'perfectly agree[d]' with his opponent John Locke that maiming and killing for spiritual offences alone was evil.[92] Throughout the period very few could stomach the view that Protestant nonconformists, who dissented from the Church of England on liturgical and ecclesiological (as opposed to doctrinal) grounds, deserved to die for their misguided opinions on mere 'things indifferent'.

These emerging doubts about employing the death penalty in cases of schism and heresy were not, however, incompatible with enthusiastic endorsement of lesser punishments like financial charges, incarceration, exile and civil discrimination, which touched the pockets and constrained the personal liberty of religious deviants but stopped short of physically mutilating or extinguishing them. The laying of such 'thorns and briars' where 'gentle admonitions' and 'earnest entreaties' failed to persuade dissenters to return to the fold continued to be supported as a form of fraternal correction, an act of Augustinian compassion for the health of their souls.[93] Judicious use of the stick was justifiable where the carrot of pastoral care proved ineffectual.

No one, moreover, disputed the right of secular officials to employ the sword where religious unorthodoxy became intermingled with subversion and conspiracy. By universal assent, genuine traitors could not be allowed to live. Bishop Joseph Hall of Exeter was clear that blood should not be shed for 'mere heresy' but where it was mixed with 'perturbances', 'malicious complotting', or 'treacherous machinations', he ventured, 'it tends to the setting of whole kingdoms on fire, and therefore may well be worthy of a fagot'.[94] Hence, the executions of a succession of Catholic laymen and priests implicated in the invasion and assassination schemes in the reigns of Elizabeth and James and the twenty-four exemplary deaths were carried out in the wake of the scared surrounding the Popish Plot in 1678. Hence too the judicial deaths of dissenters and sectarians who lent their support to thwarted uprisings and coups, including the ill-fated attempt to oust James II and replace him with the Protestant Duke of Monmouth in 1685, as a consequence of which some 150 were hung, drawn and quartered. The Baptist shopkeeper Elizabethan Gaunt was burnt at Tyburn for giving shelter to one of the rebels, who had informed against her to save his own neck – a grim reminder that, despite the repeal of the 1401 statute seven years earlier, incineration continued to be the standard sentence handed down to women convicted not just of high treason, but also of the petty treason of murdering their husbands. Gaunt was not even afforded the mercy of strangulation before she was bound to the stake.[95] As such instances reveal, in a climate of fear the hazy line that divided religious dissent from political treachery could become very blurred indeed.

Next we must turn to the issue of how far the ecclesiastical and political authorities sought to coerce the consciences of the English people. The legislation passed under Henry VIII was predicated on the notion that the king had the prerogative to dictate dogma to his subjects and to punish those who dared to deviate from it. The same presumption compelled his daughter Mary to send nearly 300 Protestants to the stake in the space of less than four years. By the reign of Elizabeth I, however, we can detect a shift of emphasis from intellectual deviation to institutional schism. The Act of Uniformity of 1559 focused attention on the outward behaviour rather than the inner belief of the laity by making failure to attend church, as opposed to adherence to heterodox opinions, illegal.[96] The queen stubbornly resisted repeated attempts by bishops and MPs to replace the statutory obligation to attend Prayer Book services with a stiffer test of theological orthodoxy such as compulsory reception of communion, swiftly scotching bills presented to the House in 1571 and 1581. Bare bodily presence at public worship was deemed a sufficient guarantee of religious fidelity and political integrity and calls for some more rigorous 'touchstone of triall' to distinguish loyal Catholics from 'rebellious calves whom the [papal] bull [of excommunication] hath begotten' were briskly dismissed. Despite the efforts of zealots like William Strickland, who cited the precedent of the prophets constraining the consciences of the Israelites in the Old Testament, official policy was designed to enforce an external uniformity of practice and conduct rather than consent or subscription to a detailed formulary like the Thirty-nine Articles, though this was, of course, required of the beneficed clergy.[97] Richard Hooker would provide a classic, retrospective defence of the precept of non-interference in private thoughts in his *Lawes of ecclesiastical politie* (1593): the Church, he insisted, had no warrant 'to dive into men's consciences'.[98]

Not until 1606 did refusal to receive the Protestant Eucharist become a criminal act, though it must be emphasised that it had always been and remained an offence under ecclesiastical law, subject to punishment by the sanctions at the disposal of the episcopal hierarchy described below.[99] However much of a paper tiger the Jacobean legislation may have proved in practice,[100] it did represent a significant encroachment by the state into an arena from which the previous queen and leading apologists for her regime had rhetorically sought to retreat. It constituted a claim to peel away the mask that disguised conforming papists, and to search the very secrets of their hearts. It asked deeply committed Catholics to cross a spiritual rubicon: to participate in a rite they regarded as a sacrilegious parody of the miraculous living sacrifice of the mass.

The principle of enforcing compulsory attendance at one's parish church would remain at the heart of the pursuit of uniformity for most of the seventeenth century. That this was not one of the issues under dispute at the Westminster Assembly makes the temporary repeal of the statutes requiring it by the Rump Parliament in 1650 all the more striking. There was a partial return to regulation in 1657 with the passage of the Act for the Observance of the Lord's Day in 1657, though this sprang more from anxiety about the profanation of the sabbath than from a desire to ensnare the sincere sectary.[101] The Elizabethan status quo was re-established by the Restoration settlement of 1662 and underpinned the Clarendon Code. Once again there were those who feared that outward conformity could be used by Catholics as a cloak for conspiracy and exploited by dissenters as a means of evading civil disabilities. One of the consequences of this was the Test Acts of 1673 and 1678, which required all office holders to receive the Anglican sacrament and make a declaration repudiating the doctrine of transubstantiation.[102] Their chief purpose was to restrict the exercise of political power to upstanding members of the Church of England rather than constrain the consciences of the laity at large. They may be regarded as a measure of how far the enforcement of uniformity across the board was already implicitly recognised as a practical impossibility.

The Tudor and Stuart state's dominant preoccupation with securing external conformity should not necessarily be regarded as indicative of a relatively mild regime of religious coercion. The logic behind this policy was, at least initially, fundamentally intolerant. Its aim was to eliminate diversity of opinion by subjecting the populace to weekly doses of indoctrination in Protestant theology: if men and women heard enough sermons and homilies and absorbed the language of Cranmer's Prayer Book over a long period, then popery and radical heresy would eventually wither out of existence. As the Wiltshire minister Nathaniel Aske would comment in 1673, 'constant hearers doe many tymes become conscientious hearers'.[103] Repeated exposure might just breed sincere conversion. Nor can official efforts to bring obstinate recusants into compliance with the law be dismissed as superficial bureaucratic manoeuvres. As Michael Questier has stressed, the enforcement of conformity was often a hard and unforgiving process. Not content with creating a mere illusion of consensus and engendering a body of hypocritical church papists, many bishops took seriously their responsibility to persuade Catholics to embrace the Protestant faith through a programme of godly persuasion and preaching. The procedures for reconciling such convicts with the Church of England were both humiliating and rigorous. At least some officials were unprepared to sanction a charade and sought instead to effect a real change of heart.[104]

Furthermore, if the official concentration upon outer conduct over inner belief provided the conditions in which mystical or spiritualist sects like the Family of Love, which privileged the spirit above the flesh, could survive if not thrive, it struck at the heart of a religion like Catholicism, which hinged upon the performance of ritual and which regarded all ceremonies as inherently sacred acts. To require men and women to yield their bodily presence at Anglican worship was to impose upon the scrupulous a painful ordeal akin to a medieval judicial test of innocence, their reaction to which could materially affect their fate in the afterlife, if not draw down divine punishment immediately upon them from heaven.[105] It was, in a sense, to require them to swear a pledge of allegiance, to signify their obedience not with their lips but with their limbs.

Nor can we afford to ignore the succession of oaths, engagements and declarations which Tudor and Stuart governments imposed upon their subjects. In an age in which God was believed to intervene regularly to strike perjurers dead, such devices were regarded as a 'provisional self-curse'.[106] Many were primarily designed to test and secure political loyalty, to divide the trustworthy from traitors and potential terrorists. But in a confessional state, such statements inevitably had spiritual implications: they were simultaneously mechanisms for separating the sheep from the goats. To be asked to consent to the Royal Supremacy or to reject the papal deposing power (as in the Jacobean oath of allegiance of 1606) was to be compelled to reveal one's beliefs about the legitimacy of the Protestant Church established by law. To Roman Catholics with particularly sensitive consciences, it could indeed be 'a diabolically effective polemical cocktail'.[107] Parliamentarians and lay people who subscribed to the Protestation of 1641 and the Solemn League and Covenant of 1643 or swore the oath of 1658 to Lord Protector were obliged to declare their commitment to maintaining and preserving 'the true, reformed, Protestant, Christian religion, in the purity thereof' recovered at the Reformation. These too were intended to operate as shibboleths to discover 'true Israelites' and identify popish 'malignants'. More implicitly, the Engagement of 1650 to the infant Commonwealth raised religious as well as political dilemmas for many Anglicans.[108]

Some declarations were more overtly doctrinal in character. A draft bill of 1586 would have forced disaffected Catholics to 'acknowledge before the Lord God of heaven and earth' that Rome was 'an Antichristian and hereticall Churche, and that it hath erred and can and doth erre'.[109] During the Civil War, a sequestration ordinance of 1643 likewise cut to the quick of Catholic convictions about the real presence of Christ in the Eucharist, supplying a precedent for the Test Acts passed under Charles II, while in 1657 the Cromwellian regime introduced a measure that compelled recusants (including women and children) to recite on demand a declaration abjuring the Pope, transubstantiation, purgatory, and image worship, though this was hardly ever enforced.[110] In time, refusal to swear an oath would itself become a litmus test of religious dissent and a criminal offence. Under a statute of 1662, anyone one who disdained or denied the legality of solemn binding statements of this kind thereby identified him or herself as a Quaker.[111]

Turning from the laity to the clergy, the Church of England likewise sought to ensure the orthodoxy of its personnel by requiring them to assent to the legality of the ecclesiastical institution by which they were employed. John Whitgift eliminated some of the ambiguity that had hitherto surrounded this in 1583 when he insisted that ministers subscribe that the Book of Common Prayer and Articles of Religion in their entirety contained nothing contrary to God's word.[112] This was to force puritans with reservations about England's imperfect and flawed Reformation to come out of shadows and reveal their true colours. It too constituted a claim to be able to sift their consciences in the interests of securing inner as well as exterior compliance.

Yet more intrusive was the notorious ex officio oath employed by the Elizabethan and early Stuart High Commission, a procedure of self-incrimination that compelled individuals under interrogation to confess to having committed ecclesiastical infractions. Used against the imprisoned Presbyterian leaders in the 1590s and the critics of the Laudian hierarchy, it embodied an aggressive assertion of power over the private sphere of the mind. Not without some justice did contemporary commentators liken it to the methods of enquiry utilised by 'the most execrable Inquisition of Spain'.[113] The so-called 'etcetera oath' imposed on clergymen by the Convocation of 1640, which bound them not to consent to alteration of the government of the Church 'by archbishops, bishops, deans and archdeacons, etc.', was designed chiefly to smoke out lurking Romanists, but its effect was to confirm general resentment of the crypto-papalist pretensions of the Caroline episcopal hierarchy. Puritans like Nehemiah Wallington regarded this 'execrable' device as another of the 'snares' devised to catch 'the poor children of God'.[114] By such means, the early modern Church and state endeavoured to bind the consciences of those over whom it claimed spiritual as well as secular jurisdiction.

Much of the debate that surrounded the Elizabethan and early Stuart campaign for clerical subscription was sparked by disagreement over the extent of the magistrate's right to legislate in the area of 'things indifferent' for the sake of public order and decorum. This problem had already reared its head under Edward VI, in the guise of the dispute over John Hooper's scruples about the use of traditional episcopal garments, but it came to a head during the Vestiarian and Admonition controversies of the 1560s and 1570s. The 'hotter sort' of Protestants tended to reduce the category of matters neither ordained nor forbidden by the Bible to a minimum, consequently limiting the scope for intervention by the civil authorities. Conformist writers, by contrast, who were inclined to read the prohibitions contained in Scripture much more literally and narrowly, and insisted that Parliament and the monarch could compel obedience on such questions as vestments and ceremonies at their discretion.[115] As we see in Chapter 5, *adiaphora* could be a mandate for pastoral latitude, but it could also legitimise drives to eradicate liturgical nonconformity as a threat to political stability.[116]

In the second half of the seventeenth century, divergent attitudes on this issue would likewise complicate and frustrate proposals for comprehending dissenters into the Church of England. Some believed that adherence to a compulsory core of fundamentals was sufficient, but others were unwilling to overlook differences of opinion on a wide penumbra of more minor topics on which the Bible offered little guidance and which were thus open to human judgement. The latter blocked successive moves to widen the criteria for membership of the Restoration Church in a manner that would have accommodated many nonconformists, convinced that this would bring dangerous schisms into the heart of it and transfer the blame for this 'from their own door to ours'. In the 1660s defensive clerics refused to budge on the question of relatively trivial matters of liturgical practice because they feared that this was merely an entrée to demands for the abolition of any set form of worship and the licensing of prayer 'by the spirit'. Faced with a choice between expanding the parameters for orthodoxy or maintaining the status quo, the architects of the Glorious Revolution themselves took the route of conservatism and caution.[117]

More delicate fault-lines developed around the question of how best to prevent the growth of dissident churches and sects. Despite calls for more systematic crusades to bring individual lay people to heel, official policy tended to concentrate on clamping down on the clerical evangelists who led them astray. In the 1660s and 1670s, dissenting ministers were the main victims of the drive against nonconformity, together with the 'seditious' conventicles they led and organised. Unobtrusive family gatherings of fewer than five people for private worship were deemed beyond the reach of the state by those who framed the Clarendon Code.[118] Similarly, in the sixteenth century it was the Catholic missionary priests and those who succoured and sheltered them who bore the brunt of capital punishment. Hearing mass merely attracted heavy fines and imprisonment,[119] to the discontent of those zealots who felt that clandestine, no less than flagrant, acts of idolatry were deserving of death. The underlying aim of this strategy was to sap the strength of the community by starving it of spiritual sustenance and undermining its capacity to replenish itself by creating new converts. This slow war of attrition did not satisfy everyone: extreme Protestants wanted more ferocious and sweeping steps to be taken to bring about its extinction. They wanted the conversion not capitulation of recusants. In this, as in other respects, the methods by which the government tried to enforce uniformity frequently fell short of the ideals and aspirations of godly activists. To quote Michael Questier, 'the state's political rhetoric of unity was not the Reformed evangelical rhetoric of grace and renewal'.[120]

All this should remind us that the early modern English Church and state were not monolithic institutions. Official policy towards religious minorities was forged in the crucible of factional conflict at court and within ecclesiastical circles. Its twists and turns reflected the complex and constantly shifting balance of power between monarchs, privy councillors and Parliament, as well as the character of those who occupied the top posts in the episcopal hierarchy. The confused rhythms of persecution during the 1530s and 1540s were a function of the king's fluctuating attitude towards evangelicals. The execution of Somerset and the rise of the Duke of Northumberland helped generate a climate of discipline and repression of the radical fringe after 1550, sweeping away the atmosphere of *glasnost* with which Edward's reign had begun.[121] Under Elizabeth, the impatience of John Whitgift and Richard Bancroft with the dilemmas of puritan ministers displaced the regime of relative leniency towards nonconformity which had been a hallmark of the episcopate of the former exile Edmund Grindal. This intensification of intolerance towards Protestant dissent was also a function of the subtly modulating theological and liturgical temper of the Church of England, of gradual shifts in how it perceived itself vis-à-vis the Church of Rome and international Calvinism. By 1600, the close affinity with the doctrine and practice of Reformed congregations abroad which had marked Edwardian and early Elizabethan Protestantism was slowly altering with the rise of a generation of divines with a different set of ideological and ceremonial priorities. English representatives were sent to the Synod of Dort in 1618 and the king strongly supported its pronouncements against Arminianism, but under Charles I the eclipse of the consensual predestinarianism and apocalyptic anti-popery that had hitherto welded together Protestants from all points on the spectrum gathered pace and was accompanied by a further reordering of the targets of intolerance – a shift in priorities that also reflected the replacement of George Abbot by William Laud at Lambeth. This fostered fresh anxiety about the radical and subversive tendencies within puritanism, which, together with a growing tendency to concede that Rome was a true if imperfect Church, helped to divert hostile attention away from the Roman Catholic community.[122] The existence of an inverse and dialectical relationship between fear of popery and fear of sectarian dissent also shaped patterns of persecution in the later Stuart period. The decades during which Presbyterians, Quakers and Baptists suffered most under the Clarendon Code were comparatively peaceful for Catholics but when zeal against the papists peaked in the later 1670s and 1680s in response to royal attempts to extend toleration to them, Protestant nonconformity in turn enjoyed some welcome respite.

Finally, we may note that official initiatives against religious dissidents were often sparked by specific events. Both the evolution and implementation of government policy tended to be reactive rather than proactive, responsive to the constraints of foreign diplomacy, to moments of domestic and international crisis, and to spasms of moral panic occasioned by natural disasters. The augmentation of the heresy legislation in 1414 followed immediately in the wake of the Oldcastle rebellion, while Bishop Alnwick's local drive against heresy in the diocese of Norwich in 1428–31 was partly spurred on by concern about the growth of Hussite movement in Bohemia.[123] The Pilgrimage of Grace of 1536 hardened Henry VIII's determination to root out conservative resistance and later surges of legislative and administrative activity against Catholics were linked with the promulgation of Pius V's bull excommunicating Elizabeth in 1570, with the launching of the Jesuit mission in 1580,[124] with the invasion threatened by the Spanish Armada in 1588, and with the Gunpowder Plot of 1605. Similarly, prosecution of puritans was stepped up in 1573 after the stabbing of the mariner John Hawkins by the disturbed law student Peter Birchet, who mistook him for the privy councillor Christopher Hatton, a well-known adversary of the godly. The proclamation of that year censuring the negligence of prelates and magistrates in suppressing nonconformity and ordering the imprisonment of anyone who defamed the Prayer Book was a direct consequence this fanatical, 'Anabaptist' act of attempted tyrannicide.[125]

The assassination of the French king Henry IV in 1610 greatly accentuated anxiety that English Catholics might mimic their Continental co-religionists: in the archdeaconry of Leicester, for instance, it prompted a vigorous campaign against local recusants designed to reduce the 'knowne enemies of Gods truth' from error and superstition and 'purge the Church of many inconveniences'.[126] The Irish massacre of 1641 resulted in another drive against priests on the English mainland: more than twenty were executed in the wave of revulsion engendered by this horrific atrocity. The fear unleashed by the millenarian rising of Fifth Monarchists in January 1661 likewise played into the hands of hard-line Anglicans who sought a conservative settlement and led to a first wave of official persecutory action against Baptists, Quakers and other sectaries. The Conventicle Act of 1664 was in many respects a by-product of the Yorkshire Plot the previous year and the Rye House conspiracy of 1683 supplied the ecclesiastical establishment with grounds for a fresh assault upon the Presbyterian and nonconformist firebrands lurking in the bowels of the realm.[127] And throughout the period, major outbreaks of plague and other catastrophes stimulated urgent exhortations from preachers and parliamentarians for action against papists, Jesuits and other perpetrators of the 'crying sins of atheism and blasphemy', who were hauling down God's judgements on the land, as if with 'cordes' and 'carte ropes'.[128] At such junctures, due execution of the laws against idolaters and dissenters seemed the best method of deflecting further devastating manifestations of divine anger with the English nation. The interpositions of Providence decisively influenced the pattern and intensity of persecution.

SPIRITUAL SANCTIONS AND CORPORAL PENALTIES

The English Church and state had an extensive machinery for enforcing uniformity and repressing dissent at its disposal, which is analysed in the second half of this chapter. In the late medieval and early modern periods, many bodies were charged with responsibility for correcting and controlling misbehaviour and false belief. At the beginning of the sixteenth century, the ecclesiastical hierarchy was undoubtedly the dominant player in efforts to mark out the boundaries of religious orthodoxy and eliminate heresy, idolatry and nonconformity. It was the bishops assembled collectively in Convocation who defined dogma and prescribed practice through canons, injunctions and special formularies such as the Thirty-nine Articles of 1563 and the Lambeth Articles of 1595. Orders were also issued on the personal authority of the Archbishop of Canterbury, for instance, the controversial 'Advertisements' on clerical dress and ceremonies set forth by Matthew Parker in 1566. This was linked with an elaborate system of justice, the key organs of which were episcopal visitations and diocesan church courts. Religious deviants were detected to these tribunals for reform and censure as a result of investigations carried out in response to lists of 'articles' issued by bishops, local clergy and churchwardens, with the assistance of sidesmen, members of the vestry and other parishioners.[129] Supported by a vast edifice of canon law and served by its own bureaucracy of clerks and 'apparitors', consistory courts exercised wide jurisdiction over spiritual and moral offences from heresy and blasphemy to sexual immorality and sabbath-breaking.[130] In 1559 they were supplemented as agents for the enforcement of uniformity by the institution of two High Commissions, based in Canterbury and York. Manifestations of the monarch's prerogative as Supreme Governor of the Church of England, these courts consisted of both clergy and laity but adopted the ex officio procedures of medieval ecclesiastical justice and employed semi-professional hunters of papists, heretics and sectaries known as pursuivants. Weapons of the Laudian drive against puritan dissent in the 1630s, they were denounced as instruments of tyranny and abolished by the Long Parliament in 1641.[131]

Overlapping with and complementing this network was a complex web of institutions of secular authority, at the centre of which stood the Crown, Privy Council and the two Houses of Parliament. The statutes, proclamations and orders issued by these bodies were implemented in the provinces by lord lieutenants, sheriffs and justices of the peace. In the absence of a paid police force, the early modern state had to rely on a voluntary magistracy to enforce its will in the localities and, as already mentioned, in the course of this period it laid an increasingly heavy burden of responsibility for prosecuting religious nonconformity upon the shoulders of these overworked individuals. City governors and town corporations also disciplined ecclesiastical heterodoxy where it interfered with the maintenance of public order and decency. In addition, some regions had special administrative arms of their own, such as the Councils of the North and the Marches and Wales. Offenders were presented to judges, justices and juries in regular county assizes and quarter and petty sessions through the efforts of village constables and other parish officials. Superimposed upon this judicial apparatus was a series of higher courts which dealt with criminal cases, most notoriously the Court of Star Chamber, a body composed of royal councillors whose role in suppressing outspoken opponents of Caroline religious policy ensured its demise at the same time as the hated High Commission.[132]

The lowest and most local level of law enforcement and justice was that of the manor. Courts leet and the stewards who presided over them were steadily losing their vitality and force as the feudal structures underpinning them were progressively eroded by the encroachments of municipal bodies and the state. Their role in protecting seigneurial rights, in arbitrating and resolving disputes between tenants, and in supervising the use of common lands had rapidly declined in the later Middle Ages. As mechanisms for regulating social misbehaviour and punishing rural affray they were also largely defunct by 1600. Nevertheless, they cannot be excluded from our survey completely. As Marjorie MacIntosh has shown, in some parts of England, especially the south-west and north, manorial courts remained energetic in preventing and prosecuting illegal, immoral and unsociable conduct throughout the sixteenth century, as witnessed by the raft of by-laws they generated.[133]

The records of all these institutions help the historian to trace the contours of official intolerance. They reveal the wide range of measures by which the early modern English Church and state, as well as the representatives of local

1 The penance imposed upon James Bainham in 1532: standing in front of the pulpit, he
bears a lighted taper and bundle of faggots: John Foxe, *Actes and monuments* (London,
1570), vol. 2, p. 1170. (By permission of The British Library, shelfmark 4705. h. 4).

authority, sought to restore Christian unity and concord and to rehabilitate, reform, punish and correct members of religious minorities.

We begin with the sanctions employed by the Church and its courts. All such censures worked on the principle of exposing offenders to public disgrace; they rested on the assumption that humiliation and shame could have salutary, didactic and (as it were) medicinal effects. Ecclesiastical punishments had a double function: they were designed to act both as a deterrent to the spectators and as an inducement to sinners to abandon their wicked ways and return to the embrace of the single true Church outside of which they could not hope to find salvation. In conjunction with clerical conference and persuasion, their aim was to wean the heterodox away from error and false belief, to reclaim and re-educate them, rather than to exact retribution or revenge.

The least severe of the penalties imposed by the consistory courts was a sharp ticking off: a simple verbal reproof or 'admonition' delivered by the presiding judge. Sometimes this consisted of a dry, formal reprimand; on other occasions it took the form of personal counselling and spiritual guidance. Varying in severity from strict to charitable, court records rarely reveal what was actually said. Next came various types of public penance. Barefooted, bareheaded and garbed in a skimpy white shift, early Tudor heretics were required to stand on a platform in front of the pulpit, abjure their false opinions and beg the forgiveness of their fellow parishioners, symbolically carrying a bundle of faggots and a wand or rod (Figure 1). Sometimes this ritual enactment of contrition had to be repeated in the marketplace of the town in which they dwelt and in front of the assembled congregation of the closest cathedral. In some such autos-da-fé, penitents threw the heretical tracts or writings they had used to seduce the populace on to a fire.

Concessions were made to lesser (as well as to weak, old and sickly) offenders, who were obliged to perform similar ceremonies dressed in ordinary clothes. In the pre-Reformation period, these often involved the recitation of paternosters and Hail Marys and focused on precisely those aspects of Catholic belief and practice which such individuals had disdained or rejected. Unlearned Lollards were frequently made to prostrate themselves in front of the altar, kneel before images, or carry out pilgrimages to the shrines of saints at which they had scoffed. In 1430, for instance, as a penance for his irreverent heretical opinions about Catholic sacraments and images, William Hardy, a tailor from Mundham in Norfolk, was ordered to perambulate the parish cemetery on three separate occasions clothed only in a skimpy shirt and carrying a wax taper, and to make a public offering to the high altar.[34] Three parishioners of Carleton Rood in Norfolk who refused to creep to the cross at Easter 1554 were made to give a shilling to the poor and declare that their penance was 'for the xample of other that such ceremonyes be not condemned'. A year later two suspected Yorkshire Protestants, William Byns and John Burkynshay, were forced to go on procession two Sundays in a row 'with either of theme a candle of a penny pece in ther hand and a boke or a paire of bedes in the other hand'. During Harpsfield's visitation of Kent in 1557 Margaret Geoffrie of Ashford was obliged to make amends for her refusal to venerate the Blessed Sacrament by kneeling in the midst of the chancel and 'devoutlie and reverentlie' worshipping the consecrated host.[135]

The stigma of having to confess one's faults in the presence of one's neighbours was quite commonly linked with the indignity of having to sew a distinctive badge onto one's outer garments. This practice, which dated back to the Fourth Lateran Council of 1215, chillingly prefigures the yellow star worn by the Jews in Nazi Germany. In the case of medieval heretics, the symbol depicted was either an embroidered faggot or a red cross: its purpose was to warn all who came into contact with such individuals of their solemn duty to shun them. Such insignia could indeed lead to social marginalisation: in the late 1490s, John Hig of Cheshunt petitioned his bishop for permission to remove his badge because no one was willing to employ him as long as he wore this ignominious emblem.[136] Some religious deviants, like a Southwark woman investigated by Bishop Richard Fox in the early sixteenth century, were permanently marked out by branding the letter 'H' on their hand or left cheek.[137] Particularly stubborn offenders could be flogged or imprisoned in monasteries, priories or episcopal gaols or prohibited from travelling beyond the boundaries of their parishes, though these corporal penalties could only be imposed with the assistance of the secular authorities.

Fasting was another component of the late medieval arsenal of ecclesiastical punishments. Several heretics convicted as a result of the investigations of Archbishop Warham in 1511–12 were forbidden to eat fish on Fridays for the rest of their lives: already bound to abstain from red meat, this further prohibition reduced them to a meagre vegetarian diet.[138] Robert Wright, a chaplain who refused to separate from his wife after Queen Mary's accession to the throne, was likewise confined to bread and water by the Chester consistory, as well as ordered to lodge at a distance of at least twenty miles from her.[139]

Protestants dismissed enforced abstention as a pointless 'popish' gesture and physical censures like whipping were rarely imposed by post-Reformation bishops, for whom such sanctions smacked rather too much of inquisitorial cruelty. Nevertheless, embarrassing forms of public apology continued to be employed by the courts against both nonconformists and notorious sinners (especially sexual delinquents) until the end of the seventeenth century. Indeed, recent work suggests that the puritan drive for godly discipline may even have inspired a partial revival of penitential rites in the public forum of the marketplace during the early Elizabethan period. As a strategy for effecting the reformation of character it was often employed by the Presbyterian consistories of the Scottish kirk.[140] Although these rituals were pruned of their more obviously Catholic elements, significant continuities with the past remained. In the early 1580s, John Woolton, bishop of Exeter, made twenty Familists recant their vile opinions in the cathedral in a collective display of ritual contrition. The abjuration of allegiance to the Church of Rome which conforming recusants were required to make was scarcely less chastening.[141] The former boxmaker and semi-professional lay prophet, John Etherington, was compelled to stand beneath the open air pulpit at Paul's Cross for three hours while Stephen Denison, minister of St Katherine Cree, denounced him as a heretic, Familist and Anabaptist. To his chest was attached a paper with his offence 'written in large letters'.[142]

Converts from Islam were subjected to equally irksome rituals of reconciliation. In 1637 William Laud ordered the drawing up of a special liturgy for the re-admission of such apostates: the renegade had to stand in the porch of the Church in a white sheet and humbly crave the prayers of the entire congregation while on his knees.[143] After the Restoration, dissenters were still occasionally singled out for exemplary punishment by means of this mortifying spectacle: in February 1683, a Quaker who had committed double adultery was required to perform penance in his parish church at Llanrost in Wales in the conventional garb of the contrite sinner. He repeated this penance at Denbigh and St Asaph, though in view of the cold weather he was allowed to wear breeches and shoes. Like his early Tudor predecessors, Bishop William Lloyd earnestly hoped that 'this severity on one of that sect' would do much good in the region.[144]

Although some Elizabethan and later puritans disparaged this procedure as 'pricking in a blanket' and 'pinning in a sheet' and complained constantly about the ineffectiveness of these 'toyishe censures',[145] there is evidence to suggest that fear of ridicule by one's peers could be acute. Thomas More told how a certain 'Holy John' of Paternoster Row in London resolved to throw himself down a well rather than face the taunts of his fellow citizens, and in the reign of Henry VIII a Lincolnshire heretic threatened to kill himself if he was subjected to this degrading ceremony.[146] In other instances, the prospect of becoming a laughing stock may well have been enough to bring about a swift change of heart. In a culture obsessed with honour, reputation and credit, we should not underestimate the power of penance to bring offenders to acknowledge the error of their ways. For men and women from the middling and upper ranks of English society, the obloquy of having to admit one's fault was particularly corrosive of the dignity and deference they claimed by virtue of their social status.

This partly explains the widespread tendency for such punishments to be commuted to fines. Repentant heretics like Gregory Newman, who displayed extreme sorrow for his offence by 'vehemently knocking upon his breast' in 1555, might be spared this shameful rite at the discretion of the judge and ordered to make a gift of charity to their parish churches or 'Christ's poor' instead.[147] Increasingly, money payments for 'pious uses' were substituted regardless of the degree of remorse shown by the defendant and critics of commutation fiercely denounced it as a travesty of true godly discipline. Such mitigations of the rigour of spiritual justice were further evidence to the authors of the Admonition to Parliament that the ecclesiastical courts of the Church of England were intolerable relics of antichristian Romanism, 'stinking ditches' flowing out of a 'great puddle' and 'poysoned plashe' of the popish 'abhominations' still infecting the realm.[148] Nevertheless, the very willingness of lay people to endure financial penalties rather than suffer public disgrace in itself reveals that ecclesiastical sanctions had not entirely lost their teeth.

In the case of recalcitrant ministers and priests, the Church could ultimately deprive them of their livings. Incorrigible clergymen who refused to respond to the paternal admonitions of their ecclesiastical superiors were liable to be barred from preaching and administering the sacraments. The early Reformation period witnessed a succession of purges of clerical personnel from all levels of the Church hierarchy: those who refused to adjust their opinions according to the prevailing theological wind all too frequently found themselves thrust out into the cold and this included a large number of bishops. Under Elizabeth, hundreds of ministers with scruples about the 'popish rag' of the surplice and other ceremonial remnants were suspended in the wake of the Vestiarian controversy of 1566 and John Whitgift's campaign for subscription in 1583 – a stubborn minority being permanently stripped of their benefices. Richard Bancroft's renewed drive for liturgical uniformity after the Hampton Court Conference led to the suspension of around eighty clergymen between 1604 and 1609, including such famous puritans as John Dod and Robert Cleaver. During the archiepiscopate of Laud, more dissenting clerics were silenced and expelled from their parishes after appearances before the High Commission for belligerent protests against the Caroline policies designed to restore the 'beauty of holiness'. Despite the exaggerated claims made by partisan commentators eager to parallel the events of the 1630s with the Marian persecutions of the 1550s, there were, however, relatively few actual deprivations. After 1640, the Long Parliament and later county committees retaliated by harassing around 2780 'scandalous and malignant ministers', some 1600 of whom were dispossessed. The Restoration settlement was accompanied by the ejection of about 1700 incumbents who refused to accept the conservative order of the newly restored Church of England: here too the mechanisms of traditional ecclesiastical discipline were supplemented and reinforced by the arm of statute law.

The highest censure at the disposal of the Church authorities was excommunication, which itself was applied in two degrees: major and minor. Usually employed in cases of contumacy, the latter, milder punishment involved deprivation of the right to attend religious services and receive the lifeblood of the sacraments; the former was more severe and far-reaching. This state of 'amputation from the body of Christ' not only entailed ritual exclusion from religious worship and fellowship and from the ministrations of the priesthood; it also exposed one to considerable legal and social disabilities. Prefiguring their terrible fate in the afterlife, excommunicates could not be married, have their children baptised or be buried in consecrated ground; they were also unable to serve as executors, administrators and guardians and could not conduct suits in the secular courts. In theory, moreover, their spiritual alienation was to be accompanied by civil ostracism. The orthodox and conformable were expected to treat such individuals like living 'corpses': until they were reconciled they would have to 'wander the earth as an outcast, a shipwrecked man and a stranger'.[149] Anyone who (except of necessity) consorted with them, bought or sold from them, or offered them succour was technically subject to the same penalties. Visitation articles repeatedly enquired if parishioners infringed these rules by favouring and cherishing those 'so cutt off' from the society of the faithful.'[150] While ecclesiastical records yield little evidence that this was systematically enforced in practice, where they were, one could be left in an unenviable state of social isolation. In a case of 1628, a contumacious woman was even deprived of the help of midwives during childbirth, while Mary Cundy, a Muggletonian from Orwell in Cambridgeshire was accorded 'the burial of an asse' outside the churchyard walls in 1686.'[151]

The effects of this interdict were most telling where religious dissenters were a beleaguered minority. In Mountmellick in Ireland, for example, the local miller was prohibited from grinding corn grown by nine excommunicated Quakers and their neighbours found themselves placed under pressure not to purchase it.'[152] To be prohibited from entering sacred buildings and attending common prayer was to be excluded from a regular gathering of one's local parish community and to some people, at least, this was still a punishment which stung. Edmund Wyland of Chipping Ongar in Essex, an excommunicate who refused to leave a service of evensong in 1590, may have been no more than a mischievous troublemaker, but we cannot rule out the alternative possibility that he sincerely wished to participate in the liturgy. The same applies to the woman from Great Badby in the same county who 'came privily to church' despite having been banned from hearing divine service on several occasions.'[153] In this regard, it is perhaps significant that the churchwardens of Cranbrook were presented in 1582 for allowing 'divers' such persons to come to church and take communion.'[154] And although many excommunicates died unreconciled, it would be wrong to ignore those who sought to absolve themselves at the first opportunity.

Nevertheless, there was more than a grain of truth in puritan claims that the sentence of excommunication was 'pronounced for every light trifle' and had consequently become a blunt and rusty sword of justice.[55] Routinely applied as the ordinary penalty for contempt of court, it had lost its force in large part through overuse. The early seventeenth-century separatist John Robinson protested that the Church of England played with excommunicates 'as children with rattles'.[56] In the 1670s, the Anglican divine Lancelot Addison likewise lamented how far 'the power of the keys' had become 'contemptible, and sunk so low in some men's opinions, that they rise not above the estimate of artificial fire or mere noisy thunder'.[57]

The high levels of contumacy and non-appearance in both the pre-Civil War and later Stuart Church reflect the extent to which this most severe of ecclesiastical sanctions had come to be regarded as an empty threat. This loss of credibility was arguably less a function of a rise of disrespect for institutional religion than a symptom of the advancing pluralism of English society.[58] The capacity of excommunication to coerce an offender depended on the assumption that he or she wished to be part of the national Church and of the parish community which represented it in microcosm and miniature. Consequently, it held few terrors for those who regarded the established Church of England as a heretical congregation or synagogue of Satan and separated from it as a matter of principle, as ecclesiastical officials came to recognise with growing dismay. One Restoration bishop frankly admitted that to proceed against such offenders 'by Church-Censures' was 'vaine'; another acknowledged that 'fanatics fear as little our excommunication as the Papists and indeed I find no sect much dreading it'.[59] To debar Catholics or dissenters from Church of England services was simply to give them a cast-iron excuse for their recusancy and refusal to partake of the polluted Anglican Holy Communion and its other 'sacrilegious' and 'superstitious' sacraments. It was to render them immune to the legislative penalties for nonconformity. The strategy of humiliating spiritual exclusion only worked in a context in which men and women believed that to remain beyond the ecclesiastical pale was to risk damnation. This was another reason why the state played an ever more significant role in the enforcement of religious uniformity in the course of the period.

Where the mechanism of 'fraternal correction' failed to bring about the desired effect, the Church, of course, had always had the option of seeking the assistance of the secular powers. Unable to impose corporal punishments like public whipping and imprisonment by its own authority, it required the co-operation of sheriffs and justices of the peace, empowered by the writ *de excommunicatio capiendo*, to carry them out. The same applied to the physical extermination of relapsed or impenitent heretics. The handing over of such persons to be burnt at the stake embodied an admission of defeat on the part of the ecclesiastical hierarchy: it represented a decision to abandon the attempt to bring a sinner back into the bosom of the Church, a belief that their error was an incurable cancer. The special commission Elizabeth issued to Sir Nicholas Bacon for the burning of the two Dutch Anabaptists in 1575 is indicative of the assumptions that conventionally underpinned such sentences. These 'corrupt members' were 'to be cut of[f] from the rest of the flocke of Christ, lest they should infect others professinge the true Christiane faythe'. Though they had 'bynne often and very charitable traveled with' by godly ministers anxious to dissuade them from their damnable opinions, yet because 'they arrogantlie and willfullie persist and continewe in the same', a warrant was to be drawn up for their incineration.[160]

Public executions by fire were highly symbolic occasions in which false believers were ritually expelled from the society which they had poisoned and profaned, exorcised from the body politic like a filthy disease or an evil possessing demon.[161] They were akin to a public health initiative designed to stop the spread of an epidemic. The reduction of a heretic's body to ashes signified the complete obliteration of his or her presence and memory from the community. It was for this reason that offenders' possessions and writings were often burnt at the same time, together with portraits or effigies of them. This also occurred when suspects escaped punishment by retreating underground or fleeing overseas: in the 1690s, for example, the radical deist John Toland, who provocatively denied the authority of the Bible, was vicariously punished when his books were publicly incinerated by the official hangman.[162] In the case of individuals like John Wyclif and the Edwardian reformer Martin Bucer who had died before being denounced for their heresies, their bones could be exhumed years later and ostentatiously cremated.[163] The same desire to cleanse society posthumously of infection explains why priests poured soap ashes on the resting place of John Petit of London in 1532, 'affirmyng that God would not suffer grasse to grow upon suche an heretykes grave', and why coals were deposited on the burial plot of the late Dr Champion of Kent.[164]

Fire was not only a cleansing and purifying agent; it foreshadowed the fate of intransigent sinners in hell. At another level, these dramatic rites of destruction were rituals of atonement and expiation, religious ceremonies intended to appease the wrath of a jealous and intolerant God. Carefully staged by the authorities for the benefit of onlookers, they might also be characterised as a kind of morality play designed to teach the populace the lesson that the wages of theological deviance were death (Figure 2). A last minute recantation could be equally edifying, a powerful advertisement for the mercy of the Church and compelling propaganda for the merits of

2 The burning of the Protestant bishops Hugh Latimer and Nicholas Ridley, 1555: John Foxe, *Acts and monuments* (London, 1570), vol. 2, p. 1938. (By permission of The British Library, shelfmark 4705. h. 4).

conversion. Friar Forrest's execution in 1538 was quite literally an act of iconoclasm, with fuel for the pyre over which he was suspended in chains being supplied by the great wooden idol of Dderfel Gardarn, once the focus of a thriving pilgrimage cult in North Wales.[165]

In pre-Reformation England bishops sought to swell the crowds present at these ceremonial burnings by granting forty days indulgence to all who attended. At the burning of a Lollard in Ipswich in 1515, for instance, everyone who threw a faggot on the fire was accorded this privilege, while the promise of a similar pardon greatly enlarged the audience that gathered to watch the evangelical Thomas Bennet perish at the stake in Exeter in 1532.[166] Increasingly, however, the authorities found that these spectacles were ceasing to operate as effective mechanisms for restoring harmony and reinforcing orthodoxy and becoming instead theatres in which the victims all too successfully constructed themselves as holy and charismatic martyrs. As the reign of Mary progressed, officials began to find that the fires of Smithfield were not healing the social ruptures wrought by heresy but rather serving to inflame and exacerbate them. As a mechanism for enforcing uniformity and restoring concord, they had become counter-productive. It became common to conduct executions early in the morning in order to avoid large and unruly assemblies and London householders were warned to keep their servants and apprentices indoors. After June 1558, public burnings were halted altogether.[167] As already noted, determined not to repeat the mistakes of her half-sister, Elizabeth's government made a point of executing Catholic priests and lay people for treasonous behaviour rather than unorthodox beliefs – some 189 between 1570 and 1603. A further 75 suffered the same fate in the seven subsequent decades to 1681. At the beginning of our period, Henry VIII had engaged in a kind of 'murderous ecumenism', epitomised by the hideous symmetry of the collective execution carried out at Smithfield on 30 July 1540, when three papists were hung on a gibbet erected alongside a pyre lit to consume the bodies of three Protestant reformers.[168]

Hanging, drawing and quartering was a punishment that left an indelible stain of disgrace upon convicted traitors and their relatives. Strangled on the gallows like common felons, their organs and entrails were removed and boiled and their corpses dismembered and exposed to the elements on pikes placed near the city gates, gruesome warnings and 'ghastly bill-boards' to onlookers of the terrible consequences of sedition and disloyalty (Figure 3).[169] To reclassify religious dissenters as enemies of the monarch and state was an attempt to dispel the aura of sanctity that tended to hover around a heretic who went courageously to his death. John Foxe claimed that the Essex hedge preacher George Eales had been executed by the Marian authorities for political dissidence rather than spiritual error in 1557 'to cause him to be more hated of the people', but this was a strategy which subsequent Protestant

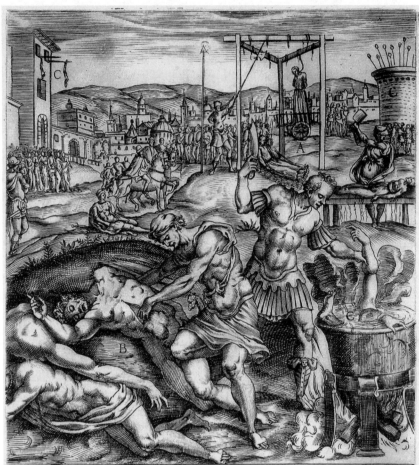

A. *Edmundus Campianus focietatis Iesu fub patibulo concionatur, ſtatimq̃ cum Alexandro Brianto Rhemensis, et Rodulpho-Sheriuño huius Collegij alumno fuspenditur.*

B. *Illis adhuc tepentibus cor et uiscera extrahuntur, et in ignem proijciuntur.*

C. *Eorundem membra feruenti aqua elixantur, tum ad urbis turres et portas appenduntur, regnante Elizabetha Anno M.D.LXXXI die prima Decēbris. Horum conſtanti morte aliquot hominum millia ad Romanam Eccleſiam cõnuerſa sunt.*

33

3 The execution of the Jesuit Edmund Campion and the seminary priests Alexander Briant and Ralph Sherwin, 1581: Giovanni Battista de Cavalleriis, *Ecclesiae Anglicanae trophaea* (Rome [1584]), plate 33. (By permission of the Syndics of Cambridge University Library, shelfmark Acton. a. sel. 21 (3)).

regimes pursued far more systematically.[170] From the early 1580s onwards, the Elizabethan government sought to discredit Catholic priests by putting them to death alongside depraved criminals like thieves, coiners and murderers. In December 1582 James Thompson was executed at York with five other felons, while Robert Drury died in February 1607 with no fewer than thirty-two common criminals.[171]

Like burning, judicial execution on the scaffold carried strong theological overtones. It too was 'a sacrificial rite that purged society'; a ceremonial demonstration of divine and secular vengeance against heinous transgressors of the human and heavenly order; a form of ordeal, the accomplishment of which supernaturally proved the guilt of the man or woman subjected to it.[172] As Michel Foucault, James Sharpe and others have argued, it was also a solemn display of the sovereign power of the state in which the victim, by means of a public admission of his or her transgression and a sincere expression of repentance, was made 'to consecrate his own punishment by proclaiming the blackness of his crimes'. The legitimacy of the authority that inflicted violence upon them was not only graphically inscribed on their bodies but affirmed by them in the course of their 'last dying speeches'.[173] However, recent work has suggested that, as instruments for exerting ideological control, such occasions also had significant weaknesses. As we see in Chapter 4, they too could be appropriated and subverted by the very individuals they were designed to annihilate, to glorify themselves and the faith for which they died.[174]

Nevertheless, it is evident that these carefully orchestrated events did have the capacity to influence the crowds which witnessed them, to convey emphatic messages about the duties of religious conformity and unconditional obedience. Edmund Campion's execution in 1582, for instance, was an elaborately contrived piece of political pageantry: paraded through the streets of London to the Tower, he was tied to a horse with a sign in large letters reading 'Campion the seditious Jesuit' pinned to his hat.[175] Pressed to death for refusing to plead, the body of the York recusant Margaret Clitherow was buried on a dunghill in a deliberate act of degradation that was also intended to deter would-be collectors of her relics.[176] Such spectacles surely did much to cement the link between treason and popery in the eyes of the populace, as well as to persuade the wayward that religious heterodoxy, like crime, simply did not pay.

Where they were suspected of having engaged in or been privy to conspiratorial activity, a few religious dissidents were subjected to forms of torture designed to extract information vital to ensuring national security and preserving the life of the sovereign. This could include deprivation of food, drink and sleep, the driving of spikes under the fingernails, compression in the iron ring called the 'Scavenger's Daughter', or the torment of being stretched and broken on the rack. In England, by contrast with the Continent, such methods were not employed in order to acquire judicial evidence or proof but rather as an aid to identifying accomplices and forestalling future plots.[177] Consequently torture remained a very exceptional practice authorised only by the highest authorities. The pseudo-Christ and radical puritan William Hacket was placed in manacles at Bridewell in July 1591 to make him 'utter and discover the bottom of his wicked and devilish purpose' to murder Queen Elizabeth and other members of her Council. However, Jesuits and seminary priests were the commonest victims of these ordeals. The torments Edmund Campion stoically endured left his body numb and mangled and on the scaffold it was noticed that all his nails had been dragged out in the course of his interrogations. John Gerard also suffered the excruciating pain induced by the device of the strappado on two occasions in 1597 and the Yorkshire missionary Thomas Bell was hung upside down for three days.[178]

Viewed through the distorting prism of modern liberal values, such practices may seem barbaric, but it must be stressed that they were a standard and legally sanctioned feature of investigations for treason and terrorism in this period. The motives of individual officials may have been more sinister, and some, like Richard Topcliffe, did act without proper warrants. Even so not many contemporaries regarded torture per se as a grotesque form of sadism. This was a context in which the notion that intense pain might be both therapeutic and a diagnostic tool, that it could help to liberate a heretic from the clutches of the devil and falsehood, and bring him or her to a startling recognition of the truth, had not entirely faded away.[179]

Only a small minority of dissenters ever experienced torture or death. Far more important for our purposes was the wide range of lesser civil penalties that the Tudor and Stuart state employed to secure compliance and to enforce uniformity. In part these were punitive and retributive, but they were also underpinned by enduring moral assumptions about the duty of the magistrate as God's lieutenant to seek to rehabilitate sinners, to deter and restrain activities that not only endangered their souls but drew down divine judgements upon the realm as a whole.

In the course of the sixteenth and seventeenth centuries, many individuals were flogged, branded or permanently crippled by order of the state for beliefs or behaviour that were deemed to be subversive or disruptive. Two women who dared to aver that Catherine of Aragon was 'ye treu queen of England' rather than the king's new wife Anne Boleyn were beaten with rods in 1533, their bodies having been stripped from the waist upwards.[180] In 1561, one William Geoffrey was publicly scourged through the streets of London for blasphemously proclaiming that a certain John More was Christ, the saviour of the world. Papers declaring his monstrous crime were stuck to his head and the cart on which he was conveyed to the lunatic hospital Bethlem.[181] Under

The manner 'how *James Naylor* ſtood in the Pilory, and was whipt from the Pallace-yard at *Weſtminſter*,to the Royall Exchange in *London*, December the 18. 1656.

4 The punishment of the Quaker James Nayler for blasphemy, after his entry into Bristol in imitation of Christ's arrival in Jerusalem on Palm Sunday in 1656: *A true relation of the life, conversation, examination, confession, and just deserved sentence of James Naylor the grand Quaker of England* (London, 1657), title-page. (By permission of The British Library, Thomason Tracts E. 1645 [4]).

the thwarted bill against Familists of February 1581, members of the mystical brotherhood would have been whipped and seared with the letters H. N.[182] In 1618 John Traske, leader of a sect of extreme Saturday sabbatarians, was flogged from the Fleet to Westminster and Cheapside, where he was nailed to the pillory through each of his ears in turn and then burnt on his forehead with J, 'in token that hee broached Jewish opynions'.[183] The outspoken puritans William Prynne, John Bastwick and Henry Burton had their ears severed on the instruction of the Star Chamber in 1637. Prynne, who had lost the lower half of his in an earlier tussle with the law, was also disfigured with S.L. (for Seditious Libeller) scorched into his cheeks. Earlier that decade a fellow critic of Caroline episcopacy, Alexander Leighton, had had his nose slit.[184]

Similar exemplary justice was dealt out to the Quaker James Nayler by Parliament in 1656: transported through the capital and placed in the stocks, his tongue was bored through with a hot iron and his brow branded with a B for blasphemer (Figure 4).[185] The authors of unorthodox books were also liable to have the offensive right hands with which they had penned them cut off at the wrist, in a manner comparable to some medieval thieves. Such physical stigmas placed their recipients on a par with vagrants and beggars, who were marked with V or R and burnt through the 'gristle' of the ears as a sign of their perpetual infamy by order of a series of savage Tudor statutes.[186] Sexual offenders could also be the subject of equally gruesome punishments. Under a vicious penal code which four godly magistrates drew up for the parishioners of St Mary's, Bury St Edmunds, in 1579, fornicators were to be tied to a post for twenty-four hours, have their hair cut off, and receive 'thirty strypes well layde on till the blood come'.[187] Here, as elsewhere, the city fathers were seeking to revive the strict moral censures laid down in the Pentateuch.

To understand the rationale for these severe corporal penalties, once again we need to set aside some of the most cherished precepts of Western civilisation. Powerfully buttressed by the Old Testament, such sanctions operated on the same principle as ecclesiastical penances and popular customs like ridings and skimmingtons.[188] Offenders were quite literally marked out as deviants by means of bodily mutilation and their exposure to the contempt and mockery of those who witnessed these gruesome rituals was intended to be an incentive to their reintegration as much as a solemn lecture to the spectators. Simultaneously acts of deterrence, retribution and ritual cleansing, they too reflected a conviction that external chastisement could be an effective mechanism of mental correction. This was a culture in which psychological mortification and physical pain were not yet sharply distinguished, despite signs of a long-term shift of priority from the former to the latter.[189]

It is in these terms that we need to interpret the carting of a woman around the town square at Walsingham in January 1538 for spreading rumours that the image removed from the nearby despoiled Marian shrine had begun to work wonders,[190] and the four booksellers who had been paraded through the capital sitting backwards on horses eight years earlier by order of the Chancellor Sir Thomas More. Their coats were 'pinned thick' with copies of

Tyndale's New Testament and other heretical books they had helped to disperse, as well as placards proclaiming '*Pecasse contra mandata regis*' ('For crimes against the king's proclamations').[191] Similarly, in 1555 a youth named William Featherstone who claimed that he was the young Protestant Josiah Edward VI *redivivus* was taken from the Marshalsea to Southwark 'in a folles cote' and there stripped naked before being whipped to Smithfield.[192] At the Surrey Assizes in Lent 1604, a Catholic spinster called Dorcas Stephen was ordered to be pilloried for two hours in market time bearing a notice inscribed with her defiant words against King James and the reformed religion.[193] In addition to his humiliation in London, James Nayler was made to enter Bristol strapped facing the back of a nag and in 1676 Lodowick Muggleton was committed to stand upon the pillory in Cornhill, Chancery Lane and Smithfield bearing a notice describing his pernicious opinions and seditious offences on his breast, while his blasphemous tracts and pamphlets were torn up and incinerated by the common hangman.[194] After the Restoration, some Quakers were even placed in a cage and exposed to public derision.[195]

As in the penances imposed by bishops, the colourful or unusual clothing worn by such offenders visibly distinguished them from their orthodox neighbours. In this regard, a motion put forward in the Addled Parliament of 1614 seems particularly striking. Reflecting fears of a fifth column of dissembling papists busily undermining the nation from within, it was seriously proposed that all Romanists should be made to wear 'yellow Cappes and Slippers'. The aim of this, observed Catholic commentators, was not merely to make their co-religionists immediately identifiable but also 'to be hooted at wherever they should appear'. It should not surprise us that such suggestions were revived in the heady atmosphere of the year 1640, at the height of the anti-popish scares that swept the metropolis and many provincial towns, poisoning attitudes towards the recusant minority.[196]

The segregation of religious dissidents from normal society was more conventionally achieved by means of imprisonment. Locked up in gaol, they could not proselytise or indoctrinate unwary lay people, while the experience of incarceration might concentrate their minds and encourage them to renounce their erroneous opinions. Had Amnesty International conducted a thorough investigation of Tudor and Stuart England, it would have discovered many individuals who would now be classified as 'prisoners of conscience'. In the first half of the sixteenth century, many Lollards, Protestants and Anabaptists spent periods in the Tower of London and other places of detention for espousing views at odds with those advocated by the reigning monarch. In Edward's reign, the radical bishop-elect of Worcester and Gloucester, John Hooper, was confined in the Fleet until he agreed to wear the vestments prescribed by the Book of Common Prayer[197] and under the Elizabethan recusancy legislation, imprisonment was imposed upon the most persistent lay offenders. Presence at illicit masses automatically earned the penalty of a year in gaol (as well as a fine of 100 marks).[198] Numerous priests were detained at Wisbech Castle in the course of the period and at times of national emergency and crisis, like the threatened invasion by the Spanish Armada, prominent Catholics such as the Northamptonshire magnate Sir Thomas Tresham were temporarily incarcerated in private houses and episcopal palaces.[199] The Blasphemy Act of 1650 prescribed six months imprisonment for the members of extreme antinomian sects like the Ranters and sentences of this length were also handed down against Quakers, Presbyterians and other dissenters under the terms of the Conventicle Act of 1664.[200] The Bedfordshire Baptist preacher John Bunyan was arrested in 1660, charged under the 1593 Act for holding 'unlawful meetings and conventicles' and committed to gaol. Consistently refusing to conform, there he remained for the space of twelve years.[201]

Conditions in prisons varied significantly. Some religious nonconformists were held in dark, filthy, stinking and overcrowded dungeons, rendered immobile by means of iron fetters, and subjected to intimidation and brutality by their hostile gaolers. The mental strain they suffered could also be acute. Nearly 100 Catholic missionaries died in captivity before 1603.[202] In 1583, the recusant John Finch was kept in the middle of a bridge at Salford where he was 'pinched ... with extreme hunger', being fed on fish days with sodden beans and the rest of the week with small morsels of liver. The Elizabethan priest Nicholas Horner was kept so long in a common gaol that one of his legs allegedly rotted and had to be cut off.[203] After the Restoration severe privations were endured by many members of the Society of Friends. The health of George Fox was permanently impaired by three years' imprisonment in Lancaster and Scarborough, where rain poured into his exposed room through an open window, and the 28-year-old Edward Burrough perished after contracting a fever in Newgate in February 1663, passing his final days on a damp straw mattress next to a flowing drain.[204]

The 'literature of suffering' in which such cases are recorded must, however, be treated with caution. Subject to martyrological hyperbole and distortion, it eclipses the considerable freedom and relative comfort enjoyed by many prisoners, not least as a consequence of the laxity and corruption of their custodians. Some had well-furnished rooms and were permitted to receive visitors and make short trips home. Elizabethan seminary priests were able to celebrate mass, hear confession and even to use their cells as sites for energetic campaigns of evangelism.[205] John Bunyan had access to pen and paper and took advantage of his enforced leisure to write *Grace abounding to the chief of sinners* and several other books, including the first part of *Pilgrim's progress*.[206] Clearly some prison governors did not take the task of rehabilitating dissenters very seriously. Others, however, certainly did. Recusants held in York Castle in the winter of 1599–1600, for instance, were force-fed Protestantism by being dragged to a series of fifty sermons, to which they responded by murmuring, heckling and blocking their ears.[207] To the most deeply committed Catholics, exposure to heretical preaching – the central medium of the Reformation – amounted to a form of psychological torture.

An alternative to imprisonment was deportation and banishment. By a proclamation of 1538, Anabaptists and sacramentarians were peremptorily ordered to depart England on pain of death and similar commands were repeatedly issued to Jesuits and seminary priests after 1574, with the intent that the realm might be 'free from the danger and infection which is derived from their continual workings upon men's consciences'.[208] In the 1550s, Stephen Gardiner found that he could achieve the same effect by exerting a subtler form of pressure. As he reputedly confided to the imperial ambassador Simon Renard, merely summoning preachers for interrogation had proved 'a good device for getting the Lutherans out of the country'.[209] The twin acts against seditious sectaries and popish recusants of 1593 both sent offenders into involuntary exile, the latter to the end that the kingdom would not be 'pestered and overcharged' with a multitude of impoverished Catholics, who being committed to prison 'do live for the most part in better case than they could if they were abroad at their own liberty'.[210] A third conviction under the Quaker and Conventicle Acts of 1662 and 1664 earned a dissenter seven years transportation to the New World, though this was only rarely carried out in practice because of the difficulty of persuading the colonies to accept such convicts.[211] Twenty-eight Friends perished of plague aboard the *Black Eagle* in 1665, while the ship lay at anchor in the Thames prior to setting sail across the Atlantic Ocean; the rest were released after the vessel was captured in the Channel by a Dutch privateer.[212] By exporting such troublemakers across the seas, Tudor and Stuart regimes hoped to defuse their potentially dangerous influence upon the English populace.

Fiscal penalties were also employed with increasing frequency. If non-conformists were unperturbed by the sanctions of the ecclesiastical courts, it was thought that they might be persuaded to comply by a systematic assault on their income and property. Under the Act of Uniformity of 1559, failure to attend Protestant services was punishable by a one shilling fine. The 1581 recusancy law raised the penalty to the crippling sum of £20 per month. Those unable to pay would lose two-thirds of their estates by sequestration. Bishop John Aylmer believed this would be more effective than imprisonment, which 'by sparing their housekeeping greatly enricheth them'.[213] Administered by the Exchequer, this system of extortion made a serious hole in the fortunes of some wealthy recusants; lower down the social scale, justices confiscated other goods and chattels.[214] In 1589, for instance, Norfolk commissioners made an indenture of the possessions of John Dike of Kelling with a view to seizing them: these included a milch cow, two workhorses, and assorted items of furniture.[215] Pecuniary pressure on nonconforming Catholics reached a dramatic peak during the Interregnum, aggravated by their Cavalier connections. In the years 1650–52 alone, some £4,466 was raised by systematic application of the recusancy statutes in Staffordshire, as compared with £927 in 1640.[216]

Fines were also used to deter Protestant separatists under the Conventicle Acts of 1664 and 1670. Both preachers and worshippers were liable to heavy exactions and, by default, forfeiture of their moveable possessions. If the sale of these items was too meagre to yield the required sum the distress was to be levied on richer members of the same congregation.[217] As the tireless Westmorland justice Sir Daniel Fleming commented about his crusade against northern Quakers, 'it is as clear as the day that nothing will convince them of their errors so soon as the drawing of money from them; for a great part of their religion – notwithstanding their great zeal and fair pretences – is tied to their purse strings'.[218] By a process of attrition, dissent would gradually disintegrate as individuals came to realise that they simply could not afford the luxury of refusing to conform to the established Church of England.

Recusants were also vulnerable to a variety of special taxes and tariffs, such as an Elizabethan levy to equip light horsemen for service in Ireland.[219] In the 1620s they had to pay double subsidies like foreign immigrants, on the grounds that, to use the words of Sir Edward Coke, they were 'aliens in heart'.[220] Under Charles I and during the Civil War, Catholics were mercilessly exploited as a monetary resource to fund the expensive military engagements of the late 1630s and 1640s. Other minorities were the targets of similar forms of expropriation. Economic protectionism had always dictated that stranger merchants and craftsmen were assessed at a higher rate that native traders and artisans and made to pay for the privilege of religious asylum by contributing extra sums to the civic defence and security of the coastal towns in which they resided.[221] The later Stuarts preyed on the readmitted Jews as a convenient source of revenue and in 1689 the Commons passed a resolution ordering a bill to be introduced to raise the sum of £100,000 from the community, quite apart from the existing fiscal obligations the English state imposed upon individuals.[222] The aim of taxing religious deviance out of existence was gradually outweighed by the Crown's increasing need to preserve such groups as a sleeping financial asset that could be tapped into at times of royal and national exigency. By this means, as we see in Chapter 5, members of minority churches and sects were effectively able to purchase immunity from persecution – to pay for the privilege of their own toleration.

Throughout the sixteenth and seventeenth centuries, dissenters were also subjected to various civil disabilities designed to induce them to rejoin the ranks of the orthodox by exposing them to the humiliating experience of being treated as second-class citizens and incipient criminals. Chief among these was disqualification from holding political office. Catholics, Quakers, Presbyterians and other sectarians were all barred from becoming members of Parliament, justices of the peace, or city governors because of their refusal to swear the oaths of allegiance and supremacy. Periodic purges of the county magistracy flushed out suspected dissemblers and after the Restoration the Corporation and Test Acts made reception of the Anglican sacrament a precondition for public employment and more particularly for entry into the hallowed halls of the House of Commons. This attempt to close off the loopholes so deftly exploited by dissenters was temporarily reinstated by the Occasional Conformity Act of 1711.[223] Under the ferocious Act against Popery of 1700, those making profession of the popish religion and refusing to take the oaths of allegiance and supremacy were also disabled from inheriting and purchasing lands and tenements.[224]

Furthermore, there were repeated attempts to ensure that false believers could not seduce and proselytise the young under cover of acting as local schoolmasters. The Parliament of 1593 debated taking the children of convicted recusants away from their unfit parents at the age of seven and placing them in homes where they would be properly instructed in the Protestant faith, though in the end this did not reach the statute book. Jacobean legislation prohibited the wealthy from sending their sons and daughters to Catholic finishing schools on the Continent on pain of £100.[225] Dissenters too were the objects of attempts to preserve an Anglican monopoly on education. Enshrined in the Schism Act of 1714, this policy retained its relevance even after 1689, its unstated aim being to extinguish such sects within a few generations.[226] Nonconformists were additionally prevented from attending the universities of Oxford and Cambridge. Recusants also suffered the indignity of being regarded as inherently untrustworthy subjects and sleeping terrorists. During the Armada scares, as well as throughout the Civil War and Interregnum, Catholics were required to hand over all the weapons they had in their possession.[227]

Disarmament was often accompanied by restrictions on dissenters' right of mobility – the Five Mile Act of 1593 kept known delinquents under virtual house arrest, banning papists from travelling beyond their places of residence without a special licence. Similar measures were passed by the Rump Parliament in February 1650 for 'the better discovery, prevention and avoyding of ... traiterous and dangerous Conspiracies'.[228] Under a statute of 1606 recusants could not enter a region within a ten-mile radius of London without written permission; this was reinforced by proclamation in 1640.[229] Legislation passed in 1665 likewise forbade deprived preachers from coming near the parishes where they had formerly been incumbents, or any corporation or borough.[230] In its pursuit of uniformity, the Tudor and Stuart state recognised few barriers to its right – indeed duty – of religious interference.

These processes of legal, social and spiritual discrimination and exclusion were linked with strategies of deliberate vilification. Ritually denounced on public occasions and in officially commissioned propaganda, heretics and dissenters were systematically stigmatised and classified as evil and dangerous others, if not literally or metaphorically denounced as agents of Satan. Thus, in the course of indicting Dorothea White and Katherine Bellamy, zealous recusants who maintained seminary priests, the judges presiding over the Middlesex Assizes in 1588 and 1592 declared that they had been 'moved and seduced by the instigation of the devil', a judicial cliché also routinely invoked in sentencing murderers and other felons.[231] Similar allegations pervaded episcopally sponsored sermons delivered from conspicuous pulpits like Paul's Cross in London, particularly on providential anniversaries like the discovery of the Gunpowder Plot in 1605. The liturgy issued for use at the yearly celebration of this miraculous deliverance also explicitly attributed the conspiracy to diabolical guile. The massacre was 'a work of iniquity' hatched in hell itself.[232]

Proclamations and the preambles of statutes against Anabaptists and separatists likewise exploited an ancient repertoire of stereotypes of deviance, including insinuations of sexual perversion and moral licentiousness. A royal edict ordering the prosecution of the Family of Love in 1580 spoke of the secretive sect as 'an evil' devised 'by the malice of the devil' and deplored the 'monstrous new kind of speech' by which it bewitched the ignorant and simple people.[233]

Printed pamphlets and treatises sponsored or endorsed by the authorities also contributed to the cultural marginalisation of religious minorities. In the 1520s, Thomas More utilised the same technique of demonisation in denouncing Luther as 'an open incestuous lecher, a plain limb of the Devil and a manifest messenger from hell' and Tyndale as 'that beast and hell-hound of the Devil's kennel'.[234] Thomas Bell received a royal pension for writing a succession of virulently anti-Catholic works with scurrilous titles like *The popes funerall*, *The woefull crie of Rome* and *The Jesuits antepast* in the early seventeenth century and Richard Bancroft was the mastermind behind a brilliant campaign against Martin Marprelate and the Presbyterians in the late 1580s and early 1590s, employing some of the leading semi-professional satirists of the day. With the aid of Samuel Harsnet, he also issued damaging propaganda against the 'fraudulent practises' and 'egregious impostures' perpetrated by puritan and Jesuit exorcists which ingeniously demonstrated that these bitter enemies actually shared the same despicable characteristics.[235] In John Rogers' *The displaying of an horrible secte of grosse and wicked heretiques*

(1578), Familists were accused of sanctioning adultery and antinomianism,[236] and puritans were often conflated with medieval heretics like Cathars and Donatists by their conformist adversaries. Laudian and later polemic, like that produced by Peter Heylyn, created a compelling caricature of Calvinists as anarchic rebels and deluded enthusiasts who legitimated tyrannicide and engaged in fanatical behaviour reminiscent of the disastrous millenarian experiment at Münster in 1534–35.[237] In turn these features were transferred onto the shoulders of the Civil War sects and they occasionally resurfaced in the works of Restoration divines like Samuel Parker and Edward Stillingfleet. In the course of a charge to a Cheshire grand jury on 2 October 1677, Sir Peter Leicester gave expression to the same ingrained assumptions, fulminating against Roman Catholics as 'engineers ... continually hatching new devices for stirring up rebellions in our nation and to disturb the peace of Israel' and insisting that puritans who repudiated Anglican ceremonies had been 'tickled in the ears by the Jesuits'.[238] The hostile rhetoric and vicious commonplaces which pervaded such texts and addresses were perhaps the most insidious manifestations of official intolerance.

An analysis of statute books and lists of edicts and ordinances allows us to sketch in outline the administrative and judicial mechanisms by which the Tudor and Stuart authorities sought to enforce religious uniformity. But it is important to recognise that such prescriptions do not necessarily provide us with an accurate guide to the realities of persecution in practice. As a speaker in the House of Commons commented in 1601, 'a law without execution is like a bell without a clapper', or to quote Sir Harbottle Grimston's charge to the Essex Grand Jury in 1638, 'execution does as it were *animare legem*, it quickens, animates and puts life into the law which otherwise of itself is but *littera mortua*, or dead letter'.[239] The implementation of government policy in sixteenth- and seventeenth-century England was dependent upon the loyalty and diligence of local representatives of the Crown and Church. In the absence of a professional civil service and police force, these institutions were forced to rely on the co-operation of a voluntary bureaucracy and this frequently hampered the due execution of justice. Some historians have been optimistic about the power of the Tudor state to enforce its will upon the populace. Geoffrey Elton's emphasis on the ruthless efficiency of the Henrician regime under Thomas Cromwell has been echoed by Ronald Hutton in his search for an explanation for the striking lack of resistance to the sweeping theological and liturgical revolution that was the English Reformation.[240] Michael Questier has likewise argued that the Elizabethan and Jacobean system for punishing recusancy was far more effective than the flimsy scare-crow of historical myth and the work of Steve Hindle, Michael Braddick and others is also alerting us to the ways in which a centralising early modern state was increasingly flexing its muscles and stretching its tentacles into the localities in the course of this period.[241]

Nonetheless, it would be a mistake to ignore the intrinsic flaws of a system of law and order which revolved around 'mutual neighbourly supervision' and which exhibited a high level of discretion and flexibility.[242] During two centuries marked by almost constant upheaval, uncertainty and turbulence, many justices and constables simply failed to share the law's fluctuating definition of an offence. The gentry and middling sort who took on the chief burden of public and parish office had their own agendas: where these clashed with the aims of government policy, the result was liable to be studied inertia if not outright defiance.[243] Bribery was not uncommon and in small, close-knit communities, officials were vulnerable to being placed under considerable pressure to overlook nonconformity by those higher up in the social hierarchy to whom they owed respect and were indebted for the exercise of patronage. The enforcement of official policy in the first half of the sixteenth century was also seriously compromised by the fact that many religious conservatives remained in post. In 1564 as many as 157 out of 852 JPs were said to be adversaries of Protestantism, with another 264 categorised as indifferent.[244] In Sussex, the crypto-Catholics Sir Thomas Palmer, Thomas Lewkenor and Richard Emley remained on the commission of the peace throughout the 1570s, neutralising episcopal initiatives to identify and discipline stubborn papists. In response to the charge that they were lax in detecting those 'backward in religion', they protested 'we cannott take knowledge of everymans … conscience that cometh into our companie'.[245] Similar complaints were made in 1581 about sympathetic Suffolk gentlemen who countenanced separatists, Familists and refractory puritans, 'winkinge at if not of pollicie procuringe the disordered sorte to go forwardes in their evill attemptes' in a manner which would ultimately 'hazarde the overthrow of all religion'.[246] The device of occasional conformity facilitated the persistence of dissenters in office after the Restoration and this too prevented many of their co-religionists from being hauled before the civil courts for attending conventicles.

Where the balance of local power was held by a defiant minority, officials intent on securing compliance faced an uphill struggle and were virtually terrorised into inactivity. The second Conventicle Act of 1670 contained a belated admission of the chronic problem that many constables and magistrates were failing to enforce persecuting legislation. Village officials were fined £5 for non-presentment, while chief magistrates who 'wilfully and wittingly omitted the performance' of their duty were stung with the massive sum of £100. As an incentive, informers were offered a third of the penalties levied on offenders by way of reward.[247] The difficulty of enforcing the laws against nonconformity persisted in the 1680s. In London and Middlesex, for instance, the refusal of grand juries to approve indictments against persons attending illicit assemblies repeatedly frustrated government attempts to hamstring dissent.[248]

Throughout the sixteenth and seventeenth centuries, as Mike Braddick has remarked, there remained an 'uncomfortable gap' between the pretensions of the persecuting confessional state and local political and social realities. Lay interference restricted the ability of the Tudor and Stuart regimes to propagate their varying visions of the 'true religion' and to prosecute those who deviated from it. Provincial evasion of central directives made uniformity an impossible aspiration and even narrow conformity hard to sustain.[249] The persecution of dissent was a process of negotiation between the Crown and its representatives in the towns and countryside. Only where and when their interests converged did the machinery of civil intolerance operate with anything approaching administrative efficiency.

Similar observations and caveats apply to ecclesiastical justice. It, too, is best characterised as selective and exemplary rather than comprehensive. Modern scholars have disagreed about the impact that the Reformation had upon the capacity of the church courts to mould liturgical observance and doctrinal opinion. Some, like Ronald Marchant and Ralph Houlbrooke, have argued that they were gravely weakened by the religious and political changes of the era and have presented a picture of progressive deterioration and obsolescence. More recent research by Martin Ingram, however, has stressed the continuing vigour of these institutions, or rather their recovery after a mid-Tudor dip, and credited them with a vital role in policing piety and devotion before the Civil War.[250] There can be little doubt that their efficacy as a mechanism for repressing religious nonconformity diminished markedly in the later seventeenth century: as John Spurr has commented, the Restoration Church of England found it exceptionally difficult to enforce uniformity on a nation which had tasted nearly two decades of liberty and licence.[251]

No less than the civil and criminal courts, their spiritual counterparts relied for their business on the good will of unpaid officials who often found it was less disruptive to communal harmony and peace to turn a blind eye to nonconformity than to take steps to draw it to the attention of the episcopal authorities. During a parliamentary debate in 1571 it was observed that many churchwardens 'would rather commit perjury then give their neighbours cause for offence'; a puritan petition of 1590 complained that they were nominated in such a way as made them 'most fit to serve the humour of the gentry and the multitude'; and the incumbents of the same office in the Lancashire village of Prescot in 1595 were said to be 'infected with papistry' and accused of 'colourable and cunning dealing' to hide the infractions of the Catholics of the parish.[252] Later Stuart churchwardens could be equally truculent, swayed by personal animosity and entrenched in local faction. In the diocese of Oxford an average of 12 per cent of parish officers summoned to visitations between 1662 and 1675 did not appear before the bishop.[253] All too often the notorious return of *omnia bene* in response to visitation articles disguised the ineradicable pluralism of urban and rural communities. Spiritual no less than secular justice was at the mercy of those whose duty it was to present refractory members of their communities to it.

There was, then, always potential for a significant gulf between the letter of the laws against religious deviance and the situation at the grass roots. Filtered through the sieve of local interests and priorities, the measures which gave teeth to the persecuting ideology of the sixteenth- and seventeenth-century Church and state could not only be tempered and mitigated by the officials charged with carrying them out. They could also be augmented and intensified by justices, constables and churchwardens whose zeal against heresy, idolatry or nonconformity drove them to exceed their brief and treat dissenters with greater severity. The conduct of such persons underlines the artificiality of drawing hard and fast boundaries between 'official' and 'popular' intolerance. It also draws attention indirectly to some of the practical ways in which early modern people condoned and tolerated the religious transgressions of neighbours who in theory were their spiritual enemies. These are issues which will be discussed at greater length in Chapters 3 and 5.

NOTES

1 Haigh, *English Reformations*, p. 86.

2 G. R. Elton (ed.), *The Tudor Constitution: Documents and Commentary* (Cambridge, 1982 edn), pp. 399–401.

3 Susan Brigden, *London and the Reformation* (Oxford, 1989), pp. 606–7.

4 *The Sermons of Edwin Sandys*, ed. John Ayre, PS (Cambridge, 1842), pp. 34–54, at pp. 54, 49 respectively.

5 Edmund Calamy, *An indictment against England because of her self-murdering divisions* (London, 1645). J. P. Kenyon (ed.), *The Stuart Constitution: Documents and Commentary* (Cambridge, 2nd edn, 1986), pp. 353–6.

6 Spurr, *Restoration Church*, p. 80.

7 Augustine, letter to Vincentius, bishop of Mauretania (408), in David George Mullan (ed.), *Religious Pluralism in the West: An Anthology* (Oxford, 1998), pp. 39–50, quotations at pp. 41 and 42. On Augustine, see above, ch. 1, n. 2.

8 Zagorin, *Religious Toleration*, pp. 30–2 and ch. 2 *passim*; Lecler, *Toleration and the Reformation*, i. 60–1.

9 Thomas Aquinas, *Summa Theologica*, pt II, 2nd part, question xi, 'Of Heresy', Article 3, in Mullan (ed.), *Religious Pluralism*, pp. 70–1. Aquinas's attitude towards non-believers (infidels and Jews) was far more indulgent on the grounds that they had never known the Christian faith: *ibid*, pp. 56–66. See Lecler, *Toleration and the Reformation*, i. 78–9, 87–9. For the medieval discourse of fraternal correction, see Shogimen, 'From disobedience to toleration', esp. 601–6.

10 Brad S. Gregory, *Salvation at Stake: Christian Martyrdom in Early Modern Europe* (Cambridge, MA, 1999), pp. 85–6 and ch. 3 *passim*.

11 Thomas More, *The confutation of Tyndale's answer*, in Louis A. Schuster, Richard C. Marius, James P. Lusardi and Richard J. Shoeck (eds), *The Complete Works of St Thomas More* (New Haven, 1973), viii. 28. Such arguments were reiterated in *A dialogue concerning heresies* (1529), in *ibid.*, vi (1), ed. Thomas Lawler *et al.*, 405–10, 415–18. See also Craig W. D'Alton, 'Charity or fire? The argument of Thomas More's 1529 *Dyaloge*', *SCJ*, 33 (2002), 51–70.

12 Dickens, *English Reformation*, p. 294.

13 Gina Alexander, 'Bonner and the Marian persecutions', in Christopher Haigh (ed.), *The English Reformation Revised* (Cambridge, 1987), p. 160; Brigden, *London and the Reformation*, p. 574.

14 Robert Persons, *A treatise of three conversions of England from paganisme to Christian religion*, 3 vols ([St Omer], 1603–4), iii. 388. See Anne Dillon, *The Construction of Martyrdom in the English Catholic Community, 1535–1603* (Aldershot, 2002), pp. 364–8.

15 Thomas Hide, *A consolatorie epistle to the afflicted Catholikes* ([London secret press], 1580), sig. EIV.

16 Helpful surveys of post-Reformation attitudes include: Dalberg-Acton, 'Protestant theory of persecution'; Goldie, 'Theory of religious intolerance'; Coffey, *Persecution and Toleration*, ch. 2.

17 *The lanterne of lyghte* (London, [1530?]), fo. 52v.

18 *Certaine sermons or homilies appointed to be read in churches* (London, 1623), pp. 44–5.

19 Davies, *Religion of the Word*, pp. 166–7; Gerald Bray (ed.), *Tudor Church Reform: The Henrician Canons of 1535 and the Reformatio Legum Ecclesiasticarum*, Church of England Record Society 8 (Woodbridge, 2000), pp. 187–213, at pp. 187, 193.

20 Thomas Bilson, *The true difference between Christian subjection and unchristian rebellion* (London, 1585), p. 17. See also Conrad Russell, 'Arguments for religious unity in England, 1530–1650', *JEH*, 18 (1967), 201–26.

21 Thomas Edwards, *The casting down of the last and strongest hold of Satan. Or, a treatise against toleration and pretended liberty of conscience* (London, 1647), p. 64.

22 Spurr, *Restoration Church*, p. 47.

23 Goldie, 'Theory of religious intolerance', pp. 348, 349, 350 and *passim*.

24 *Ibid.*, pp. 362–6, and Mark Goldie, 'John Locke, Jonas Proast and religious toleration 1688–1692', in John Walsh, Colin Haydon and Stephen Taylor (eds), *The Church of England c.1689–c.1833* (Cambridge, 1993), pp. 143–71, esp. 168.

25 Sandys, *Sermons*, ed. Ayre, p. 333.

26 Quoted in Graeme Murdock, 'The importance of being Josiah: an image of Calvinist identity', *SCJ*, 29 (1998), 1043–59, at 1054.

27 See *ibid.*, 1043–59 *passim*. See also John N. King, *Tudor Royal Iconography* (Princeton, 1989), ch. 1 and *passim*.

28 See Rex, *Henry VIII*, pp. 23–9, 103–5, 153, 173–4. For the Lambert trial see also MacCulloch, *Thomas Cranmer*, pp. 232–3.

29 MacCulloch, *Tudor Church Militant*, ch. 2.

30 Hughes and Larkin (eds), *Tudor Royal Proclamations*, ii. 57–8; ii. 481–3; James F. Larkin and Paul L. Hughes (eds), *Stuart Royal Proclamations*, vol. I, *Royal Proclamations of King James I 1603–1625* (Oxford, 1973), pp. 89, 245.

31 25 Henry VIII c. 6; Rex, *Henry VIII*, p. 173.

32 See 4 Jac. I. c. 5, 21 Jac. I. cc. 7, 20, 1 Car. I. c. 1; C. H. Firth and R. S. Tait (eds), *Acts and Ordinances of the Interregnum 1642–1660*, 3 vols (London, 1911), ii. 387–9 and see 393–6 (for a further act against swearing and cursing). See also Joan R. Kent, 'Attitudes of members of the House of Commons to the regulation of "personal conduct" in late Elizabethan and early Stuart England', *Bulletin of the Institute of Historical Research*, 46 (1973), 41–71; Keith Thomas, 'The puritans and adultery: the act of 1650 reconsidered', in Donald Pennington and Keith Thomas (eds), *Puritans and Revolutionaries: Essays in Seventeenth Century History Presented to Christopher Hill* (Oxford, 1978), pp. 257–82; Derek Hirst, 'The failure of godly rule in the English Republic', *P&P*, 132 (1991), 33–66.

33 Claydon, *William III*, ch. 1, quotations at pp. 32, 60. See also Hannah Smith, 'The idea of a Protestant monarchy 1714–1760', *P&P*, 185 (2004), 91–118.

34 D. M. Loades, *The Oxford Martyrs* (London, 1970), p. 109.

35 Horst, *Radical Brethren*, p. 106.

36 John Davis, 'Joan of Kent, Lollardy and the English Reformation', *JEH*, 33 (1982), 233; MacCulloch, *Thomas Cranmer*, pp. 475–6.

37 See Patrick Collinson, 'The Elizabethan exclusion crisis and the Elizabethan polity', *Proceedings of the British Academy*, 84 (1994), pp. 84–5; Patrick Collinson, 'The monarchical republic of Queen Elizabeth I', in his *Elizabethan Essays* (London, 1994), pp. 45–6.

38 Sandys, *Sermons*, ed. Ayre, pp. 57, 59, 69, 61, 62, 56. See my 'An English Deborah? The myth of Elizabeth I as a providential monarch', in Susan Doran and Thomas Freeman (eds), *The Myth of Elizabeth I* (Basingstoke, 2003), pp. 149–50.

39 Murdock, 'Importance of being Josiah', 1054.

40 Goldie, 'Theory of religious intolerance', p. 334.

41 Collinson, *The Religion of Protestants*, ch. 4 *passim*, quotations at pp. 153, 178.

42 Marsh, *Family of Love*, p. 150.

43 Kent, 'Attitudes', p. 43. This was in the context of a speech on drunkenness.

44 Thomas, *Religion and the Decline of Magic*, p. 107. On these convictions, see my *Providence in Early Modern England* (Oxford, 1999), esp. pp. 135–42.

45 William Hunt, *The Puritan Moment: The Coming of Revolution in an English County* (Cambridge, MA, 1983), p. 188; Conrad Russell, *Parliaments and English Politics 1621–1629* (Oxford, 1979), pp. 229–31.

46 Kenyon (ed.), *Stuart Constitution* (2nd edn), p. 240; Blair Worden, 'Oliver Cromwell and the Sin of Achan', in Derek Beales and Geoffrey Best (eds), *History, Society and the Churches: Essays in Honour of Owen Chadwick* (Cambridge, 1985), pp. 125–45.

47 Alexander Ross, *[Pansebia]. Or, a view of all religions in the world* (London, 4th edn, 1664), p. 506.

48 Russell, 'Arguments for religious unity', p. 222.

49 William Laud, *The Works of the Most Reverend Father in God, William Laud, D.D.*, ed. W. Scott, 7 vols (Oxford, 1847), i. 96; Roger L'Estrange, *Toleration discuss'd* (London, 1663), p. 86.

50 Goldie, 'Locke, Proast and religious toleration', p. 167.

51 Margaret Aston, 'Lollardy and sedition, 1381–1431', *P&P*, 17 (1960), 1–44.

52 Lake, 'Anti-popery', pp. 84–7. On Hacket, see my '"Frantick Hacket": prophecy, sorcery, insanity and the Elizabethan puritan movement', *HJ*, 41 (1998), pp. 27–66.

53 Gordon Schochet, 'Samuel Parker, religious diversity, and the ideology of persecution', in Roger D. Lund (ed.), *The Margins of Orthodoxy: Heterodox Writing and Cultural Response, 1660–1750* (Cambridge, 1995), pp. 119–48, at 132–4.

54 Russell, 'Arguments for religious unity', p. 219.

55 Murphy, *Conscience and Community*, pp. 106–8, 233–8. See also Glenn Burgess, 'Thomas Hobbes: religious toleration or religious indifference', in Nederman and Laursen (eds), *Difference and Dissent*, pp. 139–61.

56 Mark Knights, '"Meer religion" and the "church-state" of Restoration England: the impact and ideology of James II's declarations of indulgence', in Alan Houston and Steve Pincus (eds), *A Nation Transformed: England after the Restoration* (Cambridge, 2001), pp. 41–70.

57 For these developments see Gordon Leff, *Heresy in the Later Middle Ages: The Relation of Heterodoxy to Dissent c.1250–c.1450*, 2 vols (Manchester, 1967), i. 34–46; John Guy, 'Perceptions of heresy, 1200–1550', in Gordon J. Schochet with Patricia E. Tatspaugh and Carol Brobeck (eds), *Reformation, Humanism and Revolution: Papers Presented at the Folger Institute Seminar 'Political Thought in the Henrician Age, 1500–1550'* (Washington, DC, 1990), pp. 39–41; A. K. McHardy, '*De heretico comburendo*, 1401', in Margaret Aston and Colin Richmond (eds), *Lollardy and the Gentry in the Later Middle Ages* (Stroud, 1997), p. 113; Lecler, *Toleration and the Reformation*, i. 80–1.

58 The relevant acts are 5 Rich. II, st. 2, c. 5; 2 Hen. IV, c. 15; 2 Hen.V, st. 1, c. 7. See H. G. Richardson, 'Heresy and the lay power under Richard II', *EHR*, 201 (1936), 1–28; Guy, 'Perceptions of heresy', pp. 42–3; Peter McNiven, *Heresy and Politics in the Reign of Henry IV: The Burning of John Badby* (Woodbridge, 1987), ch. 3; McHardy, '*De heretico comburendo*', pp. 112–26.

59 See G. L. Harriss, 'Medieval government and statecraft', *P&P*, 25 (1963), 8–39, esp. 13–17; J. Dahmus, 'Henry IV of England: an example of royal control of the Church in the fifteenth century', *Journal of Church and State*, 23 (1981), 35–46; Rex, *Lollards*, ch. 1.

60 Elton (ed.), *Tudor Constitution*, pp. 364–7 and see pp. 338–45.

61 See esp. 25 Hen. VIII. c. 14, the 'Act to punish heresy', which removed the Church's ability to initiate heresy proceedings on its own.

62 See John Bellamy, *The Tudor Law of Treason: An Introduction* (London, 1979); G. R. Elton, *Policy and Police: The Enforcement of the Reformation in the Age of Thomas Cromwell* (Cambridge, 1972), ch. 6; Elton (ed.), *Tudor Constitution*, pp. 59–87. For later developments, see D. Alan Orr, *Treason and the State: Law, Politics and Ideology in the English Civil War* (Cambridge, 2002).

63 See Peter Marshall, 'Papist as heretic: the burning of John Forrest, 1538', *HJ*, 41 (1998), 351–74.

64 Elton (ed.), *Tudor Constitution*, pp. 433–7.

65 Collins, 'Church settlement', *passim*, at 19.

66 Coffey, *Persecution and Toleration*, p. 99.

67 Shagan, *Popular Politics*, p. 51 and *passim*.

68 William Cecil, *The Execution of Justice in England*, ed. Robert M. Kingdon (Ithaca, NY, 1965).

69 For an important discussion of these contested categories, see Peter Lake and Michael Questier, 'Puritans, papists, and the "public sphere" in early modern England: the Edmund Campion affair in context', *Journal of Modern History*, 72 (2000), 587–627.

70 See William Monter, 'Heresy executions in Reformation Europe, 1520–1565', in Grell and Scribner (eds), *Tolerance and Intolerance*, pp. 48–64. For early signs of these processes of confessionalisation, see Peter Marshall, 'The other black legend: the Henrician Reformation and the Spanish people', *EHR*, 116 (2001), 31–49.

71 See Bossy, *Christianity in the West*, pp. 153–61; Stuart Clark, *Thinking with Demons: The Idea of Witchcraft in Early Modern Europe* (Oxford, 1997), chs 39–41. See also Paul Kléber Monod, *The Power of Kings: Monarchy and Religion in Europe 1589–1715* (New Haven, 1999), esp. chs 2–3, though this book traces a trajectory of sacred monarchy giving way to the rational state.

72 *The Works of that Learned and Judicious Divine Mr Richard Hooker*, ed. J. Keble, 2 vols (Oxford, 1850), ii. 98.

73 Leland H. Carlson (ed.), *The Writings of Henry Barrow 1587–90*, Elizabethan Nonconformist Texts iii (London, 1962), p. 558. See also Collinson, *Elizabethan Puritan Movement*, pp. 24–6.

74 See Leland H. Carlson (ed.), *The Writings of Henry Barrow 1590–1591*, Elizabethan Nonconformist Texts v (London, 1966), pp. 6–10, for one articulation of this theme.

75 Collinson, *Elizabethan Puritan Movement*, pp. 348–50. This was, of course, a broader phenomenon, employed for a variety of reasons: see Christopher Haigh, 'Communion and community: exclusion from communion in post-Reformation England', *JEH*, 51 (2000), 721–40.

76 T. E. Hartley (ed.), *Proceedings in the Parliaments of Elizabeth I*, vol. I, 1558–1581 (London, 1981), p. 241. It was Francis Bacon who said of Elizabeth I that she was disinclined 'to make window into men's hearts and secret thoughts': J. E. Neale, *Elizabeth I and her Parliaments*, 2 vols (London, 1953), i. 391.

77 More, *Complete Works*, vi (1), p. 407 and pp. 405–10 *passim*.

78 For Bucer, see MacCulloch, *Thomas Cranmer*, p. 476. For Calvin, Lecler, *Toleration and the Reformation*, i. 328–32.

79 Bray (ed.), *Tudor Church Reform*, pp. 195–7, 205–7.

80 MacCulloch, *Thomas Cranmer*, p. 475.

81 Jordan, *Development of Religious Toleration*, pp. 45–52.

82 Neale, *Elizabeth I and her Parliaments*, i. 117; Sandys, *Sermons*, ed. Ayre, p. 40 and see pp. 72–3.

83 Stephen Batman, *The doome warning all men to the judgemente* (London, 1581), p. 395.

84 Henry Foley (ed.), *Records of the English Province of the Society of Jesus*, 7 vols in 8 (London, 1877–83), vii (2), p. 1066; Wallace Notestein, Frances Helen Relf and Hartley

Simpson (eds), *Commons Debates 1621*, 7 vols (New Haven, 1935), vii. 636.

85 Christopher Durston, *Cromwell's Major Generals: Godly Government during the English Revolution* (Manchester, 2001), p. 46. For the Nayler case, see Leo Damrosch, *The Sorrows of the Quaker Jesus: James Nayler and the Puritan Crackdown on the Free Spirit* (Cambridge, MA, 1996), ch. 4, at p. 213.

86 29 Charles II c. 9. See Andrew Browning (ed.), *English Historical Documents 1660–1714* (London, 1953), p. 400.

87 See Michael Hunter, '"Aikenhead the atheist": the context and consequences of articulate irreligion in the late seventeenth century', in his *Science and the Shape of Orthodoxy: Intellectual Change in Late-Seventeenth Century Britain* (Woodbridge, 1995), pp. 308–32.

88 MacCulloch, *Thomas Cranmer*, pp. 475–6; G. R. Elton, 'Persecution and toleration in the English Reformation', in Sheils (ed.), *Persecution and Toleration*, pp. 175–8.

89 Hartley (ed.), *Proceedings ... 1558–1581*, p. 539.

90 Francis Bacon, 'Of unity in religion', in *The Essayes or Counsels Civill and Morall* (London, 1906), p. 11.

91 Coffey, *Persecution and Toleration*, p. 25.

92 Goldie, 'Theory of religious intolerance', p. 365.

93 *Ibid.*, p. 364.

94 Philip Wynter (ed.), *The Works of the Right Reverend Joseph Hall, D.D.*, 10 vols (Oxford, 1863), vi. 649–50.

95 Watts, *Dissenters*, pp. 256–7; *ODNB*, xxi. 650–1. For the continuity of the burning of women, which was not abolished until 1790, see Malcolm Gaskill, *Crime and Mentalities in Early Modern England* (Cambridge, 2000), p. 113.

96 1 Eliz. I c. 2. See Elton (ed.), *Tudor Constitution*, pp. 410–13.

97 Hartley (ed.), *Proceedings ... 1558–1581*, p. 240; Neale, *Elizabeth I and her Parliaments*, i. 212–15, 386–7.

98 Hooker, *Works*, ed. Keble, i. 102.

99 It was frequently enquired after in visitations, see W. P. M. Kennedy (ed.), *Elizabethan Episcopal Administration*, 3 vols, Alcuin Club Collections 25–7 (London, 1924), ii. 14, 70, 71, 95, 120, 130; iii. 140, 148, 164, 179, 229, 248, 260, 289, 307, 320.

100 For evidence of some efforts at vigorous enforcement, see, however, Questier, *Conversion*, pp. 144–5.

101 Firth and Rait (eds), *Acts and Ordinances*, ii. 423–5, 1162–70.

102 Kenyon (ed.), *Stuart Constitution* (2nd edn), pp. 385–6.

103 Donald A. Spaeth, *The Church in an Age of Danger: Parsons and Parishioners, 1660–1740* (Cambridge, 2000), p. 159.

104 Questier, *Conversion*, pp. 120–5.

105 On ordeals, see Robert Bartlett, *Trial by Fire and Water: The Medieval Judicial Ordeal* (Oxford, 1986).

106 John Spurr, 'A profane history of early modern oaths', *TRHS*, 6th series, 11 (2001), 37–63, at 38.

107 See M. C. Questier, 'Loyalty, religion and state power in early modern England: English Romanism and the Jacobean Oath of Allegiance', *HJ*, 40 (1997), 311–29, at 311.

108 See, respectively, Kenyon (ed.), *Stuart Constitution* (2nd edn), pp. 239–42, 330–1, 307–8. Key discussions include David Cressy, 'The Protestation protested, 1641 and 1642', *HJ*, 45 (2002), 251–70; Edward Vallance, '"An holy and sacramental paction": federal theology and the solemn league and covenant in England', *EHR*, 116 (2001), 50–75; Edward Vallance, 'Oaths, casuistry, and equivocation: Anglican responses to the Engagement Controversy', *HJ*, 44 (2001), 59–77.

109 Questier, *Conversion*, pp. 114–15.

110 See Firth and Rait (eds), *Acts and Ordinances*, i. 254–6; ii. 1170–80, at 1171.

111 13 Car. II. c. 1 (1662): An Act for preventing the Michiefs and Dangers that may arise by certain Persons called Quakers and others refusing to take lawful Oaths'. On the use of oaths against Quakers, see Barry Reay, 'The authorities and early Restoration Quakerism', *JEH*, 34 (1983), 69–84, esp. 71, 73–4, 75–6.

112 Collinson, *Elizabethan Puritan Movement*, pp. 243–8.

113 John Guy, 'The Elizabethan establishment and the ecclesiastical polity', in John Guy (ed.), *The Reign of Elizabeth I: Court and Culture in the Last Decade* (Cambridge, 1995), pp. 129–49, esp. 135–7, 139–40; Ethan H. Shagan, 'The English Inquisition: constitutional conflict and ecclesiastical law in the 1590s', *HJ*, 47 (2004), 541–65.

114 Kenyon (ed.), *Stuart Constitution* (2nd edn), p. 152; Paul S. Seaver, *Wallington's World: A Puritan Artisan in Seventeenth-Century London* (London, 1985), p. 51.

115 For these divergent viewpoints, see John S. Coolidge, *The Pauline Renaissance in England* (Oxford, 1970), esp. chs 1–2; Peter Lake, *Anglicans and Puritans? Presbyterianism and English Conformist Thought from Whitgift to Hooker* (London, 1988), esp. pp. 16–17, 44–7, 146–7, and M. E. C. Perrott, 'Richard Hooker and the Elizabethan Church', *JEH*, 49 (1998), 29–60.

116 See ch. 5, below, and Ethan M. Shagan, 'The battle for indifference in Elizabethan England', in Luc Racaut and Alec Ryrie (eds), *Moderate Voices in the European Reformations* (Aldershot, 2005), pp. 122–44.

117 See John Spurr, *Restoration Church*, pp. 125–8, at p. 127, and 337; John Spurr, 'Schism and the Restoration Church', *JEH*, 41 (1990), 408–24. For the politics of comprehension in this period, see Douglas R. Lacey, *Dissent and Parliamentary Politics in England 1661–1689: A Study in the Perpetuation and Tempering of Parliamentarianism* (New Brunswick, NJ, 1969).

118 Kenyon (ed.), *Stuart Constitution* (2nd edn), p. 356, and see ch. 5, below.

119 See n. 197 below.

120 Questier, *Conversion*, p.167.

121 MacCulloch, *Tudor Church Militant*, p. 133.

122 For these developments, see Milton, *Catholic and Reformed*.

123 Malcolm Lambert, *Medieval Heresy: Popular Movements from the Gregorian Reform to the Reformation* (Oxford, 1992), p. 269.

124 See John L. La Rocca, 'Popery and pounds: the effect of the Jesuit mission on penal legislation', in Thomas M. McCoog (ed.), *The Reckoned Expense: Edmund Campion and the Early English Jesuits* (Woodbridge, 1996), pp. 249–63.

125 Collinson, *Elizabethan Puritan Movement*, pp. 150–1, 154.

126 Kenneth Fincham (ed.), *Visitation Articles and Injunctions of the Early Stuart Church*, 2 vols, Church of England Record Society 1, 5 (Woodbridge, 1994–98), i. 122–6.

127 Spurr, *Restoration Church*, pp. 38, 51, 81.

128 *Ibid.* p. 74; Walsham, *Providence*, p. 139 and ch. 3 *passim*.

129 For visitations, see Walter Howard Frere (ed.), *Visitation Articles and Injunctions of the Period of the Reformation*, 3 vols (London, 1910); Kennedy (ed.), *Elizabethan Episcopal Administration*; Fincham (ed.), *Visitation Articles*.

130 For accounts of the workings of the church courts in this period, see Ronald A. Marchant, *The Church under the Law: Justice, Administration and Discipline in the Diocese of York 1560–1640* (Cambridge, 1969), esp. ch. 1; Ralph Houlbrooke, *Church Courts and the People during the English Reformation 1520–1570* (Oxford, 1979), esp. ch. 8; Martin Ingram, *Church Courts, Sex and Marriage in England, 1570–1640* (Cambridge, 1987), esp. ch. 1; Martin Ingram, 'Puritans and the Church Courts, 1560–1640', in Christopher Durston and Jacqueline Eales (eds), *The Culture of Puritanism, 1560–1700* (Basingstoke, 1996), pp. 58–91; Spurr, *Restoration Church*, pp. 209–19.

131 See R. G. Ussher, *The Rise and Fall of the High Commission* (Oxford, 1913; repr. 1968, with preface by Philip Tyler); Elton (ed.), *Tudor Constitution*, pp. 221–6, and for the act establishing it, pp. 226–30; Kenyon (ed.), *Stuart Constitution* (2nd edn), pp. 158–60 and for the act abolishing it, pp. 206–7. For an attempt to dispel the myth of the High Commission's tyranny, see Sharpe, *Personal Rule*, pp. 374–83.

132 Central institutions of government are described in Elton (ed.), *Tudor Constitution*; Kenyon (ed.), *Stuart Constitution* (2nd edn), see pp. 204–5, for the act abolishing the Star Chamber. For the structure of the state and its administrative organs in the provinces, see Michael J. Braddick, *State Formation in Early Modern England c.1550–1700* (Cambridge, 2000), esp. ch. 7. Outlines of the criminal courts and their operations can be found in J. A. Sharpe, *Crime in Early Modern England 1550–1750* (London, 1984), ch. 2 and John Briggs, Christopher Harrison, Angus McInnes and David Vincent, *Crime and Punishment in England: An Introductory History* (London, 1996).

133 Marjorie K. McIntosh, *A Community Transformed: The Manor and Liberty of Havering, 1500–1620* (Cambridge, 1991), esp. pp. 298–314 and *Controlling Misbehaviour in England, 1370–1600* (Cambridge, 1998), esp. pp. 34–45.

134 See Tanner (ed.), *Heresy Trials*, pp. 152–6. See also Norman P. Tanner, 'Penances imposed on Kentish Lollards by Archbishop Warham 1511–12', in Aston and Richmond (eds), *Lollardy and the Gentry*, pp. 229–49.

135 Davis, *Heresy and Reformation*, p. 108; Dickens, *Lollards and Protestants*, p. 233; L. E. Whatmore (ed.), *Archdeacon Harpsfield's Visitation 1557, together with the Visitations of 1556 and 1558*, CRS 45–46 (1950–51), i. 118.

136 Davis, *Heresy and Reformation*, p. 6.

137 Houlbrooke, *Church Courts*, p. 225.

138 Tanner, 'Penances', p. 40.

139 Haigh, *English Reformations*, p. 227.

140 Dave Postles, 'Penance and the market place: a Reformation dialogue with the medieval Church (c.1250–c.1600', *JEH*, 54 (2003), 441–68; Margo Todd, *The Culture of*

Protestantism in Early Modern Scotland (New Haven, 2002), ch. 3. For some characteristic examples, see Hubert Hall, 'Some Elizabethan penances in the diocese of Ely', *TRHS*, 3rd series 1 (1907), 263–7 and F. G. Emmison, *Elizabethan Life: Morals and the Church Courts* (Chelmsford, 1973), pp. 281–91.

141 Questier, *Conversion*, p. 110, n. 46.

142 Lake, *Boxmaker's Revenge*, p. 2.

143 Matar, *Islam*, pp. 69–70; Questier, *Conversion*, p. 110.

144 Spurr, *Restoration Church*, p. 214.

145 W. H. Frere and C. E. Douglas (eds), *Puritan Manifestoes: A Study of the Origin of the Puritan Revolt with a Reprint of the Admonition to the Parliament and Kindred Documents, 1572* (London, 1907), pp. 17, 34.

146 Stefan J. Smart, 'John Foxe and "The story of Richard Hun, Martyr"', *JEH*, 37 (1986), 1–14, at p. 5, n. 20.

147 Brigden, *London and the Reformation*, p. 149.

148 Frere and Douglas (eds), *Puritan Manifestoes*, pp. 32–3.

149 Quotations are taken from the aborted revision of canon law, the 'Reformatio Legum': Bray (ed.), *Tudor Church Reform*, p. 469. For excommunciation, see Emmison, *Morals*, pp. 300–7.

150 See, for typical examples, Bishop Valentine Carey's articles for Exeter, 1625, Archdeacon Theophilus Aylmer's articles for London, 1625, and William Higgins's articles for Derby, 1641: Fincham (ed.), *Visitation Articles*, ii. 5, 16 and 256.

151 Marchant, *Church under the Law*, p. 221; Barry Reay, 'The Muggletonians: an introductory survey', in Hill, Reay and Lamont (eds), *World of the Muggletonians*, p. 43.

152 Reay, 'Authorities', p. 78.

153 Emmison, *Morals*, p. 305.

154 Collinson, *Religion of Protestants*, p. 216.

155 Frere and Douglas (eds), *Puritan Manifestoes*, pp. 17, 33–4. See also Carlson (ed.), *Writings of Barrow ... 1587–90*, pp. 623–47.

156 Colllinson, *Religion of Protestants*, p. 215.

157 Spurr, *Restoration Church*, p. 215.

158 See also F. Douglas Price, 'The abuses of excommunication and the decline of ecclesiastical discipline under Queen Elizabeth', *EHR*, 57 (1942), 106–15. But cf. Ingram, *Church Courts*, pp. 14, 52–3, 340–62. For the post-1660 period, see Spurr, *Restoration Church*, p. 215.

159 Reay, 'Authorities', p. 79; J. Anthony Williams, *Catholic Recusancy in Wiltshire 1660–1791*, CRS Monograph Series 1 (London, 1968), p. 72.

160 Thomas Rymer, *Foedera, Conventiones, Literae, et Cujuscunque Generis* (The Hague, 3rd edn, 1739–45), vi, pt iv, p. 161.

161 For suggestive discussions of the judicial rite of burning heretics, see David Nicholls, 'The theatre of martyrdom in the French Reformation', *P&P*, 121 (1988), 50–73; Jane A. Dawson, 'The Scottish Reformation and the theatre of martyrdom', in Diana Wood (ed.), *Martyrs and Martyrologies*, SCH 30 (1993), pp. 259–70.

162 Coffey, *Persecution and Toleration*, p. 200.

163 Foxe, *Actes and monuments* (1570 edn), i. 551–2 and ii. 2151.

164 John Gough Nichols (ed.), *Narratives of the Days of the Reformation*, Camden Society, 1st series, 77 (1859), p. 28; Susan Brigden, 'Religion and social obligation in early sixteenth-century London', *P&P*, 103 (1984), 67–112, at 81.

165 Marshall, 'Papist as heretic', p. 356.

166 Rex, *Henry VIII*, p. 165.

167 Loades, *Oxford Martyrs*, p. 242.

168 The phrase is Diarmaid MacCulloch's: 'Archbishop Cranmer: concord and tolerance in a changing Church', in Grell and Scribner (eds), *Tolerance and Intolerance*, p. 204.

169 Quotation from Peter Lake and Michael Questier, 'Agency, appropriation, and rhetoric under the gallows: puritans, Romanists, and the state in early modern England', *P&P*, 153 (1996), 64–107, at p. 83. See also Peter Lake with Michael Questier, *The Antichrist's Lewd Hat: Protestants, Papists and Players in Post-Reformation England* (New Haven, 2002), ch. 7, esp. 231–9.

170 David Loades, 'John Foxe and the traitors: the politics of the Marian persecution', in Diana Wood (ed.), *Martyrs and Martyrologies*, SCH 30 (Oxford, 1993), pp. 231–44, at p. 242.

171 Lake and Questier, 'Agency, appropriation, and rhetoric', p. 86.

172 Richard van Dülmen, *Theatre of Horror: Crime and Punishment in Early Modern Germany*, trans. Elisabeth Neu (Cambridge, 1990), p. 3 and ch. 6.

173 Michel Foucault, *Discipline and Punish: The Birth of the Prison*, trans. Alan Sheridan (Harmondsworth, 1977; first publ. 1975), pp. 66, 47–8; J. A. Sharpe, '"Last dying speeches": religion, ideology and public execution in seventeenth-century England', *P&P*, 107 (1985), 144–67.

174 See ch. 4, below.

175 Lake and Questier, 'Agency, appropriation and rhetoric', p. 77.

176 Philip Caraman (ed.), *The Other Face: Catholic Life under Elizabeth I* (London, 1963), p. 193.

177 John H. Langbein, *Torture and the Law of Proof: Europe and England in the Ancien Régime* (Chicago, 1977), pt 2.

178 *Ibid.*, p. 89; Caraman (ed.), *Other Face*, pp. 237–9, 241; Bellamy, *Tudor Law of Treason*, p. 114.

179 See Esther Cohen, 'The animated pain of the body', *American Historical Review*, 105 (2000), 36–68, esp. 50–2 and Lyndal Roper, 'Witchcraft and fantasy in early modern Germany', in her *Oedipus and the Devil: Witchcraft, Sexuality and Religion in Early Modern Europe* (London, 1994), pp. 203–4.

180 Martin Ingram, 'Shame and pain: themes and variations in Tudor punishments', in Simon Devereaux and Paul Griffiths (eds), *Penal Practice and Culture, 1500–1900* (Basingstoke, 2004), pp. 36–62, at p. 58.

181 Caraman (ed.), *Other Face*, p. 76.

182 Hartley (ed.), *Proceedings ... 1558–1581*, p. 536.

183 David S. Katz, *Philo-Semitism and the Readmission of the Jews to England 1603–1655* (Oxford, 1982), p. 24.

184 See J. R. Knott, *Discourses of Martyrdom in English Literature, 1563–1694* (Cambridge, 1993), pp. 134–44.

185 Damrosch, *Sorrows of the Quaker Jesus*, pp. 222–5; Coffey, *Persecution and Toleration*, p. 154.

186 A. L. Beier, *Masterless Men: The Vagrancy Problem in England 1560–1640* (London, 1985), pp. 158–60; Ingram, 'Shame and pain', pp. 46, 54.

187 John Craig, *Reformation, Politics and Polemics: The Growth of Protestantism in East Anglian Market Towns, 1500–1610* (Aldershot, 2001), pp. 87–8.

188 For these rituals, see Martin Ingram, 'Ridings, Rough Music and the "Reform of Popular Culture" in Early Modern England', *P&P*, 105 (1984), 79–113 and 'Ridings, Rough Music and Mocking Rhymes in Early Modern England', in Barry Reay (ed.), *Popular Culture in Seventeenth Century England* (London, 1988), 166–97.

189 See Ingram, 'Shame and pain'.

190 Duffy, *Stripping of the Altars*, p. 403.

191 Brigden, *London and the Reformation*, p. 183.

192 Bellamy, *Tudor Law of Treason*, p. 185.

193 J. S. Cockburn (ed.), *Calendar of Assize Records: Surrey Indictments James I* (London, 1982), p. 1.

194 Reay, *Quakers*, p. 55; T. L. Underwood (ed.), *The Acts of the Witnesses: The Autobiographical Writings of Lodowick Muggleton and Other Early Muggletonian Writings* (New York, 1999), p. 133.

195 John Miller, 'A suffering people': English Quakers and their neighbours', *P&P*, 188, (2005), 71–103, at 78.

196 Notestein, Relf and Simpson (eds), *Commons Debates 1621*, vii. 636; Foley (ed.), *Records*, vii (2), p. 1066: this account reported that Catholics would have to wear 'a red hat like Jews in Rome, or parti-coloured stockings like the clowne'. Robin Clifton, 'The fear of Catholics in England 1637 to 1645. Principally from central sources', unpubl. DPhil dissertation (University of Oxford, 1967), p. 346.

197 MacCulloch, *Thomas Cranmer*, p. 482.

198 Elton (ed.), *Tudor Constitution*, p. 432.

199 Patrick McGrath and Joy Rowe, 'The imprisonment of Catholics for religion under Elizabeth I', *RH*, 20 (1991), 415–35; G. de C. Parmiter, 'The imprisonment of papists in private castles', *RH*, 19 (1988), pp. 16–38.

200 Firth and Rait (eds), *Acts and Ordinances*, ii. 409–12; 16 Car II. c. 4.

201 Watts, *Dissenters*, p. 224.

202 McGrath and Rowe, 'Imprisonment'.

203 Bellamy, *Tudor Law of Treason*, pp. 111–12; Caraman (ed), *Other Face*, pp. 243–4.

204 Watts, *Dissenters*, pp. 235–6.

205 Peter Lake and Michael Questier, 'Prisons, priests and people', in Tyacke (ed.), *England's Long Reformation*, pp. 195–233.

206 Christopher Hill, *A Turbulent, Seditious and Factious People: John Bunyan and his Church* (Oxford, 1989), pp. 120–4.

207 BL, Additional MS 34250, esp. fos. 15v, 16r, 20r–v.

208 Hughes and Larkin (eds), *Tudor Royal Proclamations*, i. 270–2 (no. 186), iii. 250–5, at 254. The Act of 1585 ordered Jesuits and seminary priests to depart the realm within forty days of the end of the current parliamentary session: Elton (ed.), *Tudor Constitution*, p. 434.

209 Christina Hallowell Garrett, *The Marian Exiles: A Study in the Origins of Elizabethan Puritanism* (Cambridge, 1938), p. 11.

210 Elton (ed.), *Tudor Constitution*, pp. 439–41, 459–60.

211 14 Car. II. c. 1; 16 Car II. c. 4. See Kenyon (ed.), *Stuart Constitution* (2nd edn), p. 357 n. 28.

212 Braithwaite, *Second Period of Quakerism*, pp. 47–8.

213 Roger B. Manning, *Religion and Society in Elizabethan Sussex: A Study of the Enforcement of the Religious Settlement 1558–1603* (Leicester, 1969), p. 137.

214 For the Exchequer, see Questier, *Conversion*, ch. 6.

215 H. W. Saunders (ed.), *The Official Papers of Sir Nathaniel Bacon of Stiffkey, Norfolk, as Justice of the Peace 1580–1620*, Camden Society, 3rd series, 26 (1915), p. 171.

216 Terence Stephen Smith, 'The persecution of Staffordshire Roman Catholic recusants: 1625–1660', *JEH*, 30 (1979), 327–51, at p. 351. For the preceding period, see K. J. Lindley, 'The lay Catholics of England in the reign of Charles I', *JEH*, 22 (1971), 199–21, esp. 211–14.

217 16 Car II. c. 4 (1664); Kenyon (ed.), *Stuart Constitution* (2nd edn), p. 357 (1670 act).

218 Anthony Fletcher, 'The enforcement of the Conventicle Acts 1664–1679', in W. J. Sheils (ed.), *Persecution and Toleration*, SCH 21 (Oxford, 1984), p. 239.

219 Manning, *Religion and Society*, pp. 140–1.

220 Russell, *Parliaments*, p. 132.

221 See Irene Scouloudi (ed.), *Returns of Strangers in the Metropolis 1593, 1627, 1635, 1639: A Study of an Active Minority*, Huguenot Society of London, Quarto Series 57 (London, 1985), ch. 2.

222 David S. Katz, 'The Jews of England and 1688', in Grell, Israel and Tyacke (eds), *From Persecution to Toleration*, p. 236.

223 For the Corporation and Test Acts, see Kenyon (ed.), *Stuart Constitution* (2nd edn), pp. 351–3, 385–7. For the Occasional Conformity Act, see Browning (ed.), *English Historical Documents*, pp. 406–8.

224 Browning (ed.), *English Historical Documents*, pp. 405–6.

225 T. E. Hartley (ed.), *Proceedings in the Parliaments of Elizabeth I*, vol. iii 1593–1601 (London, 1995), p. 70; 3 Jac. I, c. 5. Under the 1700 Act against Popery, this fine was given to informers who reported such offenders to the authorities: Browning (ed.), *English Historical Documents*, p. 406.

226 See, *ibid.*, pp. 384 (Five Mile Act of 1665), p. 410 (Schism Act 1714). See David L. Wykes, 'Quaker schoolmasters, toleration and the law, 1689–1714', *Journal of Religious History*, 21 (1997), 178–92.

227 For instance, under acts and ordinances of 1659: Firth and Tait (ed.), *Acts and Ordinances*, ii. 1293, 1297.

228 Elton (ed.), *Tudor Constitution*, p. 438; Firth and Rait (ed.), *Acts and Ordinances*, ii. 349–54.

229 Russell, *Parliaments*, p. 160; James F. Larkin (ed.), *Stuart Royal Proclamations*, vol. 2, *Royal Proclamations of King Charles I 1625–1646* (Oxford, 1983), pp. 736–8.

230 Browning (ed.), *English Historical Documents*, p. 383 (Five Mile Act of 1665).

231 John Cordy Jeaffreson (ed.), *Middlesex County Records 1549–1603*, OS, vol. i (London, 1886), pp. 181, 207.

232 *Prayers and thanksgivings to be used by all the kings majesties loving subjects, for the happy deliverance of his Majestie, the Queene, Prince, and States of Parliament, from the most traiterous and bloody intended massacre by gunpowder the 5 of November* (London, 1606), sig. D2r–v.

233 Hughes and Larkin (ed.), *Tudor Royal Proclamations*, ii. 474–5.

234 Dickens, *English Reformation*, p. 163.

235 For Thomas Bell, see my 'Yielding to the extremity of the time: conformity, orthodoxy and the post-Reformation Catholic Community', in Peter Lake and Michael Questier (eds), *Conformity and Orthodoxy in the English Church, c.1560–1660* (Woodbridge, 2000), pp. 211–36, at pp. 77–88. For the anti-Marprelate campaign, Collinson, *Elizabethan Puritan Movement*, pp. 404–5; Samuel Harsnet, *A discovery of the fraudulent practises of John Darrell* (1599) and *A declaration of egregious popish impostures* (1603). See also F. W. Brownlow, *Shakespeare, Harsnett and the Devils of Denham* (Newark, Delaware, 1993), chs 2–3; Thomas Freeman, 'Demons, deviance and defiance: John Darrell and the politics of exorcism in late Elizabethan England', in Lake and Questier (eds), *Conformity and Orthodoxy*, pp. 34–63, esp. 44–51.

236 John Rogers, *The displaying of an horrible secte of grosse and wicked heretiques* (1578), esp. sigs D4v–6v, E8r–F1v, H3v–4r.

237 See Anthony Milton's forthcoming biography: *Altar, Sword and Pen: Peter Heylyn and the Origins of Anglican Royalism* (Manchester, forthcoming 2007).

238 Kenyon (ed.), *Stuart Constitution* (2nd edn), p. 459.

239 Neale, *Elizabeth I and her Parliaments*, ii. 398; Russell, *Parliaments*, p. 69.

240 See esp. Elton, *Policy and Police*; Ronald Hutton, 'The local impact of the Tudor Reformations', in Haigh (ed.), *The English Reformation Revised*, pp. 114–38, esp. p. 138.

241 Questier, *Conversion*, ch. 6, esp. pp. 204–5. Cf. the pessimistic view of F. X. Walker, 'The implementation of the Elizabethan statutes against recusants', unpubl. PhD thesis (University of London, 1961). Steve Hindle, *The State and Social Change in Early Modern England c.1550–1640* (Basingstoke, 2000); Braddick, *State Formation*.

242 J. A. Sharpe, 'Crime and Delinquency in an Essex parish', in J. S. Cockburn (ed.), *Crime in England 1550–1800* (London, 1977), pp. 90–109, at p. 96. For the discretionary character of law enforcement, see Cynthia B. Herrup, *The Common Peace: Participation and the Criminal Law in Seventeenth-Century England* (Cambridge, 1987); Robert B. Shoemaker, *Prosecution and Punishment: Petty Crime and the Law in London and Rural Middlesex c.1660–1725* (Cambridge, 1991).

243 The classic formulation of this case is Keith Wrightson, 'Two concepts of order: justices, constables and jurymen in seventeenth-century England', in John Brewer and John Styles (eds), *An Ungovernable People: The English and their Law in the Seventeenth and Eighteenth Centuries* (New Brunswick, NJ, 1980), pp. 21–46.

244 Mary Bateson (ed.), 'A collection of original letters from the bishops to the Privy Council 1564', *Camden Miscellany IX*, Camden Society, NS 53 (1895), p. iii.

245 Manning, *Religion and Society*, p. 88.

246 Marsh, *Family of Love*, p. 129.

247 Kenyon (ed.), *Stuart Constitution* (2nd edn), p. 359. This omits passage about rewards for informers: see 22 Car. II. c. 1 §2.

248 Shoemaker, *Prosecution and Punishment*, p. 147.

249 Braddick, *State Formation*, ch. 7, quotation at p. 335. See also Questier, *Conversion*, p. 157.

250 Marchant, *Church and the Law*; Houlbrooke, *Church Courts*; Ingram, *Church Courts*.

251 Spurr, *Restoration Church*, pp. 209–19 and xiv.

252 Neale, *Elizabeth I and her Parliaments*, i. 192; Christopher Haigh, *Reformation and Resistance in Tudor Lancashire*, pp. 18–19, 271.

253 Spurr, *Restoration Church*, p. 193.

Chapter 3

Godly zeal and furious rage:
prejudice, persecution and the populace

I n seeking to accord responsibility for past episodes of religious persecution,
historians have frequently structured their discussions around the
enduring polarity of institutionalised authority versus the ordinary populace.
Outbursts of hostility and violence against unbelievers have often been
attributed to the intolerant impulses of the masses at large, to popular
prejudice spontaneously swelling up from below and carrying the officials of
Church and state reluctantly along in their wake. In part, this tendency to
account for episodes of vicious behaviour in terms of mob rule and crowd
hysteria betrays a residual sense of embarrassment about these extreme
manifestations of the 'superstition' and 'barbarity' of pre-modern European
society, a desire to explain them away as irrational aberrations and knee-jerk
reactions. It faintly reflects the instinct of Victorian scholars to distance
themselves simultaneously from the illiberal values of their medieval
forebears and from the base conduct of the ignorant and unruly rabble. In its
more sophisticated forms it is also a function of the influential theory
propounded by the early sociologist Emile Durkheim, who saw such
manifestations of collective activity as mechanisms for reaffirming the social
cohesion and unity of divided communities.

Inspired by the thinking of Max Weber, an alternative model of interpretation has been delineated, in which the initiative for action against minority
groups originated not primarily with the common people but rather with the
ecclesiastical and political entities that ruled them. According to this argument, persecution was a bureaucratic phenomenon driven by princes, magistrates, prelates and ministers attempting to consolidate their own authority
and to buttress that of the centralising Church and state. It was part of a struggle
to professionalise the structures of power and to establish an institutional
monopoly on legitimate violence.[1] Debates about the relationship between
official antagonism and popular hatred and the relative roles of governments

and their subjects in the repression and attempted eradication of deviance have been a central theme of studies of medieval heretics, witches and Jews, as well as those of post-Reformation religious dissenters.

The polarity between the populace and their clerical and political leaders that underpins many such discussions is partly dictated by and ingrained in the primary sources. In martyrological literature, for instance, two relevant tropes may be detected: brutal officials criticised by sympathetic spectators and malicious and ignorant onlookers egging on unwilling executioners. The latter in particular can be found in blueprint in the Gospel accounts of Christ's crucifixion. While apologetic propaganda commissioned by dominant regimes tends to ascribe atrocious acts of sectarian violence to the uncontrollable instincts of the plebeian multitude, elitist condescension inclines other contemporary narratives to stress the extent to which the actions of the lower orders, incapable of developing a coherent programme of their own, were orchestrated by their social superiors. Mediated through the filter of official transcripts, the motives and behaviour of the people who perpetrated attacks on religious dissenters cannot easily be disentangled from the prejudices and presuppositions of those who witnessed and recorded them for the sake of posterity. All too often such assumptions have been absorbed uncritically into later historical analyses.[2]

However, as commented at the end of Chapter 2, to situate 'popular' attitudes in sharp opposition to legislated policies is to set up a false dichotomy. In the context of the reliance of the Church and state on the co-operation of unpaid officials, hard and fast distinctions are deeply problematical. At every level these institutions depended on the participation of the English people. Without justices of the peace, sheriffs, parish constables, churchwardens and episcopal pursuivants prepared to enforce statutes, proclamations, edicts and injunctions, these measures would have had little bite or force. The consensual nature of the implementation of law in local communities and the scope that existed for it to be used as a vehicle for settling old scores and prosecuting factional disputes make it difficult to draw a clear line between judicially sanctioned violence and illegal vigilante action. As we shall see, the manner in which informal punishments often mimicked the rituals of ecclesiastical and civil justice and vice versa further blurs the boundary between them. Efforts to distinguish between the ideological, social and emotional aspects of such sectarian outbursts are often equally unhelpful: religious bigotry, class resentment and personal animosity combined and reacted in complex ways and in many cases, 'godly zeal' and 'furious rage' are impossible to separate neatly.[3] Intolerance consisted of multiple, intertwined strands of ill-feeling.

With these caveats in mind this chapter attempts to analyse the character of popular intolerance, to explore the range of ways in which the inhabitants of sixteenth- and seventeenth-century cities, towns and villages persecuted individuals who adhered to rival beliefs and creeds. The distorting generic conventions that shape so many of our sources render futile efforts to measure the scale and extent of inter-confessional tension in early modern England precisely; instead we concentrate upon examining when, why and against whom contemporaries translated their latent animosities into action and practice. Investigating those occasions on which people refrained from displaying their distaste for, and impatience with, their dissenting neighbours, indulging their idiosyncrasies and bearing with their faults and weaknesses, is no less vital: this half of the picture is explored in Chapter 5. Inevitably, the survey offered here cannot do proper justice to the complex inner histories and dynamic micro-politics of the many individual incidents to which it refers, but it may perhaps highlight some revealing common patterns and themes.

BARBAROUS BEHAVIOUR AND UNCIVIL CONDUCT

We begin with the observation that some of the Crown's servants carried out their responsibilities with more than conventional efficiency and vigour. Many examples may be cited of ecclesiastical and civil officials who proactively pursued the adherents of heresy, idolatry and sectarian error in the regions under their jurisdiction, though it must be remembered that such evidence is frequently built upon a tissue of rumour, hearsay and myth. Intent upon stamping out false belief and sin, a few such individuals seem to have taken a perverted pleasure in searching out and disciplining their victims – at least according to the martyrologists and historians who later recorded and glori-fied their tribulations at the hands of these bloodthirsty villains.

John Longland's eagerness to uproot Lollardy in the diocese of Lincoln in the 1520s prompted John Foxe to call him 'a fierce and cruel vexer of the faithful poor servants of Christ'; his fellow Bishop John Stokesley was said to have boasted on his deathbed 'that he had sent thirty-one heretics into the infernal fire'; Stephen Gardiner also acquired a reputation for excessive severity. Edmund Bonner's alleged exploits in Marian London likewise earned him a venomous sketch in the *Actes and monuments*, which incorporated accounts of how he had held one martyr's hand over the flame of a candle until the flesh blistered and a picture of him personally whipping another in his back garden in a distinctly sadomasochistic fashion.[4] That these infamous events can be read as desperate efforts by a conscientious prelate to gain the recantations of misguided souls by employing pain as a therapeutic tool merely underlines the extent to which cruelty is a relative concept and how far the historical documents we rely upon are elaborate and subjective constructions. The same remarks may apply to Sir Thomas More, whose passionate hatred of heretics extended to imprisoning and interrogating two suspects in his house at Chelsea, probably using torture: he wrote to Erasmus that he found 'that breed of men absolutely loathsome' and wanted to be 'as hateful to them as anyone can possibly be'.[5] Nicknamed Justice Nine-Holes because of his mode of spying on the congregation, one Kentish magistrate was allegedly so determined to unmask secret Protestants that he watched from the rood screen to see if any worshippers cast their eyes down during the elevation of the host.[6] Once again it may be suspected that accuracy has been sacrificed to the ends of crude polemical caricature.

Similar stories were told about Protestant officials who maliciously molested Elizabethan Catholics: Henry Hastings, the Earl of Huntingdon, was described as a 'monster' who ruthlessly hunted down and apprehended priests; the judge who sentenced Edmund Arrowsmith to death reputedly watched him being disembowelled through a telescope and inspected his bloody quarters while sitting at the dinner table; and in 1618 a Yorkshire pursuivant called Dales was reported to have struck a recusant lady with his cudgel and forcibly removed her shoes, stockings and underclothes.[7] Richard Topcliffe was particularly notorious for his inquisitorial methods and his capacity for savagery even horrified his superiors: Lord Burghley had him imprisoned for a period on the grounds that he had exceeded his warrant.[8] In the 1650s, energetic magistrates also seem to have sometimes overstepped the mark in their efforts to restrain disorderly Quaker evangelists: at Maidstone John Stubbs and William Caton were 'cruelly whipped with cords in a bloody manner', while at Evesham the mayor Edmund Young supervised the gratuitous punishment of Margaret Newby and Elizabeth Cowart, who were made to spend seventeen hours in the stocks one cold November night with a block of wood wedged between their legs.[9] A decade earlier embittered puritans were uncompromising scourges of the Anglican parish clergy and after the Restoration there were those who positively exulted in the strictness of the Clarendon Code, such as Sir Henry Yelverton in Northamptonshire, who bombarded Archbishop Sheldon with complaints about unchecked conventicles and nonconformist ministers and resolved to do his 'utmost' to reduce the refractory 'to principles of sobriety'.[10] Sir Daniel Fleming of Westmorland not only flouted the law and continued to proceed against dissenters after the lapse of the act of 1664, but bragged about his actions in a letter to the Secretary of State.[11] Clearly the activities of such zealots were the subject of much hagiographical embellishment, but it cannot be doubted that there were officials whose convictions propelled them to treat religious deviants with extraordinary, if not excessive severity.

At the parish level, it is also evident that the impetus for the prosecution and harassment of religious dissenters often came from ordinary lay people. The readiness of men and women to turn over their Lollard, Protestant, Catholic and nonconformist neighbours to the authorities cannot pass unnoticed. In late fifteenth-century London Robert Warde menaced the suspected heretic John Boking with the words 'I shall make the[e] to bere a fagot'.[12] This turned out to be an empty threat but our sources are scattered with examples of individuals who actually carried out such chilling promises. When Thomas Collins from Ginge near Wantage admitted to his son that he did not believe in transubstantiation around 1513, his mother had to use all her powers of persuasion to prevent the young man from betraying him to the ecclesiastical hierarchy.[13]

Without people willing to pass on incriminating information, like the 'frantycke papyst of Hamshyre' who in 1551 called upon the authorities to 'hang up an hundred of such heretic knaves', the Marian burnings might not have been possible. In Norwich, for instance, a local gentleman was responsible for reporting a number of people for failing to receive the sacrament at Easter and there are several cases of heretics being reported by close relatives, including John Davis of Worcester, who was handed over to the bailiffs by his apothecary uncle in 1546. Richard Woodman was freed from prison in December 1555, only to be turned in again by his family and neighbours.[14] In Elizabeth's reign, a father in London apparently caused his son to be flogged and seared through the ear for being a Catholic. We may also note the initiative that Bartholomew Benson took in discovering recusants to the Middlesex magistrates, giving evidence at the General Sessions in April 1615 against a yeoman by the name of Lawrence Penne, who had been absent from church for nearly a year, as well as that of the 'overthwart neighbour' who uncovered the separatist congregation led by Henry Jessey to officials in 1638.[15] The second Conventicle Act of 1670 provided a further incentive to those who were prepared to blow the whistle on religious dissenters in the form of financial reward, and many of the professional informers it engendered were acknowledged even by the orthodox to be unscrupulous and callous, persons of 'mercenary tempers, or of vile dissolute lives'.[16] Moderate divines sometimes deplored the level of antagonism towards nonconformists exhibited by their parishioners: Benjamin Hoffman, minister in the city parish of St George, Botolph Lane, did not doubt that the penal laws should be put in operation, but was shocked to find that many did 'rejoyce in their Brothers' sufferings'.[17] Once again caution is needed in assessing evidence derived so largely from the records and chronicles kept by molested minorities themselves, but such examples do help to sustain the view that religious intolerance had popular as well as official foundations and roots.

Instances of congregations working collectively to present nonconformist clergy to the church courts provide reinforcement for this point. Christopher Haigh and Judith Maltby have drawn to our attention cases in which villagers reported their puritan ministers to the ecclesiastical authorities for failing to wear the surplice, use the sign of the cross in baptism, administer communion according to the rubrics, and conduct proper funerals. They disagree, however, about whether such people should be identified as crypto-Catholic 'parish Anglicans' or committed 'Prayer Book Protestants'. The vicar of Flixton in Suffolk, Thomas Daynes, was deprived of his living in 1590 after his parishioners launched a concerted campaign against him. Accused of a predictable list of liturgical lapses, including refusal to church women, allow godparents, and pray for the queen, he had also rebuked those who brought their prayer books to church to ensure that he followed the official service to the letter, calling them 'papists and atheists'. Articles were presented against William Hieron of Hemingby in Lincolnshire towards the end of that decade for omitting set prayers or hastening through them 'in [an] unreverent manner' and in 1639 the curate of Tarporley, Cheshire, was hauled up for leaving out the Ten Commandments to the 'scandal of well affected people'.[18] Parishioners excluded from the Eucharist by ministers determined to preserve it from profanation by the unregenerate could be the targets of particular antagonism and not a few were reported for withholding the sacraments from all but the 'saints'.[19]

Sometimes the consensus of local opinion could result in the prosecution of conforming rather than nonconforming clergy. Protests against preachers and pastors who refused to comply with the prescribed conventions can be parallelled by protests against those who slavishly followed them. Before 1643, much of the initiative in ejecting 'scandalous' and 'malignant' Laudian ministers was taken by outraged parishioners, as indexed by several hundred surviving petitions to Parliament. Thirty years later, the bishop of Salisbury received a series of complaints from inhabitants of the Wiltshire village of Somerford Magna about their rector, a contentious and unpopular man from whose hands they felt unable to receive the holy Eucharist.[20] Whatever underlying ecclesiastical preferences such cases reveal, they also indicate that pressure to discipline clerical misdemeanours was not infrequently exerted by the laity rather than the episcopal hierarchy. In this increasingly litigious society, people were evidently quite prepared to harness the arm of the law in their struggle to bring recalcitrant clergymen into conformity with the injunctions and canons.

These orderly and systematic attacks on conformist and dissident ministers contrast with the turbulent behaviour of some of those who witnessed the executions of convicted heretics and traitors. The London goldsmith who bequeathed 6s. 8d. for faggots for the burning of Lollards in 1463 demonstrated his support for these gruesome *autos-da-fé* from the distance of his grave,[21] but some contemporaries plainly wished to take a more active part in official rites of purification by fire. The crowd which witnessed Thomas Bennet go to the stake at Exeter in 1532 raged as a furze-bush on a pike was thrust into his face, threw sticks and branches at him, and taunted him as a 'whoreson heretic'.[22]

Those who saw Catholic priests hung, drawn and quartered in the reigns of Elizabeth and James I were also often not content to be passive spectators. People shouted 'a devil, a devil' when Father Richard Simon was found to be wearing a hair shirt and the Latin prayers of John Nelson were interrupted by the catcalls of the crowd that had gathered beneath the gallows: 'away with thee and thy Catholic Romish faith'. A common porter placed his foot on the throat of the recusant gentlemen John Rigby to stop him calling upon Jesus to receive his soul. At Gloucester in 1586, Stephen Rowsham was assailed by 'a graceless company of apprentices and youths' who pelted the martyr with excrement collected from the local dunghill. Even more grotesquely, onlookers in Oxford iconoclastically disfigured the faces of Richard Yaxley and George Nicholls with knives and Hugh Green's decapitated head was kicked around in an impromptu football match organised by witnesses of his execution in Dorchester in 1642.[23] The response to religious enthusiasts prosecuted under the blasphemy laws could be nearly as brutal: Lodowick Muggleton was showered with stones, mud, rotten eggs and turnips when he was carted through the streets and publicly pilloried in Cornhill, Chancery Lane and Smithfield in 1676.[24]

Such episodes were doubtless embroidered in the telling, with the crowd typically being compared with the biblical rabble at whose behest the thief Barabbas had been spared over Christ. But beneath the veneer of pious invention, these incidents suggest that some individuals enthusiastically endorsed the intolerant policies of the Tudor and Stuart state. In a number of cases, displays of hostility towards its victims were stimulated by executioners, prison chaplains and other officials; in others, the cruelty of the crowd spilled out far beyond the legitimate boundaries of these occasions for licensed carnivalesque violence.[25]

These acts were carried out within, or at least on the edges of an established framework of judicial persecution. But physical attacks on the adherents of false religions also occurred in other contexts. Many examples can be assembled of individuals who were heard articulating homicidal thoughts. In the early sixteenth century the Lollard Alice Hignell said that whenever she saw devout parishioners offering a candle to the image of a saint she wished she 'had a hatchet in my hand And wer behynde theim to knoke theim on their heddis'. Robert Bing recalled how a Protestant friend had turned on him for attending a popish service in the 1530s, declaring, 'if I knew him that would go to mass I would thrust my dagger in him'. Perhaps a little more light-heartedly, in 1538 a neighbour of the Whitechapel bricklayer John Harrydance threatened to throw a bowling ball at him if he did not stop expounding the Gospel from a tree in his garden. When Edward Underhill removed the pyx from the altar at Stratford le Bow later in the reign of Henry VIII the Catholic wives of Stepney allegedly 'conspired to have murdered me'.[26] However, probably only a small minority translated such plots and statements into

5 Providential persecution. In the Blackfriars accident of October 1623 a Jesuit preacher
and over ninety members of his audience died when a makeshift chapel in the French
ambassador's residence collapsed: many Protestants interpreted this as a divine judgement
for the *ad hoc* toleration of Catholics during the negotiations for the Spanish match. The
tragedy prompted the London crowd to commit violent attacks on the victims. *No plot, no
powder 1623* (London, [c. 1623]). (© The British Museum, Department of Prints and
Drawings, Satires, no. 95).

action. An evangelical preacher who arrived in the Dorset town of Poole in 1548 to denounce idolatry met with an angry reception by three local men and was only saved from having his guts 'drawn out' by the intervention of the mayor, who pushed him into the chancel out of harm's way.[27]

Other striking cases of sectarian activism and violence may be cited. In the West Midlands during Elizabeth's reign a local 'persecutor' not only intimidated a crippled Catholic with a loaded pistol; he also took milk that had been given to 'one Mother Taylefathes, aged and decrepit', and 'washed his hands in it, saying that she was unworthy to have alms, and that whosoever gave her anything should repent it all the days they had to live'.[28] One of the most intense and dramatic incidents occurred when a large garret in Blackfriars collapsed in October 1623, killing over ninety people who had gathered to hear a Jesuit preach, and injuring hundreds of others. The London crowd savagely set upon the victims of the 'fatall vesper', assaulting them with curses, as well as with rubble and rocks, besieging a distressed gentlewoman as she was driven away in a coach and dragging an unconscious girl from the wreckage, ostensibly with the intent of beating her to death. The Venetian ambassador wrote back to the Doge and Senate that the disaster had provided the occasion for 'a general and bloody riot' and condemned the cruelty of the Calvinist fanatics – '*infuriati Protestanti*' – who had perpetrated these outrages (Figure 5).[29]

In the early 1640s, examples of confessional conflict multiplied. In the late summer of 1642, parliamentarian crowds numbering several thousand destroyed and plundered the property of wealthy recusants in parts of Essex and Suffolk. The Countess of Rivers, Lady Elizabeth Savage, fled her seat in St Osyth for fear of her life only hours before the arrival of a horde of Colchester townsmen, who proceeded to attack her servants and tear the house to pieces, leaving 'not a doore, nor so much as a barre of a window behind them'. Pursuing her to her other mansion at Long Melford in Suffolk, a multitude of 'Essex schismatics' reputedly threatened her with death and then ransacked the property. When the home of Sir Francis Mannock of Stoke-by-Nayland was pillaged, the furious crowd refused to spare his beloved hounds. In these cases, although the attackers utterly terrified their targets, they stopped short of slaughtering them. A recusant officer in charge of a company of men on their way north to fight the Scots a few years earlier had not been so lucky: his troops mutinied and 'barbarously murthered' him 'for his Religion only', it was said, and then dragged his mangled body through the streets of Wellington.[30] The collapse of royal control in Charles I's three kingdoms provided the occasion for even more heinous crimes, not least the atrocities committed by Irish Catholics against Protestants in Ulster in 1641, where ethnic and confessional hatred converged with truly ghastly results. The worst incidents involved the deliberate drowning of a group of settlers at a bridge at Portadown and the calculated burning of a band of refugees in a thatched cottage in Kilmore.

Others were subjected to the degrading ordeal of being stripped naked and searched internally for money (Figure 6).[31]

Even once allowance is made for the layers of legend that have accumulated around them, such isolated episodes are horrifically reminiscent not only of the terrorist violence that has accompanied the troubles in Northern Ireland and the Balkans in recent memory, but also of the clashes between Catholics and Protestants in France which culminated in the carnage of St Bartholomew's day in 1572, when heretics were treated equally obscenely and unspeakably. They lend support to John Morrill's argument that the English Civil War should be seen as part of Europe's Wars of Religion.[32] It was not merely the puritan leaders of the parliamentary cause who conceived of it in apocalyptic terms, as an epic battle between Christ and Antichrist, a final showdown with the Scarlet Whore of Babylon, a kind of Armageddon. Many soldiers and civilians were likewise fired by anxiety about the creeping rise of popery in the kingdom, not least in the guise of Laudian ceremonialism. Hence the spate of spontaneous vandalism of altar rails, images, stained glass windows, and other detested remnants of 'Romish idolatry' which coincided with the formal outbreak of fighting. Sometimes these acts of ritual iconoclasm overflowed into assaults on the human representatives of Caroline ecclesiastical policy: at Halstead, for instance, not only were the surplice, hood and Prayer Book seized and burnt in the marketplace, but the curate himself was beaten up for christening an infant with the superstitious sign of the cross.[33] On the royalist side, there were raids on separatist conventicles: a pregnant woman in Henry Jessey's London congregation died as a result of the harsh treatment meted out to her during a siege led by the lord mayor Sir John Wright, and the building in which Praise-God Barebones and fellow worshippers met in Fleet Street took a severe battering at the hands of the crowd.[34]

Following Patrick Collinson, we may link such incidents with the heated 'street wars' that had periodically arisen in towns and villages throughout the previous century over the attempts of the godly to suppress popular recreations and impose a culture of sober discipline. Collisions over the contested symbols of 'merry England' were also symptomatic of a kind of religious intolerance – the mutual intolerance of the advocates of sweeping moral reform and the defenders of traditional pastimes. On occasion, they too could end in bloodshed. In Warbleton, Sussex, in 1572 a young carpenter called Noah who had walked six miles to assist in sawing down a maypole in the middle of the night was shot and killed by an invisible assailant. Similar confrontations in Shrewsbury in the 1590s over customary festive practices surrounding the 'Shearmen's Tree' led to the death of the servant of a local draper.[35] These are examples of interconfessional conflict interpreted in the broadest sense, conflict between the hotter sort of Protestants and those they were inclined to condemn as impious reprobates and residual papists.

At one Mr Atkins house 7 Papistes brake in
& beate out his braines, then riped upe his
wife with Childe, after they had rauished her,
& Nero like vewed natures bed of conception
then tooke they the Childe & sacrificed it
in the fire

English Protestantes striped naked & turned
into the mountaines, in the frost, & snowe, whe:
reof many hundreds are perished to death,
& many lyinge dead in diches & Sauages
upbraided them sayinge now are ye wilde
Irish as well as wee,

6 The atrocities committed during the Irish rising of 1641 etched themselves on the
English imagination as a symbol of Catholic cruelty and persecutory violence: [James
Cranford], *The teares of Ireland* (London, 1642), p. 23. (By permission of The British
Library, shelfmark c. 21. b. 42).

During the Interregnum, antagonism towards the sects also led to outbursts of aggression. Emotive reporting aside, it is clear that the earliest Quakers often met with an extremely hostile reception. At Mansfield, where George Fox tried to speak out in church, the congregation fell upon him in a rage, hitting him with hands, sticks and bibles and very nearly smothering him. In Bishop Auckland in 1653, 'a rude multitude' pulled Thomas Holmes down from the seat in which he was proclaiming 'the Gospell of Truth' and laid heavy blows on his companion John Durham 'as if it had been on a Beast'. The following year a group of Oxford undergraduates pumped water upon the necks and into the mouths of two female Friends, 'till they were allmost stifled', while their colleagues at Sherborne, Dorset, were 'unhumanely abussed' by a 'rude Multitude' who bespattered them with filth and encompassed them 'like the Sodomites in the dayes of old'.[36] Not far away at Broad Cerne in May 1660, 'rude people of the baser sort' beat a drum to summon a crowd, fired guns beneath the windows of a building in which the Quakers were assembled and then attacked them as they left the village. In Cambridge, students ran through a meeting house like 'wild Horses', stamping to drown out the speakers, pulling off the women's bonnets and 'daubing their faces with Filth and Excrements'.[37] At Colchester in Essex in 1655 one 'blind zealot' was so outraged by the exhortations of James Parnell that he 'struck him a violent Blow with a great Staff, saying, 'There, take that for Christ's Sake'.[38] This individual clearly saw himself as engaged in a kind of crusade to defend the orthodox Protestant faith.

The Restoration prompted a fresh surge of prejudice against religious dissenters. There were widespread attacks on separatist meeting houses. Upon hearing of the sacking of a Baptist church on St Dunstan's Hill in May 1660 a woman from Wapping allegedly announced that 'it had done her more good, than if two hundred pounds had been flung in her lap'. In the wake of the Fifth Monarchist rising, a vintner from the same district called for all 'Fanaticks' to be hanged.[39] When a Quaker who attempted to disturb the consecration of the new Archbishop of Canterbury was set upon by a mob, a former royalist urged them to 'dash out his braines', saying, 'Marke they are like dogs in time of plague they are to be killed ... yt they do not infect'.[40] In the tense atmosphere of 1662 another member of the sect was beaten to death, against the backdrop of dramatic acts of sacrilege such as the pouring of blood on the high altar of St Paul's Cathedral by two female Friends.[41] Similar scenes of wanton destruction of nonconformist places of worship were witnessed following James II's Declaration of Indulgence in 1687, after the death of William III in 1702, and most famously during the Sacheverell Riots of 1710, when half a dozen Presbyterian churches were all but demolished by Anglican crowds. Huge bonfires were made of their contents and some of the participants threatened to throw the builder of the meeting house in Leather Lane into the

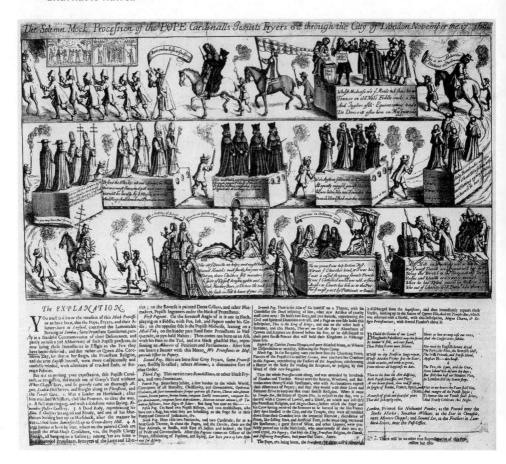

7 Ritual persecution: pope-burning procession on 17 November 1680: *The solemn mock procession of the pope cardinals jesuits fryers etc through the city of London November the 17th 1680* (London, 1680). (© The British Museum, Department of Prints and Drawings, catalogue of satires, no. 1085).

pyre, on the grounds that his efforts had contributed to drawing people away from conformity to the Church of England.[42]

These anti-nonconformist outrages had a mirror image on the other side of the late seventeenth-century religio-political divide. Ritual assaults on Roman Catholicism were a prominent feature of the period of the Popish Plot and the Exclusion Crisis, as the pioneering work of Tim Harris has revealed. Catholic chapels were wrecked before and after James II's accession and again at the time of the Glorious Revolution, and not merely in London. In Cambridge priests were set upon and massing equipment and vestments were systematically destroyed and in Oxford 'the rabble and boyes', as many as two hundred in number, 'went to every popish house and broke there windows'.[43] The Gordon Riots of 1780, when the metropolitan crowd rose again in defiance of a parliamentary bill alleviating the plight of recusants, saw a belated resurgence of the same type of confessional violence.[44]

Despite the many statements of murderous intent recorded by contemporary chroniclers of the sufferings of minority groups, it is notable that those involved in these episodes rarely went to the length of killing their victims. Vicarious punishment of the adherents of false religions, in the form of attacks on effigies and emblems, was far more typical. The famous Pope-burning processions organised by the Whigs in the late 1670s and early 1680s found a counterpart in the public incineration of figures of Jack Presbyter, dressed in appropriate garb and bearing a scroll marked 'solemn league and covenant' (Figure 7). In 1682, there were plans to set alight a model of the arch puritan rebel Oliver Cromwell, though these were frustrated by a royal order prohibiting bonfires.[45]

Also relevant here are the rites of violence to which the corpses of religious deviants were sometimes subjected posthumously. In mid-seventeenth-century Ireland insurgents showed a frightening disrespect for the dead. Corpses were desecrated and denied Christian burial and decapitated heads stabbed, cut and slashed. In one particularly harrowing case the bodies of a Protestant clergyman and his wife were disinterred from the churchyard of Waterford Cathedral, boiled in a furnace until they had been reduced to saltpetre, and then converted into gunpowder.[46] Nothing quite matching this incident has been uncovered on the British mainland, but a Catholic missionary who fell from a roof as he tried to escape a band of pursuivants and sustained further fatal injuries at the hands of those waiting below was buried at a crossroads with a stake through his heart, like a suicide. A similar fate awaited the corpse of a young Baptist woman after the Restoration, exhumed from its grave in a Breconshire churchyard and transferred to an intersection on the common highway.[47]

The fact that Catholics and nonconformists were often persecuted, as it were, at one step removed should not necessarily be regarded as evidence that the temperature of religious intolerance in England was significantly lower than that reached in sixteenth-century France or seventeenth-century Germany. A capacity to displace hatred on to inanimate objects or (less frequently) lifeless cadavers might help to explain why this country never experienced a massacre like that which engulfed Paris and other provincial towns and cities in 1572. But it may also reflect Protestantism's obsession with eradicating anything that might become an 'abominable idol' by contrast with Catholicism's enhanced sense of the persons of heretics as the sources of danger and defilement.[48] We should not, however, underestimate the depth of negative sentiment embodied in these ceremonies of symbolic assassination.

RITUAL AND VERBAL VIOLENCE

It is equally important to recognise how intensely the humiliation and shame of being subjected to structured forms of ridicule could be felt by dissenters. The carnivalesque ritual of the skimmington or charivari was sometimes directed against those who transgressed religious as well as moral norms: popular hostility towards killjoy puritans could find expression in ridings, as at Wells in 1607, where the constable John Hole and his supporters were mercilessly traduced following strenuous attempts to suppress the city's May games.[49] 'Rough music' was also a common element in anti-Quaker violence, the cacophony of saucepans and kettles reflecting local outrage at the inversion of social order embodied by the Society of Friends. Horns were thrown into a meeting at Evershot in 1656 and a mob beset those who had gathered to hear Edward Burroughs speak at Glastonbury Cross 'beating their drum, whooping, hallooeing and thrusting the Friends to and fro in a wild and barbarous manner'.[50] Other forms of street theatre could be quite sinister: according to a Jesuit report, a priest captured at Dover in the Jacobean period was not only showered with insults but sewn into a bear or bull's skin and exposed in the town centre 'to be torn in pieces by dogs and sported with as a monster'. At least some residents felt that the perpetrators had crossed the line into gratuitous cruelty because the man was rescued 'through the interference of some humane persons standing by'.[51] Such mocking performances were no less menacing for being disguised as festive pastimes.

Indeed, laughter in general could be a devastating weapon. Religious dissidents often taunted their adversaries in scurrilous libels and railing rhymes. The hilarious Marprelate tracts against the Elizabethan bishops are perhaps the best-known example, but Catholics were equally adept at employing them as instruments for inflicting injury upon their heretical enemies.[52] In turn, persecutors appropriated this style of invective to pillory unpopular minorities. One such composition read aloud at the market cross in Dorchester in 1606 was addressed 'To the execrable Companie of Puritans and the deepest desemblinge Anabaptistes of this tyme', while a set of unflattering verses entitled 'A Satyre to the Cheife Rulers of the Synagogue of Stratford [upon Avon]' was dispersed in 1619.[53] Similar squibs accompanied the heated religious politics of the 1670s and 1680s. Anonymous poems and verses circulated orally and scribally on both sides of the Exclusion Crisis. Supporters of the Duke of York travestied his Protestant rival Monmouth and the nonconformists, while those opposed to a Catholic succession poured contempt upon the prince and his fellow papists. Not all of these ephemeral pieces were the work of elite propagandists.[54]

Although such lampoons were usually directed at particular individuals, sometimes only general types were targeted, as in the case of many topical comedies. These expressions of prejudice may have been impersonal but they hardly lacked potency and it would be a mistake to exclude them from our survey. During the early Reformation, monks, priests and credulous lay people were often the butt of derisive playlets, skits, farces and interludes: surviving texts by the printer-poet and vituperative ex-Carmelite friar John Bale probably represent only the tip of an iceberg of robustly anti-Catholic popular pastimes.[55] From the 1580s onwards, this tradition continued more insidiously in the guise of Italianate revenge tragedies, which, as Alison Shell has shown, perpetuated enduring images of popish deceit, sexual depravity and satanic conspiracy.[56] The sanctimonious, hypocritical piety of the self-styled saints was similarly satirised in informal jigs. Patrick Collinson suggests that these were forerunners of the stock figure of the stage puritan, which emerged in commercial drama in the late 1580s, the most memorable examples of which are Malvolio in *Twelfth Night* and the rabid scourge of puppet plays who stars in Ben Jonson's *Bartholomew Fair*, Zeal-of-the-Land Busy.[57] Thomas Middleton's play *The Family of Love*, written and enacted around 1603–4, described itself as a piece of 'harmless mirth' but in depicting the secretive activities of the fellowship as a cover for carnal lust and in emphasising its predilection for dissimulation it helped to perpetuate ancient stereotypes of heretical deviance.[58] When the theatres closed in 1642, tracts in dialogue form like Samuel Sheppard's *The jovial crew or, the devil turned ranter* (1651) performed a similar function. After their reopening at the Restoration, the genre enjoyed a rapid renaissance. Jonson's classic anti-puritan comedy was re-staged in 1661; two years later Abraham Cowley's *Cutter of Coleman Street* savagely parodied the Fifth Monarchist movement; and during the 1680s, lecherous popes and pregnant nuns made an appearance in a number of London plays.[59]

Some historians have argued that the appearance of such entertainments indicates that amused contempt had begun to outweigh fear in contemporary attitudes towards such groups, but it may be, on the contrary, that they helped to sustain it, by constructing them as bizarre and frightening 'others'. As Frank Felsenstein has pointed out, in the absence of actual Jews, dramatic representations of them, notably in the guise of Shylock in *The Merchant of Venice*, played a powerful role in keeping traditional anti-Semitic attitudes alive. In Christopher Marlowe's *The Jew of Malta* (c.1591), for instance, the eponymous hero Barabas confesses that 'sometimes I go about and poison wells' and the Portuguese converso physician, Dr Roderigo Lopez, executed for attempting to kill Elizabeth with a toxic potion, had a walk-on part in a number of sixteenth- and seventeenth-century productions.[60] The Elizabethan and Jacobean theatre also familiarised Englishmen and women with the figure of the Muslim renegade, a Machiavellian villain which it conflated with the generic evil of the Catholic Antichrist. Lack of contact with real Turks did not render these representations void of anxiety. Indeed, Nabil Matar insists that it actually intensified apprehension, fostering the demonisation of Islam.[61] Such entertainments sublimated but perhaps also stimulated ingrained biases against those who practised other religions, providing a reservoir of tropes that could help to transform individual nonconformists into scapegoats at times of crisis.

Popular literature operated in a comparable way. Ballads and ephemeral newsbooks publicised the monstrous natures and antinomian behaviour of religious deviants, elevating isolated aberrations into universal characteristics. Sensational pamphlets about 'parricide papists' in Cornish villages and axe-murdering puritans in the wilds of Wales painted a lurid picture of the malicious criminal instincts of dissidents to the left and right of the ecclesiastical mainstream. Familists and Anabaptists were constantly depicted as promiscuous libertines and polemicists remorselessly exploited Catholicism's metaphorical equation with the Whore of Babylon.[62] The spectre of the amoral excesses of the millenarian kingdom of Münster was constantly invoked in the anti-sectarian tracts that proliferated in the Civil War and Interregnum and the heresiographer Thomas Edwards's *Gangraena* (1646) dissected the errors, blasphemies and pernicious and depraved practices of the enthusiasts in such exhaustive detail and with such unseemly relish that it ran to some 700 pages.[63] Internecine conflict within and between the various radical sects played no inconsiderable part in creating and perpetuating such images. By choosing to conduct these very personal struggles through the medium of print, they themselves helped to fashion the very stereotypes that were used against them. J. C. Davis has controversially argued that the Ranter scare of 1650–1 was essentially a journalistic fiction, a projection of contemporary disquiet about pluralism, anarchy, and atheism and of a conservative desire to reinforce traditional moral boundaries – a literary inversion of everything that constituted true godliness. It is not necessary to get entangled in the debate about whether the Ranters existed before they were invented by the yellow press to appreciate the extent to which older stories about obscene orgies, clandestine plotting and diabolical intervention were mapped and superimposed upon them (Figure 8).[64]

The same points can be made in connection with the Adamites, so-called because of their antinomian tendency to take off their clothes. Denounced in *A nest of serpents discovered* and various other lurid tracts, this elusive nudist sect may have been more a product of paranoid imaginations than a real phenomenon, but this does not detract from its significance as a symptom of the fears and assumptions about deviance that occupied the minds of the time.[65] Print also gave currency to medieval tales of child murder, host desecration, sorcery and usury which clouded and contaminated contemporary perception of Jews following their readmission to England from the 1650s: in this case stereotypes did precede and shape encounters with actual Judaisers.[66]

The Ranters Ranting: [8]

W ɪ ᴛ ʜ

The apprehending, examinations, and confession of *Iohn Collins*,
I. Shakespear, *Tho. Wiberton*, and five more which are to answer
the next Sessions. And severall songs or catches, which were sung
at their meetings. Also their several kinds of mirth, and dancing.
Their blasphemous opinions. Their belief concerning heaven and
hell. And the reason why one of the same opinion cut off the
heads of his own mother and brother. Set forth for the further
discovery of this ungodly crew.

Behold our joy
to our Fellow-
Creature.

Welcome Fel-
low-Creature.

Let us eat while
they dance.

Decemb: 2   *L O N D O N*
Printed by *B. Alsop*, 1650.

8 The mid-seventeenth century reaction against sectarian enthusiasm invoked ancient
stereotypes of deviance, including allegations of sexual promiscuity: sects such as the
Ranters were used to illustrate the evils to which religious liberty gave rise: *The Ranters
ranting* (London, 1651), title-page. (By permission of The British Library, Thomason Tracts,
E 618 [8]).

Visual satire and the vogue for Theophrastian characters further cemented distinctive religious identities. Witty pen portraits of the 'she puritan' and 'church papist' had a sharp edge, and together with crude woodcut images and engraved prints, they contributed to the creation and consolidation of confessional polarities. The pictures of bloodthirsty persecutors in Foxe's *Actes and monuments* exerted strong influence on the popular imagination, as did depictions of Catholic conspirators scheming with the papacy and foreign powers, typically in tandem with Satan himself. The figure of Guy Fawkes with his lantern and long flowing cloak became a familiar shorthand for popish deception and guile, and during the 1640s Archbishop Laud and his fellow 'tottering prelates' were the subject of savage graphic parodies.[67] The sects also acquired a pictorial life of their own. The frontispiece to Daniel Featley's *Dippers dipt* (1645) showed vignettes of fifteen different species of radical Protestant heretics and the crude woodcuts that adorned cheap pamphlets dwelt on their libertinism and promiscuity (Figure 9). A more elaborate broadside engraving dating from c.1653 shows a Quaker woman arrogantly seeking guidance from her 'inner light' with a lustful horned devil standing behind her (Figure 10). The later Stuart period saw a fresh proliferation of familiar pictorial tropes of 'hell-bred' Catholic cruelty and tyranny and non-conformist conspiracy and subversion.[68] The circulation of such images supplied contemporaries with the ingredients for stigmatising and dehumanising their enemies. Just as the stock figure of the ugly, wart-ridden hag surrounded by her animal familiars may have assisted in engendering accusations of witchcraft against impoverished elderly women who lived on the margins, so too, it might be suggested, did the iconography of religious minorities help to entrench latent prejudices.

Drawing on beliefs rooted in folklore, over time the commonplaces embedded in texts and pictures were absorbed or reabsorbed into oral culture and collectively internalised. Sir Thomas Browne dedicated an entire chapter of his *Pseudodoxia epidemica* (1646) to disproving the vulgar error and 're-ceived opinion' that 'the Jews stink', and various other anti-Semitic assumptions were immersed in widely used proverbs.[69] By the early eighteenth century tales of popish atrocities had likewise become legendary. According to Daniel Defoe, popery was 'the Hobgoblin, the Spectre with which the Nurses fright the Children, and entertain the old Women all over the Country'.[70] Such myths and narratives not only crystallised contemporary anxieties, they also provided what Miri Rubin has called 'a blueprint for action'. Their presence is important in explaining 'the terrifying mechanisms which move or facilitate that awful transformation of neighbour into persecutor, of community into murderous crowd, of tolerated other to the object of all phobic energy and destructive desire'.[71]

This brings us to the wider phenomenon of verbal abuse, which Archbishop

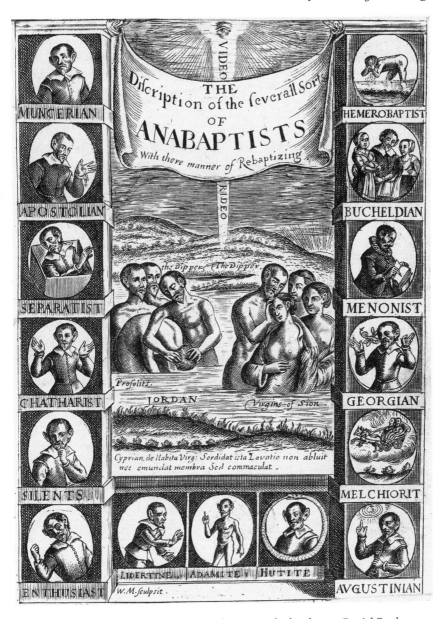

9 The anatomy of enthusiasm: the Anabaptists and related sects: Daniel Featley,
The dippers dipt (London, 1645; 1660 edn), frontispiece. (By permission of The British
Library, Thomason Tracts, E 1012 [2]).

A QVAKER

Weake as you say we are, yett woel command,
all flesh to fall, that doth against us stand.
The light within us, of such force is fownd,
showld satan come, twill lay him on the grund.

The Light they talke of keepes a heavy rout,
ile search all corners, but ile find it out.
By yea and nay, she is a dareing Gule,
ile try a fall, or els I am a Chirle.

With face of brass, this woman that you see
most Impudently doth afirm, that shee.
The mind of God, in all poynts, more doth know,
then from the Sacred Scriptures, ere could flaw.
Presumptious wretch: it were more fitt that shee.
at home showld keepe, and mind hir howsewifery.
And if noe meanes to live on, woorke for bread,
then idlye gossop with hir magot head.
Their light within doth so prevayle.
it makes them hot about the tayle.
Exsept afreind that poynt doth cleare,
they could them selves in pecces teare.

10 Visual satire of female Quaker, driven on by the devil: engraving dating from c. 1653?
(© The British Museum, Department of Prints and Drawings, Satires, no. 158).

John Whitgift once described as 'the persecution of the tongue'.[72] Like sticks and stones, vicious words could hurt and wound. As instances of individuals prosecuting their neighbours for defamation and slander reveal, Englishmen and women were extremely sensitive to the slight of being branded a heretic. Several suits were launched in the diocese of Norwich in the early sixteenth century against people who had impugned the plaintiffs as Lollards and casual and not so casual accusations of Lutheranism were a source of much litigation and conflict both in and out of court in the early part of the reign of Henry VIII.[73] The rhetorical assaults that early modern men and women made upon nonconformists crop up frequently in our sources. They both accompanied corporal punishment and physical violence and operated as a surrogate and substitute for it. For instance, a poor Catholic woman from Yorkshire exposed in the marketplace like 'an owl in the daytime' was hissed at by local boys who shouted 'A papist, a papist' before being set in the stocks. In London in the 1650s, children scoffed and spat upon playmates with recusant parents, saying 'Papist, Papist, pray to the Pope, Your neck in a halter, your heels in a rope'. The Duke of York himself was publicly denounced as a 'popish dog' when he arrived at the Temple to assist in putting out a fire in 1679.[74]

Those against whom the odious label 'puritan' was deployed complained about being made a 'byword' and a 'mocking stock'. Carrying overtones of the ancient Cathar and Donatist heresies, it came to encapsulate contempt for men and women who had earned a reputation as officious busybodies and self-righteous zealots. This was not the only unkind nickname invented by their enemies: if the records of the church and civil courts are any indication, the godly of Elizabethan Essex were constantly being traduced as 'pratling-stants', 'trim mates' and 'pickthankly knaves'.[75]

'Quaker' too began as a cutting term of abuse, though contemporaries hurled the full range of derogatory epithets at members of the sect. Of particular interest is the case of the Friend from Woodbridge in Suffolk disparaged as 'Rogue, Witch, Devil, Papist, and whatever else … drunken Rage did suggest' as he was beaten by a minister.[76] Restoration clergymen likewise lamented the damage that had been done by 'bespattering and aspersing' worthy men with insinuations like 'latitudinarian' and 'rationalist': these too were 'engines devised by [the] spiteful' and those with 'a very aking tooth'.[77]

Flung out loosely and often indiscriminately, such nicknames index the irritation and hostility that could mark everyday interaction with those who espoused different faiths. As Patrick Collinson has remarked, they draw our attention to 'one half of a stressful relationship'.[78] As contemporaries recognised, their application was corrosive of cordial and harmonious relations. Thus, in a speech lamenting the divisions that afflicted his kingdom delivered to Parliament on Christmas Eve 1545, Henry VIII reproved the tendency of his people to inveigh against one another 'without charity or discrecion': 'the one calleth the other Hereticke and Anabaptist, and he calleth hym again, Papist, Ypocrite and Pharisey'.[79] Injunctions against 'devilish terms' and 'con-tumelious words' were issued by both Mary and Elizabeth I and in 1626 John Yates wished that a statute might be passed outlawing 'this offensive name of a Puritan ... for certainly Satan gains much by the free use of it'.[80] In the state of Maryland, founded on the principle of toleration, just such a law was instituted in 1649. It banned the words heretic, schismatic, idolater, puritan, Independent, Presbyterian, popish, priest, Jesuit, Jesuited papist, Lutheran, Calvinist, Anabaptist, Brownist, antinomian, Barrowist, roundhead, separatist, together with any other term employed 'in a reproachful manner relating to matter of religion'.[81] As we have seen, vitriolic language always had the capacity to trigger conflict and to erupt into violent acts.

At the opposite extreme, dissenters could suffer the ultimate indignity of being treated as if they did not exist. In accordance with the biblical injunction to shun and flee sinners and idolaters (Titus 3: 10–11), the faithful were expected to segregate themselves from excommunicates and heretics. Susan Brigden has argued that in the early sixteenth century 'utter social ostracism awaited the unorthodox'. But it remains difficult to gauge how far contem-poraries complied with canon law in this regard, how far they deliberately and systematically avoided the company of their confessional enemies. By its very nature, frosty silence does not impinge much on the historical record. However, we do occasionally catch sight of nonconformists being sent to Coventry. When Humphrey Monmouth began to gain a reputation as a 'Scrip-ture man' in the reign of Henry VIII his poor neighbours in Barking gave him the cold shoulder, declining to accept charity from him or to borrow money. When Richard Hunne's apostasy became known in the city of London he was apparently unable to find anyone willing to trade with him. In several instances parishioners prevented the burial of people suspected of holding erroneous beliefs, as in the case of William Glover at Wem in Shropshire in the mid-1550s.[82] Serious tumults surrounded attempts to inter the recusant Alice Wellington in a Herefordshire churchyard under cover of night in 1607, after the vicar of the parish refused point blank to perform the funeral.[83] Those who chronicled the 'sufferings' of Quakers, Baptists and other dissenters in the late seventeenth century naturally concentrated on the most acute manifestations of popular hostility, passing over the many lesser discourtesies to which they were probably subjected by their Anglican neighbours. Indivi-dually, such incivilities may have been a minor irritant to social equilibrium; cumulatively they had the capacity to erode cordial relations between members of different churches and sects.

Religious intolerance in early modern England, then, took diffuse and tacit as well as precisely targeted forms. The range of negative responses to minority groups we have reviewed need to be seen not as clear alternatives but as part of a finely graded spectrum and a continuous cycle. Persecution was a circular and incremental process fuelled by the existence of stereotypes of deviance and by wars of words between the adherents of competing faiths and creeds. It manifested itself both in virulent language and in real and ritualised violence. In the next section, we look more closely at what motivated such outbursts of bigotry and try to identify the occasions on which men and women were driven to take spontaneous action against the fellow inhabitants of their local communities – people with whom, as we shall see later in this book, they seem generally to have lived in relative harmony and peace.

INCENTIVES FOR ACTION AND OCCASIONS FOR CONFLICT

There is a temptation to dismiss many episodes of persecution and prejudice as examples of crowd psychopathology, as distasteful instances of collective hysteria and irrational frenzy. But this is to sidestep the challenge of interpreting and explaining them. Careful investigation reveals that such attacks were not random and indiscriminate but had a underlying logic and structure. Those involved in them were provoked by specific sets of circumstances and inspired by particular goals.

Undoubtedly some such assaults and encounters were driven by malice. The laws against religious nonconformity could be a useful weapon to those intent upon harming their neighbourhood rivals and enemies. Alice Taylor of Bisham may herself have had a hidden agenda when she insisted in 1503 that 'the heretickis brande at Wikecombe wer put to deathe for il will and their goodis', but it is clear that some contemporaries were quite prepared to make false allegations as part of private vendettas. Complaints that innocent men were being accused of doctrinal error out of sheer spite led to the revisions in the indictment procedure ordered by the Henrician statutes of 1533 and 1543. The authorities evidently suspected that the Colchester servant who reported his employer for sheltering Protestants in 1556 did so for less than pious reasons, since they placed him in the stocks to teach him 'to speak good of his master'.[84] Some cases of clerical infraction presented to the authorities in early seventeenth-century Lincolnshire seem to have had less to do with a desire to enforce conformity to the Prayer Book rubrics than with deep-seated personal animus: John Robotham of Manton had fought several protracted law suits with various parishioners and alleged that the proceedings against him were rooted in the enmity of one of his tenants.[85] A man who informed against John Cotton of Boston in the early 1630s seems to have been a disgruntled victim of the local drive for moral discipline: he took revenge by giving evidence to the High Commission against the town's renowned puritan preacher. The work of the parliamentary Committee for Plundered Ministers in the 1640s was also hampered by the mischief wrought by witnesses aroused by festering resentment or envy: as one incumbent remarked bitterly, too many evil aspersions came 'from the Chimney-corner, or Table'. The clergy themselves were not above manipulating ecclesiastical justice to pursue private grudges and prosecute interpersonal disputes: the litigious Restoration rector Nathaniel Aske from Wiltshire assured his superiors that in his presentments 'there shall not be one drop of revenge, No such vinegar or gall in our ink', but he resorted to the courts on a regular basis to punish those who crossed him.[86]

As research on the Reformation in its local context has shown, factional competition for power in market towns could also be clothed in the garb of confessional conflict. In Elizabethan Thetford, for example, an essentially secular squabble over office-holding was transformed into a spiritual war between the 'godly' and the 'frowardly and popishly inclined', those 'very cold in the cause of religion'.[87] Corporate politics in the second half of the seventeenth century was likewise often conducted in terms of clash between Anglicanism and nonconformity: in Bristol and other towns, underlying tensions about matters of finance and property were expressed in the language of sectarian rivalry, which itself merged and crystallised in time into the vocabulary of party, 'Tory' and 'Whig'.[88] We may learn something here from case studies of the conditions in which accusations of witchcraft arose. A struggle for political control in Jacobean Rye was played out in these terms, as Annabel Gregory has shown, and Malcolm Gaskill and others have emphasised how fraudulent claims about malevolent sorcery and maleficium could be a function of village feuds in Kent and elsewhere.[89] In the mid-1650s, similar allegations of diabolism were levelled at the radical minister, John Pordage, as part of a concerted effort by local puritan authorities to dispossess him of the rich living of Bradfield. Ironically the very frequency with which false charges of demonic conspiracy were laid against groups and individuals in this period may be one reason why the discourse of witchcraft eventually lost credibility: the politicisation of the crime undermined its usefulness as a tool of partisan dispute.[90]

Greed also had a role in promoting assaults on members of minority groups. Pursuivants were a breed of men who often ransacked the homes of wealthy recusants in the process of arresting them, regarding their spoils as a perquisite of their unsavoury profession. At least one example of a criminal forging a warrant and escutcheon, so that he could commit robbery under the pretence of searching for priests, has been discovered.[91] Money was clearly a motive for many of those who informed under the provisions of the Second Conventicle Act of 1670 and we cannot ignore the element of fortuitous looting carried out by those involved in religious rioting. The anti-Catholic disturbances linked with the Glorious Revolution of 1688–89 seem to have provided some with a cover for common theft and not all those who sacked opulent Presbyterian meeting houses in the wake of Henry Sacheverell's sermon in 1710 surrendered the expensive furnishings they had removed to the flames.[92]

Nor can we rule out the possibility that such episodes simply provided an outlet for youthful high spirits and an excuse for drunken fun and unruly hooliganism. As unpleasant as it may sound to modern ears, executions were a form of popular entertainment.[93] It is significant that many verbal and physical assaults on religious dissenters and their churches and dwellings occurred on holidays and holy days such as Christmas, Easter, Corpus Christi and Whitsun. It can be no coincidence that a band of 500 Londoners chose the great Catholic feast day of the body of Christ to attack visiting Spaniards in 1555, nor that the contested seasons of Yuletide and May provided the back-drop for some of the anti-puritan tumults that accompanied the restoration of the monarchy in 1660–1.[94] These were occasions when a degree of saturnalian disorder was not merely sanctioned but also in some sense expected: turning the world topsy-turvy and setting wrongs playfully to right was all part of the game and contemporary reports suggest alcohol often fired the bellies of both participants and spectators. The festive aspect of such attacks is also illustrated by the case of the Catholic chapel in Newcastle raided in 1688 and used by 'Jack Pudding and his brethren for a Play-House'.[95]

Key dates in the Protestant calendar of providential deliverance and thanks-giving also provided the backdrop for spasms of persecution and intolerance. The London crowd that acted so aggressively towards those injured in the Blackfriars accident had only just finished celebrating the failure of the Spanish match and the return of the Prince of Wales to England without a popish bride.[96] In the reign of Charles I, commemoration of Elizabeth's accession on 17 November sparked pointed expressions of hostility towards the French Princess Henrietta Maria, whose own birthday fell on the sixteenth, some of it in the form of overly enthusiastic sessions of bell-ringing.[97] It was also the day on which the famous pope-burning processions organised by the Whigs in the years 1678–81 took place – a custom still practised annually at Lewes in Sussex on 5 November. The anniversary of the discovery of the Gunpowder Plot was another prompt for action against popery and papists, whether open or secret. During the Civil War, several incidents of iconoclasm took place on Guy Fawkes Day and in 1642 the Essex royalist Sir Humphrey Mildmay and his family stayed at home 'in all fears', apprehensive about the passions which the date might unleash.[98] These red-letter days could be dangerously liminal.

The prominence of young people in conflicts and confrontations with religious nonconformists deserves notice. Adolescent servants and appren-tices were conspicuous by their presence in the anti-Catholic episodes of the sixteenth and seventeenth centuries and rumours spread by small girls were responsible for searches of the homes of recusants in Colchester instigated by vigilante bands.[99] 'Rude boys' were likewise alleged to be behind many attacks on the early Quakers, and in Cambridge and Oxford students showed little mercy to visiting evangelists in the 1650s.[100] Youths were also at the forefront of risings against Huguenot strangers and aliens, as they had been in the notorious outrages against foreign merchants that took place on Evil May Day 1517.[101] The impulse to cock a snook at one's elders and rebel against the symbols and representatives of established authority was a feature of Protestantism in its initial phase as an illicit protest movement but it was surely also a strand in incidents of antagonism towards these same religious minorities.[102] As Natalie Zemon Davis demonstrated in a classic essay, young men and women had other reasons for misrule: acting as moral custodians of the community, they sought to rectify affronts to its sense of order. Like the London apprentices who ritually attacked city brothels every Shrove Tuesday, those who engaged in outrages against Catholic and Protestant dissenters were involved in some sense in a rite of passage from Carnival to Lent, from childish frivolity into responsible adulthood.[103]

The repeated appearance of young artisans and craftsmen in such incidents is also indicative of the fact that they contained undercurrents of economic jealousy and tension. This does much to explain sporadic attacks on industrious Protestant emigrants from the Netherlands and France. Ill-feeling against them was aroused by the perception that they were stealing the livelihoods of local people. Sympathy for afflicted co-religionists was inclined to wear thin in the context of anxieties about food shortages, high prices and declining wages and it is no coincidence that the troubled decades of the 1590s and 1620s, marked by harvest failure, scarcity and industrial depression, saw some of the most intense manifestations of these sentiments. In 1593 a pamphlet pinned to the wall of the Dutch church in Austin Friars warned of the mass slaughter of Flemish asylum seekers unless they left the capital, and two years later the yeoman weavers lamented 'We nourish Serpents in our bosomes, who stinge us to the harte'.[104] It is striking that in Southampton, where there was less competition for employment, unrest against exiles was limited by comparison with that experienced in other coastal towns and Cinque Ports where they settled. Native support for immigrants likewise remained strong in Canterbury, where they played a key role in reversing the fortunes of their host community; this also largely explains the failure of a crypto-Catholic conspiracy in Norwich in 1570, which planned to rally the common people to 'beat the strangers out of the city'.[105]

Later in the century the refugees' prosperity and superior technical expertise once again became a major source of grievance: in the 1680s the company of silk weavers spoke of their looms as 'devilish inventions' and there were sporadic Luddite-like attacks on their machines. Others threatened that if they could 'get a sufficient number together they will rise and knock them on the head'.[106] Such commotions owed little to the Calvinist religion which these foreigners professed, though occasionally allegations were made that they had gained admission to England by virtue of 'feigned hypocrisy and counterfeit show of religion'.[107] It is true that the Fenland riots against Dutch and Walloon Calvinists engaged in draining the boggy East Anglian landscape in the 1640s and 1650s involved assaults on their chapel at Sandtoft, but this had less to do with their faith than with the fact that the building had become an architectural symbol of engineering schemes that were depriving the local inhabitants of their common agricultural rights.[108]

In the case of other groups, however, economic anxiety fused powerfully with confessional prejudice – not least in relation to wealthy Jewish merchants and financiers, whose prominence and prowess in the field of money-lending had fostered jealousy in many countries in the Middle Ages. Both sentiments were present in the Stour Valley riots: it was given out by some of the Colchester plunderers that recusants were 'the occasion that they, their wives and children were brought into great want and extremity (by the great decay of trading)'. In 1641–42 there was grumbling resentment of the Catholic soap monopoly and concessions to papists in the Forest of Dean and it was rumoured among the poor that the Queen Mother had been granted an imposition on shoe leather.[109] At other junctures, recusants were also blamed for scarcity, recession and crisis and in their capacity as landlords they could find themselves the focus of the hatred of exasperated tenants. Sir Thomas Tresham, who practised ruthless enclosure and rack-renting on his estate in Northamptonshire, seems to have been 'vulgarly odious' to his social inferiors.[110] The crowd politics of the reign of Charles II likewise had an economic dimension, though no simple equation can comprehend the complexity of the links between ideological anxiety and the unrest of workers suffering from unemployment or reduced to penury by low wages.[111] While it would be reductionist to ascribe incidents of persecution merely to material hardship, the role of the latter in stirring up religious disorder must be acknowledged.

Spasms of anti-Catholic and anti-nonconformist activity also frequently occurred at times of natural disaster. Wolfgang Behringer has suggestively explored the connection between the chronology of the witch-hunt and long-term changes in the European climate which culminated in the so-called 'Little Ice Age' and there are some grounds for arguing that the vulnerability of English society to bad weather was also one of the preconditions for episodes of intolerance towards religious dissenters.[112] Severe frosts, harsh winters and terrible floods inevitably added strain to relationships with heretical neighbours and outbreaks of fire and epidemics of plague were sometimes linked directly with false believers. Just as witches were accused of causing fatal accidents and whipping up storms, so too were those who espoused unorthodox opinions sometimes alleged to have spread disease and started conflagrations. Mostly these catastrophes were believed to be man-made but occasionally wild insinuations were made about the use of black magic and the intervention of the devil.

Famously, the Great Fire of London of 1666 was traced to the machinations of Catholics, though rumours flew about the involvement of the Fifth Monarchists and stranger communities – a French watchmaker who confessed to having ignited it as part of a scheme hatched in Paris was quickly dispatched to the gallows. But the monument erected to the 'Perpetuall Remembrance of that most Dreadfull Burning of this Protestant City' in 1681 declared confidently that it had been 'Begun and Carried on by the Treachery and Malice of the Papists'.[113] Such stories were part of a long tradition stretching back to the previous century: in 1591 Richard Verstegan received letters in Antwerp saying 'There is no evil publikely done but streyt they father it on Papists' and 'bloody news' about Catholic attempts to consume Norwich by fire was published in 1641. The same year false reports that Parliament had been set alight by recusants prompted Nehemiah Wallington and others to go 'thither with swords and other weapons'.[114] In 1659 Quakers were said to have burnt houses in Oxford and to have threatened to do the same in Middlesex.[115] Bernard Capp has made the intriguing point that the inflammatory rhetoric employed by the Society of Friends and other sects made them, in part, the source of their own misfortunes. In *A fiery flying rolle*, for instance, Abeizer Coppe predicted terrible fires and detected the Lord's hand behind a number of recent conflagrations, claims that may have aroused suspicions that he was the agent and author, as well as the eyewitness, of these events.[116] Similar rumours about fire-raising circulated alongside Titus Oates's other feverish fabrications and the arrest of several maidservants on suspicion of igniting their masters' residences at the instigation of priests only exacerbated the situation. Elizabeth Oxley, hung in 1679, confessed to setting her employer's home in Fetter Lane alight, blaming a man who had converted her to Rome and promised her £5. The execution of individual arsonists gave credibility to the wider conspiracy theories about popish pyromania that so often provided the pretext for vigilante action, just as triumphant declarations by a few outspoken Catholics that the Great Fire was a manifestation of God's wrath against heresy had fed the panic surrounding that calamity.[117]

Religious deviants were also occasionally accused of a kind of germ warfare. In 1569 the conduit heads in Southampton were covered and locked for fear that the newly arrived Walloons might contaminate the water supply. Some believed that Catholic sorcerers were responsible for the Oxford gaol fever of 1577, which wiped out the entire judicial bench and several hundred others besides, and vicious papists were also supposed to have sent plague-sores to the parliamentary leader John Pym in 1641.[118] Admittedly such allegations were rare in England, as on the Continent: a recent study of plague-spreading conspiracies in sixteenth- and seventeenth-century Swiss cities notes that remarkably few of those convicted of this offence were supposed to have a confessional motivation for their activities, even in the Calvinist citadel of Geneva.[119] Yet claims of this kind did rear their heads at critical junctures. As late as 1745 a virulent cattle murrain was blamed on Catholics deliberately corrupting pools and before the Gordon Riots it was alleged that Benedictine monks had poisoned all the flour in Southwark.[120] When the Poor Palatines arrived in England from the Rhineland in 1709 some not only questioned their Protestant credentials but accused them of introducing small pox.[121] In general, though, mass epidemics which killed vast swathes of the population were hard to pin upon minority groups because the arrow of death was no discriminator of particular faiths. These improbable tales of biological sabotage had a taproot in the myth that Jews, in collaboration with lepers, had brought about the Black Death of 1347 by infecting wells – a myth which must have silently contributed to Roderigo Lopez's conviction for treasonously plotting to poison Queen Elizabeth in 1594.[122] An index of well-entrenched anxieties, such rumours were simultaneously an attempt to find an explanation that could provide closure for these fears.[123] They find a telling modern echo in the anthrax scares which rocked the US in the wake of the terrorist attacks of 11 September 2001. Whether imaginary or real, such incidents increased distrust of religious deviants, sowing the seeds for further episodes of violence.

Even where minority groups escaped the charge of actively conspiring such catastrophes, a causal link was often made between calamity and their passive but polluting presence. Aliens in early Elizabethan London were thought to be 'comonlie unclenly people' who bred 'filthynes, infection and pestilence' and in Norwich the spread of plague in 1578–79 was likewise put down to the dirty habits of Calvinist refugees and the crowded conditions in which they lived.[124] For many contemporaries the overlap between literal and spiritual infection was instinctive: in Devon and Cornwall the courts ordered watches to be set on highways and bridges to catch wandering Quakers, 'for the preventing of this great contagion, that infects almost every corner of this Nation'.[125]

On a second level, providentialism inspired the conviction that natural disasters were divine punishments of communities that permitted heretics and idolaters to abide among them. In 1563 God was believed to have visited plague on the capital because of the 'superstitious religion of Rome ... so much favoured by the citizens' and when the disease devastated Barnstaple in 1646 some inhabitants called for members of the local congregation of Independents to be turned out of town.[126] The assumption that entire villages and towns would suffer if steps were not taken to expel or eliminate non-conformists could be a powerful incentive to collective crowd action. The logic of scapegoating was informed by the Bible: the story of how the throwing of Jonah overboard had calmed the ferocious storm (Jonah 1: 15) and the chapter in the book of Joshua (Joshua 7) in which the stoning of Achan induced the Lord to turn away from Israel 'the fierceness of his anger'. Just as it consistently triggered fresh initiatives in the crusade against the sins of swearing, drunkenness, sexual promiscuity and sabbath-breaking, so too, it seems, did the desire to deflect and avert providential wrath underpin some popular attacks on papists, Quakers and other dissenters.[127] As Bob Scribner has remarked, prejudice against ideological 'others' was most intense when it was linked to a process of diagnosis and explanation. It was at these moments of moral panic that the volcano of intolerance was most likely to erupt.[128]

No less striking is the relationship between episodes of verbal and physical aggression and times of acute political crisis. Lay people were most often stirred to hostile behaviour towards their heterodox neighbours in the context of threats of rebellion and of plots to overturn the status quo. The recent Oldcastle Rising may account for the animosity displayed towards the eccentric Margery Kempe in 1414, when women came running from their houses crying 'Brennyth this fals heretyk'.[129] Much anti-Catholic activity likewise synchronised with domestic emergencies and dangerous developments in foreign affairs, as Robin Clifton has emphasised. The rhythm of local alarms closely matched the ebb and flow of worrying occurrences both at the centre and on the Continent. It was generally in the aftermath of events like the Gunpowder Treason that provincial communities turned against recusants, though seven months prior to its discovery, Sir Thomas Tresham was said to be the leader of an impending purge of Northamptonshire Protestants, in which the houses of the victims were to be marked with the sign of the cross. Such scares drew sustenance from the memory of St Bartholomew's Day 1572, which no less a figure than Robert Beale, clerk of the Privy Council, believed to be the work of the organ of the Counter-Reformation itself, a 'conjuration of the Council of Trent to root out all such as contrary to the Pope's traditions, make profession of Christ's Gospel'.[130] The assassinations of William of Orange and Henry IV in 1584 and 1610 were also a stimulus to panics, not to mention the attempted naval invasion by Philip II's Armada.

Even before news of the Ulster rising of 1641 filtered through to England, concern was raised by reports of intemperate speeches made by recusants, such as that uttered by Elizabeth Shipley, who boasted that there were sufficient Romanists to hang all the heretics and puritans in the Middlesex town in which she lived.[131] The massacre itself (which some zealous souls supposed had been committed on the orders of Charles I and Henrietta Maria) spawned fears that Catholics in dozens of English communities were planning similar atrocities. In Ipswich, stories circulated of a hidden army ready to slit the throats of the inhabitants. In Leicester, Lichfield and Ashby-de-la-Zouche people volunteered to keep night watches following talk of 'a plot intended to be done by the Papists on the Protestants'. In Norwich, the mayor received a tip-off that the city was to be attacked by 12,000 papists.[132] Indeed, it was the belief that the king had secretly commissioned the Earl of Antrim and other Catholics to carry out the rebellion in Ireland, which convinced many fervent Protestants that 'there was no other way of safety' other than to take up arms against him in 1642. By doing otherwise, Richard Baxter reflected in retrospect, one would have been 'giving up the land to blood'.[133]

The second half of the seventeenth century was covered in a rash of such rumours. In the ferment of anti-Catholic feeling that followed the Great Fire of London in 1666, the discovery of a sinister collection of 'desperate kinds of knives or daggers' prompted official no less than popular speculation: in the event they turned out to be intended for use upon whales off the coast of Greenland, rather than the capital's Protestants.[134] These fears reached their apex in Titus Oates's revelation in the autumn of 1678 that 20,000 Catholics were to rise up and kill 100,000 people. Repudiating the tradition of historiography which sees the Popish Plot as an astonishing example of mass credulity, Jonathan Scott has stressed that the episode reflected genuine and well-informed anxieties about the menace presented by the resurgent Counter-Reformation in Europe, especially in the form of French absolutism.[135] The accession of James II led to fresh trepidation: in April 1685, the wife of a London shoemaker speculated that a great massacre of Protestants would follow within days of the coronation.[136] Incidents of bigotry linked with trepidation about national events continued in the eighteenth century: the ship carpenters of Whitby 'took there Axes and Cleavers to hack and hew the said papists to pieces' upon hearing of the 'great rejoicings' of the Catholics of Egton on the Yorkshire moors over the defeat of the government's forces by the Jacobites at Prestonpans in September 1745.[137]

Time and again people were prompted to take pre-emptive action against religious dissenters by concerns about the security of the country at large and the safety of their local communities. Intolerance was often a defensive reaction to keenly-felt (but poorly substantiated) threats of slaughter by a fifth column of papists or sectaries. In 1641, for instance, Protestants in Staffordshire were afraid to go to church unarmed in case their enemies took the opportunity to kill them en masse, and the many contemporaneous incidents of ordinary lay people breaking into the homes of recusants to confiscate their personal weapons reflected similar fears.[138] It was alleged in 1660 that, in order to win popular support for suppressing the saints, the malignant of Tiverton in Devon had aroused the whole town in the middle of night with an invented story that the Fifth Monarchists, Quakers and Baptists were shortly to murder them. Venner's rising the following year appears to have been partly incited by the belief that 'The Devil and the Pope hath at this day a great design upon England' and that their agents in England were plotting to 'suck out our very heart blood'.[139] Many persecutors did not see themselves as belligerent aggressors so much as hapless victims engaging in acts of self-protection.

To this extent, crowds were often imbued with a strong sense of the legitimacy of their vicious and uncivil conduct. What Natalie Zemon Davis has observed of Catholics and Protestants who perpetrated assaults on their confessional enemies during the French Wars of Religion is no less true of those who participated in similar incidents in sixteenth- and seventeenth-century England.[140] Just as many Parisians were convinced that orders for the St Bartholomew's Day massacre had been issued by the king himself, so too can instances be found on this side of the Channel of individuals claiming merely to be following the instructions of higher authorities. The Colchester rioters believed they were effecting the will of the Long Parliament and on two occasions anti-Catholic gangs possessed an authenticated warrant for their disorderly actions. At least some of those who had sworn the oath of Protestation of 1641 felt themselves bound by a solemn covenant to defend the Church, king and state 'against all Popery and popish innovations' by taking up swords and cudgels against its representatives in their own neighbourhoods.[141] The involvement of magistrates and constables also lent an air of legality to the proceedings, as did the beating of drums and the tendency for the crowd to mimic the rituals of civic and Mosaic justice. Preachers also tacitly sanctioned or openly advocated violence in rousing sermons: Stephen Marshall's *Meroz cursed*, preached more than sixty times, may have been one spur to attacks on Essex papists. Other texts were equally incendiary, including David's words in 1 Chronicles 22: 16 ('Arise and be doing') and the tale of the zeal of Phineas in Numbers 25: 11, who stayed the plague by driving a spear through the copulating bodies of an Israelite and a Midianite. The Bath minister who declared during the Interregnum that if St Paul had been alive he would have stoned the Quakers, saying this was merely 'Christian zeal', may have helped some to justify their brutality towards members of the Society of Friends.[142]

Other participants in such episodes appear to have been motivated by the notion that if officials failed in their duty to root out deviance it fell to ordinary people to take the law into their own hands. If the authorities were lax and complacent and legislation was inadequate it was up to obscure individuals to discipline heretics and wicked idolaters. In this sense their violence was 'didactic and coercive as well as vindictive'.[143] Spontaneous acts of iconoclasm by godly zealots like Henry Sherfield and Sir Robert Harley owed something to frustration at the state's defective policy with regard to the wholesale removal of 'superstitious' and 'idolatrous' images and similar feelings surfaced in a number of cases of persecution.[144] Concern about the excessive leniency of the government towards recusants was one of the ingredients in the savage reaction of Londoners to the Blackfriars accident and it may also account for their response to the king's reprieve of the condemned priest John Goodman in January 1641: according to one Catholic writer, they were so enraged that had he been recognised he would have been stoned. The case of the South-ampton cobbler who gathered a band to disarm local papists is also revealing: he did so on the grounds that the town's officials were too slack and would 'suffer theire throats to be cut'.[145]

The Lancashire minister who told local Quakers in 1659 that magistrates were 'Faulty in that they did not sheath their swords in the Bowells of such Blasphemers as you are' also seems to have been articulating a more widely held sentiment. It is certainly interesting that popular aggression against this group was most pronounced in the Interregnum, when legal remedies against them were lacking, and that its decline coincided with the introduction of the sharp Clarendon Code. The violence of the crowd, argues John Miller, might be seen as a form of 'self help in the absence of effective laws'.[146] In the 1680s there were likewise those who felt that nonconformists were treated too gently: Bishop Sparrow of Norwich found many 'loud[ly] complaining that we do not proceed violently beyond the rule of law'.[147] The tumults associated with the Popish Plot sprang partly from anger about tolerance of Catholics and, in their own eyes, the Gordon Rioters were simply making up for the negligence of the Anglican establishment, which should never have allowed the passage of the Catholic Relief Act in 1778.[148]

These assumptions flourished in a context in which the populace played an active role in detecting and policing crime. This may account for the fact that officials were not infrequently willing to condone or tolerate the quasi-judicial initiatives of the crowd. Just as city masters were unwilling to condemn the activities of the apprentices who sacked brothels in the bawdy house riots of 1668 on the grounds that they did 'but the magistrates drudgery',[149] so too, it may be supposed, did the authorities sometimes turn a blind eye to attacks on individuals who infringed the Act of Uniformity and met in corners and conventicles. How could they find fault with those who filled the gaps left by a still flimsy, if ever-growing government bureaucracy?

There is, finally, a distinct sense in which some individuals who carried out attacks on dissenters regarded themselves as agents of divine wrath. Studies of the St Bartholomew's Day massacres by Denis Crouzet and Barbara Diefen-dorf have emphasised how people were driven to kill heretics by the conviction that they were soldiers of God, *les guerriers de dieu*, an interpretation that Nicholas Canny has also recently used to illuminate the Ulster risings of 1641.[150] Although passions never quite reached the same peak in England, where few people seem to have been callously murdered in the name of religion alone, it seems clear that similar concerns about purity, defilement and danger inspired a minority of men and women to take up arms against their heretical, papist or sectary neighbours, not only during the Civil War but also at other critical junctures. It was in precisely these terms that the regicides justified the execution of Charles I himself: insisting that they had been 'extraordinarily carried forth to desire justice upon the King, that man of blood', they saw themselves as the Lord's instruments to cleanse the land of sin and to avenge the evil wrought against the saints by 'he and his monarchy' in the name of the Beast.[151] Like many lesser acts of animosity towards the unorthodox, this too was a type of holy violence.

THE TARGETS OF INTOLERANCE: THE SOCIAL PROFILE OF THE PERSECUTED

Having established that religious intolerance was highly structured and informed by coherent motives and objectives, we now turn to consider the nature and the identity of its victims. It would be a mistake to suppose that they were randomly chosen. Against whom did crowds channel their aggression? What kinds of people were most vulnerable to being made into scapegoats? And which individuals did voluntary civic and ecclesiastical officials single out for exemplary punishment in a context in which justice could only ever be selective? Such questions have more often been asked by historians of the witch-hunt and the Reformation of Manners than they have by scholars of interconfessional relations, but they are no less relevant. The task of the last part of this chapter is to offer a preliminary sketch of the social profile of the persecuted.

There is very little to suggest that attacks on nonconformists were a masked form of class war. The recurrent description of those involved in religious rioting as the 'rude multitude' should not be taken at face value: this was less an indication of hierarchical rank than it was a comment on the barbarity and incivility of the crowd's actions. Although such incidents did sometimes conceal friction between the rich and the poor and entail attacks on the property of the privileged, it would be a mistake to read them, on Marxist lines, as self-conscious attempts at social levelling. This is not, however, to rule out the possibility that such events contributed to the construction of embryonic class identities. It is even more difficult to sustain an argument that such episodes were part of a drive by elites to police and discipline the poor. Despite the topos of the illiterate heretic, dissent was socially heterogeneous in character. No less than orthodoxy, it drew the support of people from all parts of the spectrum of status and wealth. We must conclude that, like the crusade against sin, waves of religious persecution cut vertically rather than horizontally across communities and neighbourhoods.[152]

What stands out from the sources far more conspicuously is the frequency with which the individuals who became the focus of collective enmity were foreigners and strangers. It was usually outsiders and intruders who inflamed the prejudices of the ordinary populace rather than the familiar inhabitants of particular localities. The xenophobic dimension of contemporary intolerance is perhaps most clearly reflected in the regular uprisings of the native residents of towns and cities against refugees in the mould of Evil May Day 1517, when economic resentment of emigrés swelled into a movement to slay them. Even Calvinist exiles who had lived many years in England could find it hard to shed the stigma of birth beyond its shores: a newsbook of 1653 noted that many were 'very hot in persecuting … [their] alien friends'.[153] The same strand of hatred is also manifest in the attacks on ambassadors and members of their households that disturbed London in the early 1620s against the backdrop of the Spanish match. James I was compelled to issue two proclamations suppressing the 'Insolencies of rude & savage barbarisme' committed by 'the inferiour and baser sort of people' and ordering that such persons were shown due reverence and courtesy 'both in speech, gesture and otherwise'.[154]

Chauvinistic outrages continued in the metropolis after the Restoration and again on the eve of the Glorious Revolution, though they often seem to have been a kind of holiday pastime: the coaches of the Spanish and Dutch envoys were besieged on the 5 November 1668 and 1683, respectively, and on the same date in 1673 a Frenchman was burnt in effigy.[155] Irish immigrants and soldiers were similarly a source of much fear in the early 1640s and again in the 1680s – both their Catholicism and their nationality giving rise to exaggerated anxiety.[156] If by the mid-seventeenth century, the tendency to conflate popery with foreignness was already pronounced, by the eighteenth it was quite inescapable – an observation that helps to render more intelligible the apparently absurd belief that the Huguenots fleeing after the revocation of the Edict of Nantes were actually papists in disguise, agents of the absolutist Catholic King Louis XIV.[157]

In a context in which people commonly spoke of their county as their 'country' and in which parishes took pride in annually beating (and so reasserting) their boundaries, the category 'stranger' could be very encompassing. Heretics, Catholics and dissenters who had no connections with a community or had only recently arrived were far more likely to find themselves the objects of envy and loathing than those who were indigenous to it. It was when Lollards left the localities in which they habitually resided that they were most at risk of detection for their unorthodox opinions. 'What was tolerable idiosyncrasy in one parish', observes Richard Rex, 'could be unacceptable deviance a few miles away'. This may explain why most Bristol Lollards were hauled before courts some distance from that city: their odd behaviour and unusual views attracted attention in no small part because they were intruders.[158] Hence, too, the hostility towards itinerant Quaker evangelists and those who harboured these unwelcome incomers. The fact that many early members of the sect were northerners helps to account for the opposition they met with in the West Country and south, where they were judged to be 'men of a strang humor'.[159]

Early modern society's profound distrust of mobility is another factor that must be brought into the equation. Friends were sometimes indicted as vagrants and both recusants (who posted from parish to parish to avoid detection for non-attendance at church) and puritans (who gadded about the countryside in search of godly sermons) stimulated unease for similar reasons. This is also why seminary priests and Jesuits bore the brunt of the penal laws: tainted by their training in Rome and the Low Countries, they also lacked the ties that bound many recusants and church papists to their Protestant neighbours.[160] It is striking that when alarms did arise, they often centred on Catholic gentry who lived on the edges of villages and just beyond urban precincts, their physical marginality being matched by a semi-detached relationship with local inhabitants. Their spatial separation added to the menace they appeared to present.[161] There are interesting points of comparison here with the prosecution not only of witches, but of criminals in general: records show that outsiders were more prone to be indicted and sent to the gallows as felons than those who had family or friends nearby able to vouch for them.[162] Part of the explanation for this pattern of persecution lies in the observation that stereotypes of deviance tend to be suspended by personal contact, while in its absence they develop and grow.[163] In times of high domestic tension or disaster, it was much easier to blame individuals around whom there was an aura of mystery than people with whom one interacted on a daily basis.

Ironically, the geographical concentration of dissenters on the fringes of parishes or in ghettos in particular quarters of cities was often a consequence of official policies of repression. But their remote and aloof relationship with their orthodox neighbours was also to an extent self-imposed. As we see in more detail in Chapter 4, in an attempt to preserve the purity of their faith and to ensure their very survival in a hostile environment, some minorities were drawn to practise strict social as well as ecclesiastical segregation from the wicked unbelievers by whom they were surrounded. The voluntary apartheid of those who lived in deliberate isolation and dissociated themselves culturally from the adherents of other religions contributed to the fear and suspicion that could coagulate around them. The insularity of much seigneurial Catholicism is embodied in a remark made by Lord Vaux of Harrowden, who claimed his household 'to be a parish by itself', and Patrick Collinson has argued that the 'drastic doctrine of shunning' adopted by many puritans was a strategy which 'in principle, maximised social stress'.[164] One of the complaints made against stranger communities in London in Elizabeth's reign was that they kept 'a commonwealth within themselves ... though they be denized or borne heere amongst us, yett they keepe themselves severed from us in church, in government, in trade, in language and marriage'.[165] Disdainfully estranging oneself from the wider community was hardly conducive to good neighbourly relations.

It is also apparent that what most often incited intolerance against heretics, papists and sectaries was insolent and provocative behaviour. It was not so much quiet lay people who aroused the anger of the orthodox as bold confessors and defiant proselytisers. Lollards who took it upon themselves to reprove their peers for honouring images, lighting candles, or swearing were apt to find themselves angrily reported to the authorities. Agnes Cole of Phillips Norton in the diocese of Bath and Wells, for instance, did little to endear herself to her neighbours when she reprehended them for going on pilgrimage to the tomb of St Oswald in Salisbury in the mid-fifteenth century, wishing their way 'ful of bremmel [brambles] and thornes as eny wode is to lette [impede] theym to goe thidre'. Alice Tailor of Bisham gave Agnes Miller a major incentive to bear witness against her when she publicly rebuked her for kneeling before the cross, saying 'Stonde up olde foole!'[166]

In the initial phases of the Reformation, both excessive religious fervour and lack of respect for traditional symbols could try a community's patience. Three days of psalm-singing by Thomas Hudson of Aylsham in Norfolk frayed the nerves of his neighbours, who summoned the constable to apprehend him, and when John Lithall refused to kneel before the rood in St Paul's Cathedral, onlookers allegedly spat on him, crying 'Fie on thee, heretic', saying 'it was pity [he] was not burned already'.[167] The vociferous piety of other early Protestants and separatists was equally offensive to the sensibilities of their contemporaries. A young shearman from Dewsbury who called the font a 'stinking tarn' and extreme unction 'a sibberty sauce' in 1542 soon found himself delated before the Archbishop of York and compelled to carry out a humiliating penance. Several men who denounced the Church of England as false and the bishops as antichristian in 1590 were indicted for uttering seditious words in St Albans.[168] These were situations in which individuals must have actively co-operated with constables and churchwardens to enforce the laws against heresy and nonconformity.

Catholics too were most likely to be proceeded against when they disturbed the common peace by vicious words or impudent behaviour. This is suggested by cases such as those of Dorcas Stephen, presented at the Surrey Assizes in 1604 for flourishing her rosary beads about her head and declaring her contempt for the king and all authority, and of the spinster Catherine Meabourne, summoned before the northern High Commission in 1635 for calling the children of local Protestants 'heretickes and hell ratchettes'.[169] It is also indicated by citations of church papists who disrupted sermons or, like the

Yorkshire matron Mrs Kath Lacy, removed the sacrament from her mouth and 'did treade the same breade under her fote'.[170] Officials focused their efforts on punishing recusants who openly flaunted their religion or who busied themselves seducing the ignorant, and it was often the same individuals who came under attack at times of crisis like the early 1640s.

Likewise it was dissenters who disrupted the social fabric and offended against established customs and values who found themselves the targets of popular antagonism. Richard Bauman and Adrian Davies have persuasively argued that the hostility with which the early Quakers were greeted owed much to their vocal repudiation of the rules governing interpersonal conduct. Their plain speech and refusal to give hat honour to their elders and betters violated the conventions of accepted etiquette and could cause extreme irritation. Richard Davies's mistress was so infuriated by his discourteous use of 'thee' and 'thou' that she took up a stick and dealt him a severe blow on the head.[171] Acts of flamboyant evangelism like the practice of going naked for a sign or lying trouserless on a communion table were a serious affront to the sexual mores of the time, as well as a form of sacrilege, and those who ignored sabbatarian precepts, profaned holy days by going about their everyday business, and disturbed parish worship also exposed themselves to the indignation of loyal members of the Church of England. A Huntingdon Quaker was pelted with dirt and mire when he opened his shop on Christmas Day in 1661, while a widow who interrupted a service in Sidney Sussex College chapel in the late 1650s had 'a piss pot of Urine' thrown over her by an outraged local tailor.[172]

Other nonconformists who engaged in overt displays of religiosity or broke ecclesiastical taboos also became the subject of local resentment. Popular sensitivity about sabbath-breaking may explain the citation of otherwise untroubled members of the reclusive Family of Love like Edward Rule, who was presented to the Ely consistory court in 1591, for suffering his servants to work on the feast day of St Bartholomew and for binding corn one August Sunday in divine service time. A group of London Baptists who engaged in a day of fasting and prayer in the months immediately surrounding the Restoration were disturbed by a vintner who warned that 'the King is coming now, to hang you all up'. During the Republic, Anglicans who tactlessly appeared in public in mourning dress on the anniversary of the regicide sometimes provoked an angry reaction. Preaching in 1665, Henry King recalled (perhaps with some exaggeration) that some were 'assaulted merely for their habit ... hardly escaping with their lives'.[173] Conspicuously bearing witness to an embattled faith and commemorating its martyrs carried definite hazards.

Aggressive attempts to win converts were no less double-edged, alienating and exasperating more than they persuaded. Sometimes they inspired resentment that could boil over into verbal if not physical violence. When Ludowick Muggleton tried to co-opt a certain Thomas Tanner to his sect, for instance, the man's wife said that 'she would run a Spit in his guts'.[174] To those who believed in the institution of an ordained ministry, lay people who assumed the mantle of preachers were subversive rebels. Even more upsetting to supporters of the existing social and patriarchal order were militant female missionaries. The treatment meted out to Quaker women reveals that they were often seen as a threat to the established gender hierarchy. Like scolds, they were sometimes ducked or subjected to the shaming punishment of the charivari, and when Dorothy Waugh 'published the truth' in Scotby, Cumberland, in 1653 and rebuked the local mayor impertinently, his wrath was so kindled that he caused the iron collar known as the bridle to be placed on her.[175] The indiscipline of recusant wives and matriarchs like Margaret Clitherow who defied their conformist husbands and energetically proselytised their servants and neighbours also troubled conservative observers and may account for some acts of aggression against them.[176] The conduct of such women stoked old prejudices, reaffirming the ingrained assumption that the weaker sex were spiritually frail and especially prone to fall into heresy and sin.[177] While religious persecution can no more be seen as a war against women than the witch-hunt, misogyny was nevertheless an element that occasionally helped to shape and complicate it.

All these points link neatly with the insight that the individuals whom communities were least willing to tolerate were those whose doctrinal error was combined with other forms of social and moral deviance. People seem to have been most vulnerable to prosecution for their ecclesiastical infractions when they breached charity and behaved in unneighbourly ways and when they had committed flagrant, indecent or criminal acts. Ministers who insulted and quarrelled with their congregations were likely to find themselves charged with liturgical nonconformity or scandalous malignancy, like the puritan vicar of Sherborne, David Dee, who allegedly dealt 'rather contentiously than lovingly with his parishioners', and the Suffolk rector who assaulted his flock with a long list of colourful pejorative epithets, saying they were 'Black-mouthed hell-hounds, Limmes of the Devill, Fire-brands of Hell, Plow joggers, Bawling doggs, weaverly Jacks, and Church-Robbers'.[178] Godly clergy who acted as busy controllers, suppressing popular sports and condemning the unifying sociability of the alehouse, were also commonly the victims of petitions, libels and mocking rhymes, as noted earlier. The presentment of a Catholic husbandman of South Ockenden in Essex in 1624 for harbouring 'strange popish recusants' from London probably had something to do with his reputation as a poacher who stole his neighbours' fish, fowl and bees.[179] A century earlier, when Protestants were reported to Marian officials, it was often because they were known troublemakers or were disliked for other reasons. Gregory Newman, for instance, had scandalised his neighbours by committing adultery with his maid, who was also a gospeller.[180]

Of course, there is a sense in which people were predisposed to believe that heretics and sectaries were licentious and promiscuous. Sexual aberration was an inextricable part of the stereotype. The rumour that semi-separatists in early seventeenth-century Bristol who gathered for supplementary worship in private houses 'met together in the night to be unclean' was entirely in keeping with this tradition. Like the many allegations of fornication, incest, sodomy and bestiality made against Anabaptists, Ranters and Quakers, it should be taken with a large pinch of salt.[181] What it does highlight is the repeated convergence of intellectual unorthodoxy with immorality in people's minds.

It will be apparent that there are some interesting parallels between the social dynamics of prosecuting witches and the persecution of religious dissenters. The similarities are often more than superficial and occasionally these categories directly overlapped and intersected. Although Hugh Trevor Roper's thesis that trials for witchcraft were instruments of confessional conflict has been widely criticised, in some instances it still has some validity as an explanatory tool, though the causal connection between the two was invariably indirect.[182] Village cunning men and women were quite frequently smeared as papists, a connection which drew strength from the commonplace that Catholicism was a kind of sorcery and that Latin prayers were little more than charms and spells. In turn suspicions of residual or crypto-popery could help to stimulate anxieties about particular individuals that sometimes culminated in accusations of maleficia. The allegations of false religion made against John Lowes, vicar of Brandeston in Suffolk, who, together with a fellow minister Thomas Fowkes was said to have purchased popish trinkets at a fair, for instance, probably tell us more about the wider climate of distrust which the Laudian policies of the previous decade aroused among their puritan parishioners than about any covert commitment to the Church of Rome. Neverthless they show that, while religious difference (perceived or real) alone cannot explain such incidents, it clearly exercised subliminal influence in creating unsavoury reputations and in poisoning relations between neighbours.[183]

More striking are the many examples of Quakers being conflated with witches, assembled by Peter Elmer. George Fox and other evangelists were believed to use enchanted bottles and ribbons to ensnare the unwary and Mary White of Suffolk was reputed to have become distracted by an evil spirit after reading Quaker pamphlets in 1655. Some Friends were formally accused of this diabolical crime and there are documented cases of individuals being subjected, officially and unofficially, to the ordeals of pricking and swimming. Quakers arrested after a meeting in Sherborne allegedly confessed to a compact with the devil and to having bewitched the town's two ministers, and depositions made against a Cambridge widow in 1659 told how she had been transformed into a bay mare and ridden by two other Friends to a ritual feast at

Madingley Hall.[184] There was both a literal and a symbolic aspect to these allegations, which echo those levelled at the medieval heretical sect of the Waldensians in the fourteenth and fifteenth centuries.[185] Some contemporaries were clearly convinced that the Quakers were actually agents of Satan but their cultural construction as surrogate witches may also be read as part of a process by which the language of demonology was both symbolically relocated and radically destabilised at a time of rapid and intense religio-political change.[186]

The assimilation of ordinary men and women with such stereotypes of deviance was simultaneously a cause, an instrument and an effect of persecution. It was a cause in the sense that in order for people to carry out atrocities against religious minorities they had to be able to dehumanise their victims, to define them as evil and intolerable others, to stigmatise them as dangerous enemies of which it was necessary to rid Christian society. Natalie Zemon Davis has seen these as the necessary 'conditions for guilt-free massacre' and they were also crucial in facilitating the many lesser manifestations of sectarian prejudice that we have explored in the course of this chapter.[187]

It was an instrument because the process of labelling and classifying individuals as heretics, papists, puritans, witches or Quakers was often itself deeply painful and humiliating. Through polemical pamphlets, visual propaganda and satirical plays, mocking rhymes, vicious rumours and hurtful nicknames, contemporaries expressed feelings of contempt, resentment and rancour that contributed to corroding cordial relations between those of different faiths, to marginalising the members of dissident churches and sects, and ultimately to precipitating tangible physical attacks against them.

And it was an effect because intolerance served to reinforce and consolidate the distinctive and alarming characteristics of groups that rejected and separated themselves from the beliefs and/or practices of the established Church of England. Oppressed and isolated by official policies and harassed and ostracised by unsympathetic neighbours, their response was frequently to become yet more secretive, inward-looking and detached from the wider community. In turn, this made them obvious targets for fresh outbursts of persecution.

In conclusion, we return to the difficult question of how far early modern England can be characterised a 'persecuting society'. Many historians are confident that it was. Lawrence Stone has described the English village as 'filled with malice and hatred'; Keith Thomas has emphasised 'the tyranny of local opinion and the lack of tolerance displayed towards nonconformity or social deviation'; Christopher Haigh speaks of 'a McCarthyite atmosphere of antagonism and distrust'; and Malcolm Gaskill writes that social relations in this period were all too often marked by the 'dark reverse side' of neighbourliness, an enduring enmity and 'prickly hostility' that regularly manifested itself in disputes prosecuted in the forum of the courts.[188] Clearly intolerance in early modern England took many and varied forms and its destructive and disruptive force must not be underestimated. The array of examples assembled above testifies eloquently to these points and casts some doubt on the tendency to draw a sharp contrast between the moderation of the English populace in this period and the ferocity of its French and German counterparts. There were significant variations in the intensity and frequency of intolerance in these regions but it may argued that these were differences of degree rather than kind.

At the same time, however, we must take care not to exaggerate either the incidence or effects of intolerance. Far from random, chaotic and all-encompassing, violence and aggression in this society appears to have been tightly focused, structured and circumscribed. Its objects were carefully selected and it was only very rarely that its participants were driven to commit cold-blooded murder. Persecution was perhaps not so much epidemic as endemic. To echo an insight of the late Bob Scribner, like a latent virus or germ, it was ever present, but it was only when the conditions were right that it became virulent.[189] Adopting a different metaphor, it was less a raging lion than a sleeping giant, which was only occasionally woken from its slumber to wreak havoc in local society.

We need to consider seriously the possibility that the episodes of persecution which leap out at us from the historical record were actually unusual, that they represent ruptures of normal neighbourly relations rather than accurate cameos of their typical character. How else are we to account for the paradox that for years Catholics could live peacefully with Protestants and then be transformed overnight into sinister figures? How can we otherwise resolve the puzzle of the two Ely Familists who were suddenly presented to the church court in 1609, when others living in the town who had followed H. N.'s mysterious teachings had avoided presentment for more than three decades?[190] Equally deserving of attention are the circumstances in which people abstained from taking spontaneous action against nonconformists and refrained from making use of the legal machinery at their disposal. It is also necessary to reassess the relationship between hostility to individuals and hostility to the creeds they confess. Was abstract abhorrence of a false religion always accompanied by an allergy to its human adherents? Or did contemporaries have the capacity to divorce wicked ideologies from the innocuous and unthreatening people who espoused them, whom they lived alongside? To what extent did they set aside their confessional differences in their day-to-day dealings with Lollards, Catholics, dissenters and separatists? How many people practised the 'charitable Christian hatred' recommended by the Caroline puritan vicar of Boughton, Northamptonshire, Joseph Bentham, in a tract published in 1630: how many were able 'to hate knowingly, loving the person, [but] loathing his evil properties'?[191]

There is much to suggest that such distinctions were critical. Familiarity, friendship and regular interaction counterbalanced the fear and anxiety that were prerequisites for sectarian prejudice and bigotry. They defused the power of the mythical spectres of heresy, popery and dissent which preachers and propagandists constructed and attacked from pulpit and press. And it was in the gap between these frightening theoretical entities and quotidian practical realities that tolerance spread its delicate but vigorous roots.

In Chapter 5 we look further at the factors which militated against inter-confessional conflict and facilitated the relatively peaceful coexistence of different creeds, as well as revisit the suggestion that toleration itself could stimulate persecution. But next we must turn to analyse how religious minorities responded to intolerance, how they reacted to campaigns of official repression and spasms of popular animosity and indignation.

NOTES

1   See Moore, *Persecuting Society*, esp. pp. 106–9. Emile Durkheim, *The Elementary Forms of Religious Life*, trans. J. W. Swain (London, 1915), esp. p. 427. Max Weber, *The Theory of Social and Economic Organisation*, trans. A. M. Henderson and Talcott Parsons (New York, 1947), pt III, ch. 2.

2   See John Walter, *Understanding Popular Violence in the English Revolution: The Colchester Plunderers* (Cambridge, 1999), esp. p. 337. For the concept of 'official transcripts', see James C. Scott, *Domination and the Arts of Resistance: Hidden Transcripts* (New Haven, 1990), esp. p. 87.

3   The contrast between 'godly zeal' and 'furious rage' was made by George Gifford with reference to accusations of witchcraft made by the 'common sort' of people against their neighbours: *A discourse of the subtill practises of devilles by witches and sorcerers. By which men are and have bin greatly deluded* (London, 1587), sig. H4r.

4   Margaret Bowker, *The Henrician Reformation: The Diocese of Lincoln under John Longland 1521–1541* (Cambridge, 1981), p. 59; Brigden, *London and the Reformation*, p. 308; Alec Ryrie and Michael Riordan, 'Stephen Gardiner and the making of a Protestant villain', *SCJ*, 34 (2003), 1039–63; see Alexander, 'Bonner and the Marian Protestants'. For the Foxe illustration of Bonner, *Actes and monuments* (1570 edn), ii. 2242.

5   John Guy, *Thomas More* (London, 2000), pp. 107, 120.

6   Davis, *Heresy and the Reformation*, p. 22.

7   John Morris (ed.), *The Troubles of our Catholic Forefathers Related by Themselves* , 3 vols (London, 1872–77), iii. 65; Philip Caraman (ed.), *The Years of Siege: Catholic Life from James I to Cromwell* (London, 1966), pp. 75, 61.

8   Bellamy, *Tudor Law of Treason*, p. 116.

9   Watts, *Dissenters*, p. 199; Stephen Roberts, 'The Quakers in Evesham 1655–1660: a study in religion, politics and culture', *Midland History*, 16 (1991), 63–85, at 73.

10   Ian Green, 'The persecution of "scandalous" and "malignant" parish clergy during the English Civil War', *EHR*, 94 (1979), 507–31, at 517; Spurr, *Restoration Church*, p. 60.

11   Fletcher, 'Enforcement', p. 238.

12 William Hale (ed.), *A Series of Precedents and Proceedings in Criminal Causes, Extending from the Year 1475 to 1640* (Edinburgh, 1847), p. 35.

13 Haigh, *English Reformations*, p. 52.

14 Clayton J. Drees, *Authority and Dissent in the English Church: The Prosecution of Heresy and Religious Non-conformity in the Diocese of Winchester, 1380–1547* (Lewiston, NY, 1997), p. 162; Houlbrooke, *Church Courts*, p. 233; Nichols (ed.), *Narratives of the Reformation*, pp. 62–5; Haigh, *English Reformations*, p. 232.

15 Caraman (ed.), *Other Face*, p. 85; William Le Hardy (ed.), *Middlesex Sessions Records*, NS, vol. ii *1615–1615* (London, 1936), p. 282; Tolmie, *Triumph of the Saints*, p. 37.

16 Miller, 'Suffering people', 87; Shoemaker, *Prosecution and Punishment*, p. 243.

17 Tim Harris, *London Crowds in the Reign of Charles II: Propaganda and Politics from the Restoration to the Exclusion Crisis* (Cambridge, 1987), p. 225.

18 Christopher Haigh, 'The Church of England, the Catholics and the people', in Christopher Haigh (ed.), *The Reign of Elizabeth I* (London, 1984), pp. 195–219; Maltby, *Prayer Book and People*, pp. 43–5, and ch. 2 *passim*.

19 Maltby, *Prayer Book and People*, pp. 50–2; Nuttall, *Visible Saints*, pp. 135–8.

20 Morrill, 'The Church in England, 1642–9', pp. 101–2; Green, 'Persecution of ... parish clergy', p. 515; Donald A. Spaeth, 'Common prayer? Popular observance of the Anglican liturgy in Restoration Wiltshire', in Susan Wright (ed.), *Parish, Church and People: Local Studies in Lay Religion 1350–1750* (London, 1988), pp. 125–51.

21 Thomson, *Later Lollards*, p. 152.

22 Haigh, *English Reformations*, p. 68.

23 Caraman (ed.), *Other Face*, pp. 256, 253–5; Lake and Questier, 'Agency, appropriation and rhetoric', pp. 97, 101–2.

24 Underwood (ed.), *Acts of the Witnesses*, p. 134.

25 Thomas W. Laqueur, 'Crowds, carnival and the state in English executions, 1604–1868', in A. L. Beier, David Cannadine and James M. Rosenheim (eds), *The First Modern Society: Essays in English History in Honour of Lawrence Stone* (Cambridge, 1989), pp. 305–55.

26 Brown, *Popular Piety*, p. 215; Peter Clark, *English Provincial Society from the Reformation to the Revolution: Religion, Politics and Society in Kent 1500–1640* (Hassocks, 1977), p. 154; Brigden, *London and the Reformation*, pp. 273, 431.

27 Nichols (ed.), *Narratives of the Reformation*, p. 78.

28 Morris (ed.), *Troubles of our Catholic Forefathers*, iii. 30.

29 Alexandra Walsham, '"The fatall vesper": providentialism and anti-popery in late Jacobean London', *P&P*, 144 (1994), esp. 55–62.

30 Walter, *Understanding Popular Violence*; pp. 37–8, 46; Lindley, 'Lay Catholics', 218.

31 Nicholas Canny, *Making Ireland British 1580–1650* (Oxford, 2001), pp. 485, 542, and ch. 8 *passim*. See also Hilary Simms, 'Violence in County Armagh, 1641', in Brian Mac Cuarta (ed.), *Ulster 1641: Aspects of the Rising* (Belfast, 1993), pp. 123–38.

32 John Morrill, 'The religious context of the English Civil War', *TRHS*, 5th series, 34 (1984), 155–78. See also Fletcher, *Outbreak of the English Civil War*, pp. 417–18. But note the

caution expressed by Ian Green in 'England's "wars of religion"? Religious conflict and the English Civil Wars', in J. Van den Berg and P. G. Hoftijzer (eds), *Church, Change and Revolution: Transactions of the Fourth Anglo-Dutch Church History Colloquium* (Leiden, 1991), pp. 100–21.

33 Walter, *Understanding Popular Violence*, p. 185. For civil war iconoclasm, see John Walter, ' "Abolishing superstition with sedition"? The politics of popular iconoclasm in England', *P&P*, 183 (2004), 79–123 and Margaret Aston, 'Puritans and iconoclasm, 1560–1660', in Durston and Eales (eds), *Culture of Puritanism*, pp. 110–21.

34 Watts, *Dissenters*, pp. 80–1.

35 In general, see Patrick Collinson, *The Birthpangs of Protestant England: Religious and Cultural Change in the Sixteenth and Seventeenth Centuries* (New York, 1988), ch. 5; David Underdown, *Revel, Riot and Rebellion: Popular Politics and Culture in England 1603–1660* (Oxford, 1985), ch. 4. For the Warbleton incident, see Jeremy Goring, *Godly Exercises or the Devil's Dance? Puritanism and Popular Culture in Pre-Civil War England*, Friends of Dr Williams's Library, 37th Lecture (London, 1983), p. 3; for the Shrewsbury event, Collinson, 'The shearmen's tree and the preacher: the strange death of merry England in Shrewsbury and beyond', in Patrick Collinson and John Craig (eds), *The Reformation in English Towns 1500–1640* (Basingstoke, 1998), pp. 205–20.

36 Braithwaite, *Beginnings of Quakerism*, p. 53; Norman Penney (ed.), *'The First Publishers of Truth': Being Early Records (Now First Printed) of the Introduction of Quakerism into the Counties of England and Wales* (London, 1907), pp. 89, 211, 86 respectively.

37 Underdown, *Revel, Riot and Rebellion*, p. 254; Joseph Besse, *A collection of the sufferings of the people called Quaker, for the testimony of a good conscience*, 2 vols (London, 1753), i. 86–7.

38 Penney (ed.), *First Publishers*, p. 91. For anti-Quaker violence, see also Barry Reay, 'Popular hostility towards Quakers in mid-seventeenth-century England', *Social History*, 5 (1980), 387–407; Miller, 'Suffering people'.

39 Harris, *London Crowds*, p. 52.

40 Reay, *Quakers*, p. 106.

41 Reay, 'Authorities', p. 74.

42 Tim Harris, 'Was the Tory reaction popular? Attitudes of Londoners towards the persecution of dissent, 1681–6', *London Journal*, 13 (1988), 106–20, esp. 117; David L. Wykes, 'James II's religious indulgence of 1687 and the early organisation of dissent: the building of the first nonconformist meeting-house in Birmingham', *Midland History*, 16 (1991), 97; Geoffrey Holmes, 'The Sacheverell riots: the crowd and the church in early eighteenth-century London', in Paul Slack (ed.), *Rebellion, Popular Protest and the Social Order in Early Modern England* (Cambridge, 1984), pp. 232–62.

43 Harris, *London Crowds*; William L. Sasche, 'The mob and the Revolution of 1688', *JBS*, 4 (1964), 23–40, at 28 n. 26.

44 Colin Haydon, *Anti-Catholicism in Eighteenth-Century England, c.1714–80: A Political and Social Study* (Manchester, 1993), ch. 6. For interpretations which place less emphasis on the religious dimension of the riots, see George Rudé, 'The Gordon riots: a study of the rioters and their victims', *TRHS*, 5th series 6 (1956), 93–114; Nicholas Rogers, *Crowds, Culture and Politics in Georgian Britain* (Oxford, 1998), ch. 5.

45 O. W. Furley, 'The pope-burning processions of the late seventeenth century', *History*, 44 (1959), 16–23; Sheila Williams, 'The pope-burning processions of 1679–81', *Journal*

of the Warburg and Courtauld Institutes, 21 (1958), 104–18; Harris, *London Crowds*, pp. 103–6, 169.

46 Canny, *Making Ireland British*, pp. 510, 515.

47 Foley (ed.), *Records of the English Province*, vii (2), p. 1035; Watts, *Dissenters*, pp. 233–4.

48 Natalie Zemon Davis, 'The rites of violence', in her *Society and Culture in Early Modern France* (Stanford, 1975), p. 174.

49 Underdown, *Revel, Riot and Rebellion*, p. 55. Generally on this subject, see Ingram, 'Ridings, rough music and the "reform of popular culture" ' and 'Ridings, rough music and mocking rhymes'.

50 Underdown, *Revel, Riot and Rebellion*, p. 254.

51 Caraman (ed.), *Years of Siege*, p. 83.

52 Patrick Collinson, 'Ecclesiastical vitriol: religious satire in the 1590s and the invention of puritanism', in Guy (ed.), *The Reign of Elizabeth I*, pp. 150–70. A forthcoming book by Alison Shell will illuminate the subject of Catholic satire.

53 Adam Fox, 'Religious satire in English towns, 1570–1640', in Collinson and Craig (eds), *Reformation in English Towns*, pp. 237–8 and *passim*.

54 Harris, *London Crowds*, chs 5 and 6 *passim*.

55 Collinson, *Birthpangs*, pp. 103–4.

56 Shell, *Catholicism, Controversy and the English Literary Imagination*, ch. 1.

57 Collinson, 'Ecclesiastical vitriol' and 'Bartholomew Fair: the theatre constructs puritanism', in David Bevington, David Smith and Richard Strier (eds), *The Theatrical City: London's Culture, Theatre and Literature 1576–1649* (Cambridge, 1995), pp. 157–69; Lake with Questier, *Antichrist's Lewd Hat*, ch. 14. See also William P. Holden, *Anti-Puritan Satire 1572–1642* (London, 1954) and L. A. Sasek (ed.), *Images of English Puritanism: A Collection of Contemporary Sources 1589–1649* (Baton Rouge, LA, 1989).

58 See Marsh, *Family of Love*, pp. 205–13, but note his own more subtle reading of the play as a satire on anti-Familism itself.

59 Jerome Friedman, *Miracles and the Pulp Press during the English Revolution: The Battle of the Frogs and Fairford's Flies* (London, 1993), pp. 107–9; Capp, *Fifth Monarchy Men*, p. 14; Harris, *London, Crowds*, pp. 103, 109, 110.

60 Frank Felsenstein, *Anti-Semitic Stereotypes: A Paradigm of Otherness in English Popular Culture, 1660–1830* (Baltimore, MD, 1995), pp. 161–3 and ch. 7 *passim*; Katz, *Jews*, pp. 102–4.

61 Matar, *Islam*, ch. 2; Matar, *Turks, Moors and Englishmen*, pp. 12–13.

62 G. Closse, *The parricide papist, or, cut-throat Catholike* (London, 1606); Peter Lake, 'Puritanism, Arminianism and a Shropshire axe-murder', *Midland History*, 15 (1990), 37–64; Watts, *Dissenters*, pp. 81–3; Frances E. Dolan, *Whores of Babylon: Catholicism, Gender and Seventeenth-Century Print Culture* (Ithaca, NY, 1999).

63 Watts, *Dissenters*, pp. 111–17; Hughes, *Gangraena*, esp. ch. 2.

64 Davis, *Fear, Myth and History*. For critiques of this interpretation, see G. E. Aylmer, 'Did the Ranters exist?', *P&P*, 117 (1987), 208–19; Christopher Hill, 'The lost Ranters? A critique of J. C. Davis', *History Workshop*, 24 (1987), 134–40.

65 David Cressy, 'The Adamites exposed: naked radicals in the English Revolution', in his *Travesties and Transgressions in Tudor and Stuart England: Tales of Discord and Dissension* (Oxford, 2000), pp. 251–80.

66 Felsenstein, *Anti-Semitic Stereotypes*, chs 2–3.

67 Helen Pierce, 'Anti-episcopacy and graphic satire in England, 1640–1645', *HJ*, 47 (2004), 809–48.

68 On character literature, see Patrick Collinson, *The Puritan Character: Polemics and Polarities in Early Seventeenth-Century English Culture*, William A. Clark Memorial Library Lecture (Los Angeles, 1989). For a sample of the visual material, see John Miller, *Religion in the Popular Prints 1600–1832* (Cambridge, 1986), esp. nos 2, 14, 16, 23, 28, 30.

69 Thomas Browne, *Pseudodoxia epidemica* (London, 1646), bk 4, ch. 10, in *The Major Works*, ed. C. A. Patrides (Harmondsorth, 1977), pp. 226–30. On proverbs, see Felsenstein, *Anti-Semitic Stereotypes*, p. 49.

70 Haydon, *Anti-Catholicism*, p. 43.

71 Miri Rubin, *Gentile Tales: The Narrative Assault on Late Medieval Jews* (New Haven, 1999), pp. 108 and 5, and *passim*.

72 John Ayre (ed.), *The Works of John Whitgift*, 3 vols (Cambridge, 1851–53), iii. 320.

73 Thomson, *Later Lollards*, pp. 84, 135; Davis, *Heresy and Reformation*, p. 7; Peter Marshall, *The Catholic Priesthood and the English Reformation* (Oxford, 1994), pp. 219–21.

74 Caraman (ed.), *Years of Siege*, p. 57; Foley (ed.), *Records of the English Province*, iv. 697; Harris, *London Crowds*, pp. 157–8.

75 Patrick Collinson, 'A comment: concerning the name puritan', *JEH*, 31 (1980), 483–8; Spurr, *English Puritanism*, ch. 2. For the Essex epithets, Emmison, *Morals*, pp. 66, 117.

76 Besse, *Collection of sufferings*, i. 666.

77 John Spurr, ' "Latitudinarianism" and the Restoration Church', *HJ*, 31 (1988), 61–82, at 62–3.

78 Collinson, *Birthpangs*, p. 143.

79 Peter Marshall, 'Mumpsimus and sumpsimus: the Intellectual origins of a Henrician bon mot', *JEH*, 52 (2001), 512–20, at 512.

80 Hughes and Larkin (eds), *Tudor Royal Proclamations*, ii. 6, 128; Webster, *Godly Clergy*, p. 3.

81 Thomas H. Clancy, 'Papist-Protestant-Puritan: English religious taxonomy 1565–1665', *RH*, 13 (1976), 227–53, at 248.

82 Brigden, 'Religion and social obligation', 82; Haigh, *English Reformations*, pp. 68, 232.

83 *The late commotion of certaine papists in Herefordshire. Occasioned by the death of one Alice Wellington* (London, 1605); Foley (ed.), *Records of the English Province*, iv. 452–3.

84 Hudson, *Premature Reformation*, p. 470; Davis, *Heresy and Reformation*, pp. 11–12, 16; Mark Byford, 'The birth of a Protestant town: the process of Reformation in Tudor Colchester, 1530–80', in Collinson and Craig (eds), *Reformation in English Towns*, p. 34.

85 Maltby, *Prayer Book and People*, p. 70.

86 Webster, *Godly Clergy*, p. 157; Green, 'Persecution of ... parish clergy', pp. 520–1; Spaeth, 'Common prayer?', p. 129.

87 Craig, *Reformation, Politics and Polemics*, ch. 5. See also generally Collinson and Craig (eds), *Reformation in English Towns*.

88 This could also happen in reverse, with religious disputes cloaked in the language of 'secular' conflict. See Jonathan Barry, 'The politics of religion in Restoration Bristol', in Harris, Seaward and Goldie (eds), *The Politics of Religion in Restoration England*, pp. 163–89.

89 Annabel Gregory, 'Witchcraft, politics and "good neighbourhood" in early seventeenth-century Rye', *P&P*, 133 (1991), 31–66; Malcolm Gaskill, 'Witchcraft in early modern Kent: stereotypes and the background to accusations', in Jonathan Barry, Marianne Hester and Gareth Roberts (eds), *Witchcraft in Early Modern Europe: Studies in Culture and Belief* (Cambridge, 1996), esp. pp. 281–3.

90 Peter Elmer, '"Saints or sorcerers": Quakerism, demonology and the decline of witchcraft in seventeenth-century England', in Barry, Hester and Roberts (eds), *Witchcraft in Early Modern Europe*, p. 167 and 145–79 passim.

91 Caraman (ed.), *Other Face*, p. 213.

92 Sasche, 'Mob and the Revolution', 35.

93 See esp. Laqueur, 'Crowds, carnival and the state'.

94 Brigden, *London and the Reformation*, p. 597, Harris, *London Crowds*, p. 54.

95 Sachse, 'Mob and the Revolution', p. 28. On inversion, see R. W. Scribner, 'Reformation, carnival and the world turned upside-down', in his *Popular Culture and Popular Movements in Reformation Germany* (London, 1987), pp. 71–101.

96 Walsham, 'Fatall vesper', 59.

97 See David Cressy, *Bonfires and Bells: National Memory and the Protestant Calendar in Elizabethan and Stuart England* (London, 1989), pp. 136–8. Ronald Hutton qualifies Cressy's conclusions in *The Rise and Fall of Merry England: The Ritual Year 1400–1700* (Oxford, 1994), pp. 186–7.

98 Walter, *Understanding Popular Violence*, esp. pp. 218–21, 329; Cressy, *Bonfires and Bells*, p. 157.

99 See Harris, *London Crowds*, p. 23; Walter, *Understanding Popular Violence*, p. 206; Clifton, 'Fear of Catholics', pp. 83, 304.

100 See Miller, 'Suffering people', 79, 83, 97–100; Reay, 'Popular hostility', 403–5; Penney (ed.), *First Publishers*, pp. 13–15, 209–14.

101 See R. H. Tawney and Eileen Power (eds), *Tudor Economic Documents*, 3 vols (London, 1924), iii. 82–90, esp. 85.

102 See Susan Brigden, 'Youth and the English Reformation', *P&P*, 95 (1982), 37–67; Patrick Collinson, 'From iconoclasm to iconophobia: the cultural impact of the second English Reformation', repr. in Peter Marshall (ed.), *The Impact of the English Reformation 1500–1640* (London, 1997), pp. 278–307, at p. 279. See also K. V. Thomas, 'Age and authority in early modern England', *Proceedings of the British Academy*, 62 (1976), 205–48.

103 Natalie Zemon Davis, 'The reasons of misrule', in her *Society and Culture*, pp. 97–123; S. R. Smith, 'The London apprentices as seventeenth-century adolescents', repr. in Slack (ed.), *Rebellion, Popular Protest and the Social Order*, pp. 219–31; S. R. Smith, 'Almost revolutionaries: the London apprentices during the Civil Wars', *Huntington Library Quarterly*, 42 (1979), 313–28.

104 Cottret, *Huguenots*, p. 77; Lien Bich Luu, 'Assimilation or segregation: colonies of alien craftsmen in Elizabethan London', in Randolph Vigne and Graham C. Gibbs (eds), *The Strangers' Progress: Integration and Disintegration of the Huguenot and Walloon Refugee Community, 1567–1889: Essays in Memory of Irene Scouloudi*, Proceedings of the Huguenot Society of Great Britain and Ireland, 26(2) (1995), p. 163. For the 1620s, see Grell, *Dutch Calvinists*, p. 23. See also Marcel F. Backhouse, 'The strangers at work in Sandwich: native envy of an industrious minority, 1561–1603', *Immigrants and Minorities*, 10 (1991), 70–99.

105 Spicer, *French-Speaking Reformed Community*, p. 162; Patrick Collinson, 'Europe in Britain: Protestant strangers and the English Reformation', in Randolph Vigne and Charles Littleton (eds), *From Strangers to Citizens: The Integration of Immigrant Communities in Britain, Ireland and Colonial America, 1550–1750* (Brighton and Portland, 2001), p. 61.

106 Gwynn, *Huguenot Heritage*, pp. 147–9.

107 Laura Hunt Yungblut, *Strangers Settled Here Amongst Us: Policies, Perceptions and the Presence of Aliens in Elizabethan England* (London, 1996), p. 41.

108 Andrew Spicer, '"A place of refuge and sanctuary of a holy temple": exile communities and the stranger churches', in Nigel Goose and Lien Luu (eds), *Immigrants in Tudor and Early Stuart England* (Brighton, 2005), pp. 91–109.

109 Robin Clifton, 'The popular fear of Catholics during the English Revolution', *P&P*, 51 (1971), 23–55, at 41; Clifton, 'Fear of Catholics', pp. 312–13. See also Walter, *Understanding Popular Violence*, ch. 7.

110 Mary E. Finch, *The Wealth of Five Northamptonshire Families 1540–1640*, Northamptonshire Record Society 19 (Oxford, 1956), pp. 72–4; Historical Manuscripts Commission, *Various Collections*, iii (London, 1904), p. 97.

111 Harris, *London Crowds*, ch. 8.

112 Wolfgang Behringer, 'Weather, hunger and fear: the origins of the European witch persecutions in climate, society and mentality', *German History*, 13 (1995), 1–27. A number of essays in William G. Naphy and Penny Roberts (eds), *Fear in Early Modern Society* Manchester, 1997) are illuminating on the theme of this and the following paragraphs.

113 Harris, *London Crowds*, pp. 78–9, 111.

114 Anthony G. Petti (ed.), *The Letters and Despatches of Richard Verstegan c.1550–1640*, CRS 52 (1959), p. 2; Walter, *Understanding Popular Violence*, p. 320, n. 101; Seaver, *Wallington's World*, p. 151.

115 Reay, *Quakers*, p. 92.

116 Bernard Capp, 'Arson, threats of arson, and incivility in early modern England', in Peter Burke, Brian Harrison and Paul Slack (eds), *Civil Histories: Essays Presented to Sir Keith Thomas* (Oxford, 2000), pp. 197–213, at p. 210.

117 *Ibid.*, pp. 208–9, 210.

118 Spicer, *French-Speaking Reformed Community*, p. 149; Walsham, *Providence*, pp. 234–5; Thomas, *Religion and the Decline of Magic*, p. 667.

119 William G. Naphy, *Plagues, Poisons and Potions: Plague-Spreading Conspiracies in the Western Alps c.1530–1640* (Manchester, 2002), p. 164 and *passim*.

120 Haydon, *Anti-Catholicism*, p. 250.

121 Gwynn, *Huguenot Heritage*, pp. 160–1.

122 See Rosemary Horrox (ed.), *The Black Death* (Manchester, 1994), pp. 207–26.

123 As remarked by Walter, *Understanding Popular Violence*, p. 229.

124 Luu, 'Assimilation', p. 162; Backhouse, 'Strangers at work', p. 87.

125 Reay, *Quakers*, p. 52.

126 Brigden, *London and the Reformation*, p. 634, and Caraman (ed.), *Other Face*, pp. 30–1 for similar claims the following year; Thomas, *Religion and the Decline of Magic*, p. 668.

127 Thomas, *Religion and the Decline of Magic*, pp. 107–8; Walsham, *Providence*, pp. 135–42.

128 Bob Scribner, 'Preconditions of tolerance and intolerance in sixteenth-century Germany', in Grell and Scribner (eds), *Tolerance and Intolerance*, pp. 41–2.

129 Thomson, *Later Lollards*, p. 195.

130 The National Archives, London, SP 14/12/96; A. G. Dickens, 'The Elizabethans and St Bartholomew', in A. Soman (ed.), *The Massacre of St Bartholomew* (The Hague, 1974), p. 63.

131 Lindley, 'Lay Catholics', 215–16.

132 Walter, *Understanding Popular Violence*, p. 229; Clifton, 'Fear of popery', p. 160; Sharpe, *Personal Rule*, p. 910. See also Keith J. Lindley, 'The impact of the 1641 rebellion upon England and Wales, 1641–5', *Irish Historical Studies*, 18 (1972), 143–76.

133 William Lamont, 'Richard Baxter, "popery" and the origins of the English Civil War', *History*, 87 (2002), 336–52, at 341 and 348.

134 Williams, *Catholic Recusancy*, p. 19.

135 See J. P. Kenyon, *The Popish Plot* (London, 1972); Jonathan Scott, 'England's troubles: exhuming the Popish Plot', in Tim Harris, Paul Seaward and Mark Goldie (eds), *The Politics of Religion in Restoration England* (Oxford, 1990), pp. 107–31.

136 Harris, *London Crowds*, p. 158.

137 Haydon, *Anti-Catholicism*, p. 154.

138 Clifton, 'Popular fear', p. 30 and *passim*.

139 Capp, *Fifth Monarchy Men*, p. 125; Bernard Capp, 'The Fifth Monarchists and popular millenarianism', in MacGregor and Reay (eds), *Radical Religion*, pp. 165–89, at p. 175.

140 Davis, 'Rites of violence', esp. pp. 164–9.

141 Clifton, 'Popular fear', p. 51; Walter, *Understanding Popular Violence*, pp. 291–6; Cressy, 'Protestation protested', 262–3.

142 Walter, *Understanding Popular Violence*, pp. 296, 325–6; Reay, *Quakers*, p. 91.

143 Barbara Diefendorf, *Beneath the Cross: Catholics and Huguenots in Sixteenth-Century Paris* (New York, 1991), p. 103.

144 Aston, 'Puritans and iconoclasm'.

145 Walsham, 'Fatall vesper', 58; Clifton, 'Fear of Catholics', pp. 112–13, 218.

146 Reay, *Quakers*, p. 91; Miller, 'Suffering people', 80 and *passim*.

147 Spurr, *Restoration Church*, 82.

148 Rogers, *Crowds, Culture and Politics*, p. 165.

149 Tim Harris, 'The bawdy house riots of 1668', *HJ*, 29 (1986), 537–74, at 539. See also

the comments of Robert B. Shoemaker, 'The London "mob" in the early eighteenth century', *JBS*, 26 (1987), 273–304, at 287–90.

150 Denis Crouzet, *Les guerriers de dieu: la violence au temps des troubles de religion, vers 1525–vers 1610*, 2 vols (Paris, 1990); Diefendorf, *Beneath the Cross*; Canny, *Making Ireland British*, ch. 8.

151 Kenyon (ed.), *Stuart Constitution* (1966 edn), pp. 325–7 and see pp. 318–19.

152 For a discussion of the debates about the Reformation of Manners, see Collinson, *Religion of Protestants*, ch. 5.

153 Cottrett, *Huguenots*, pp. 140–1. On levels and the limits of xenophobia, see Yungblut, *Strangers*; Joseph P. Ward, 'Fictitious shoemakers, agitated weavers and the limits of popular xenophobia in Elizabethan London', in Vigne and Littleton (eds), *From Strangers to Citizens*, pp. 80–7.

154 Larkin and Hughes (eds), *Stuart Royal Proclamations*, i. 508–11, 588–90 (1621 and 1624).

155 Harris, *London Crowds*, pp. 30–1.

156 Clifton, 'Popular fear', pp. 49–50; G. H. Jones, 'The Irish fright of 1688: real violence and imagined massacre', *Bulletin of the Institute of Historical Research*, 55 (1982), 148–53.

157 Gwynn, *Huguenot Heritage*, p. 147. See Colin Haydon, ' "I love my king and my country, but a Roman Catholic I hate": anti-Catholicism, xenophobia and national identity in eighteenth-century England', in Tony Claydon and Ian MacBride (eds), *Protestantism and National Identity: Britain and Ireland, c.1650–c.1850* (Cambridge, 1998), pp. 33–52. On xenophobia, see also William S. Maltby, *The Black Legend in England: The Development of Anti-Spanish Sentiment, 1558–1660* (Durham, NC, 1971); Michael Duffy, *The Englishman and the Foreigner* (Cambridge, 1996), introduction.

158 Rex, *Lollards*, pp. 97–8.

159 Reay, 'Popular hostility', pp. 392–4.

160 Braddick, *State Formation*, p. 306.

161 Clifton, 'Popular fear', pp. 47–8; Walter, *Understanding Popular Violence*, p. 210.

162 Herrup, *Common Peace*, pp. 178–9; J. A. Sharpe, 'Enforcing the law in the seventeenth-century English village', in V. A. C. Gatrell, Bruce Lenman and Geoffrey Parker (eds), *Crime and the Law: The Social History of Crime in Western Europe since 1500* (London, 1980), pp. 97–119, at 118–19; Martin Ingram, 'Communities and courts: law and disorder in early-seventeenth-century Wiltshire', in Cockburn (ed.), *Crime in England*, pp. 110–34, at 129–34.

163 Haydon, *Anti-Catholicism*, p. 11.

164 Godfrey Anstruther, *Vaux of Harrowden* (Newport, 1953), p. 113. Collinson, *Birthpangs*, p. 143. See also ch. 4, below.

165 Luu, 'Assimilation', p. 160.

166 Hudson, *Premature Reformation*, p. 165; Brown, *Popular Piety*, p. 215.

167 Haigh, *English Reformations*, p. 232.

168 A. G. Dickens, 'Heresy and the origins of the English Reformation', in J. S. Bromley and E. H. Kossman (eds), *Britain and the Netherlands*, vol. ii (Groningen, 1964), p. 62; Haigh, *English Reformations*, pp. 69, 231; J. S. Cockburn (ed.), *Calendar of Assize Records: Hertfordshire Indictments: Elizabeth I* (London, 1975), p. 77.

169 Cockburn (ed.), *Surrey Indictments James I*, p. 1; *The Acts of the High Commission Court within the Diocese of Durham*, Surtees Society, 34 (Durham, 1858), pp. 119–21.

170 J. S. Purvis, *Tudor Parish Documents of the Diocese of York* (Cambridge, 1948), p. 68.

171 Richard Bauman, *Let your Words be Few: Symbolism of Speaking and Silence among Seventeenth-Century Quakers* (Cambridge, 1983), p. 51 and ch. 4 *passim*; Davies, *Quakers*, esp. ch. 3.

172 Reay, *Quakers*, p. 92; Bill Stevenson, 'The social integration of post-Restoration dissenters, 1660–1725', in Margaret Spufford (ed.), *The World of Rural Dissenters 1520–1725* (Cambridge, 1995), pp. 360–87, at 366. See also Miller, 'Suffering people'.

173 Christopher Marsh, 'The gravestone of Thomas Lawrence revisited (or the Family of Love and the local community in Balsham, 1560–1630)', in Spufford (ed.), *World of Rural Dissenters*, p. 218; Harris, *London Crowds*, p. 52; Lacey, *Cult of King Charles the Martyr*, p. 132.

174 Underwood (ed.), *Acts of the Witnesses*, p. 53.

175 Penney (ed.), 'First Publishers', p. 69. See also David Underdown, *A Freeborn People: Politics and the Nation in Seventeenth-Century England* (Oxford, 1996), p. 106 and David Underdown, 'The taming of the scold: the enforcement of patriarchal authority in early modern England', in Anthony Fletcher and John Stevenson (eds), *Order and Disorder in Early Modern England* (Cambridge, 1995), pp. 116–36.

176 See Peter Lake and Michael Questier, 'Margaret Clitherow, Catholic nonconformity, martyrology and the politics of religious change in Elizabethan England', *P&P*, 185 (2004), 43–90, esp. 45–54.

177 See McSheffrey, *Gender and Heresy*, esp. p. 139.

178 Ingram, 'Puritans and the church courts', p. 79; Green, 'Persecution of ... the parish clergy', p. 520.

179 Hunt, *Puritan Moment*, p. 184.

180 Brigden, *London and the Reformation*, p. 627.

181 Tolmie, *Triumph of the Saints*, p. 29.

182 Hugh Trevor Roper, *The Witch-craze of the Sixteenth and Seventeenth Centuries* (Harmondsworth, 1978 edn).

183 For connections between cunning folk and popery, see the cases of Agnes Waterhouse of Hatfield Peverel in Essex and John Walsh of Netherbury in Dorset, both indicted in 1566 (the early Elizabethan context may well be significant): C. L'Estrange Ewen, *Witchcraft and Demonianism* (London, 1933), pp. 145–7. For the Lowes and Fowkes case, see C. L'Estrange Ewen, *Witchcraft in the Star Chamber* (n.p., 1938), pp. 44–54. I am grateful to Malcolm Gaskill for bringing this case to my attention and for a helpful discussion of this point.

184 Elmer, 'Saints or sorcerers'. Underdown, *Revel, Riot and Rebellion*, p. 254; Stevenson, 'Social integration', p. 367. For other allegations, see Braithwaite, *Beginnings of Quakerism*, pp. 67, 102, 181, 220, 487, 574; Reay, 'Popular hostility', pp. 396–9.

185 Wolfgang Behringer, 'Detecting the ultimate conspiracy, or how Waldensians became witches', in Barry Coward and Julian Swann (eds), *Conspiracies and Conspiracy Theory in Early Modern Europe: From the Waldensians to the French Revolution* (Aldershot, 2004), pp. 13–34.

186 Elmer, 'Saints and sorcerers', esp. pp. 174–9.

187 Davis, 'Rites of violence', p. 181.

188 Lawrence Stone, *The Family, Sex and Marriage in England 1500–1700* (London, 1977), pp. 94–8, at 98; Thomas, *Religion and the Decline of Magic*, p. 629; Haigh, *English Reformations*, p. 52; Gaskill, 'Witchcraft', p. 287.

189 Scribner, 'Preconditions', p. 47.

190 Clifton, 'Popular fear', p. 49; Marsh, *Family of Love*, p. 214.

191 Peter Lake, ' "A charitable Christian hatred": the godly and their enemies in the 1630s', in Durston and Eales (eds), *Culture of English Puritanism*, pp. 145–83, at 168–9.

Chapter 4

Living amidst hostility:
responses to intolerance

The experience of being a persecuted minority posed a wide range of practical and moral problems for the religious dissenters of sixteenth- and seventeenth-century England. At the centre lay the question of how true believers should behave when they found themselves immersed in an ideologically hostile environment. What were their obligations when confronted by demands for conformity to a false religion and when faced with the prospect of fierce repression by the established Church and state? Could they leave their native country or should they stay and suffer whatever might be inflicted upon them for openly professing their faith? Was flight into exile a legitimate alternative to martyrdom? Did those who participated in the liturgical and sacramental rites of their confessional enemies always commit mortal sin, or could one join outwardly in worship with heretics and idolaters without compromising one's inner convictions? Was it necessary to separate oneself completely from the wicked in the mundane transactions that marked everyday life? Or might some concessions be made with regard to interacting with them in purely secular affairs – in the spheres of business, finance, leisure and hospitality? In an Erastian context, the predicament of those who adhered to a different creed to that espoused by their ruler also inevitably had a political dimension. Should one submit passively to the wrath and violence of the authorities or was active resistance or rebellion against one's sovereign the correct course of action? How could the duty of obedience to a divinely ordained monarch be reconciled with one's higher allegiance to God?

The dilemmas and perplexities surrounding what the Protestant reformer Peter Martyr Vermigli called 'the cohabitacyon of the faithfull with the unfaithfull' found frequent expression in contemporary documents and texts.[1] The ministers and leaders of underground churches and sects constantly addressed these difficult ethical questions in the printed and manuscript tracts they circulated to stiffen the resolve and bolster the morale of their beleaguered congregations and they featured prominently in the private letters they sent to, and received from, their troubled lay disciples. Such 'cases of conscience' are also reflected in the formal casuistry of the age, in the manuals prepared for Catholic priests to use in the confessional and in classic works of practical divinity written by puritan divines like William Perkins and Richard Baxter.[2] As well as engendering much discomfort and anxiety in the minds of individuals, the issue of how people should conduct themselves in the context of official repression and proscription also precipitated much division and friction within the ranks of dissenting communities. It provoked heated debates and conflicts that sometimes seriously jeopardised their internal solidarity and unity.

This chapter explores how religious minorities responded to the intolerance of English society and the Tudor and Stuart state. It examines the full spectrum of positions adopted by dissenters in their attempts to negotiate the restrictions and challenges of civil and ecclesiastical prosecution and popular prejudice – from martyrdom, insurrection and emigration to dissimulation, equivocation and forms of partial and occasional conformity. We consider the factors and assumptions that influenced the choices made by individuals, the tensions to which these various strategies of resistance and compromise gave rise, and their wider implications for, and effects upon, interconfessional relations. Two further themes of the discussion which follows are the often counter-productive effects of persecution and the prominent part which it played in the forging and shaping of sectarian identities.

Once again our sources are a hindrance as well as a help. They tend, on the one hand, to highlight people who took a defiant and stubborn stance against the authorities and who engaged in heroic acts of separation and self-sacrifice. On the other, they ignore or eclipse those who complied with the law in order to evade its penalties and to mitigate the resentment and distrust of their neighbours. Celebrated in the hagiographies and histories produced by minority religions, nonconformists and martyrs are also conspicuous in official records of ecclesiastical and civil infractions. Those who reacted more pragmatically and prudently to persecution, by contrast, are far less easy to detect. Almost by definition, men and women who yielded to the temptation to comply with the legal requirements are invisible in the reports and presentments made to the courts. Regarded as an embarrassment by their more zealous co-religionists, they were often air-brushed out of martyrological narratives. One of the main aims of this chapter is to correct the historiographical imbalance, to emphasise the importance of the phenomenon of conformity for understanding the history of tolerance and intolerance in early modern England.

TAKING UP THE CROSS OF CHRIST: MARTYRDOM

It makes sense, however, to start with those who staunchly refused to renounce their dissident beliefs and to conform with secular and ecclesiastical law, with individuals who willingly suffered the penalties for holding heretical precepts, for withdrawing from their parish churches, for secretly assembling to practise an alternative religion, and for aiding and abetting its evangelists and pastors. It is not hard to find compelling examples of men and women prepared to take up the cross of Christ: to risk everything to sustain and defend their prohibited faith, to withstand torture and interrogation, and to face up courageously to the consequences of their adherence to an illicit creed. For some this meant crippling fines and civil disabilities, for others the rigours of imprisonment or corporal punishment, and for a small minority it entailed the ultimate sacrifice of dying on the stake or the gallows. Vociferously resisting the temptation to abjure or conform, such people immediately draw themselves to the attention of historians.

As we shall discover later, a great many Lollards renounced their opinions under pressure from the episcopal authorities, but the sect nevertheless produced a small contingent of martyrs. Joan Boughton, an 'old cankered heretic' of 80, was burnt in April 1494 after rejecting offers of mercy in exchange for abandoning her errors and perversities: she went bravely to her death saying 'she was so beloved with God and his holy angels, that all the fire in London should not hurt her'.[3] Immortalised in John Foxe's *Actes and monuments*, England's earliest Protestants were often equally unflinching when confronted with the choice between betraying their faith or the horrific prospect of being slowly incinerated. Anne Askew, executed late in the reign of Henry VIII for denying the doctrine of transubstantiation, rebuked her persecutors and turned back the chance of a last-minute pardon with 'a countenance stout, mighty and earnest'. Weighing up the options before her in the 1550s – 'to flee, or abide and deny my God (which the Lord forbid), or else to be cast into prison and suffer death' – Elizabeth Longshaw hoped she would not shrink from the truth if put to the final test. Offered freedom in return for penitent submission in 1557, Cicely Orme, wife of a Norwich weaver, resolutely refused, declaring that if she did 'God would surely plague her'.[4] Two years earlier the protomartyr of Marian evangelicals, John Rogers, had likewise resisted the temptation to repudiate his Protestant faith, insisting that he was content 'most gladly to resign up his life and to geve his flesh to the consumyng fyre, for the testimonie of the same'.[5]

After Elizabeth's accession, Catholic priests and lay people convicted as felons and traitors were often just as unwavering. Thus William Hart, executed at York in March 1583, embraced his fate without flinching: writing to his mother shortly before his death, he declared 'The joy of this life is nothing, and the joy of the afterlife is everlasting' and urged her to rejoice that he was soon to become 'a most glorious and bright star in heaven'. Arrested in the midst of celebrating mass, Edmund Geninges persuaded his companions 'not to yield one iota to any of their enemies' allurements, animating them with the saying of St James, *Appropinquate Deo, et appropinquabit vobis*: Approach to God, and he will approach to you'. Persevering in their faith, he and several others suffered stoically at Tyburn in November 1591.[6] Ralph Milner, father of a large family, refused to conform in 1591, saying that the loss of his soul was too high a price to pay for his temporal liberty, and so 'went merrily to his death'. Eight or nine young women who had committed the same crimes of attending mass and harbouring a missionary priest pleaded in vain to be allowed to share his sentence 'with open outcries and exclamations'.[7] Those incarcerated or compelled to pay extortionate sums to the government often regarded their sufferings as a lesser form of martyrdom. The Northampton-shire gentlemen Sir Thomas Tresham stoically endured many months in captivity and handed over some £8000 to the Exchequer for his noncon-formity in the twenty-five years prior to his death in 1605. To him this 'triple prenticeship ... in direst adversity' was far preferable to the 'everlasting fier' of hell into which the faithless would descend. 'No manne,' he wrote, 'canne make himselfe a cushine to leane uppon to ease his elboes'.[8]

Radical Protestants, who regarded the Church of England as an arm of Antichrist, were no less ready to stand firm against determined attempts to reclaim them from the wilderness of schism. Urged to attend Common Prayer by the Dean of Westminster in 1593, a feltmaker by the name of Quintine Smith said he would never attend Anglican services 'till suche time as the churche may bee reformed from the wicked'. He had made a covenant with his brethren 'that as longe as they did walke in the lawes of God hee would forsake all other assemblies'. Detention in one of London's notoriously filthy and infectious prisons had evidently failed to sway him from his separatist principles.[9] Others showed no less mettle in their clashes with the authorities, clinging stiffly to the belief that mingling promiscuously with the profane in public worship was quite insupportable. Writing to his followers after his arrest and appearance before the Court of High Commission, Henry Barrow prayed that he might not 'hinder this gratious work of the Lord', 'who begineth to sommone me owt of this world' and who, through the agency of Arch-bishop Whitgift, was 'preparing me a fyrye chariot to passe in'.[10]

Other acts of constancy deserve a mention in this survey of conscientious objection. Puritan clergymen forced to choose between complying with the rubrics of the Book of Common Prayer and subscribing to the Thirty-nine Articles or being stripped of their livings were often unwilling to be cowed into submission. Parker's drive to enforce the surplice in the 1560s and the cam-paigns of Whitgift, Bancroft and Laud for liturgical conformity consequently claimed many victims. Stephen Turner was suspended from his cure at Arlington in Sussex in 1584 because he would and could not swear that the Prayer Book contained nothing contrary to the Word of God; Thomas Carew of Hatfield Peverell, was another 'painfull' preacher who suffered at the hands of these 'Antichristian prelates' and other 'popish adversaries' in his parish for the sake of his liturgical scruples and Presbyterian convictions.[11]

During the Elizabethan period, several godly ministers spent periods in insalubrious London gaols for their opposition to the surplice and bishops, including Thomas Cartwright himself. Submitting to imprisonment did not merely mean forgoing one's liberty: it was also to expose oneself knowingly to discomfort, disease and even the danger of death. Robert Johnson, vicar of St Clement's without Temple Bar, who complained to Edwin Sandys in the 1570s that such places were 'more unwholesome than dunghills, more stinking than swine sties', was only one of those who expired in the Gatehouse.[12] In the 1630s, a fair number of ministers likewise went to the wall rather than read out the notorious Book of Sports from the pulpit – a document which, in their eyes, did nothing less than sanction the profanation of the sabbath and the violation of the fourth commandment. Hauled before the Star Chamber for reading Henry Burton's provocative sabbatarian tract, *A divine tragedy lately acted* (1636), the London turner Nehemiah Wallington was 'glad ... that I should be put among them and ... be made a partaker of [the] Saint's sufferings'.[13] In their own small way, such lay people showed that they too were not afraid to stand up and be counted.

During the Interregnum, it was the turn of Anglicans to defy the authorities by continuing to use Cranmer's liturgy. The clergy were most at risk of prosecution and few lay people were troubled for their conduct, though John Evelyn was briefly taken prisoner at Christmas 1657 for frequenting an illicit service in London, which was interrupted by soldiers who 'held their muskets against us as we came up to receive the Sacred Elements'.[14] As the mass ejections at the Restoration reveal, hundreds of Presbyterian and Independent pastors also stuck fast by their scruples, preferring to resign their posts rather than give their unfeigned assent to the contents of the reinstated Prayer Book or to retract the Solemn League and Covenant, which explicitly condemned the institution of episcopacy. Well aware of the harsh penalties they were likely to suffer for doing so, numerous dissenters and their ministers boldly continued to gather for worship in defiance of the Clarendon Code. The Quakers were particularly noted for refusing to hide their light under a bushel. When the Second Conventicle Act came into force in May 1670 George Fox deliberately thrust himself into danger by attending the meeting in London's Gracechurch Street, where he 'expected the storm ... most likely to begin'. He was duly apprehended and thrown into prison.[15] Many dissenters bore the cross of long periods of incarceration with remarkable fortitude. Abraham

Cheare, the Baptist pastor of Plymouth who died in confinement on Drake's Island in 1668, wrote that he had 'never been under an hour's temptation, to relinquish or repent of my testimony in word or deed to any persecuted truth of Christ for which I suffer'. John Bunyan spent more than a decade in Bedford County Gaol: neither separation from his wife and children (an experience he described as 'the pulling the flesh from my bones') nor awareness of the hardships they suffered on his behalf could deter him from his determination to persist in stubborn nonconformity.[16] On the contrary, his experience of imprisonment was the catalyst of a singularly resolute commitment to the Baptist faith.

It takes a considerable leap of the imagination to comprehend the mentality and motives of these men and women, especially those whose convictions carried them all the way to Smithfield or Tyburn. Some have attempted to use the tools of modern psychoanalytical theory to explain such behaviour, but to describe the burning desire of such individuals for a martyr's death as obsessive, pathological, insane or fanatical is not only to fall into the trap of viewing it from the distorting perspective of the secular twenty-first century; it also replicates the polemical strategy employed by hostile contemporaries who branded such people suicides and madmen.[17] Instead, we need to understand the theological assumptions that underpinned the implacable stance that such people adopted in response to intolerance. Conscious of Christ's warning that 'whosoever shall deny me before men, him will I also deny also before my Father which is in heaven' (Matthew 10: 33), they believed that every Christian had a solemn and binding duty to bear open witness to the truth. To conceal it out of cowardly fear was to commit the heinous sin of religious apostasy and to expose oneself to the mental torment of a guilty conscience, if not to the terrors of eternal damnation. What was at stake was their spiritual health, if not their fate in the afterlife.

Late medieval writers had sometimes presented martyrdom as a counsel of perfection and warned against the temerity of seeking it without a proper vocation. The Familist Hendrick Niclaes struck a similar note of caution in the advice he issued to 'two daughters of Warwick' in a manuscript epistle in the 1550s. Some members of the Family of Love even claimed that men 'ought not to suffer their bodyes to be executed bycause they are the temples of the holly gost'.[18] Privately, the danger of crossing the fine line between passively embracing and presumptuously courting death on the scaffold or stake continued to trouble early modern religious minorities. So too, especially in the early, highly fluid stages of the English Reformation, did uncertainty about whether particular points of doctrine were sufficiently important to necessitate making the ultimate sacrifice. Thus Hugh Latimer warned James Bainham in 1532: 'Let not vain-glory overcome you in a matter that men deserve not to die for; for therein you shall neither please God, do good to yourself, nor your neighbour: and better it were for you to submit yourself to the ordinances of men, than so rashly to finish your life without good ground.'[19] However, the rhetorical thrust of most post-Reformation literature published on this subject was towards the idea that confessing one's faith, even unto death, was a universal obligation. 'No manacynge wordes, no imprysonment, no chenes, no fetters, no sweard, no faggot, no fyre ought to plucke us from this Confession', declared the Henrician evangelical Thomas Becon in a tract of 1542, 'No tyranny ought so to be feared, that God & hys trueth shoulde not be confessed'.[20] The lesson of Matthew 10: 33 likewise suffused many catechisms and treatises issued by Counter-Reformation and Dissenting writers: 'Whosoever shall deny me before men, I also will deny him before my Father which is in heaven.' No worldly consideration should hinder one from fulfilling this obligation, not even the importunate pleas of one's nearest and dearest relatives. '[P]asse by thy father, passe by thy mother with drie eyes, and hasten to the Cross of Christ', exhorted the seminary priest Thomas Hide in 1579, 'crueltie in this case, is the onelye kinde of pietie, and pietie for God, is no crueltie'.[21]

Key passages in the Bible encouraged the assumption that enduring pain in the name of the Gospel was sacred and holy. Through affliction, the faithful glorified God and earned the prize of his love and approbation. For Catholics martyrdom was nothing less than a guarantee of salvation, a direct route to paradise. An act of oblation and the highest work of piety a human being could ever undertake, it was also a means by which ordinary lay people might become enrolled in the hallowed company of saints. In the third century Cyprian had declared that imprisoned Christians would proceed 'by the lingering of torments to more ample titles of merit' and 'have so many rewards in the heavenly payment as there are days reckoned in present pains'. This was echoed by many early modern priests: 'Doubtless you be daily crowned, the longer you fight, the more is your victory.'[22] A growing conviction that only the blood of martyrs could atone for England's apostasy from the Holy Mother Church provided an additional and powerful impetus. The 'lively sacrifice' of the priesthood was the price that had to be paid to redeem the country from heinous sin of heresy. 'There is nothing ... which we ought not readily to suffer rather than see the evils of our nation', William Allen told his missionaries; 'bloud so yelded maketh the forciblest meane to procure mercie that can be'.[23]

For Protestants adversities and trials were the mechanism by which the Almighty purified and tested His flock and winnowed out wicked reprobates. The supreme sacrifice of those who died on the pyre was a testimonial of the saving faith that the Lord had graciously bestowed upon the predestinate elect. As William Tyndale wrote in the *Obedience of a Christian man*, it was a 'sure' sign that a person was 'sealed with Gods spirit unto everlasting life'.[24] Some positively yearned to face this ultimate test: in 1588 an old woman from Essex told the puritan minister Richard Rogers on her deathbed that 'if she should be burned at a stake, she should set light by it, for the hope of the glory which was set before her'.[25] The clerical leaders of minority churches and sects constantly impressed upon their congregations that to take up the cross and suffer for Christ was a peculiar honour and privilege, the prospect of which should fill them with solace and strength rather than horror or anguish. 'Prefer not the world to your heavenly byrthright', wrote Henry Barrow in the early 1590s.[26] These were the themes of a long line of works stretching from Thomas More's *Dialogue of comfort against tribulation* (1534) and Richard Tracy's *Of the preparation to the crosse* (1540) to John Bunyan's *Seasonable counsell* (1684). The latter consoled sufferers with the comment that 'chastisements are a sign of sonship, a token of love'. The examples cited above suggest that they were tenets that at least some religious dissenters deeply internalised.[27]

On both sides of the confessional divide, those who stood firm against their oppressors were inspired by a common set of precedents.[28] They found justification for their actions in both the Old and New Testaments, in the stories of the three children of Israel thrown into a fiery furnace for refusing to bow down to idols and of the apostle Stephen, stoned to death in Jerusalem for denouncing the Jews. They looked to the legends of the early Christian martyrs thrown to the lions at the behest of Roman emperors, and of Polycarp, Bishop of Smyrna, burnt in 155 by order of Caesar. They were emboldened by the heroic example set by their own co-religionists, by the recent victims of persecution, in England, Europe, the New World and the Far East. But the ultimate paradigm for martyrdom was, of course, the Crucifixion. As Donald Kelley has remarked, this was *'imitatio Christi* with a vengeance'. It was a sublime form of mimesis.[29]

On the stake and the gallows, some seem to have self-consciously modelled their conduct on Christ's Passion on the Cross at Calvary, seeking what Brad Gregory has called 'an intoxicating intimacy' with him.[30] Emulating earlier confessors, ancient and modern, they transformed their punishments and deaths into an arresting dramatic spectacle. The stamina that the Henrician and Marian Protestants displayed in the midst of the flames, for instance, was often astonishing. John Rogers calmly extended his arms and implored 'Lord receive my spirit'; half consumed by the blazing fire, James Bainham of Gloucestershire informed the spectators that 'I feele no more payne then if I were in a bead of downe: but it is to me as swete as a bead of roses'; and John Bradford was equally ecstatic about the prospect of meeting his Maker, exhorting the young apprentice who was his companion on the pyre: 'Bee of good comfort, brother, for we shall have a mery supper with the Lord this night'.[31] As immortalised in a graphic illustration in Foxe's *Actes and monuments* and in subsequent prints, Archbishop Thomas Cranmer used the

11 The memory of the Marian burnings of 1555–56 lived long in the Protestant imagination. This print, sold by Thomas Jenner, a printseller who catered for customers with puritan inclinations, dates from the early seventeenth century, possibly the 1620s. In the centre, Archbishop Thomas Cranmer thrusts the hand with which he had earlier signed his recantation into the flames, with the words: 'Burne unworthie right hand'. *Faiths victorie in Romes crueltie.* (© The British Museum, Department of Prints and Drawings, Satires, no. 11).

occasion of his own burning to counteract the effects of his earlier recantation, thrusting the very hand with which he had signed it into the flames (Figure 11).[32] The accounts that have come down to us betray clear traces of rhetorical emendation if not invention, but it would be a mistake to dismiss the possibility that some individuals were indeed inspired to use the pyre as their stage.

Many Catholic priests and their lay helpers faced the ordeal of being hung, drawn and quartered no less triumphantly. Richard Kirkman and John Boste allegedly greeted their sentences with the hymn of thanksgiving '*Te deum laudamus*'; Margaret Clitherow poignantly adopted a cruciform posture in preparation for her gruesome death in 1586 by the method of *peine forte et dure*, in which the body of the convict was crushed under a series of unbearable weights. William Freeman, a missionary in the West Midlands executed in August 1595, was said to have approached the scaffold 'very chearfully' and 'in joyfull manner', 'smilinge as thoughe he had ben goinge to a banquett' and 'lawghinge' as he was turned off the ladder.[33] A woman who was 'sett upon two laddars lyke a cuckyngstole' for hooting at the bishop of London during the Vestiarian controversy in 1566 also rejoiced in her punishment, praising the Lord 'for that He had made hir worthy to soffer persecution for ryghtwysnes, and for the truths sake'.[34] The puritan pamphleteer Alexander Leighton likewise gloried in the mutilation he suffered for his outspoken critique of the crypto-popish policies of the Caroline regime: as he placed his neck in the pillory he said 'this is Christes yoke' and as his eare was sliced off he declared 'Blessed be God. Iff I had 100 I would loose them all in the cause.'[35] In a similar fashion, at the scene of his humiliation in 1637 William Prynne beseeched all Christian people to 'stand firm and zealous for the cause of God and his true religion to the shedding of your dearest blood' and he later reinterpreted the two letters burnt into his cheeks (S. L. for 'Seditious Libeller') as 'Stigmata Laudis or Laud's Scars'.[36]

Quakers too endured their persecutions with exemplary patience. In 1653, for instance, two female Friends sang and praised God while they were whipped by an unruly band of Cambridge undergraduates, asking the forgiveness of their attackers and bearing their terrible trials 'without the least Change of Countenance'. More famously, James Nayler embraced his savage punishment for blasphemy with a Christ-like serenity which (in the eyes of hostile observers) matched the sacrilegious audacity of his re-enactment of the entrance of Jesus of Nazareth into Jerusalem: precisely mimicking the events of the crucifixion three women followers gathered at his feet and a placard in front of him proclaiming 'This is the King of the Jews'.[37] Elizabeth Gaunt, the Baptist woman burnt for her role in the Monmouth rebellion, 'died with a constancy, even to a cheerfulness, that struck all that saw it', calmly arranging the straw around her to hasten her death and behaving 'in suche a manner that all the spectators melted in tears'.[38]

Our knowledge of such incidents is inevitably coloured by the martyrological patterning of the narratives through which they were filtered. Nevertheless, they are suggestive of the ways in which the victims of popular and judicial violence could appropriate rituals designed to discredit them as heretics, subversives and traitors and use them to affirm their status as martyrs. Hijacking occasions intended to crush them into oblivion and silence, they turned them into opportunities for preaching the Gospel and demonstrating the integrity of the doctrines for which they suffered and died. To echo Jane Dawson, 'by a virtuoso solo performance', convicted religious dissidents 'could change the theatre of death into the theatre of martyrdom'.[39] Hence the attempts of the Marian regime to restrict their impact by burning Protestants at daybreak and banning servants and apprentices from attending and Stephen Gardiner's growing suspicion that it might be better to banish than burn obstinate Protestants, so pernicious was the influence that they exerted in their last hours.[40]

English officials never quite went to the lengths of their counterparts in France, where from at least 1528 the tongues of heretics were slit or cut out,[41] but in some cases Elizabethan seminary priests had their mouths gagged with a cloth to stop them from addressing the crowd.[42] As the authorities came increasingly to realise, the edifying speeches and gestures they made as they awaited execution could be an extraordinarily powerful form of counter-propaganda. It became a commonplace among the persecuted to speak of martyrdom as a kind of preaching. 'Our innocent blode for the gospell', declared the Henrician Protestant George Joye in 1545, 'shall preache it with more frute ... than ever did our mouthes and pennes'.[43] Cardinal Allen echoed the same sentiments in a letter to Rome in 1582, insisting that the recent deaths of three missionaries had affected the people far more deeply than many rousing sermons. The Jesuit poet Robert Southwell spoke no less eloquently of the effects of these 'books' written not in ink but in the lifegiving liquid that effused from the bodies of martyrs.[44] Certainly, more than a few who witnessed such events were thereby inspired to embrace the religion of those whom they had just seen expire: in 1601 the charismatic bravery of the priest John Pybus reputedly induced the horse thief due to be executed immediately after him to make a public gallows conversion to Roman Catholicism.[45] While it is intractably difficult to disentangle fact from fiction in such narratives, the courage and depth of commitment exhibited by many men and women in defence of their faith can hardly be doubted.

Such acts of suffering and self-sacrifice supplied religious minorities with an instant pantheon of heroes and fostered the spontaneous creation of cults to their memory. Sixteenth- and seventeenth-century lay people who stood by the scaffold as Catholic priests were executed eagerly gathered up and venerated fragments of their flesh, bone, hair and teeth, together with pieces of clothing, spectacles, handkerchiefs, rosaries and other blood-stained objects. Energetically reporting the thaumaturgic cures that were subsequently effected by them, they helped to engender a busy traffic in relics both in England and on the Continent, which was condoned if not actively encouraged by the Tridentine hierarchy. They also played a key role in shaping and circulating (both orally and scribally) reports of the prodigious signs that had accompanied their deaths, from the haloes seen hovering above their heads on the eve of their martyrdoms to the sweet smells which emanated from their incorruptible bodies and incombustible organs. Familiar from medieval hagiography, such phenomena linked the Counter-Reformation martyrs created by the Elizabethan and early Stuart state inextricably with the Christian saints of old.[46]

Such cults were not, however, merely confined to the Catholic community. Despite the ferocious attacks which the reformers launched against miracles and pilgrimages, the instinct to collect gory souvenirs from the fires of Smithfield and erect ad hoc shrines to Protestants who died in firm defence of their faith is attested by both hostile and sympathetic sources. The Marian controversialist Miles Huggarde commented savagely on those who lay 'wallowing like pigs in a sty to scrape in that heretical dunghill' for remnants of the corpses of these 'holy gospellers' and even grated them into powder for medicinal purposes, but a similarly frenzied scramble for relics of bone, scalp and tongue was recorded in the account of John Hullier's execution on Jesus Green in Cambridge in 1556 which John Foxe incorporated in his *Actes and monuments*.[47] In the fifteenth century the sites at which several relapsed Lollards were burnt had no less ironically become the focal points for 'superstitious' piety of a type fiercely criticised by John Wyclif and his disciples. The ashes of the octogenarian Joan Boughton were collected the night after her demise in April 1494 and 'kepyd for a precious relyk in an erthyn pott'.[48] Even more strikingly, stones were piled upon the place on Tower Hill where Richard Wyche had been incinerated in 1440 and the authorities had a hard time suppressing resort to the spot, as well as reports of the posthumous wonders that he had worked. Richard Rex's recent suggestion that popular reverence for Wyche was rooted less in sympathy for his alleged heretical views than in his perceived status as an innocent and orthodox victim of judicial violence deserves serious consideration, but it is hard to agree with him that the episode 'throws into even higher relief' Lollardy's complete lack of any kind of martyrological tradition. Rather, such instances of syncretism may bear witness to the cultural continuities that blurred and complicated confessional boundaries in a period of upheaval and to the inconsistencies and contradictions that were part and parcel of the messy process of ideological assimilation and change.[49]

Furthermore, other persecuted sects and churches that overtly repudiated all forms of 'popish' idolatry revered individuals who suffered for their religious convictions in strikingly similar ways. A coffin bearing the corpse of the Southwark separatist Roger Rippon, who died in prison in February 1593, was paraded in front of the home of the justice Richard Young with an inscription proclaiming him 'the last of sixteen or seventeen which that great enemy of God, the Archbishop of Canterbury with his High Commissioners have murdered in Newgate within these five years, manifestly for the testimony of Jesus Christ'; a button maker who perished in the same gaol in 1639 was celebrated as another martyr by the 200 'Brownists and Anabaptists' who turned out for his funeral.[50] Nor did radical sectarians disdain to gather physical mementoes of their heroes. When the Arian Francis Kett was executed as a heretic in Norwich for denying the divinity of Christ and the Holy Spirit in 1587 his bones and ashes were rapidly whisked away by his followers within a short space – so eager, it was said, were 'these foes of holy relics' to gain possession of his remains.[51] Handkerchiefs were dipped in the blood that dripped from the pillory on which Prynne, Bastwick and Burton lost their ears and carried away as 'a thing most precious'. The puritan triumvirate were widely lauded as 'holy living martirs' and the godly regarded their release from prison in 1640 as 'the returne of the captivity from Babilon'.[52] Similarly, a woman present at the deathbed of John Reeve, co-founder of the Muggletonian movement, in 1658 cut off a lock of his hair to keep 'for a Memorial of one of the two last Prophets that God will ever send while his World endureth'.[53]

Yet more evocative of Catholic patterns of sanctity, in the wake of the regicide relics of Charles I were reported to have cured a number of people of scrofula and to have restored the eyesight of a young maid from Deptford.[54] In the eyes of ardent royalists, such healing miracles proved that the Stuart king, once the Lord's lieutenant on earth, now sat in heaven on the right hand of God. To their enemies they were further evidence that Anglicanism was a thinly veiled form of Antichristian Romanism – and these manifestations of the royal martyr's cult are indeed particularly hard to reconcile with Reformed Protestant theology. The spontaneous cults that sprang up around dissenters following the renewed drive against nonconformists in the 1660s and 1670s were more restrained in character, but they were underpinned by similar impulses. When the seven bishops imprisoned for refusing to read the Declaration of Indulgence from their pulpits in 1688 were let out on bail people flocked to see and touch them thinking 'it a blessing to kiss any of [their] hands or garments'. After they were eventually acquitted of libel, crowds surged the streets of London to congratulate them, falling upon their knees in the hope of receiving a personal benediction from these celebrated prelates.[55] Persecution bestowed a kudos upon its victims which elevated them, literally or metaphorically, into a league of superhuman beings.

Commemorated in martyrological narratives and catalogues, such individuals had a long and powerful afterlife. Manuscripts describing the interrogations and trials of William Thorpe, Richard Wyche and Sir John Oldcastle appear to have circulated widely within Lollard circles in the fifteenth century, just as in the 1540s and 1550s accounts of the lives and deaths of Thomas More and John Fisher would be disseminated scribally among religious conservatives.[56] The 'divine art of printing', together with the tireless efforts of the indefatigable John Foxe and his host of collaborators and correspondents, ensured that the inspiring sacrifice of the Henrician and Marian martyrs was etched forever on collective Protestant consciousness. Linking these men and women with a brotherhood of believers from the Cathars and Waldensians to the followers of Wyclif and Hus who had stood fast against the Roman Antichrist throughout the Middle Ages, the *Actes and monuments* simultaneously supplied the 'new religion' with a much needed history and lineage – with an emphatic answer to the perennial Catholic taunt 'where was your Church before Luther?' However, more than a little creative editing and rewriting was required to ensure that the embarrassing eccentricities of these heretical predecessors did not mar the overall impression of consensus and unity.[57]

During Elizabeth's reign, the English Catholic leaders likewise exploited the typographical medium to publicise the heroism of the missionary priests and lay people whom the Tudor regime had unjustifiably executed for treason both at home and abroad. Alongside texts such as the William Allen's *Briefe historie of the glorious martyrdom of twelve reverend priests* (1582) and John Wilson's *English martyrologe* (1608) swirled a mass of documents prepared by eye-witnesses and copied out by hand or passed on by word of mouth, becoming increasingly embellished and embroidered in the process.[58] The tribulations of godly puritan ministers from the 1570s to 1590s were recorded in the first and second 'Partes of a Register'.[59] These may be accounted forerunners of the Congregationalist minister Edmund Calamy's account of the dissenting ministers ejected at the Restoration, which was eventually published in 1702, followed twelve years later by the Tory rector John Walker's rival anthology of the harrowing experiences of the Church of England clergy during the 'Grand Rebellion'.[60] The separatists and sects engendered similar books of 'sufferings', especially the Quakers, for whom the compilation of such chronicles came to be regarded as a crucial act of witness itself. Many of these fed into Joseph Besse's two-volume collection published in 1753, another classic of the genre.[61] The apotheosis of Anglican martyrology was the famous *Eikon basilike* (1649), a series of memoirs, meditations and prayers purportedly written by Charles I himself after his capture, which depicted him as a Christ-like figure and a heavenly martyr.[62] Among sixteenth- and seventeenth-century religious minorities, only the Family of Love failed to generate its own literature of persecution. Consciously or unconsciously, all such texts were shaped by a common set of conventions, motifs and tropes, which can be traced back to the first ecclesiastical historian Eusebius, and from thence to the accounts of Christ's crucifixion in the canonical Gospels.

Similar processes of myth-making surrounded the random and innocent victims of occasional outbursts of religious violence. The sectarian circumstances and contexts of their deaths likewise imbued them with an aura of sanctity and transformed their perpetrators into evil agents of Satan. Although England itself lacked a massacre on the scale of that which occurred on St Bartholomew's Day 1572 in Paris and other French cities, the incident left cauterising scars on the Calvinist mind all over Europe. Incorporated in the martyrological writings of John Foxe, Samuel Clarke and others, it provided contemporaries with a framework for understanding the horrific events of November 1641, when tens of thousands of Protestant settlers were slaughtered by Irish Catholics in Ulster. Propagandists deftly elevated these unfortunate men and women into a cloud of witnesses for the Reformed faith in a flood of pamphlets and tracts which ensured that this atrocity too became an enduring paradigm of popish brutality, fanaticism and inhumanity – a constant reminder of what could happen if Roman Catholicism was not kept under tight rein.[63]

In an age of limited literacy, pictures were particularly crucial in embedding martyrs in the popular memory. The elaborate and gratuitously detailed engravings of Protestant torture and cruelty which made up Giovanni Battista de Cavalleriis's *Ecclesiase Anglicanae trophaea* (1584) and Richard Verstegan's *Theatrum crudelitatum haereticorum nostri temporis* (1587) in particular played a critical part in shaping the ethos of the recusant community. Painted on the walls of the English College at Rome, such images inflamed and nurtured the vocation of the priests who risked their lives to succour the faithful at home; dispersed in the heartlands and on the embattled frontiers of Catholic Europe, they also provided the Tridentine Church militant with its own set of glistening heroes. Anne Dillon describes them as 'an international ... banner' behind which countries loyal to Rome were urged to assemble in the war against heresy (see Figure 3, p. 78).[64] The compelling woodcuts of men and women being consumed by the flames with which John Day illustrated the pages of the *Actes and monuments* likewise left an enduring impression on the unlearned and illiterate (see Figure 2, p. 76).[65] Although the increasingly iconophobic temper of the Reformed Protestantism in the seventeenth century militated against further extension of this visual tradition, it is notable that portraits of Prynne, Bastwick and Burton seem to have commissioned by some of their godly supporters (Figure 12).[66] Their capacity to provide a rallying point for dissidents is testified by the determined efforts of the Caroline authorities to subject them to iconoclastic destruction. In turn, the frontispiece of *Eikon basilike*, which showed the king kneeling before an altar, grasping a crown of thorns, and bathed in a shaft of supernatural light, would become nothing less than a royalist icon, while Edmund Godfrey, the putative martyr of Titus Oates's Popish Plot, was later depicted in a series of patriotic prints and on sets of playing cards.[67] Medals were even struck in honour of the seven bishops locked up in the Tower of London for resisting James II's Declaration of Indulgence (Figure 13).[68]

Such episodes were vital in forging a sense of sectarian identity and in providing a focus for solidarity at times of crisis. Repeatedly read and recounted, martyrological texts and images fortified dissenters to face fresh bouts of intimidation and pressure and shook the orthodox out of their complacency. Accompanied by tales of the sudden providential punishments that befell those who tormented God's servants, they helped to create black legends about the barbarity of their enemies which hardened confessional boundaries, exacerbated conflict and tension, and intensified their conviction that the institution which afflicted them could not be the true religion. In many

12 Puritan saints: the harsh corporal punishments suffered by Prynne, Bastwick and Burton at the hands of the Star Chamber in 1637 made them into martyrs of the Laudian regime in the eyes of godly. John Bastwick is depicted here in the guise of a Christian soldier. This engraving by John Goddard is probably from a broadside published some time after his trial. (By permission of the Ashmolean Museum, Oxford, Sutherland Collection, C. I. 540).

13 Portraits of the seven bishops prosecuted for refusing to read James II's Declaration of Indulgence of 1688 who were widely revered as Protestant heroes. Their acquittal led to popular celebrations: (© The British Museum, Department of Prints and Drawings, Satires, no. 1168).

respects, the posthumous legacy that martyrs left to the religious movements they represented far outweighed the influence they had exerted during their lifetimes. Their blood watered and fertilised the seed of a minority Church and the searing memory of their sufferings fanned the flames of hatred and prejudice for many generations. The potent myths that sprang up around them help to explain why historians have accorded them a significance out of all proportion to their actual numbers.

GRASPING THE SWORD AND FLEEING THE PLAGUE: RESISTANCE AND EXILE

At root, martyrdom was a form of passive resistance. It rested upon an acceptance by its victims of the legitimacy of the regime that inflicted capital punishment upon them. In accordance with the biblical dictum of 'render unto Caesar' and with the political theology embodied in official propaganda, such individuals believed they were bound to submit meekly to the persecution meted out by an ungodly ruler. Since monarchs were the Almighty's anointed lieutenants on earth, subjects had no right to mount a rebellion against them, even when their edicts were in breach of divine law. As William Tyndale wrote in his treatise on the subject published in 1528, kings stood 'in the room of God'. 'Whosoever therefore resisteth that power resisteth the commandment of God'. 'If [they] command [us] to do evil we must then disobey and say we are otherwise commaunded of God: but not to rise against them.'[69] Instead, as the official homily on obedience of 1547 admonished, people had to accept the consequences of their insubordination stoically, leaving the Lord to inflict providential vengeance upon their sovereign in due course.[70] Furthermore, wicked princes were 'the rod and scourge wherewith God chastiseth us, the intruments wherewith God searcheth our wounds': just as a sick man who resisted the harsh remedies prescribed by physicians and surgeons was endangering his health, so too was the subject who took steps to deliver him or herself from the cruel bondage of persecution. As several Marian Protestant writers remarked, it might be that the Almighty was using such a tyrant to scourge the sins and test the faith of his flock, in which case it would be nothing less than sacrilege to resist.[71] Fifty years later, the separatist John Penry spelt out the implications of his acceptance of Elizabeth's civil supremacy: 'I hold it to be the duty of private men to suffer patiently the stroke of her sword, and in no wise to withstand the power thereof, either by open force, or secret practices.'[72] On the scaffold, many Roman Catholic priests likewise pointedly professed their loyalty to the English monarchy: Thomas Cottam wished Elizabeth 'prosperity as my liege and sovereign Queen' and John Nelson even managed to pray for her during his dismemberment.[73] This ideology also lay at the heart of the response of many seventeenth-century dissenters to religious intolerance, not least the pacifist Quakers. As Edward Burroughs wrote in two papers addressed to the Interregnum regime in the winter of 1659, 'in His season' the Lord would sway the English government to set up righteousness and overthrow all oppressors. In the meantime His people had no intention of warring against it with 'carnal weapons'. '[W]e have not the spirit of mischief and rebellion in our hearts towards thee.'[74]

Despite the tendency of contemporaries to conflate sedition with heresy, few of the later Lollards followed in the footsteps of Sir John Oldcastle, who attempted to raise an ill-fated revolt in January 1414, though some were implicated in the more localised risings of 1431.[75] It is unlikely that the authorities were justified in supposing that the Protestant George Eagles, convicted of treason in 1557 after he was overheard imploring God to 'turn Queen Mary's heart, or else take her away', was a dangerous dissident.[76] Nor perhaps should we take too seriously the threatening words of the Essex husbandman, David Brown, who declared in January 1581 that 'yt was a mery worlde when the servyce was used in the latten tunge' and went on to indicate that he 'wolde doe the beste he colde' to assist an invading army led by the late Earl of Westmorland, whom he believed to be alive, well and biding his time in Ireland.[77] This may just be a case of an exasperated papist letting off steam. Likewise Laudian and later seventeenth-century fears about the existence of a confederation of Presbyterian incendiaries and conspiratorial dissenters intent upon undermining the civil and ecclesiastical status quo were greatly exaggerated: at the grassroots level, as Patrick Collinson has argued, puritanism was for the most part 'as factious and subversive as the Homily on Obedience'.[78]

Yet there were individuals prepared to take militant action against an intolerant prince. Marching under banners bearing the symbols of the crucifix and the five wounds, the participants in the Pilgrimage of Grace in 1536 and the Prayer Book Rebellion in the West Country in 1549 clearly believed they were engaged in a crusade against a heretical regime. Sir Thomas Wyatt's Protestant insurrection against Mary I in 1554 also deserves to be mentioned, together with the Northern Rising of 1569 led by the Earls of Northumberland and Westmorland.[79] The beheading of these aristocratic rebels seems to have led some conservatives in Yorkshire to revere them as near-saints themselves: a few even cut off pieces of their beards to preserve for posterity while their severed heads were displayed on the tollbooth.[80] The series of assassination plots linked with Mary Queen of Scots that marked the following two decades were likewise stimulated by the conviction that drastic measures were necessary to bring England back into communion with the Church of Rome. A recent study by John Bossy concludes that Robert Persons was willing to contemplate tyrannicide and Cardinal William Allen also appears to have actively collaborated in foreign invasion schemes.[81] Adding weight to Peter Holmes's doubts about the assumed quiescence of the recusant laity, Michael Questier has uncovered evidence that the Elizabethan government was quite justified in fearing that the Catholic nobility and gentry in the dark corners of England were a fifth column intent upon securing assistance from Scotland or

Spain to unseat the Tudor queen.[82] The rhetorical protestations of loyalty made by magnates like Sir Thomas Tresham, Sandeep Kaushik has argued, disguise a far more ambivalent attitude towards the legitimacy of the English state that oppressed them. Sometimes they contain 'veiled expressions of potentially subversive ideas'.[83] Likewise, Jacobean attempts to enforce the oath of allegiance should not be seen as mere paranoia on the part of the Stuart authorities: clearly there were some individuals prepared to defend the power of the Pope to depose an ungodly monarch very energetically. We can only wonder how many might have lent a hand to Philip II's forces had the Armada succeeded, while the Gunpowder Plot of 1605 provides further support for the suggestion that frustration and desperation could drive Catholics to devise ambitious plans to topple the Protestant regime. Partly prompted by a deter-mination to throw off the yoke of an oppressive colonial power, the bloody massacre in Ireland in 1641 perhaps represented the high point of sectarian violence designed to eradicate heresy and reunite one part of Charles I's triple kingdom with Rome. Magnified yet further by the contemporary media, it too wound up the English establishment into a frenzy of anti-popish panic.

The hotter sort of Protestants also proved themselves capable of conspiring against governments they regarded as idolatrous and antichristian. With the assistance of Edmund Coppinger and Henry Arthington, the Northampton-shire maltster William Hacket, for instance, devised a half-baked plot in the early 1590s to assassinate Elizabeth and several of her Privy Councillors, and reform the Church of England in a radical Genevan direction.[84] Though the leaders of the Presbyterian movement vehemently dissociated themselves from this piece of political extremism, the insurrection serves to remind us that puritanism (as Peter Lake has repeatedly stressed) had a distinctly subversive edge.[85] The Restoration did not mark the end of incidents reminiscent of the Anabaptist debacle in Münster in 1534–35. In 1661, a wine-cooper by the name of Thomas Venner led a rising of Fifth Monarchists in the city of London, killing twenty people: he had also been arrested four years earlier for plotting a revolt against Oliver Cromwell.[86] The bawdy house riots of 1668 seem also to have been in part a protest against the religious policies of the restored Stuart regime: on Easter Tuesday the crowd bayed 'that if the king did not give them liberty of conscience, that May-day must be a bloody day'.[87] In the wake of the Conventicle Act of 1670, one Cheapside stationer defended his meeting from suppression, threatening to kill anyone who harmed the nonconformist preacher. As the London and Middlesex sessions records reveal, others too readily resorted to brickbats and stones.[88] Despairing of obtaining redress of their grievances by legal means, in the mid-1680s some dissenters once again resorted to arms. The ejected Presbyterian minister Robert Ferguson and three prominent Baptists were the main figures behind the abortive Rye House Plot of 1683, which allegedly involved a plan to kill Charles II and his brother as they returned from the races at Newmarket. Two years later non-conformists were also heavily implicated in Monmouth's thwarted rebellion against James II, making up a considerable proportion of the 150 who sub-sequently died on the gallows for the crime of high treason.[89] Had they succeeded, such individuals might have become the heroes of a revised history of the triumph of Protestantism over the evil forces of popery. Because they failed, they are mostly remembered as terrorists and traitors. In the case of the Duke of Monmouth and his accomplices, the ousting of the Catholic king, whom they had tried to overthrow in 1688–89 cemented their reputation as martyrs for the Whig cause.

It is not always clear how far those who engaged in these acts of attempted tyrannicide were inspired by a coherent ideology, but it would be wrong to ignore the fact that the ingredients for a fully-formed resistance theory were in circulation in sixteenth- and seventeenth-century England. This had one set of roots in the Catholic response to Henry VIII's bold schism from Rome, but the seed of the idea of lawful rebellion against an ungodly king also lurked beneath the surface of early Protestant thinking. Conditions in the reign of Edward VI were not conducive to their germination, but they burst forth and blossomed profusely in the mid-1550s. The works of the exiles John Knox, Christopher Goodman and especially John Ponet informed Marian Protestants that there were circumstances in which magistrates and even ordinary people had a right, indeed obligation, to depose if not kill an idolatrous princess who persecuted the adherents of the true religion. Invoking the example of the Old Testament tyrants Jezebel and Athaliah executed by their subjects, they insisted that such acts were necessary to save the entire nation from divine judgement.[90]

These same biblical stories reared their heads in the context of the campaign to induce Elizabeth I to order the execution of her Catholic cousin in 1572 and Gerald Bowler and Patrick Collinson have discerned in the Parliamentary debates on the subject a chilling if subtle warning to the queen herself. These hints of the conditionality of Protestant allegiance to the queen have provoked Collinson to coin the suggestive phrase 'the monarchical republic of Elizabeth I'.[91] In the period between 1584 and 1595, inspired by the militancy of the Catholic League in France, Jesuits and seminary priests developed their own justifications for mounting a holy war against the unjust government of an illegitimate and excommunicated Protestant monarch who had violated 'the universal moral law of Christendom'. Published under the cover of a pseudonym, Robert Persons's *Conference about the succession to the crowne of England* (1584) can be read as a provocative charter for revolt.[92] Recent work is discovering a more pervasive if hidden discourse on resistance embedded in the polemical theology of this period, one marked by allusion and evasion rather than overt confrontation.[93]

The radicalisation of Huguenot political thought in the wake of the St Bartholomew's Day massacre also caused ripples in England: Hotman's *Francogallia*, Beza's *Du droit des magistrats* and the anonymous *Vindiciae contra tyrannos* supplied arguments for constitutional and (by default) popular resistance which were to re-emerge in the early 1640s. Beza had even concluded that those who took up their sword against a tyrant and 'devoted their strength to the defense of the true religion' should be honoured as sacred martyrs, no less than those who conquered their enemies by patiently submitting to their own execution.[94] Together with familiar passages from Scripture, such arguments may have helped to convince at least some individuals that they could legitimately take up arms against their king. In the eyes of the godly warriors who fought for Parliament, they were not rebels and traitors but instruments of the Lord's avenging justice against a man who had polluted the land with the blood of the saints. In retrospect, they declared that they had been 'extraordinarily stirred up by the Lord' and 'called forth ... to be instrumental to bring about ... the destruction of Antichrist and the deliverance of his Church and people'.[95] It was eager anticipation of the imminent millennium and the conviction that they had a duty to assist in ushering it in which propelled Fifth Monarchists to take aggressive action against their enemies in 1661. Conceiving of themselves as 'souldiers in the Lambs Army', they vowed they would not sheathe their swords again 'untill Mount Zion became the joy of the whole earth ... untill Rome be in ashes, and Babylon become a hissing and a curse'.[96] Five years earlier a debate on the question 'whether God's people must be a bloody people' had ended in the motion being carried with enthusiasm, while a tract of 1667 argued that 'If Government break Covenant with the People, they break the bond of Relation, and the People are disingaged, on their part from Subjection.'[97] Such episodes and texts served to feed and reinforce the anxieties about religious minorities explored in Chapter 3. They provided the backdrop against which, in times of crisis, the orthodox were induced to take pre-emptive steps to restrain individuals suspected of plotting to assassinate their neighbours, if not their sovereign. Themselves a radical response to persecution, the militant measures adopted by such dissidents in turn provided a powerful incentive and excuse for further manifestations of official intolerance. There was a dangerous and inescapable circularity about this process.

Of course, the vast majority of religious dissenters lacked the temperament necessary to be martyrs or militants. Conspiracy was a very risky strategy and the chances of being caught and hung, drawn and quartered were high. Such terrorists must have participated in these missions fully aware that they could be executed for treason as a consequence. Unlike Islamic suicide bombers they did not physically strap explosives to their bodies and turn themselves into human bombs. There is very little evidence to suggest that self-destruction was part of their intention. But many must have known that there was a distinct possibility that they might die in the act of rebellion. Nor could any amount of rousing rhetoric disguise or neutralise the fact that death on the stake or the gallows entailed excruciating pain: it is hardly surprising that only a handful had the stomach to face it.

Rather more responded to persecution by seeking asylum in a foreign land. To leave one's native country and flee into exile was itself in many respects a heroic act of self-sacrifice. It was to sever oneself from one's roots, to abandon friends, family, property and material possessions, to opt for an insecure and introverted life among strangers who spoke an unknown tongue. In embarking overseas, religious refugees exposed themselves to financial hardship, xenophobia, civil disabilities and economic restrictions: the experience of French and Dutch stranger communities in England provided a mirror in which they might have seen their own condition had they cared to take a closer look. Poverty, homesickness and isolation could take a heavy toll. Nor were religious migrants ever entirely safe from arrest: there remained a real danger that the authorities might cooperate with the English government and imprison or deport them to face justice at home. Nevertheless, in the course of the sixteenth and seventeenth centuries, a steady stream of individuals crossed the Channel and the Atlantic in order to be able to practise their faith openly.

One of the earliest to do so was the Lutheran William Tyndale, whose translation of the New Testament in 1525, smuggled back to England in multiple copies, ignited a desire for the vernacular Scriptures which it proved impossible to extinguish. In his case, exile was not so much an alternative to martyrdom as a prelude to it: he was arrested and executed in Antwerp in 1537.[98] The reactionary final decade of Henry VIII's reign prompted around 37 evangelicals to seek a safe haven in more emphatically Protestant lands, including Miles Coverdale, John Bale, William Turner and John Hooper, all of whom would later return to become leading lights in the ecclesiastical hierarchy of the young Josiah, Edward VI. Not a few of the priests who fled did so because they had defied the rules about clerical celibacy and married. To escape the heat generated by a local reputation for heresy, others simply took refuge elsewhere in England. Robert Ferrar, future bishop of St Davids, for instance, sought shelter in Yorkshire and Anthony Gilby too chose rural obscurity rather than confrontation.[99] After the accession of Mary I nearly 800 men, women and children, some accompanied by their servants, left the country for reformed cities in Germany and Switzerland. A few also settled in Italy, Holland and France. Most of these immigrants were of gentle birth, though there were some merchants and artisans. The martyrologist John Foxe, the printer John Day and the intemperate Scotsman John Knox numbered among them. Many departed with conflicting emotions: Rose Hickman, for instance, recalled how she had left behind two residences in Essex and

London, 'both of them well furnished with houshould stuffe, yet I accompted nothing in comparison of liberty of conscience for the profession of Christ'. The exiles were not, however, united in their theological outlook and a series of unseemly squabbles, which have since become known as the 'Troubles at Frankfurt', ensued. On their return after Elizabeth's accession, several, including Sir Francis Knollys, Edmund Grindal, and John Jewel filled key posts in Elizabeth's Privy Council and episcopate.[100]

In the reign of Henry VIII a few stalwart papists who saw the writing on the wall travelled north to Scotland, particularly in the wake of the Pilgrimage of Grace, and under Edward some resolute Catholics were 'content to forsake, like slaves their country' in order 'to see a Mass freely in Flanders'.[101] However, their numbers were negligible in comparison with the scale of the exodus after 1558. Again many of these individuals were members of the noble and educated classes. A sizeable contingent of conservative theologians from the universities swiftly established bases in Louvain and Rheims from which to fire back a constant volley of propaganda to England; others founded schools, colleges and seminaries. Hundreds of young men left to be trained as missionaries in Douai, Rome and Spain and it is striking how often lay people who sought asylum in the Low Countries simultaneously adopted a religious vocation, their entry into a monastery or convent a symbol of their serene retreat from all worldly tribulations and vanities.[102] However, for some the experience of exile was just too much of a wrench: a Latin inscription in the church of S. Gregorio tells us that Robert Peckham 'left England because he could not live in his country without the Faith and, having come to Rome, died there because he could not live apart from his country'.[103] From the 1590s onwards, the outflow of Catholics abroad lessened considerably, though the foundation of the colony of Maryland by George Calvert, first Lord Baltimore, as a haven for Catholics in 1632 led to a fresh wave of emigration.[104]

The Catholic community on the Continent also had its rifts, mainly over the strategy to be employed with regard to England's reclamation to the bosom of Rome, an issue that locked the secular clergy and Society of Jesus and their lay supporters in bitter and protracted contention. No less fractious were the quarrels which beset the various separatist communities that grew up in the Netherlands in the late sixteenth and early seventeenth centuries. In the 1580s Robert Browne and his followers took refuge in Middelburg convinced that 'the Lord did call them out of England' and in the succeeding decade other congregations sprang up in Amsterdam and Leiden around the figures of Francis Johnson, John Smyth, Thomas Helwys, John Robinson and Henry Jacob. Relations between these groups were anything but amicable and the injection of Anabaptist ideas into the equation proved especially conducive to division and strife. Some hoped to start again in the New World: in 1619 most of Johnson's flock perished in the course of a voyage to Virginia.[105]

During the Caroline period, these radical Protestants were joined by puritans fleeing the inhospitable climate which William Laud's growing influence over ecclesiastical policy was creating for godly ministers with scruples of conscience. Thomas Hooker, lecturer at Chelmsford in Essex, escaped across the Channel in 1630 on being summoned before the High Commission, and John Davenport, vicar of St Stephen's Coleman Street, in London, left for the Dutch capital shortly after Laud's translation to Canterbury in 1633. Both men subsequently set sail for Massachusetts, accompanied by zealous members of their flocks.[106] Others followed in their footsteps. The Hertfordshire tailor John Dane reached the difficult decision to embark for New England with the aid of bible divination. The first passage upon which his eye alighted upon randomly opening the book was 2 Corinthians 6: 17: 'Cum out from among them, touch no unclene thing'.[107] Michael Metcalf of Norwich took flight after repeated clashes with episcopal apparitors. It may be that few lay people who travelled to America were direct victims of the wrath of the Laudian authorities, but many went in anticipation that true professors of the Gospel would soon suffer far worse forms of persecution.[108] According to William Bradford the Pilgrim Fathers 'shook off this yoke of antichristian bondage' and John Norton, minister at Ipswich, wrote that the puritan migration was 'an open profession, that our faith is dearer to us than all that we flie from, for the defence therefore'.[109] Many pious and patriotic legends have been woven around this sacred 'errand into the wilderness' and David Cressy is right to emphasise the need for a degree of scepticism about the process of retrospective myth-making. Perhaps many made their way over the Atlantic for a mixture of motives, but as Susan Hardman Moore has remarked, it is misleading to play off economic incentives too sharply against spiritual impulses.[110] In 1662 there was once again 'great Talke of many Ministers with their congregations' removing to New England, but in fact only fifteen crossed the Atlantic, with another ten taking up residence in Holland.[111]

Such exiles instinctively assimilated their experience with the exodus of the Israelites into Egypt in the Old Testament. Other biblical diasporas added cachet to their actions. The metaphor of the Flood and the apocalyptic injunction in Revelation to abandon Babylon provided ample justification for their egress out of England, as did the story of Lot's timely withdrawal to Zoar from the wicked city of Sodom. Moreover, Christ himself had advised his disciples: 'when they persecute you in this city, flee ye into another' (Matthew 10: 23). Patristic discussions about the legality of flight to evade religious molestation were also widely rehearsed, notably those of the early fathers Athanasius and Tertullian.[112] John Knox admonished Marian Protestants that God was 'not to be tempted but is to be hard, feared, and obeied, whan thus earnestlye he calleth and thretenth not without cause, passe from the middes of her O my people ... that you bee not partakers of her plages'.[113]

English writers echoed Calvin, himself long an exile from France, in insisting that the words in Genesis 12: 1 ('Get thee out of thy country and from thy kindred') applied equally to their own situation: 'as long as we are there constrained to act against our conscience, and cannot live for the glory of God', it was necessary to leave one's homeland. It was far better to 'submit to a voluntary exile than remain entangled among the defilements which contaminate you'.[114] Indeed, to embrace the adversities of flight into a foreign nation was acknowledged to be a kind of martyrdom itself. John Ponet remarked that it was to be 'weighted down with various crosses from the Lord' and in his *Actes and monuments* Foxe had accounted the mental anguish suffered by the exile John Glover almost equivalent to suffering the ultimate sacrifice.[115] John Bale likewise constructed his experience as an act of ascetic denial, declaring that he had exiled himself 'from myne own native contrye, kyndred, fryndes, acquayntaunce (which are the great delyghtes of this lyfe) and am well contented for Jesus Christes sake & for the comforte of my brethren there, to suffre poverte, penurye, abjeccion, reprofe, and all that shall come besydes'.[116] The same themes were taken up by the seminary priest Thomas Hide, who warned of the infectious air in Protestant countries and compared religious immigrants with martyrs and confessors.[117]

A further argument employed by those who urged their co-religionists to retreat across the seas included an emphasis on the virtues of caution. It was 'spiritual wisdom' to withdraw from a context in which one might be tempted to fall into apostasy – St Paul himself had been let down by basket out of a window to avoid persecution. Thomas Becon defended his decision to retreat to the Midlands in the late 1540s and cease preaching and writing in similar terms, saying 'I thoughte it best not rashly to throwe my self into the ravenyng pawes of these gready wolves, but for a certaine space to absent my selfe from theyr tyrannye accordynge to the doctrine of the Gospell.'[118] Others stressed that it was presumptuous to neglect the means provided by the Almighty for the safe deliverance of the faithful. Seventeenth-century puritans were especially drawn to the idea that 'the Lord had opened a door of escape' in New England, which he meant 'to be a refuge for many, whom he means to save out of the general destruction', 'a rock and shelter for his righteous ones to run unto'.[119] To flee was simply to act in concert with Providence, to concur with God's plans for the preservation of the elect.

More pragmatically, exile conserved a cohort of the faithful who might form the backbone of a restored godly regime. Certainly some immigrants used their safe havens on the Continent as headquarters for organising subversive activity against the Tudor and Stuart government or as launching pads for polemic or pastoral literature designed to sustain and console their co-religionists at home. Sleeping cells of potential terrorists beyond English borders represented a frustratingly diffuse threat to national security which

Tudor and Stuart espionage lacked the resources to identify and uproot successfully, while the printing press provided the persecuted with a powerful if imperfect substitute for the pulpit, enabling them to carry out their duty of preaching and evangelising at one remove.

Although many exile communities played a key role in sustaining minority churches, the influence of these groups should not be exaggerated. Later celebration of the Henrician and Marian evangelicals as keepers of the Protestant flame has served to disguise the fact that they essentially remained on the sidelines, cut off from developments in England, their internal divisions hampering their efforts to reverse the Reformation and ensure that it had a permanent future. The cohesion and impact of Catholic expatriates can also be questioned. Scattered in cities, monasteries and seminaries across the Continent and torn in different directions by the competing priorities of their Spanish, Italian and French patrons and benefactors and of the rival religious orders to which they adhered, their capacity to shape events across the Channel was limited.

At the same time, it is important to recognise that the social experience of diaspora and displacement often helped to strengthen the religious commitment of those who undertook it. We have already noted that isolation and privation in an alien environment galvanised the faith of many English Catholics. Ole Grell has similarly argued that even where commercial and mercantile incentives outpaced religious zeal as an incentive for emigration, the effect of leaving one's native country for a foreign one was to reinforce a Calvinist's sense of belonging to an international movement and to intensify and catalyse the conviction that one was a member of the predestinate elect.[120] It imbued many men and women who made the long journey to New England in the first half of the seventeenth century with the belief that they were God's chosen people engaged in a divine mission – a notion that helped to give birth to the United States as a separate nation and that remains a crucial ingredient of American patriotism to the present day. Among both the 'stranger churches' in England and their English counterparts on the Continent exile also characteristically promoted a preoccupation with internal discipline and doctrinal definition which played a critical role in the ongoing process of confessionalisation.[121] The endogamy that was so often a feature of these expatriate communities was a further stimulus to their consciousness of having a separate and special religious identity.

Despite the many persuasive arguments and precedents that could be cited in support of it, not all dissenters were convinced that exile was a legitimate response to official intolerance. Both ministers and lay people nurtured niggling doubts about the moral defensibility of abandoning their pastoral and civic obligations. Deserting one's congregation at a time of such danger might be deemed a terrible dereliction of one's clerical duty, while failure to discharge one's magisterial commission or to succour one's family and friends could be seen as a sinful abdication of one's paternal and patriarchal responsibilities. The same qualms surrounded the question of whether or not it was permissible to flee from an outbreak of plague: in this case the risk of infection by the pestilence was not symbolic but literal. Theodore Beza had stressed that anyone torn about whether to stay or to go should calculate 'what he oweth unto another, whether they be bound by the common bond of humanity and society' and Hugh Latimer fiercely reproved those preachers who left their posts, saying 'Out upon thee! The wolf cometh upon thy flock to devour them, and when they have most need of thee, thou runnest away from them!'[122] After all, not everyone could afford to forgo their earnings or to pay for a passage and an extended stay abroad.

The puritan John Davenport was more than a touch defensive about his decision to flee to Amsterdam, insisting he had not 'forsaken my ministry, nor resigned up my place ... but am onely absent for a while to wayte upon God, upon the settling and quieting of things, for light to discerne my way, being willing to lye and dye in prison, if the cause may be advantaged by it, but choosing the rather to preserve the liberty of my person and ministry for the service of the church elsewhere if all dores are shutt against mee here'.[123] In the late 1630s, Samuel Ward sought to dissuade his colleagues from embarking for America by insisting that the righteous were the leaven in the lump, a remnant whose presence might just redeem the rest from a devastating judgement: 'if such as you, & all the Godly of the Land because of persecution should presently leave ... what doe you think will become of our poor native Country? It will be even as Sodom and Gomorrah. I pray you lay by these thoughts.'[124]

Such arguments had an ecclesiological dimension. Though some like William Ames saw physical and geographical dislocation as a valid – indeed preferred – alternative to separation, as 'a lawfull secession, or a heavenly translation', others regarded flight as an uncharitable act of schism from a true, if faulty Church. It was on these grounds that Thomas Helwys and his tiny Church prepared to return to England in 1612.[125] The Elizabethan Catholic hierarchy seems to have been reluctant to encourage mass emigration for fear that it might weaken the community at home, which would be crucial if the country were ever rescued from heresy by a foreign army or a successful domestic coup.[126] Finally, there were those who regarded exile as a form of cowardly evasion, the resort of the weaker brethren. Even Calvin had conceded that those who remained at home and held firmly to their faith regardless of the risks were morally superior to those who sought refuge further afield: 'when a man lives purely and serves God as he should in the midst of papist tyranny, I esteem him a hundred times more, point for point, than we who enjoy freedom and peace'.[127] Exile, it appears, was often accompanied by guilt.

But this was a side of the refugee experience that was frequently written out of confessional histories: celebrated as brave witnesses to the truth and intrepid pilgrims into the wilderness, there was a distinct tendency in such texts to elevate them to the status of secondary saints.

STRATEGIES FOR SURVIVAL AND WAYS OF LYING: CONFORMITY AND DISSIMULATION

We now turn to responses to persecution that involved a degree of concession to the demands of a repressive regime. For obvious reasons, individuals who concealed their faith or conformed in order to weather the storm and avoid falling foul of the law have left little impression on the historical record. Like those who collaborated with the Nazis in the Second World War, their presence was frequently suppressed both by the leaders of the religious minorities to which they adhered and by those who later chronicled the defiant survival of such churches and sects. Privately deplored as hypocrites and quislings, they were either roundly condemned as an insignificant fringe or quietly swept under the carpet by contemporary and later apologists. Until recently, historians have largely followed the lead of these writers in ignoring and neglecting them.

This section of the chapter should be read with a number of caveats in mind. We must take care not to mistake the sincerely committed but timid for those who were merely bewildered and confused. The ambiguity and fluidity that marked the early decades of the Reformation makes it particularly difficult to draw a distinction between cautious Catholics and prudent Protestants: the rigid confessional polarities which were the end product of these events should not be read back anachronistically into the period before they had formed. It is also vital to realise that there was a whole spectrum of positions between resistance and compromise. Some dissenters made only the slightest gesture of compliance with the requirements of the Tudor or Stuart state; others almost completely disguised themselves as orthodox members of their parish communities, outwardly behaving in accordance with the various Acts of Uniformity but inwardly espousing a completely different set of beliefs. The boundaries between conformity and nonconformity, furthermore, were porous rather than fixed. Individuals moved easily between the various degrees of separation and detachment from the established Church, adjusting their behaviour in accordance with changing circumstances. At times of relative calm, when the preoccupations and priorities of policy makers and provincial justices focused upon other issues, to display one's faith or reveal one's scruples openly carried fewer risks; when the ecclesiastical and political authorities stepped up their efforts to restrain those who infringed the canons and statutes many lapsed back into less bold and daring modes of dissent. As the Jesuit John Gerard commented about Catholics in Elizabethan Lancashire, there were many people who practised their religion when conditions permitted 'but they fall away the moment persecution blows up'.[128] Likewise, during the 'troublous times' of 1668, 'many of the friends' of the Bedford congregation withdrew themselves 'from close walking with the church'; when the pressure eased their commitment to overt dissent no doubt stiffened accordingly.[129] The relationship of puritan clergy and laity with the Church of England depended heavily on who held the balance of power in their local communities and, as both Donald Spaeth and John Spurr have pointed out, distinguishing Restoration 'Anglicans' from 'nonconformists' is consequently by no means always straightforward.[130] It is in any case problematic to erect clear lines of demarcation between categories of conduct whose definition, to use the words of Peter Lake and Michael Questier, was 'an inherently political and contingent process'.[131] We must also be careful to avoid seeing conformists as faint-hearted and spineless: as we shall see, often their behaviour was underpinned by strongly-held convictions. Compromise itself could be a stance built upon the foundations of principle.

Like the Waldensians before them, the Lollards were renowned for adopting the wisdom of the serpent and dissembling their Wycliffite opinions. Clandestinity was a congenital feature of this sect. The man from King's Lynn who sat at work on Easter Sunday 1430 saying 'he would not go to church to show himself a scribe or pharisee' was something of a rarity.[132] Few Lollards went so far as to absent themselves from their parish assemblies and there is evidence to the effect that where they felt under particular pressure they assumed a pose of impeccably orthodox piety. In the early sixteenth century it was said that 'they, above all others in Coventry, pretended most show of worship and devotion at the holding of the sacrament'. In Amersham, by contrast, where they dominated the town, this level of disguise was unnecessary and some displayed ostentatious contempt when the sacrament was elevated.[133] Notwithstanding their rejection of the doctrine of transubstantiation, many – perhaps most – participated in the annual Eucharist, as a trial from the diocese of Salibury in 1498 reveals. Thomas Boughton, a shoemaker and woolwinder from Mungerford, stated that 'I have every yere receyved the said holy sacrament, not for that I had any stedfast byleve therin, but that I shuld not be noted and knowen of the people', adding that 'I feyned with myn hondys to honoure it as Cristen men use to doo, but my mynd and entent was nothing therto.'[134] This kind of internal dissociation from medieval Catholicism was virtually impossible to detect from the outside but some marked themselves out from their misguided neighbours by means of small gestures – attendance at church was not incompatible with asserting that one had a separate religious identity. Agnes Frank, for instance, averted her face from the cross as it was carried in procession and there were those who, 'especially at the elevation time, would say no prayers, but did sit mum ... like beasts'. The behaviour of Agnes Grevill and her two sons was at once insidious and audacious: in 1511 they admitted that on several occasions they had secretly brought home consecrated wafers and eaten it with 'noon other regard unto it but as to other brede'.[135] Such cases may represent only the tip of the iceberg of Lollard conformity: we can only speculate how many men and women managed to camouflague their illegal convictions even more completely.

Henrician and Marian evangelicals appear to have employed many similar strategies in their attempts to evade prosecution while still adhering in their hearts to the new religion. Ironically we only know about these shifts and subterfuges because the authorities gradually came to recognise them as the tell-tale signs of a 'mass gospeller' or 'nicodemite', so called after Nicodemus, the Jew who came to Jesus under the cover of night. In the late 1540s, for instance, a Canterbury barber by the name of Thomas Makeblyth was detected when he retreated into a corner and read the Bible during the procession time.[136] During his visitation of the diocese of London in 1554 Edmund Bonner instructed churchwardens to identify 'any that at the sacring time, do hang down their heads, hide themselves behind pillars, turn away their faces, or do depart out of the church', evidently suspecting that they were closet heretics.[137] John Bradford described the same phenomenon from the other side of the Reformation divide, noting disapprovingly that many a Protestant tried to qualify his presence at the popish service by refusing to look up when the priest held up the host or by kneeling down in 'hys pue or fourme sadlye & hevelye, as one of small devocion to the masse'.[138] Even some members of the 'privy' or underground congregations which sprang up in London were not immune to the potential advantages of occasional outward conformity, and more than one stalwart succumbed to this temptation after a stint in captivity. Nicholas Grimwald, for instance, was released from the Marshalsea 'not without some becking or bowing, alas, of his knee to Baal'.[139] As in France and the cities of Northern Italy, crypto-Protestantism was a natural reaction to the threat and reality of discovery and punishment by hostile officials.[140]

When Catholics found themselves the target of intolerance, they too frequently responded by seeking to shade into the background. Even in remote parts of Cornwall, it was reported in 1537, 'popish' sympathisers 'do show outward, for avoiding the danger of the law'.[141] In the second half of the sixteenth century, a large number of those who continued to support the Church of Rome attended Prayer Book services in their parish churches in order to comply with the Act of Uniformity and escape the increasingly harsh penalties for repeated non-appearance – extortionate fines, sequestration of land, mobility restrictions and extended imprisonment.[142] It is hardly suprising that forms of partial and occasional conformity flourished in a climate in which government policy focused almost exclusively on controlling recusancy. In a very real sense, Elizabethan legislation condoned and encouraged these tactics: the principle of not making windows into men's souls provided the Catholic laity with an opportunity to maintain their religion without attracting persecution. A variety of ingenious methods of exploiting these legal loopholes evolved.

Some appeared at church on a handful of carefully chosen Sundays, just enough to convince magistrates of their political loyalty and to secure a certificate giving them immunity.[143] In many upper-class households, a shrewd domestic arrangement prevailed, whereby the husband periodically conformed to protect the family's social respectability and financial security, while his wife and children safeguarded its spiritual integrity by strictly separating themselves from heretical worship. Others attended more regularly but paid no attention to the proceedings and instead sat clicking their rosary beads, or like Sir Thomas Cornwallis, reading psalters, primers and other devotional books, sometimes silently but quite often aloud.[144] John Vicars, a Hereford brewer, walked up and down the outer aisles of the cathedral in order to avoid hearing the sermon.[145] Unlike many Lollards, however, most of these so-called 'church papists' drew the line at receiving communion. An even more hair-splitting solution described by the Jesuit Henry Garnet in 1593 was to send a proxy to inhabit an enclosed wooden pew with the aim of deceiving the congregation and vicar.[146] Well into the seventeenth century crypto-Catholicism was a force to be reckoned with. John Earle's witty pen portrait of the 'church papist' of 1628 remarks that 'Once a moneth he presents himselfe at the Church, to keep off the Church-warden, and brings in his body to save his bail', and in 1659 Richard Baxter was lamenting the continuing presence of such men and women in English parishes. As late as 1681 a tract was published alerting contemporaries to their characteristic circumventions.[147] Of course, the success of these strategies for deflecting harassment and evading monetary penalties hinged upon the predilections of local officials. It required a willingness on their part to collaborate with their Catholic neighbours in the art of dissimulation.

Other dissenting groups also employed evasive practices. In the case of the small community of Sephardic Jews who settled in London in the mid-sixteenth century, the *converso* habits that had enabled them to escape the all-seeing eye of the Inquisition were readily adapted to fit the requirements of their new Protestant environment. In 1548 a Spaniard reported to the authorities in Madrid that many observed Judaic rites in private but publicly 'they attend Lutheran churches, and listen to the sermons, and take the bread and wine in the manner and form as do the other heretics'.[148] Deceit and dissimulation were likewise interwoven into the very fabric of Familism. To borrow a phrase from Patrick Collinson, the whole ethic of the Family was 'a kind of cryptic Nicodemite masquerade, elevated to casuistry, a way of life'.[149]

Hendrick Niclaes's disciples saw no contradiction between adherence to their mystical creed and full compliance with the statutes ordering attendance at Church of England services – a fact which explains why so few appeared before ecclesiastical tribunals.[150] During the Civil War and Interregnum, some extreme sectarians avoided confrontation with the authorities by behaving in equally devious ways. The Muggletonians, for instance, seem to have kept out of trouble by resorting to the technique of occasional conformity. In the 1660s Thomas Tompkinson was 'loth to loose my preferment as the world' and, bowing to the wishes of his father, wife and parish officials, attended church 'by fits'. A Derbyshire follower who hid her books from the rest of her household also went 'some times' to mattins 'but never to the Sacrement'.[151] Itinerancy was another way of avoiding prosecution and some sought to lessen the financial impact of excommunication by selling movable property which might be confiscated, in a manner reminiscent of recusants who encumbered their estates with fictitious debts, trusts and mortgages to prevent them being sequestered by the Exchequer.[152] By such time-honoured devices, this wily group proved adept at eluding and resisting the effects of repressive legislation.

Dissenting Protestant clergymen likewise attempted to square their consciences with the law in an intriguing range of ways. During Laud's archiepiscopate some puritan ministers adroitly sidestepped offensive 'popish' ceremonies by employing 'conformable' curates to perform baptisms using the sign of the cross or read the hated Book of Sports. Following the lead of their Elizabethan and Jacobean predecessors, others omitted the word Jesus during the blessing so that they did not have to bow at his name or claimed that the surplice was in the wash or old and unfit for use. Stephen Marshall was apparently 'so supple a soul that he brake not a joint, yea, sprained not a Sinew, in all the alterations of times'. As Henry Jessey commented, many 'good men' were 'fain to stoop' to the bishops to dodge persecution by the High Commission.[153] After 1642 the shoe was on the other foot and it was Anglican vicars who contrived to keep in favour with the prevailing Presbyterian regime while simultaneously indicating their disapproval of it, for example by reading out the declarations of Parliament 'with a low voyce' or in a muddled fashion.[154] Similar prevaricating strategies enabled many puritans to maintain a toehold within the Church of England after the Restoration. The attitude of the Cambridgeshire vicar Isaac Archer to liturgical conformity may well be indicative: his strategy was to do 'as little as was possible, without incurring danger, and so [I] kept myself very moderate, and displeased, I think, none by so doing.'[155] Those who led supplementary or alternative forms of worship also found ways of getting around the severe restrictions of the Clarendon Code. Gathering under the guise of holding a banquet or feast was one such ruse, while Adam Martindale cleverly frustrated the intention of the Conventicle

Act by dividing his flock into small groups and preaching the same sermon four or five times a day.[156]

In the case of the laity, accommodation with the Restoration Church and state usually took the form of partial or occasional conformity. Mark Stoneham of Aldbourne in Wiltshire, who attended the local Presbyterian meeting, attended church twice a year, but would not remove his hat during the service or receive the Eucharist.[157] Anxious to qualify for civic office, dissenting gentlemen circumvented the Corporation and Test Acts by annually receiving communion. This practice had acquired considerable infamy by the late seventeenth century: in 1701 Daniel Defoe accused occasional conformists of 'playing Bo-peep with God Almighty'.[158] In some instances it was clearly no more than a nominal gesture: the Lord Mayor of London Sir Humphrey Edwin caused a scandal in 1697 by attending the Anglican Eucharist in the morning and then tactlessly processing in full regalia to a nonconformist meeting, preceded by the city's swordbearer.[159]

Though Quakers often scorned the expedients employed by other dissenters, not all could resist the temptation to compromise themselves. Despite the Society's clear policy with regard to the duty of Friends to refuse to pay tithes, for instance, it is apparent that a considerable number did so surreptitiously in order to avoid imprisonment. In Essex some overcame the practical difficulties presented by their opposition to swearing oaths by asking their relatives and neighbours or employing poor women to do so on their behalf.[160] Unwilling to choose the path of exile, resistance or martyrdom, in the midst of persecution the instinct of many was to reach some kind of modus vivendi with the early modern Church and state. Likewise, perhaps only a small and intrepid minority refused to take advantage of the official initiatives designed to comprehend, accommodate, or offer a modest form of relief to dissenters, which we discuss in Chapter 5. However much they may have resented the humiliation of accepting the clemency of the Anglican regime and distrusted the motives of the monarchs who extended it, many swallowed their pride and made the most of royal dispensations and declarations of indulgence.

Such practices might be seen as behavioural equivalents of the verbal techniques of equivocation and mental reservation. The first of these devices involved answering questions under interrogation ambiguously, in a manner intended to deceive the questioner. The second entailed saying one thing and adding a qualifying or contradictory clause under one's breath. Such practices were employed by many dissenting groups in the course of the sixteenth and seventeenth centuries. The later Lollards were renowned for recanting rather than burning and the strategy of responding evasively when under official inquisition was apparently taught in the sect's underground schools. Anne Hudson estimates that 98 per cent of those arrested abjured their beliefs.[161] Driven by a similar instinct for self-preservation, Familists too had no scruples about dissembling under oath: when a commission was appointed to investigate the community in Wisbech in 1580, for instance, its members were advised to deny ever having seen the works of the mysterious 'H. N.'[162] Ranters like Abiezer Coppe also superficially retracted their opinions when under arrest and this seems to have been positively recommended in the face of persecution.[163]

In the early modern period, however, equivocation and mental reservation were most notoriously linked with the Jesuits. A number of priests utilised these linguistic tricks during their trials for treason, notably Robert Southwell (1595) and Henry Garnet (1606), but it is less well known that they were also sometimes employed by the Catholic laity. Papers circulated advising learned recusants how to reply to the question 'doe you, or will you goe the church' sufficiently enigmatically to evade prosecution and it is revealing that the Jacobean authorities felt the need to insert a clause in the oath of allegiance of 1606 explicitly prohibiting the use of equivocation.[164] At a lower level, it may be suspected that some of the individuals who explained their absence from matins by saying that they were ill, babysitting, or lacked proper apparel, were actually prevaricating.[165] While some church papists quite openly displayed their contempt for Calvin's blasphemous supper, others were more circumspect about their motives for abstaining from the sacrament: claiming to be out of charity with one's neighbours was a common excuse and William Shakespeare's father pleaded fear of arrest as a debtor. Perhaps the Yorkshire serving maid Elizabeth Coulson presented at her local church court for surreptitiously removing the sacrament from her mouth and slipping it into her sleeve was also disguising her true convictions when she alleged she had not swallowed it 'by reason of a pain in her side and a cough'.[166]

It is additionally now clear that both Catholics and Protestants utilised the technique of oral dissimulation during the reigns of Henry VIII and Edward VI. In the late 1530s, the Observant Franciscan friar John Forrest equivocated over the oath of supremacy and many early evangelicals like Dr Edward Crome became skilled in the art of ambivalent retraction.[167] Alec Ryrie has recently illuminated the full extent and significance of this 'culture of recantation' in the last decade of Henrician rule and argued vigorously that some kind of link with Lollardy cannot be entirely discounted. Despite the efforts of later Protestant apologists to iron out evidence of these practices from their historical narratives, in the later 1540s, he concludes, conformism was 'the rule rather than the exception'. These dissemblers were not marginal figures but men of exceptional prominence and calibre like Robert Wisdom, Thomas Becon and Nicholas Shaxton.[168]

In Elizabethan Northamptonshire some puritan ministers subscribed or submitted by adding qualifying phrases or tacit reservations. Carefully worded concessions about the lawfulness of indifferent ceremonies also enabled John

Burgess, rector of Waddesdon in the diocese of Lincoln, to evade conviction for his liturgical nonconformity, even during Bancroft's determined drive against it in 1604–5. Such 'shadow boxing' with the authorities usually resulted in a draw.[169] A Paul's Cross preacher would complain in 1608 that too many of the puritan 'faction' imitated Arius who 'subscribed but haltingly, and dissemblingly, retaining the poison of his opinion at heart', while Laudian officials in East Anglia remarked of the godly clergy that 'although they let their tongues speake and traduce ye Jesuits, yet their practices in many things have Identity & equypage'.[170]

In the 1640s, however, the supporters of episocopacy can themselves be found equivocating: Robert Sugden of Benhall took the ambiguously phrased Protestation, but only 'with reservation that the Church might be governed by bishops', and Nathaniel Ward of Staindrop in County Durham confided to a friend that 'if I might interpret that sacred form of words in my own way, I could take an oath and call God to witness the cause'.[171] Face-saving formulae also allowed later nonconformists to endorse the Thirty-nine Articles without completely abandoning their principles.[172] Nor were Quakers entirely above exploiting such legal casuistries. In fact, as Craig Horle has shown, they shrewdly subverted attempts to prosecute them by quibbling about procedural minutiae and by deliberately leading their opponents into the darker and obscurer thickets of the law.[173] By means of these devious techniques, clergy and laity alike sought to elude the attempts of the Tudor and Stuart state to bind their consciences.

Religious minorities, then, frequently responded to intolerance by becoming as cunning as the fox. The practices we have been describing were, however, often highly controversial. The leaders of many, though not all, minority churches and sects vehemently condemned conformity and compromise as a perilous threat to the souls of their followers and to the survival of the faith as a whole, as well as an appalling stain upon its collective integrity. Uncompromising reformers on both sides of the Reformation divide reviled their 'wordlye wyse brethren' who hovered between truth and falsehood and seventeenth-century dissenters were no less critical of those who sought to 'to make our knees feeble ... by creeping into corners, and meeting by fours' to evade the full force of the laws regarding conventicles.[174] The urgency with which such 'trimmers' and 'temporisers' were denounced by their more rigorous co-religionists testifies indirectly to the scale of the problem the latter believed they confronted. It also reflected an awareness that such behaviour could tarnish the image of resilient defiance and moral righteousness projected by martyrs and exiles and supply the enemy with ammunition with which to attack one's religion as inherently false and hypocritical. Hence the endeavours of martyrologists like Henry Bull and John Foxe to suppress evidence of godly Protestants who had faltered in the face of persecution and succumbed after being bitten by 'the old serpente our auncient enemy', and to omit letters which cast the reformers in a less than heroic light from the collections of their 'monuments' which they edited and published for posterity.[175]

During this period a large body of literature designed to discourage such 'cowardly' forms of conduct circulated in manuscript and print. Calvin's tracts against the French nicodemites were translated into English in the 1540s and 1550s and native reformers like John Bradford, John Hooper and William Tyms constantly admonished members of their flocks about the 'hurte of heringe masse'.[176] In Elizabeth's reign seminary priests and Jesuits produced a series of treatises about the evils of 'schism', the most famous of which were Gregory Martin's book of that title (1578) and Robert Persons's *Brief discourse* or 'Reasons of Refusal' (1581).[177] Separatists too exhorted their followers to 'keep themselves from idols'; puritan clergymen like Daniel Rogers abhorred the forms of 'Jesuiticall evasion' that had kept his colleagues in Caroline pulpits; and many of the same themes pervade the polemical writings of Restoration dissenters who deplored the lax and supine morality of 'latitudinarians' and 'neuters' who conformed rather than embrace persecution and punishment.[178] The arguments these authors used to dissuade people from concealing and disguising their faith were remarkably similar. They cut across the doctrinal barriers that divided Catholics from Protestants and transcended the fierce disagreements which fractured relations between the various sects. Indeed, sometimes writers even cited texts by their confessional adversaries, insisting that the general principles they expounded were sound even though they were 'very badly applied'. In so doing, it may be argued, they contributed, albeit unwittingly, towards laying the foundations for a recognition of the rights of the subjective and erroneous conscience. As we see in Chapter 5, this was to become a key thread in arguments mounted to defend toleration.[179]

In such works, conformity was presented as a despicable and damnable act of apostasy, a dereliction of every Christian's duty to confess his or her religion plainly and openly. Those whose outward behaviour was at odds with their inner convictions were no less guilty of perjury than those who denied or dissembled them under interrogation, for as Peter Martyr Vermigli explained in his tract *The cohabitacion of the faithfull with the unfaithfull* (1555), 'the doinges of men be as it were a tongue'. The Lord expected true believers to keep their bodies pure and unpolluted as well as their souls. He was 'not content with halfes'.[180] As William Perkins put it in his *Cases of conscience*, 'we robbe him of his due, when we reserve our hearts to him, and give our bodies to Idolls'.[181] To participate in the public rites of a false religion was to expose oneself to the risk of infection, as well as to give scandal to the weaker brethren – much emphasis was placed on the dangers of casting stumbling blocks in the path of the ignorant. Quoting 2 Corinthians 6, those who opposed such duplicitous practices declared that there could be no fellowship between light and darkness or Christ and Belial: true professors were bound to segregate themselves from unbelievers: they could not drink simultaneously from the cup of the Lord and the cup of the devil. '[A]bove all things', exhorted Henry Barrow, the Lord 'abhoreth a dubell minded man; halt not, therefor, betwixt tow [two] opinions'.[182]

This was the hallmark of an indifference and apathy which contemporaries typically conflated with atheism. Those who were too scared to face up to the consequences of defending their principles, said Henry Garnet in his *Treatise of Christian renunciation* (1593), effectively made 'Gods either of their belly and ease, or of the wicked mammon'.[183] After the Restoration, the nonconformist pamphleteer Ralph Wallis similarly deplored the insincerity of dissenters who 'stab'd their own consciences, and there's an end of the Persecution with them', while John Bunyan crystallised his contempt for such feeble piety in the characters of Pliable, Mr Worldly Wiseman and Mr By-Ends.[184] Like the lukewarm Church of Laodicea in Revelation 3: 15–16, warned the Reformation and Counter-Reformation clergy alike, because they were neither hot nor cold, such people would be spewed out of God's mouth. This was a biblical passage that continued to have profound resonance well into the seventeenth century.

It is wrong to read these tracts as evidence of a simple clash between the strict counsels of preachers and ministers and the more pragmatic and flexible instincts of the ordinary lay people they served. Historians must be wary of subscribing to the argument that those who conformed were cowards who lacked any shred of moral fibre. Undoubtedly many did so for the reasons enunciated by a group of Lollards in 1499: 'oonly for dreed of the people, and to eschew the iuberdye [jeopardy] and daunger that we dredd to falle in if we had not doon as other crysten people dyd'.[185] But it is clear that resorting to such strategies for survival often involved much mental anguish. Like the Italian apostate Francis Spiera, whose deathbed torments became nothing less than a literary topos, some suffered acute pangs of spiritual anxiety after succumbing to the temptation to dissemble their beliefs.[186] Overcome by remorse after recanting and performing penance, the Marian Protestant Gertrude Crockhay was unable to settle until she had confessed her fault in front of her entire congregation; James Bainham was likewise 'never quiet in mind ... until the time he had uttered his fall to all his acquaintance, and asked God and all the world forgiveness, before the congregation in those days, in a warehouse in Bow-Lane'; and Rose Hickman's husband 'could not sleep for grief to think that he was on the morrow to go ... to that idolatrous service'.[187]

The commonplace that the church papist had a 'Conscience ... so large, that he could never wander out of it' also belies the very real distress that many schismatics felt.[188] The Norfolk recusant Francis Wodehouse, for instance, was reputedly consumed by a searing thirst, which felt like a 'raging furnace', after entering a Protestant church.[189] For puritans and dissenters, deciding whether to wear the surplice, subscribe to Thirty-nine Articles or to receive the Anglican sacrament could be equally agonising. In a few extreme cases, the psychological torment experienced by those torn apart by conflicting impulses and allegiances had tragic consequences. The Protestant Sir James Hales of Kent was so haunted by his recantation during the reign of Queen Mary that he stabbed himself repeatedly with a pen-knife in his cell in the Fleet. Thwarted in these attempts to take his own life, he later succeeded by throwing himself into a shallow pond. In 1583, a 'very seditious' Manchester Catholic also tried to drown himself after capitulating to the authorities and appearing at Common Prayer.[190] In the eyes of the uncompromising, such incidents of suicide were themselves a judgement from God, divine punishments for the sin of apostasy.

Moreover, although their leaders tried hard to create an illusion of consensus, many religious minorities in this period were troubled by internal conflicts about the legitimacy of dissembling in order to survive. Like their counterparts on the Continent and within the stranger churches of the metropolis, the Marian Protestants quarrelled among themselves on this and other topics[191] and disputes about partial and occasional conformity racked the Catholic camp from the 1580s onwards. The 'comfortable advertisements' of the Yorkshire priest Thomas Bell, who advocated the lawfulness of attending church with a protestation prior to his defection to Protestantism in 1592, won the support of more than a handful of the missionary clergy. Moreover, Jesuits in England and Scotland seem to have adopted contrasting positions on the question of conformity: south of the border members of the Society insisted that it was anathema, but north of the Tweed their colleagues taught that 'a man might lock up his conscience, after he had h[e]ard masse, and then goe to the Protestants Churches'.[192]

Debate on this subject, as well as upon the related issue of taking the oath of allegiance, also contributed to the virulence of the Appellant and Archpriest controversies at the turn of the century. The use of equivocation and mental reservation by captured priests, as sanctioned in manuscript tracts by the Jesuits Robert Southwell and Henry Garnet, proved no less contentious, for comparable reasons: such practices were liable to expose the Church of Rome to charges of Machiavellian deception.[193] The introduction of the Clarendon Code similarly precipitated serious disagreements within the higher ranks of the Baptists and the Society of Friends. The former wrangled about the legality of taking oaths and during the persecution of the 1680s those who were prepared to attend Anglican services were 'most heinously censured by those that do not'. One of the matters in contention during the Wilkinson-Story Controversy of the late 1660s was the question of how Quakers should react to persecution. The orthodox 'Foxonians' charged the so-called separatists with slackness for meeting secretly in fields rather than boldly in open assemblies and for paying or condoning the payment of tithes.[194] Conformity had articulate lay and clerical advocates who justified their conduct with persuasive and plausible arguments, even if these were all too often suppressed and censored by the rival factions whose priorities in the end prevailed.

The picture is further complicated by the fact that, despite their public insistence upon the necessity of external confession, in private the leaders of underground churches and sects often relaxed and qualified these hard-line strictures. In responding to the moral dilemmas of their troubled followers, they tacitly conceded that there were particular circumstances in which lying or concealing one's faith might be excusable. John Bale regarded recantation as evidence of the devil's power, but when dealing with actual cases he tended to treat individuals as victims of heretical pressure rather than unforgivable criminals.[195] In counselling and absolving contrite sinners in the confessional, Catholic priests were guided by casuistical manuals which implicitly condoned occasional conformity as an interim strategy in the lead up to the overthrow of the Protestant regime and in 1593, with the support of Pope Clement VIII, Cardinal Allen urged missionary priests to show compassion for those who sometimes, out of 'meere feare', committed the sin of 'schism' and attended heretical services.[196] Elizabethan casuists even sanctioned the practice of bribing constables, 'catchepoles', guards and gaolers, on the grounds that this was a lesser evil than the unjust persecution to which Catholics were subjected.[197] During the Interregnum a manuscript tract by the Anglican divine Robert Sanderson similarly gave encouragement to episcopalian incumbents struggling to reconcile taking the Engagement with maintaining an untroubled conscience, and in dozens of individual letters puritan and dissenting clergymen tempered and mitigated the message that any kind of compromise with the establishment was quite insupportable.[198] Such writers recognised that to rule out all forms of dissimulation and accommodation might be to doom a persecuted religion to complete annihilation. They acknowledged that such tactics and techniques were a necessary evil if it was to outlive its trials and tribulations. In other words, a balance had to be struck between prudence and passion, discretion and zeal.

A range of reasoning could be employed to defend or excuse conformity and equivocation. On a purely practical level, some made the point that dissemblers might actually be more useful to an oppressed Church or sect than a band of dead martyrs and stubborn confessors. Robert Southwell justified the disguises assumed by Jesuit missionaries by saying that 'the salvation of souls' was 'much more weighty' than 'the external decency of our apparel' and the same arguments could be used to vindicate lying under oath. Attendance at Protestant services could, furthermore, be a smokescreen behind which to conduct undercover operations, as well as a vital method of preserving the personnel upon which a successful reversion to Rome would ultimately depend. If 'occasion serve', declared the Essex gentleman Sir John Petre, schismatics like himself would 'be able to do better service than they which refuse to go to the church'.[199] Behind the scenes clerical casuists were bound to agree that church papists were critical to the very survival of the Catholic community: 'Once these men have gone', it was candidly admitted, 'religion in England will be finished, or virtually finished'.[200] Conformity could be an astute 'form of estate management', a way of protecting the resources of wealthy recusants so that in due course they could assume the reins of power.[201] Though they rarely acknowledged it explicitly, early Protestants also recognised that individuals who chose to hide their real colours and remain in their posts could perform signal service to the cause of the Gospel. Without timeservers like William Cecil, remarks Andrew Pettegree, the restoration of Protestantism in 1559 would have been unthinkable: 'To a very large extent the Elizabethan settlement was a Nicodemite Reformation'.[202]

Other defenders of conformity found prototypes for their behaviour in Scripture. Nicodemus was much cited by Marian 'mass gospellers' and reference was also made to the case of Joseph of Arimathea, the counsellor who quietly concealed his faith while he awaited the advent of the Kingdom of God (Luke 23: 50–3). A particular favourite was the example of Naaman the Syrian, the courtier permitted by the prophet Elishah to assist his king at worship in the idolatrous temple of Rimmon as a token of civil obedience (2 Kings 5: 18–19). Catholic writers recurrently invoked this text to justify attendance at church as a mere mark of loyalty to one's monarch and country, implicitly instigating a split between an individual's political and religious obligations.[203] Even the outspoken John Hooper wondered if it implied that a man might legitimately conceal his faith and submit to royal authority: it is clear that respect for the latter induced many evangelicals to avoid confrontation in the 1540s.[204] Indeed, the theme of 'rendering unto Caesar' was prominent in many defences of conformity, with the passage in 1 Peter 2: 13 ('Submit your selves to every ordinance of man ...') being frequently quoted. In a confession of faith published in 1575 the Family of Love declared that in this as in other areas it was 'meete and right' for all subjects to defer to the demands of their earthly governors. Members of the sect in Surrey deposed that 'they were al bounde to come unto the church, and to doe outwardly, there, all such thinges as the lawe required'.[205]

It was also common to insist that outward actions did not compromise inner belief, that presence at false worship was immaterial provided one remained steadfast to the truth in one's heart. Protestant nicodemites frequently deployed the argument that God was concerned only with one's private convictions and church papists too were often accused of believing that their external actions had no bearing provided they were faithful in the sacrosanct sphere of their consciences. The same logic could readily be adapted to sanction superficial verbal recantation. Elizabethan and Jacobean Englishmen captured by Barbary pirates who converted to Islam to escape enslavement were likewise apt to plead that they had 'received the abominable circumcision in their flesh, but not in their hearts'.[206] However, this line of thought came most naturally to the Familists and the spiritualist sects of the Civil War whose mystical theology inclined them to elevate the spirit over the flesh and to devalue all forms of external ceremonial.[207]

In the case of dissenting groups whose attitude to the established Church was not one of outright condemnation, it is equally important to point out that conformity was often a matter of principle as much as of thinly-veiled pragmatism. For those who believed that the institution that persecuted them was imperfect rather than damnable, a measure of co-operation with it could, somewhat paradoxically, be regarded as a positive obligation. This, rather than mere abject fear, may help to explain why so few Lollards abstained from the Catholic mass and why so many meekly submitted to ecclesiastical discipline and renounced their heresies. The followers of Wyclif did not reject the medieval Church and conceive of themselves as a separate sect as such; they expected to achieve salvation within it. They did not share the totalitarian claims to possess the truth that would become a badge of the gathered congregations of Anabaptists and Brownists.[208] The same assumptions are also vital to understanding the mentality of puritan ministers faced with a stark choice between suspension and deprivation or casuistical accommodation with the Church of England, and of semi-separatist lay people who continued to participate in parish services with their reprobate neighbours. Zealous Protestant preachers regarded the moral discomfort of conformity to Anglican rubrics as the necessary price to be paid for their liberty to preach the Gospel to the people. Compromise was to be preferred above the evils of schism and the 'quicksands of separation'.[209] Rather than make 'needless rents in the Church' over adiaphora or 'things indifferent' – matters omitted from the canon of Scripture upon which a ruler had a right to legislate for the sake of order and decency – moderate puritans such as Nicholas Byfield and Joseph Bentham believed they had a responsibility to 'yeeld to some things inconvenient for the peace of this society' and for the sake of weak.[210] If men agreed on the fundamentals, wrote Edward Reynolds in 1638, it was 'impudent and immoderate pertinacity', to 'disturbe or hazard the worke which God hath set us to doe' over issues that were 'meerely notionall and curious'.[211] Emphasising the 'grievous discommodities' of any 'rash departure' from a Church that still had 'the least breathings of Christ', Independents like Henry Jacob and William Ames saw it as not merely acceptable but even as imperative for the godly 'to communicate with the public ordinary Congregations assembled for the exercise of religion in England', provided that 'neither assent, nor silent presence is given to any mere human tradition'.[212] For puritans, worshipping alongside the impious multitude, rather than withdrawing from them, was the real act of self-sacrifice.

As Christopher Hill and John Ramsbottom have argued, the behaviour of Presbyterians and other dissenters who partially conformed with the Restoration Church thus had 'a very respectable intellectual ancestry'.[213] Many of those who continued to attend Prayer Book services seem to have considered it their duty, in the words of Richard Baxter and Thomas Goodwin, to 'loveingly joyne in the publike congregation' and 'break down' the 'partition wall' dividing the self-consciously godly from involuntary Protestants. As Edmund Calamy claimed in the early eighteenth century, nonconformist ministers who had maintained communion with the Church of England after 1662 did so from ecumenical motives, 'with a design to show their charity' towards it, 'notwithstanding they apprehended themselves bound in conscience ordinarily to separate from it'.[214] Such arguments were not simply 'a cobweb of sophistry'.[215] By keeping a foot in both camps, individuals like Oliver Heywood and his flock were not cynically circumventing the constraints of the law so much as clinging to the concept of an inclusive national Church. Rather than reflecting hypocrisy or a lack of commitment the practice of occasional conformity may often be an index of a sincere conviction that separation was sinful. Proceeding not from a 'mercenary' but a 'Catholick spirit', it was a way of keeping bridges open between different Protestant groupings which did not yet regard themselves as distinct denominations.[216] Against the backdrop of continuing efforts to achieve ecclesiastical comprehension of scrupulous dissenters, it was a tangible commitment to the elusive possibility of a revised Restoration settlement.

In this and other respects it is possible to argue that ecclesiastical conformity and compromise fostered a kind of de facto pluralism and tolerance. Alec Ryrie has suggested that the propensity for Henrician evangelicals to concur with the demands of the Tudor regime rather than take the path of open opposition contributed towards a temporary 'lowering of the ideological temperature' in this critical period.[217] Similarly after 1559, it may be suggested that the willingness of both Catholic and Protestant dissenters to make a nominal and symbolic gesture of compliance with the Act of Uniformity helped in a small way to ease confessional tensions. It not only afforded them a legal space within which to coexist with the orthodox and paved the way for negotiations that might have redefined the parameters of the Church of England itself; it may also have earned them a kind of grudging respect and acceptance from at least some of their Anglican neighbours.

Simultaneously, and somewhat paradoxically, however, it is apparent that such behaviour often evoked distrust and anxiety. The secrecy and invisibility of the Family of Love was one chief cause of the disproportionate fear that surrounded it. Alarm about this enigmatic sect peaked when it was revealed that outward religious conformity had even enabled them to infiltrate the Queen's personal guard of yeomanry.[218] Camouflaged behind the cloak of conformity, church papists also came to be seen as a potential fifth column, undermining the established Church from within. Protestant magistrates began to suspect that they were far 'more dangerous and hurtfull to the state' than 'symple recusants' who stuck out like a sore thumb and wore their colours on their sleeves.[219] Andrew Willet wished that all papists would withdraw themselves from parish services 'that we might the better take heede of them': it was much harder to keep an eye upon those who were 'content for a while to temporize, watching for an houre'. There was a dawning realisation that mere attendance at church was no guarantee of political loyalty. The puritan agitator John Field regarded such 'timeserving Hipcrites' as 'the bane of this lande', 'prickes and thornes in our sides', and other preachers and writers likewise thought that the 'good outward civill carriage' of such individuals was too often a mask for treasonous intentions. Even John Earle's light-hearted character of the church papist left him hatching plots and expecting an invasion by Catholic General Spinola.[220] In the reign of James I, Catholics prepared to take the oath of allegiance provoked equal dismay: Richard Bernard thought this 'farre more pernicious to the State, then open and profest Recusancie'.[221] During a debate in the House of Lords in 1642, a speaker likewise complained that too many 'dangerous Papists' came to church 'with Purpose (as is conceived) to make themselves capable of Employment'.[222]

Similarly, the Quaker principle of public witness made the Society of Friends seem less insidious than groups like the Ranters and Muggletonians and in the 1680s the Anglican divine John Shaw expressed concern about the corrupting influence of 'Church-Puritans' who participated in the public liturgy, but nursed Presbyterian or Congregationalist opinions, averring that 'a declared enemy without is not so dangerous as a pretended traitorous friend within'.[223] Widespread vilification of the phenomenon of 'latitudinarism' in the later seventeenth century suggests that there were many who believed with Jeremy Taylor that an honest error was better than hypocritical profession of the truth and who were troubled by the readiness of some of their contemporaries to 'transform themselves into any shape for their Secular Interests'.[224] By 1700, when Henry Sacheverell complained of 'crafty, faithless, and insidious persons … [who] slyly creep to those altars they proclaim idolatrous', 'to qualify themselves for a paltry place', resentment rather than apprehension may have been the dominant sentiment prompted by the practice of occasional conformity, but it remained a source of grievance and irritation that could and sometimes did spill over into verbal and even physical violence.[225] In a world which defined itself in terms of polarities and contrarieties, nicodemism and dissimulation were deeply disturbing.

The concerns about crypto-popery reviewed above greatly illuminate puritan preoccupations in the 1620s and 1630s, when the godly began to believe that Arminianism and Laudianism constituted a Trojan Horse 'ready to open the gates to Romish tyranny and Spanish monarchy'.[226] The perceived Catholicising tendencies of the Caroline Church – its ceremonialism, neo-clericalism, questioning of predestination and assault on the sabbath – were all regarded as proof of an underhand plot to bring in popery by the back door. Laudian bishops were said to have 'a Pope in their bellies' and to be 'Papists in grain' and dissident preachers increasingly conflated the threat presented by church papists and anti-Calvinists.[227] By the early 1640s this rhetorical linkage had acquired a literal reality in the eyes of John Pym and his party in Parliament: the Grand Remonstrance gave graphic expression to the conviction that the ecclesiastical policies of the king's counsellors amounted to a 'malicious', 'malignant' and 'mischievous design' to introduce a Counter-Reformation by stealth.[228] In a very real sense unease about the unseen Romanists lurking within the bowels of the nation assisted in precipitating the English Revolution.

Such anxieties may also shed light upon the proliferation of bizarre rumours during this period that Baptists, Brownists, Levellers, Ranters and other sectarians were Jesuits and papists in disguise. The tendency to jumble all deviants into a single category of evil was rooted in an outlook that viewed history in terms of an unending duel between Satan and Christ. It was a time-honoured polemical tactic to discredit a sect by alleging that it was actually in secret league with its own mortal enemies. In the 1540s, Anabaptist refugees were reported to have been sent from Rome as agents of the Pope and Cardinal Pole to disrupt the unity of the Protestant Church in England and the charge of being papist spies was also sometimes levelled at the French and Walloon Calvinist communities.[229] Elizabethan Familists were compared with covert Catholics and Presbyterians and separatists likewise found themselves being habitually condemned as agents of the papacy. John Cosin and others spoke of 'the Puritane Antichrist' and Christopher Hill has traced the process by which this label unerringly transferred itself on to a variety of targets.[230]

During the Civil War and Interregnum, such claims reached a new height of what can seem, with the benefit of hindsight, to be hysterical absurdity. Seekers, Quakers and other sectaries were said to be the puppets of the Jesuits, fears fed by their rejection of predestinarian doctrine and downgrading of Scripture to the status of secondary revelation, as well as their repudiation of the oaths of allegiance and supremacy.[231] William Prynne and William Baxter both believed that the regicide had been engineered by the Society of Jesus and other papal agents and in 1659 it was reported to the Massachusetts governor John Winthrop that the same order had deposed Richard Cromwell and, in the guise of the Quakers, was negotiating the purchase of Whitehall for future use

14 An Anglican-Tory engraving embodying the polemical commonplace that the dissenters, in league with the papists, were plotting to overthrow the Church and state: *The committee, or popery in masquerade* (London, 1680). (© The British Museum, Department of Prints and Drawings, Satires, no. 1080).

as a seminary.[232] Nor did the Restoration put the lid on wild conspiracy theories of this kind. Anglican churchmen continued to warn that there was 'a papacy in every sect or faction' and Robert South spoke for many in suggesting that 'puritanism … is only reformed Jesuitism, as Jesuitism is nothing else but popish puritanism'. A statement made at the Bath Assizes in 1681 solemnly warned that conventicles themselves provided shelter for seditious priests intent upon subverting the realm. It was also a commonplace to discern 'a vein of Judaism' running throughout the pharisaical religion of dissenters.[233] The Popish Plot was said to be the result of collaboration between papists and Fifth Monarchists; in reply the famous Meal Tub Plot during the Exclusion Crisis sought to lay the blame at the door of another set of enemies of 'true Protestants', the Presbyterians, the allegations being laid against a leading Whig by Elizabeth Cellier, a Catholic midwife.[234] A Tory print published in the 1680s showing the Committee on Popery in Masquerade provides visual testimony to the destablisation of categories which was a feature of this as of earlier eras of acute political upheaval: here we see Catholicism being brought in under Jack Presbyter's cloak (Figure 14).[235] Similar stories about crypto-popery continued to circulate throughout the eighteenth century, with the charge settling, among others, on John Wesley and the Methodists.[236]

Concern about wolves wearing sheep's clothing was a constant ingredient of the religous culture of early modern England: it was both a product and a precipitant of official and popular intolerance. Persecution drove minorities underground and encouraged them to hide behind a façade of outward conformity, so creating a new and more slippery problem for the authorities. Just as the focus of the activities of the Spanish Inquisition had shifted, following the mass expulsions of 1492, from Jews and Muslims to the crypto-religion of the *conversos* and *marranos*, so too in England did disguise and dissimulation come to be regarded forms of deviance themselves. It became necessary to take steps to unmask those who conformed in order to avoid discrimination and detection and to impose more rigorous tests of orthodoxy. Hence the act for the 'better discovering and repressing of Popish Recusants' of 1606, which made non-reception of communion a criminal offence, and the short-lived legislation of 1711, which disabled dissenters who engaged in occasional conformity from taking office and made triannual reception of the Eucharist a requirement for public employment.[237] Ironically these were in large part evils of the Tudor and Stuart regime's own making: they were a legacy of the Elizabethan settlement's treatment of dissent and the legislation of 1662 and 1689 that built upon and buttressed it.

THE COHABITATION OF THE FAITHFUL WITH THE UNFAITHFUL

Conformity, then, was a highly ambiguous phenomenon. It could be a cover for terrorism or rebellion, but it could also indicate an instinct for conciliation and compromise or a simple desire to keep out of the heat and the limelight. However, apart from the hope of defusing suspicion and deflecting persecution, there were other compelling reasons why dissenters might feel the need to remain part of their parishes. It is important to recognise that this was a social as well as an ecclesiastical unit: to withdraw from it was, therefore, to dissociate oneself quite deliberately from one's neighbours, to situate oneself conspicuously on its outer edges and margins. People who seceded from the established Church into recusant households and separatist conventicles were choosing a life of frosty isolation above one of genial integration. As Susan Brigden has remarked, 'for those who valued religious truth more highly than social unity there could be no concord'. Individuals who abstained from Common Prayer and Holy Communion quite literally placed themselves 'out of charity' with fellow inhabitants of their local communities.[238] For many, though, the contrary impulse for peace and harmony must have been overriding. Partial and occasional conformity might be seen as a powerful manifestation of what John Bossy has called the 'moral tradition', one embodiment of a deeply rooted instinct to avoid ostracisation and preserve fraternal Christian relations.[239] Alongside those who came to church, as the Lollard Margery Swayne confessed, 'to avoyde the Romour of the [pepul]', were those who came in order to interact with them. As the Protestant John Chapman of Appledore admitted in the latter part of the reign of Henry VIII, 'he did creep to the Cross more for company than for devotion'.[240] Church papistry too often expressed a wish to remain on cordial and amicable terms with one's neighbours and a sense of alienation was also an incentive for dissenters who gradually drifted back to the establishment during the Interregnum and Restoration. In 1654, for instance, one Jasper Docraw explained to the elders of the Baptist congregation in Fenstanton that 'he being alone a long time was much discouraged, and at length did go to the Church of England'.[241]

The same combination of factors prompted many members of religious minorities to ignore or modify St Paul's precept in 1 Corinthians 5: 11 that Christians should not 'keep company together' with idolaters and fornicators. Recent work has drawn our attention to the concessions which sixteenth- and seventeenth-century dissenters often made to their confessional enemies in the sphere of day-to-day relations. On the evidence that is now beginning to be assembled, the 'cohabitacion of the faithfull with the unfaithfull' was not always characterised by the antagonistic segregation of the heterodox from the rest of society. Derek Plumb's research on the later Lollards in the Thames

Valley has revealed that many heretics in this area actively assimilated themselves into the urban and rural communities in which they resided and his findings are confirmed by the work of other historians. Some Lollards were nothing less than pillars of the establishment, serving as churchwardens, guild officers and burgesses, assisting with the upkeep of civic and ecclesiastical buildings, and bequeathing money in their wills for the maintenance of highways and paupers. In 1544, Roger Bennet, for instance, not only left 4*d* to the high altar of Amersham, but donated a cloth to cover it worth 3*s* 4*d*, while a year earlier Roger Collins of East Hendred in Oxfordshire had willingly contributed to a collection for a new casting of the parish church's great bell.[242] Like William Sweeting of Colchester, several heretics seem to have been quite happy to occupy the post of holy water clerk and in 1518 one Henry Phip of Hughenden was appointed keeper of the rood light.[243] Such examples bear out Richard Davies's claim that few Lollards seem to have sought 'to operate against the grain of local society'.[244]

The case of the Family of Love provides further support for this insight. Chris Marsh has meticulously reconstructed the multiple ways in which Hendrick Niclaes's disciples participated in the life of Balsham and other villages in the diocese of Ely. Familists may have pursued a strictly endogamous marriage policy, seeking partners within the incestuous circle of their secretive sect, but their 'collective introversion' in the sphere of interpersonal relations was balanced by an equally energetic integration with the world around them. They too duly paid their church rates, made gifts to the poor, helped to run manorial courts and charities, and took on a variety of temporal and ecclesiastical offices from bailiff and constable to questman and churchwarden. Their involvement in these social and political networks not only had 'a significant self-protecting effect'; it also reflected a genuine sense of belonging to the community.[245]

When their activities are subjected to close scrutiny, Catholics too often prove to be far from the insular and aloof figures of popular myth. Wealthy gentlemen with large country estates may have had the resources and disposition necessary to live a secluded existence, but there is much to suggest that those who inhabited villages and market towns immersed themselves fully in the regular round of parochial and civic activities. Here the hypothetical cases of conscience studied by seminary priests in the course of their training to return as missionaries to England are especially revealing. They suggest indirectly that in the spheres of business, hospitality, law, entertainment and local government zealous Catholics could find ways of rubbing along legitimately with the heretics who lived all around them. To read between the lines of these documents is to catch sight of recusants acting as godparents to the children of Protestants, presenting ministers to benefices, involving themselves in local politics, serving meat to their Calvinist visitors on fast days, and turning a tactful deaf ear to sacrilegious prayers and graces said when they sat down to meals in mixed company. It is to see them paying tithes, repairing windows in ecclesiastical buildings, and participating in seasonal pastimes in church buildings and yards.[246] The Yorkshire recusant Richard Shanne evidently played a full part in the annual perambulation of the parish of Methley, an event accompanied by the hearty partaking of 'good store of Cakes', 'beare' and 'Ayle' with his Protestant neighbours: he described the circuit in his commonplace book in detail and lamented the demise of this traditional ceremony after a 'yonge headed fellowe' who objected to its drunken and disorderly elements was installed as the curate.[247]

The prevalence of mixed marriages is another index of the extent to which recusants and church papists were bound to the communities within which they lived by ties of affection and obligation. The missionary priests frowned upon this sinful practice, declaring it a 'profanation of the sacrament', but the prohibition was commonly disregarded. A casuist's claim around 1580 that it was 'nowe a dayes made no matter of Conscience, or a Trifle' is amply borne out by the evidence that can be extracted from parish registers and the matriculation records of novice seminarians, whose parents not infrequently came from both sides of the confessional fence. The continuing disapproval of the clergy did little to inhibit such matches in late seventeenth-century Wiltshire, as in many other counties.[248]

Such gestures of good will undoubtedly made it difficult for the orthodox to identify these individuals as alien outsiders. It is also clear that many Catholics continued to utilise the Church of England's social services, baptising their children, wedding their spouses and burying their dead, using Anglican rites of passage.[249] This had a double purpose: as well as deflecting the charge of 'fornication' that might befall those who married clandestinely and avoiding the eschatalogical perils of being interred in unconsecrated ground, it simultaneously wove them into a wider network of neighbourly relations. In a microscopic study of Linton in Cambridgeshire, Andrzej Bida has discovered that Elizabethan papists made bequests to alleviate poverty, appointed Protestants as the executors of their wills, and even left small legacies to the vicar, while Malcolm Wanklyn has shown that in late seventeenth-century Madeley in Shropshire recusants consistently sent their wives to be churched after childbirth.[250] In these ways Catholics fulfilled their responsibilities as good citizens and neighbours and prevented themselves from becoming social pariahs.

Historians of nonconformity in its local context have reached similar conclusions. Careful analysis of county archives has led Bill Stevenson and Adrian Davies to question the traditional picture of Restoration dissenters as closed sects living in self-imposed apartheid. Once again these groups seem to have pursued deliberate strategies of social integration. Drawing back from the aggressive and outrageous evangelism which had characterised the first decade of the movement, the Society of Friends began to devise methods of reconciling faithful witness with participation in secular affairs. Scaling down 'the Lamb's War' and seeking to repackage themselves as a peaceable people, from the 1660s onwards, they too accepted parish office, witnessed Anglican wills and made charitable bequests to the sick and needy. The clothier John Freeborn, for instance, set aside funds for 'four score sixpenny loaves' for the hungry of Witham in 1674. In Harwich and Kirby in Essex in the 1680s Quaker cobblers did not disdain to mend the shoes of Church of England ministers and in Stanstead a Quaker chandler supplied the vicar with paper and candles for sixteen years from 1692. As Richard Barclay assured the Friends in 1678, they could mix and converse with the world because they were 'inwardly redeemed out of it'.[251]

Baptists likewise forged bonds with their neighbours in a variety of areas, offering their services as surveyors of highways, vermin destroyers, overseers of the poor and law enforcers. Richard Marchant, a yeoman of Ditchling whose house was licensed for meetings in 1672 served in a succession of such offices during that decade. Nor did many spurn social gatherings: the Fenstanton Baptist John Blowes was 'one of the principal appointers' of a village football match in 1658 and cases may be cited of others joining with 'vain' and 'carnal' non-believers on outings to fairs and alehouses.[252] If, like the Familists, members of both of these sects tended to marry fellow believers, this evidently did not mean that they isolated themselves from their peers and led secluded and sequestered lives. It is apparent that large numbers of Baptists continued to be married in parish churches: John Caffyn, who has calculated that in Sussex some 70 per cent were conducted in Anglican buildings in the period up to 1754, is emphatic that this was less a formality than a measure of their wish to remain part of village society.[253] In part these policies of collaboration and fraternisation were a conscious attempt to limit and alleviate dissenters' sufferings under the Clarendon Code, but they also both reflected and fostered a sincere commitment to the wider community, which in turn must have functioned as a powerful disincentive to outbursts of hostility against them. In short, they may have helped to neutralise the impulse to persecute and to nurture a climate of tolerance.

On the other hand, dissenters who systematically spurned interaction with orthodox society for fear of spiritual defilement were likely to provoke the irritation and anger of the communities in which they resided. To separate oneself from false believers in the mundane transactions that marked every-day life was to behave in a way which was inimical to good neighbourly relations. The Catholic Anne Petre, for instance, can hardly have endeared herself to local Protestants by blessing herself and uttering prophylactic prayers every time their minister approached, 'as apprehending such persons [were] attended with numbers of evill spirits'.[254] The anti-social stance of Quakers and Baptists who sought to keep themselves 'unspotted of the world' by disdaining to participate in communal activities and in the rituals which surrounded birth, marriage and death must likewise have rankled.[255] Evidence of this 'severe ethic of exclusivism' can also be found among the early Protestants: in the 1550s, for instance, the Kentish Freewillers 'affirmed as a generall doctryne that they oughte not to salute a synner'.[256]

But it was among puritans that rejecting fellowship with the 'unfruiful works of darkness' took its most classic form. As early as 1586 John Udall's flock refused to mix with the impious and took communion separately, and in a Star Chamber case of 1591, a London minister commented upon 'those seekers of reformation' who refrained ('as much as they might convenyently') from interacting with 'persons which are not of their faccion and opynions or inclyning that waye'. A particular manifestation of this attitude was refusal to join with the unregenerate in holy communion. As Richard Bancroft remarked sarcastically, 'most of them will not communicate with anye, but such as are of their owne crew'.[257] Where a parish was served by a puritan incumbent this could result in the wholesale exclusion of the visibly ignorant and unworthy from the Lord's Table, as in the Essex village of East Hanningfield in the mid-1580s.[258] In 1623 a self-selected congregation of the godly in Chelmsford went one step further towards ghettoisation, resolving to nail shut the gates in the fence that segregated the houses of profane tipplers and carnal professors from the children of light, lest they be disturbed during divine worship.[259]

This policy of ostracism was a curious by-product of puritan ecclesiology. Separatists who obeyed the command to 'come out from among them ... and touch no unclean thing' by formally withdrawing from the Church of England were taught that in 'civill affayres' it was permissible to converse with the wicked in peace, 'as to eat and drink with them, buy and sell, make covenants of peace, shew kindness to them, pity their estate, love them, relieve their wants, and receive from them for our own relief ...' For puritans compelled by their own principles to mingle promiscuously with the impious multitude in public worship, by contrast, it was necessary to avoid 'voluntary society with the incorrigible'. Only by ostentatiously shunning the ungodly, by strictly eschewing 'familiar accompanying in private conversation', could they comply with the biblical injunction to quarantine themselves from sin and idolatry. The Gloucestershire minister John Sprint explained: '[W]e suffer for separating in the Church', 'We professe separation from known evilles, but not from the churches of Christ for evilles among them'.[260] As Patrick Collinson has argued, the puritan position was probably far 'more threatening to the general tranquillity and wellbeing of society' than that of their separatist brethren.[261] The Presbyterian Richard Baxter would recall how he and his family were derided 'under the odious name of a puritan' by fellow inhabitants of Kidderminster, irked by their ardent piety and god-fearing lifestyle. This in turn did much to 'alienate me from them'. By renouncing dancing and drinking for sermon-gadding and Scripture-reading, such individuals were implicitly setting themselves up as 'alternative societies'.[262] Like inward-looking stranger communities who sought to preserve their separate identity by marrying within their own ranks and who clung on to their own language and customs as talismans, puritans who called their children by peculiar baptismal names like Flee-Sin, Much-Mercy, Obedience and Praise-God were exposing themselves and their offspring to allegations of self-righteous insularity, not to say contempt and mockery.[263] As we saw in Chapter 3, people who deliberately estranged themselves from their neighbours were liable to be made into scapegoats. Rigid application of the precept that it was 'extreme perilous to be sociable with wicked men, their society being dangerous and infectious'[264] can only have been corrosive of social concord. Provoking resentment and friction, it surely created the preconditions in which periodic outbursts of aggression arose. Patrick Collinson suggests it was a crucial catalyst to England's wars of religion.[265]

It is wrong, then, to set up the impulses of assimilation and segregation, resistance and compromise, in opposition, as they operated in tandem and were dialectically linked. All minorities had to negotiate the tension between the competing imperatives of survival and the need to maintain a firm sense of their separate identity. The various strategies they developed in response to this both fostered and defused religious intolerance. In complex and contra-dictory ways, they simultaneously laid the foundations for renewed spasms of persecution and for peaceful coexistence and toleration.

One further paradox deserves some attention before this chapter can be brought to a close. As we have seen, the challenges involved in living in a context of official and popular hostility often precipitated significant frictions and divisions within the ranks of minority churches and sects. In the minds of individuals, they gave rise to delicate and difficult moral dilemmas that only added to the stresses and strains of adhering to an illegal creed. And yet the experience of persecution was at the same time immensely empowering. A sense of suffering at the hands of ruthless authorities and a rabid populace became a critical element in the self-definition of dissenting communities. It gave them what Gabriel Audisio has called a 'superiority complex'.[266] Armed with consoling passages from the Bible, such groups believed that their trials and tribulations were evidence of divine approbation: as the Gospels taught them, Christ's disciples could only expect to be hated, repressed and despised. Those 'whom the Lord loveth he chasteneth, and scourgeth every son whom he receiveth' (Hebrews 12: 6). Following the example of Job, they embraced their afflictions with patience, as proof of their adherence to the single true religion. Equating themselves with the Old Testament Israelites and with the congregations of primitive Christians, they regarded their adversities as an indisputable sign that they alone were God's chosen people.

Such convictions find constant expression in the literature engendered by sixteenth- and seventeenth-century religious minorities. Poignantly echoing the language of St Paul's epistles to the congregations of the early Christians in Corinth, Ephesus, Galatia and Thessalonika, the pastoral letters which the leaders of such movements sent to their flocks imbued their recipients with the belief that they too would be rewarded for their constancy. Coloured by a spirit of defiance against the oppressions of the 'prelati', Lollard writings began in 'apostollycal fashyon'; the early Protestants, puritans and separatists addressed many similar missives to their afflicted brethren; so too did Catholic priests, Presbyterian pastors, Quaker evangelists and Baptist ministers.[267] The potent themes of suffering and redemption suffused the poetry and prose such men and women wrote in prison and exile, as well as the ballads, motets, psalms and songs they composed and performed in private homes and conventicles to console themselves. In the internal histories they compiled to inspire later generations, the metaphors of catacombs and upper rooms are ever present. Many dissenters seem to have positively relished their afflictions and gloried in what they thought of as the 'Lord's winnowing and sifting'.[268] A sense of suffering at the hands of their confessional enemies was a critical element of the self-definition of such communities. In short, there is a distinct sense in which religious minorities thrived on persecution.

The consequence of this was that many found it difficult to adjust to victory. Reversals of fortune that transformed a repressed sect into a dominant church brought their own trials and tribulations. Illegality gave dissident faiths like early Protestantism a charisma and cachet that was difficult to retain or recapture when institutionalisation set in: they lost the appeal of an exotic forbidden fruit which had initially made them such a magnet for the youthful and adventurous. With the triumph of the Reformation this mantle passed to the Catholics and contributed significantly to swelling the ranks of the Jesuits and seminary priests intent upon returning to their native land as missionaries, notwithstanding the formidable risks.[269] Half a century earlier, Edwardian Protestants were reluctant to relinquish the image of being the 'poor persecuted flock of Christ' which had sustained them during their years in the wilderness, despite the fact that it did not fit with their objective situation. The tensions associated with the transition from embattled creed to official religion were temporarily resolved when the young Josiah died and his implacably Catholic half sister acceded.[270] The predestinarian tenets that shaped the outlook of puritans also gave rise to a kind of siege mentality: the sense of being a tiny remnant surrounded by a sea of hostile adversaries and engaged in a constant struggle to vanquish the forces of the devil and Antichrist was no less essential to their identity. 'This experience of oppression, real or imagined, was needed as convincing evidence of election.'[271] Temperamentally and theologically, Calvinism was particularly well suited to the condition of adversity.[272]

Anglicans too revelled in their troubles during the Civil War, Republic and Interregnum. The relative tolerance they enjoyed at the hands of the Cromwellian regime was no bar to the development of a sense of 'mental exile'. Ejected ministers averred that the sufferings of the Church would make it 'appear more glorious and celestial, when these black clouds and fogs shall be dissolved and scattered into nothing' and the beleaguered Book of Common Prayer was celebrated as a work of inspired creativity forged in the crucible of the Marian persecutions by Thomas Cranmer.[273] The cult of the royal martyr proved a huge asset to this institution after it reassumed the reins of power in 1662. It allowed it to perpetuate a sense of that heroic suffering from which the dissenters it would soon begin to oppress more frequently benefited.[274] Finally, we may note that the Act of Toleration presented many nonconformists with particular psychological challenges. Accustomed to taking up the cross in defence of their faith, Baptists, Presbyterians and Quakers were disconcerted by their new-found, albeit relative, liberty and freedom. As I suggest in Chapter 6, in the absence of persecution, they were often obliged to reinvent or imagine it. Firstly, however, we turn to examine the chequered careers of the theory and practice of tolerance in the sixteenth and seventeenth centuries.

NOTES

1 Peter Martyr Vermigli, *A treatise of the cohabitacyon of the faithfull with the unfaithfull* ([Strassburg, 1555]).

2 See Thomas Wood, *English Casuistical Divinity during the Seventeenth Century* (London, 1952); Edmund Leites (ed.), *Conscience and Casuistry in Early Modern Europe* (Cambridge, 1988); Lowell Gallagher, *Medusa's Gaze: Casuistry and Conscience in the Renaissance* (Stanford, 1991); Keith Thomas, 'Cases of conscience in seventeenth-century England', in John Morrill, Paul Slack and Daniel Woolf (eds), *Public Duty and Private Conscience in Seventeenth-Century England* (Oxford, 1993), pp. 29–56.

3 Brigden, *London and the Reformation*, p. 86; Hudson, *Premature Reformation*, p. 161.

4 Knott, *Discourses of Martyrdom*, p. 58; A. Townsend (ed.), *The Writings of John Bradford*, PS, 2 vols (Cambridge, 1848, 1853), ii, p. 227; Muriel McClendon, *The Quiet Reformation: Magistrates and the Emergence of Protestantism in Tudor Norwich* (Stanford, CA, 1999), p. 175.

5 Foxe, *Actes and monuments* (1563 edn), p. 1036.

6 Gregory, *Salvation at Stake*, p. 279; [John Geninges], *The life and death of Mr Edmund Geninges priest, crowned with martyrdome at London* (St Omers, 1614), pp. 76–7.

7 J. H. Pollen (ed.), *Unpublished Documents Relating to the English Martyrs. I. 1584–1603*, CRS 5 (London, 1908), pp. 200, 203.

8 Historical Manuscripts Commission, *Various Collections*, p. 124; BL, Additional MS 39830, fo. 87r.

9 Leland H. Carlson (ed.), *The Writings of John Greenwood and Henry Barrow 1591–1593*, English Nonconformist Texts 6 (London, 1970), pp. 380–1.

10 Carlson (ed.), *Writings of ... Barrow 1587–1590*, p. 117.

11 Albert Peel (ed.), *The Second Parte of a Register Being a Calendar of Manuscripts under that Title Intended for Publication by the Puritans about 1593*, 2 vols (Cambridge, 1915), i. 221; ii. 28–35, 261.

12 Collinson, *Elizabethan Puritan Movement*, p. 152.

13 Seaver, *Wallington's World*, p. 150.

14 Maltby, "'The good old way'", pp. 240–1.

15 Watts, *Dissenters*, p. 227.

16 White, *English Baptists*, p. 114; John Stachniewski with Anita Pacheco (ed.), *Grace Abounding with Other Spiritual Autobiographies* (Oxford, 1998), pp. 87–93, at p. 89.

17 See, for instance, Seymour Bryan, 'Ritualistic acts and compulsive behaviour: the pattern of Tudor martyrdom', *American Historical Review*, 83 (1978), 625–43.

18 Marsh, *Family of Love*, p. 94, n. 67; Hamilton, *Family of Love*, p. 127.

19 Hugh Latimer, *Sermons and Remains*, ed. G. E. Corrie (Cambridge, 1845), pp. 222–3.

20 Ryrie, *Gospel and Henry VIII*, p. 72.

21 Hide, *Consolatorie epistle*, sig. B2r.

22 Gregory, *Salvation at Stake*, pp. 280–1.

23 Dillon, *Construction of Martyrdom*, p. 372.

24 William Tyndale, *The Obedience of a Christian Man*, ed. David Daniell (Harmondsworth, 2000), p. 10. See also Robert Kolb, 'God's gift of martyrdom: the early Reformation understanding of dying for the faith', *Church History*, 64 (1995), 399–411.

25 Hunt, *Puritan Moment*, p. 88.

26 Carlson (ed.), *Writings of ... Barrow 1587–1590*, p. 113.

27 Thomas More, *Dialoge of comfort against tribulacion* (London, first publ. 1553); Richard Tracy, *Of the preparation to the crosse* (London, 1540); John Bunyan, *Seasonable counsel: or, advice to sufferers* (London, 1684), sig. A4r.

28 Gregory, *Salvation at Stake*, esp. ch. 4.

29 Donald R. Kelley, 'Martyrs, myths, and the massacre: the background of St Bartholomew', *American Historical Review*, 77 (1972), 1328.

30 Gregory, *Salvation at Stake*, p. 277.

31 Foxe, *Actes and monuments* (1570 edn), ii. 1662, 1172, 1804 respectively.

32 Foxe, *Actes and monuments*, ii. 2067.

33 Lake and Questier, 'Agency, appropriation, and rhetoric', p. 77; John Mush, 'A true report of the life and martyrdom of Mrs Margaret Clitherow', in Morris (ed.), *Troubles of our Catholic Forefathers*, iii. 432; Pollen (ed.), *Unpublished Documents*, pp. 357–8.

34 Ingram, 'Shame and pain', p. 50.

35 Stephen Foster, *Notes from the Caroline Underground: Alexander Leighton, the Puritan Triumvirate and the Laudian Reaction to Nonconformity* (Hamden, CT, 1978), pp. 33–4.

36 Seaver, *Wallington's World*, p. 159; Samuel Rawson Gardiner (ed.), *Documents Relating to the Proceedings against William Prynne in 1634 and 1637*, Camden Society, NS 18 (1877), p. 90.

37 Knott, *Discourses of Martyrdom*, p. 220; J. Deacon, *An exact history of the life of James Naylor* (London, [1657]), pp. 35–6.

38 *ODNB*, xxi. 650–1.

39 Dawson, 'Scottish Reformation and the theatre of martyrdom', p. 263.

40 Loades, *Oxford Martyrs*, p. 242; David Loades, *The Mid-Tudor Crisis, 1545–1565* (London, 1992), p. 154.

41 Nicholls, 'Theatre of martyrdom', 58.

42 Bellamy, *Tudor Law of Treason*, p. 191.

43 Ryrie, *Gospel and Henry VIII*, p. 70.

44 T. F. Knox (ed.), *Letters and Memorials of William Cardinal Allen 1532–1594* (London, 1882), p. 148; Nancy Pollard Brown, 'Robert Southwell: the mission of the written word', in Thomas M. McCoog (ed.), *The Reckoned Expense: Edmund Campion and the Early English Jesuits* (Woodbridge, 1996), pp. 193–213, at p. 195.

45 Gregory, *Salvation at Stake*, p. 283.

46 Dillon, *Construction of Martyrdom*, ch. 2; Alexandra Walsham, 'Miracles and the Counter Reformation Mission to England', *HJ*, 46 (2003), 779–815, esp. 789–96.

47 Miles Huggarde, *The displaying of protestantes* (London, 1556), p. 54; Foxe, *Actes and Monuments* (1583 edn), p. 2004.

48 Hudson, *Premature Reformation*, p. 172.

49 Richard Rex, 'Which is Wyche? Lollardy and sanctity in Lancastrian London', in Thomas S. Freeman and Thomas Mayer (eds), *Sanctity and Martyrdom in Early Modern England* (Woodbridge, forthcoming). I am grateful to the author for allowing me to read this in advance of publication.

50 Petti (ed.), *Letters and Despatches of Richard Verstegan*, pp. 114, 117; Spurr, *English Puritanism*, p. 91.

51 Caraman (ed.), *Other Face*, p. 79.

52 Alastair Bellany, 'Libels in action: ritual, subversion and the English literary underground, 1603–42', in Tim Harris (ed.), *The Politics of the Excluded, c.1500–1850* (Basingstoke, 2001), pp. 111–12; John Fielding, 'Opposition to the Personal Rule of Charles I: the diary of Robert Woodford, 1637–1641', *Historical Journal*, 31 (1988), 769–88, at 780.

53 Underwood (ed.), *Acts of the Witnesses*, p. 77.

54 *A miracle of miracles: wrought by the blood of King Charles the first* (London, 1649). See also Lacey, *Cult of King Charles the Martyr*, pp. 62–4.

55 Spurr, *Restoration Church*, pp. 96–7.

56 Hudson, *Premature Reformation*, pp. 220–2; Dillon, *Construction of Martyrdom*, pp. 45–7; A. G. Dickens and John Tonkin, 'Weapons of propaganda: the martyrologies', in *The Reformation in Historical Thought* (Oxford, 1985), pp. 39–57, at pp. 52–3.

57   Cameron, 'Medieval heretics as Protestant martyrs'; Collinson, 'Truth and legend'.

58   Dillon, *Construction of Martyrdom*, ch. 2.

59   *A parte of a register, contayninge sundrie memorable matters* (Middelburg, [1593?]); Peel (ed.), *Seconde Parte of a Register*.

60   Edmund Calamy, *An abridgement of Mr Baxter's history of his life and times ... With an account of many others of those worthy ejected ministers who were ejected, after the restauration of King Charles the second* (London, 1702); John Walker, *Attempt towards recovering an account of the numbers and sufferings of the clergy of the Church of England ... who were sequestr'd, harass'd, etc, in the late ... grand rebellion* (London, 1714). On the former, see David L. Wykes, ' "To let the memory of these men dye is injurious to posterity": Edmund Calamy's "Account" of the Ejected Ministers', in R. N. Swanson (ed.), *The Church Retrospective*, SCH 33 (Oxford, 1997), pp. 379–92. On the latter, which consciously sought to eschew the Foxeian martyrological tradition in favour of Baconian empiricism, see Burke W. Griggs, 'Remembering the puritan past: John Walker and Anglican memories of the English Civil War', in McClendon, Ward and MacDonald (eds), *Protestant Identities*, pp. 158–91.

61   Joseph Besse, *A collection of the sufferings of the people called Quakers*, 2 vols (London, 1753). See also J. R. Knott, 'Joseph Besse and the Quaker Culture of Suffering', in T. Corns and D. Loewenstein (eds), *The Emergence of Quaker Writing: Dissenting Literature in Seventeenth Century England* (London, 1995), pp. 126–41.

62   *Eikon Basilike. The portraiture of his sacred majextie in his solitudes and suffering* (1649). See Lacey, *Cult of King Charles the Martyr*, esp. ch. 4.

63   For some aspects of the English response, see Dickens, 'Elizabethans and St Bartholomew'. On the Irish Rebellion, MacCuarta (ed.), *Ulster 1641*; Canny, *Making Ireland British*, ch. 8.

64   Dillon, *Construction of Martyrdom*, chs 3–5, quotation at p. 276. See also Christopher Highley, 'Richard Verstegan's Book of Martyrs' and Richard Williams, '"Libels and payntinges": Elizabethan Catholics and the international campaign of visual propaganda', both in Christopher Highley and John N. King (eds), *John Foxe and his World* (Aldershot, 2002), pp. 183–97 and 198–215 respectively. For a more cautious assessment, and emphasis on the ways in which the representation of martyrdom became a tool of intra-confessional dispute between Jesuits and Appellants, see Thomas M. McCoog, 'Construing martyrdom in the English Catholic community 1582-1602', in Shagan (ed.) *Catholics and the Protestant Nation'*, pp. 95–127.

65   Elizabeth Ingram and Margaret Aston, 'The iconography of the *Acts and Monuments*', in David Loades (ed.), *John Foxe and the English Reformation* (Aldershot, 1997), pp. 66–142.

66   See, for instance, Arthur M. Hind, *Engraving in England in the Sixteenth and Seventeenth Centuries*, 3 vols (Cambridge, 1952–64), iii. 333 (plate 178); Frederick George Stephens, *Catalogue of Political and Personal Satires Preserved in the Department of Prints and Drawings in the British Museum*, vol. I, *1320–1689* (London, 1870), nos 137–40.

67   Alan Marshall, 'To make a martyr: the Popish Plot and Protestant propaganda', *History Today*, 47 (March, 1997), 39–45.

68   Stephens, *Catalogue of Satires*, nos 1169–73.

69   Tyndale, *Obedience*, pp. 36, 181.

70   Elton (ed.), *Tudor Constitution*, p. 15.

71 Tyndale, *Obedience*, pp. 57–8; Joy Shakespeare, 'Plague and punishment', in Peter Lake and Maria Dowling (eds), *Protestantism and the National Church in Sixteenth-Century England* (London, 1987), pp. 103–23, esp. 115–16.

72 White, *English Separatist Tradition*, p. 89.

73 Lake and Questier, 'Agency, appropriation, and rhetoric', pp. 78–9.

74 Braithwaite, *Beginnings of Quakerism*, pp. 466–7.

75 Aston, 'Lollardy and sedition'; Hudson, *Premature Reformation*, ch. 8, esp. pp. 363–7.

76 White, *English Separatist Tradition*, p. 10.

77 J. S. Cockburn (ed.), *Calendar of Assize Records: Essex Indictments: Elizabeth I* (London, 1978), pp. 213–14.

78 Lake, 'Anti-popery', pp. 86–7; Collinson, *Religion of Protestants*, p. 177.

79 For a survey of the debates surrounding the character of these episodes, see Anthony Fletcher and Diarmaid MacCulloch, *Tudor Rebellions* (Harlow, 4th edn, 1997), chs 4, 5, 7, 8.

80 One William Tessimond was presented to the High Commission for this offence in 1572: Borthwick Institute of Historical Research, York, High Commission Act Book 1572–4, fo. 40r–v.

81 John Bossy, 'The heart of Robert Persons', in Thomas McCoog (ed.), *The Reckoned Expense: Edmund Campion and the Early English Jesuits* (Woodbridge, 1996), pp. 141–58; Eamon Duffy, 'William, Cardinal Allen, 1532–1594', *RH*, 22 (1995), 265–90. See also Michael L. Carrafiello, 'English Catholicism and the Jesuit mission of 1580–1581', *HJ*, 37 (1994), 761–74, for the more extreme claim that the avowedly political aims of the mission were cunningly disguised by spiritual language.

82 P. J. Holmes, *Resistance and Compromise: The Political Thought of the Elizabethan Catholics* (Cambridge, 1982), ch. 16; Michael Questier, 'Practical anti-papistry during the reign of Elizabeth I', *JBS*, 36 (1997), 371–96; idem 'Elizabeth and the Catholics' in Shagan (ed.), *Catholics and the Protestant Nation*, pp. 69–94. For the older view that lay Catholicism was essentially quiescent, see, for instance, Arnold Pritchard, *Catholic Loyalism in Elizabethan England* (London, 1979), esp. ch. 3.

83 Sandeep Kaushik, 'Resistance, loyalty and recusant politics: Sir Thomas Tresham and the Elizabethan state', *Midland History*, 21 (1996), 37–72, at 63.

84 See Walsham, ' "Frantick Hacket" '.

85 See Peter Lake, 'Defining puritanism – again?', in Francis J. Bremer (ed.), *Puritanism: Transatlantic Perspectives on a Seventeenth-Century Anglo-American Faith* (Boston, 1993), pp. 3–29; Lake, *Boxmaker's Revenge*.

86 Watts, *Dissenters*, pp. 222–3; Capp, *Fifth Monarchy Men*, pp. 115–18. See also Richard L. Greaves, *Deliver us from Evil: The Radical Underground in Britain, 1660–1663* (New York, 1986).

87 Harris, 'Bawdy house riots', 540 and *passim*.

88 Gary S. De Krey, 'The first Restoration crisis: conscience and coercion in London, 1667–73', *Albion*, 25 (1993), 565–80, at 570–1.

89 Watts, *Dissenters*, p. 256. See also Peter Earle, *Monmouth's Rebels: The Road to Sedgemoor, 1685* (London, 1977); Robin Clifton, *The Last Popular Rebellion: The Western Rising of 1685* (London, 1984).

90 Gerry Bowler, 'Marian Protestants and the idea of violent resistance', in Lake and Dowling (eds), *Protestantism and the National Church*, pp. 124–43; Quentin Skinner, *The Foundations of Modern Political Thought*, 2 vols (Cambridge, 1978), ii, ch. 7, esp. pp. 227–30; Robert M. Kingdon, 'Calvinism and resistance theory, 1550–1580', in J. H. Burns with Mark Goldie (eds), *The Cambridge History of Political Thought 1450–1700* (Cambridge, 1991), pp. 194–200.

91 Gerald Bowler, '"An axe or an acte": the parliament of 1572 and resistance theory in early Elizabethan England', *Canadian Journal of History*, 19 (1984), 349–59; Collinson, 'Elizabethan exclusion crisis', 84–5; Collinson, 'Monarchical republic', esp. pp. 43–6.

92 Holmes, *Resistance and Compromise*, chs 11–14; J. H. M. Salmon, 'Catholic resistance theory, ultramontanism, and the royalist response, 1580–1620', in Burns with Goldie (eds), *Cambridge History of Political Thought*, pp. 241–4, quotation at p. 242.

93 I refer to a forthcoming doctoral dissertation entitled 'Early Elizabethan resistance thinking, 1558–c.1587', by Elisabeth von Glinski of the University of Heidelberg, with whom I have benefited from discussing this subject.

94 Beza quoted in Kelley, 'Martyrs', p. 1340. For the French literature, see Skinner, *Foundations*, ch. 9, esp. pp. 302–38; Kingdon, 'Calvinist resistance theory', pp. 206–14.

95 Crawford, ' "Charles Stuart, that man of blood" '; 'A declaration of the English army now in Scotland, 1 August 1650', in Kenyon (ed.), *Stuart Constitution* (1st edn), pp. 325–6. For a concise account of civil war resistance theory, see Glenn Burgess, 'The impact on political thought: rhetorics for troubled times', in John Morrill (ed.), *The Impact of the English Civil War* (London, 1991), pp. 67–83.

96 Champlin Burrage, 'The Fifth Monarchy insurrections', *EHR*, 25 (1910), 722–47, at 740.

97 Capp, *Fifth Monarchy Men*, p. 116; Gary S. de Krey, 'Rethinking the Restoration: Dissenting Cases for Conscience, 1667–1672', *HJ*, 38 (1995), 53–83, at 71.

98 David Daniell, *William Tyndale: A Biography* (London, 1994), chs 5–6, 15.

99 Ryrie, *Gospel and Henry VIII*, ch. 3, at p. 111.

100 Maria Dowling and Joy Shakespeare (eds), 'Religion and politics in mid Tudor England through the eyes of an English Protestant woman: the recollections of Rose Hickman', *Bulletin of the Institute of Historical Research*, 55 (1982), 94–108, at 100. More generally, see Garrett's (now somewhat dated) *Marian Exiles*; Frederick Abbott Norwood, *Strangers and Exiles: A History of Religious Refugees*, 2 vols (Nashville, TN, 1969), pt ii, ch. 13; Nicola M. Sutherland, 'The Marian exiles and the establishment of the Elizabethan regime', *Archive für Reformationsgeschichte*, 78 (1987), 253–87; Andrew Pettegree, 'The Marian exiles and the Elizabethan Settlement', in his *Marian Protestantism*, pp. 129–50; Andrew Pettegree, *Emden and the Dutch Revolt: Exile and the Development of Reformed Protestantism* (Oxford, 1992), ch. 8.

101 On Henrician exiles, see Shagan, *Popular Politics*, pp. 124–6; Peter Marshall, 'Catholic exiles', in his *Religious Identities in Henry VIII's England* (Aldershot, forthcoming 2005) For the Edwardian exiles, see Brigden, *London and the Reformation*, pp. 453–4.

102 Catherine Gibbons is currently completing a York PhD thesis on 'The experience of exile and English Catholics: Paris in the 1580s, which promises to revise completing confessional depictions of Catholics abroad as either martyrs or traitors and offer a more nuanced picture of their significance for and within the English Catholic

community. Older studies include Peter Guilday, *The English Catholic Refugees on the Continent 1558–1795* (London, 1914); A. J. Loomie, *The Spanish Elizabethans: The English Exiles at the Court of Philip II* (New York, 1963); Norwood, *Strangers and Exiles*, pt ii, ch. 15. On female religious, see Claire Walker, *Gender and Politics in Early Modern Europe: English Convents in France and the Low Countries* (Basingstoke, 2003), esp. ch. 1.

103 Caraman (ed.), *Other Face*, p. 141.

104 J. D. Krugler, 'Lord Baltimore, Roman Catholics and toleration: religious policy in Maryland during the early Catholic years, 1634–1649', *Catholic Historical Review*, 65 (1979), 49–75.

105 White, *English Separatist Tradition, passim*, quotation p. 49; Tolmie, *Triumph of the Saints*, p. 2. See also Keith L. Sprunger, *Dutch Puritanism: A History of English and Scottish Churches of the Netherlands in the Sixteenth and Seventeenth Centuries* (Leiden, 1982).

106 Watts, *Dissenters*, pp. 63–4 and see pp. 62–6.

107 'John Dane, 'A declaration of remarkabell provedenses in the corse of my lyfe', *New England Historical and Geneaological Register*, 8 (1854), 147–56, at 154.

108 David Cressy, *Coming Over: Migration and Communication between England and New England in the Seventeenth Century* (Cambridge, 1987), pp. 87–8.

109 Avihu Zakai, *Exile and Kingdom: History and Apocalypse in the Puritan Migration to America* (Cambridge, 1992), pp. 208 and 193–4 respectively.

110 See *ibid.*, chs 5–7; Cressy, *Coming Over*, ch. 3; Susan Hardmann Moore, 'Popery, purity and providence: deciphering the New England experiment', in Anthony Fletcher and Peter Roberts (eds), *Religion, Culture and Society in Early Modern Britain: Essays in Honour of Patrick Collinson* (Cambridge, 1994), pp. 257–89, esp. 271–2. See also Sharpe, *Personal Rule*, pp. 751–7.

111 N. H. Keeble, *The Literary Culture of Nonconformity in Later Seventeenth Century England* (Leicester, 1987), p. 48.

112 On biblical and patristic precedents, see Norwood, *Strangers and Exiles*, pt I, chs 1–4; Alvyn Pettersen, '"To flee or not to flee": an assessment of Athanasius's *De fuga sua*', in Sheils (ed.), *Persecution and Toleration*, pp. 29–42.

113 Garrett, *Marian Exiles*, p. 40.

114 Carlos M. N. Eire, *War against the Idols: The Reformation of Worship from Erasmus to Calvin* (Cambridge, 1986), pp. 260–4; Jonathan Wright, 'Marian exiles and the legitimacy of flight from persecution', *JEH*, 52 (2001), 220–43, at 229.

115 Wright, 'Marian exiles', 237–8.

116 Ryrie, *Gospel and Henry VIII*, p. 96.

117 Hide, *Consolatorie epistle*, sig. E7r.

118 Wright, 'Marian exiles', p. 232; Ryrie, *Gospel and Henry VIII*, p. 75.

119 See Webster, *Godly Clergy*, p. 274; Zakai, *Exile and Kingdom*, pp. 63–4.

120 Ole Peter Grell, 'Merchants and ministers: the foundations of international Calvinism', in Andrew Pettegree, Alastair Duke and Gillian Lewis (eds), *Calvinism in Europe 1540–1620* (Cambridge, 1994), pp. 254–73.

121 See, esp. Pettegree, *Emden*, pp. 237, 243, 249 and *passim*.

122 Wright, 'Marian exiles', pp. 224–5.

123 Webster, *Godly Clergy*, pp. 165–6. See also ch. 14.

124 Hardmann Moore, 'Popery, purity and providence', p. 284.

125 Collinson, 'Towards and a broader understanding of the early dissenting tradition', p. 533; Tolmie, *Triumph of the Saints*, pp. 70–1.

126 Holmes, *Resistance and Compromise*, p. 110.

127 Eire, *War against the Idols*, p. 263.

128 See John Gerard, *The Autobiography of an Elizabethan*, ed. Philip Caraman (London, 1951), pp. 32–3. See also Walsham, *Church Papists*, pp. 73–6.

129 Spurr, *English Puritanism*, p. 142.

130 Spaeth, *Church in an Age of Danger*, esp. p. 171; Spurr, *Restoration Church*, pp. 186–90.

131 Editorial preface to section III of Lake and Questier (eds.), *Conformity and Orthodoxy*, p. 209. See also Questier's essay, 'Conformity, Catholicism and the Law', pp. 237–61, in the same volume.

132 Hudson, *Premature Reformation*, p. 150. On Waldensian practices, see Gabriel Audisio, *The Waldensian Dissent: Persecution and Survival c. 1170–c.1570*, trans. Claire Davison (Cambridge, 1999), ch. 5.

133 John Fines, 'Heresy trials in the diocese of Coventry and Lichfield, 1511–12', *JEH*, 14 (1963), 160–74, at 167; Collinson, 'Night schools', p. 222.

134 Anne Hudson, 'A Lollard mass', repr. in her *Lollards and their Books* (London, 1985), pp. 111–23, at 118.

135 Hope, 'Lollardy', p. 15; Hudson, *Premature Reformation*, pp. 150–1.

136 Davis, *Heresy and Reformation*, p. 94.

137 Alexander, 'Bonner', p. 169.

138 John Bradford, *The hurte of heringe masse* ([London, 1561?]), sig. A4r.

139 Bridgen, *London and the Reformation*, p. 572.

140 On which see John Martin, *Venice's Hidden Enemies: Italian Heretics in a Renaissance City* (Berkeley, 1993), ch. 5; Eire, *War against the Idols*, ch. 7.

141 Robert Whiting, 'Local responses to the Reformation', in MacCulloch (ed.), *Reign of Henry VIII*, pp. 203–26, at 226.

142 See Walsham, *Church Papists*, esp. ch. 4.

143 For example, Cockburn (ed.), *Essex Indictments: Elizabeth I*, p. 428. See also Dorothy M. Clarke, 'Conformity certificates among the King's Bench records: a calendar', *Recusant History*, 14 (1977), 53–63.

144 Patrick McGrath and Joy Rowe, 'The recusancy of Sir Thomas Cornwallis', *Proceedings of the Suffolk Institute of Archaeology and History*, 28 (1961), 224–71, at 242. For another example, see James Raine (ed.), *Depositions and other Ecclesiastical Proceedings from the Courts of Durham, Extending from 1311 to the Reign of Elizabeth*, Surtees Society (London, 1845), p. 231.

145 Patrick Ryan, 'Diocesan returns of recusants for England and Wales 1577', in *Catholic Record Society Miscellanea XII* , CRS 22 (London, 1921), p. 79.

146 Henry Garnet, *An apology against the defence of schisme* ([London, 1593]), p. 62.

147 John Earle, *Microcosmography: or, a piece of the world discover'd* (London, 1732 edn; first publ. 1628), p. 28; Richard Baxter, *A key for Catholicks* (London, 1659), p. 337; [John Underdown], *The church papist* (London, 1681).

148 Edgar Samuel, 'London's Portuguese Jewish Community, 1540–1753', in Randolph Vigne and Charles Littleton (eds), *From Strangers to Citizens: The Integration of Immigrant Communities in Britain, Ireland and Colonial America, 1550–1750* (Brighton and Portland, 2001), pp. 239–46, at 239. See also Beverley Nenk, 'Public worship, private devotion: the crypto-Jews of Reformation England', in David Gaimster and Roberta Gilchrist (eds), *The Archaeology of Reformation 1480–1580* (Leeds, 2003), pp. 204–20, at 210.

149 Patrick Collinson, 'The cohabitation of the faithful with the unfaithful', in Grell, Israel and Tyacke (eds), *From Persecution to Toleration*, pp. 51–76, at p. 76.

150 As revealed by Marsh's detailed study of the records of Cambridgeshire Familism: see *Family of Love*, esp. p. 214.

151 Barry Reay, 'The Muggletonians: an introductory study', in Hill, Reay and Lamont (eds), *World of the Muggletonians*, pp. 45–6.

152 Smith, 'Staffordshire Roman Catholic recusants', 338–9.

153 Webster, *Godly Clergy*, pp. 228, 247–50.

154 Green, 'Persecution of … parish clergy', p. 513.

155 Spurr, *Restoration Church*, p. 206.

156 Watts, *Dissenters*, pp. 229–30; Spurr, *English Puritanism*, p. 135.

157 Spaeth, *Church in the Age of Danger*, p. 171.

158 David L. Wykes, 'Religious dissent and the penal laws: an explanation of business success?', *History*, 75 (1990), 39–62, at 48. See Keeble, *Literary Culture of Nonconformity*, pp. 36–7; Christopher Hill, 'Occasional Conformity and the Grindalian Tradition', repr. in his *Collected Essays*, vol. 2, *Religion and Politics in Seventeenth-Century England* (Hassocks, 1986), pp. 301–20; John Flaningham, 'The occasional conformity controversy: ideology and party politics, 1697–1711', *JBS*, 17 (1977–78), 38–62.

159 Wykes, 'Religious dissent', 48.

160 Davies, *Quakers*, pp. 183, 193.

161 Hudson, *Premature Reformation*, pp. 158–60.

162 Hamilton, *Family of Love*, p. 126.

163 Hill, *World Turned Upside Down*, pp. 209, 212–3; Aylmer, 'Did the Ranters exist?', 210.

164 See Johann P. Sommerville, 'The "new art of lying": equivocation, mental reservation, and casuistry', in Edmund Leites (ed.), *Conscience and Casuistry in Early Modern Europe* (Cambridge and Paris, 1988), pp. 159–84; Michael L. Carrafiello, 'Robert Parsons and equivocation, 1606–1610', *Catholic Historical Review*, 79 (1993), 671–80; Perez Zagorin, *Ways of Lying: Dissimulation, Persecution and Conformity in Early Modern Europe* (Cambridge, MA, 1990), ch. 9. For one such manuscript tract, see The National Archives, State Papers Domestic 12/136/15. The complexities of clerical dissimulation and equivocation will be further illuminated by Stefania Tutino in 'The Society of Jesus in England: between nicodemism and "honest dissimulation"', *Historical Research* (forthcoming).

165 See Walsham, *Church Papists*, p. 75.

166 *Ibid.*, p. 86; J. C. H. Aveling, *Northern Catholics: The Catholic Recusants of the North Riding of Yorkshire 1558–1790* (London, 1966), p. 195.

167 Marshall, 'Papist as heretic', 361–71; Wabuda, 'Equivocation and recantation'. For some ingenious manoeuvres by conservation Henrician clergymen, see Ethan Shagan, 'Confronting compromise: the schism and its legacy in mid-Tudor England', in Shagan (ed.) *Catholics and the Protestant Nation*, pp. 51–3.

168 Ryrie, *Gospel and Henry VIII*, pp. 69–89, esp. 80–1, 85.

169 W. J. Sheils, *The Puritans in the Diocese of Peterborough 1558–1610* , Northamptonshire Record Society 30 (Northampton, 1979), pp. 82–3; Peter Lake, 'Moving the goal posts? Modified subscription and the construction of conformity in the early Stuart Church', in Peter Lake and Michael Questier (eds), *Conformity and Orthodoxy in the English Church, c.1560–1660* (Woodbridge, 2000), pp. 179–205, at 183. See also Collinson, *Elizabethan Puritan Movement*, p. 266, 344.

170 Kenneth Fincham, 'Clerical conformity from Whitgift to Laud', in Lake and Questier (eds), *Conformity and Orthodoxy*, p. 144; Webster, *Godly Clergy*, p. 247.

171 Cressy, 'Protestation protested', 276–7.

172 Spurr, 'Latitudinarianism', p. 78.

173 Craig W. Horle, *The Quakers and the English Legal System 1660–1688* (Philadelphia, 1988).

174 Ryrie, *Gospel and Henry VIII*, pp. 132–3; Watts, *Dissenters*, p. 228.

175 Wabuda, 'Henry Bull ... and the making of Foxe's Book of Martyrs', pp. 257–8; Thomas S. Freeman, 'Publish and perish: the scribal culture of the Marian martyrs', in Julia Crick and Alexandra Walsham (eds), *The Uses of Script and Print 1300–1700* (Cambridge, 2004), pp. 235–54.

176 Bradford, *The hurte of heringe masse*. See Carlos M. N. Eire, 'Prelude to sedition? Calvin's attack on nicodemism and religious compromise', *Archiv für Reformationsgeschite*, 76 (1985), 120–45; Eire, *War against the Idols*, ch. 7; Zagorin, *Ways of Lying*, chs 4, 10; Andrew Pettegree, 'Nicodemism and the English Reformation', in his *Marian Protestantism*, pp. 86–117; M. A. Overell, 'Vergerio's anti-nicodemite propaganda and England, 1547–1558', *JEH*, 51 (2000), 296–318.

177 Walsham, *Church papists*, ch. 2; Zagorin, *Ways of Lying*, ch. 7.

178 See Carlson (ed.), *Writings of ... Barrow 1587–1590*, pp. 108–17; Webster, *Godly Clergy*, p. 245; Spurr, 'Latitudinarianism', esp. 62–8.

179 See my 'Ordeals of conscience: casuistry, conformity and confessional identity in post-Reformation England', in Harald Braun and Edward Vallance (eds), *Contexts of Conscience in Early Modern Europe 1500–1700* (Basingstoke, 2004), pp. 32–48.

180 Vermigli, *Treatise*, fos 23r, 24v.

181 William Perkins, *The whole treatise of the cases of conscience* (Cambridge, 1606), pp. 363–4.

182 Carlson (ed.), *Writings of ... Barrow 1587–1590*, p. 111.

183 Henry Garnet, *A treatise of Christian renunciation* ([London, 1593]), p. 13.

184 Keeble, *Literary Culture of Nonconformity*, p. 48; John Bunyan, *The Pilgrim's Progress*, ed. Roger Sharrock (Harmondsworth, 1965).

185 Hudson, *Premature Reformation*, p. 468.

186 See Michael MacDonald, 'The fearefull estate of Francis Spira: narrative, identity, and emotion in early modern England', *JBS*, 31 (1992), 32–61; M. A. Overell, 'The exploitation of Francesco Spiera', *SCJ*, 26 (1995), 619–37.

187 Bridgen, *London and the Reformation*, p. 602; Clebsch, *England's Earliest Protestants*, pp. 281–2; Dowling and Shakespeare (eds), 'Recollections of Rose Hickman', p. 101.

188 Earle, *Microcosmography*, p. 29.

189 *William Weston: The Autobiography of an Elizabethan*, trans. and ed. Philip Caraman (London, 1955) pp. 148–50.

190 Sarah Covington, *The Trail of Martyrdom: Persecution and Resistance in Sixteenth-Century England* (Notre Dame, 2003), p. 75; *Calendar of State Papers Domestic 1581–1590*, p. 131.

191 Freeman, 'Publish and perish', pp. 245–6; Pettegree, 'Nicodemism', pp. 86–117.

192 Walsham, *Church Papists*, ch. 3; Walsham, '"Yielding to the extremity of the time"'; Michael Questier, 'The politics of conformity and the accession of James I', *Historical Research*, 71 (1998), 14–30, at 27.

193 Sommerville, 'New art of lying', esp. pp. 177–8.

194 Harris, *London Crowds*, p. 69; Richard T. Vann, *The Social Development of English Quakerism 1655–1755* (Cambridge, MA, 1969), pp. 95–6, 103; Watts, *Dissenters*, p. 302. See also Braithwaite, *Second Period of Quakerism*, pp. 294–323.

195 Ryrie, *Gospel and Henry VIII*, p. 87.

196 Walsham, *Church Papists*, pp. 64–9.

197 P. J. Holmes (ed.), *Elizabethan Casuistry*, CRS 67 (London, 1981), pp. 51–2, 124.

198 Vallance, 'Oaths, casuistry and equivocation', 72–3; Zagorin, *Ways of Lying*, pp. 246–53.

199 Holmes, *Resistance and Compromise*, p. 118; Walsham, *Church Papists*, p. 82.

200 Holmes (ed.), *Elizabethan Casuistry*, p. 61.

201 Questier, *Conversion*, p. 113. See also Aveling, *Northern Catholics*, pp. 266–7.

202 Pettegree, 'Nicodemism', p. 106.

203 Walsham, *Church Papists*, pp. 64–5, 67–8; Elliot Rose, *Cases of Conscience: Alternatives Open to Recusants and Puritans under Elizabeth I and James I* (Cambridge, 1975), pp. 75–7, 242–50.

204 Ryrie, *Gospel and Henry VIII*, p. 72.

205 Hamilton, *Family of Love*, p. 121; Acheson, *Radical Puritans*, p. 15.

206 Matar, *Islam in Britain*, pp. 67–8.

207 Zagorin, *Ways of Lying*, pp. 116–19, 127–30.

208 See Collinson, 'Night Schools', pp. 223–5. For Lollard ecclesiology, see Hudson, *Premature Reformation*, ch. 7, esp. p. 319.

209 Patrick Collinson, 'The English conventicle', in W. J. Sheils (ed.), *Voluntary Religion*, SCH 23 (Oxford, 1986), pp. 223–59, at 251. For puritan anti-separatism, see also Collinson, 'Cohabitation'. Rather similar arguments were employed by Martin Bucer: see Pettegree, 'Nicodemism', p. 93.

210 Webster, *Godly Clergy*, pp. 159, 224–5.

211 *Ibid.*, pp. 225–6.

212 White, *English Separatist Tradition*, p. 166. See also Tolmie, *Triumph of the Saints*, ch. 5.

213 Hill, 'Occasional Conformity', p. 301; John D. Ramsbottom, 'Presbyterians and "partial conformity" in the Restoration Church of England', *JEH*, 43 (1992), 249–70.

214 Ramsbottom, 'Presbyterians', p. 256; Hill, 'Occasional Conformity', p. 316; Spaeth, *Church in an Age of Danger*, p. 170.

215 Perry Miller, *Orthodoxy in Massachusetts, 1630–1650: A Genetic Study* (New York, 1970 edn; first publ. 1933), p. 84 and ch. 4 *passim*.

216 As the non-juror Charles Leslie claimed in the early eighteenth century: Keeble, *Literary Culture of Nonconformity*, p. 37. W. J. Sheils, 'Oliver Heywood and his Congregation', in Sheils (ed.), *Voluntary Religion,*, pp. 261–77. See also Flaningham, 'Occasional conformity controversy'.

217 Ryrie, *Gospel and Henry VIII*, pp. 9, 89.

218 Marsh, *Family of Love*, pp. 116–22, 163–6.

219 Clare Talbot (ed.), *Miscellanea: Recusant Records*, CRS 53 (London, 1961), p. 66.

220 Milton, *Catholic and Reformed*, p. 44; Wiener, 'Beleaguered isle', p. 38; Earle, *Microcosmography*, p. 29.

221 Milton, *Catholic and Reformed*, p. 258.

222 Walter, *Understanding Popular Violence*, p. 215.

223 Spurr, *Restoration Church*, p. 201.

224 Worden, 'Toleration and the Cromwellian Protectorate', p. 207; Spurr, 'Latitudinarianism', esp. p. 65.

225 Watts, *Dissenters*, p. 265.

226 Russell, *Parliaments and English Politics*, p. 407.

227 Brian Manning, *The English People and the English Revolution* (Harmondsworth, 1976), p. 52; Walsham, *Church Papists*, pp. 115–18.

228 Kenyon (ed.), *Stuart Constitution* (2nd edn), pp. 207–17. See also Hibbard, *Charles I and the Popish Plot*.

229 Jasper Godwin Ridley, *Nicholas Ridley: A Biography* (London, 1957), p. 164; Cottret, *Huguenots*, p. 192 and Eileen Barrett, 'Huguenot integration in late seventeenth- and eighteenth-century London: insights from records of the French Church and some relief agencies', in Vigne and Littleton (eds), *From Strangers to Citizens*, pp. 375–82, at p. 376.

230 Hamilton, *Family of Love*, p. 134; Milton, *Catholic and Reformed*, p. 118. See also Christopher Hill, *Antichrist in Seventeenth-Century England* (London, 1990 edn; first publ. 1971).

231 Reay, *Quakers*, pp. 59–60; Elmer, 'Saints or sorcerers', p. 160; S. A. Kent, 'The papist charges against the Interregnum Quakers', *Journal of Religious History*, 2 (1982–3), 180–90; Braithwaite, *Beginnings of Quakerism*, pp. 170n, 172, 193, 214, 229, 356, 362, 407, 446.

232 Clifton, 'Popular fear of Catholics', 33–4; W. M. Lamont, *Marginal Prynne, 1600–69* (London, 1963), pp. 138–48.

233 Spurr, *Restoration Church*, pp. 49, 65, 264–5; Williams, *Catholic Recusancy*, p. 26.

234 Harris, *London Crowds*, p. 148; Dolan, *Whores of Babylon*, ch. 4.

235 Capp, *Fifth Monarchy Men*, p. 219; Harris, *London Crowds*, pp. 119, 137.

236 Haydon, *Anti-Catholicism*, p. 127.

237 Kenyon (ed.), *Stuart Constitution* (2nd edn), pp. 168–71; Browning (ed.), *English Historical Documents 1660–1714*, pp. 406–8.

238 Brigden, 'Religion and social obligation', pp. 110–11. See also Spaeth, 'Common prayer?', pp. 130–1.

239 John Bossy, *Peace in the Post-Reformation* (Cambridge, 1998), esp. pp. 87–91.

240 McSheffrey, *Gender and Heresy*, p. 72; Davis, *Heresy and Reformation*, p. 94.

241 John Caffyn, *Sussex Believers: Baptist Marriage in the Seventeenth and Eighteenth Centuries* (Worthing, 1988), p. 156.

242 Derek Plumb, 'A gathered church? Lollards and their society', in Spufford (ed.), *World of Rural Dissenters*, pp. 132–63, at 147; Brown, *Popular Piety*, p. 218.

243 Hope, 'Lollardy', p. 7; Davies, 'Lollardy and locality', p. 206, n. 68.

244 Davies, 'Lollardy and locality', p. 211.

245 Marsh, *Family of Love*, pp. 96, 147, 170–3, 182–7, and ch. 7 *passim*; Marsh, 'Gravestone of Thomas Lawrence revisited', p. 212 and *passim*.

246 Holmes (ed.), *Elizabethan Casuistry*.

247 BL, Additional MS 38599, fo. 78r–v.

248 Walsham, *Church Papists*, pp. 76–7; Holmes (ed.), *Elizabethan Casuistry*, p. 30; Williams, *Catholic Recusancy*, p. 7.

249 Bossy, *English Catholic Community*, ch. 6 §3.

250 Andrzej Bida, 'Papists in an Elizabethan parish: Linton, Cambridgeshire. c.1560–c.1600', unpubl. Diploma in Historical Studies dissertation (University of Cambridge, 1992), pp. 31–3; Malcolm Wanklyn, 'Catholics in the village community: Madeley, Shropshire, 1630–1770', in Rowlands (ed.), *Catholics of Parish and Town*, pp. 210–36, at 225.

251 Davies, *Quakers*, pp. 203, 209, 210–11, and ch. 14 *passim*; Stevenson, 'Social integration', pp. 360–87.

252 Caffyn, *Sussex Believers*, p. 162; Stevenson, 'Social integration', p. 376.

253 Caffyn, *Sussex Believers*, p. 101, and see pp. 157–66.

254 Clifton, 'Fear of Catholics', pp. 294–5.

255 See Davies, *Quakers*, ch. 2.

256 Collinson, *Religion of Protestants*, p. 253.

257 Foster, *Notes*, p. 8; Collinson, *Religion of Protestants*, p. 269, and ch. 6 *passim*. See also Collinson, 'Cohabitation', *passim*.

258 Collinson, *Elizabethan Puritan Movement*, pp. 349–50.

259 Hunt, *Puritan Moment*, p. 150.

260 Collinson, 'Cohabitation', pp. 60–1. See also Lake, 'Charitable Christian hatred', esp. pp. 165–74.

261 Collinson, *Birthpangs*, p. 145.

262 *The Autobiography of Richard Baxter*, ed. J. M. Lloyd Thomas (London, 1925), p. 6.

263 See Nicholas Tyacke, 'Popular Puritan Mentality in Late Elizabethan England', in P. Clark, A. G. R. Smith and N. Tyacke (eds), *The English Commonwealth 1547–1640* (Leicester 1979), pp. 77–92; Collinson, *Birthpangs*, p. 149.

264 Lake, 'Charitable Christian hatred', p. 165.

265 Collinson, *Birthpangs*, pp. 143–51, and ch. 5 *passim*.

266 Audisio, *Waldensian Dissent*, p. 37.

267 Quotation from Hudson, *Premature Reformation*, p. 222. For this epistolary tradition, see Alexandra Walsham, 'Preaching without speaking: script, print and religious dissent', in Julia Crick and Alexandra Walsham (eds), *The Uses of Script and Print 1300–1700* (Cambridge, 2004), pp. 211–34.

268 John Spurr, 'From puritanism to dissent 1660–1700', in Durston and Eales (eds), *Culture of English Puritanism*, pp. 234–65, at 249. For the literary culture of persecution, see John Stachniewski, *The Persecutory Imagination: English Puritanism and the Literature of Religious Despair* (Oxford, 1991); Shell, *Catholicism, Controversy, and the English Literary Imagination*; Keeble, *Literary Culture of Nonconformity*.

269 Brigden, 'Youth and the English Reformation', esp. 67; Alison Shell, '"Furor juvenilis": post-Reformation English Catholicism and exemplary youthful behaviour', in Shagan (ed.), *Catholics and the 'Protestant Nation'*, pp. 185–206. I am grateful to the author for allowing me to read this in advance of publication.

270 Catharine Davies, '"Poor persecuted little flock" or "commonwealth of Christians": Edwardian Protestant concepts of the Church', in Peter Lake and Maria Dowling (eds), *Protestantism and the National Church in Sixteenth Century England* (London, 1987), pp. 78–102, esp. p. 84; Davies, *Religion of the Word*, esp. pp. 231–3.

271 Collinson, 'Cohabitation', p. 56. See also Hunt, *Puritan Moment*, p. 146; Lake, 'Charitable Christian hatred', esp. pp. 156–65; and Frank Luttmer, 'Persecutors, tempters and vassals of the devil: the unregenerate in puritan practical divinity', *JEH*, 51 (2000), 37–68.

272 As commented by Andrew Pettegree, 'Coming to terms with victory: the upbuilding of a Calvinist church in Holland, 1572–1590', in Andrew Pettegree, Alastair Duke and Gillian Lewis (eds), *Calvinism in Europe 1540–1620* (Cambridge, 1994), p. 160 and pp. 161–80 *passim*.

273 Lacey, *Cult of King Charles the Martyr*, p. 57; Maltby, *Prayer Book and People*, pp. 115–16. See also Maltby, '"The good old way"'.

274 Lacey, *Cult of King Charles the Martyr*, ch. 5.

Chapter 5

Loving one's neighbours:
tolerance in principle and practice

It would be wrong to underestimate the influence that the Augustinian theory of persecution exerted in sixteenth- and seventeenth-century England. Had a random poll been conducted in the year 1500, probably a considerable majority of people would have subscribed to the view that it was the solemn duty of the reigning monarch and state to take steps to correct, if not to eliminate individuals and groups who held heterodox opinions and beliefs, even where these did not manifest themselves in forms of behaviour that were subversive of public order or inimical to the settled rhythms of everyday life. Driven by the conviction that God would punish communities and nations which winked at the deviants living within their midst and persuaded that religious pluralism was a recipe for political chaos and social anarchy, perhaps most would have endorsed the proposition that intolerance was not merely a practical necessity but also doctrinally right and morally just. As we have seen, some even supposed that where the authorities failed in their obligation to separate the sheep from the goats, it was the responsibility of private citizens to take the sickle of divine justice into their hands and to wield it unflinchingly as the appointed instruments of the Lord's stringent but loving discipline. As propounded by its most articulate and eloquent advocates, persecution was at once an expression of the passionate zeal that the faithful were expected to display for the truth and an act of charity and kindness to those who would otherwise slide unwittingly into the quagmire of irredeemable error, and from thence headlong into the abyss.

For those locked inside this compelling set of assumptions, the concept of toleration was nothing less than anathema. Knowingly to permit individuals to continue to profess a false religion was not merely a deplorable dereliction of one's responsibilities as a Christian; it was also an act of disobedience to the deity, a failure to carry out the ringing scriptural injunction to 'compel them to come in'. As such it constituted a form of spiritual murder or soul-killing –

hence, the repeated and emphatic condemnations of 'toleration' by contemporaries from all parts of the ecclesiastical spectrum. In the tradition of medieval Catholic theologians such as Thomas Aquinas, Tridentine writers repudiated the notion of conniving at heresy as a sinful and diabolical policy. 'I think no one thing to be so dangerous, dishonourable, or more offensive to Almighty God in the World', declared the Jesuit Robert Persons around 1596, 'than that any Prince should permit the Ark of Israel and Dagon, God and the Devil, to stand and be honoured together, within his Realm or Country.'[1] Across the confessional divide, the sentiment was shared by leading Protestant reformers like Jean Calvin, who lectured magistrates uncompromisingly on the evils of lapsing into 'a most cruel "humanity"' and allowing themselves 'to be enervated by a superstitious attachment to clemency into a soft and dissolute indulgence, to the destruction of many'.[2]

Many puritan writers of the seventeenth century reiterated the claim that this was an unholy, not to say antichristian arrangement. '[T]o authorise an untruth, by Toleration of State', wrote the New England pastor Nathaniel Ward in a tract published in London in 1647, 'is to build a Sconce against the walls of Heaven, to batter God out of his Chair'. A Church that permitted a general liberty of conscience would 'sooner become the Devills Dancing-Schoole, than Gods-Temple': it would exchange its status as 'Christs Academy' for the title of 'the Devils University'.[3] The same year the Presbyterian Thomas Edwards thundered that toleration was the 'very thing for which God hath a controversie with the Parliament and Land', 'the last and strongest hold of Satan', while Richard Baxter warned the Interregnum regime that to grant such a licence would be to bear the burden of having enticed thousands to follow the road to damnation: 'Thousands might curse you for ever in Hell'. Protesting their 'utter dislike and abhorrence' of this policy, the Independents of Yarmouth declared in 1659 that it was 'contrary to the mind of God in His Word'.[4] One of the first presidents of Harvard University likewise looked upon unbounded religious freedom 'as the first-born of all abominations'.[5] Early Restoration clergymen similarly spoke of schemes designed to achieve the comprehension of Protestant dissenters as a 'a dragnet, that will fetch in all kinds of fish, good or bad, great or small', and that would provide 'room enough for Leviathan'.[6] According to the Anglican propagandist Sir Roger L'Estrange 'Toleration of Religion' was 'Cousin-German to a License for Rebellion', while in 1680 Edward Stillingfleet, Dean of St Paul's, described it in a famous sermon entitled the <i>Mischief of separation</i> as 'that Trojan Horse, which brings in our enemies without being seen'.[7]

Nevertheless, the two hundred years covered by this book witnessed a growing, if still trickling stream of calls for the toleration of religious minorities. The most outspoken of those who championed this cause turned the polemical rhetoric employed by its opponents on its head, writing of persecution as '*stratagematum satanae*' ('Satan's stratagems') for undermining true religion, a 'mistery of iniquity', and a 'bloudy tenent' that had no place in the Christian faith and reasoning that licensing some form of religious coexistence might in fact better serve the interests of the kingdom than concerted efforts to eradicate it.[8] Inverting the providential logic that provided such a powerful incentive for religious coercion, they argued that, far from appeasing the Lord's wrath, this was 'a very sure and certain way of bringing National Judgements upon a People'. Indeed, some were 'verily perswaded' that the chaos and bloodshed of the civil wars of the 1640s were a punishment for 'the generall obstinacie and aversenesse' of the English to 'tollerate, and beare with ... [the] different opinions of their brethren'. Leaving 'every man to the liberty of his conscience', by contrast, was 'the way to make the blessing of God upon a nation'.[9]

At the end of the seventeenth century, English society was not only more familiar with the case for toleration; an increasing proportion of the populace appears to have been far more sympathetic and amenable to the key arguments that constituted it. As a tract of 1689 remarked, many seem to have come round to the view 'that heaven is not entail'd upon any particular opinion'.[10] This gradual, subtle and partial shift in the outlook of educated men and women who enshrined their opinions on paper took place against the backdrop not only of the rampant, de facto pluralism that was the consequence of the Reformation nearly everywhere it spread, but also of legal concessions and political initiatives that involved tentative, temporary, and often unpopular steps towards the official recognition or accommodation of the conscientious dilemmas of certain groups of religious dissidents or at least a measure of grudging acceptance that they were a permanent, if regrettable, presence. The endeavour to enforce ecclesiastical uniformity that had been central to the enterprise of the established Church was reluctantly abandoned. While the idea of creating consensus had always been something of an idealistic fiction, by 1700 many intellectuals tacitly if not openly acknowledged it to be a practical impossibility.

Engaged in a more or less self-conscious quest to uncover the origins and forerunners of modern secular liberalism, the Whig historians who explored the 'rise of toleration' from Lord Macaulay forwards accorded great importance to the ideas expounded by an illustrious company of 'enlightened' thinkers and exaggerated the significance of the legislative landmarks of the period – notably, the famous statute passed in the wake of the so-called Glorious Revolution in 1689. As reviewed in the introduction, recent revisionist work has done much to qualify and complicate this grand narrative of steady progress away from bigotry and darkness towards freedom and light and to stress both the limited and conservative nature of many celebrated intellectual statements and institutional developments, and the degree to which these were frequently products of particular political, ecclesiastical and social circumstances. Indeed, often they were side effects of concentrated episodes of intolerance itself. Scholars have underlined the fortuitous element of events that retrospectively appear to be turning points and milestones and cut the rousing cries of leading advocates of toleration down to size by carefully restoring them to their original discursive contexts. It was 'not the noble nature of tolerationist ideas or the mean-spirited obstinacy of their opponents' that ensured their partial realisation of religious liberty in the 1640s and the 1680s, writes Andrew Murphy, but the military victory of the New Model Army and the pressing need for Protestant unity in the face of Stuart absolutism.[11]

Yet the temptations and conveniences of an implicitly teleological approach to this topic continue to prove hard to resist. Even while emphasising the enormous vitality of the theory of religious intolerance and resisting crude models that connect toleration inexorably with the onward march of secularisation, John Coffey still speaks of the period as 'a critical era of transition', which witnessed 'a dramatic movement' towards the notions that we regard as hallmarks of the 'modern' world. Perez Zagorin too sees it as the crucible in which a 'very momentous, far-reaching change in Western civilisation' took place and in which a positive commitment not merely to toleration, but more fundamentally to religious freedom, was forged.[12]

Such a narrative has enduring relevance and undoubted value, but it will not be reproduced here. The discussion that follows deliberately discards any attempt to trace a path 'from persecution to toleration' and suggests that it is an error of perspective to set up these categories in polar opposition, when they are best seen as part of a complex continuum that could flow in both directions. It rests on the twin premises that enmity and amity, prejudice and benevolence, are impulses that persistently coexisted in the minds of individuals and in English society at large and that the relationship between them was cyclical rather than linear. Tackling the subject in a thematic rather than chronological fashion, this chapter seeks to examine the triangular interaction between ideology, official edict and the 'tolerance of practical rationality' exhibited at the grass roots. Notwithstanding the difficulties of detecting this elusive phenomenon in our sources, there is much to suggest that historians have underestimated both the extent and the capacity of an instinct for concord, harmony and peace to shape social relations. As we shall see, the evolution of principled defences of toleration was not necessarily a precondition of its realisation in practice: sometimes they may have been post-facto justifications of changes that were already proceeding apace. Nor was an abstract commitment to confessional hatred of an illegitimate faith incompatible with a charitable disposition to love one's neighbours despite their religious idiosyncrasies. The implications of the recurrent disjunction between polemical rhetoric and parochial reality deserve much attention.

Could it be that a willingness to accept and accommodate diversity and difference was actually a long-term feature of the experience of living in the towns, villages and cities of medieval and early modern England? – not so much a consequence of local efforts to ease and heal the destructive divisions precipitated by the Reformation as the continuation of a state of affairs that had previously prevailed? How far was this precarious equilibrium between the adherents of rival creeds affected by the way in which minorities responded to their treatment by the populace and state? And what role did the perception that toleration was being extended and exercised play in precipitating fresh outbreaks of persecution and violence? While our answers to such questions will often be merely suggestive and speculative, if we are to reach a greater understanding of the dialectical link between tolerance and intolerance it is still vital to ask them.

ADVOCATES AND ARGUMENTS

For obvious reasons, early modern individuals who called for religious liberty and freedom of conscience pluck at the historian's sleeve. Our ears naturally prick up when we hear voices that speak a language that echoes the values we cherish in theory, even if we do not always honour them in practice. It is easy to give way to the feeling that they embody an oasis of 'reason' and 'sanity' in a landscape of the past marked by destructive and 'hysterical' sectarian passions – notwithstanding the fact that nearly every news broadcast brings forth fresh and harrowing evidence that the instinct to persecute is far from extinct. It is thus not surprising that the historiography of this subject has often resulted in the construction of a gallery of European heroes and worthies who espoused ideas 'in advance of their time'. Typically, this chamber of 'pioneering' thinkers encompasses eirenic humanists like Desiderius Erasmus, Sebastian Castellio, Jacob Acontius and Dirck Coornhert; spiritualist writers and mystical Anabaptists such as Balthasar Hubmaier, Menno Simons and Sebastian Franck; the Italian evangelicals Lelio and Fausto Sozzini and their Socinian disciples; the French politiques Michel de L'Hôpital and Jean Bodin; the Dutch Armininian (or Remonstrant) theologians Johannes Uyttenbogaert, Simon Episcopius and Hugo Grotius; the exiled Huguenot academic Pierre Bayle and the Jewish freethinker Benedict Spinoza; and the great Enlightenment philosophers of the eighteenth century François-Marie Arouet Voltaire, Jean-Jacques Rousseau and Immanuel Kant.[13]

In this hall of fame, English figures occupy a prominent place: the Henrician Lord Chancellor Sir Thomas More,[14] the Elizabethan and Jacobean separatists Henry Jacob and Thomas Helwys, the latitudinarians John Hales and William Chillingworth and the Deist John Toland. Particular importance is attached to the participants in the intense tolerationist debates of the 1640s and 1650s, to the tracts and speeches of radical puritans and dissenters like the Baptist Roger Williams, the Independent John Goodwin, the Quaker William Penn, the Levellers Richard Overton and William Walwyn, and the poet John Milton, who all condemned persecution and called for varying degrees of liberty of conscience.[15] The Whitehall Debates of 1648, the campaign surrounding the 'Humble Proposals' set forth by the parliamentary Committee for the Propagation of the Gospel in 1652,[16] and the formal discussions that took place three years later regarding the readmission to England of the Jews are justifiably regarded as the high-water marks of intellectual activity on this topic during the revolutionary decades.[17] Above all, however, the spotlight falls upon John Locke, a man who espoused Socinian opinions but remained a devout member of the Church of England, and whose *Letter concerning toleration*, published in 1689, is the subject of a substantial academic industry in its own right. Although Roman Catholics such as the Jesuit Robert Persons and the Appellant and Irish Blackloist writers of the seventeenth century did assemble powerful arguments in favour of it on occasion themselves,[18] the indisputable dominance of reformed writers in this lineage has lent itself all too readily to a rather triumphalist and self-congratulatory Protestant reading of the evolution of tolerationist thought in England, as in Europe as a whole.

The impulse to assemble such a pedigree has commonly been beset by other problems and perils. Not least among these is the danger of misapprehending what exactly contemporaries meant when they called for 'toleration', 'religious freedom', and 'liberty of conscience': we must beware of anachronistically confusing the modern connotations of these words with the significance they had in the sixteenth and seventeenth centuries. For the most part, the rhetoric employed by the architects of the American and French Revolutions, the Victorian philosopher John Stuart Mill in his renowned tract *On Liberty* of 1859, or twentieth-century theorists like John Rawls and Ronald Dworkin has little place in the texts and utterances of the period under examination.[19] It is a mistake to suppose that the later notion of toleration as a universal natural right or 'the prerogative of humanity' was self-evident to early modern thinkers.[20] During the 1640s, some puritan writers, including Oliver Cromwell and Sir Henry Vane, did speak in these highly resonant terms. Similarly, the Quaker William Penn would later declare that persecution deprived individuals of a principal 'privilege of nature', while both John Locke and Bishop Gilbert Burnet maintained that it was 'one of the rights of human nature, antecedent to society'.[21] But the frame of reference of all these writers was theological rather than secular. With a very few exceptions, early modern intellectuals were not demanding equality without discrimination or advocating the frank embrace of religious pluralism, let alone propounding the advantages and merits of a multi-faith or multi-cultural society. C. H. George once warned of the 'alchemistic tricks' perpetrated by scholars such as A. S. P.

Woodhouse and William Haller who transmuted the 'base stuff of puritan piety into the gold of egalitarianism', a theme taken up with vigour by William Lamont with regard to such towering figures as Roger Williams, Oliver Crom-well and John Milton. These men, he insists, were 'not interested in such wishy-washy nineteenth-century concerns as personal freedoms and equality'.[22] The 'religious liberty' of which they wrote so movingly, says J. C. Davis, was paradoxically a liberty to be able to submit themselves wholly to the will of God Almighty. It was the Christian liberty of the Protestant soul that was utterly helpless to save itself without the external interposition of supernatural grace.[23]

Equally, it is important to distinguish calls for 'toleration' from calls for 'concord' and 'comprehension'. The latter, which lay at the heart of much moderate Anglican and latitudinarian thinking, entailed a search for an ecclesiastical settlement that could accommodate differences of opinion on non-essential issues within the context of a single institution. It still enshrined a theoretical commitment to the indivisibility of religious truth. The former had long been an ideal to which governments and communities aspired: a desire to conserve and uphold unity of faith and the peace of a Christian society which implied temporary forbearance but never approval of, or even resignation, to diversity per se.[24] To add to the difficulties created by these subtle linguistic nuances and ambiguities, it must be noted that *tolerantia* was a highly-developed political and judicial concept in medieval Latin scholastic theology and canon law. As István Bejczy has shown, it was a word used to denote the self-restraint of a civil power in the face of groups like lepers, prostitutes and especially non-believers and infidels such as Muslims and Jews, a precept of non-interference that offered authorities 'the possibility of coming to terms with the outer world'. Those who employed it never doubted that they alone pursued the path of righteousness, but they utilised it as a means of justifying the existence of beliefs and practices which they unequi-vocally considered to be evil and insupportable.[25]

A further area where careful discrimination is required relates to the question of the constituencies to which its proponents intended 'toleration' to be extended. It would be wrong to overlook the small contingent of individuals who did mount a case for tolerating all forms of religious faith and opinion without exception. There were those who would have permitted the coexistence of the Christian and non-Christian religions. Such views were rarely articu-lated before the 1640s, though in two key tracts of 1612 and 1614 the Baptists Thomas Helwys and Leonard Busher argued that earthly powers should grant liberty not merely to heretics, but 'yea to Jews, Turks, and pagans, so long as they are peaceable, and no malefactors'.[26]

After the collapse of consensus in the middle decades of the century, a small chorus of godly voices including Roger Williams, Samuel Fisher, John

Lilburne and Richard Overton reiterated the opinion that heathen and Semitic sects should be allowed to live without molestation. John Saltmarsh said that 'misbeleefe of particular Scripture mysteries' was no grounds for persecution and William Walwyn also insisted that those 'so far mis-informed as to deny a Deity' or the Bible should be immune from prosecution. Transcending their ingrained hatred of popery and idolatry, some of these radical Protestants believed that Catholics too ought to be tolerated.[27] The Quaker George Fox advocated the 'universal liberty' of mankind in the sphere of religious conviction, whether Protestant, papist, or pagan – 'such as worship sun or moon or stocks and stones'.[28] A few individuals, including the New Model Army chaplain Thomas Collier, even went so far as to claim that the magistrate had no right to take action against blasphemy or atheism, though he later retracted this opinion on the grounds that these positions contradicted natural reason and moral law.[29]

Such views cannot be dismissed as the 'random eccentricities' of a handful of maverick thinkers,[30] but it must be stressed that throughout the period they were confined to a tiny minority. The Jesuit Persons would have countenanced Jews and infidels but not heretics, on the grounds that the latter had wilfully abandoned their primitive faith while the former, in their ignorance, might still accept it.[31] Similarly, most Protestants who championed the cause of 'toleration' automatically excluded atheists and Romanists from their calculations. This applies to both Milton and Locke: the author of *Areopagitica* (1644) explicitly refused to countenance Catholics because they were guilty of superstition and idolatry, while the writer of the *Letter on toleration* adopted the politique view that both groups represented a serious threat to the state and to the sinews of civil society and as such could not be suffered in a well-governed commonwealth.[32] Not until Pierre Bayle was the assumption that an inherent link existed between the possession of religious faith and a predilection for political rectitude and moral virtue seriously questioned: perhaps his most significant contribution to the debate was the insight that atheists no less than believers could be good citizens.[33]

Similar concerns about stability inspired many to rule out the sanctioning of flagrant immorality and profane apostasy and then, as now, almost no one contested the right of the authorities to take steps to restrain religious dissidents who committed acts of violent rebellion or terrorism. As Oliver Cromwell declared emphatically to the first Protectorate Parliament in 1654, anything that abused liberty of conscience 'for the patronising of villanies' could not be permitted on principle.[34] Such reasoning induced Bayle himself to approve the use of torture, pillories and burning against religious enthusiasts whose convictions spilled over into subversive action that threatened state security. He did not doubt that it was 'the duty of princes to enact wholesome laws against heretics who disturb the public peace, who are of a turbulent persecuting spirit'. Such arguments formed the basis of what John Christian Laursen has termed his 'intolerance of intolerance'.[35]

Furthermore, upon closer scrutiny, some of the most vocal of the puritan 'revolutionaries' who attacked the pillars of persecution theory in the course of the Civil War would have barred all but a small core of Calvinists from exercising freedom of belief and worship in practice. The Independents in particular never contemplated anything more than a limited indulgence for Protestant dissenters with scruples about Presbyterian ecclesiology: this did not stretch to either episcopalian Anglicans or heretical sectaries who dissented from Trinitarian orthodoxy and questioned the authority of the canonical Scriptures. As Thomas Goodwin told the House of Commons in a sermon of 1645, 'I only plead for [the] Saints'.[36] Notwithstanding their reputation for moderation, most latitudinarian writers were likewise unwilling to support any relaxation of the laws restraining sectarian and Catholic dissent.[37]

This brings us to the point that the majority of those who called for toleration in the sixteenth and seventeenth centuries were not disinterested outsiders but the victims of some form of religious persecution themselves. Toleration was largely, though not solely, the slogan and creed of minorities who found themselves on the receiving end of judicial coercion and popular violence and one which they felt little sense of ideological contradiction or discomfort about discarding when they in turn took political control.[38] Tactical, tendentious and contingent in character, it was a position from which many hastily retreated once they were restored or exalted to institutional dominance. At root, it was a strategy for ensuring survival rather than an end in and of itself. The Edwardian Anabaptist Robert Cooche observed the effects of this double standard on the early Protestant reformers at first hand, noting that 'afore they came to authoritie, they were of an other judgement, and did bothe say and write, that no man ought to be persecuted for his conscience saik; but now they are not onely become persecutors, but also they have given, as far as lieth in them, the sword into the hands of bloodie tyrantes'.[39]

With the notable exceptions of Adrian van Haemstede and Jacob Acontius, the experience of exile also did little to breed a commitment to ecclesiastical tolerance among the Dutch and Walloon refugees who temporarily settled in Denmark and Emden during the reign of Mary I: they had little sympathy for the plight of their erring radical brethren and defended the harsh discipline which the local authorities meted out to them.[40] The Elizabethan separatists Robert Browne, Henry Barrow and John Greenwood loudly asserted their right to hold views at odds with those of the Church of England establishment but felt under no obligation to fight for those of the non-elect. As the Civil War would later prove, nor did the Presbyterians: Thomas Cartwright openly supported rigorous punishment of false teachers and preachers, declaring that 'if this be bloudie and extreme, I am contente to be so counted with the holie goste'.[41] The Leveller William Walwyn provided a particularly acute analysis of what he saw as the hypocritical about-face performed by the self-styled godly in his tract *The vanitie of the present churches* (1649): 'Do they not freely discover a serpentine disposition hankering after persecution? Do they not dayly spet their venom privately and publickly, against any that either separate from them, or joyne not with them, and that in as foul aspertions, as ever the Pope uttered against Luther, the Bishops against the Puritans, or the Presbyter against the Independents'.[42] The same is true of Bishop Jeremy Taylor: during the difficult years of the 1640s and 1650s he wrote powerfully in favour of the 'liberty of prophesying', but after the Restoration of the monarchy and Church he significantly modified his liberal opinions.[43]

It is also clear that Catholics like Robert Persons, who eloquently argued the case for freedom of conscience in more than one treatise, would not have practised what they preached had they achieved the overthrow of the Protestant regime. At root they too were unwilling to relinquish the principle that the true Church had a duty to restrain the 'furye and pryde' of those who forsook the faith of Rome and schismatically rent holes in the corporate body of Christ.[44] As for the Appellant writers who sought to negotiate toleration for politically quiescent laypeople and priests with the Elizabethan and Jacobean government, this embodied a grudging acceptance of the permanence of Catholicism's status as a minority sect. Proceeding from a position of weakness, there is no reason to suppose that it entailed a repudiation of the tradition of persecution inaugurated by Augustine and systematised by Aquinas.[45]

In this connection, it is also vital to stress that many of those who espoused toleration envisaged it as nothing more than a temporary measure, a prelude to conversion and a mechanism for restoring the religious uniformity they saw as a bulwark of the social order. This was the conviction that underpinned the eirenical stance of Erasmus and other humanists, for whom leniency towards Protestants was a provisional solution and a lesser evil than descent into full-scale religious war. It informed the outlook of Thomas Starkey and Cardinal Reginald Pole, who emerges from recent work as a reluctant persecutor,[46] and it strongly influenced that of Thomas Cranmer, whose initiative in securing the admission of the stranger churches to Edwardian England sprang from a pious hope that ecumenical contact between different communities would in the end all but eliminate the points of contention between them.[47] In his memorandum of 1596 sketching a programme for the reconciliation of England to Rome following the hypothetical overthrow of Queen Elizabeth, the Jesuit Persons advocated a period of amnesty in which stubborn but peaceable heretics would be treated gently and efforts made to bring them over by persuasion: 'a certain Connivence or Toleration of Magistrates only for a certain time'.[48] If or when such endeavours failed to heal the schism in the Church and nation, it would be quite legitimate to resort to force as an alternative means of restoring religious consensus. This was a strand of thinking about tolerance that lingered long in Protestant England: it lay behind the search for both 'concord' and 'comprehension'. Less common, but in the same vein, was the suggestion that toleration could be a cunning but effective method of fostering the mutual destruction of a mass of fissiparous sects: 'if they could not be suppressed', said the Polish Cardinal Stanislaus Hosius, it was better to suffer them all 'so that, attacking and denouncing each other they would ruin themselves'.[49]

By 1700, the case for toleration was no longer a near monopoly of the marginalised and repressed; nor was it merely regarded as an interim stage prior to the re-establishment of doctrinal and ecclesiastical unity. Yet we may still question the extent to which it reflected opinion or exercised influence outside the circles of the literate intellectuals who articulated it. How far the views expressed in recorded speeches and published tracts were representative of a wider body of opinion remains hard to assess: were such individuals lone voices crying in the wind or did they enunciate views that enjoyed fairly broad, if unspoken, assent? The reception of the key texts that have generated a disproportionate share of scholarly attention presents equally intractable difficulties to the intellectual historian: did their readers bristle with hostility to these subversive opinions or nod with emphatic approval?

With these caveats in mind, we now examine the various arguments put forward in the early modern period for concord, comprehension, 'liberty of conscience', and 'toleration'. Such arguments were overwhelmingly theological and scriptural in substance, texture and tone, although a more pragmatic brand of reasoning grounded on considerations of political and economic utility did grow in importance over the course of these two centuries. Nevertheless, it is generally impossible to draw a neat line between the 'religious' and 'secular' elements of contemporary discourse on this controversial issue: the prudential, no less than the philosophical points made by its advocates can rarely be abstracted from the Christian framework within which they were enunciated.[50]

The most powerful weapon that the proponents of toleration had at their disposal was the New Testament, especially the testimony of Christ's teachings contained in the Gospels. In commanding his disciples to love their enemies, turn the other cheek, and treat others as they would wish to be treated themselves, it was argued, the Messiah had superseded the intolerant ethos of Deuteronomic law, fulfilling the predictions of the Hebrew prophets who had foretold the coming of a kingdom of peace in which swords would be beaten into ploughshares and spears into pruning hooks (Matthew 5–7, Luke 6, Isaiah 2:4). His injunctions to show charity, patience and mercy towards the misguided and weak proved that persecution was contrary to the original tenor of the Christian religion and a mark of the falsehood rather than truth of a Church.

Thus a Familist whose words were recorded by John Rogers in his tract exposing this 'horrible secte' declared that it was 'not Christian-like, that one man should envie, belie, and persecute an other, for any cause touching conscience'. Separatists and Independents also repeatedly invoked these texts in support of their calls for toleration and Henry Robinson regarded intolerance as 'an infallible character of unsound Christians'.[51] So did George Villiers, the second Duke of Buckingham, close ally of the Earl of Shaftesbury, declaring in a parliamentary speech of 1675 that religious coercion was 'positively against the express doctrine and example of Jesus Christ'.[52] For Pierre Bayle, it was repugnant to the 'dominant and essential spirit of the Gospel itself': 'nothing can be more opposite to this spirit than dungeons, exiles, pillage, galleys, insolence by soldiers, torture and suffering'.[53] In the 1650s, Ludowick Muggleton had condemned persecution in no uncertain terms as a sin against the Holy Ghost.[54] This too was a commonplace.

Many authors marshalled the parable of the wheat and the tares (Matthew 13: 24–30) in defence of the tenet that Christ intended the godly and ungodly to live together unmolested until the day of judgement. Only then would the weeds be uprooted from the field of the world and separated from the good seed by the Almighty. It was consequently presumptuous for mere men to usurp the Lord's prerogative to carry out this formidable task of demarcation. In the Middle Ages this passage had often been taken to apply to moral offenders; in the sixteenth and seventeenth centuries it was increasingly employed to justify the coexistence of the heretical and orthodox, though opinion varied about whether the field referred to the commonwealth at large or to the visible Church.[55] The Baptists incorporated it into one of their confessions of faith and Roger Williams devoted a whole chapter of his *Bloudy tenent of persecution* (1644) to showing that this allegory revealed that men ought to exercise patience towards false believers and reprobates alongside whom they lived in society, even while they were to be expelled from the gathered congregations of the elect. The ministers and messengers of Jesus Christ were to leave these people untroubled and 'neither seeke by prayer or prophesie to pluck them up before the Harvest': their fate was fixed and 'their doome is fearfull ... even gathering, bundling, and everlasting burnings by the might hand of the Angels in the end of the world'. Heresy, in any case, was a form of temporal vengeance itself: to have 'the right eye of the mind and spirituall understanding' struck out by the finger of God was 'ten thousand times a greater punishment then if the Magistrate should command both the right and left eye of their bodies to bee bored or pluckt out'.[56] The lessons of this parable also came easily to the lips of many other dissenters in the later seventeenth century.

The Pauline epistles provided further ammunition for the view that the Son of God intended spiritual rather than 'carnal' and physical instruments to be used to bring people to embrace the faith that he preached. Pacifist Anabaptists and spiritualists were particularly insistent that the application of corporal and capital punishment was inconsistent with the will of the Lord, but this was a precept reiterated by many early Protestant writers, not all of whom, however, would have been prepared to carry it through to its logical conclusions. In the 1530s the Henrician evangelical John Frith can be found asserting that 'To say that Christ would have his disciples to compel men with prisonment, fetters, scourging, sword and fire is very false and far from the mildness of a Christian spirit'. A decade and a half later the Edwardian physician and cleric William Turner similarly insisted that religious error was 'no material thing that we must fight withall, but ghostly'.[57]

This, indeed, was a central tenet of Sebastian Castellio's well-known tract written in protest at the burning of Michael Servetus in Geneva in 1553, as it had been of the early pronouncements of Martin Luther, who had written in 1523 that 'heresy is a spiritual matter which you cannot hack to pieces with iron, consume with fir[e], or drown in water'.[58] John Foxe famously averred that it was 'tyrannical to constrain by faggots' and that 'the most effective master of teaching was love' and the separatist martyr John Penry told his accusers in 1593 that 'imprisonments, judgements, yea, death itself, are not meet weapons to convince men's consciences'.[59] In 1615 Thomas Helwys similarly declared it a 'a sure word in divinity' that 'God loves not to plant his church by violence & bloodshed'. Ironically, in view of his imprisonment by the Jacobean regime, Helwys was echoing a statement made to Parliament a year earlier by King James I, who told assembled members that no 'relygeone or heresye was ever exterpated by ... the swoarde'.[60] 'Prisons and swords are no Church-officers', John Goodwin informed his parishioners in 1644, reinforcing it with the astute observation that execution and incarceration all too often had counterproductive effects: 'an Heretique being dead ... speaketh in his surviving heresie with every whit as much authoritie ... as he could do if he were alive, if not with more'. '[F]etters ... put upon the feet of errors ... to secure and keep them under' too often proved 'wings whereby they raise themselves the higher in the thoughts and minds of men, and gain an opportunitie of a further and ranker propagation of themselves in the world'.[61] The only sword that had the capacity to conquer obstinacy and error, wrote Roger Williams, was the 'soule-piercing' sword of God's word as wielded by the Holy Spirit. Violence could prevail 'no more than the vapour of wind that blows, to hinder the heat of the fire', remarked John Musgrave.[62] Locke too reminded his readers that Christ had 'sent out his soldiers to the subduing of Nations' armed not with 'Instruments of Force, but prepared with the Gospel of Peace, and with the Exemplary Holiness of their Conversation': 'it was much more easie for him to do it with Armies of Heavenly Legions, than for any Son of the Church how potent soever, with all his Dragoons'.[63]

All this was closely linked with the notion that religious belief was inherently voluntary and that force could never produce a genuine commitment to the truth. Instead, it encouraged clandestinity and dissimulation. In the words of Luther, it forced 'the tongue to lie'.[64] Persecution, complained the Baptist Leonard Busher in 1614, created not a congregation of the faithful but 'a confused Babel, full of every unclean and hateful bird, even a hold of foul spirits'.[65] According to the Independent William Bartlet in 1647, it was 'the High-way to make more hypocrites then sound Christians'; 'compulsion can no more gain the heart', insisted his colleague John Cook, 'than the fish can love the fisherman'.[66] In emphasising the futility of seeking to enforce external conformity, Henry Robinson pointed to the unedifying spectacle of the Portuguese Jewish *conversos* whose Christianity was merely skin-deep, of Protestant merchants and travellers in Italy and Spain 'which ordinarily goe to Masse and Vespers, to avoid suspition of the Inquisition', and of English church papists who attended services 'when they were strictly lookt too, stopping their eares with wooll because they would not heare at all, or heare with an intention to beleeve the contrary'.[67]

The same convictions were articulated by Henry Stubbe in 1659: 'Terrour may bring men to an outward complyance but not to alter their judgements, it doth not abate their wickedness, but heightens it with the aggravation of hypocrisy'.[68] Such arguments regularly reasserted themselves in the post-Restoration period, appearing in the context of the parliamentary debates about toleration in the mid-1670s[69] and occupying a prominent place in Locke's *Letter concerning toleration*. Corporal sufferings and outward penalties had no 'such Efficacy as to make Men change the inward Judgement that they have framed of things'. 'Far from being any furtherance', the false profession and practice wrought by coercion were 'indeed Great Obstacles to our Salvation'. Rather than expiating the sins that displeased the Almighty, they added to them an impious contempt of His divine majesty.[70] In the eyes of the oppressed and oppressors alike this was to open a door for the entry of atheism and thus damnation.

An alternative strand of thinking about tolerance revolved around what may be called a 'theology of reduction'.[71] This involved paring down the body of canonical dogma to a minimum with the aim of accomplishing the goal of religious reunion. The instinct to foster reconciliation by reducing religious faith to a core of truths essential to salvation, around which hovered a wider penumbra of secondary issues upon which Christians might agree to differ, was Erasmian and humanist in origin. As developed by Philip Melanchthon and Martin Bucer, the concept of *adiaphora* or 'things indifferent', could, of course, cut both ways. As we saw in Chapter 2, it was an area in which the magistrate could claim the right to legislate for the sake of order and decency and to discipline those who infringed these human rules, and in which the

Pauline imperative for edification could impel the godly to take coercive action to avoid scandal. On the other hand, however, it could provide the basis for a case for ecclesiastical comprehension. This was a feature of the proposals which Robert Beale, clerk of the Privy Council, put forward in 1584 in an effort to ease the plight of puritan minsters with liturgical scruples: an element of flexibility with regard to ceremonies was to be preferred above ecclesiastical fission and schism over these peripheral issues.[72]

Later in the period moderate Anglican and latitudinarian writers likewise invoked *adiaphora* to argue that cordial disagreement on non-doctrinal matters could be accommodated within the parameters of the national Church. This was the essence of a massive tract published by Daniel Whitby, Precentor of Salisbury Cathedral, in 1682 entitled *The Protestant reconciler, humbly pleading for condescension to dissenting brethren, in things indifferent and unnecessary, for the sake of peace.*[73] In the 1650s, the Independent Vavasour Powell believed that differing views on baptism could 'consist with brotherly love and Christian communion', while the Presbyterian Richard Baxter called for 'unity in all things necessary and liberty in things unnecessary, and charity in all', a cry he renewed in his *Proposal for union among Protestants* addressed to Parliament in the wake of the Popish Plot in 1679.[74] Indeed, a willingness to allow room for discretion was often inspired by a determination to present a united front against the Romish Antichrist. As such it rarely embodied a real break with the paradigm of persecution which the reformed shared with their Catholic enemies. More radically, puritans like Samuel Rutherford insisted that *adiaphora* constituted a sphere in which the consciences of individuals could not be bound by any external power, except where this interfered with the stability of civil society or contravened moral law. Christ's rule over this faculty, which was widely conceived to be the spiritual deputy or lieutenant He placed in the soul of each believer, had to be direct and unmediated.[75]

This leads us neatly on to the contention that conscience was inviolable, even where it was manifestly misguided and erroneous. This became an increasingly insistent feature of tolerationist writing in the course of the post-Reformation period. Robert Persons urged respect for the recusant's refusal to attend Protestant services on the grounds that a person who acted in defiance of his inner beliefs commited a grievous sin and that a civil authority which sought to compel him to do so was itself guilty of a diabolical crime. To force a Jew to swear to the existence of the Holy Trinity, he insisted, would be no less unpardonable.[76] It was to become an accessory to the innocent blood of that soul. Similar claims had been made by Edward Aglionby in the context of a parliamentary debate on the enforcement of conformity in 1570, when he declared that 'the conscience of man is internall, invisible, and not in the power of the greatest monarch of the worlde; in no lymittes to be streightened, in no bondes to be conteyned'.[77]

During the Civil War, the Leveller John Lilburne echoed the point that God alone was lord over this inner kingdom, 'it being too high a throne for all the creatures of the world to raigne in'. Those who dared 'to plucke his Crowne from his head' and 'his Scepter out of his hand' should quake and tremble at their own temerity.[78] The same opinions were frequently restated during the Whitehall debates of 1648. Leonard Busher and Richard Overton both employed the emotive metaphor of rape to describe external violation of the individual conscience, the latter remarking emphatically that this was 'worse than to ravish the bodies of women and Maides against their wills'.[79] The Cambridge Platonist Henry More would also stress in a treatise of 1666 that in hindering 'the sincere Religionist from the Profession of his Religion' civil authorities were '*ipso facto* guilty of rebellion against their Maker, by corrupting this liege Subjects, and urging them to faithlessness and neglect of their duty'. This was to question the 'unerring Wisedom' of God who had his reasons for allowing them to be seduced by false opinions, whether by way of 'Punishment' or 'Probation'.[80]

Such claims were frequently connected with an insistence that magistrates had neither responsibility for the salvation of the souls of men and women nor any jurisdiction over them. The principle that the state and Church were not coterminous and that the former had no business meddling in the sphere of the Holy Spirit was a shibboleth of Anabaptist and separatist thinking in the sixteenth century. In the seventeenth the assault on the notion that the godly ruler and nation had an unshirkable obligation to prevent its subjects from taking a high road to hell was joined by other sectarian voices. This was the point where the sects parted from Presbyterians and Independents. The purposes of government were 'merely civil', said Roger Williams, confined to 'the defence of persons, estates, families, liberties of a city or civil state, and the suppressing of uncivil or injurious persons or actions'. It was an entirely separate entity from the Church, which was a purely private association consisting of the free and voluntary congregation of the gathered saints, 'like unto a Body or College of Physitians' or 'a Corporation, Society or Company of East Indie or Turkie-Merchants'.[81] In urging the abolition of the confessional state and its constitutional separation from any kind of ecclesiastical institution, such writers were certainly not denying disestablished, independent churches the right to impose internal discipline upon their members. On the contrary, rigorous application of sanctions against errant and heretical brethren was all the more necessary. Nevertheless, they were simultaneously laying the ideological foundations for a secular society. This axiom that civil powers had no dominion over the private religious opinions of human beings and that 'no Man by nature is bound unto any particular Church or Sect' would also be one of the cornerstones of John Locke's thesis about toleration.[82]

Embedded in some statements on this theme, furthermore, was the germ of the modern idea that 'conscience' is a relative concept and that what matters is the sincerity of one's convictions rather than their concordance with an absolute and objectively defined body of 'truth'. This came to be intimately connected with the argument that Christians should refrain from persecution on the grounds that their ability to identify what constituted that truth was inherently fallible. In expressing doubt about the validity of the wave of contemporary trials for diabolical witchcraft, the sixteenth-century French humanist Michel de Montaigne famously observed that 'it is putting a very high price on one's conjectures to have a man roasted alive because of them'.[83] Applied to the question of theological heterodoxy, the same precept seriously undercut the imperative for religious coercion and judicial violence.

Uncertainty about the possibility of arriving at certain knowledge was already present in Castellio's *Concerning heretics* (1554), but it grew in prominence as the period progressed. According to the Independent John Goodwin, men ran 'the hazard of fighting against God in suppressing any way, doctrine, or practice, concerning which they know not certainly whether it be from God or no'. The foundation on which William Walwyn placed his case for toleration in *The compassionate samaritan* (1644) was also the claim that 'no man, nor no sort of men can presume of an unerring spirit: 'tis known that the Fathers, General Councells, Nationall Assemblies, Synods, and Parliaments in their times have been most grosly mistaken'.[84] Eirenical Anglican writers like Henry More and Benjamin Whichcote also inclined to the view that persecutors took a huge risk in punishing people for opinions which could not be definitively verified: More warned against 'affixing any of our own Inventions or Interpretations of Scripture for Christian Truths' and Whichcote said that he would 'not break the certain Laws of Charity, for a doubtful Doctrine'.[85] Locke and Bayle too spoke of the weakness of the human capacity to comprehend the nature of divine teaching and this was one of the streams that fed into the fashionable philosophical doubt of the early Enlightenment. Nevertheless, scepticism per se has little place in the discourse of 'toleration' in early modern England. Despite our tendency to assume an 'emotional kinship' between indifference towards or rejection of the existence of God and the acceptance of religious pluralism, there is little to support such a link before the eighteenth century. In fact sceptics like Thomas Hobbes were just as frequently advocates of repression as they were of the removal of sanctions, both on purely political and pragmatic grounds.[86]

In the preceding period, tolerance was far more likely to grow from the soil of Protestant zeal. From the mid-sixteenth century onwards, there were those who argued that heresy and diversity were actually good for the cause of Christian truth since they catalysed discussion that would clarify its content. Following this logic, the Italian exile Jacob Acontius insisted in his Latin treatise of 1565 that 'Satan's kingdom cannot long continue where there is liberty of opinion in regard to religion'.[87] Writing eighty years later, Henry Robinson was also convinced that 'if the Gospel had but a free passage, and the true Professours liberty to teach and publish it, this only as a sovereigne remedy and counterpoyson, would prevaile against all heresies'.[88] Toleration was not the enemy of religious unity but its trusty ally and friend. As John Milton yet more eloquently contended, far from inhibiting the victory of the truth, it would in fact facilitate it.[89]

More surprisingly from the perspective of the twenty-first century, extreme millenarianism can be shown to have inspired calls for toleration. An over-whelming sense of the imminence of Christ's reign on earth gave the Fifth Monarchist movement an ecumenical dimension. Latitude could and should be permitted in the lead up to it, even to Turks and infidels: it was the duty of the saints to participate actively in ushering in this messianic kingdom.[90] William Lamont has commented that apocalyptic expectation of the heavenly discrimination of the sheep and the goats which would accompany the end of the world was a 'supreme comfort' to men like Roger Williams – both an incentive to and a justification for their rousing cries for human governments to grant liberty of conscience to all.[91] Chiliasm also helped to create a climate of opinion conducive to serious discussion about the readmission of the Jews in the mid-1650s. The philo-semitism of intellectuals such as Samuel Hartlib and John Dury and of self-styled prophets like Thomas Tany and Arise Evans was underpinned by the conviction that the Jews had a leading part to play in the great cosmic drama that was unfolding before them and that their con-version would precede the Second Coming. For both groups the ultimate aim of this enterprise was the reunification of the scattered body of God's chosen people and the 'deliverance' of the Jewish race from 'captivity' in ignorance and sin. The same (ultimately intolerant) assumptions had shaped the policy of *convivencia* in the Middle Ages and they were also an element in the benign attitude that some contemporary Protestant and Catholic churchmen displayed towards the American Indians.[92]

The Bible and Christian theology were undoubtedly the dominant sources of early modern thinking on liberty of conscience and toleration. But the case was sometimes also buttressed with more pragmatic arguments. Prominent here was the idea of *raison d'etat* or 'reason of state'. Absorbing the precepts developed by *politiques* like Michel de L'Hôpital, Jean Bodin and William of Orange in the context of the destructive religious wars in France and the Netherlands, some began to elevate the preservation of the monarchy and nation above the pursuit of ideological purity. Looking across the English Channel, they saw both the anarchy engendered by the attempt to enforce uniformity and the mollifying effects that could be wrought by a policy of official toleration. The renewed conflicts of the Thirty Years War (1618–48) underlined the point that mutual intolerance was often pernicious to the survival of the political establishment and to the peace of society, while England's own troubles in the middle decades of the seventeenth century drove the lesson home yet more emphatically to many, including Thomas Hobbes.[93] Making a priority of state stability, however, was not incompatible with a commitment to restoring the monopoly of a single form of truth when a change in circumstances permitted; it could also furnish a clear warrant for persecution.

Even those who did not subscribe to *politique* views could still invoke the example of neighbouring countries to prove that licensing pluralism and denominational diversity did not necessarily consume a nation or community from within. In his dialogue *The arraignment of Mr Persecution* (1645), Richard Overton memorably embodied this insight in the characters of Mr Unity of Kingdoms, Mr Nationall-Strength, Mr Setled-Peace, Mr United Provinces, Mr Desolate-Germany, Mr Publique-Good, Mr Nationall-Wealth and Mr Domestick-Miseries, who were all called to testify against this 'great Enemie and Incendiary of mankind' who had an infinite variety of sly aliases and disguises, including Mr Spanish-Inquisition, Mr High-Commission, and Mr Classicall Presbytrie.[94] Practical experience of travel in Holland, Poland, Transylvania and North Africa showed that adherents of heretical and even non-Christian religions could still be loyal, reliable and peaceable citizens and that their presence inhibited neither the security nor the prosperity of a state.

There were also some who stressed the disruptive effects which the pursuit of unity had upon commerce and trade. Such arguments were frequently largely negative and defensive in character, but as the period progressed greater emphasis fell upon the positive economic benefits attendant upon toleration. The Baptist Thomas Helwys appealed to the flourishing state of the Dutch economy in his *Humble supplication* to the Jacobean regime of 1609. In the 1640s Henry Robinson offered an even more sustained analysis of the advantages religious *laissez-faire* would bring to England, this time from the hand of a leading businessman who had watched the steady defection of Protestant merchants to America and elsewhere and who would later advise the Commonwealth in this area of policy. If his own country did not follow the example of Turkey, Morocco and the United Provinces, he predicted, it would very rapidly find itself lagging behind its capitalist rivals. In the latter region, setting consciences free had proved 'a great meanes to prevaile with God Almighty to prosper them'. Henry Parker's *Of a free trade* (1648) and Slingsby Bethell's *The present interest of England stated* (1671) continued in the same mercantilist vein. The latter condemned 'imposing upon conscience, in matters of religion' as 'a mischief unto trade transcending all others whatsoever', remarking upon the particular industriousness of the dissenters in passing.[95] Quakers like William Penn also warned that religious repression would lead inexorably to commerical decline: 'it cannot be in the Interest of

England', he argued in 1679, 'to let a great part of her Sober & Useful Inhabitants be destroy'd about things that concern another World'.[96] Similar reasoning was employed by some proponents of the readmission of the Jews, and in the eighteenth century by Daniel Defoe.[97]

Once again, it is important to emphasise the degree to which such arguments were still couched in the theological language, and underpinned by the doctrine, of divine providence. Their advocates still regarded the material well-being of society as a blessing bestowed by the Lord. Toleration, rather than persecution, came to be viewed as a mechanism for ensuring that a benevolent deity continued to smile kindly upon it. To this extent, as Blair Worden has suggested, the development of thinking on this issue may reflect a gradual shift in how in God Himself was conceptualised. It may be evidence of the process by which He was increasingly seen less as an 'awesome dictator' and tyrannical judge and more as a 'friendly monitor', tender father and magnanimous creator.[98] In short, it may index the way in which charity and tolerance eclipsed rigour and severity as the chief attributes of the divine personality.

To stress the theological as opposed to the secular and sceptical roots of tolerationist thought and to underline the contingent and limited character of many calls for 'liberty of conscience' in this period is not in the end to deny their significance. Even if they touched a chord with only a minority of people in early modern England, even if they often evaporated in the face of a sudden reversal of fortune, the crystallisation and articulation of such ideas in writing and print had important implications. At the very least those who dared to dissent from the Augustinian consensus on persecution were providing future generations with the linguistic and conceptual resources to explain the gap between ideal and practice created by the circumstances in which they increasingly found themselves. Eventually, they may have helped people to come to terms with the unstoppable spread of religious pluralism that was the most powerful legacy left by the long Reformation itself. However, they did not prevent renewed outbreaks of hatred and violence. Indeed, as I argue in the concluding part of this chapter, on occasion they may even have contributed to precipitating them.

OFFICIAL EDICTS AND POLITICAL INITIATIVES

The theories and arguments in support of toleration that we have been discussing had an ambiguous and ambivalent relationship with evolving legal and practical realities. Examining them in isolation has the disadvantage of dislocating them from the institutional and sociological settings in which they developed organically. The aim of the next two sections is to sketch the ecclesiastical, political and social dimensions of tolerance in early modern England – firstly, the official edicts and initiatives that provided space for dissent to exist, and secondly, the personal and parochial manifestations of the instinct to bear patiently with the misguided beliefs and illicit observances of one's neighbours. In the former case, once again care must be taken in describing the character and assessing the objectives of such measures, and in unravelling their actual intentions and empirical effects from the elaborate web of rhetoric woven around them. In the case of the latter, we must train our ears and eyes to detect the absences, silences and omissions in our sources – to identify the occasions on which lay people refrained from overtly expressing their implicit disapproval of the outlook and lifestyle of religious minorities. Dividing these two areas of activity (or inactivity) into separate analytical categories has its heuristic uses, but, in the context of a voluntary bureaucracy, it is by no means always straightforward.

We may begin with the point that a degree of strategic and temporary leniency was explicitly built into the ecclesiastical procedures designed to bring about uniformity with the established Church. It was the responsibility of bishops and ministers to use every endeavour to dissuade dissenters from their erroneous opinions before resorting to spiritual or physical sanctions. Gentle persuasion was to precede persecution. Amicable dialogue with the wayward was one end of the spectrum that concluded with excommunication and execution – and it was a process that involved give and take on both sides. This is often overlooked by historians drawn to those moments when these efforts at conciliation and arbitration fell short of achieving the goal of recantation or conversion, as a consequence of which men and women who stubbornly refused to relinquish their heterodox convictions were imprisoned, corporally punished, or consigned to the gallows or stake. To echo Alec Ryrie, it is important to remember that 'to burn a baptised Christian for obstinate heresy represented a catastrophic pastoral failure'.[99] Where this was averted and dissidents yielded to the arguments of the episcopal and clerical authorities, by contrast, we would do well to focus less on the 'weakness' and 'hypocrisy' of the former and more on the discretion and flexibility exhibited by the latter in their attempts to restore religious concord.

Undoubtedly, much depended on the temperaments of the particular individuals involved, but it should not be forgotten that the duty of private conference with heretics, schismatics, recusants, and separatists was an obligation of office. Visitation articles frequently asked if the clergy had laboured to reclaim those of their parishioners who stood 'in hazard of salvation' and to bring them 'into the faith, profession, body and bosome of the Church'. Ministers were enjoined to undertake 'quiet and temperate conference' to dissuade nonconformists from the errors that induced them to forsake the ecclesiastical establishment.[100] A memorandum from the late 1570s recommended that those 'backward and corrupt in relligion' be 'conferred withall by the space of two moneths, by men sufficientlie learned after a Charitable sorte'.[101]

Approached from this angle, the frequency with which the fifteenth- and early sixteenth-century Lollards abjured may be an indirect tribute to the extent to which prelates and pastors succeeded in coaxing and negotiating rather than forcing straying sheep back into the fold. Heretics in the Thames Valley were mildly treated by Bishop William Atwater who rarely imposed full public penance upon offenders, preferring friendly admonition above stern correction. As one Lollard testified, when 'known-men' were called before him, he often 'sent them home again, bidding them that they should live among their neighbours as good Christian men should'.[102] Not all of his colleagues carried these tactics as far as Atwater but it would be a mistake to attribute the large number of Lollard recantations recorded in ecclesiastical registers merely to the nicodemite inclinations of the movement. This was 'a game for two players'.[103]

Equally earnest attempts to persuade evangelicals, sacramentarian radicals and intransigent Catholics were a feature of the early Reformation period – a period when confessional boundaries were particularly porous and fluid. During the reigns of Henry VIII, Edward VI and Mary I, both conservative and Protestant bishops can be found bending over backwards to find common ground with lay and clerical dissidents. Craig D'Alton has recently illuminated the humanist strategy of *caritas* that Cardinal Wolsey and his colleagues adopted in the 1520s when dealing with academic Lutheran heretics like Robert Barnes. Those whose inclinations towards the novel ideas of the German monk sprang from intellectual curiosity and who showed little propensity for public proselytising were counselled secretly, 'behind closed doors', in a manner that seems to have minimised their impact and reclaimed not a few from travelling a defiant road to the stake.[104] Eager to heal the breach within the English Church brought about by the formal break with Rome, Archbishop Thomas Cranmer also displayed considerable forbearance in his dealings with the 'sects' on both the right and the left. In 1533 he summoned John Frith 'three or four times to persuade him to leave ... his imagination' on the vexed question of the Eucharist, so anxious was he to avoid consigning him to the flames. Two years later he pleaded for two monks to be spared death for denying the Royal Supremacy, 'that their consciences may be clearly averted from the same by communication of sincere doctrine', a task he offered to undertake himself.[105]

Despite the reputation of bloody persecutor posthumously constructed for him by John Foxe, Edmund Bonner was no less industrious in his efforts to win round heretics like Robert Wisdom and Anne Askew, while Cuthbert Tunstall took such pains with Thomas Bilney that the law was 'so far stretched forth that the leather could scant hold'.[106] Reginald Pole too seems to have seen doctrinal instruction rather than sanguinary force as the key to the reunification of Christendom: famously his solicitous treatment of Edward VI's former tutor, John Cheke, saved him from the fires of Smithfield.[107]

Elizabethan ministers were likewise conscious of the advantages of approaching recalcitrant papists and sectaries with kindness, courtesy and tact. Such tactics were adopted by Andrew Perne in tackling the problem of Familist dissent in the Cambridgeshire parish of Balsham, and by Edmund Bunny and John Dove in their encounters with the Catholics of the north. Both believed that, rather than seeking 'to breake the brused reede' and 'quench the smoaking flax', the most effective evangelical strategy was often 'gentlenesse'.[108] Early seventeenth-century divines like William Bedell and John Reading also saw moderation as the best method of luring those 'snarled by this perswasion of separation' back towards Protestant orthodoxy. As the latter preached in 1641, 'lenity can doe more than rigour, a mild hand maketh better impression than a rigid and imperious injunction can; sanctity cannot be forced neither will opinion ...'[109]

Similar convictions underpinned the conduct of bishops and ministers after the Restoration: Nathaniel Aske, rector of Somerset Magna in Wiltshire, delayed presenting dissenters to the church courts in the 1670s, hoping 'to overcome them by love', and Bishop William Nicholson of Gloucester's conciliatory attitude towards the Quakers of his diocese induced at least some to rejoin the Church of England. One Friend whom he summoned from his prison cell, 'sometimes keeping him to dinner' and 'reasoning the case with him, that he had no other argument for his principles than that the Spirit said it must be so', desired to be absolved from the excommunication and readmitted to the Anglican communion.[110] In none of these cases, however, was there ever any question of according religious dissidents a permanent right to exist. The aim of such eirenicism was always to bring them into complete conformity with the status quo – it was merely a technique for persuading them to embrace a single version of the truth. When it failed, few had any difficulty with exchanging charity for rigour and moving from cordial discussion to punitive coercion: these were two sides of the same coin. Nor should a willingness to employ such tactics be used as a litmus test for dividing 'humanist' from 'Tridentine' Catholics, militant puritans from 'latitudinarian' Protestants, or Calvinists from Laudians, and projecting them onto a graph which maps 'persecution' against 'toleration'. Although it could, and as we shall see did, become caught up in polemical disputes about different styles of churchmanship, ecclesiastical tolerance as a mechanism for achieving Christian unity transcended denominational barriers.

This is apparent if we look at the central documents of the English Reformations of the mid-sixteenth century. Much of the legislation of this period embodied a desire to create conditions in which communities fractured by the spread and imposition of Protestant ideas could reach eventual agreement. Alongside statutes designed to abolish 'diversity in opinions', we find proclamations, ordinances and injunctions offering a form of temporary amnesty to dissenters and urging people to exercise restraint and forbearance in response to their neighbours at a time of bewildering theological change and liturgical upheaval. Thus in 1539 Henry VIII issued a proclamation pardoning simple persons seduced by foreign Anabaptists and sacramentarians who would retract their opinions, presenting himself as 'a most loving parent much moved with pity, tendering the winnowing of them again to Christ's flock ... and fearing also that great fear of extreme punishment might turn their simplicity to obstinacy, whereby they might perish and be lost out of [it] forever'.[111]

The fatherly mercy of the king did not last long, as the passing of the Act of Six Articles the same year reveals, but it is important to recognise that at root both were a means to the same end – national concord. This objective also underpinned Mary's first declaration on the subject of religion in August 1553, which promised short-term freedom of conscience to all her subjects, declaring that 'of her most gracious disposition and clemency' she would not compel any man or woman to embrace Catholicism until 'such time as further order by common assent may be taken therein', and charging them to set aside 'those new-found devilish terms of papist or heretic' and 'live together in quiet sort and Christian charity' for the sake of maintaining the 'tranquility of the realm'.[112] A similar ban on words of 'disdainful names of reproach' had been ordered in royal injunctions issued in the year of Edward VI's accession in 1547, which also admonished that people should not 'in any wise refuse or exclude' those who held different views from themselves 'from their companies, at any time when occasion shall be offered that they may come together charitably and Christianly'.[113]

In a proclamation issued before the promulgation of the official settlement of religion of July 1559, Elizabeth charged mayors, sheriffs and justices to restrain those 'disordered persons' who sought 'willingly to break, either by misordered deed or contemptuous speech, the common peace and bond of charity'. The Elizabethan Injunctions themselves echoed earlier statements in prohibiting those 'slanderous words and railings, whereby charity, the knot of all Christian society, is loosed' and declaring that none were 'to use in despite or rebuke of any person these convicious words, papist, or papistical heretic, schismatic, or sacramentary'.[114] Until such time as religious consensus was restored, the discord that invariably accompanied such ecclesiastical 'alterations' was to be remedied by mutual tolerance and moratorium.

To highlight the strategies to contain chaos that marked the initial phases of the English Reformation is emphatically not, however, to endorse the idea that this was a movement that deliberately set out to forge a middle way between Catholicism and Reformed Protestantism,[115] let alone to 'tolerate' all those who avoided these extremes. That said, it must be acknowledged that the ambiguous, incremental and piecemeal character of Henrician developments was inadvertently conducive to the accommodation of a broad spectrum of views. A product both of the tussle of competing factions and of the king's own idiosyncratic vision (memorably described by Diarmaid MacCulloch as 'a weird jackdaw's nest containing a jumble of theological ideas from tradition- alist and evangelical sources'),[116] the confusions, anomalies and apparent reversals of religious policy in the 1530s and 1540s sent out a very mixed message to contemporaries, which itself provided considerable scope for diversity of opinion. Although the brief reign of Edward VI represented the high-water mark of the Church of England's alignment with the Swiss Reformed tradition, it too involved an element of compromise on certain key issues, which was emblematic of its chief architect Thomas Cranmer. As one commentator informed Heinrich Bullinger in Zurich in 1549 'some puerili- ties have been still suffered to remain, lest the people should be offended by too great an innovation'.[117]

Elizabeth's religious settlement was also the outcome of some vigorous horse-trading in Convocation and Parliament and it too rested on a peculiar hybrid of Calvinist doctrine and conservative liturgy and discipline. The queen's temperamental caution, combined with the squabbles within the clerical establishment, resulted in a gradualist and fabian strategy for effecting England's wholesale conversion into a Protestant nation. Slightly modified from its predecessor of 1552, the language of the Book of Common Prayer on the critical question of a real presence in the Eucharist was 'a masterpiece of theological engineering',[118] which afforded room for divergent points of view, while its rubrics permitted the continuing use of time-honoured ceremonies and vestments in a manner that was primarily intended to conciliate and accommodate Lutheran opinion,[119] but which indubitably supplied Catholics and conservatives with much room for manoeuvre too.

A degree of pastoral latitude was also permitted with regard to the use of unleavened wafers or 'common bread' during the administration of com- munion. Eager to appease the 'division and bitterness' that had arisen over the issue, in one incident in 1580, the Privy Council advised the bishop of Chester 'charitabley to tollerate' those who preferred the former 'as children, with milke'.[120] The Church of England was to be a nursery in which the people were to be gently weaned, rather than roughly snatched, from popery. Confessional pluralism might have to be condoned for a period, but it would soon evaporate under the influence of Protestant preaching and teaching of the true religion. This had to be given time to do its work: hence the regime's avoidance of coercion for more than a decade. The problem as the godly saw it was that the queen demonstrated no commitment to replacing this ad hoc, pragmatic and interim settlement with a more thorough-going Reformation. As John Jewel wrote to Peter Martyr Vermigli in February 1562, things that could be 'toler- ated by sovereigns by reason of the times' and were at first 'not attended with inconvenience' had to be removed once 'the full light of the gospel' had 'shone forth', lest 'the very vestiges of error' perpetuate the weak in false belief.[121] Instead, Elizabeth allowed the 1559 settlement to harden into permanence. Later writers like Richard Hooker who played a key part in 'the invention of Anglicanism' would retrospectively celebrate this as the original intention and claim that the unique moderation of the English Church was a singular achievement. This process was paralleled and complicated by the reinvention, not to say canonisation, of Hooker himself by Laudian and Anglo-Catholic commentators.[122] But we should not allow their rhetoric to disguise the fact that the inclusiveness that became its hallmark was initially, at least in part, the offspring of expediency. Its capacity for comprehension was a function less of design than of an 'accidental genius'.[123] Without reproducing the flawed notion of an Anglican 'via media', it can still be observed that in the long term this created a peculiarly accommodating institution.

We shall return to the question of the ability and willingness of the post-Reformation Church to absorb some forms of Roman Catholic dissent later, but first we consider how leading figures within it strove to contain the hotter sort of Protestants within its ranks, even those who yearned to replace the episcopal hierarchy with a system of elders, deacons and synods. Here again the concept of *adiaphora* was critical. Even as some bishops were determined to enforce conformity on matters of clerical dress and liturgical gesture which they regarded as necessary for order and decency, others were willing to bear with precisians for the good of the Church to which, on the grounds of the purity of its doctrine, they remained firmly committed. Concentration on episodes such as Bancroft's and Whitgift's drive for subscription has deflected attention from those occasions, especially, but by no means exclusively during the archiepiscopates of Grindal and Abbot, when the authorities treated puritan ministers with scruples of conscience about the surplice, articles or canons with a degree of indulgence and condoned the evolution of quasi-Presbyterian forms of training and discipline like prophesyings, classes and conferences. Bishop Parkhurst of Norwich was commended to Bullinger for his 'kind forbearance' to nonconformists during the Vestiarian Controversy, a strategy of 'love and favore' which he defended to Matthew Parker as far more likely to produce compliance than a 'rough and austere forme and maner of ruling'. Thomas Bentham of Coventry and Lichfield was also willing to make concessions to dissenting brethren whose contribution to the evangelical programme of the Church was too valuable to consider forgoing, and Grindal himself granted informal and verbal licences to diligent ministers who would not wear the 'rag of Rome'.[124] Likewise the good service that many puritan preachers did in the fight against Catholic recidivism in 'dark corners of the land' like Lancashire earned them a degree of dispensation within the sphere of things indifferent. Lawrence Chaderton told James I at the Hampton Court

Conference in 1604 that this policy was necessary to prevent those won to the gospel from backsliding to popery once more.[125] In Elizabethan Kent, magistrates pleaded against the suspension of the Presbyterian radical John Strowd on the grounds that 'neither our county be deprived of so diligent a labourer in the Lord's harvest nor that the enemies of God's truth ... may herein find matter of joy and triumph'.[126]

The need for solidarity against the popish or sectarian menace could also prompt the extension of an olive branch to those with powerful polemical skills which the Church could ill afford to lose: George Gifford survived in large part because of his energetic efforts against the East Anglian separatists and in exile the disgraced Thomas Cartwright was encouraged to produce a comprehensive refutation of the marginal notes of Douai-Rheims New Testament with the suggestion that it might make 'an overture for your further favour'.[127] While he remained out in the cold, many other puritans of more moderate views were kept within the pale by the judicious exercise of discretion by their local ordinaries. The famous Blackfriars preacher William Gouge was handled with kid gloves, as was the talented pastor Richard Bernard, who was awarded a West Country living despite his ejection in 1605.[128] Some members of the later Stuart episcopate likewise turned a blind eye towards the liturgical quirks of those who had conformed far enough to escape suspension in 1662, as a result of which puritan piety continued to infuse the religion of England's Protestants. Patrick Collinson speaks of the Jacobean Church as an institution that had 'the capacity to contain within its loose and sometimes anomalous structures vigorous forms of voluntary religious expression' – a characterisation that applies equally well to its Restoration successor.[129] Without the de facto tolerance of godly ministers with reservations about the religious settlement that remained a feature of church life throughout this period this would not have been possible.

This form of Protestant ecumenism within the established Church was parallelled by a limited and equivocal Protestant ecumenism without. The decision of the Edwardian regime to permit the setting up of autonomous Dutch and French 'stranger churches' in London in 1550 had the effect of legitimising the existence, alongside the English episcopal hierarchy, of a series of separate congregations organised on quite different lines. Under the superintendence of the Polish evangelical John à Lasco, these foreign churches were originally envisaged as a providing a shining model of the kind of Reformed polity to which the still evolving Church of England should itself aspire. The underlying aim of some at least seems to have been convergence and fusion, though consideration of the economic benefits that might be brought by the immigrants was also a prominent factor. Their royal charter of independence was restored under Elizabeth I, who confirmed their privilege of separate worship, but placed them loosely under the oversight of the bishop of the diocese. There was no longer any intention of using them as a blueprint for a radical overhaul of the prevailing ecclesiastical structures and increasingly they were suspected of being havens and nurseries of Presbyterian dissent. They played 'the part of a Trojan horse, bringing Reformed worship and discipline fully armed into the midst of the Anglican camp'[130] and their irregular status remained a source of inspiration to separatists, who saw them as a prototype for the religious 'liberty' they themselves wished to be accorded by the authorities. To Henry Jacob these congregations in 'brotherly communion with the rest of our English churches' were examples of how a broader denominational parity might work in practice.[131] This was not a principled form of 'toleration' but it did represent a significant concession born out of a commitment to the concept of the Calvinist International – a brotherhood of churches joined by a shared body of doctrine, even if they differed in outward governance. It is no wonder that William Laud set his sights on reducing later generations of these 'outlandish' congregations to conformity in the 1630s. Other targets of the Archbishop's drive for bureaucratic standardisation were the churches of Guernsey and Jersey, whose Calvinist synods were compelled to accept the Book of Common Prayer and submit to the jurisdiction of the bishop of Winchester.

As the Caroline Church distanced itself from its Protestant sisters on the Continent the pressure to eliminate these un-, even anti-, episcopal anomalies grew. The threat was lifted by the onset of the Civil War and, although there were ongoing Restoration attempts to impose the Anglican liturgy upon the stranger communities, they continued to facilitate an element of religious diversity on the edges (both geographical and metaphorical) of the Protestant establishment.[132] This was to be greatly rejuvenated by the fresh influx of refugees from France in the wake of the revocation of the Edict of Nantes in 1685, despite the intention of James II and his advisers to offer relief only to those who could provide a certificate of their reception of communion. The Act of Toleration would release the Huguenots, no less than other separate congregations, from the constraints of the Act of Uniformity.[133]

From initiatives for accommodating foreign Protestants within the English commonwealth we now return to legal efforts to comprehend dissenting ones within the Church of England itself. This had long been an objective of puritan members of Parliament and the hijacking by the ecclesiastical authorities of the statute of 1571 ordering clerical subscription to the Thirty-nine Articles should not eclipse the fact that this began as a bill designed not to detect crypto-Catholics but to ease the scrupulous consciences of the godly. Nicholas Tyacke has christened it 'the first toleration act'. The casuistical phrasing of the requirement that the clergy subscribe to those articles which '*onely* concerne the confession of the true Christian faithe and the doctrine of the sacraments' admitted of a range of interpretations on the part of those charged with enforcing it. This, of course, cut both ways, with the consequence that there were continued attempts to introduce legislation that would provide a more secure outlet for puritan ministers with doubts about the Prayer Book and other aspects of the Elizabethan settlement. Bills for limited subscription and for excusing those who made 'omissions or changes of some portions or ryte' in the liturgy commanded fairly wide parliamentary support but were angrily vetoed by the queen. Similar measures were floated in 1614, 1625, 1626 and 1628, all without success.[34]

Passing over for the present the disorderly experiments of the Civil War and Cromwellian Interregnum, we may note that a new window of opportunity for comprehension opened with the return of Charles II. The Declaration of Breda of 4 April 1660 declared 'a liberty to tender consciences' and promised that he would look favourably upon confirming this in statute shortly.[35] Hopes were high in the months that followed that a new religious settlement could be negotiated in which bishops would co-govern the Church with presbyters and in which latitude would be allowed to individual ministers on the divisive question of 'indifferent' ceremonies and vestments. These plans, together with proposals for a revision of the Book of Common Prayer, reached their peak in the Worcester House Declaration issued by the king in October, which reiterated the principle of reduced episcopacy.[36] Thereafter, however, the tide in favour of a broad-bottomed Church receded swiftly and in the wake of events, including the Fifth Monarchist uprising of January 1661 and the deadlocked Savoy Conference later that year, a more intolerant breed of Anglicanism reasserted itself vigorously. The latitudinarian moment was lost and under the Act of Uniformity of 1662 Protestant dissenters were placed firmly beyond the fence. Nevertheless, further comprehension bills briefly reared their heads in the Parliaments of the following three decades. In the face of the looming menace of popery some felt that it was 'high time to leave off insisting on little punctilio's of honour'; others, however, were convinced that this would 'introduce a Schism into the very Bowels of the Church and lay a foundation for perpetual feuds'.[37] The coup that brought William and Mary to the throne in 1689 afforded one last chance for legally expanding the terms of the Anglican communion. But this too was to be thwarted by circumstances, sacrificed to save the second bill on 'toleration' that would ultimately find a place on the statute book – an act we shall return to examine in more detail. It remains to remark that had these initiatives to comprehend dissenting Protestants not collapsed and evaporated, the Church of England as we now know it would be a very different creature.[38]

It is necessary to stress that the pursuit of comprehension rested on a continuing commitment to the notion of the confessional state. None of those who sought to stretch the parameters of Protestant orthodoxy would have denied the right of the magistrate to compel people by law to attend the services of the Church that emerged. Nor was this a point of contention between the Presbyterians and Independents within the Westminster Assembly who struggled to construct a satisfactory religious settlement in the mid-1640s. This changed, at least on paper, in 1650, when the Rump Parliament passed a statute for the relief of 'religious and peaceable people' which effectively repealed the Elizabethan Act of Uniformity and removed the penalties for non-attendance at one's parish church. People were expected to participate in some form of Christian worship but they were no longer under a civil obligation to conform to an exclusive ecclesiastical establishment. This probably did no more than legalise the religious free-for-all that followed the breakdown of political control and the descent into Civil War, but it nevertheless represents a juncture of some importance. It marked a departure, albeit temporary, from the notion of the national Church as a monopolistic and compulsory institution, towards an explicit recognition of a world in which competition with other denominations was a constant fact of life. The act of 1650 laid the groundwork for Cromwell's Instrument of Government of 1653, which granted freedom of belief and practice to all 'such as profess faith in God by Jesus Christ', provided they did not abuse their liberty to the injury of others or to the disturbance of the public peace. It did not extend, however, to 'popery', 'prelacy' or any type of 'licentiousness'. This was not a universal 'toleration' so much as a somewhat constrained union of the 'saints'. It was also one that the Lord Protector's Parliament subsequently sought to limit yet further in the Humble Petition and Advice of 1657, by exempting Quakers, Socinians and other socially disruptive and blasphemous sectaries from its dispensations and ordering the drawing up of a formal confession of faith, which it was to be an offence to denounce or revile. Ministers, preachers and others who were not prepared to acknowledge the Trinity and accept the Scriptures as the 'revealed will and Word of God' would be disabled from receiving public maintenance or holding positions of trust and responsibility.[39] While little was done to implement these recommendations they did signal a withdrawal from the policy of partial ecclesiastical de-regulation towards the re-establishment of Calvinist orthodoxy which would gather further momentum under Richard Cromwell.

Enforcement of religious uniformity returned with the Act of 1662. Like its Edwardian and Elizabethan predecessors it rested on the principle that outward conformity with the Church of England was a sufficient index of commitment and loyalty to it, and to the monarch who was its supreme governor or head. We should recognise the efforts that many ecclesiastical officials made to ensure the full internal conversion of the lay people under their charge, but it remains true that Tudor and Stuart governments largely resisted the pressure exerted by Protestant zealots for the political imposition of more rigorous tests of doctrinal compliance such as reception of Holy Communion or an oath on the tenet of transubstantiation, though these did later become requirements for holding civil office. Official propaganda which celebrated this refusal 'to make windows into men's hearts and secret thoughts' and subject them to an 'inquisition of their opinions' as evidence of the 'clemency' and 'tolerance' of the Elizabethan regime should not seduce us into speaking of its relative 'mildness' as a persecuting state.[140] Nor should Hooker's later philosophical defence of using exterior observance as the sole criterion for inclusion in the visible Church on the grounds that Christ alone had the power to divide the sincere and the sound[141] – an argument that, as we have seen, could itself be marshalled to support 'toleration'. As observed in Chapter 2, we should not underestimate the extent to which attendance at a Protestant Church could quite literally be an ordeal for deeply committed adherents of a religion which believed in the sacred instrumentality of ritual.

That said, it would be foolish to deny that the official focus on ensuring mere church attendance – a focus upheld in later recusancy legislation – did make room for the proliferation of religious pluralism in practice. It gave tacit approval to lay people who were prepared to make a minimal gesture of obedience to the state and to keep their dissident opinions to themselves, whether they were Familists, Protestant radicals, or indeed Roman Catholics. Although it must be acknowledged that the leeway permitted by the statutes was always dependent on the attitude to the task of implementing them adopted by individual officials, they did in effect create space for the politique, pragmatic and sometimes even the conscientious to continue to retain a toehold within the national Church. They created space within English society for dissent to exist.

This is also apparent if we turn to consider the financial penalties imposed by successive regimes for refusal to attend Church of England services. The initial intention of these sanctions was to drive recusancy into extinction by touching the pockets of those who practised it: unable to afford their non-conformity, it was supposed, Catholics would eventually drift of necessity into the harbour of orthodoxy.[142] Over time, though, it is clear that governments became content to contain rather than eliminate this problem. In the context of the growing desire of the Stuart kings to supplement their dwindling income they came to rely on the revenue which recusants regularly poured into the coffers of the English treasury – an annual average of between £7000 and £13,000 for the years 1605–13. They had no wish for this lucrative source of money to evaporate. As Mike Braddick remarks, 'heavy-handed administration would have killed, if not a golden goose, at least one that produced reasonably nutritious eggs'. Sir Henry Spiller, the Jacobean director of recusant finance, opposed repeated prosecution and sequestration of the lands of the recalcitrant for this very reason.[143] As a consequence, recusancy fines arguably evolved into a kind of luxury tax. Rather like those which the current Chancellor of the Exchequer attaches to cigarettes and alcohol, they became a sum of money that Catholics could pay, as it were, in exchange for the privilege of misbehaving, though this did not render them immune to civil discrimination. Despite their satirical intent, the words which Beaumont and Fletcher put in the mouth of a character in their comedy of 1615, *Cupids revenge*, were probably not far from the mark: 'Would I had gi[ve]n 100 pound for a tolleration. That I might but use my conscience in mine Owne house'.[144] To this extent it is possible to see refusal to conform, no less than conformity itself, as a tolerated vice, albeit one that carried an official health warning. However, the authorities still took exception to anyone who had the impertinence to point this out publicly: a weaver from Braintree was indicted at the Essex assizes in 1603 for sedition after he provocatively declared that 'The kinge hath received fower scoore pounds of Mr [Thomas] Southcoate for the usage of his Conscience in his religion.'[145]

The exploitation of recusants as a milch cow for a cash-strapped regime was not confined to this form of extortion: perceptions of the usefulness of the Catholic gentry as a fiscal asset also lay behind the sale of the title of baronet to 26 with 'popish' credentials or connections in 1611.[146] Nor did these rather mercenary transactions cease with the Civil War. Recusants were also seen as a solution to the financial straits in which the Commonwealth government found itself, which systematically confiscated and sold off royalist Catholic estates and then sometimes leased them back to them at hefty rents.[147] It is somewhat ironic that what began as a method of persecution ended up, to echo Pauline Croft, forming part of 'that series of measures which offered, not toleration, but a limited degree of tolerance' to England's Catholics.[148] Stranger merchants performed a similar economic function, providing the English government with money in the form of the higher subsidies and alien duties that were levied upon them. This was also no doubt a factor in the informal readmission of Jews following the failure of the Whitehall Conference of 1656. In the 1680s and 1690s they were the victims of a forced loan and a special poll tax, pressure being placed upon them to demonstrate their loyalty to the new Williamite regime financially.[149] As in the medieval past, the Jewish community was allowed to reside within the realm in large part because it was an invaluable monetary resource.

The persistent – and frequently stated – priority of the ecclesiastical and political authorities with rooting out active evangelism rather than passive adherence may also be argued to have indirectly facilitated conditions in which some members of religious minorities might survive, if only temporarily, within English society. To focus on those who were spreading a dissident faith was, of course, a perfectly logical strategy for eradicating a heresy or sect en masse. The underlying assumption was that if an illicit religion was deprived of ministers or priests (and the books that they disseminated), it would soon wither away. This was clearly the intention of the royal mandate of 1555 which ordered JPs in Norfolk to focus their attention on 'preachers and teachers of heresy' who were leading the ignorant masses astray, as it had been of the earlier initiatives undertaken against the Lollards by late medieval bishops.[150] It also underpinned the preoccupation of Elizabethan and Jacobean legislators and magistrates with removing Jesuit and seminarian missionaries and with clamping down on the lay people who aided, abetted and sheltered them, or endeavoured 'to infect and poison' their neighbours with the 'dregs of popery' themselves.[151]

A determination to eliminate energetic recruiters likewise lay at the heart of drives against later seventeenth century sects. Such measures carried an implicit hint that members of religious minorities who remained circumspect and introverted and who refrained from pursuing an aggressive programme of expansion, concentrating instead on the less disruptive goal of inward growth, might be left in relative peace. Chris Marsh thinks that this is one reason why the Familists remained more or less unmolested in the Cambridgeshire parishes he has investigated,[152] and we may well wonder how far the adoption of a non-evangelical endogamy enabled other groups and sects to escape the wrath and scrutiny of the authorities, even if in the long run this meant that they might fade quietly out of existence. At least some officials may have been willing to draw the distinction made in a proclamation of 1606 banishing Catholic priests, between 'such as be caried onely with blinde Zeale, and such as sinne out of presumption, and under pretext of zeale make it their onely occupation to perswade disobedience, and to practise the ruine of this Church and Common-wealth'.[153]

While there is once again a danger in taking the propaganda of politicians and prelates too much at face value and supposing that it accurately reflects what was happening at parish level, we should not overlook the ways in which a policy of annihilation gradually gave way to one of containment. The restoration of religious unity remained the ultimate aim, but as time progressed this came to be recognised as an unattainable ideal.[154]

A further manifestation of the accommodations that evolved in response to this realisation is the emergence of a tendency to regard the family home as an inviolable private sphere sharply demarcated from the communal space in which the public acts of worship of the dominant Church took place. This process was far more advanced in the Dutch Republic, where clandestine Catholic and Anabaptist churches (*schuilkerken*) outwardly disguised as domestic residences were widely tolerated by the authorities. As Benjamin Kaplan has recently argued, this open secret represented tacit acceptance that the household was an arena in which the confessional state should refrain from intervening and where the dissenting conscience could operate without fear of interference. It embodied a 'fiction of privacy' which superficially maintained the monopoly of the ecclesiastical establishment, while simultaneously carving out room for those who felt unable to subscribe wholeheartedly to it.[155] A similar principle was enshrined in the Treaty of Westphalia of 1648, which granted certain religious minorities the right of *devotio domestica*, based on the notion of the *conscientia libera*, or free conscience.[156]

In England this development took less concrete forms and was never extended to encompass adherents of the Church of Rome, with the very temporary exception of a clause inserted in Charles II's Declaration of Indulgence of 1672.[157] But early signs of its crystallisation can be detected in the definition of puritan 'conventicle' adopted by the Elizabethan and Stuart regimes. In 1583 Archbishop Whitgift had 'utterly inhibited' all assemblies for preaching, reading or catechising in private houses involving members of more than one family, declaring these 'a manifest sign of schisme, and a cause of contention'.[158] The Conventicle Acts of the 1660s and 1670s worked within essentially the same parameters. By prohibiting private gatherings of more than five people who did not belong to a single household, the Restoration establishment was seeking to strike a blow at the very structures that sustained and perpetuated dissenting communities, but it was also indirectly designating the physical arena coterminous with the family unit as a social and cultural zone within which practices that were otherwise forbidden might safely be exercised. It was anticipating the modern principle – albeit one always hedged about with qualifications and exceptions – that what goes on behind the doors of private citizens is more or less their own business, provided that it does not threaten the political or social order.[159]

Another symptom of the process by which pluralism was grudgingly accepted to be ineradicable is the growing insistence by governments that they sought merely to differentiate 'true-hearted' and peaceable subjects from seditious firebrands and rebels. One aspect of this was the increasing reluctance of the Tudor and Stuart state to execute religious dissidents for heresy and the trend towards to condemning them to death under the laws of treason. Desire to avoid bad publicity obviously played a large part here. The Protestant regimes of Elizabeth and her Stuart successors were anxious to avoid comparison with the harsh brutalities reputedly practised by the Spanish Inquisition on the Continent and in their own country by 'bloody' Queen Mary I, and late seventeenth-century Anglicans contined to seek to distance themselves from 'the monstrous cruelty of the Holy Office'.[160]

It is easy to be cynical about the hair-splitting claims made by contemporary spokesmen from William Cecil onwards that people were punished not for their heterodox beliefs but rather for the political consequences of holding them. This was the language of political prudence not of a deep-seated commitment to freedom of thought: its aim was to pull the wool over the eyes of the menacing Catholic states that hovered round this vulnerable island. At the same time, however, such statements do signal the fact that the basis for punitive action was very slowly shifting. A sharper line was emerging between unwarrantable 'persecution' and legitimate political measures to restrain 'terrorism' – one that is still maintained by modern Western governments today. That such a distinction was often specious in practice should not detract from its potential significance. As stressed in Chapter 2, the politicisation of dissent in many ways intensified intolerance; paradoxically, though, it perhaps also assisted in crystallising the view that holding opinions at odds with those of the established Church did not necessarily mean that one was a bad subject.

Considered in this light, those pieces of anti-Catholic legislation which professed to differentiate between loyal and disobedient 'papists' deserve fresh attention. Although it enraged zealous puritans, this was one way of interpreting the recusancy laws: those who came to church were giving a sign of their political quiescence; those who didn't were marking themselves out as suspicious and unreliable. If some Catholics were unwilling to take advantage of this loophole in the law, as we have seen, others did find it possible to square outward conformity with their consciences and to separate off their religious from their civil allegiance – and it is clear that there were many within the commission of the peace who were quite happy to concur with the casuistical accommodations made by church papists.

The same observation may be made about the Jacobean oath of allegiance of 1606. This too was clothed in the soothing rhetoric of 'favour and clemencie' and presented itself as a moderate attempt to detach politically quiescent from radical Romanists, who could then be indicted under the penalties of *praemunire*: the king declared 'we had never any intention in the forme of that Oath to presse any point of Conscience for matter of Religion, but only to make some discoverie of disloyall affection'.[161] Whether or not those who framed it actually intended it as an extremely 'lethal measure against Romish dissent' (as Michael Questier has vigorously contended), it remains true that on both sides of the confessional fence many were prepared to accept it as a gesture towards creating a framework in which some Catholics could legitimately exist as second-class citizens within a Protestant state.[162] In effect, if not objective, it may have made the position of at least some of those who were willing to repudiate the papal deposing power openly a little less precarious. In reacting against Whiggish tributes to James I's efforts to establish 'toleration', there is no need to throw the baby out with the bath-water. In the light of Brown Patterson's definitive study of the king's energetic and life-long commitment to achieving religious reconciliation between English Protestants, Lutherans, Calvinists, Catholics and Greek Orthodox and to establishing a stable and peaceful Christendom, we cannot afford to dismiss this attempt to lay the foundations for a kind of confessional coexistence – even if the controversy that it catalysed had the unforeseen effect of forging a broad anti-

Catholic alliance in England and of making James a celebrated figure in militant Protestant circles on the Continent.[163]

Continuing, and yet more discriminating, attempts to distinguish between loyal and disloyal Catholics can be discerned in the later seventeenth century. A bill of 1677 'for the more effectual conviction and prosecution of popish recusants' would have let some nonconformists off with a nominal fine while exposing others to the full force of the penal code. Neither its peremptory dismissal by the Commons nor the disdain of critics who complained that it put 'but twelve pence a Sunday difference betwixt the best Protestant and severest Papists' should distract us from recognising that this too represented a negative and back-handed effort to reach a kind of modus vivendi with some members of a highly variegated community.[164]

Other developments suggest that the climate in which persecution occurred was subtly changing. We cannot ignore the fact that a declining number of individuals who adhered to 'false' religions and illicit sects were executed as the period progressed: nearly 300 Protestants suffered at the stake under Mary; Elizabeth had 187 Catholics hung, drawn and quartered (or otherwise despatched as traitors), and a handful of heretics burnt; in James's admittedly shorter reign around twenty-five met one of these fates. While two priests suffered the ultimate penalty in Lancaster in 1628, none did so during the eleven years of Charles I's Personal Rule. In relative terms, fewer still went to the gallows in the second half of the seventeenth century. The early 1640s witnessed a concentrated outburst of judicial violence with twenty-four Catholic missionaries being put to death between 1641 and 1646, but this was a product of wartime panic and an aberration from a developing pattern. Only two were executed during the Interregnum and one of those, the Jesuit John Southworth, who had been banished on pain of death 26 years earlier, only because he stubbornly refused to utilise the escape route which the Cromwellian government offered to him. The Lord Protector went through the motions of strangulation and dismemberment, but paid for the body to be sewn back together by a surgeon and returned to Douai for a proper burial. In the reign of Charles II, once again it was only the frenzied purge that followed the furore surrounding the alleged Popish Plot that created a spike on a graph that was otherwise flat. Hobbes heard rumours that he was to be 'burn't for a Heretique' but in the event only his book *Leviathan* was consumed by the flames.[165]

Comparisons of this kind are treacherous but there do seem to be grounds for arguing that putting members of religious minorities to death (by whatever method) was coming to be seen not merely as counter-productive and inexpedient, but also to some degree distasteful, at least to those who comprised the political nation. Charles II was to express his 'little liking' of 'sanguinary' laws, which imposed this penalty on the basis of doctrinal belief,[166] and this was a sentiment which he seems to have shared with some members of his

Parliament. While the abolition in 1678 of the fifteenth-century statute *De haeretico comburendo* was an indication as much as anything of its practical redundancy, it is nevertheless not without symbolic significance. The right of the church courts to punish offenders in cases of atheism, blasphemy, heresy or schism by 'excommunication, deprivation, degradation, and other ecclesiastical censures not extending to death' remained intact but there was no longer any spiritual cause for extinguishing life.[167] We may see this not so much as evidence of the decline of a persecuting society as of a transmutation in its nature.

As the preceding paragraphs emphasise, positive and proactive legal and political initiatives which paved the way for religious pluralism are decidedly thin on the ground: for the most part the official measures we have so far reviewed were pragmatic and reactive. Drawing a hard and fast boundary between 'tolerance' and 'intolerance' is both intractably difficult and a matter of perspective: measures which look like 'persecution' through one lens can bear a faint resemblance to 'toleration' when inspected through another set of spectacles. Furthermore, there are distinct pitfalls in using the statute book as a guide to what was occurring at the grass roots: the texts of ordinances, proclamations, acts and injunctions could be variously interpreted by those responsible for their implementation and many lost their teeth as a result of incompetence, inefficiency, or general disorder and turmoil.

To this may be added the point that monarchs, ecclesiastical officials and civil magistrates sometimes deliberately allowed the law to fall into abeyance and justice to lie 'in a slumber'.[168] How the decision of constables, church-wardens and justices *not* to enforce the law ameliorated the experience of religious minorities in cities, towns and villages is addressed in the following section; here we focus on those occasions when legislative measures were suspended by direct order of the sovereign. This could take the form of a temporary amnesty: a period of grace during which missionary priests or disruptive heretics or dissenters were to conform or to make their way to ports and book themselves a berth on the first ship. On other occasions a pause in enforcement was dictated by the needs of foreign policy and dynastic alliance. During the negotiations in the 1620s for a match between Prince Charles and the Spanish Infanta, for instance, the recusancy laws were allowed to lapse. A similar goodwill gesture towards the religion professed by the intended bride of the future king of England was made in the lead up to his betrothal to Princess Henrietta Maria. French negotiators were to be disappointed in their efforts to press for 'no less than a direct and public toleration, not by con-nivance, promise or *escrit secret*, but by a public notification to all the Roman Catholics in all kingdoms': Charles I was forced to promise the Parliament of 1624 that liberty would only be extended to the person of his wife.[169] However, after his accession the following year, the royal court remained an arena of sanctuary from the (dying) heat of persecution.[170] Much frequented by London papists, the Catholic chapels attached to foreign embassies enjoyed a similar diplomatic immunity: they were a space in which the general ban on Romanist masses did not apply. In theory, individuals who attended services at these locations were deemed to be temporarily outside the jurisdiction of English law. Like European dissenters who crossed state borders on a weekly basis in order to worship freely, their activities technically took place on foreign territory and were thus beyond the reach of the civil authorities. The evolution of this principle represented a post-facto justification of a well-established ad hoc form of toleration.[171]

At a more individual level, it was always within the power of the monarch to pardon and exempt particular individuals and interrupt the legal process against them. Thus in 1601 proceedings against the recusant gentleman Thomas Watton of Addington were terminated by the assize judges at Seven-oaks on the queen's instructions; four years later, judges at Southwark were shown letters from the Privy Council signifying that it was the 'king's pleasure' that Catherine, widow of Sir Thomas Cornwallis, was not to be further troubled on this account; and in 1613 the trial of Elizabeth Guildford was stayed by order of Henry Montague, sergeant, 'for some causes known unto me'.[172]

Such interventions represented instances of the direct use of the royal pre-rogative. The documents and proclamations in which they were announced – especially those of James I – typically made much of the natural inclination of kings and queens to patience and leniency and their genuine desire 'to avoid the effusion of blood' in imitation of the 'divine mercy' of the Almighty. Employing familiar formulae and manifesting a mastery of the ancient art of political spin, they insisted that it belonged 'to our Royall Clemency, to moder-ate and mitigate the rigour of our Lawes, where we find the same over-burdensome to Our loving Subjects'. They also stressed, however, that where such 'mildness', 'forbearance' and 'pity' was presumptuously abused or misconstrued it could, and would, just as easily be withdrawn and removed. Anyone who supposed that royal zeal for the truth was abated was seriously mistaken: where 'Princely Policie and care' required, monarchs were also duty-bound to 'procure and quicken' the execution and observation of the statutes that were designed to protect it.[173] This was not 'toleration' either; it was a manifestation of kingly magnanimity.

These were the precedents for the more notorious Declarations of Indul-gence issued by the later Stuarts. But by then the world had changed. In the aftermath of the constitutional and religious struggles of the Civil War and Interregnum the whole issue of the regal dispensing power was fraught with potential controversy. In an atmosphere increasingly sensitive to signs of the rise or resurgence of absolutism, monarchs who sought to exercise it were venturing into very dangerous territory. In 1662, stressing his intent to remedy 'the non-performance of our promises' regarding liberty of conscience made at Breda and reiterated in the Worcester House Declaration of October 1660, Charles II asked Parliament to 'concur with us in the making of some such act … as may enable us to exercise with a more universal satisfaction that power of dispensing which we conceive to be inherent in us'. More particularly his aim was to find a way of exempting both Protestant and Catholic nonconformists from the penalties and 'fetters' of the newly promulgated Act of Uniformity. Fearing that religious pluralism would be but a prelude to the wholesale re-imposition of popery, the Commons politely declined to 'incline their wisdom' and 'cheerfully co-operate' with the king in bringing this apparently well-meant but ill-judged scheme to fruition.[74] His right to discharge the occasional individual from statutory obligations, however, was not seriously questioned.

A decade later Charles II was less wary of 'invading the freedom of parliament'. In March 1672, referring to the failure of the 'forcible courses' used 'for reducing all erring or dissenting persons' to conformity to compose the 'unhappy differences' of religious opinion between his subjects, he suspended the penal legislation by virtue of his 'supreme power in ecclesiastical matters' in a personal proclamation. Members of erstwhile puritan conventicles would be permitted to meet publicly for devotional exercises led by properly vetted preachers under licence, while popish recusants were allowed to hold masses only in private domestic settings. This too met with fierce resistance and in February of the following year he capitulated obsequiously after the Lower House delivered him a sharp slap on the wrist for infringing the terms of his office as supreme head of the Church.[75]

Charles's overtly Catholic brother James II was no less insensitive to the prickliness of the Commons on the controverted issue of the royal prerogative, setting forth in April 1687 a similar edict granting his subjects constrained in conscience 'the free exercise of their religion'. This not only placed the recusancy laws in mothballs; it also disabled the Test Act by ordering that the oaths of allegiance and supremacy and certificates of reception of the Anglican communion were not to be tendered or demanded of those employed in a municipal or military position of trust. Again, these 'gracious' dispensations applied equally to papists and dissident Protestants and this time no restrictions were imposed with regard to their freedom to assemble and worship. The declaration was reissued a year later, with a promise that it would be enshrined in parliamentary statute when this (increasingly obstreperous) body next met. James justified these measures on the grounds that persecution not only spoilt trade, depopulated countries and discouraged the immigration of talented strangers but was an ineffectual method of bringing a kingdom 'to an exact conformity in religion'. As the reigns of his four predecessors had proved, the difficulty in achieving this was nothing less than 'invincible'.[76]

The prudential arguments James employed reflect the extent to which the rhetoric of tolerationist writers was entering into the mainstream of contemporary thinking, but they belied his own evidently sincere conviction that in a situation of free competition the truth of the Catholic faith would become apparent to all, leading to an ever-growing volume of voluntary conversions, as a consequence of which the Church of Rome would eventually be restored to its rightful position of dominance. Though his opponents saw the declaration as a piece of popish duplicity – a cunning and underhand plan to reintroduce popery – it is perhaps better characterised as an instance of his political naivety.[77] However mixed the king's motives may have been, it is important to note that once again this was an act of condescension and 'indulgence' on the part of an autocratic monarch who regarded himself as the Lord's anointed representative on earth. Like the earlier initiatives that were its generic precursors, it contained the explicit threat that anyone who abused this liberty to stir up sedition in the commonwealth or 'alienate the hearts of our people' would be proceeded against with 'all imaginable severity'.[78] In other words, this policy of 'pardon and indemnity' was intrinsically reversible. It was also one for which James II expected to (and did) receive the humble and 'unfeigned' thanks of its beneficiaries for the 'princely pity' that had rescued them from their 'long sufferings' and 'put an end to the groans and lamentations of many thousands' of 'innocent and industrious' citizens.[79] Temporarily and theoretically, it sanctioned religious pluralism to an extent unmatched elsewhere in Europe.

The misnamed Act of 'Toleration' of 1689 was in fact a notable step backwards from the position attained under the sovereign infamously toppled by the constitutional coup that is now equally misleadingly celebrated as the 'Glorious Revolution'. 'Toleration' is a word that is conspicuous by its absence from the text of the statute, the actual title of which plainly revealed its real intent and very significant limits: to 'exempt their Majesties' Protestant subjects dissenting from the Church of England from the penalties of certain laws' that had been passed and employed against them. The laws designed to enforce uniformity were not repealed but remained in force. However, registered congregations of dissenters were granted freedom to worship in public meeting houses on the condition that both lay people and their ministers swore the oaths of allegiance and supremacy and the 1678 Test against transubstantiation, with the latter also being required to subscribe to all but four of the Thirty-nine articles – those concerning the system of ecclesiastical government. Additional dispensations were made for Baptists on the point of infant baptism and for the Quakers, who were permitted to substitute a simple affirmation of loyalty in place of the oaths they so abhorred on principle. Dissenters were not, however, relieved of their civil disabilities. They were excluded from admission to the universities, and office-holding too was technically to remain an Anglican monopoly: to qualify for it necessitated receiving the Eucharist in a parish church. Nor were they treated with respect as the equals of their conformist neighbours: to guard against these gatherings being used as a cover for plotting subversion and rebellion, a further clause specified that during service time the doors of their meeting houses were to remained unlocked, unbarred and unbolted. Furthermore, Catholics, atheists and anti-Trinitarian radicals were explicitly excluded from the privilege that was the 'toleration' of which the act never spoke. There was not the slightest hint or whisper of the notion that this might be a natural right or human entitlement.[180]

Once lauded as a towering constitutional landmark, recent historians have done much to hack away the legends surrounding it and to underline the cluster of contingencies that brought it about. For John Miller it is 'the product of an unedifying mixture of ecclesiastical backtracking and political horse-trading', while John Spurr sees it as 'a generally unwelcome, and slightly disreputable, compromise born out of ... deadlock'. Nicholas Tyacke has written of it as the result not of evolution but of revolution, and Mark Goldie describes it as 'the broken-backed reminder of a large package of reform which came to grief at the hands of High Churchmen'.[181] In part a reflection of the *politique* outlook of William III, its professed purpose was to provide 'some ease to scrupulous consciences' as a means to unite the fragmented Protestant nation 'in interest and affection' behind a new and upstart regime.[182] The sorry remnant of a two-pronged parliamentary programme which would have fundamentally restructured the Church, it embodied something of a marriage of convenience between Tories and Whigs, Anglicans and nonconformists anxious to rout and vanquish the evil spectre of popish tyranny. In essence this too was a declaration of indulgence: it differed from preceding ones only in being issued by the King-in-Parliament rather than by the king acting on his own behest. What it shared with the Edict of Nantes of 1598, revoked by Louis XIV of France just four years earlier, was the hidden proviso that the exemptions for which it legislated were not necessarily perpetual.

It took less than a generation for regret about this measure to set in: the Occasional Conformity and Schism Acts of 1711 and 1714 were serious attempts to further limit its dispensations. Only with the benefit of hindsight does their repeal in 1718 appear to be the end of the struggle to secure this much qualified form of 'liberty of conscience'. Implicitly, religious uniformity remained the ideal. Nevertheless, it would be wrong to whittle away the Act of Toleration into complete insignificance. To say that it represented belated official recognition of a situation that had prevailed since at least the 1640s – a condition of religious pluralism within English society that had become endemic and ineradicable – is not to belittle it. On the contrary, it is to underline how far the political establishment had come to rectify the mismatch between legal principle and practical reality – to closing the gap between the de jure tolerance of the statute book and the de facto tolerance that appears to have generally prevailed between the adherents of different faiths on a day-to-day basis.

Nor can we ignore the fact that this 'somewhat ungainly compromise congealed into a durable system' and in time became revered as a sacrosanct part of what William Warburton called 'our matchless constitution in Church and state'. Hallowed by the patina of prescription as well as by a century of proven utility, eighteenth-century writers now heralded the act as the embodiment of 'a sovereign Law of Nature', 'certainly of divine original'.[183] Posthumously reinterpreted in the image of their own Enlightenment outlook, it proudly entered into the annals of patriotic Whig historical mythology.

THE TOLERANCE OF PRACTICAL RATIONALITY

In a context in which the implementation of policy was dependent upon the co-operation of a host of unpaid officials, it would be erroneous to suppose that acts and edicts promulgated by the monarch, Privy Council and Parliament were necessarily translated into action at the parochial level. Equally, though, we should not automatically assume that such measures represented a fundamental challenge or affront to the prevailing texture of social relations in the towns, villages and cities of early modern England. Was confessional hostility, prejudice and antagonism in fact the dominant characteristic of the multiple, mundane interactions that made up everyday life? Or were forbearance and cordiality the real keynotes of the conduct of the orthodox towards their heterodox neighbours? The chief difficulty we face in seeking to answer these questions is evidential. To tolerate is to permit or endure, to abstain from taking steps to restrain something and to refuse to make a fuss: it is a conscious act of omission, the only external trace of which is often the resounding silence of our sources. As a consequence, it can all too easily be mistaken for mere indifference or apathy, and vice versa. Notwithstanding the dangers of misidentification, this dimension of contemporary experience deserves far more attention than it has hitherto received.

The first point to make is that the successive religious upheavals and reversals of the mid-sixteenth century created a degree of theological and ecclesiastical uncertainty that was not inherently conducive to intolerance. Reformations carried out from above by official mandate inevitably left large numbers of people lingering in a prolonged state of transition and limbo, unsure about what exactly constituted divine truth. The fact that the vast majority of the English populace were initially involuntary professors of the Gospel – men and women converted to the reformed faith, as one Elizabethan separatist noted, 'by the blowing of her majesty's trumpet at her coronation'[184] – arguably encouraged a form of amicable confusion in which many individuals felt unable to take a strong stand against conservatives who fiercely resisted the general drift towards conformity with the Church of England. The same fluidity inhibited and delayed ideological and cultural clashes with those who would later mark themselves out as the 'hotter sort of Protestants'. The polarisation of opinion and processes of classification and stigmatisation that were the preconditions of persecution at the grass roots seem to have been slow to develop. This was not 'tolerance' so much as an inertia born of a combination of bewilderment and resignation in the face of an era of change. Such observations may help to account for the relative absence of spontaneous attacks by lay people against 'heretics' and 'papists' in the four decades between 1530 and 1570. They may also partly explain the patchy, haphazard and selective enforcement of legislation designed to bring about uniformity by churchwardens, constables and justices in the muddled early phases of the English Reformations.

A willingness on the part of local officials and the communities they served to turn a blind eye to religious offences they should have reported to the secular and ecclesiastical courts was, however, a feature of the entire period under review. Visitation articles consistently enquired about those who failed to present delinquents or 'wincked at and suffered any faults punishable by ecclesiasticall censure', 'for bribe, reward, pleasure, friendship, feare, or any other partiall respect'.[185] Complaints about ineffectual execution of the statutes against Catholicism and Dissent also litter contemporary administrative documents and private memoranda. It is apparent that many magistrates ignored heretical deviance and popish infractions, that parishioners withheld from prosecuting their vicars and curates for puritan nonconformity, and that the crippling potential of the Clarendon Code against Presbyterians, Baptists and Quakers was likewise much moderated in practice. In 1557, for instance, a series of letters was sent to sheriffs and bailiffs in various counties demanding to know why sentences for heresy had not been executed and the Privy Council fined Sir John Butler of Essex the sum of £10 for condoning the reprieve of a woman who should have been burnt on the stake at Colchester.[186] In 1600, the entire body of constables and churchwardens of one Yorkshire parish was imprisoned for refusing to certify what kind of education the children of local recusants were receiving.[187] At Braintree in 1631 John Dedman and Samuel Smith were cited before the archdeacon for failing to present the incumbent of the parish, Samuel Collins, for disdaining the standard liturgical vestments and ceremonies.[188]

Later in the century, the role of 'mongrel justices' in frustrating the prosecution of dissenters was widely noted: at Great Yarmouth in Norfolk in 1667 it was said that the mayor and magistrates did little to check the flocking of people to illicit meetings of the Congregationalists.[189] In Essex in 1684 a correspondent of Bishop Compton noted that borough officers were loath to execute warrants against Quakers 'without many and great threats' from those above them. Despite intense pressure from JPs, their counterparts in Tower Hamlets obstinately refused to present their neighbours for attending illegal meetings. Not a few village constables were themselves prosecuted in the Court of Assize and Quarter Sessions for conniving at local conventicles and misleading the authorities about the number of nonconformists in their respective parishes.[190] In Lancashire and Cheshire, the presence of Thomas Fell and John Bradshaw within the commission of the peace likewise ensured that many Friends were treated leniently and released from prison, despite the concerted efforts of their colleagues to crush the sect in this region.[191]

Such examples can be replicated from all parts of the country. Zealots and politicians frequently scoffed at the 'lukewarmness' of those who thus undermined the intent of the law and lamented their corruption and ineptitude. As in the Dutch Republic, there were no doubt those who quite literally 'payd off the sheriff', buying the accommodation of local authorities with money or gifts.[192] But room should also be made for a wider variety of motives. Some such instances of inaction by officials reflect the degree to which local office holding continued to be infiltrated by members of religious minorities themselves. Over time the presence of crypto-Catholics in the ranks of local government may have decreased, though it never disappeared entirely – a situation which shielded many conservatives from the force of the law. In the period 1624–28 (when Catholicism was on the ascendant at court), it is estimated that eighty-one justices and two high sheriffs were Romanists and under Charles II several were granted commissions, including Sir Thomas Strickland, who had been expelled from the House of Commons in 1677 as a convicted recusant.[193]

Sympathy or support for the scruples of puritan and dissenting ministers also continued to interfere with the implementation of the Crown's policies right up until the end of the seventeenth century. Many such officials pulled strings for their co-religionists, speciously pleaded their inability to repress them, or sheltered conventicles in their own homes. A constable of Stepney penalised for refusing to execute a warrant in 1685 had previously been found guilty of attending a Quaker meeting himself.[194] On other occasions, neglecting to employ the machinery of persecution may have been a reflection of the power exerted by noble and gentry patrons. Catholic peers like the Petres and Montagues could put pressure on those below them in the social hierarchy and the attempts of the archdeacon of Suffolk to stamp down on dissent in Yoxford in the mid-1660s were similarly thwarted by one Lady Brooke, who kept her own nonconformist chaplain and was declared to be intent upon ruling 'that parish in spight of my teeth'.[195]

Swinging to the other extreme, we cannot dismiss the possibility that lax implementation of legislation was animated by a sincere commitment to the ideas articulated in tracts which argued the case for principled 'toleration'. The restraint of such magistrates may conceivably reflect the influence exerted by texts written by men like Thomas Helwys, Roger Williams, William Penn and John Locke, and embody a determination to put the 'liberty of conscience' for which they called into practice in spite of the slow and halting progress that was being made on this front by the English monarchy and Parliament. Just as the inadequacies of official policy could lead to unauthorised and personal campaigns of persecution, so too perhaps did its perceived iniquities inspire some individuals to suspend the statutes against those who dissented from the Church of England. Just as some took the sword of justice into their own hands in default of the magistrates, so others may have deliberately taken the decision to return it unused to the scabbard, and to exercise clemency in defiance of the fact that this was a jealously guarded aspect of the royal pre-rogative. On most occasions, however, this can be no more than a hypothesis. People rarely articulated the reasons for their actions verbally.

The discretion exercised with regard to religious deviance must also be set in the context of a culture where rigorous enforcement of the law in general was so frequently tempered by a preference for informal arbitration and reconciliation that it was probably the exception rather than the rule. Close studies by social historians such as Keith Wrightson, Jim Sharpe, Cynthia Herrup, Martin Ingram and Robert Shoemaker have emphasised the extent to which maintenance of 'order' was equated with an impulse to avoid disruption and contain conflict rather than carry through the judicial priorities of the Church and state in a manner that might actually increase tension and friction. In communities that placed a premium on preserving harmonious relations, prosecution and presentment were a last resort. They were themselves poten-tially a breach of the peace. Only when offenders had repeatedly failed to respond to 'gentle and neighbourly admonitions' were steps taken to expose them to the disciplinary sanctions of the civil and ecclesiastical courts. Suf-fused with a common set of moral values, and conscious of the propensity of all men and women to fall into sin, the inhabitants of sixteenth- and seventeenth-century England displayed a striking capacity for differentiating dangerous crimes from forgivable errors and for tolerating the presence of deviant but well-intentioned residents for fairly long periods.[196] Churchwardens, constables and magistrates exercised a judicious pragmatism, which sometimes required them to subordinate the aim of restoring religious uniformity to the end of ensuring social stability. In sixteenth-century Norwich, for instance, the ruling hierarchy seems to have been reluctant to jeopardise civic order by proactively hounding and punishing dissidents. However, Muriel McLendon goes too far in attributing it to a precocious ability to 'compartmentalise religion in relation to other political concerns' and in according this process importance in the emergence of 'a practical secularisation' and 'toleration'.[197] Norwich's 'quiet Reformation' is perhaps better explained in terms of a pursuit of the *pax et concordia* prized by European cities like Basle and Strasbourg in the medieval and early modern era alike. This was never a policy of choice, but one designed to suppress conflicts that could all too easily explode into a major conflagration in a circumscribed urban environment.[198]

At a yet more local level, the priority that contemporaries placed upon the exercise of true Christian charity and the ideal of 'good neighbourhood' was a powerful disincentive to taking action against those religious dissenters whose beliefs and activities were not in themselves too disruptive or corrosive of social relations. A determination to avoid confrontation and an aspiration towards communal concord evidently prompted many benignly to ignore the heterodoxy of those who lived nearby them. The scripturally enjoined duty of loving one's neighbours appears to have outweighed the conflicting spiritual obligation incumbent upon true believers to root out and restrain those who adhered to falsehood. Evidently, more than a few internalised the words of the Elizabethan homily on this topic, which declared that to behave charitably towards one's enemies 'was the proper condition of them that bee the children of God'.[199]

One indirect measure of this is the fact that local support for externally driven campaigns against the Lollards was often absent. In East Anglia in the 1420s very few members of the sect were identified as a result of proactive complaints made by the Catholic majority: most of the impetus for prosecution came from above. In early sixteenth-century Sussex parishioners of Bosham even proceeded against their vicar for public defamation after he called one of their number a 'heretic'.[200] In the late 1530s, as the apprentice merchant tailor Richard Hilles explained, many were unwilling to inform against evangelicals for fear of being 'regarded in the sight of all as guilty of treachery against their neighbours'.[201] In 1556, Walter Staplehead, the mayor of Exeter, behaved kindly towards local Protestants 'and did, both friendly and lovingly, bear with them and wink at them'.[202] In turn, similar considerations of amity and peace prevented many from reporting Elizabethan and Stuart recusants to the authorities: research on Havering in Essex reveals how reluctant people were to betray those bound to them by ties of friendship and neighbourhood, not to say kin.[203] Here and elsewhere they intervened to protect Catholics from indictment, colluded in fictive sales and mortgages to prevent their estates from being sequestered, and turned a deaf ear to the activities of resident chaplains and visiting missionary priests. Nor did they stand back and watch while their inoffensive Catholic neighbours were subjected to abuse by intrusive officials or unruly outsiders. For example, when a group of drunken soldiers plotted to extort money from two recusant ladies in Corscombe in Dorset in 1626 local people warned the household of impending trouble and the village constable succeeded in arresting some of the culprits. In the Lancashire town of Wigan a crowd protected a poor Catholic widow from distraint in 1681 in a remarkable show of solidarity in this divided community.[204]

Dissenters of all kinds benefited from the same overriding desire to maintain social harmony. Anglicans displayed sympathy in their dealings with nonconformist ministers and lay people, mitigating the impact of statutory persecution not merely by slack enforcement of the legislation but also by actively sheltering them from harassment or by roughing up amateur and professional informants.[205] A Quaker labourer imprisoned in 1658 for non-payment of tithes was freed when the townspeople of Leverton in Lincolnshire paid his debt; in Fenstanton in Huntingdonshire local officers would not execute a warrant against a grocer of the sect who owed £10, being 'Convinced in their Consciences' of his 'Innocency'; in London a carrier refused to obey the constables' command to bring his cart and horses to carry a group of Quakers to prison in August 1664.[206] Neighbours of other Friends helped harvest their crops while they were in gaol and obstructed magistrates who came to break up their meetings. Commanded by the justice to break down the door of the Quaker John Adams of Haddenham, in order to distrain his goods in October 1670, John Bishop, a poor man, refused with 'tears tricklin dowen his Cheekes', saying he was 'Loath to wrong his peacabl nibours'.[207] When Quakers were shut out of London meeting houses in the bitter winter of 1683–84, watchmen and constables did them small kindnesses, allowing them into the locked-up buildings and providing them with forms to sit upon. Those who sought to expel members of this and other sects from parish life could find themselves accused of unneighbourly conduct.[208]

Such evidence supports Keith Wrightson's recent contention that reports of the death or decline of 'neighbourliness' in early modern England have been greatly exaggerated. This ideal was certainly placed under severe strain by the religious upheavals and conflicts of the period, as well as by demographic and economic pressure, but it retained a vitality that ensured it was never entirely extinguished.[209] The clashes that culminated in England's street wars of religion in the 1640s should not blind us to the fact that there were evidently many who shared Nehemiah Wallington's regret that some of his contemporaries were so 'ready to devour one another' over 'differences in judgements'.[210]

Indeed, a growing body of detailed archival research is highlighting the surprising degree to which 'the bonds of love and duty' often 'paper[ed] over the chasms of ideology'. Local studies are casting serious doubt upon our instinctive assumption that religious minorities were usually ostracised and habitually surrounded by a chilly atmosphere of hostility and suspicion. They are drawing attention to what Norman Jones has called 'the private treaties of toleration' that characterised inter-confessional relations in England, as on the Continent.[211] The work of Derek Plumb on Lollards in the Chiltern Hundreds, Chris Marsh on East Anglian Familists, and Bill Stevenson and Adrian Davies on dissenters and Quakers in Bedfordshire, Cambridgeshire, Huntingdon-shire, Hertfordshire, Buckinghamshire and Essex highlights the extent to which many people engaged in normal social intercourse with Protestant sectaries and nonconformists.[212] Similar patterns of regular interaction have emerged from careful reconstructions of the experience of Roman Catholics in the villages of Linton, Cambridgeshire, Egton on the North York moors, and Madeley in Shropshire by Andrzej Bida, W.J. Sheils and Malcolm Wanklyn.[213]

It is increasingly evident that people recurrently ignored standard injunctions to shun their spiritual enemies. Just as they apparently 'kept company' with other 'excommunicated and aggravated persons' in defiance of canon law, 'favouring and cherishing' those who '(being so cutt off) care not to be restored, nor to satisfy the church', so too did they 'buy, sell, eat, drink, talk, set on worke, converse and otherwise communicate' with men and women who disdained the services of the Anglican establishment and/or rejected its central theological tenets.[214] These were people whom they regularly trusted to witness and execute their wills and to act as godparents to their children; people with whom they engaged in business, employed as servants, enter-tained to dinner, enjoyed a pint in the alehouse, played football and bowls, and even intermarried; people whom they were happy to elect to parish office and whom they regarded as worthy recipients and dispensers of poor relief.

In the 1540s differences of doctrinal opinion did not stop John Bradford's mother from receiving the conservative priest Thomas Hall as a regular visitor; nor in 1557 did they prevent the Catholic Richard Rothwell from spending his final illness at the home of the Protestant John Crompton, who summoned the vicar of Bolton to administer the last rites to his friend.[215] In Elizabethan Stratford-upon-Avon, the physician John Hall, husband of Shakes-peare's daughter, did not disdain to treat recusant and church papist patients who sought his professional advice. In Essex, the Protestant gentry willingly accepted the hospitality of the local Catholic family of the Petres, as did the Dean of Westminster and his entourage in 1606.[216] In Caroline Madeley, the Catholic bricklayers Thomas Wigmore and Abraham Ankers and the landlady of The Crown, Alborough Turner, could not have made a living had Protes-tants not set aside their religious convictions in their day-to-day dealings.[217] Nor could Richard Churnock and Anthony Jues and their wives, who kept inns in the vicinity of Gray's Inn and St Giles-in-the-Fields, respectively.[218] Joseph Hall might deplore the carelessness with which his contemporaries conversed and consulted with 'our Romish Samaritans', allowing them 'to haunt our tables, our closets, our ears', but some clerical writers like William Bedell sanctioned social intercourse with Catholics where civility and polite-ness required.[219] The Northamptonshire lawyer Robert Woodford did not shrink from supping and mixing with papists he encountered in the course of his professional duties or with whom he travelled on long journeys, or refrain from discoursing with them of 'divinity'.[220] Ideological disagreement was also no bar to scholarly exchange between educated Catholic and Protestant divines: James Ussher, the implacably anti-papal Archbishop of Armagh corresponded with David Rothe, the Romanist Bishop of Ossory, and Robert Cotton permitted the Benedictine Augustine Baker to make use of his incomparable library while he was writing his history of medieval English monasticism.[221]

Class loyalty, economic links and family ties likewise militated strongly against popular intolerance of later seventeenth-century dissenters. Anglicans did not merely collude with the ingenious compromises nonconformists made to avoid the penalties laid down by the statutes. They interacted with them in ways which suggest that the animosities within the Protestant camp enshrined in the Clarendon Code bore little relation to how lay people behaved towards those who refrained from joining them in Common Prayer each Sunday and worshipped illicitly. In Essex between 1660 and 1700 some 80 per cent of Quaker wills were witnessed by people who were not members of the Society, while a considerable proportion of these were written by conformist scribes.[222] The funerals of Friends respected in their neighbourhoods could attract many non-Quaker mourners: some 200 villagers assembled at the funeral of Robert Falkner of Somersham in Huntingdon in 1675, for instance, risking prosecution under the Conventicle Act, to pay their last respects to a man who had clearly been an esteemed figure in the local community.[223]

Religious affiliation with an extreme and idiosyncratic sect did not prevent overseers in the Cambridgeshire parish of Orwell from financially supporting the excommunicated Muggletonian widow Mary Cundy in her old age.[224] Nor did it generally stand in the way of securing employment: parents were quite willing for their offspring to take up places as serving maids and apprentices in dissenting households. The prosperity enjoyed by nonconformist tradesmen and artisans would not have been possible had their neighbours and peers bought goods and services exclusively from the orthodox. In Harwich in 1666 a Quaker draper mended the clothes of the town's sergeant; at Southminster in 1672 and 1681 a Quaker cordwainer was employed to repair the shoes of the pauper children of the parish; in the North-east, the Quaker builder and stonemason John Langstaffe was employed by the Restoration bishop of Durham himself, John Cosin.[225] Anglicans admitted Quaker midwives to assist them through the rigours of childbirth and in turn attended female Friends through the last painful phases of pregnancy. In the village of Ashton-in-Makerfield in Lancashire the Presbyterian shopkeeper Roger Lowe was much in demand for his skills in accounting and literacy among a broad cross-section of society, preparing bonds, writing up presentments to the assize, and even composing love letters for those who lacked the ability to translate their most intimate thoughts into writing.[226] And, despite the obstacles placed in the way by ecclesiastical officials, intermarriage between rival denominations was evidently rife. It too indexes the extent to which the stark polarities etched so acidly on paper were in practice softened by affection and obligation.[227]

Such examples provide further support for the view that the English populace had a far greater capacity for tolerating difference within its midst than has hitherto been assumed. As in confessionally divided parts of France, the Netherlands and the Holy Roman Empire, people seem to have exhibited a remarkable ability to 'play simultaneously on several fields of commitment or engagement'.[228] To quote Willem Frijhoff's observation about the Netherlands, 'everyday ecumenism' and 'interconfessional conviviality' coexisted with and counterbalanced 'a tenacious mentality of socio-religious exclusivism'.[229] The formal vows taken by communities in Dauphiné, Nyons and Saint-Laurent-des-Arbes in the 1560s to 'live in peace, friendship and confederation' despite the 'diversity of religion that is among them' may have few if any direct counterparts on this side of the English Channel. Nor can equivalents be found for the mid-seventeenth-century confraternities of Utrecht whose stated objective was the 'removal of all mistrust' between Calvinists and Catholics 'in order henceforth to live with one another with greater trust, correspondence and unity, as inhabitants of one state, brothers of one brotherhood ought to do'.[230] But they embody the spirit of the many tacit and unspoken agreements that seem to have been made between those who espoused different creeds in the villages, towns and cities of Tudor and Stuart England.

The underlying incentives for this tolerance are once again extremely difficult to pinpoint, but it cannot be unconnected with the efforts which many religious dissenters themselves made to reach a kind of modus vivendi with their Protestant neighbours. The partial, occasional and sometimes comprehensive gestures of social compliance and ecclesiastical conformity discussed in Chapter 4 surely helped to defuse antagonism, neutralise potential conflicts, and foster a climate in which people felt able to condone beliefs and observances of which they disapproved. The corresponding endeavours which magistrates, constables, churchwardens and parishioners made to meet heretics, papists, and sectaries halfway permitted perhaps most of the latter to live in relative equilibrium with men and women who neither shared nor approved of their doctrinal views or their conscientious scruples. Such reciprocal expressions and tokens of good will were mutually reinforcing: sympathy for minority groups was in part a consequence of the strategies of assimilation they adopted for dealing with persecution and suffering, which in turn reinforced the willingness of the orthodox to interact with them according to the rules of Christian charity and good neighbourhood. Those who deliberately separated themselves from wider society and spurned the company of the reprobate or non-believing majority were likely to find themselves the targets of hostility, resentment and further marginalisation, but dissenters who actively integrated themselves within the networks of communal sociability were rarely identified or treated as threatening outsiders or aliens. It may be proposed that these interrelated processes facilitated forms of coexistence which desensitised individuals to the presence of deviance and contributed to creating a religious environment in which pluralism became accepted as a fact of life.

These practical experiences seem to have both facilitated and reflected an ability on the part of the populace to accommodate a considerable degree of inconsistency between physical behaviour and internal opinion. The many mundane compromises people made with those who were technically their confessional enemies bear out Chris Marsh's suggestion that at the local level outward conduct was instinctively regarded as a better basis for judging an individual's worth than his or her adherence to precise theological formu-lations enshrined in catechisms and confessions of faith. He may, however, push the evidence beyond the limits of what it can yield in arguing that social relations in early modern England were marked by 'a lack of prying interest in matters of inward belief', which is indicative of the emergence of 'something approaching a concept of privacy'.[231] Norman Jones's claim that the post-Reformation period created 'a multi-denominational world in which each individual was recognised to have some choice in how he or she related to God' is no less difficult to prove.[232] What can be said is that the doctrinal beliefs upon which historians of this period have traditionally focused so much attention do not seem to have always or inevitably driven a wedge between those who held them and those who did not.

It is also apparent that passionate abhorrence of a false religion or deviant sect in the abstract was by no means incompatible with cordial relations with its human adherents. This too was both a cause and an effect of the de facto coexistence and pluralism engendered by England's long Reformation. Personal contact eroded the menacing stereotypes depicted and elaborated in propagandist tracts and prompted men and women to display towards their dissident neighbours the 'Charitable Christian hatred' recommended by Joseph Bentham. In their everyday interactions with heretics, papists and dissenters people demonstrated a repeated ability to distinguish between individuals and the ideologies they espoused.[233] In 1624 Sir William Pelham maintained that it was impossible for a Romanist to be a true subject because no man could serve two masters, but he nevertheless admitted that 'some of my best friends are papists'.[234] Roger Lowe could engage in a heated dispute with a Catholic neighbour about the integrity of the Protestant religion without coming to blows with his opponent: despite their zeal, the two were 'in love and peace in our discourse'.[235] An even clearer instance of this split between mental attitudes and practical realities comes from the eighteenth century. During the Gordon Riots in 1780, a crowd, called upon to attack a house where recusants resided, tellingly replied 'What are Catholics to us? We are only against Popery!'[236]

In such instances contemporaries temporarily suspended the beliefs that were central to their social identity in a manner which could itself generate anxiety and tension. To adapt an insight of Anthony Milton, in a context in which minorities were widely tolerated in practice it was particularly vital to assault their religion stridently at the level of theory. The fact that confessional polarities were so frequently ignored or contradicted did not invalidate the abstract ideological constructs that preachers and propagandists attacked; rather it enhanced the desirability, even necessity of constantly re-articulating opposition to them.[237] Polemical hostility helped to ease the inner discomfort that was often associated with the decision to refrain from taking action against one's spiritual adversaries. It is important to recognise that for many people tolerance itself was in some sense a moral dilemma and a case of conscience. It was socially possible but not yet ideologically acceptable.

At the same time, however, we must consider the possibility that this 'tolerance of practical rationality' contributed to effecting a gradual sea change in contemporary thought. Could it be that the parochial experience of confessional coexistence and social ecumenism helped not just to pave the way for the edicts and statutes that retrospectively licensed it, but also for the intellectual insights of those who mounted a case for toleration in the key tracts and speeches we have already reviewed? These were not produced in a social or cultural vacuum. At the end of his book on Essex Quakers, Adrian Davies speculates that the pluralism which the movement both symptomised and succoured encouraged 'a greater preparedness to recognize freedom of conscience in religious matters', 'a revolution in attitudes ... which constituted the roots of Enlightenment tolerance'.[238] By their very nature, such suggestions cannot be precisely substantiated but they remain worthy of serious consideration. We need to be conscious of the ways in which specific social conditions may have played a part in stimulating new thinking. Could it be that the growing willingness of tolerationist writers to detach political loyalty from religious allegiance sprang from the mounting body of evidence that most papists and dissenters were not subversive rebels and firebrands? How far was the commitment of Anglican divines like Jeremy Taylor to the concept of a core of fundamentals surrounded by a penumbra of 'inessentials' upon which people could legitimately disagree a product of the ad hoc latitudinarianism that prevailed at the grass roots? To what extent was Locke's insistence that coercion produced hypocrisy rather than sincere conversion a function of studied reflection on the limitations of the policy of enforcing outward conformity? And in what ways did contemporary observation of the horrific consequences of persecution during the wars of religion in both England and Europe assist in encouraging the view that only toleration could prevent society and the state from implosion?

Over time, the gap between the official ideology of intolerance and the sociological reality of tolerance may have gradually narrowed, but it never closed completely. To question the assumption that tolerance was in short supply in early modern England is not to imply that there was an absence of persecution. Contradictory impulses towards concord and conflict, integration and apartheid, coexisted both within individuals and within communities as a whole. There was 'a continuous interplay between the urge to despise, shun and victimise, and the urge to love, tolerate and embrace'.[239] And it is this unstable compound that may provide the key to reconciling the evidence presented here with that examined in Chapter 3 – to explaining why the generally peaceful surface of English society was periodically rocked by spontaneous outbreaks of prejudice and violence. It was the extent to which confessional polarities were compromised in practice that propelled men and women to commit belligerent acts of intolerance against heretics, papists and sectaries at critical junctures when the safety and integrity of their communities or of the country at large was thought to be in jeopardy. Subconscious anxiety about their own overly close contacts with those who had taken the side of the devil and error had the latent capacity to erupt into aggression and terrorism. These were the means by which individuals psychologically deflected and appeased their own guilt about consorting with people who wilfully adhered to a false and evil Church, sect or creed. It was also often a consequence of a deep-seated conviction that if the authorities neglected to take steps to eliminate God's enemies, the responsibility for doing so fell to ordinary lay people. The very perception that 'toleration' or 'tolerance' was being extended or exercised by either individuals or institutions could itself spark off fresh episodes of persecution. This supplies the theme of the next and final section.

THE CONSEQUENCES OF TOLERATION

In a climate of commitment to the principle that religious diversity was a recipe for social disorder, political dissolution and providential disaster, any form of laxity or leniency towards deviance was liable to prompt unease, friction and even public outrage. In many respects, this was the root of puritan dissatisfaction with the 'halfly reformed' Church of England. At the heart of the Presbyterian movement was the claim that the English Church (by constrast with its Genevan, French and Scottish counterparts) lacked the proper machinery for persecution – the system of ecclesiastical discipline that would facilitate the severe correction of faults that was one of the 'outwarde markes' of the true Christian religion. In an institution in which the elect and the reprobate mingled in worship promiscuously, it was essential that the holy sacrament was protected from profanation by the unworthy and that offenders were bridled and brought to humble repentance. Overuse and abuse of the supreme sanction of excommunication and episcopal corruption had reduced the pure regiment of admonition and correction outlined in the Bible to a flimsy shadow and a mere parody. It was time, insisted Wilcox, Field and other puritan spokesman, for Christ to be 'restored into his kyngdome, to rule in the same by the scepter of his worde' and the sword of godly coercion.[240]

The failure of Elizabeth I to respond to the calls for further reform issued by ministers and members of Parliament, and her angry determination to put an end to attempts to redefine the status quo, was one source of grievance stemming from the ideology of intolerance that stored up trouble for the future. The willingness of her regime to settle for mere conformity and to detach inner belief from outward conduct also greatly dissatisfied the godly, who made more than a few cutting comments about the integrity of a state that was ready to embrace hypocritical Familists and dissimulating papists. They regarded its repudiation of repeated attempts to impose stiffer tests of 'uniformity' such as reception of communion as yet more evidence that it did not take seriously the solemn obligations that had been laid upon it by God. Their opponents, by contrast, were disturbed by the latitude allowed to puritans within the Church of England – by the tacit and explicit concessions made by individual bishops and politicians to clergymen with scruples of conscience about the surplice, sign of the cross and subscription to the Thirty-nine Articles, by its foolhardy readiness to comprehend potential subversives and revolutionaries within its ranks. The umbrella-like capacity of the ecclesiastical settlement that Elizabeth bequeathed to her successors to accommodate what James I called 'sects' on both the right and left – to harbour within it groups who regarded its tolerance of each other as a threat to themselves – was to sow the seeds of the conflicts that ignited the Civil Wars of the 1640s and rumbled on until the Glorious Revolution.

At the local level, passive or active toleration of religious minorities not infrequently resulted in protests and petitions for greater rigour. In the 1580s, 'professors' of the Gospel from the Essex village of Dunmow pleaded with Lord Rich that the 'traitorous brood and dangerous sect' of papists might be more tightly controlled, while the vicar of Prescot in Lancashire complained that 'they that have the sword in their hands under Her Majesty to redress abuses among us suffer it to rust in the scabbard'.[241] In 1605, the minister and churchwardens of Lamberhurst in Sussex humbly begged East Grinstead justices to take 'due proceedings' against recusants, since by 'the sufferaunce' of too many of their number 'others doe refuse and more are likelye to withdraw themselves'.[242] Others addressed their petitions to the House of Commons itself. Such worries were echoed by Protestant divines like Richard Bernard, who issued a damning indictment of the 'toleration, connivencie, or remisnesse, and paralyticall distemper of the arme of justice' in a tract of 1617.[243] Similar anxieties could be animated by sympathetic attitudes towards and indulgent treatment of nonconforming Protestants. In a case from the

1680s, Edward Fowler, rector of St Giles in Cripplegate – a man who called for Anglicans to show compassion for 'Peaceable and Modest dissenters' and was outspoken in his condemnation of those who harassed and molested them – caused such discontent among his parishioners that they prosecuted him in court for negligence in his duties.[244]

If insufficient zeal on the part of magistrates and ministers inspired concern, much more so did ill-judged acts of clemency performed by the monarch and his immediate advisers and deputies. Rumours that James I might yield to Appellant pleas for toleration inspired several tracts in the years 1603–5 reminding the king that the Pope was Antichrist and that his seduced minions should not be suffered to live in his dominion. By 1610, despite the punitive legislation that followed the Gunpowder Plot, practical tolerance of moderate Catholics was beginning to provoke public expressions of disappointment from locations as prominent as Paul's Cross: William Sclater complained 'where is that ancient severity and strict hand over Papists? ... And who ever saw the fruite of lenity this way, that the number hath bin any more abated, and not rather increased by forbearance?'[245]

More damagingly, the relaxation of the recusancy laws in the 1620s in the context of the negotiations for the Spanish and French dynastic matches led to an outpouring of criticism from the pulpit and underground press. Requiring not just de facto toleration of Catholics but also English aid in suppressing their Huguenot brethren at La Rochelle, fervent Protestants found the terms of the marriage treaty between Charles I and Henrietta Maria utterly repellent and many interpreted the outbreaks of plague and the military debacles of this period as the Lord's judgement upon these ungodly policies. John Preston told Parliament that only by 'cleansing the land from the sins wherewith he is provoked' would His punitive hand be lifted.[246] Some writers provocatively interpreted the tragic accident at the French ambassador's residence in Blackfriars in October 1623 as another manifestation of divine wrath against the 'lenative courses' of the Caroline government with regard to its Catholic subjects (see Figure 5, p. 113).[247] A proclamation issued in February of the following year gave lip-service to growing concerns that the king's 'Zeale and Constancy in Our Religion were cooled or abated' and acknowledged that there was a danger that 'Our Clemency and Moderation might bee misconstrued'.[248] But this evidently had little effect. By 1629 a parliamentary subcommittee was lamenting the 'extraordinary growth of Popery' brought about 'a bold and open allowance' of popery and demanding due execution of the statutes.[249]

In the 1630s these anxieties intensified as royal connivance allowed court Catholicism to grow in strength and vigour. The policy of mercilessly exploiting recusants as a source of revenue to be carefully husbanded and protected aroused opposition among those who wanted effective persecution of what they considered a dangerous and evil minority.[250] To fine Catholics for their nonconformity was implicitly to license the existence of idolatry in a manner that the hotter sort of Protestants found insupportable. The period also saw the revival of complaints about the Laodicean lukewarmness of an institution that rested content with securing merely external compliance and did not require people to turn their souls inside out. Yet this was a point on which the establishment would brook no criticism: a man who abused a recently conformed recusant as a 'base turne coate' was prosecuted by the northern High Commission in 1635 and ordered to perform public penance in Durham Cathedral for his 'rash and unadvised speeches which tended to the scandal of religion'.[251]

Such incidents probably only increased fear about the real intentions of the Laudian regime. In this heightened atmosphere, eirenical tactics for persuading Catholics to come over to the Protestant camp that had once been employed with impunity became surrounded by an aura of suspicion. Championed in the public domain by figures like Richard Montagu, they were invested with controversial significance. It is ironic that initiatives which were ostensibly underpinned by a desire to restore uniformity by converting papists to Protestantism were mistaken for an insidious scheme to introduce toleration of a false religion.[252]

That those who controlled the Church of England were simultaneously beginning to reconceptualise their relationship with the Church of Rome was no less of a stimulus to renewed calls for persecution. Stepping back from their 'immortal fewde' with Antichrist, leading churchmen stifled apocalyptic anti-Catholic discourse by censoring both preaching and publishing in a way which, as Anthony Milton has shown, many contemporaries found deeply unsettling.[253] 'Bitter invectives' and 'indecent railing speeches' by the clergy and intemperate statements by the laity were prohibited by proclamation and authors who defied the new rhetorical conventions were subjected to censure, if not imprisonment.[254] According to the Scots Covenanter Robert Baillie, to suppress polemical attacks on the papacy in these terms was to dismantle the 'chiefe bulwark' to keep the people 'from looking back towards that Babilonish Whore'.[255] That the evolution of this more qualified intolerance of Roman Catholicism coincided with a gradual severing of close ties with the sisterhood of Reformed churches on the Continent and an attempt to downplay the Church of England's Calvinist heritage only fuelled the flames of puritan alarm and indignation. Even more destabilising were revelations that Richard Montagu was actively involved in discussions with the papal agent Gregorio Panzani regarding reconciliation and reunion with Rome.[256] These ecumenist ventures to restore a measure of unity to Christendom further fed paranoia that Laud and his colleagues were intent upon carrying out a complete Counter-Reformation, assumptions that radicalised the godly and revitalised calls for the abolition of episcopacy.

'Toleration' was thus one of the iniquities of which the Long Parliament convicted the Caroline regime: the authors of the Grand Remonstrance of 1641[257] were outraged that popery could be condoned in a Christian commonwealth and the conviction that this had stirred up God's wrath against the nation was to be one of the principal motors of the decision to take up arms against the king in 1642. Just as Catherine de Medici's edicts of pacification contributed to launching France into bloody conflict in the 1560s, so did the ad hoc indulgence and tolerance of the Stuart king help to propel England towards her own bloody showdown between two sides equally convinced that they were doing God's will. The speeches and writings of William Prynne and other parliamentarians resonate with a passionate conviction that any form of collaboration with or concession to Antichrist was an invitation to catastrophe – a conviction which can seem peculiarly alien to the modern secular historian. Yet these sentiments are still alive and well in some outlying quarters of twenty-first century British society. In March 2001, an elder of the Free Presbyterian Church of Scotland interpreted the recent floods, rail chaos and the foot and mouth epidemic as divine retribution for the queen's visit to the Vatican and meetings with the Pope the previous autumn.[258]

During the Civil Wars and Interregnum, 'toleration' was also blamed for the spread of radical sects like Ranters, Seekers, Fifth Monarchists and Muggletonians. The proliferation of such 'false prophets' following the collapse of political and ecclesiastical control seemed to many observers a sign that the last days were nigh; calls for this unruly pluralism to be belatedly sanctioned by law were thought to be the height of impiety, a satanically inspired scheme to subvert the true Church. Some of the most insistent articulations of this theme came from the Presbyterians, who claimed that to license diversity was to place 'a sword in a madman's hand'.[259] In 1647 it was said that toleration would 'open a floodgate unto all licentious Liberty'. A year earlier the heresiographer Thomas Edwards had declared in his *Gangraena* that this 'monster' was 'the grand designe of the Devil, his Masterpeece and Chiefe Engine ... to uphold his tottering Kingdome; it is the most compendious, ready, sure way to destroy all Religion'.[260]

A broadside published around the same time to expose 'the sandy foundation of a general toleration' depicted the double-faced figure of 'Profane Libertin' holding a book entitled 'loose liberty', trampling the Bible underfoot and united with popery and prelacy to wound honest hearts (Figure 15).[261] Nehemiah Wallington identified the 'many strange false forms of worship that are tolerated in the midst of us' as one of the chief causes of a devastating fire in London in 1655 and regarded Cromwellian 'liberty of conscience' as a source of 'national sin' that was drawing down divine judgements upon the land.[262] The Ranter movement proved a tremendous asset to royalist propagandists and popular pamphleteers intent on discrediting religious enthusiasm

Proper Perſecution, or the ſandy Foundation of a general Toleration,

Diſcovered and Portrayed in its proper Colors.

By the fruit ye ſhal know the tree; And by the waters the fountain. Read and Conſider what the Envious man hath done.

80

If ſhall begin with Martins curſed ſhrill Eccho. pag. 5, 6.

1. THe life of Sir *John Preſbyter* is like neither to be long nor good.
2. That he will be brought to a ſudden untimely end, perhaps to hanging.
3. That Preſbytery ſhall live but a ſhort time to do miſchief, and then the common people will ſing, *Hey toſſe the Devils dead.*
4. The Synod will ſoon be diſſolved, the devill chain'd up.
5. Clap thy hands for joy, O *England*, Preſbytery ſhal have never a child to vex thee ſhortly, or impriſon thy free Deniſons, and to ſuck up thy fat.
6. Then farewel perſecution for *conſcience*, then farewel *Ordinance for tithes*; farewel *Eccleſiaſtical ſupremacy*; farewel *Pontifical revenue.*
7. Farewel *Aſſembly of Divines*, Diſſembled at *Weſtminſter*, Sir *Simon Synod*, and his ſon *Preſbyter Jack.*

In Perſecution Araignment, Pag. 2.

8. Perſecution hath a thouſand *Jack* tricks above all the reſt to block up all paſſages and ſtop all mouths.
9. He turned Reverend *Imprimatur* and here all was as ſure as the Devil and Preſbyter could make it.

Pag. 14. We imploy Dr. *Featlyes* Devil-a very reverend ten pound Sir *John*, to make up a deſcription of the Anabaptiſts, &c.

Againſt Tithes in a ſcurrilous Libel.

11. Time hath been wholy taken up in the Procurement of that ſacred Ordinance of Tithes, wiſely thought on before the *Directory*; for *he is an Infidel and denyeth the faith that doth not provide for his Family.*
12. My Lord the Defendant ſmels of a fat benefice; ſee his pockets are ful of *Preſbyterian* ſteeples, the ſpires ſtick under his girdle, *ha, ha, ha,* inſtead of weathercocks, every ſpire hath got a black box on it.
13. Inſtead of *Moſes, Aaron*, and the two tables, we ſhal have Sir *Simon* and Sir *John* holding the late ſolemn League and Covenant.
14. And then that demure, ſpotleſs, pretty, lovely, ſacred, divine, and holy *Ordinance* for Tithes. The two *tables* of our Preſbyterian Goſpel painted upon all the Churches in *England.*
15. O brave Sir *Simon* the Bels in your pocket chime all in, ours chime all out.
16. I pray you give a funeral homily for your friends here before you depart, heres twenty ſhillings for your pains.
17. Yea tis ſacriledge to bring down the *priſas it was in the beginning is now, and ever ſhal bee, world without end,* Amen.
18. Our Temporizing Doctors are not ſo ſimple to ſwim againſt the ſtream, they are wiſer in their generation and know moſt ſtate goes that way.
19. Their Religion moves upon the wheel of the State.
20. I would your Lordſhips would cal in your Ordinance for tithes & turn them to the peoples goodwils; Then a tithe pig would be ſold for a penny.

In the Sacred Decretal, or Hue and Cry.

21. From his ſuperlative holineſs Sir *Simon Synod, &c.* In the front whereof is the picture of a Bul toſſing Sir *Simon Synod* on his horns, Trampling the Ordinance for tithes under his feet, with

this Inſcription upon it. *Ordinance for Tithes.*

22. That the Ordinance permitting none to preach, but ſuch as are ordained is a pattern of the ſpirit worſe then the Monopoly of Sope, hereby to get all trading into their own hands.
23. Sir *John Gurnt* being lately rob'd with a Parliament Corall, that late Ordinance is made to put his boariſh Tuſks, his great huge iron fangs in execution, to divorce, rend and teare theſe Hereticks.
24. Therefore we wiſely conſulted of a Committee of examination to be choſen out of us, it muſt not be eſteemed a Court of Inquiſition thats popery, not a Renovation of the High Commiſſion, thats Antichriſtian, only an Inlet to a through Reformation, thats a godly name that may doe much good, &c.
25. The Claſſicall Clarks and Sextons of the three Kingdoms demoliſh and put down all the Martins neſts from your Church-wals and Steeples. that no birds build, chatter, or doe their buſineſs there.
26. But Church owles, Jack-dawes, otherwayes called Sir *John* blind *Batt* Preſbyterian Wood cocks.
27. O yee two Houſes of Parliament make another Ordinance, that all the meetings may be made to fly the three Kingdoms the next Mid-ſummer with Cuckowes and Swallows.
28. That ſo we may have a blew Cap Reformation, amongſt *Bats, Owles,* Jack-dawes and Wood cocks and the blew Cap for us.

Araignment of Perſecution, pag. 13, 14.

29. Perſecution is thy name, Perfect Reformation.

Perſecu. Yes my Lord, *Iudge*. Who gave you that name? *I. Reaſon*, his God fathers and God-mothers in his Baptiſm wherein he was made a member of the Aſſembly, and an Inheritor of the Kingdom of Antichriſt.

30. *Iudg.* Who are your God-fathers, and God-mothers?

Perſecu. My Lord, Maſter Eccleſiaſticall Supremacy, and Maſter Scotch government my God-fathers, Miſtris State ambition, and Church Revenue are my God-mothers.

31. And I was ſprinkled into the Aſſembly of Divines, at the taking of the late ſolemn League and Covenant.

32. *Iudge.* Tis ſtrange, that at the making of the late ſolemne league and Covenant, blood Thirſty Perſecution ſhould be Anabaptiſt preſent before Reformation.

33. Then here's a deſigne of blood in the Covenant, if under the name of Reformation the Clergy have infuſed the ſpirit of Perſecution into it.

34. My Lord there was never any National or Provincial Synod, but ſtrengthned the hand of Perſecution under the vizard of Religion.

35. *I. Reaſon*, as ſoon as theſe underling Divites are from under their Epiſcopal Task-maſters, and begin to incroach your Lordſhips power, they preſently take this notorious bloody Traytor *Perſecution*, ſtript by your Lordſhips of his High Commiſſion habit, and out of their zeal dreſſe him in a Synodical garb, and change his name from *Perſecution* to *Reformation.*

Pag. 39. By the late ſolemn League and Covenant, Good Lord deliver us.

Araignment of perſecution in the Epiſtle.

36. A Reverend Aſſembly ſuch a quagmire of croaking skipjack Preſbyters &c.
37. New upſtart trifling Preſbyters, Synodian Cormorants; the Synodian whore of *Babylon*, The trayterous Synod called the Aſſembly of *Divines.*
38. Preſbyterian Horſe leeches, blood-thirſty cattel.
39. The great gore-bellyed Idol, called the Aſſembly of Divines.
40. Jeſuitical Traytors, deſigns of the Synod.
41. Our diſſembly Doctors a Conſiſtory of Devils.
42. *Pag.* 1. The Synod is guided by the holy Ghoſt, ſent in Cloakbag from *Scotland.*
43. Becauſe the Aſſembly have ſadled the *Parliament*, it is unlawful for the Preſbyterians to go on foot.
44. *Pag.* 25, 26. It is moſt certain that this fellow, whoſe name Sir *Simon* faines to be *Reformation*, is abſolute *Perſecution*; ſo that had theſe Reformers as much power as Queen *Maries* Clergy, their Reformation would conclude in fire and faggot.
45. Judge, oh inſufferable Aſſembly, I ſee tis dangerous for a State to pin their faith upon the ſleeve of the Clergy.
46. Others are impoveriſht and loſe their lives in the Quarrel, that theſe are inricht and advanced by it, ſave their purſes and perſons, cram their filthy greedy guts too il to carry to a bear.
47. Yea my Lord this great gore belly Idoll called the Aſſembly of Divines is not aſhamed in this time of neceſſity to devour more at one Meal then *Bel* and the *Dragon.*
48. Beſides all their fat Benefices forſooth they muſt have four ſhillings a peece by the day, &c.
49. They move your Lordſhip that all the Clergy may be freed from taxations that now the trade of *Preſbytery* is the beſt.
50. All are taxt and it goes free, thus theſe Church-lubbers live at eaſe.
51. Let all that ſuffer oppreſſion conſider this and no longer be Riden and Jaded by Clergy-maſters.
52. But to give the Devil his due, they are zealouſly affected to the honor of the cloth, that it is pity to diſrobe them of the caſſock garb to be led in ſtrings from *Weſtminſter* to *Algate* in leathern Jackets and mattrock on their ſhoulders.
53. *Pag.* 26, 27. Primacy, Metrapolitaniſm, Prelacy &c. are ſhrunk into the *Preſbytery*, and the High Commiſſion court turned into an *Aſſembly of Divines.*

With ruinerous ſuch like curſed expreſſions the like whereof I perſwade my ſelf all our Jeſuiticall State-deſtroying Romiſh enemies are no way able to paralel, thus in plain Engliſh we ſee a goodly Foundation laid for a Toleration, pretended for tender conſciences but contradicted by helliſh, heatheniſh and curſed carnal practiſes.

A Reply to DICTATED *thoughts by a more* **Proper Emblem**

*Dictater heere behould in proper place
Three joynd as one to blemiſh and diſgrace
Heere wants noe chayne to linke each to other
you ſee how loueingly they gree together
Sweet peace and Truth how gladly would they meet
Yet for theſe enimies they Cannot greet*

London, Printed for *Joſeph Potts*, and are to be ſold at his ſhop, in the *Old Bayly*, neer the Seſſions houſe 1646.

---

15 A Presbyterian indictment of the evils of toleration: in the centre the two-faced figure of 'Profane Libertin' holds a book entitled 'loose liberty', tramples the Bible underfoot and unites with Popery and Prelacy to wound honest hearts. This broadside was a reply to an earlier anti-Presbyterian publication which pleaded the case for 'tender consciences', in which the central figure was 'Antichristian Presbiter'. *Proper persecution or the sandy foundation of a general toleration* (1646). (By permission of The British Library, Thomason broadsides, shelfmark 669 f 10/104).

and illustrating the acute dangers of toleration – if they did not actually manu-facture it to fulfil this objective.[263] The pluralism that was the unexpected side effect of this war between two groups of persecutors fostered a renewed sense that strict enforcement of uniformity was the best way of preventing English society from disintegrating.

This culminated in the Restoration itself. The harsh penalties dealt out to dissenters under the Clarendon Code were a backlash against the anarchy that the religious laissez-faire of the previous two decades was perceived to have promoted. Ecclesiastical comprehension was seen as an underhand method of legitimising schism within the boundaries of the established Church and accordingly rejected and it is important to recognise that 'latitudinarianism' was above all a term of abuse – less a description of a coherent outlook than another symptom of contemporary distrust of tendencies that seemed to favour conciliation and compromise rather than bold confrontation.[264]

The attempts of Charles II and James II to extend a form of toleration via declarations of indulgence were equally ill-received. One contemporary called them 'the pope's mousetrap to catch the simple'[265] and it was widely supposed that this was a device for re-imposing monopolistic control by the Church of Rome, as well as a serious threat to England's balanced constitution and the legislative role of Parliament. Hence, the dilemma which many Protestant nonconformists felt about taking advantage of the liberties granted to them, and the celebrated refusal of the seven Anglican bishops to read the proclam-ation of 1687 from their pulpits. The latter's insistence that this did not spring 'from any want of due tenderness to Dissenters' was a measure of how far the religious landscape had changed in half a century.[266] Reigniting fears that had brought the nation to war in the 1640s, such initiatives intensified anti-Catholic feeling in Parliament and in the streets at large and supplied the ingredients for the spasms of intolerance and scapegoating that took their most virulent form in the furore surrounding the alleged Popish Plot of 1678. Welding together Protestants from all parts of the ecclesiastical spectrum, they also led directly to James II's explusion in 1688 and the constitutional coup which brought William and Mary to the throne, a paradoxical by-product of which was the Act of 'Toleration'.[267]

In turn, this legislation inspired its own conservative reaction, in the guise of the Sacheverell riots of 1710 and the Occasional Conformity and Schism Acts of 1711 and 1714. The repeal of the latter in 1718 by no means represented the end of attempts to resolve the tensions between tolerance and intolerance that had shaped English culture in the post-Reformation era. The passage of an Act for the Naturalisation of the Jews in 1753, and its cancellation later that year following resentment and tumult around the country,[268] provides further evidence that this vicious circle had not yet been broken, as do the Gordon Riots in London incited by the Catholic Relief Act of 1778. The inconsistencies between continuing intellectual commitment to the Augustinian theory of persecution and the parochial reality of pluralism and practical tolerance continued to test the stability of eighteenth-century England. It remained a powerful undercurrent in an age that regarded 'Enlightenment', 'civility' and 'reason' as its defining characteristics.

It is, then, misleading to attempt to trace a linear path 'from persecution to toleration', to seek to delineate the process by which a 'persecuting society' gave way to one in which liberty of conscience and freedom of worship were accepted as basic principles. Tolerance and intolerance interacted with and fed off each other in a recurrent and unending cycle. Prejudice and violence were tempered and restrained, but also sometimes stimulated and intensified, by an instinct to preserve peace and concord and to turn a blind eye to heterodox beliefs and practices that did not interfere with normal social relations. The complex legacy of the long Reformation was to reinforce both these impulses. It fostered fierce campaigns to eradicate the pluralism unleashed by it, but it also catalysed a body of ideas, theories and legal measures that sanctioned, justified, and defended this. It both facilitated and complicated the conditions in which people coexisted with difference.

NOTES

1 Robert Persons, *The Jesuit's memoriall for the intended Reformation of England*, ed. Edward Gee (London, 1690), p. 33.

2 Harro Höpfl (ed.), *Luther and Calvin on Secular Authority* (Cambridge, 1991), p. 62.

3 Avihu Zakai, 'Orthodoxy in England and New England: puritans and the issue of religious toleration, 1640–1650', *Proceedings of the American Philosophical Society*, 135 (1991), 401–41, at 435–6.

4 Edwards, *Casting down*, title-page and sig. A2r; Worden, 'Toleration and the Cromwellian Protectorate', p. 201; Christopher Hill, 'History and denominational history', in his *The Collected Essays of Christopher Hill*, vol. 2 *Religion and Politics in Seventeenth-Century England* (Hassocks, 1986), pp. 3–10, at 7.

5 Kamen, *Rise of Toleration*, p. 182.

6 Spurr, *Restoration Church*, p. 71.

7 Gordon J. Schochet, 'From persecution to "toleration"', in J. R. Jones (ed.), *Liberty Secured? Britain before and after 1688* (Stanford, CA, 1992), pp. 122–57, at 128, 122 respectively.

8 These were the titles of key tolerationist tracts by Jacobus Acontius, *Stratagematum satanae* (1565); Thomas Helwys, *A short declaration of the mistery of iniquity* (1612); Roger Williams, *The bloudy tenent, of persecution, for cause of conscience* (1644).

9 To quote Sir Charles Wolseley, in De Krey, 'Dissenting cases for conscience', p. 66; Henry Robinson, *Liberty of conscience: or the sole means to obtaine peace and truth* (London, 1643), sig. A3v; and Colonel Holland in Kamen, *Rise of Toleration*, p. 175.

10 Knights, '"Meer religion" and the "church-state"', p. 59.

11 Murphy, *Conscience and Community*, chs 3, 4 and 6 passim, esp. pp. 77–8, 124, 127. See ch. 1 above. Much of this rethinking has been loosely inspired by Quentin Skinner's approach to the history of ideas. See especially his 'Meaning and understanding in the history of ideas', *History and Theory*, 8 (1969), 3–53.

12 Coffey, *Persecution and Toleration*, esp. pp. 5, 7–10; Zagorin, *Idea of Religious Toleration*, p. 3.

13 See, for instance, Zagorin, *Idea of Religious Toleration*, and the list appended to Laursen (ed.), *Religious Toleration*, pp. 231–45. Note also Anthony Milton's comments about parallel tendencies in the history of ecumenism and eirenicism: this too has been characterised by a tendency to construct an 'apostolic succession of moderate, fair-minded people who urged projects for Christian unity': 'The unchanged peacemaker? John Dury and the politics of irenicism in England, 1628–1643', in Mark Greengrass, Michael Leslie and Timothy Raylor (eds), *Samuel Hartlib and Universal Reformation: Studies in Intellectual Communication* (Cambridge, 1994), pp. 95–117, esp. pp. 96–7.

14 More's reputation as a tolerationist rests uneasily on his engimatic fiction *Utopia* (1516).

15 See Haller, *Liberty and Reformation*.

16 See Caroline Polizzotto, 'Liberty of conscience and the Whitehall debates of 1648–9', *JEH*, 26 (1975), 69–82 and 'The campaign against *The Humble Proposals* of 1652', *JEH*, 38 (1987), 569–81.

17 Katz, *Philo-Semitism*, esp. chs 5–6.

18 See Jordan, *Development of Religious Toleration*, ii. 492–521; Lecler, *Toleration and the Reformation*, ii. 365–78; T. H. Clancy, *Papist Pamphleteers* (Chicago, 1964), ch. 6; Elton, 'Persecution and toleration in the English Reformation', in Sheils (ed.), *Persecution and Toleration*, pp. 180–4; Pritchard, *Catholic Loyalism*, pp. 171–3; Holmes, *Resistance and Compromise*, pp. 211–14. On the Blackloists, see Anthony Brown, 'Anglo-Irish Gallican-ism *c.*1635–*c.*1685', unpubl. PhD thesis (Cambridge, 2004).

19 See, among others, John Rawls, *A Theory of Justice* (Oxford, 1972) and his *Political Liberalism* (New York, 1993); Ronald Dworkin, *Taking Rights Seriously* (London, 1977) and his *Law's Empire* (London, 1986).

20 Voltaire, *Philosophical Dictionary* (1764), in Mullan (ed.), *Religious Pluralism*, p. 188.

21 Kamen, *Rise of Toleration*, pp. 170, 178, 205. For Penn, see Krey, 'Dissenting cases of conscience', p. 64.

22 C. H. George, 'Puritanism as history and historiography', *P&P*, 41 (1968), 77–104, at p. 102; William Lamont, 'Pamphleteering, the Protestant consensus and the English Revolution', in R. C. Richardson and G. M. Ridden (eds), *Freedom and the English Revolution: Essays in History and Literature* (Manchester, 1986), pp. 87 and 72–92 passim. Such assumptions inspired the publication of works like Woodhouse (ed.), *Puritanism and Liberty*; Haller, *Liberty and Reformation*; and his facsimile edition of *Tracts on Liberty in the Puritan Revolution 1638–1647*, 3 vols (New York, 1933–34).

23 J. C. Davis, 'Religion and the struggle for freedom in the English Revolution', *HJ*, 35 (1992), 507–30, esp. 517–19.

24 Turchetti, 'Religious concord and political tolerance'. See also Nederman and Laursen (eds), *Difference and Dissent*, introduction, pp. 9–12.

25 Bejczy, '*Tolerantia*: a medieval concept', 383.

26 Leonard Busher, *Religions peace or a plea for liberty of conscience* (London, 1646 edn), in Edward Bean Underhill (ed.), *Tracts on Liberty of Conscience and Persecution 1614–1661* (London, 1846), p. 33. This was not universal. The Baptist John Tombs would not have tolerated papists, worshippers of false gods, or those who denied Scripture: see Timothy George, 'Between pacifism and coercion: The English Baptist doctrine of religious toleration', *Mennonite Quarterly Review*, 58 (1984), 30–49, at 48–9.

27 John Coffey, 'Puritanism and liberty revisited: the case for toleration in the English Revolution', *HJ*, 41 (1998), 961–85, at 968, 970 respectively. Norah Carlin, 'Toleration for Catholics in the puritan revolution', in Grell and Scribner (eds), *Tolerance and Intolerance*, pp. 216–30.

28 Coffey, *Persecution and Toleration*, p. 55.

29 *Ibid*, p. 56; Coffey, 'Puritanism and liberty revisited', 967.

30 As Carlin remarks in 'Toleration', p. 221.

31 See Walsham, 'Ordeals of conscience', p. 44; Clancy, *Papist Pamphleteers*, p. 146. This, of course, was the position adopted by Thomas Aquinas.

32 John Milton, *Areopagitica: a speech ... for the liberty of unlicenc'd printing, to the parliament of England* (London, 1644); John Locke, *A letter concerning toleration* (London, 1689).

33 John Dunn, 'The claim to freedom of conscience: freedom of speech, freedom of thought, freedom of worship?', in Grell, Israel and Tyacke (eds), *From Persecution to Toleration*, p. 188.

34 Kamen, *Rise of Toleration*, p. 170.

35 Pierre Bayle, *A philosophical commentary* (1686), in Mullan (ed.), *Religious Pluralism*, p. 172. John Christian Laursen, 'Baylean Liberalism: tolerance requires intolerance', in Laursen and Nederman (eds), *Beyond the Persecuting Society*, p. 198 and *passim*.

36 Zakai, 'Orthodoxy', p. 428. See also Avihu Zakai, 'Religious toleration and its enemies: the Independent divines and the issue of toleration during the English Civil War', *Albion*, 21 (1989), 1–33.

37 See Richard Ashcraft, 'Latitudinarianism and toleration: historical myth versus political history', in Richard Kroll, Richard Ashcraft and Perez Zagorin (eds), *Philosophy, Science and Religion in England 1640–1700* (Cambridge, 1992), pp. 151–77.

38 As noted by Pettegree, 'Politics of toleration', p. 198. See ch. 1, pp. 3–4, above.

39 Horst, *Radical Brethren*, p. 119.

40 Ole Peter Grell, 'Exile and tolerance', in Grell and Scribner (eds), *Tolerance and Intolerance*, pp. 164–81.

41 Thomas Cartwright, *The second replie of Thomas Cartwright: agaynst Maister Doctor Whitgiftes second answer, touching the church discipline* ([Heidelberg], 1575), p. CXV. See also Lecler, *Toleration and the Reformation*, ii. 392–5, and 390.

42 Morton, *World of the Ranters*, p. 173.

43 Kamen, *Rise of Toleration*, p. 180.

44 Robert Persons, *A briefe discours contayning certayne reasons why Catholiques refuse to goe to church* (Douai [London secret press], 1581), sig. ±± 4r. See Walsham, 'Ordeals of Conscience', p. 44; Elton, 'Persecution and toleration', pp. 182–3.

45 Jordan, *Development of Religious Toleration*, ii. 505–21, esp. 512.

46 Thomas F. Mayer, '"Heretics be not in all things heretics": Cardinal Pole, his circle, and the potential for toleration', in Laursen and Nederman (ed.), *Beyond the Persecuting Society*, pp. 107–24. On Starkey, A. G. Dickens, 'Religious toleration and liberalism in Tudor England', in his *Reformation Studies* (London, 1982), pp. 427–42, at 430.

47 Diarmaid MacCulloch, 'Archbishop Cranmer: concord and tolerance in a changing Church', in Grell and Scribner (eds), *Tolerance and Intolerance*, pp. 199–215, esp. pp, 213–14.

48 Persons, *Memoriall*, p. 33.

49 Lecler, *Toleration and the Reformation*, i. 392.

50 For a concise analysis of the range of arguments employed, see Hans R. Guggisberg, 'The defence of religious toleration and religious liberty in early modern Europe: arguments, pressures, and some consequences', *History of European Ideas*, 4 (1983), 35–50.

51 Marsh, *Family of Love*, p. 188; Carlson (ed.), *Writings of ... Barrow 1587–1590*, p. 4; Robinson, *Liberty of conscience*, p. 55.

52 Nicholas Tyacke, 'The "rise of puritanism" and the legalizing of dissent', in Grell, Israel and Tyacke (eds), *From Persecution to Toleration*, p. 36. See also Bruce Yardley, 'George Villiers, second duke of Buckingham and the politics of toleration', *Huntington Library Quarterly*, 55 (1992), 317–37.

53 Bayle, *Philosophical commentary*, in Mullan (ed.), *Religious Pluralism*, p. 169.

54 Underwood (ed.), *Acts of the Witnesses*, p. 201.

55 Roland H. Bainton, 'The parable of the tares as the proof text for religious liberty to the end of the sixteenth century', *Church History*, 1 (1932), 67–89.

56 Tyacke, 'Legalizing of dissent', p. 30; Williams, *Bloudy Tenent*, in Mullan (ed.), *Religious Pluralism*, pp. 136–7, 139.

57 John Frith, *A disputacio[n] of purgatorye* (Antwerp, 1531), sig. I5r; Dickens, *English Reformation*, p. 379.

58 Sebastian Castellio, *Concerning Heretics: Whether they are to be Persecuted and how they are to be Treated*, trans. Roland H. Bainton (New York, 1965; first publ. 1554). Castellio quoted from Luther extensively: pp. 141–54; Martin Luther, 'Temporal authority: to what extent it should be obeyed (1523), in Mullan (ed.), *Religious Pluralism*, p. 92.

59 Dickens, 'Religious toleration', p. 438; Watts, *Dissenters*, p. 39.

60 Coffey, 'Puritanism and liberty revisited', 974; Kamen, *Rise of Toleration*, p. 164.

61 John Goodwin, *The grand imprudence of men running the hazard of fighting against God* (London, 1644), pp. 34, 36–7.

62 Kamen, *Rise of Toleration*, p. 188; Murphy, *Conscience and Community*, p. 111.

63 Locke, *Letter concerning toleration*, in Mullan (ed.), *Religious Pluralism*, p. 177.

64 Luther, 'Temporal authority', in Mullan (ed.), *Religious Toleration*, p. 92.

65 Busher, *Religions Peace*, p. 30.

66 Nuttall, *Visible Saints*, p. 104.

67 Robinson, *Liberty of conscience*, pp. 6–7.

68   Coffey, *Persecution and Toleration*, p. 68.

69   Tyacke, 'Legalizing of dissent', p. 36.

70   Locke, *Letter concerning toleration*, in Mullan (ed.), *Religious Pluralism*, p. 179.

71   Guggisberg, 'Defence', p. 38.

72   Shagan, 'Battle for indifference'.

73   Spurr, *Restoration Church*, p. 84.

74   Watts, *Dissenters*, p. 160; Cross, 'Church in England', p. 119; Spurr, *Restoration Church*, p. 78.

75   Johann Sommerville, 'Conscience, law, and things indifferent: arguments on toleration from the vestiarian controversy to Hobbes and Locke', in Braun and Vallance (eds), *Contexts of Conscience*, pp. 166–79, esp. pp. 168–70.

76   Persons, *Briefe discours*, fo. 5v. See also Clancy, *Papist Pamphleteers*, pp. 142–7.

77   Hartley (ed.), *Proceedings ... 1558–1581*, p. 240.

78   John Lilburne, *A copie of a letter ... to Mr William Prinne Esq* (London, 1645), p. 5.

79   Richard Overton, *The araignement of Mr Persecution* (London, 1645), p. 15. He was closely echoing Busher, *Religions Peace*, p. 34.

80   Henry More, *An explanation of the grand mystery of godlines* (1660), in Mullan (ed.), *Religious Pluralism*, pp. 163–4.

81   Williams, *Bloudy tenent*, pp. 79–80, 25 respectively.

82   Locke, *Letter concerning toleration*, in Mullan (ed.), *Religious Pluralism*, p. 180, and pp. 178–81 *passim*.

83   Michel de Montaigne, 'Of cripples', in Alan C. Kors and Edward Peters (eds), *Witchcraft in Europe 1100–1700* (Philadelphia, 1972), p. 337.

84   Goodwin, *Grand imprudence*, title-page and *passim*; [William Walwyn], *The compassionate samaritane* (London, 1644), pp. 10–11.

85   G. A. J. Rogers, 'Locke and the latitude men: ignorance as a ground of toleration', in Kroll, Ashcraft and Zagorin (eds), *Philosophy, Science and Religion*, pp. 230–52, at 239; Kamen, *Rise of Toleration*, p. 180.

86   As Richard Tuck has argued, scepticism could also lead to intolerance: 'Scepticism and toleration in the seventeenth century', in Mendus (ed.), *Justifying Toleration*, pp. 21–35. See also Murphy, *Conscience and Community*, pp. 233–8, 106–10.

87   Acontius, *Stratagematum satanae*, in Mullan (ed.), *Religious Pluralism*, p. 116.

88   Robinson, *Liberty of conscience*, p. 61.

89   Milton, *Areopagitica*, esp. pp. 4, 29, 36.

90   Capp, *Fifth Monarchy Men*, pp. 181–4.

91   Lamont, 'Pamphleteering', p. 82.

92   See Katz, *Philo-Semitism*, chs 3, 5; Richard Popkin, 'Hartlib, Dury and the Jews', in Greengrass, Leslie and Raylor (eds), *Samuel Hartlib and Universal Reformation*, pp. 118–36; Richard Popkin, 'Skepticism about religion and millenarian dogmatism: two sources of toleration in the seventeenth century', in Laursen and Nederman (eds), *Beyond the Persecuting Society*, pp. 232–50, at pp. 242–6. See also H. C. Porter,

'Anglicans, puritans and American Indians: persecution or toleration', in Sheils (ed.), *Persecution and Toleration*, pp. 189–98.

93 Burgess, 'Thomas Hobbes', pp. 139–61.

94 Overton, *Araignement*, p. 1 and *passim*.

95 Thomas Helwys, *A most humble supplication* (1620), in Underhill (ed.), *Tracts*, pp. 224–5; Robinson, *Liberty of conscience*, p. 48. For Bethell, Tyacke, 'Legalizing of dissent', pp. 34–5.

96 Richard L. Greaves, 'Seditious sectaries or "sober and useful inhabitants"? Changing conceptions of the Quakers in early modern Britain', *Albion*, 33 (2001), 24–50, at 38.

97 Daniel Brühlmeier, 'Daniel Defoe: dissent, economics and toleration', in Laursen (ed.), *Religious Toleration*, pp. 211–27.

98 Worden, 'Toleration and the Cromwellian Protectorate', p. 233.

99 Ryrie, *Gospel and Henry VIII*, p. 81.

100 These were the formulae used by Richard Montagu in the diocese of Norwich in 1638 and Tobie Matthew in York in 1607: Fincham (ed.), *Visitation Articles*, ii. 197; i. 57 respectively. Many other clauses to this effect can be found in the records of episcopal administration throughout the period.

101 BL Lansdowne MS 155, fo. 62r–v.

102 Thomson, *Later Lollards*, p. 90; Margaret Bowker, *The Secular Clergy in the Diocese of Lincoln 1495–1520* (Cambridge, 1968), pp. 21–2.

103 Ryrie, *Gospel and Henry VIII*, p. 81.

104 Craig W. D'Alton, 'The suppression of Lutheran heretics in England, 1526–1529', *JEH*, 54 (2003), 228–53.

105 MacCulloch, 'Archbishop Cranmer', pp. 205–6, 208–9.

106 Ryrie, *Gospel and Henry VIII*, pp. 83–4.

107 Mayer, 'Cardinal Pole', pp. 116–17.

108 Christopher Marsh, 'Piety and persuasion in Elizabethan England: the Church of England versus the Family of Love', in Tyacke (ed.), *England's Long Reformation*, pp. 141–65; Anthony Milton and Alexandra Walsham (eds), 'Richard Montagu: "Concerning recusancie of communion with the Church of England"', in Stephen Taylor (ed.), *From Cranmer to Davidson: A Miscellany*, Church of England Record Society 7 (Woodbridge, 1999), pp. 74–5.

109 William Bedell, *An examination of certaine motives to recusancie* (London, 1628), sig. A4r; Acheson, *Radical Puritans*, pp. 38–9.

110 Spaeth, *Church in an Age of Danger*, p. 159; David L. Wykes, 'They "assemble in greater numbers and [with] more dareing then formerly": the bishop of Gloucester and nonconformity in the late 1660s', *Southern History*, 17 (1990), 24–39, at 26.

111 Horst, *Radical Brethren*, p. 90.

112 Hughes and Larkin (eds), *Tudor Royal Proclamations*, ii. 5–6.

113 Frere (ed.), *Visitation Articles*, ii. 149.

114 Frere (ed.), *Visitation Articles*, iii. 23. Cf. the compromise reached between conflicting

confessions in Eastern Switzerland *c.*1610, which stressed the responsibility neighbours had not to 'touch one another with disdainful or burdensome words, but to live in good peace according to our alliance': Randolph C. Head, 'Religious coexistence and confessional conflict in the Vier Dörfer: practices of toleration in eastern Switzerland, 1525–1615', in Laursen and Nederman (eds), *Beyond the Persecuting Society*, pp. 145–65, at p. 156.

115 See Diarmaid MacCulloch, 'The myth of the English Reformation', *JBS*, 30 (1991), 1–19. Cf. G. W. Bernard, 'The Church of England *c.*1529–*c.*1642', *History*, 75 (1990), 183–206; *ibid.*, 'The making of religious policy, 1533–1546: Henry VIII and the search for the middle way', *HJ* 41 (1998), 321–49; Wooding, *Rethinking Catholicism, passim.*

116 MacCulloch, 'Archbishop Cranmer', p. 204.

117 Francis Dryander to Henry Bullinger (25 March 1549), in Hastings Robinson (ed.), *Original Letters Relative to the English Reformation*, vol. I, *1537–1558*, PS (Cambridge, 1846), p. 350.

118 MacCulloch, *Later Reformation*, p. 30.

119 Diarmaid MacCulloch, *Reformation: Europe's House Divided 1490–1700* (London, 2003), p. 289.

120 K. R. Wark, *Elizabethan Recusancy in Cheshire*, Chetham Society, 3rd series, 19 (1971), p. 18n; Christopher Haigh, ' "A matter of much contention in the realm": parish controversies over communion bread in post-Reformation England', *History*, 88 (2003), 393–404, esp. 399–400. Haigh examines the contradictions in official policy and charts the declining use of wafers.

121 Hastings Robinson (ed.), *The Zurich Letters 1558–1579*, PS (Cambridge, 1842), p. 100.

122 Lake, *Anglicans and Puritans?*, p. 230 and ch. 4 *passim*; Diarmaid MacCulloch, 'Richard Hooker's Reputation', *EHR*, 117 (2002), 773–812.

123 Jones, *English Reformation*, p. 202. For another attempt to tackle these vexed questions, see Louise Campbell, 'A diagnosis of religious moderation: Matthew Parker and the 1559 settlement', in Racaut and Ryrie (eds), *Moderate Voices*, pp. 32–50.

124 Hastings Robinson (ed.), *The Zurich Letters 1558–1602*, 2nd series, PS (Cambridge, 1845), p. 151 and R. A. Houlbrooke (ed.), *The Letter Book of John Parkhurst, Bishop of Norwich, Compiled During the Years 1571–5*, Norfolk Record Society 43 (1974–5), p. 222; Collinson, *Elizabethan Puritan Movement*, pp. 66–7. See also Fincham, 'Clerical conformity', pp. 125–58.

125 Collinson, *Elizabethan Puritan Movement*, p. 406.

126 Clark, *English Provincial Society*, p. 166.

127 The National Archives, London, State Papers 12/154/48 (5 July 1582).

128 Spurr, *English Puritanism*, p. 62.

129 Collinson, *Religion of Protestants*, pp. 282–3; Green, *Re-Establishment of the Church of England*, esp. ch. 8; Spurr, *Restoration Church*, pp. 163–5.

130 Patrick Collinson, 'The Elizabethan puritans and the foreign reformed churches in London', in his *Godly People*, p. 248 and pp. 245–72 *passim*. See also Pettegree, *Foreign Protestant Communities*.

131 Grell, *Calvinist Exiles*, pp. 55–6.

132 See Pettegree, 'The French and Walloon communities in London, 1550–1688', in Grell, Israel and Tyacke (eds), *From Persecution to Toleration*, pp. 77–96, at 88–96; Grell, *Dutch Calvinists*, ch. 6; Milton, *Catholic and Reformed*, pt II *passim*, and for the Channel Islands, pp. 479, 496; Sharpe, *Personal Rule*, pp. 348–51.

133 Robin D. Gwynn, 'James II in the light of his treatment of Huguenot refugees in England, 1685–1688', *EHR*, 92 (1977), 820–33, esp. 828; G. C. Gibbs, 'The reception of the Huguenots in England and the Dutch Republic 1680–1690', in Grell, Israel and Tyacke (eds), *From Persecution to Toleration*, pp. 275–306.

134 Tyacke, 'Legalizing of dissent', pp. 19–24.

135 Kenyon (ed.), *Stuart Constitution*, (2nd edn), p. 332.

136 Browning (ed.), *English Historical Documents 1660–1714*, pp. 365–70.

137 John Spurr, 'The Church of England, comprehension and the toleration act of 1689', *EHR*, 104 (1989), 927–46, at 941–2, 943. See also Spurr, 'Schism and the Restoration Church'. For local initiatives for comprehension, see Newton E. Key, 'Comprehension and the breakdown of consensus in Restoration Herefordshire', in Harris, Seaward and Goldie (eds), *Politics of Religion*, pp. 191–215.

138 Spurr, 'Church of England', *passim*; Roger Thomas, 'Comprehension and indulgence', in Geoffrey F. Nuttall and Owen Chadwick (eds), *From Uniformity to Unity 1662–1962* (London, 1962), pp. 191–253; Gordon J. Schochet, 'The Act of Toleration and the failure of comprehension: persecution, nonconformity and religious indifference', in Hoak and Feingold (eds), *World of William and Mary*, pp. 165–87.

139 Kenyon (ed.), *Stuart Constitution* (2nd edn), pp. 32–13, 328–9. See Worden, 'Toleration and the Cromwellian Protectorate', p. 227.

140 Neale, *Elizabeth I and her Parliaments*, i. 191, 391.

141 Hooker, *Works*, ed. Keble, ii. 96–103.

142 See ch. 2, pp. 85–6.

143 Michael Questier, 'Sir Henry Spiller, recusancy and the efficiency of the Jacobean Exchequer', *Historical Research*, 66 (1993), 251–66. It should be noted that Spiller himself may have had Catholic inclinations and sympathies. Braddick, *State Formation*, p. 305.

144 Francis Beaumont and John Fletcher, *Cupids revenge* (London, 1615), sig. B3r.

145 J. S. Cockburn (ed.), *Calendar of Assize Records: Essex Indictments James I* (London, 1982), p. 3.

146 Pauline Croft, 'The Catholic gentry, the earl of Salisbury and the baronets of 1611', in Lake and Questier (eds), *Conformity and Orthodoxy*, pp. 262–81.

147 Smith, 'Persecution of Staffordshire Roman Catholic recusants', esp. 333–44.

148 Croft, 'Catholic gentry', p. 281.

149 Roth, *History of the Jews in England*, p. 187; Katz, *Jews in England*, pp. 162–3.

150 Davis, *Heresy and Reformation*, p. 108.

151 Cockburn (ed.), *Essex Presentments: James I*, p. 206.

152 Marsh, 'Piety and persuasion', esp. pp. 144, 156–7.

153 Larkin and Hughes (ed.), *Stuart Royal Proclamations*, i. 145.

154 See ch. 2, pp. 63–4.

155 Benjamin J. Kaplan, 'Fictions of privacy: house chapels and the spatial accommodation of religious dissent in early modern Europe', *American Historical Review*, 107 (2002), 1031–64.

156 Joachim Whaley, *Religious Toleration and Social Change in Hamburg 1529–1819* (Cambridge, 1985), p. 5.

157 See below, p. 266.

158 Collinson, *Religion of Protestants*, p. 248. See also his 'English conventicle'.

159 For a subtle account of the blurred boundaries between domestic piety and the illegal conventicle, see Andrew Cambers and Michelle Wolfe, 'Reading, family religion, and evangelical identity in late Stuart England', *HJ*, 47 (2004), 875–96.

160 See Goldie, 'Locke, Proast and religious toleration', pp. 168–9. The quotation is from a letter written by Locke in 2 June 1692.

161 Larkin and Hughes (eds), *Stuart Royal Proclamations*, i. 184–5.

162 Questier, 'Loyalty', 313 and *passim*, and the critique of Questier in Johann P. Sommerville, 'Papalist political thought and the controversy over the Jacobean oath of allegiance', in Shagan (ed.), *Catholics and the Protestant Nation*, pp. 162–84. Cf. the different interpretation of John J. La Rocca, '"Who can't pray with me, can't love me": toleration and the early Jacobean recusancy policy', *JBS*, 23 (1984), 22–36, esp. 33–6.

163 W. B. Patterson, *King James VI and I and the Reunion of Christendom* (Cambridge, 1997).

164 Spurr, *Restoration Church*, p. 73.

165 Coffey, *Persecution and Toleration*, pp. 122, 142, 157, 186, 178. See also Albert J. Loomie, 'Oliver Cromwell's policy towards English Catholics: the appraisal by diplomats, 1654–1658', *Catholic Historical Review*, 90 (2004), 29–44. For Southworth, see *ODNB*, li. 723–4.

166 Kenyon (ed.), *Stuart Constitution* (2nd edn), p. 381.

167 Browning (ed.), *English Historical Documents 1660–1714*, p. 400. See ch. 2, pp. 57–8.

168 A phrase employed in a proclamation of 1602: Hughes and Larkin (eds), *Tudor Royal Proclamations*, iii. 253.

169 Patterson, *James VI and I*, p. 358; Russell, *Parliaments*, pp. 153–4.

170 See esp. Hibbard, *Charles I and the Popish Plot*.

171 See Benjamin J. Kaplan, 'Diplomacy and domestic devotion: embassy chapels and the toleration of religious dissent in early modern Europe', *Journal of Early Modern History*, 6 (2002), 341–61.

172 J. S. Cockburn (ed.), *Calendar of Assize Records: Kent Indictments Elizabeth I* (London, 1979), p. 469; Cockburn (ed.), *Surrey Indictments: James I*, pp. 10, 17; J. S. Cockburn (ed.), *Calendar of Assize Records: Kent Indictments James I* (London, 1980), p. 127.

173 See, for examples, Hughes and Larkin (eds), *Tudor Royal Proclamations*, iii. 250–4; Larkin and Hughes (eds), *Stuart Royal Proclamations*, i. 142–5, 329–32; Larkin (ed.), *Stuart Royal Proclamations*, ii. 128–31, 580–1. See K. J. Kesselring's recent study of pardons in the judicial process in general: *Mercy and Authority in the Tudor State* (Cambridge, 2003).

174 Kenyon (ed.), *Stuart Constitution* (2nd edn), pp. 379–82; Spurr, *Restoration Church*, pp. 50–1.

175 Kenyon (ed.), *Stuart Constitution* (2nd edn), pp. 382–4.

176 *Ibid.*, pp. 389–91.

177 See John Miller, 'James II and toleration', in Eveline Cruickshanks (ed.), *By Force or by Default? The Revolution of 1688–9* (Edinburgh, 1989), pp. 8–27, esp. p. 16.

178 Kenyon (ed.), *Stuart Constitution* (2nd edn), pp. 390, 383.

179 See the two addresses of thanks from the Presbyterians of London and the city of Gloucester, in Browning (ed.), *English Historical Documents 1660–1714*, pp. 397–9.

180 Browning (ed.), *English Historical Documents 1660–1714*, pp. 400–3. For a discussion of the incorporation of Quakers into the act, see David L. Wykes, 'Friends, Parliament and the Toleration Act', *JEH*, 45 (1994), 42–63.

181 Miller, 'James II', p. 23; Spurr, *Restoration Church*, p. 376; Tyacke, 'Legalizing of dissent', p. 12; Goldie, 'Locke, Proast, and religious toleration', p. 156. See also Scott Mandelbrote, 'Religious belief and the politics of toleration in the late seventeenth century', *Nederlands archief voor kerkgeschiedenis/Dutch Review of Church History*, 81 (2001), 93–114; Murphy, *Conscience and Community*, ch. 4.

182 Browning (ed.), *English Historical Documents 1660–1714*, p. 400. On William's politique outlook, see Jonathan I. Israel, 'William III and toleration', in Grell, Israel and Tyacke (eds), *From Persecution to Toleration*, pp. 129–70.

183 John Walsh and Stephen Taylor, 'Introduction: the Church and Anglicanism in the "long" eighteenth century', in Walsh, Haydon and Taylor (eds), *Church of England*, p. 61.

184 White, *English Separatist Tradition*, p. 71.

185 Fincham (ed.), *Visitation Articles*, ii. 48, 95, 144.

186 *Acts of the Privy Council 1542–1631*, 46 vols (London, 1890–1964), vi. 135, 144.

187 D. M. Palliser, *Tudor York* (Oxford, 1979), p. 257.

188 Webster, *Godly Clergy*, p. 198.

189 Watts, *Dissenters*, pp. 244–5.

190 Davies, *Quakers*, p. 176; Shoemaker, *Prosecution and Punishment*, p. 222.

191 Barry Reay, 'Quakerism and Society', in MacGregor and Reay (eds), *Radical Religion*, p. 156.

192 Christine Kooi, 'Paying off the sheriff: strategies of Catholic toleration in Golden Age Holland', in Hsia and van Nierop (eds), *Calvinism and Religious Toleration*, pp. 87–101.

193 Williams, *Catholic Recusancy*, pp. 12–13.

194 Harris, *London Crowds*, p. 72.

195 Wykes, 'Bishop of Gloucester and nonconformity', p. 35.

196 Ingram, 'Communities and courts'; J. A. Sharpe, 'Crime and delinquency in an Essex parish 1600–1640', in J. S. Cockburn (ed.), *Crime in England 1550–1800* (London, 1977), pp. 90–109; Sharpe, 'Enforcing the law', pp. 97–119; Wrightson, 'Two concepts of order'; Herrup, *Common Peace*; Shoemaker, *Prosecution and Punishment*, ch. 4.

197 McClendon, *Quiet Reformation*, pp. 17, 28, 253 and *passim*. See also her 'Religious toleration and the Reformation: Norwich magistrates in the sixteenth century', in Tyacke (ed.), *England's Long Reformation*, pp. 87–115.

198 Lorna Jane Abray, 'Confession, conscience and honour: the limits of magisterial tolerance in sixteenth-century Strasbourg', in Grell and Scribner (eds), *Tolerance and Intolerance*, pp. 94–107, esp. 96–7.

199 *Certaine sermons or homilies*, p. 43.

200 McSheffrey, *Gender and Heresy*, p. 73; Thomson, *Later Lollards*, pp. 84, and see comments on p. 190.

201 Brigden, *London and the Reformation*, p. 321.

202 Robert Whiting, *The Blind Devotion of the People: Popular Religion and the English Reformation* (Cambridge, 1989), pp. 169–70.

203 McIntosh, *Community Transformed*, pp. 196–7.

204 Underdown, *Revel, Riot and Rebellion*, p. 129; Braddick, *State Formation*, p. 325.

205 Harris, 'Attitudes of Londoners', 110–11.

206 Reay, *Quakers*, p. 62; Stevenson, 'Social integration', p. 373; Shoemaker, *Prosecution and Punishment*, p. 99.

207 Stevenson, 'Social integration', pp. 372–3.

208 Miller, 'Suffering people', 95; Davies, *Quakers*, p. 201.

209 Keith Wrightson, 'The "decline of neighbourliness" revisited', unpubl. conference paper delivered at Exeter, July 2003.

210 Seaver, *Wallington's World*, p. 144.

211 Jones, *English Reformation*, pp. 33, 135.

212 Plumb, 'Gathered church?'; Marsh, *Family of Love*, esp. ch. 7; Stevenson, 'Social integration'; Davies, *Quakers*, esp. ch. 14. See also Caffyn's briefer remarks in *Sussex Believers*, pp. 162–6. The other half of this equation (dissenters' willingness to interact with the orthodox) is discussed in Chapter 4 above.

213 Bida, 'Papists in an Elizabethan parish'; Sheils, 'Catholics and their neighbours'; Wanklyn, 'Catholics in the village community'.

214 Fincham (ed.), *Visitation Articles*, i. 21, 41, 82, 89, 105, 135, 144, 145, 175, 186, 201, 207; ii. 5, 18, 92, 101, 143, 239, 256. See also Marchant, *Church and the Law*, p. 221; Marsh, *Popular Religion*, p. 190.

215 Haigh, *Reformation and Resistance*, p. 193.

216 Joan Lane, *John Hall and his Patients: The Medical Practice of Shakespeare's Son-in-Law* (Stratford-upon-Avon, 1996), pp. xvii, 61, 50–2, 74–5, 184, 216, 225, 226–8, 227–9; Felicity Heal, *Hospitality in Early Modern England* (Oxford, 1990), pp. 171–2.

217 Wanklyn, 'Catholics in the village community', pp. 211–12. See also Malcolm Wanklyn, 'Shropshire recusants in 1635', *Midland Catholic History*, 3 (1993), 8–14.

218 Lindley, 'Lay Catholics', p. 204.

219 Bedell, *Examination of certaine motives*, pp. 1–6.

220 Fielding, 'Diary of Robert Woodford', 773–4.

221 Anthony Milton, 'A qualified intolerance: the limits and ambiguities of early Stuart anti-Catholicism', in Arthur F. Marotti (ed.), *Catholicism and Anti-Catholicism in Early Modern English Texts* (Basingstoke, 1999), pp. 85–115, at 95.

222 Davies, *Quakers*, p. 202.

223 Stevenson, 'Social integration', p. 375.

224 *Ibid.*, pp. 386–7.

225 Davies, *Quakers*, pp. 208–9; *ODNB*, xiii. 537.

226 Davies, *Quakers*, p. 203; Stevenson, 'Social integration', pp. 385, 377 respectively.

227 This is a much neglected subject in the English context. For a suggestive discussion of the German evidence, see Dagmar Freist, 'One body, two confessions: mixed marriages in Germany', in Ulinka Rublack (ed.), *Gender in Early Modern German History* (Cambridge, 2002), pp. 275–304 and 'Toleranz und Konfessionspolitik. Konfessionell gemischte Ehen in Deutschland 1555–1806' (unpubl. Habilitation, Osnabrück, March 2003). For the Netherlands, see Benjamin J. Kaplan, '"Mixed marriage" and the practice of religious toleration in the Dutch Republic: a comparative approach', in Marc R. Foster and Benjamin J. Kaplan (eds), *Piety and Family in Early Modern Europe: Essays in Honour of Steven Ozment* (Aldershot, forthcoming 2005).

228 Hanlon, *Confession and Community*, p. 11.

229 Willem Frijhoff, 'The threshold of toleration: interconfessional conviviality in Holland during the early modern period', in his *Embodied Belief: Ten Essays on Religious Culture in Dutch History* (Hilversum, 2002), pp. 39–65, at p. 44. See also his 'Dimensions de la coexistence confessionnelle', in Berkvens-Stevelinck, Israel and Posthumus Meyjes (eds), *Emergence of Toleration*, pp. 213–37.

230 Benedict, 'Parameters for the history of Catholic-Reformed co-existence', p. 78 and see Olivier Christin, '"Peace must come from us": friendship pacts between the confessions during the Wars of Religion', in Whelan and Baxter (eds), *Toleration and Religious Identity*, pp. 92–103; Benjamin J. Kaplan, *Calvinists and Libertines: Confession and Community in Utrecht 1578–1620* (Oxford, 1995), pp. 288–9. See also Keith P. Luria, 'Separated by death? Burials, cemeteries, and confessional boundaries in seventeenth-century France', *Catholic Historical Review*, 90 (2004), 29–44.

231 Marsh, *Family of Love*, pp. 187, 190; Marsh, 'Gravestone of Thomas Lawrence', p. 233. See also Hanlon, *Confession and Community*, p. 194: 'Tolerance was the outgrowth of a piety in which few people were highly sensitive to theological distinctions or else were reluctant to emphasize their importance'.

232 Jones, *English Reformation*, p. 34.

233 See Chapter 3, p. 148.

234 Russell, *Parliaments*, p. 120.

235 Stevenson, 'Social Integration', p. 378.

236 Haydon, *Anti-Catholicism*, p. 13.

237 Milton, 'Qualified intolerance', pp. 98, 108.

238 Davies, *Quakers*, p. 223.

239 Marsh, *Family of Love*, p. 231.

240 Frere (ed.), *Puritan Manifestoes*, pp. 15–18, at 18.

241 Hunt, *Puritan Moment*, p. 101; Haigh, *Reformation and Resistance*, p. 285.

242 J. S. Cockburn (ed.), *Calendar of Assize Records: Sussex Indictments James I* (London, 1975), p. 18.

243 Milton, 'Qualified Intolerance', p. 101.

244 Harris, 'Attitudes of Londoners', p. 113. Mark Goldie and John Spurr, 'Politics and the Restoration parish: Edward Fowler and the struggle for St Giles Cripplegate', *EHR*, 109 (1994), 572–96.

245 Milton, *Catholic and Reformed*, pp. 100, 57, respectively.

246 Hunt, *Puritan Moment*, pp. 187–8.

247 Walsham, 'Fatall vesper', p. 44.

248 Larkin (ed.), *Stuart Royal Proclamations*, ii, pp. 128–30, at 130.

249 Kenyon (ed.), *Stuart Constitution* (2nd edn), pp. 140–2.

250 Smith, 'Persecution of Staffordshire Roman Catholic recusants', p. 331.

251 *Acts of the Durham High Commission Court*, p. 142.

252 See Milton and Walsham (eds), 'Richard Montagu: "Concerning recusancie"', pp. 71–86.

253 Milton, *Catholic and Reformed*, pt I.

254 For instance the Directions to Preachers of 1622, from which the phrases quoted are taken: Kenyon (ed.), *Stuart Constitution*, (2nd edn), pp. 128–30.

255 Milton, *Catholic and Reformed*, p. 127.

256 *Ibid.*, pp. 345–73.

257 Kenyon (ed.), *Stuart Constitution* (2nd edn), pp. 207–17, esp. pp. 210–11.

258 As reported in *The Scotsman* (12 March 2001). I am very grateful to Dr Stephen Lee for this reference.

259 Spurr, *English Puritanism*, p. 111.

260 Davis, *Fear, Myth and History*, p. 103. For a very similar pronouncement, see Overton, *Araignement*, p. 21.

261 Stephens, *Catalogue of Satires*, no. 657. This Presbyterian print was a retort to an earlier anti-Presbyterian version (see nos 647 and 653).

262 Seaver, *Wallington's World*, pp. 66, 171.

263 Davis, *Fear, Myth and History*, pp. 107–25, esp. p. 123.

264 Spurr, 'Latitudinarianism', *passim*.

265 Scott, 'England's Troubles', p. 117.

266 Spurr, *Restoration Church*, p. 94. See also G. V. Bennett, 'The seven bishops: a reconsideration', in Derek Baker (ed.), *Religious Motivation: Biographical and Sociological Problems for the Church Historian*, SCH 15 (Oxford, 1978), pp. 267–87; Murphy, *Conscience and Community*, pp. 134–42.

267 See the similar comments of Murphy, *Conscience and Community*, p. 125.

268 Felsenstein, *Anti-Semitic Stereotypes*, ch. 8.

Chapter 6

———◆———

Coexisting with difference: religious pluralism and confessionalisation

The central theme of this book has been the idea that the histories of tolerance and intolerance in early modern England are not inversely related but rather closely interwoven. Narratives that seek to chart a clear path 'from persecution to toleration' do not merely run the risk of eclipsing the cyclical and reversible character of this development; they also habitually privilege legislative events and ideological advances over the practical realities of social relations between the adherents of rival sects and faiths. If the period between 1500 and 1700 witnessed hesitant steps towards insititutional recognition of the fact of religious pluralism and a steadily swelling stream of voices in favour of 'toleration', it was also marked by many powerful restatements of the Augustinian thesis that Christian rulers and churches had a God-given responsibility to restrain and discipline the wayward, and by recurrent outbursts of popular prejudice, hostility and violence. And if it saw continuing attempts on the part of the Tudor and Stuart state to eradicate or contain dissenting minorities, these were constantly moderated and alleviated by the deep-seated instinct for peace and concord that shaped the texture of life in the multiple local communities that comprised it.

It may be argued that these tensions and contradictions were in large part a consequence of the English Reformation. Designed as they were to restore religious consensus and uniformity, paradoxically the successive religious settlements of the mid-sixteenth century ended up by promoting the opposite. It was not simply that official initiatives to replace a settled and well-entrenched body of doctrine and practice with a novel alternative met with widespread resistance; nor that the political instability of 1540–1560 left many struggling to keep pace with the latest set of variations on change, and stranded in a no-man's-land somewhere between medieval Catholicism and Reformed Protestantism. One of the more distinctive features of the peculiar, hybrid species of Reformation that evolved in England was the extent to which it unwittingly facilitated the immersion and accommodation of dissent within the established Church and, by extension, within English society itself. By focusing on outward conformity as a sign of consent and by committing itself to an ecclesiology that embraced both the elect and the reprobate as legitimate members of its congregations, it nurtured an environment in which bi- or multi-confessionalism became permanently entrenched.

This had diverse and curious side effects. On the one hand, it may be said to have fostered a climate in which people became accustomed to coexisting with religious difference and to reaching a kind of modus vivendi with their neighbours – a climate of opinion that encouraged reciprocal gestures of good will and temporarily kept the lid on internecine conflicts of the kind that engulfed other parts of sixteenth-century Europe. On the other, it can be suggested that the pluralism accidentally fostered by the Elizabethan settlement laid the foundations for the wars of religion that broke out in the British Isles eighty years later. By creating conditions in which dissimulation and clandestinity could flourish, it stimulated anxieties which culminated in the conviction that radical constitutional measures and military action had to be taken to prevent English Protestantism from being undermined from within.

The outcomes of this struggle to defend and relocate the boundaries of 'orthodoxy' were equally ironic. As well as unleashing a mass of radical sects upon the scene, the Civil War and Interregnum served only to strengthen and exacerbate ecclesiastical frictions and divisions – frictions and divisions which continued to trouble the Church of England after its restoration in 1662. Thirty-seven years later these fused with fears about the threat presented by Catholic absolutism on the Continent to force the abandonment of the policy of uniformity and the granting of a limited liberty of conscience and worship to Protestant dissenters, who, nonetheless, remained subject to various forms of civil discrimination. The Test Acts ensured that Anglicans alone possessed the rights of full citizenship. In theory, Roman Catholics remained beyond the official pale. In practice, however, many enjoyed the effects of the legislation from which they had been specifically excluded. Some local officials seem to have mistakenly supposed that the statute extended to them.[1] Others simply acknowledged that there was no longer any hope of hounding this minority out of existence either. Confessional diversity was now so deeply embedded in English society that it was impossible to eliminate. Nor was this increasingly believed to be necessary: more than a century of experience had proved that living alongside people who believed in different visions of Christian truth did not lead inevitably to social implosion, political dissolution or providential catastrophe.

The task of this final chapter is to explore the long-term consequences of the religious pluralism engendered and reinforced by the events of the sixteenth and seventeenth centuries and, in particular, to consider the relationship between the state of relatively stable *convivencia* that seems to have generally prevailed in this period and the processes by which competing churches and sects defined, maintained and protected their collective identities in a context in which the parameters within which tolerance and intolerance operated were slowly changing. It seeks to examine the ways in which England participated in that series of wider religious and cultural developments that historians have come to call 'confessionalisation' and to suggest how these may have influenced the character and complexion of English society, especially in the century after the passage of the Act of Toleration in 1689.

CONFESSIONALISATION AND THE EUROPEAN REFORMATIONS

In the recent historiography of the European Reformations, the concept of 'confessionalisation' has become a key interpretative tool. First coined by E. W. Zeeden, but much elaborated and developed by the German historians Heinz Schilling and Wolfgang Reinhard, the phrase refers to the interrelated and mutually reinforcing processes by which the political and territorial consolidation of the early modern state, the imposition of moral discipline, and the formation of separate Erastian churches transformed society. Resting on the premise that the Catholic and Protestant movements for spiritual renewal were structurally parallel, this model emphasises the way in which the rivalry of different faiths converged with administrative centralisation and a growing preoccupation with moulding 'civilised' and orderly subjects to create a series of self-consciously competing confessional cultures demarcated by particular dogmas, rituals, languages, customs and codes of personal conduct.[2] In the hands of other scholars, however, the notion of confessionalisation has widened its ambit and come to be used more loosely to describe how the confusion and fluidity of the early decades of the Reformation gave way in later generations to the crystallisation and institutionalisation of formal churches and creeds. In part, this reflects growing cognisance of the fact that the absence of a dominant political regime was not necessarily a bar to these developments, which could occur both independently of and also often in tension with bureaucratic initiatives. Shedding its more explicit links with theories of state-building and 'modernisation', the term is increasingly applied to define the ongoing processes by which social and cultural barriers were erected around alternative religious communities and groups and by which distinct and often antagonistic confessional identities and sensibilities were forged.[3] Symptomatic of these processes were the emergence of explicit 'confessions', statements or formularies of doctrine and faith and the evolution of liturgical rites and ceremonies that distinguished particular Churches from the rival organisations with which they competed.[4]

Intriguingly, there is much to suggest that a heightened instinct for distinction was less a feature of the era in which Europe was torn apart by vicious spasms of war and violence than of those periods when governments and individuals tacitly accepted and even officially sanctioned or licensed the coexistence of two or more religions. As religious pluralism became recognised as a permanent feature of parochial life, people began instinctively to differentiate themselves ever more overtly from neighbours whose doctrinal beliefs or modes of worship diverged from their own. Confessionalisation in this sense appears to have been a function not so much of persecution as of truce and 'toleration', whether de facto or de jure.

This interesting hypothesis is beginning to be borne out by detailed studies of towns and cities in France in the wake of the Edict of Nantes of 1598. Careful analysis of the archives of Montpellier has enabled Philip Benedict, for instance, to demonstrate that Huguenots and Catholics in this urban community grew increasingly insular and endogamous after Henry IV's proclamation laying out the conditions for peace and political equilibrium. Even as cordial interaction and commercial collaboration knitted members of the two faiths together on many occasions, other forces worked in favour of enhancing their sectarian character and reinforcing social and cultural segregation. Intermarriage diminished and networks of neighbourly relations fractured more sharply along confessional lines. Catholics and Protestants ceased to stand as godparents for each others' children and insisted upon educating their offspring separately. Forms of economic interaction and interdependence diminished: people increasingly chose notaries of their own religion to handle their legal transactions. Vigorous catechising and indoctrination raised consciousness of the ideological differences that divided individuals, as did the hardening of the very labels used to identify them. At the same time as physical clashes were decreasing in intensity and incidence, self-imposed apartheid appears to have been on the rise.[5] In Aquitaine too, the forms of assimilation, amity and sociability that had marked the initial fluid stages of the Reformation and blunted its passions were very gradually attenuated. Despite continued transgression of confessional boundaries, in seventeenth-century Poitou, dispute over religious practices and beliefs likewise accentuated the differences between Catholics and Protestants, especially in the wake of a vigorous Capuchin mission to reclaim heretics.[6] Such developments make the 1685 revocation of the rights of worship granted to the Huguenots, and more particularly its ready acceptance in the provinces, even less surprising: the resurgence of official intolerance arguably parallelled tendencies that were pulling in the same direction at the level of local society.[7]

Within the Holy Roman Empire similar processes of dissociation can be discerned at work. The Peace of Augsburg of 1555 established the judicial framework for the coexistence of Lutheranism and Catholicism within the

Reich, though this was restricted by the principle of *cuius regio, eius religio*, whereby princes chose the faith of their subjects. The Treaty of Westphalia, which closed a door on the Thirty Years War in 1648, extended the recognition of denominational parity within the German territories to Calvinism and created a detailed legal code governing interconfessional relations, resting on a distinction between the public and private exercise of religion.[8] Especially in the imperial and free cities and in areas that underwent successive phases of Protestantisation and re-Catholicisation, the result was a pluralism that proved a fertile breeding ground for the emergence of self-consciously separate confessional cultures. Thus, following the fall of the Anabaptist kingdom in Münster, a religious life marked by an easy intermingling of confessions gave way over several generations to a stronger sense of competing Tridentine and Lutheran bodies of belief and practice, which was also catalysed by Jesuit evangelism.[9]

Similarly Marc Forster speaks of the 'mania for differentiation' that characterised Catholic–Protestant relations in the diocese of Speyer between 1650 and 1720, as a deeper awareness of, and emphasis upon doctrinal, liturgical and ritual differences emerged. From the books they read to the manner in which they decorated their homes, people deliberately set themselves apart from fellow members of their communities. A tendency to confine charitable giving, carry out trade, and seek employment within the ranks of one's coreligionists also became more pronounced.[10] In eighteenth-century Augsburg, Lutherans and Catholics acquired separate schools, cemeteries, and social institutions, and mixed marriages once again declined perceptibly. Peaceful coexistence of these groups did not so much inhibit, as arguably assist, the erection of an invisible border between the two.[11] Or, to reverse the argument, 'to coexist, the communities had to be set apart', not least in terms of the urban space they inhabited.[12] In Hamburg, Joachim Whaley notes that official celebration of Lutheran centenaries took off only after 1700, reflecting a renewed awareness of the city's Protestant heritage and a determination to assert its orthodoxy, even at a time when it was becoming a more complex, multi-faith society. If these festivities eventually congealed into a mere 'reiteration of tradition', the parading of a 'completed façade' behind which sizeable Catholic, Calvinist and Jewish minorities lived, worshipped and developed their own distinctive habits and outlooks, this does not mean that they lost their cultural significance.[13]

In the Dutch Republic, a country in which Calvinist hegemony paradoxically combined with a high degree of pragmatic coexistence, religious affiliations likewise solidified after 1600, assisted by a more systematic policy of confessional endogamy.[14] The following century saw the emergence of 'a "pillarised" society of separate communities under the watchful supervision of a strong civil authority'. Nevertheless, as Judith Pollman has stressed, we must recognise the extent to which people throughout the period demon-strated an ability to participate in two cultures simultaneously: both in an intolerant discourse of confessionalism and in a piety that subordinated polemical enmities to a wish to preserve Christian concord.[15]

The Eastern frontiers of Europe provide a different but no less revealing picture. In a reversal of the usual chronology, the remarkable tolerance that had hitherto prevailed in Prussia and Poland-Lithuania was replaced in the late seventeenth century by a return to an official policy of unity and exclu-sionism. According to Michael Müller, this was a direct consequence of confessionalisation: 'Once the confessional frontlines had become "visualised", and the dispute had turned into a conflict over the symbolic practices of popular religiosity, the project of supra-confessional toleration seemed no longer defensible.'[16]

In the long run, the impulses towards separation appear to have proved at least as powerful as the factors encouraging integration. The dynamic tension and constant interaction between the two is crucial in explaining the shape of the religious landscape in the latter stages of Europe's long Reformation.

SEPARATION AND ASSIMILATION, INTROVERSION AND INTEGRATION

Can comparable trends and tendencies be detected in the context of England? In the absence of many detailed local studies, any response to this question can only be tentative. Nevertheless, some of the evidence that has been assembled suggestively parallels the developments that have observed across the Channel.

Within the Catholic community, for instance, there is a sense that total alienation from heretics became more necessary once it had become resigned to its minority status and once the Protestant majority had reconciled itself to the presence of recusants within its midst – though it was not, of course, until 1829 that this would receive the formal imprimatur of an act of Parliament.[17] Church papistry was a phenomenon that lasted longer than many historians have recognised, but it cannot be denied that over time the strategies of occasional and partial conformity did eventually fade into oblivion. This was not just because attendance at church had become virtually unenforceable. Dissimulation might be condoned as an acceptable short-term strategy for deflecting persecution, but once all but a residual danger of losing life, limb and livelihood had been eliminated, such forms of 'adroit casuistry'[18] were denuded of their legitimacy. Compromise and circumspection could be sanctioned while there was still hope of reclaiming institutional control, but by the mid-seventeenth century, when this battle was generally acknowledged to have been been lost, such concessions were seen as a threat to its very survival. Gradually, the community moved towards 'a pattern of systematic regularity at variance with the habits of its primitive phase' – a pattern that underpins and justifies John Bossy's depiction of it as 'a branch of the English nonconforming tradition'.[19]

As Bossy has documented, formal segregation from Protestant society assumed growing importance as the period progressed. Particularly at the level of the gentry and nobility, recusant families severed some of the bonds of collective behaviour that had united them to other Englishmen and women, detached themselves from Anglican rites of passage, turned in upon themselves incestuously, and at times transformed their households into something approximating private ghettos. Marriages were arranged within the narrow circle of the faithful; baptisms were recorded in separate congregational registers; the dead were buried in specially consecrated Catholic graveyards; and ascetic rites like fasting and abstinence helped to foster 'a caste-like consciousness of superior purity'.[20] It is significant that these shifts were a feature of the era in which the penal laws had all but lost their teeth and in which the chief handicaps suffered by Catholics were economic and professional: what David Mathew once described as 'the long strain of inactivity'.[21] We must take care, however, not to overstate these tendencies, which were continually counterbalanced by the generally harmonious relations that pertained between individual Protestants and 'papists' and by the unpredictable emotional attachments that perpetuated the practice of intermarrying. Moreover, they were probably more common in seigneurial congregations than in independent ones like the rural North Yorkshire chapelry of Egton recently explored by Bill Sheils, where strong kinship links militated against the polarisation of parish life along confessional lines.[22] Both separation and co-operation remained critical to guaranteeing the durability of the community. These were the means by which post-Reformation English Catholics sought to pitch upon what Bossy calls 'the optimum line': one which provided 'the maximum of self-determining capacity and the minimum of destructive isolation'.[23]

If we turn to Protestant dissent a picture with many similarities, but also subtle differences, emerges. As we saw in Chapter 4, sixteenth- and seventeenth-century puritans were taught to negotiate the dilemmas involved in the 'cohabitation of the faithful with the unfaithful' by ostentatiously shunning the ungodly in secular affairs. Exactly how far the anti-social policy recommended by godly writers was applied in practice cannot be determined without further empirical research, but at least some individuals seem to have followed this advice through to its logical conclusions. While their principles obliged them to intermingle with the carnal worldlings of their parish in weekly services, they preserved a sense of their special identity by deliberately refraining from voluntary concourse and contact with the unfaithful in the sphere of day-to-day relations. Out-and-out separatists who repudiated the Church of England as a false and Antichristian institution, by contrast, may have had less need to embrace this ethic of exclusivism.[24] Free of the persecution which Brownists and Barrowists suffered as a consequence of their ecclesiastical nonconformity, not a few Elizabethan and early Stuart puritans were compelled to reproduce artificially the experience of oppression and estrangement that they regarded as crucial evidence of their spiritual election. They deliberately cultivated habits that divided, even alienated them from their more moderately Protestant neighbours. Gadding to sermons with a Geneva bible under one's arm, turning one's eyes upwards to heaven in prayer, liberally lacing one's speech with scriptural allusions and godly catchphrases like 'Christian liberty' and 'edification', withdrawing from harmless communal pastimes and recreations, and dressing with exaggerated decorum and sobriety all became telltale marks of those who were resented, disparaged and branded with the derogatory nickname 'puritan'. By the mid-seventeenth century, at least within the circles in which the London artisan Nehemiah Wallington moved, the precept that there could be 'no fellowship between light and darkness' was evidently translating itself into a tendency for marriage to take place within the narrow ranks of the community of saints itself.[25] As Patrick Collinson has remarked, committed Calvinists required some degree of martyrdom: 'if not the stake then death by the thousand cuts of civil ostracism'.[26] If the state failed to inflict this upon them, then they felt themselves obliged actively to set themselves at loggerheads with the local society within which they resided.

Perhaps this is why those of their later seventeenth-century descendants who had been forced into overt dissent by the Restoration settlement found it so hard to adjust to the parliamentary act granting them toleration in 1689. If this offered Presbyterians greater safety, it also posed greater challenges. To quote John Spurr, '[t]hey had to organize themselves for freedom and to sustain a zeal hitherto honed by persecution'.[27] The price they had to pay for liberty was the abandonment of their long-standing hope of rejoining and reshaping a single, inclusive national Church. As a consequence, they shuffled only very reluctantly towards a congregational structure, grumpily and begrudgingly resigning themselves to a future among the spectrum of sects with whom they shared little but the experience of being former victims of the Stuart drive to impose ecclesiastical conformity.[28]

If we turn to examine the evolution of other religious minorities which, in due course, would benefit from the dispensations of the Williamite legislation, we find further intricate variations on this striking set of themes. The Quakers provide a particularly illuminating case in point. Though this sect rejected the predestinarian theology that imbued the hotter sort of Protestants with such an empowering sense of righteous suffering and splendid isolation, in its earliest phases as a rebellious protest movement, it too courted trouble and tribulation. Provocatively iconoclastic of established norms, its adherents defiantly disdained to doff their hats to their superiors and comply with the conventions governing social encounters, refused to pay tithes, ran 'naked for a sign', and adopted a distinctive dialect and attire that marked them out from their peers and was designed to mortify the flesh and humble the inherent human sin of pride.[29] They passively endured arrest and placed themselves in peril of persecution in the conviction that this was the best method of bearing 'witness' to the truth. Yet within a generation we find the Society of Friends curbing the edge of its antinomian enthusiasm and moving towards a position of political quiescence and social respectability in an effort to limit the corrosive and damaging effects of the Clarendon Code. Without some kind of accommodation with the world, it was instinctively realised, the sect would soon be driven into extinction. But the unforeseen side effect of these strategies of integration and assimilation was to erode its uniqueness in a way that led to the decline of the movement.[30] The Act of Toleration further encouraged the process by which the cohesion and distinctiveness of the Quakers was gradually effaced. Immunity from the Conventicle Acts brought a security and prosperity that paralysed its missionary spirit and weakened its sectarian identity.

It is thus not surprising to find signs of a partial retreat from the intense engagement with wider society that had enabled the Friends to weather the perils of the previous three decades. These took the form of renewed efforts to raise the walls of ritual separation. In the 1690s and early 1700s, fresh emphasis was placed upon the dangers of association with those outside the sect. Official and parental intervention to prevent the evils of being 'unequally yoked' with non-believers became more pronounced and in the eighteenth century the movement took steps to jettison and eject those who failed to heed its injunctions against ungodly matches. Even if this marital code was frequently infringed in practice and if offenders received only token reprimands and temporary suspensions, as an 'abstract aspiration' it retained, if not enhanced, its status as an emblem of dissociation from the rest of society.[31]

Furthermore, the public 'testimonies' of plainness and simplicity that had made the first generation of Quakers the objects of such distrust and hatred were invested with disproportionate significance. Linguistic eccentricities like the use of the increasingly archaic formulation 'thou' became a veritable badge of membership and austerity of costume a shibboleth that marked Friends out from the multitude of sinners that surrounded them. The fossilised mid-seventeenth dress that was still being prescribed by Quakers one hundred years later became a kind of uniform: repudiation of lace, ribbons, cuffs, buttons, and other fashionable trimmings acquired such symbolic importance that some began to feel that it was a mere shell or husk, an external substitute for sincere commitment and genuine inward spiritual growth. As Richard Vann puts it, there was a sense in which 'the pathway to heaven commenced in a tailor's shop'.[32] Hat honour too was preserved as what Christopher Hill once called 'an intriguing museum piece', yet another self-conscious mannerism that set Friends conspicuously apart from their neighbours.[33] A studied antipathy to the gregarious, recreational culture centred on the village alehouse and to rural entertainments and customs were other aspects of an evolving counter-culture.[34] The Welsh Quaker John Kelsall carried his determination to keep himself 'unspotted' by contact with outsiders to quite remarkable extremes: he wrote in his journal in 1714 how he ritually cleansed himself each time he came out from among the multitude, his body polluted by interaction with worldlings and his heart 'sick with the smell and fume of vanity, irreligion and prophaneness that abounded among them'.[35]

Reminiscent of the distinctive sumptuary code and dietary practices still retained by Hasidic and ultra-Orthodox Jews and of the extraordinary nineteenth-century culture and lifestyle of the present-day North American Amish, Mennonite and Hutterite communities,[36] such attempts to reassert group endogamy and to erect cultural barriers between the sect and 'the people of the world' may be seen as elaborate mechanisms for guarding it from the insidious influences of a potentially corrupting environment.[37] Elevated to the status of sacred acts of self-sacrifice, they also helped it to retain that sense of separateness and suffering that was so integral to Quaker self-perception. It is no wonder that Georgian Friends referred to their continuing vexations in the area of oaths and tithes as 'sufferings' and the agents of the law who enforced them as 'persecutors'; nor that they spoke of adopting the plain testimonies as 'taking up the cross'.[38] If over time the latter had a tendency to degenerate into mere or rigid convention, this should not blind us to the psychological purposes they served.

These insulating devices were all the more important against the backdrop of the Friends' active involvement in the institutions and practices at the heart of English society: in business, industry, philanthropy, hospitality and, not-withstanding the restrictions technically designed to exclude them, in parish administration and local politics. As we have seen, far from being deviant outsiders, Quakers, and indeed other dissenters, were highly integrated members of both urban and rural communities: people who were regarded as responsible and reliable by their Anglican neighbours and who remained bound to them by ties of love, friendship, family and neighbourhood that blurred and cut across the confessional divisions that theoretically divided them. Throughout the 1700s the practice of occasional conformity enabled members of minority churches and congregations to slip through the net of civil discrimination that still surrounded them and qualify for public office. This could not have occurred without the tacit consent and approval of those of their peers who belonged to the dominant Church. This is yet another demonstration of the way in which competing impulses towards resistance and compromise, assimilation and separation, persisted in shaping the experience of such groups well into the eighteenth century.

Torn between a desire to interact with society and a contradictory instinct to recoil and shrink from it, erstwhile sects like the Baptists also continued to pursue what Patrick Collinson has called 'a benign double strategy of endogamous and exogamous integration'.[39] They too engaged in an ongoing process of boundary demarcation by admonishing their followers to choose their spouses from within the ranks of the faith. From the 1640s onwards Baptist leaders were consistent in their opposition to 'Mixt Marrige' to 'visible unbeleevers', a precept spelt out by the General Assembly of 1668 and debated in many of its subsequent meetings. They remained vigilant in their attempts to promote a quasi-incestuous pattern of marital union, casting out those who took husbands and wives 'contrary to the minds of the congregation' and outside 'the fellowship of the Gospel'. Genealogical research on Sussex Baptists has shown that some 96 per cent obeyed these injunctions up until 1750, after which date the figure slowly declines.[40] The same ingrained instinct towards separation provided the incentive for ensuring that the welfare of poor Baptists was provided for by the congregation itself: otherwise the needy would seek the support of their parishes and thereby become seduced into returning to the Church of England.[41] And yet throughout the period in question there is little evidence that Baptists were isolationist. Ironically, the vast majority of their marriages were performed in Anglican churches and few people segregated themselves off from society at large or from the collective activities that bound it together. John Caffyn remarks that 'their separatism in religion, with its concomitant requirement of marrying within the communion (which was so faithfully observed), by its very strength set up a counter-drive towards social conformity'.[42] An element of introversion was recognised to be necessary if the cohesion of the sect was to be prevented from suffering a slow death by attrition, but to avoid all forms of extroversion was to invite alienation of a kind that was equally inimical to its success and survival.

The separatist and assimilationist instincts of dissenting groups coexisted continually both before and after the Act of Toleration, even if the quantities of each in the equation changed over time. If some aspects of their development suggest that in sociological terms they were gravitating towards the status of a denomination, other tendencies and practices reveal a determination to react vigorously against it and to protect their sectarian identity and heritage. Wealth and peace may have dinted the spontaneity and spirit of mission that had initially animated them, but few, if any, wholly relinquished their claim to possess or have unique access to supernatural truth. Most continued to seek to expel the wayward and to specify exacting standards of ethical rectitude for those who voluntarily adhered to them. It was not until at least the nineteenth century or later that they surrendered the notion that their institutional borders constituted 'the one ark of salvation'.[43] To echo the conclusions drawn by Elizabeth Isichei, Adrian Davies and Michael Mullett from their in-depth studies of the Quakers, their patterns of behaviour defy any theory of unilinear and unqualified progress from sect to denomination. Instead, they reflect recurrent and reciprocally interacting phases of inward and outward orientation. 'Denominational' and 'sectarian' traits continued to struggle for ascendancy.[44]

A similar dialectic has been discerned by historians of the stranger churches and exile communities, which found a haven and sanctuary in England in the early modern period. These too found themselves pulled in two contrary directions. Determination to preserve their indigenous religious and linguistic traditions and to prevent the haemorrhage of their members to the half-reformed Church of England dictated a policy of strict endogamy, but as the period progressed a trend towards integration gathered momentum, fraying the clear boundaries between the Protestant refugees and their host societies. As long as these foreigners nursed a realistic hope of returning to their homelands, the forces in favour of maintaining the cultural and social barriers that divided them from Englishmen and women exerted a powerful inhibiting influence. Fresh waves of immigration from the Continent also served to remind exile groups of their shared inheritance, as did the financial support they sent back to those who had not yet escaped from the fire of persecution. The tendency of French and Dutch immigrants to concentrate in particular quarters of the towns and cities that had taken them in further enhanced their insularity. Anxious to maintain their internal cohesion, such communities made careful provision for the welfare and education of their members and clung resolutely to their native tongues. Elders and consistories sharply rebuked those who attended Anglican services and married outside their congregations. The biblical names they chose for their children and the peculiarities of national custom and apparel they retained likewise reinforced both their own sense of separation and the propensity for observers to perceive them as 'a common wealth within themselves'.

Yet, as the sixteenth and seventeenth centuries progressed, a number of factors combined to foster and speed the processes of assimilation. The proportion of members of stranger churches born abroad naturally declined over time, weakening the attachment of later generations to the Flemish and Francophone culture of their parents and encouraging their Anglicisation. More importantly, events across the Channel, notably Louis XIV's revocation of the Edict of Nantes in 1685, finally shattered the lingering expectation that the exiles might be able to retrace their steps and resume the lives they had reluctantly left behind in France. In the case of the Walloons and Flemings who had fled the war-torn Netherlands in the 1560s, the possibility of return had evaporated much earlier, when Habsburg control of the southern provinces was consolidated around 1600. Testamentary and other records

reveal the steady development of closer engagement with the native population, not merely in the sphere of trade but also the fields of personal and social
relations. Economic contacts encouraged the employment of English servants
and apprentices in stranger households and facilitated the entry of foreigners
into burgess ranks. Increasingly, the refugees forged links beyond the immediate circles of their fellow aliens, appointing English neighbours and friends
as the witnesses and overseers of their wills, choosing them as godparents to
their children, displaying their affection and respect for them in bequests, and
intermarrying with them. Spiritual affinity with puritans who admired the
purity of their ecclesiastical discipline and deplored the deficiencies of the
Church of England may also have contributed to cementing the ties binding
refugees and members of their host communities. Such exiles successfully
kept a foot in both camps for a prolonged period, but in London, Sandwich,
Southampton and East Anglia the opportunities for leading a double life were
gradually diminishing.[45]

Similar observations may be made about the evolution of many of the
groups of Sephardic Jews who settled in England from the mid-seventeenth
century. Although they held tightly to their religious beliefs and rituals in the
privacy of their homes, in public they too slowly lost their cultural and social
distinctiveness as they became assimilated into English society, conformed
with its fashions of dress and established codes of civil interaction, and
embedded themselves in its business affairs.[46] In the case of the Portuguese
conversos who had arrived in the 1540s, generations of dissimulation led to the
gradual incorporation of aspects of Christian culture into Jewish life and to the
blending and amalgamation of ethnic characteristics.[47] The manner in which
foreign Protestants and Jews handled the competing pressures towards and
against acculturation offers both illuminating parallels and instructive contrasts
with the development of native religious minorities. In each case, achieving a
homeostatic balance between integration and separation was a formidable
challenge: the former was necessary to keep the latent intolerance of the
orthodox majority in check and the latter vital to ensuring that the community
did not disappear or disintegrate completely. Oscillation between these two
instincts ensured that there was no easy transition 'from stranger to citizen'.[48]
But while the dilemmas of immigrants revolved around the problem of naturalisation, those of dissenters turned on the unexpected trials of toleration.

It may be commented that adjusting to the condition of non-persecution
proved more difficult for some nonconformist sects and churches than for
others. While the Presbyterians, Congregationalists, Baptists and Quakers
negotiated this passage with varying degrees of skill and in a range of different
ways, the Familists and Muggletonians steadily and inexorably lost ground to
their rivals after 1689. In part this was because of their retreat from or
aversion to the tasks of proselytism and conversion; in part because the

secrecy and deceit that was integral to the identities of these groups was rendered anomalous and unnecessary by the Act of Toleration.[49] What is noticeable about those that survived as more than a tiny and scattered remnant in the eighteenth century is the way in which they too turned away from their earlier preoccupation with outreach and evangelism and began to concentrate on consolidating their hold over and educating the next generation. The ecumenical co-operation between beleaguered groups of dissenters that had characterised the period after 1662 also evaporated: the ties of common self-interest that had bound together those who shared the searing experience of proscription, who united 'as poor sheep driven together by wolves',[50] lost relevance and gave way to greater exclusiveness. The separate churches and sects that comprised the loose coalition of Protestant 'Dissent' began to turn against each other and develop mutually derogatory and acrimonious stereotypes.[51] Among the Lancashire Quakers, for instance, respect for 'sober people of other persuasions' was displaced by a growing determination to divide themselves liturgically and ideologically from other nonconformists. The advent of Methodism as a dangerous competitor merely reinforced these trends and by the end of the eighteenth century the Yearly Meeting ruled against lending meeting houses to other religious societies.[52]

Related features of this process of transition were the growing systematisation of theology and doctrine, the formalisation of worship, the emergence of a professional trained ministry, and the crystallisation of an ecclesiastical hierarchy mimicking that of other settled Churches. Simultaneously outdoor preaching and clandestine prayer meetings were replaced by sermons and services in established chapels and assembly-houses, which became symbols both of their independence and their institutionalisation.[53] Such developments may be seen as symptoms of the routinisation of charisma to which, so Max Weber famously argued, all religious and political movements eventually succumb.[54] They were also legacies and by-products of the legalisation of pluralism.

It is probably no coincidence that the period after 1689 was marked by a drive on the part of formerly persecuted minorities to chronicle the sufferings and tribulations that had been heroically endured by their predecessors. During the eighteenth century the tradition of writing denominational history began to flourish and take firm root. Building upon the classic martyrological narratives produced by those who had actually experienced or witnessed state persecution, Quaker, Baptist, Presbyterian and Congregationalist writers sought to re-capture the fervour that had inspired the founders and first disciples of their faiths, and to instil in their co-religionists a fresh awareness of the origin and evolution of the churches to which they belonged. Committed to buttressing contested positions and imbued with a robust conviction of the righteousness of the cause that was the subject of their enquiry, these histories fostered a powerful illusion of continuity between past and present and contributed significantly to sustaining confessional and sectarian identity in an age in which the less arduous conditions of coexistence could easily breed complacency.[55] In the guise of Richard Challoner and others, recusant historiography likewise laid the foundations for the future, setting a mould that even now much Catholic history still has difficulty in successfully breaking out of. The impulse of the members of dissenting and stranger churches to transcribe and compile collections of documents detailing the legendary troubles of their forefathers, together with their acquisition in the nineteenth century of specialist in-house journals and scholarly societies dedicated to providing a forum for investigation and discussion, are further manifestations of the acute sense of historical consciousness and empathy that became a feature of many religious minorities in the era following the acts of Toleration and Catholic emancipation.[56] It is striking that this was a sphere of intellectual activity in which Anglicanism, spared from persecution save for the brief period of the Interregnum, lagged behind its denominational rivals. It was also one which highlighted and exacerbated the internal divisions within the Church of England, setting in concrete the conflicting visions of its origins and the rival myths about the character of the English Reformation that continue to afflict it.[57]

Arguably, the literary cultures of Catholicism and nonconformity were even more important to later generations than they were to those who had inaugurated them amidst the adversities of the sixteenth and seventeenth centuries. Reading and re-reading texts about the ennobling travails of one's forerunners was a way of compensating for the fact that one had never personally suffered them. It enabled the descendants of dissenters to experience vicariously the empowerment that accompanied victimisation, to reproduce the plight of the martyr or exile within their own minds. The end of persecution did not herald the demise of the persecutory imagination or the cult of memory; on the contrary there is much to suggest that it may actually have given it a new lease of life. John Bunyan's immortal *Pilgrim's Progress*, which was itself one of the books that fulfilled this surrogate function, provides an apt metaphor of the fresh tests that faced those who enjoyed toleration: once Christian and his companion Faithful had passed safely through Vanity Fair, surviving violent abuse and physical vilification and escaping a sentence to be scourged and burnt at the stake, they reached 'a delicate Plain, called Ease', where they met with the even greater temptations of doubt and lucre.[58]

It can, then, be contended that the ordeals of conscience that had afflicted the members of marginal churches and sects in the Tudor and Stuart period did not so much disappear after 1700 as recreate themselves in a new guise. The moral anxieties that surrounded ecclesiastical conformity and 'the cohabitation of the faithful with the unfaithful' were not assuaged by the disabling of the penal legislation but in some sense intensified. Once the risk of real pain and oppression was more or less removed, zealous men and women were obliged to reinvent it internally, with the consequence that they became prisoners not of external organisations but of their own consciences. In the mental space vacated by the ethical dilemmas provoked by the demands of the official Church and state, they engendered new ones. In other words, with liberty, choice and freedom came guilt.[59] Toleration, in short, was no less, if not more of a psychological threat to the identity and hence survival of religious minorities than the judicial and ritual terrorism of persecution.

THE RISE OF A DENOMINATIONAL SOCIETY?

Finally, we return our attention to the conforming Protestant majority, those who consciously, even proudly accounted themselves part of the reformed Church of England. Over the previous century, these men and women, whom, with Mark Goldie, we may label 'voluntary Anglicans', had developed a genuine and stubborn affection for the Prayer Book and a tenacious attachment to the very liturgical rites and ceremonies which were symbolic of the discontents and conflicts that had helped to divide the nation in the 1640s and 1650s. Energetically defending the ambiguous legacy of the English Reformation, such lay people prosecuted their incumbents in court for disdaining or transgressing it and played an active and creative role in shaping the nature of parochial religion in the long eighteenth century.[60] Far from being passive or apathetic occupants of their allocated pews, they too were caught up in, and contributed significantly to, the steady advance of confessionalisation. In the wake of the deregulation promulgated by the legislation of 1689, it was not coercion but persuasion, not inertia but sincere commitment, which brought these Christians to church week after week. The religious culture of this constituency continued to be characterised by the uneasy mixture of contradictory instincts that had arguably been a hallmark of English society time out of mind. Resentment and reconciliation, antagonism and compassion, bitterness and benevolence counterbalanced but also catalysed each other in ways that soothed and yet simultaneously strained and irritated social relations. As suggested towards the end of Chapter 5, the degree to which a desire to preserve local harmony and concord overrode the impulses in favour of confrontation was itself a source of subliminal discord and friction. It was in the gap between people's ideological principles and the practical realities of cooperation that prevailed at the local level that the intertwined roots of both tolerance and intolerance lay. There is much to suggest that the picture of subtlety and depth we have sketched for the period between 1500 and 1700 remains valid for much of the following century.

Nevertheless, some of its features did perhaps become more pronounced. There are grounds for arguing that the licensing of pluralistic coexistence with men and women who adhered to different creeds both necessitated and promoted more emphatic manifestations of polemical hostility. There had, of course, been many earlier junctures when this tendency acquired importance and relevance. As Anthony Milton has commented about the early Stuart decades, the very fact that the absolute divisions between Catholics and Protestants were so often compromised in practice did not invalidate but rather increased the desirability of vocal anti-papistry, especially at moments of crisis.[61] Occasionally, we can even find this being articulated: preaching against the backdrop of the negotiations for the Spanish match in 1623, the Jacobean divine Richard Sheldon thought virulent propaganda against the Romish Antichrist all the more vital at a time when *raison d'etat* required pragmatic concessions to individual Catholics.[62] Ritual denunciation of Catholicism as a false religion in sermons delivered on patriotic anniversaries like Elizabeth I's Accession Day and regular perusal of works like Foxe's 'Book of Martyrs' probably performed an equally reassuring service, reconciling the tensions between abstract hatred of idolatry and daily engagement with idolaters. So too did the annual revels involving bonfires and bells on 5 November.[63]

Moreover, the incentive to display implacable hostility to the ideological entities of 'popery' and indeed 'dissent' surely increased as official persecution of these systems of belief and practice diminished and eventually ceased. This may help to explain why, as Colin Haydon, E. R. Norman and D. G. Paz have shown, anti-Catholicism retained such vibrancy and intensity in the eighteenth and nineteenth centuries, despite the fact that evidence of antagonism and violence towards recusants is sporadic, slight, and appears to have been declining. Its persistence in Victorian, as in early modern England testifies to its adaptability and to its ongoing significance as a method of resolving the contradictions engendered by religious pluralism.[64]

This may also be why traditional commonplaces about 'deviant' minorities survived and even thrived for so long in ballads, plays, literary caricatures, folk tales and graphic satires. Far from losing their currency in popular and learned culture after 1700, the stereotypes of the papist, Presbyterian, sectarian enthusiast and Jew showed remarkable resilience. Their persistence in textual, visual and dramatic form may be seen as a means by which contemporaries expressed, channelled and controlled their negative confessional feelings in an environment that can by no means be described as religiously indifferent or neutral. To echo Frank Felsenstein, they might be viewed as the 'defence mechanisms' by which people sought to protect their most deeply rooted assumptions and come to terms with what they perceived as in some sense different, threatening and inferior.[65]

In the guise of history, literature and political prints, such prejudices remained endemic in the cultural vocabulary and outlook of the era. A profusion of images and books kept alive the legends of popish plots and 'fanatic' rebellions that had inspired and stirred up the conflicts of the previous century. As long as these continued to be reproduced and rearticulated, Anglicans could not wholly forget or forgive the passions that had driven puritan revolutionaries to launch the nation into civil war and cut off the head of a divinely anointed king. Nor could they be fully convinced that Roman Catholics did not harbour a tacit wish to commit atrocities against their Protestant neighbours or that their faith was not a charter for domination and enslavement. Together with the Jacobite challenge and the prospect of a Catholic pretender, such texts and pictures did much to keep these anxieties alive. As an anonymous correspondent urged in a letter written to a local newspaper in the late 1740s, 'as long as Guy Fawks and his dark La[n]thorn stand conspicuous in your Common Prayer Books, never be persuaded that Popery can be a harmless Religion'.[66] Such legends and sentiments endured because they remained crucial to defining the identity and defending the values that constituted eighteenth-century Anglicanism. If laughter and mockery rather than fear became the predominant notes of this discourse, this should not lead us to underestimate either its significance or its latent virulence. Comedy could be no less corrosive than vituperative condemnation.

Nor can we afford to ignore the continuing vitality of religious nicknaming and labelling, which were themselves an index of the growing self-consciousness of contemporary confessional identities. Religious minorities may have slowly embraced as a badge of honour and self-identification names that had initially been hurled at them as terms of abuse and denigration,[67] but when employed in particular contexts such words could still carry a sharp sting and confer a powerful stigma. They could still operate as a shorthand and conduit for antipathy and intolerance and they retained their potential to trigger incidents of physical abuse against alien outsiders. They remained a critical component in the perennial process of scapegoating. In the eighteenth, as in the sixteenth and seventeenth centuries, inflammatory language did not shed its capacity to spill over into and precipitate persecution. If the process of confessionalisation appears in some respects to have led to the reduction or suppression of anger and violence, in others it seems to have served to foster fresh outbursts of militancy.[68] In essence, it was double-edged. Religious bigotry was a germ that was still deeply embedded in English society, as the unruly popular response to the emergence of Methodism would all too clearly reveal. Having settled into social decorum and middle-class respectability, 'Old Dissent' may have lost its power to disturb and terrify, but the Wesleyan movement soon stepped in to fill its shoes. Accused of splitting families and providing a cover for grotesque sexual orgies, it became the target of collective action designed to defend traditional values and communal solidarity against disruptive and divisive outsiders.[69]

Yet, this is not to ignore other signs of transmutation and change. Jan Albers's research on Lancashire suggests that aggression was becoming redirected away from people onto property. This may reflect the fact that religious difference was crystallising in competing physical structures. London crowds of the later seventeenth century concentrated on destroying buildings, disrupting worship and burning effigies rather than attacking actual persons, and David Hempton observes that the weapons employed by later anti-Methodist protesters were 'those of ritual humiliation rather than crude violence'.[70] Although the 1780s and 1790s witnessed outbursts of hostility towards both 'popery' and 'dissent' in the guise of the Gordon and Priestley Riots, in some places even symbolic attacks on Catholic chapels and nonconformist meeting houses seem themselves to have been waning. '[S]ectarian conflict had become more polite', Albers writes, 'as it had become rhetorically florid'.[71] Tempers continued to flare but did not always so readily explode into belligerent and destructive behaviour.

There may also be some substance in the claim that by the final quarter of the eighteenth century Anglicans were coming to regard their recusant, Quaker, and other dissenting neighbours less as potential subversives and ruthless enemies than as bands of harmless eccentrics. This shift should not, however, be overstated. As we have seen, an ability to differentiate between individuals and the 'isms' to which they adhered predated this period. Many sixteenth- and seventeenth-century Englishmen and women seem to have manifested a 'charitable Christian hatred' that combined a fervent commitment to truth with friendly treatment of those they knew who remained wedded to falsehood. People had long been capable of engaging in theological controversy and debate with members of rival churches without these culminating in bloody conflict. Like the Restoration Presbyterian apprentice Roger Lowe, Anglicans too could participate in ardent but still amicable and 'loving' dialogues with dissenters and papists about the doctrines that comprised their respective faiths.[72] Nevertheless, it is possible that the tone of such parochial engagements was more generally abating. While it would be a mistake to take the idiosyncratic self-taught Somerset maltster exciseman, and schoolmaster John Cannon as in any sense representative, it is interesting that here was a man who could read Catholic books, consume the devotional literature produced by puritan ministers, indulge a curiosity about the principles of other churches and creeds, and profess in 1738 that he had 'with St Peter ... Charity for all people & sects, & that they may be saved thro' Gods mercy at the last day', all without feeling as if he had betrayed or left the 'bosom' of the Church of England.[73]

Yet we must be wary of endorsing the thesis that Hanoverian England was a peculiarly tolerant, as opposed to a persecuting society. Like its Tudor and Stuart predecessors, it was both at the same time: religious animosities were ubiquitous but they did not generally interfere with harmonious relations.[74]

Furthermore, it is still too early to speak of the displacement of a confessional by a denominational outlook. This development was underway, but few contemporaries were yet willing to concede that religious 'truth' was plural and that its variant forms had equal validity. They could not yet accept that the door to the mansion of Christian salvation could be unlocked by many different keys: most still believed that they possessed, if not the only password to opening it, then at least the best and most effective.[75]

What is noticeable is the extent to which prejudice towards religious minorities came increasingly to be focused around their social exclusiveness and foreignness. If ecclesiastical and doctrinal differences rankled less than the snobbish insularity of Presbyterians and the clannish character of some Roman Catholic communities and families,[76] this was hardly a significant departure from the state of affairs that had prevailed in the sixteenth- and seventeenth centuries, as described in Chapter 3. But it may well have been accentuated by the sectarian and separatist impulses that appear to have been a paradoxical consequence of the granting of toleration and the spread of pluralism.

Enhanced by the Erastian nature of the English Reformation and the Royal Supremacy, the patriotic element of intolerance had always been present, particularly, but not solely, in the case of recusants, whose stance against the Protestant state was progressively defined as a species of the crime of treason. The black legend constructed by John Foxe and other propagandists cast a long chronological shadow which stretched far beyond the year 1700 and, as Linda Colley and other historians have stressed, anti-popery was a crucial ingredient of the English and British myth of nationhood in this period. Although some commentators may have underplayed its fractious potential, the vision of a godly Protestant island standing fast on the shores of a dark popish Continent was certainly critical to constituting and unifying this 'imagined community'.[77] And if anything the xenophobic dimension of stereotypes of deviance appears to acquire growing prominence in the long eighteenth century. In visual and literary satire papists are inextricably linked with England's old enemy Spain, and her new adversary absolutist France, while nonconformists are depicted as the pawns of Germany and Geneva.[78] Less attention is paid to their theological error than to their political orientation and their association with 'strangers' and 'aliens'. Hence the fierce popular resistance to the act of 1708 for the naturalisation of foreign Protestants.[79] In these respects, as in others, England did indeed remain a confessional society and state. It also retained more than a residual sense of its status as an elect nation.[80] The contours and parameters of its intolerance were, however, gradually evolving and changing.

A no less ambivalent symptom of this shifting climate of opinion is the emergence by the end of the eighteenth century of the discipline of comparative religion. The sceptical influences of the Enlightenment combined with a growing knowledge of and fascination with the world beyond Europe to produce a situation in which quasi-scientific investigation of different faiths became a possibility. Even so, the authors of such tracts rarely conceded the viability or authenticity of these alternative religions. Indeed, the motive for undertaking such studies was all too often implicitly or explicitly to prove the superiority of Christianity over Islam or Judaism or to cast aspersions at Catholics or Socinians.[81] No more than unlearned lay people beneath them in the social scale, educated scholars and gentlemen could not yet accept the existence of religious diversity with complete equanimity, but their literary and academic endeavours do nevertheless reveal that the paradigms of deviance were being reconstituted.

This is apparent in the rising concern about atheism and deism. The perception that a wave of scepticism was sweeping the country may be seen as a symptom of the fact that denominational difference was very slowly losing its power to stimulate anxiety. In the post-Reformation period, the idea of 'atheism' had provided a focus for worries about lukewarm commitment to the Protestant and Catholic religions. Contemporaries readily conflated immorality and 'godlessness' with overt philosophical hostility to orthodox Christianity, one typical component of which was an open-minded attitude to variant systems of religious observance and opinion. Their preoccupation with this phenomenon was, in a sense, a product and function of their struggle to come to terms with the unruly pluralism that had been inaugurated by the advent of Protestantism – to face up to the problem of spiritual choice.[82]

However, by the end of the seventeenth century, against the backdrop of a real growth of intellectually sophisticated and articulate irreligion, the cultural significance of 'atheism' had subtly shifted. It can be argued that 'atheists' were beginning to take the place of religious dissidents. The abolition of the statute *De heretico comburendo* and the licensing of a limited form of toleration, at least for Protestant dissenters, was rendering the medieval theological concept of heresy more or less redundant. Nonconformists and papists might begrudgingly be suffered, but freethinkers who questioned standard assumptions about providence and creation, rejected the authority of the Bible, denied the immortality of the soul, and repudiated the mysteries of traditional religion as superstitious and irrational offered profound offence to a society that still conceived of itself as a Christian polity. Far more than religious minorities, who were growing ever more respectable and tame, they were believed to present a serious danger to society and the state: Pierre Bayle alone could see that their outlook was not necessarily incompatible with being loyal and reliable citizens. To this extent, the heightened visibility of and unease about atheism neatly reflected the fears and aspirations of what was still fundamentally an age of faith. It comprises a revealing mirror image and photographic negative of how eighteenth-century England envisaged and defined itself. Not until much later would the words 'atheist' and 'Deist' come to be used in a more neutral sense and drop their derogatory connotations; only in 1870 would they be joined by the term 'agnostic', a label which came into being to designate the growing number of people who held the view that nothing is or can be known of the existence of God or of anything beyond material phenomena, and who were equally indifferent to the cultures of church, confessional box, chapel and meeting house.[83] In the era covered by this discussion, there is little evidence of the onset of the widespread secularisation that now characterises modern British society.

A few final, and very tentative, observations may be made. It may be no accident that the transformations in the nature of religious intolerance that we have been delineating coincided with renewed surges of moral and social intolerance. Without resorting to an extreme version of anthropological functionalism or subscribing to crude theories of class conspiracy, it can be noted that the late seventeenth and eighteenth centuries saw the rise of the Societies for the Reformation of Manners and related drives to control prostitution and vagrancy by the 'middling' and 'better sorts' of people.[84] The ongoing cycle of anxiety about sin, disorder and vice reached another of its periodic peaks of activity.[85] Toleration stimulated revived efforts to promote personal godliness not least because conservatives feared that it had 'let loose the reins' to 'licentious practices', including fornication, adultery, incest and blasphemy.[86] This was a sentiment voiced by Humphrey Prideaux, Dean of Norwich in 1692: the Act of 1689, he said, 'hath almost undon us ... in increaseing [the] number of ... wicked and profane persons: for it is now difficult almost to get any to church, all pleading [the] licence, although they make use of it only for [the] alehouse'.[87]

Equally, this seems to have been an age in which insanity and madness acquired a new prominence and purchase within contemporary consciousness. The growing preoccupation of Georgian society with the manifestations of mental aberration and delusion, and the expansion of these categories to include both the behaviour of 'enthusiastic' sects and the assumptions about the intervention of the supernatural that had once underpinned the theory of persecution may be seen as further facets of the process by which 'deviance' is repeatedly redefined and reinvented.[88] Learned opinion apparently began to worry less about the theological heterodoxy of Quakers, Methodists and other religious 'fanatics' than about their psychological instability. There may be some truth in Michael MacDonald's provocative claim that the rise of psychiatry should be seen less as a result of advances in medical science than as a complex backlash against the religious chaos and strife unleashed by the events of the previous century.[89] Simultaneously, in some educated circles witches and the victims of demonic possession were coming to be regarded not as the agents or objects of satanic malice but as hapless sufferers from melancholy and depression. With the advent of pluralism and the demise of the ideal of religious uniformity they ceased to carry their symbolic weight as enemies of God and the state and were reconceptualised as part of a literally lunatic fringe.[90] What had once been subsidiary features of 'otherness' became, for the time being, the chief targets of alarm and hostility. More provocatively, it might be remarked that once Christians had agreed to differ, they instinctively found new outlets for the interconnected instincts to persecute and tolerate that are an innate part of human nature. One last consequence of the cultural and intellectual changes and the transmutations in fashion and taste that occurred in this period was, somewhat ironically, to make intolerance itself increasingly intolerable.

However impressionistic and contentious, such developments further illustrate the problems inherent in linear models that seek to trace the 'decline of persecution' and the 'rise of toleration'. They underline the extent to which the conventional opposition of tolerance and intolerance is a false dichotomy and how far the relationship between them is fundamentally dialectical and symbiotic. These two impulses were caught up in a kind of vicious circle: persecution could be a side effect and by-product of toleration and vice versa. Separation and assimilation, introversion and integration, were similarly interwoven features of social experience, cross-currents that constantly muddled and muddied the waters of interpersonal and interdenominational relations. We need to avoid one-sided accounts which approach the topics covered by this book from the perspective of either aggressors or victims, bestowers of Christian charity or its recipients. As I have tried to suggest, these must be explored and analysed in tandem. How the dominant regime and majority treated dissenters is critical to accounting for their conduct in the face of persecution. In turn, without examining how these religious minorities responded to intolerance we cannot hope to explain either official policy or the way in which they were habitually treated by their neighbours. Early modern England remained a context in which the Augustinian ideology of persecution exerted enduring influence and in which moves towards the theorisation and institutionalisation of toleration were severely limited. But it was also an environment in which pluralism was ineradicable and in which people regularly chose concord and patience over conflict and confrontation. This itself was a state of affairs that contained within it the seeds both of harmonious interaction and of bitter friction. In conclusion, perhaps we should abandon the attempt to chart the demise of a 'persecuting society' and the progress of the ideal of 'toleration' and concentrate instead on explaining the circumstances in which, with striking and frightening regularity throughout history, the relatively peaceful coexistence of rival confessions, races and creeds has been shattered by vicious outbreaks of prejudice and horrific epidemics of violence.

NOTES

1 Williams, *Catholic Recusancy*, pp. 77–8.

2 See R. Po-Chia Hsia, *Social Discipline in the Reformation: Central Europe 1550–1750* (London, 1989), esp. pp. 1–9; Wolfgang Reinhard, 'Reformation, Counter-Reformation and the early modern state: a reassessment', *Catholic Historical Review*, 75 (1989), 383–404; Heinz Schilling, 'Confessionalisation in the Empire: religious and societal change in Germany between 1555 and 1620', in his *Religion, Political Culture and the Emergence of Early Modern Society: Essays in German and Dutch History* (Leiden, 1992), pp. 205–45; Heinz Schilling, 'Confessional Europe', in Thomas A. Brady, Heiko A. Oberman and James D., Tracy (eds), *Handbook of European History, 1400–1600*, 2 vols (Leiden, 1995), ii. 641–75; Heinz Schilling, 'Confessionalisation and the rise of religious and cultural frontiers in early modern Europe', in Eszter Andor and István Tóth (eds), *Frontiers of Faith: Religious Exchange and the Constitution of Religious Identities 1400–1750* (Budapest, 2001), pp. 21–35; Philip Benedict, 'Confessionalization in France? Critical reflections and new evidence', in Raymond A. Mentzer and Andrew Spicer (eds), *Society and Culture in the Huguenot World 1559–1685* (Cambridge, 2002), pp. 44–61, esp. pp. 46–53; Benjamin Kaplan, *Calvinists and Libertines: Confession and Community in Utrecht 1578–1620* (Oxford, 1995), introduction; M. R. Forster, 'With and without confessionalisation', *Journal of Early Modern History*, i (1998), 315–43; Marc R. Forster, *Catholic Revival in the Age of the Baroque* (Cambridge, 2001), esp. pp. 13–15; Ute Lotz-Heumann, 'The concept of "confessionalisation": a historiographical paradigm in dispute', *Memoria y Civilisación*, 4 (2001), 93–114.

3 See Benedict, 'Confessionalization', esp. p. 48; Hanlon, *Confession and Community*, esp. p. 193.

4 Schilling, 'Confessional Europe', p. 641. On ritual as a confessional marker, see Peter Burke, 'The repudiation of ritual in early modern Europe', in his *The Historical Anthropology of Early Modern Italy* (Cambridge, 1989), esp. p. 230; Bodo Nischan, 'Ritual and Protestant Identity in Late Reformation Germany', in Bruce Gordon (ed.), *Protestant History and Identity in Sixteenth-Century Europe*, 2 vols (Aldershot, 1996), ii. 142–58; Edward Muir, *Ritual in Early Modern Europe* (Cambridge, 1997), ch. 6.

5 Benedict, 'Parameters for the history of Catholic-Reformed coexistence', pp. 84–93; Benedict, 'Confessionalisation', pp. 53–61.

6 Hanlon, *Confession and Community*, p. 222 and ch. 8; Keith P. Luria, 'Rituals of conversion: Catholics and Protestants in seventeenth-century Poitou', in Barbara B. Diefendorf and Carla Hesse (eds), *Culture and Identity in Early Modern Europe 1500–1800* (Ann Arbor, 1993), pp. 65–81; *idem*,'Separated by death?'.

7 Benedict, 'Parameters for the history of Catholic-Reformed coexistence', pp. 92–3.

8 See Whaley, *Religious Toleration and Social Change*, pp. 4–5. The *cuius regio, eius religio* principle did not extend to those cities where more than one religion was already practised.

9 R. Po-Chia Hsia, *Society and Religion in Münster, 1535–1618* (New Haven, 1984).

10 Marc R. Forster, *The Counter Reformation in the Villages: Religion and Reform in the Bishopric of Speyer, 1560–1720* (Ithaca, NY, 1992), p. 225 and ch. 7.

11 Etienne François, 'De l'uniformité à la tolérance: confessions et société urbaine en Allemagne, 1650–1800', *Annales: Economies, sociétés, civilisations*, 37 (1982), 783–800;

Etienne François, *Protestants et catholiques en Allemagne: identités et pluralisme, Augsbourg 1648–1806* (Paris, 1993; first publ. in German 1991).

12 C. Scott Dixon, 'Urban order and religious coexistence in the German imperial city, 1548–1608', unpublished essay. I am grateful to the author for permission to cite this in advance of publication.

13 Whaley, *Religious Toleration and Social Change*, pp. 186–96, 203–5.

14 Hanlon, *Confession and Community*, p. 272.

15 Ronnie Po-Chia Hsia, 'Introduction' and Judith Pollmann, 'The bond of Christian piety: the individual practice of tolerance and intolerance in the Dutch Republic', both in Hsia and van Nierop (eds), *Calvinism and Religious Toleration*, p. 5, and pp. 53–71, esp. pp. 58 and 71, respectively. See also Pollmann, *Religious Choice in the Dutch Republic: The Reformation of Arnoldus Buchelius (1565–1641)* (Manchester, 1999).

16 Michael G. Müller, 'Protestant confessionalisation in the towns of Royal Prussia and the practice of religious toleration in Poland-Lithuania', in Grell and Scribner (eds), *Tolerance and Intolerance*, pp. 262–81, esp. p. 277.

17 For the effective toleration of Catholics after 1688, see John Bossy, 'English Catholics after 1688', in Grell, Israel and Tyacke (eds), *From Persecution to Toleration*, pp. 367–87.

18 Collinson, 'Cohabitation', p. 63, quoting Perry Miller.

19 Bossy, *English Catholic Community*, pp. 144 and 7 respectively.

20 *Ibid.*, ch. 6, quotation at p. 109. Holmes, *Resistance and Compromise*, pp. 113–15.

21 David Mathew, *Catholicism in England: The Portrait of a Minority: Its Culture and Tradition* (London, 1948 edn), p. 123.

22 Sheils, 'Catholics and their neighbours', esp. p. 129.

23 Bossy, *English Catholic Community*, p. 143.

24 See esp. Collinson, 'Cohabitation'; and Chapter 4 above.

25 Seaver, *Wallington's World*, p. 189.

26 Collinson, 'Cohabitation', p. 76.

27 Spurr, *English Puritanism*, p. 149.

28 Ramsbottom, 'Presbyterians', p. 270.

29 See Baumann, *Let Your Words be Few*; Davies, *Quakers*, chs 2–3.

30 Davies, *Quakers*, ch. 13, esp. pp. 189–90. See also Braithwaite, *Second Period of Quakerism*, pp. 630–47; Greaves, 'Changing conceptions of the Quakers'.

31 Vann, *Social Development*, pp. 181–8 and ch. 5 *passim*; Davies, *Quakers*, p. 221; Michael Mullett, 'From sect to denomination? Social developments in eighteenth-century English Quakerism', *Journal of Religious History*, 13 (1984), 177–8.

32 Vann, *Social Development*, pp. 192–6, quotation at p. 194; Davies, *Quakers*, p. 46.

33 Hill, *World Turned Upside Down*, p. 256.

34 Mullett, 'From sect to denomination?', 172–3.

35 Davies, *Quakers*, p. 37.

36 See Bryan Wilson, *Religious Sects: A Sociological Study* (London, 1970), esp. ch. 7 'Introversionists'.

37 Elizabeth Isichei, 'From sect to denomination among English Quakers', in Bryan R. Wilson (ed.), *Patterns of Sectarianism: Organisation and Ideology in Social and Religious Movements* (London, 1967), pp. 161–81, esp. pp. 169, 170–1.

38 Mullett, 'From sect to denomination?', p. 180; Vann, *Social Development*, p. 202.

39 Collinson, 'Critical conclusion', in Spufford (ed.), *World of Rural Dissenters*, pp. 388–96, at 391.

40 See Tolmie, *Triumph of the Saints*, p. 81; White, *English Baptists*, p. 106; Stevenson, 'Social Integration', pp. 361–2; Caffyn, *Sussex Believers*, p. 99.

41 Margaret Spufford, *Contrasting Communities: English Villagers in the Sixteenth and Seventeenth Centuries* (Cambridge, 1974), pp. 347; White, *English Baptists*, p. 49.

42 Caffyn, *Sussex Believers*, p. 129.

43 D. A. Martin, 'The denomination', *The British Journal of Sociology*, 13 (1962), 1–14, quotation at p. 11. I am grateful to my colleague Grace Davie for drawing this article to my attention. See also Bryan R. Wilson, 'An analysis of sect development', in Wilson (ed.), *Patterns of Sectarianism*, pp. 22–45; Betty R. Scharf, *The Sociological Study of Religion* (London, 1970). The classic works describing the transition from sect to denomination and church are Ernst Troeltsch, *The Social Teachings of the Christian Churches*, trans. Olive Wyan (London, 1931), esp. pp. 331–43; and H. Richard Niebuhr, *The Social Sources of Denominationalism* (New York, 1929).

44 Davies, *Quakers*, p. 221; Elizabeth Isichei, 'From sect to denomination', esp. pp. 176, 181. See also Mullett, 'From sect to denomination?', pp. 176, 191 and *passim*.

45 For the processes discussed in this and the previous paragraph, see Cottret, *Huguenots in England*, esp. pp. 258–60; Gwynn, *Huguenot Heritage*, ch. 10; Mark Greengrass, 'Protestant exiles and their assimilation in early modern England', *Immigrants and Minorities*, 4 (1985), 68–81; Grell, 'From persecution to integration: the decline of the Anglo-Dutch communities in England, 1648–1702', in Grell, Israel and Tyacke (eds), *From Persecution to Toleration*, pp. 97–127; Pettegree, *Foreign Protestant Communities*, ch. 9; Andrew Pettegree, ' "Thirty years on": progress towards integration among the immigrant population of Elizabethan London', in John Chartres and David Hey (eds), *English Rural Society, 1500–1800: Essays in Honour of Joan Thirsk* (Cambridge, 1990), pp. 297–312; Spicer, *French-Speaking Reformed Community*, ch. 8; Andrew Spicer, 'A process of gradual assimilation: the exile community in Southampton, 1567–1635', in Vigne and Gibbs (eds), *Strangers' Progress*, pp. 186–98; Charles Littleton, 'Social interaction of aliens in late Elizabethan London: evidence from the 1593 return and the French Church consistory acts', in *ibid.*, pp. 147–59; Lien Bich Luu, 'Assimilation or segregation: colonies of alien craftsmen in Elizabethan London', in *ibid.*, pp. 160–72; Backhouse, *Flemish and Walloon Communities*, esp. pp. 55–9; Nigel Goose, 'The Dutch in Colchester in the sixteenth and seventeenth centuries: opposition and integration' and Eileen Barrett, 'Huguenot integration in late seventeenth- and eighteenth-century London: insights from records of the French Church and some relief agencies', both in Vigne and Littleton (eds), *From Strangers to Citizens*, pp. 88–98 and 375–82 respectively.

46 See Bernard Susser, *The Jews of South-West England* (Exeter, 1993), ch. 10; Endelman, *Jews of Georgian England*, esp. chs 4, 8; Endelman, *Jews of Britain, 1656 to 2002*, esp. pp. 56–60, 65–7, 71–2; Todd Endelman, *Radical Assimilation in English Jewish History, 1656–1945* (Bloomington, Illinois, 1990).

47 Nenk, 'Crypto-Jews', esp. pp. 211–12.

48 Barrett, 'Huguenot integration', esp. pp. 375–6.

49 Underwood (ed.), *Acts of the Witnesses*, p. 12; Marsh, *Family of Love*, pp. 247–8.

50 Spurr, *English Puritanism*, p. 143.

51 See Jan Albers, '"Papist traitors" and "Presbyterian rogues": religious identities in eighteenth-century Lancashire', in Walsh, Haydon and Taylor (eds), *Church of England*, pp. 317–33, at 322–3.

52 Mullett, 'From sect to denomination?', pp. 175–6.

53 See Jonathan Barry, 'The seventeenth and eighteenth centuries', in Nicholas Orme (ed.), *Unity and Diversity: A History of the Church in Devon and Cornwall* (Exeter, 1991), pp. 104–6.

54 Weber, *Theory of Social and Economic Organisation*, pp. 363–73.

55 See Collinson, 'Towards a broader understanding of the early dissenting tradition'; Hill, 'History and denominational history'.

56 Examples include the Catholic Record Society and *Recusant History*; the Huguenot Society of Great Britain and Ireland and its *Proceedings*; the Congregational History Society and its *Transactions*; the Presbyterian Historical Society and its *Transactions*; the Friends' Historical Society and its *Journal*; the Baptist Historical Society and its *Transactions*.

57 Founded in 1992, by comparison with other similar societies the Church of England Record Society is still in its infancy, though the Parker Society and British Reformation Society do date from the nineteenth century. MacCulloch, 'Myth of the English Reformation'.

58 Bunyan, *Pilgrim's Progress*, ed. Sharrock, p. 144.

59 Walsham, 'Ordeals of Conscience', pp. 46–8, from which I reproduce a few phrases here.

60 Maltby, *Prayer Book and People*; Morrill, 'The Church of England'; Spaeth, *Church in an Age of Danger*; Mark Goldie, 'Voluntary Anglicans', *HJ*, 46 (2003), 977–90.

61 Milton, 'Qualified intolerance', p. 108.

62 Milton, *Catholic and Reformed*, pp. 59–60.

63 See Cressy, *Bonfires and Bells*.

64 Haydon, *Anti-Catholicism*; E. R. Norman, *Anti-Catholicism in Victorian England* (London, 1968); D. G. Paz, *Popular Anti-Catholicism in Mid Victorian England* (Stanford, CA, 1992).

65 Felsenstein, *Anti-Semitic Stereotypes*, p. 12 and *passim*. For the persistence of other traditional imagery, see Miller, *Religion in the Popular Prints*.

66 Albers, '"Papist traitors" and "Presbyterian rogues" ', p. 325, and *passim*. For eighteenth-century anti-popery, see also Haydon, *Anti-Catholicism*, esp. pp. 246–7 and his 'I love my king and my country', esp. pp. 38–43.

67 See Clancy, 'Papist-Protestant-Puritan'; Collinson, 'Comment: concerning the name puritan'.

68 Scribner, 'Preconditions of tolerance', pp. 45–6.

69 John Walsh, 'Methodism and the mob in the eighteenth century', G. J. Cuming and D. Baker (eds), *Popular Belief and Practice*, SCH 8 (Cambridge, 1972), pp. 213–27; David Hempton, 'Methodism and the law, 1740–1820', *Bulletin of the John Rylands University*

Library of Manchester, 70 (1988), 93–107; David Hempton, *Religion and Political Culture in Britain and Ireland: From the Glorious Revolution to the Decline of Empire* (Cambridge, 1996), p. 18; Henry D. Rack, *Reasonable Enthusiast: John Wesley and the Rise of Methodism* (London, 1992), pp. 271–5.

70   Miller, *Popery*, pp. 182–8, esp. p. 182; Hempton, *Religion and Political Culture*, p. 18.

71   Albers, ' "Papist traitors" and "Presbyterian rogues" ', p. 332; Rudé, 'The Gordon riots'; Haydon, *Anti-Catholicism*, ch. 6; Rogers, *Crowds, Culture and Politics*, ch. 5; R. B. Rose, 'The Priestley riots of 1791', *P&P*, 18 (1960), 68–88.

72   Cited above ch. 5, and see Marie B. Rowlands, 'Surviving the times, 1625–90', in Rowlands (ed.), *Catholics of Town and Country*, pp. 61–77, at 67.

73   Somerset Record Office, Taunton, 'Memoirs ... of John Cannon [1684–1743]', fos 449 and 443 respectively. I am grateful to Helen Weinstein for discussions of Cannon and for providing me with a transcription of these passages.

74   Note the subtle differences of interpretation and emphasis between Albers, ' "Papist traitors" and "Presbyterian rogues" ', p. 333; and Haydon, *Anti-Catholicism*, pp. 259–60.

75   Adapting a metaphor of Martin, 'The denomination', 5.

76   Albers, ' "Papist traitors" and "Presbyterian rogues" ', pp. 322–3.

77   Linda Colley, *Britons: Forging the Nation 1707–1837* (New Haven, 1992) and 'Britishness and otherness, an argument', *JBS*, 31 (1992), 309–29. See also Wiener, 'Beleaguered isle'; Maltby, *Black Legend*.

78   Haydon, *Anti-Catholicism*, pp. 246–7; Duffy, *Englishman and the Foreigner*, introduction.

79   Duffy, *Englishman and the Foreigner*, p. 16.

80   J. C. D. Clark, *English Society 1660–1832* (Cambridge, 2nd edn, 2000; first publ. 1985) and see the debates on this book in *P&P*, 115 and 117 (1987) and *Albion*, 21 (1989); Penelope Corfield, 'Georgian England: one state, many faiths', *History Today* (April, 1995), 14–21; Jeremy Black, 'Confessional state or elect nation? Religion and identity in eighteenth-century England', in Claydon and MacBride (eds), *Protestantism and National Identity*, pp. 53–74.

81   David A. Pailin, *Attitudes to Other Religions: Comparative Religion in Seventeenth- and Eighteenth-Century Britain* (Manchester, 1984), esp. pp. 3–6, 45.

82   Michael Hunter, 'The problem of atheism in early modern England', *TRHS*, 5th series 35 (1985), 135–57; Michael Hunter and David Wootton, *Atheism from the Reformation to the Enlightenment* (Cambridge, 1992).

83   See *OED*, s.v. 'agnostic' and 'atheist'.

84   Dudley W. R. Bahlman, *The Moral Revolution of 1688* (New Haven, 1957); Tina Isaacs, 'The Anglican hierarchy and the reformation of manners 1688–1738', *JEH*, 33 (1982), 391–411; T. C. Curtis and W. A. Speck, 'The Societies for the Reformation of Manners', *Literature and History*, 3 (1976), 45–64; John Spurr, 'The Church, the societies and the moral revolution of 1688', in Walsh, Haydon and Taylor (eds), *Church of England*, pp. 127–42; R. B. Shoemaker, 'Reforming the city: the reformation of manners campaign in London, 1690–1738', in L. Davison, T. Hitchcock, T. Kiern and R. B. Shoemaker (eds), *Stilling the Grumbling Hive: The Response to Social and Economic Problems in England, 1688–1750* (Stroud, 1992), pp. 99–120; Tim Hitchcock, *English Sexualities, 1700–1800* (Basingstoke, 1997), ch. 7.

85 Martin Ingram, 'Reformation of manners in early modern England', in Paul Griffiths, Adam Fox, and Steve Hindle (eds), *The Experience of Authority in Early Modern England* (Basingstoke, 1996), pp. 47–88.

86 Knights, ' "Meer religion" and the "church-state" ', pp. 65–6.

87 Mandelbrote, 'Religious belief and the politics of toleration', p. 107.

88 Roy Porter, *Mind Forg'd Manacles: A History of Madness in England from the Restoration to the Regency* (London, 1987).

89 Michael MacDonald, 'Insanity and the realities of history', *Psychological Medicine*, 11 (1981), 11–25.

90 Gary K. Waite, *Heresy, Magic, and Witchcraft in Early Modern Europe* (Basingstoke, 2003), ch. 6. For the tendency to see witches and victims of alleged witchcraft as melancholic or deluded, see Roy Porter, 'The Enlightenment crusade', in Marijke Gijswijt-Hofstra, Brian P. Levack and Roy Porter (eds), *Witchcraft and Magic in Europe: The Eighteenth and Nineteenth Centuries* (London, 1999), pp. 219–36, at pp. 226–35; Owen Davies, *Witchcraft, Magic and Culture 1736-1951* (Manchester, 1999), pp. 39–44.

Select bibliography of secondary sources

Acheson, R. J., *Radical Puritans in England 1550–1660* (London, 1990).

Ashcraft, Richard, 'Latitudinarianism and toleration: historical myth versus political history', in Richard Kroll, Richard Ashcraft and Perez Zagorin (eds), *Philosophy, Science and Religion in England 1640–1700* (Cambridge, 1992), pp. 151–77.

Aston, Margaret, *Lollards and Reformers: Images and Literacy in Late Medieval Religion* (London, 1984).

Aston, Margaret, 'Lollardy and sedition, 1381–1431', *P&P*, 17 (1960), 1–44.

Aston, Margaret, 'Lollardy and the Reformation: survival or revival?', *History*, 49 (1964), 149–70.

Aston, Margaret and Richmond, Colin (eds), *Lollardy and the Gentry in the Later Middle Ages* (Stroud, 1997).

Aveling, J. C. H., *The Handle and the Axe: The Catholic Recusants in England from Reformation to Emancipation* (London, 1976).

Aveling, J. C. H., *Northern Catholics: The Catholic Recusants of the North Riding of Yorkshire 1558–1790* (London, 1966).

Aylmer, G. E., 'Did the Ranters exist?', *P&P*, 117 (1987), 208–19.

Backhouse, Marcel, *The Flemish and Walloon Communities at Sandwich during the Reign of Elizabeth I (1561–1603)* (Brussels, 1995).

Bahlman, Dudley W. R., *The Moral Revolution of 1688* (New Haven, 1957).

Bainton, Roland H., 'The parable of the tares as the proof text for religious liberty to the end of the sixteenth century', *Church History*, 1 (1932), 67–89.

Baldwin Smith, Lacey, 'English treason trials and confessions in the sixteenth century', *Journal of the History of Ideas*, 15 (1954), 471–98.

Bauman, Richard, *Let your Words be Few: Symbolism of Speaking and Silence among Seventeenth-Century Quakers* (Cambridge, 1983).

Bejczy, István, '*Tolerantia*: a medieval concept', *Journal of the History of Ideas*, 58 (1997), 365–84.

Bellamy, John, *The Tudor Law of Treason: An Introduction* (London, 1979).

Benedict, Philip, 'Confessionalization in France? Critical reflections and new evidence', in Raymond A. Mentzer and Andrew Spicer (eds), *Society and Culture in the Huguenot World 1559–1685* (Cambridge, 2002), pp. 44–61.

Benedict, Philip, '*Un roi, une lois, deux fois*: parameters for the history of Catholic-Reformed co-existence in France, 1555–1685', in Ole Peter Grell and Bob Scribner (eds), *Tolerance and Intolerance in the European Reformation* (Cambridge, 1996), pp. 65–93.

Bennett, G. V., 'The seven bishops: a reconsideration', in Derek Baker (ed.), *Religious*

Motivation: Biographical and Sociological Problems for the Church Historian, SCH 15 (Oxford, 1978), pp. 267–87.

Berkvens-Stevelinck, Christiane, Israel, Jonathan I. and Posthumus Meyjes, G. H. M. (eds), *The Emergence of Tolerance in the Dutch Republic* (Leiden, 1997).

Bernard, G. W., 'The Church of England c.1529–c.1642', *History*, 75 (1990), 183–206.

Bernard, G. W., 'The making of religious policy, 1533–1546: Henry VIII and the search for the middle way', *HJ*, 41 (1998), 321–49.

Bida, Andrzej, 'Papists in an Elizabethan parish: Linton, Cambridgeshire. c.1560–c.1600', unpubl. Diploma in Historical Studies dissertation (University of Cambridge, 1992).

Black, Jeremy, 'Confessional state or elect nation? Religion and identity in eighteenth-century England', in Tony Claydon and Ian MacBride (eds), *Protestantism and National Identity: Britain and Ireland, c.1650–c.1850* (Cambridge, 1998), pp. 53–74.

Bossy, John, *Christianity in the West, 1400–1700* (Oxford, 1985).

Bossy, John, *The English Catholic Community 1570–1850* (London, 1975).

Bossy, John, *Peace in the Post-Reformation* (Cambridge, 1998).

Bowker, Margaret, *The Henrician Reformation: The Diocese of Lincoln under John Longland 1521–1541* (Cambridge, 1981).

Bowler, Gerald, '"An axe or an acte": the parliament of 1572 and resistance theory in early Elizabethan England', *Canadian Journal of History*, 19 (1984), 349–59.

Bowler, Gerry, 'Marian Protestants and the idea of violent resistance', in Peter Lake and Maria Dowling (eds), *Protestantism and the National Church in Sixteenth-Century England* (London, 1987), pp. 124–43.

Braddick, Michael J., *State Formation in Early Modern England c.1550–1700* (Cambridge, 2000).

Braithwaite, William C., *The Beginnings of Quakerism* (Cambridge, 1970 edn; first publ. 1912).

Braithwaite, William C., *The Second Period of Quakerism* (Cambridge, 1961 edn; first publ. 1919).

Braun, Harald and Vallance, Edward (eds), *Contexts of Conscience in Early Modern Europe 1500–1700* (Basingstoke, 2004).

Brigden, Susan, *London and the Reformation* (Oxford, 1989).

Brigden, Susan, 'Religion and social obligation in early sixteenth-century London', *P&P*, 103 (1984), 67–112.

Brigden, Susan, 'Youth and the English Reformation', *P&P*, 95 (1982), 37–67.

Brown, Andrew D., *Popular Piety in Late Medieval England: The Diocese of Salisbury 1250–1550* (Oxford, 1995).

Brown, P. R. L., 'St Augustine's attitude to religious coercion', *Journal of Roman Studies*, 54 (1964), 107–16.

Burns, J. H. with Goldie, Mark (eds), *The Cambridge History of Political Thought 1450–1700* (Cambridge, 1991).

Butterfield, Herbert, 'Toleration in early modern times', *Journal of the History of Ideas*, 38 (1977), 573–84.

Caffyn, John, *Sussex Believers: Baptist Marriage in the Seventeenth and Eighteenth Centuries* (Worthing, 1988).

Canny, Nicholas, *Making Ireland British 1580–1650* (Oxford, 2001), ch. 8.

Capp, B. S., *The Fifth Monarchy Men: A Study in Seventeenth-Century English Millenarianism* (London, 1972).

Carlin, Norah, 'Toleration for Catholics in the puritan revolution', in Ole Peter Grell and Bob Scribner (eds), *Tolerance and Intolerance in the European Reformation* (Cambridge, 1996), pp. 216–30.

Champion, Justin, *The Pillars of Priestcraft Shaken: The Church of England and its Enemies, 1660–1730* (Cambridge, 1992).

Clancy, Thomas H., 'Papist-Protestant-Puritan: English religious taxonomy 1565–1665', *RH*, 13 (1976), 227–53.

Clark, J. C. D., *English Society 1660–1832* (Cambridge, 2nd edn, 2000; first publ. 1985).

Clark, Peter, *English Provincial Society from the Reformation to the Revolution: Religion, Politics and Society in Kent 1500–1640* (Hassocks, 1977).

Claydon, Tony, *William III and the Glorious Revolution* (Cambridge, 1996).

Claydon, Tony and McBride, Ian (eds), *Protestantism and National Identity: Britain and Ireland, c.1650–c.1850* (Cambridge, 1998).

Clebsch, William A., *England's Earliest Protestants 1520–1535* (New Haven, 1964).

Clement, C. J., *Religious Radicalism in England 1535–1565* (Carlisle, 1997).

Clifton, Robin, 'The fear of Catholics in England 1637 to 1645 principally from central sources', unpubl. DPhil dissertation (University of Oxford, 1967).

Clifton, Robin, *The Last Popular Rebellion: The Western Rising of 1685* (London, 1984).

Clifton, Robin, 'The popular fear of Catholics during the English Revolution', *P&P*, 51 (1971), 23–55.

Cockburn, J. S. (ed.), *Crime in England 1550–1800* (London, 1977).

Coffey, John, *Persecution and Toleration in Protestant England 1558–1689* (Harlow, 2000).

Coffey, John, 'Puritanism and liberty revisited: the case for toleration in the English Revolution', *HJ*, 41 (1998), 961–85.

Colley, Linda, *Britons: Forging the Nation 1707–1837* (New Haven, 1992).

Collins, Jeffrey R., 'The Church settlement of Oliver Cromwell', *History*, 87 (2002), 18–40.

Collinson, Patrick, *The Birthpangs of Protestant England: Religious and Cultural Change in the Sixteenth and Seventeenth Centuries* (New York, 1988).

Collinson, Patrick, 'The cohabitation of the faithful with the unfaithful', in Ole Peter Grell Jonathan I. Israel and Nicholas Tyacke (eds), *From Persecution to Toleration: The Glorious Revolution and Religion in England* (Oxford, 1991), pp. 51–76.

Collinson, Patrick, 'The Elizabethan exclusion crisis and the Elizabethan polity', *Proceedings of the British Academy*, 84 (1994), 51–92.

Collinson, Patrick, *The Elizabethan Puritan Movement* (Oxford, 1990 edn; first publ. 1967).

Collinson, Patrick, 'The English Conventicle', in W. J. Sheils (ed.), *Voluntary Religion*, SCH 23 (Oxford, 1986), pp. 223–59.

Collinson, Patrick, *Godly People; Essays on English Protestantism and Puritanism* (London, 1983).

Collinson, Patrick, 'The monarchical republic of Queen Elizabeth I', in his *Elizabethan Essays* (London, 1994), pp. 31–57.

Collinson, Patrick, 'Night schools, conventicles and churches: continuities and discontinuities in early Protestant ecclesiology', in Peter Marshall and Alec Ryrie (eds), *The Beginnings of English Protestantism* (Cambridge, 2002), pp. 209–35.

Collinson, Patrick, *The Religion of Protestants: The Church in England 1559–1625* (Oxford, 1982).

Collinson, Patrick, 'Truth and legend: the veracity of John Foxe's Book of Martyrs', in A. C. Duke and C. A. Tamse (eds), *Clio's Mirror: Historiography in Britain and the Netherlands* (Zutphen, 1985), pp. 31–54.

Como, David, R., *Blown by the Spirit: Puritanism and the Emergence of an Antinomian Underground in Pre-Civil-War England* (Stanford, 2004).

Como, David R., 'The kingdom of Christ, the kingdom of England, and the kingdom of Traske: John Traske and the persistence of radical puritanism in early Stuart England', in Muriel C. McClendon, Joseph P. Ward and Michael MacDonald (eds), *Protestant Identities: Religion, Society, and Self-Fashioning in Post-Reformation England* (Stanford, CA, 1999), pp. 63–82.

Cottret, Bernard, *The Huguenots in England: Immigration and Settlement c.1550–1700* (Cambridge and Paris, 1991).

Covington, Sarah, *The Trail of Martyrdom: Persecution and Resistance in Sixteenth-Century England* (Notre Dame, 2003).

Craig, John, *Reformation, Politics and Polemics: The Growth of Protestantism in East Anglian Market Towns, 1500–1610* (Aldershot, 2001).

Crawford, Patricia, '"Charles Stuart, that man of blood"', *JBS*, 16 (1977), 41–61.

Cressy, David, 'The Adamites exposed: naked radicals in the English Revolution', in his *Travesties and Transgressions in Tudor and Stuart England: Tales of Discord and Dissension* (Oxford, 2000), pp. 251–80.

Cressy, David, *Bonfires and Bells: National Memory and the Protestant Calendar in Elizabethan and Stuart England* (London, 1989).

Cressy, David, *Coming Over: Migration and Communication between England and New England in the Seventeenth Century* (Cambridge, 1987).

Cressy, David, 'The Protestation protested, 1641 and 1642', *HJ*, 45 (2002), 251–70.

Cross, Claire, 'The Church of England 1646–1660', in G. E. Aylmer (ed.), *The Interregnum: The Quest for Settlement 1646–1660* (London, 1972), pp. 99–120.

Crouzet, Denis, *Les guerriers de dieu: la violence au temps des troubles de religion, vers 1525–vers 1610*, 2 vols (Paris, 1990).

Dalberg-Acton, John E. E. (Lord Acton), 'The Protestant theory of persecution', in *The History of Freedom and Other Essays* (London, 1919 edn), pp. 150–87.

D'Alton, Craig W., 'Charity or fire? The argument of Thomas More's 1529 *Dyaloge*', *SCJ*, 33 (2002), 51–70.

D'Alton, Craig W., 'The suppression of Lutheran heretics in England, 1526–1529', *JEH*, 54 (2003), 228–53.

Damrosch, Leo, *The Sorrows of the Quaker Jesus: James Nayler and the Puritan Crackdown on the Free Spirit* (Cambridge, MA, 1996).

Davies, Adrian, *The Quakers in English Society 1655–1725* (Oxford, 2000).

Davies, Catharine, *A Religion of the Word: The Defence of the Reformation in the Reign of Edward VI* (Manchester, 2002).

Davies, Julian, *The Caroline Captivity of the Church: Charles I and the Remoulding of Anglicanism 1625–1641* (Oxford, 1992).

Davies, Richard G., 'Lollardy and locality', *TRHS*, 6th series, 1 (1991), 191–212.

Davis, J. C., *Fear, Myth and History: The Ranters and the Historians* (Cambridge, 1986).

Davis, J. C., 'Religion and the struggle for freedom in the English Revolution', *HJ*, 35 (1992), 507–30.

Davis, John F., *Heresy and Reformation in the South-East of England, 1520–1559* (London, 1983).

Davis, Natalie Zemon, *Society and Culture in Early Modern France* (Stanford, 1975).

De Krey, Gary S., 'The first Restoration crisis: conscience and coercion in London, 1667–73', *Albion*, 25 (1993), 565–80.

De Krey, Gary S., *London and the Restoration 1659–1683* (Cambridge, 2005).

De Krey, Gary S., 'Rethinking the Restoration: dissenting cases for conscience, 1667–1672', *HJ*, 38 (1995), 53–83.

Dickens, A. G., *The English Reformation* (London, 2nd edn 1989; first publ. 1964).

Dickens, A. G., *Lollards and Protestants in the Diocese of York 1509–1558* (London, 1982 edn; first publ. Oxford, 1959).

Dickens, A. G., 'Religious toleration and liberalism in Tudor England', in his *Reformation Studies* (London, 1982), pp. 427–42.

Dickens, A. G. and Tonkin, John, 'Weapons of propaganda: the martyrologies', in *The Reformation in Historical Thought* (Oxford, 1985), pp. 39–57.

Diefendorf, Barbara, *Beneath the Cross: Catholics and Huguenots in Sixteenth-Century Paris* (New York, 1991).

Dillon, Anne, *The Construction of Martyrdom in the English Catholic Community, 1535–1603* (Aldershot, 2002).

Dolan, Frances E., *Whores of Babylon: Catholicism, Gender and Seventeenth-Century Print Culture* (Ithaca, NY, 1999).

Drake, H. A., 'Lambs into lions: explaining early Christian intolerance', *P&P*, 153 (1997), 3–36.

Drees, Clayton J., *Authority and Dissent in the English Church: The Prosecution of Heresy and Religious Non-conformity in the Diocese of Winchester, 1380–1547* (Lewiston, NY, 1997).

Duffy, Eamon, *The Stripping of the Altars: Traditional Religion in England 1400–1580* (New Haven, 1992).

Duffy, Eamon and Loades, David (eds), *The Church of Mary Tudor* (Aldershot, 2005).

Duffy, Michael, *The Englishman and the Foreigner* (Cambridge, 1996).

Dures, Alan, *English Catholicism 1558–1642* (Harlow, 1983).

Durston, Christopher, *Cromwell's Major Generals: Godly Government during the English Revolution* (Manchester, 2001).

Durston, Christopher and Eales, Jacqueline (eds), *The Culture of English Puritanism, 1560–1700* (Basingstoke, 1996).

Select bibliography of secondary sources

Earle, Peter, *Monmouth's Rebels: The Road to Sedgemoor, 1685* (London, 1977).

Eire, Carlos M. N., *War against the Idols: The Reformation of Worship from Erasmus to Calvin* (Cambridge, 1986).

Elmer, Peter, '"Saints or sorcerers": Quakerism, demonology and the decline of witchcraft in seventeenth-century England', in Jonathan Barry, Marianne Hester and Gareth Roberts (eds), *Witchcraft in Early Modern Europe: Studies in Culture and Belief* (Cambridge, 1996), pp. 145–79.

Elton, G. R., 'Persecution and toleration in the English Reformation', in W. J. Sheils (ed.), *Persecution and Toleration*, SCH 21 (Oxford, 1984), pp. 163–87.

Elton, G. R., *Policy and Police: The Enforcement of the Reformation in the Age of Thomas Cromwell* (Cambridge, 1972).

Endelman, Todd, *The Jews of Britain, 1656 to 2002* (Berkeley, CA, 2002).

Endelman, Todd, *The Jews of Georgian England 1714–1830: Tradition and Change in a Liberal Society* (Philadelphia, 1979).

Endelman, Todd, *Radical Assimilation in English Jewish History, 1656–1945* (Bloomington, Indiana, 1990).

Felsenstein, Frank, *Anti-Semitic Stereotypes: A Paradigm of Otherness in English Popular Culture, 1660–1830* (Baltimore, MD, 1995).

Fincham, Kenneth, 'Clerical conformity from Whitgift to Laud', in Peter Lake and Michael Questier (eds), *Conformity and Orthodoxy in the English Church, c.1560–1660* (Woodbridge, 2000), pp. 125–58.

Fincham, Kenneth (ed.), *The Early Stuart Church, 1603–1642* (Basingstoke, 1993).

Fines, John, 'Heresy trials in the diocese of Coventry and Lichfield, 1511–12', *JEH*, 14 (1963), 160–74.

Flaningham, John, 'The occasional conformity controversy: ideology and party politics, 1697–1711', *JBS*, 17 (1977–8), 38–62.

Fletcher, Anthony, 'The enforcement of the Conventicle Acts 1664–1679', in W. J. Sheils (ed.), *Persecution and Toleration*, SCH 21 (Oxford, 1984), pp. 235–46.

Fletcher, Anthony, *The Outbreak of the English Civil War* (London, 1981).

Forster, Marc R., *The Counter Reformation in the Villages: Religion and Reform in the Bishopric of Speyer, 1560–1720* (Ithaca, NY, 1992).

Foster, Stephen, *Notes from the Caroline Underground: Alexander Leighton, the Puritan Triumvirate and the Laudian Reaction to Nonconformity* (Hamden, CT, 1978).

Foucault, Michel, *Discipline and Punish: The Birth of the Prison*, trans. A. Sheridan (London, 1977).

François, Etienne, 'De l'uniformité à la tolérance: confessions et société urbaine en Allemagne, 1650–1800', *Annales* (1982), 783–800.

François, Etienne, *Protestants et catholiques en Allemagne: identités et pluralisme, Augsbourg 1648–1806* (Paris, 1993; first publ. in German 1991).

Freeman, Thomas S., 'Dissenters from a dissenting Church: the challenge of the Freewillers, 1550–1558', in Peter Marshall and Alec Ryrie (eds), *The Beginnings of English Protestantism* (Cambridge, 2002), pp. 129–56.

Frijhoff, Willem, 'The threshold of toleration: interconfessional conviviality in Holland during the early modern period', in his *Embodied Belief: Ten Essays on Religious Culture in Dutch History* (Hilversum, 2002), pp. 39–65.

Gallagher, Lowell, *Medusa's Gaze: Casuistry and Conscience in the Renaissance* (Stanford, 1991).

Garrett, Christina Hallowell, *The Marian Exiles: A Study in the Origins of Elizabethan Puritanism* (Cambridge, 1938).

George, Timothy, 'Between pacifism and coercion: The English Baptist doctrine of religious toleration', *Mennonite Quarterly Review*, 58 (1984), 30–49.

Goldie, Mark, 'John Locke, Jonas Proast and religious toleration 1688–1692', in John Walsh, Colin Haydon and Stephen Taylor (eds), *The Church of England c.1689–c.1833* (Cambridge, 1993), pp. 143–71.

Goldie, Mark, 'The search for religious liberty 1640–1690', in John Morrill (ed.), *The Oxford llustrated History of Tudor and Stuart Britain* (Oxford, 1996), pp. 293–309.

Goldie, Mark, 'The theory of religious intolerance in Restoration England', in Ole Peter Grell, Jonathan I. Israel and Nicholas Tyacke (eds), *From Persecution to Toleration: The Glorious Revolution and Religion in England* (Oxford, 1991), pp. 331–68.

Goldie, Mark, 'Voluntary Anglicans', *HJ*, 46 (2003), 977–90.

Goldie, Mark and Spurr, John, 'Politics and the Restoration parish: Edward Fowler and the struggle for St Giles Cripplegate', *EHR*, 109 (1994), 572–96.

Greaves, Richard L., *Deliver us from Evil: The Radical Underground in Britain, 1660–1663* (New York, 1986).

Greaves, Richard L., 'Seditious sectaries or "sober and useful inhabitants"? Changing conceptions of the Quakers in early modern Britain', *Albion*, 33 (2001), 24–50.

Green, Ian, 'The persecution of "scandalous" and "malignant" parish clergy during the English Civil War', *EHR*, 94 (1979), 507–31.

Green, Ian, *The Re-establishment of the Church of England 1660–1663* (Oxford, 1978).

Greengrass, Mark, 'Protestant exiles and their assimilation in early modern England', *Immigrants and Minorities*, 4 (1985), 68–81.

Gregory, Brad S., *Salvation at Stake: Christian Martyrdom in Early Modern Europe* (Cambridge, MA, 1999).

Grell, Ole Peter, *Calvinist Exiles in Tudor and Stuart England* (Aldershot, 1996).

Grell, Ole Peter, *Dutch Calvinists in Early Stuart London: The Dutch Church in Austin Friars 1603–1642* (Leiden, 1989).

Grell, Ole Peter, 'Merchants and ministers: the foundations of international Calvinism', in Andrew Pettegree, Alastair Duke and Gillian Lewis (eds.), *Calvinism in Europe 1540–1620* (Cambridge, 1994), pp. 254–73.

Grell, Ole Peter Israel, Jonathan I. and Tyacke, Nicholas (eds), *From Persecution to Toleration: The Glorious Revolution and Religion in England* (Oxford, 1991).

Grell, Ole Peter and Porter, Roy (eds), *Toleration in Enlightenment Europe* (Cambridge, 2000).

Grell, Ole Peter and Scribner, Bob (eds), *Tolerance and Intolerance in the European Reformation* (Cambridge, 1996).

Griggs, Burke W., 'Remembering the puritan past: John Walker and Anglican memories of the English Civil War', in Muriel C. McClendon, Joseph P. Ward, and Michael MacDonald (eds), *Protestant Identities: Religion, Society, and Self-Fashioning in Post-Reformation England* (Stanford, CA, 1999), pp. 158–91.

Guggisberg, Hans R., 'The defence of religious toleration and religious liberty in early modern Europe: arguments, pressures, and some consequences', *History of European Ideas*, 4 (1983), 35–50.

Guilday, Peter, *The English Catholic Refugees on the Continent 1558–1795* (London, 1914).

Guy, John, 'Perceptions of heresy, 1200–1550', in Gordon J. Schochet with Patricia E. Tatspaugh and Carol Brobeck (eds), *Reformation, Humanism and Revolution: Papers Presented at the Folger Institute Seminar 'Political Thought in the Henrician Age, 1500–1550'* (Washington, DC, 1990), pp. 39–61.

Guy, John (ed.), *The Reign of Elizabeth I: Court and Culture in the Last Decade* (Cambridge, 1995).

Gwynn, Robin D, *Huguenot Heritage: The History and Contribution of the Huguenots in Britain* (Brighton, 2001 edn; first publ. 1985).

Gwynn, Robin D., 'James II in the light of his treatment of Huguenot refugees in England, 1685–1688', *EHR*, 92 (1977), 820–33.

Haigh, Christopher (ed.), *The English Reformation Revised* (Cambridge, 1987).

Haigh, Christopher, *English Reformations: Religion, Politics and Society under the Tudors* (Oxford, 1993).

Haigh, Christopher, 'From monopoly to minority: Catholicism in early modern England', *TRHS*, 5th series, 31 (1981), 129–47.

Haigh, Christopher, *Reformation and Resistance in Tudor Lancashire* (Cambridge, 1975).

Haller, William, *Liberty and Reformation in the Puritan Revolution* (New York, 1955).

Hamilton, Alastair, *The Family of Love* (Cambridge, 1981).

Hanlon, Gregory, *Confession and Community in Seventeenth-Century France: Catholic and Protestant Coexistence in Aquitaine* (Philadelphia, 1993).

Hardmann Moore, Susan, 'Popery, purity and providence: deciphering the New England experiment', in Anthony Fletcher and Peter Roberts (eds), *Religion, Culture and Society in Early Modern Britain: Essays in Honour of Patrick Collinson* (Cambridge, 1994), pp. 257–89.

Harris, Tim, 'The bawdy house riots of 1668', *HJ*, 29 (1986), 537–74.

Harris, Tim, *London Crowds in the Reign of Charles II: Propaganda and Politics from the Restoration to the Exclusion Crisis* (Cambridge, 1987).

Harris, Tim, 'Was the Tory reaction popular? Attitudes of Londoners towards the persecution of dissent, 1681–6', *London Journal*, 13 (1988), 106–20.

Harris, Tim, Seaward, Paul and Goldie, Mark (eds), *The Politics of Religion in Restoration England* (Oxford, 1990).

Haydon, Colin, *Anti-Catholicism in Eighteenth-Century England, c.1714–80: A Political and Social Study* (Manchester, 1993).

Haydon, Colin, '"I love my king and my country, but a Roman Catholic I hate": anti-Catholicism, xenophobia and national identity in eighteenth-century England', in Tony

Claydon and Ian MacBride (eds), *Protestantism and National Identity: Britain and Ireland, c.1650–c.1850* (Cambridge, 1998), pp. 33–52.

Hempton, David, 'Methodism and the law, 1740–1820', *Bulletin of the John Rylands University Library of Manchester*, 70 (1988), 93–107.

Hempton, David, *Religion and Political Culture in Britain and Ireland: From the Glorious Revolution to the Decline of Empire* (Cambridge, 1996).

Herrup, Cynthia B., *The Common Peace: Participation and the Criminal Law in Seventeenth-Century England* (Cambridge, 1987).

Heyd, David (ed.), *Toleration: An Elusive Virtue* (Princeton, 1996).

Hibbard, Caroline M., *Charles I and the Popish Plot* (Chapel Hill, NC, 1983).

Hibbard, Caroline, 'Early Stuart Catholicism: revisions and re-revisions', *Journal of Modern History*, 52 (1980), 1–34.

Highley, Christopher and King, John N. (eds), *John Foxe and his World* (Aldershot, 2002).

Hill, Christopher, *Antichrist in Seventeenth-Century England* (London, 1990 edn; first publ. 1971).

Hill, Christopher, 'The lost Ranters? A critique of J. C. Davis', *History Workshop*, 24 (1987), 134–40.

Hill, Christopher, 'Occasional conformity and the Grindalian tradition', repr. in his *Collected Essays*, vol. 2, *Religion and Politics in Seventeenth-Century England* (Hassocks, 1986), pp. 301–20.

Hill, Christopher, *A Turbulent, Seditious and Factious People: John Bunyan and his Church* (Oxford, 1989).

Hill, Christopher, *The World Turned Upside Down: Radical Ideas during the English Revolution* (Harmondsworth, 1975 edn; first publ. 1972).

Hill, Christopher, Reay, Barry and Lamont, William (eds), *The World of the Muggletonians* (London, 1983).

Hirst, Derek, 'The failure of godly rule in the English Republic', *P&P*, 132 (1991), 33–66.

Hoak, Dale and Feingold, Mordechai (eds), *The World of William and Mary: Anglo-Dutch Perspectives on the Revolution of 1688–1689* (Stanford, CA, 1996).

Holden, William P., *Anti-Puritan Satire 1572–1642* (London, 1954).

Holmes, Geoffrey, 'The Sacheverell riots: the crowd and the church in early eighteenth-century London', in Paul Slack (ed.), *Rebellion, Popular Protest and the Social Order in Early Modern England* (Cambridge, 1984), pp. 232–62.

Holmes, P. J., *Resistance and Compromise: The Political Thought of the Elizabethan Catholics* (Cambridge, 1982).

Hope, Andrew, 'Lollardy: the stone the builders rejected', in Peter Lake and Maria Dowling (eds), *Protestantism and the National Church in Sixteenth-Century England* (London, 1987), pp. 1–35.

Horle, Craig W. *The Quakers and the English Legal System 1660–1688* (Philadelphia, 1988).

Horst, Irvin Buckwater, *The Radical Brethren: Anabaptism and the English Reformation to 1558* (Nieuwkoop, 1972).

Select bibliography of secondary sources

Houlbrooke, Ralph, *Church Courts and the People during the English Reformation 1520–1570* (Oxford, 1979).

Hsia, R. Po-Chia and van Nierop, Henk (eds), *Calvinism and Religious Toleration in the Dutch Golden Age* (Cambridge, 2002).

Hudson, Anne, *The Premature Reformation: Wycliffite Texts and Lollard History* (Oxford, 1988).

Hughes, Ann, *Gangraena and the Struggle for the English Revolution* (Oxford, 2004).

Hunt, William, *The Puritan Moment: The Coming of Revolution in an English County* (Cambridge, MA, 1983).

Hunter, Michael, '"Aikenhead the atheist": the context and consequences of articulate irreligion in the late seventeenth century', in Michael Hunter, *Science and the Shape of Orthodoxy: Intellectual Change in Late-Seventeenth Century Britain* (Woodbridge, 1995), pp. 308–32.

Hunter, Michael, 'The problem of atheism in early modern England', *TRHS*, 5th series, 35 (1985), 135–57.

Hunter, Michael and Wootton, David, *Atheism from the Reformation to the Enlightenment* (Cambridge, 1992).

Hutton, Ronald, *The Restoration: A Political and Religious History of England and Wales, 1658–1667* (Oxford, 1985).

Iogna-Prat, Dominique, *Order and Exclusion: Cluny and Christendom Face Heresy, Judaism and Islam (1100–1150)*, trans. Graham Robert Edwards (Ithaca, NY, 2002; first publ. 1998).

Ingram, Martin, *Church Courts, Sex and Marriage in England, 1570–1640* (Cambridge, 1987).

Ingram, Martin, 'Puritans and the church courts , 1560–1640', in Christopher Durston and Jacqueline Eales (eds), *The Culture of English Puritanism, 1560–1700* (Basingstoke, 1996), pp. 58–91.

Ingram, Martin, 'Shame and pain: themes and variations in Tudor punishments', in Simon Devereaux and Paul Griffiths (eds), *Penal Practice and Culture, 1500–1900* (Basingstoke, 2004), pp. 36–62.

Isichei, Elizabeth, 'From sect to denomination among English Quakers', in Bryan R. Wilson (ed.), *Patterns of Sectarianism: Organisation and Ideology in Social and Religious Movements* (London, 1967), pp. 161–81.

Jones, J. R. (ed.), *Liberty Secured? Britain Before and After 1688* (Stanford, CA, 1992).

Jones, Norman, *The English Reformation: Religion and Cultural Adaptation* (Oxford, 2002).

Jones, Norman, *Faith by Statute: Parliament and the Settlement of Religion, 1559* (London, 1982).

Jordan, W. K., *The Development of Religious Toleration in England*, 4 vols (London, 1932–40).

Kamen, Henry, *The Rise of Toleration* (London, 1967).

Kaplan, Benjamin J, *Calvinists and Libertines: Confession and Community in Utrecht 1578–1620* (Oxford, 1995).

Kaplan, Benjamin J., 'Diplomacy and domestic devotion: embassy chapels and the toleration of religious dissent in early modern Europe', *Journal of Early Modern History*, 6 (2002), 341–61.

Kaplan, Benjamin J., 'Fictions of privacy: house chapels and the spatial accommodation of religious dissent in Early Modern Europe', *American Historical Review*, 107 (2002), 1031–64.

Katz, David S., *The Jews in the History of England 1485–1850* (Oxford, 1994).

Katz, David S., *Philo-Semitism and the Readmission of the Jews to England 1603–1655* (Oxford, 1982).

Kaushik, Sandeep, 'Resistance, loyalty and recusant politics: Sir Thomas Tresham and the Elizabethan state', *Midland History*, 21 (1996), 37–72.

Keeble, N. H., *The Literary Culture of Nonconformity in Later Seventeenth Century England* (Leicester, 1987).

Keeble, N. H., *The Restoration: England in the 1660s* (Oxford, 2002).

Kelley, Donald R., 'Martyrs, myths, and the massacre: the background of St Bartholomew', *American Historical Review*, 77 (1972), 1323–42.

Kent, S. A., 'The papist charges against the Interregnum Quakers', *Journal of Religious History*, 2 (1982–3), 180–90.

Kenyon, J. P., *The Popish Plot* (London, 1972).

Knights, Mark, '"Meer religion" and the "church-state" of Restoration England: the impact and ideology of James II's declarations of indulgence', in Alan Houston and Steve Pincus (eds), *A Nation Transformed: England after the Restoration* (Cambridge, 2001), pp. 41–70.

Knott, John R., *Discourses of Martyrdom in English Literature 1563–1694* (Cambridge, 1993).

Kolb, Robert, 'God's gift of martyrdom: the early Reformation understanding of dying for the faith', *Church History*, 64 (1995), 399–411.

Lacey, Andrew, *The Cult of King Charles the Martyr* (Woodbridge, 2003).

Lacey, Douglas R., *Dissent and Parliamentary Politics in England 1661–1689: A Study in the Perpetuation and Tempering of Parliamentarianism* (New Brunswick, NJ, 1969).

Lake, Peter, *Anglicans and Puritans? Presbyterianism and English Conformist Thought from Whitgift to Hooker* (London, 1988).

Lake, Peter, 'Anti-popery: the structure of a prejudice', in Richard Cust and Ann Hughes (eds), *Conflict in Early Stuart England: Studies in Religion and Politics 1603–1642* (Harlow, 1989), pp. 72–106.

Lake, Peter, *The Boxmaker's Revenge: 'Orthodoxy', 'Heterodoxy' and the Politics of the Parish in Early Stuart London* (Manchester, 2001).

Lake, Peter, '"A charitable Christian hatred": the godly and their enemies in the 1630s', in Christopher Durston and Jacqueline Eales (eds), *The Culture of English Puritanism, 1560–1700* (Basingstoke, 1996), pp. 145–83.

Lake, Peter, *Moderate Puritans and the Elizabethan Church* (Cambridge, 1982).

Lake, Peter, 'Moving the goal posts? Modified subscription and the construction of conformity in the early Stuart Church', in Peter Lake and Michael Questier (eds), *Conformity and Orthodoxy in the English Church, c.1560–1660* (Woodbridge, 2000), pp. 179–205.

Lake, Peter and Dowling, Maria (eds), *Protestantism and the National Church in Sixteenth Century England* (London, 1987).

Lake, Peter and Questier, Michael, 'Agency, appropriation, and rhetoric under the gallows: puritans, Romanists, and the state in early modern England', *P&P*, 153 (1996), 64–107.

Lake, Peter with Questier, Michael, *The Antichrist's Lewd Hat: Protestants, Papists and Players in Post-Reformation England* (New Haven, 2002).

Lake, Peter and Questier, Michael, 'Puritans, papists, and the "public sphere" in early modern England: the Edmund Campion affair in context', *Journal of Modern History*, 72 (2000), 587–627.

Lake, Peter, and Questier, Michael (eds), *Conformity and Orthodoxy in the English Church, c.1560–1660* (Woodbridge, 2000).

Lambert, Malcolm, *Medieval Heresy: Popular Movements from the Gregorian Reform to the Reformation* (Oxford, 1992).

Lamont, William, *Godly Rule: Politics and Religion 1603–1660* (London, 1970).

Lamont, William, *Marginal Prynne, 1600–69* (London, 1963).

Lamont, William, 'The Muggletonians 1652–1979: a "vertical" approach', *P&P*, 99 (1983), 22–40.

Lamont, William, 'Pamphleteering, the Protestant consensus and the English Revolution', in R. C. Richardson and G. M. Ridden (eds), *Freedom and the English Revolution: Essays in History and Literature* (Manchester, 1986), pp. 72–92.

Lamont, William, 'Richard Baxter, "popery" and the origins of the English Civil War', *History*, 87 (2002), 336–52.

Langbein, John H., *Torture and the Law of Proof: Europe and England in the Ancien Régime* (Chicago, 1977).

Laqueur, Thomas W., 'Crowds, carnival and the state in English executions, 1604–1868', in A. L. Beier, David Cannadine and James M. Rosenheim (eds), *The First Modern Society: Essays in English History in Honour of Lawrence Stone* (Cambridge, 1989), pp. 305–55.

La Rocca, John J., '"Who can't pray with me, can't love me": toleration and the early Jacobean recusancy policy', *JBS*, 23 (1984), 22–36.

Laursen, John Christian (ed.), *Religious Toleration: 'The Variety of Rites' from Cyrus to Defoe* (New York, 1999).

Laursen, John Christian and Nederman, Cary J. (eds), *Beyond the Persecuting Society: Religious Toleration before the Enlightenment* (Philadelphia, 1998).

Lecler, Joseph, *Toleration and the Reformation*, trans. T. L. Westow, 2 vols (New York, 1960).

Leff, Gordon, *Heresy in the Later Middle Ages: The Relation of Heterodoxy to Dissent c.1250–c.1450*, 2 vols (Manchester, 1967).

Leites, Edmund (ed.), *Conscience and Casuistry in Early Modern Europe* (Cambridge, 1988).

Lindley, Keith J., 'The impact of the 1641 rebellion upon England and Wales, 1641–5', *Irish Historical Studies*, 18 (1972), 143–76.

Lindley, K. J., 'The lay Catholics of England in the reign of Charles I', *JEH*, 22 (1971), 199–221.

Loades, David, 'Anabaptism and English sectarianism in the mid-sixteenth century', in Derek Baker (ed.), *Reform and Reformation: England and the Continent c.1500–c.1750*, SCH Subsidia 2 (Oxford, 1979), pp. 59–70.

Loades, David, *The Oxford Martyrs* (London, 1970).

Loades, David, *The Reign of Mary Tudor: Politics, Government and Religion in England, 1553–1558* (London, 1979).

Loades, David (ed.), *John Foxe and the English Reformation* (Aldershot, 1997).

Loomie, A. J., *The Spanish Elizabethans: The English Exiles at the Court of Philip II* (New York, 1963).

Luria, Keith P., 'Rituals of conversion: Catholics and Protestants in seventeenth-century Poitou', in Barbara B. Diefendorf and Carla Hesse (eds), *Culture and Identity in Early Modern Europe 1500–1800* (Ann Arbor, 1993), pp. 65–81.

Mac Cuarta, Brian (ed.), *Ulster 1641: Aspects of the Rising* (Dublin, 1993).

MacCulloch, Diarmaid, *The Later Reformation in England 1547–1603* (Basingstoke, 1990; 2nd edn 2001).

MacCulloch, Diarmaid, 'The myth of the English Reformation', *JBS*, 30 (1991), 1–19.

MacCulloch, Diarmaid, *Thomas Cranmer: A Life* (New Haven, 1996).

MacCulloch, Diarmaid, *Tudor Church Militant: Edward VI and the Protestant Reformation* (London, 1999).

MacCulloch, Diarmaid (ed.), *The Reign of Henry VIII: Politics, Policy and Piety* (Basingstoke, 1995).

MacFarlane, K. B., *Wycliffe and the Beginnings of English Nonconformity* (London, 1952).

MacGregor, J. F. and Reay, Barry (eds), *Radical Religion in the English Revolution* (Oxford, 1984).

Maltby, Judith, '"The good old way": prayer book Protestantism in the 1640s and 1650s', in R. N. Swanson (ed.), *The Church and the Book*, SCH 38 (Woodbridge, 2004), pp. 233–56.

Maltby, Judith, *Prayer Book and People in Elizabethan and Early Stuart England* (Cambridge, 1998).

Maltby, William S., *The Black Legend in England: The Development of Anti-Spanish Sentiment, 1558–1660* (Durham, NC, 1971).

Mandelbrote, Scott, 'Religious belief and the politics of toleration in the late seventeenth century', *Nederlands archief voor kerkgeschiedenis/Dutch Review of Church History*, 81 (2001), 93–114.

Manning, Roger B., *Religion and Society in Elizabethan Sussex: A Study of the Enforcement of the Religious Settlement 1558–1603* (Leicester, 1969).

Marchant, Ronald A., *The Church under the Law: Justice, Administration and Discipline in the Diocese of York 1560–1640* (Cambridge, 1969).

Marsh, Christopher W., *The Family of Love in English Society, 1550–1630* (Cambridge, 1994).

Marsh, Christopher W., *Popular Religion in Sixteenth-Century England: Holding their Peace* (Basingstoke, 1998).

Marshall, Peter, 'Papist as heretic: the burning of John Forrest, 1538', *HJ*, 41 (1998), 351–74.

Marshall, Peter and Ryrie, Alec (eds), *The Beginnings of English Protestantism* (Cambridge, 2002).

Martin, D. A., 'The denomination', *The British Journal of Sociology*, 13 (1962), 1–14.

Martin, J. W., *Religious Radicals in Tudor England* (London, 1989).

Matar, Nabil, *Islam in Britain 1558–1685* (Cambridge, 1998).

Matar, Nabil, *Turks, Moors and Englishmen in the Age of Discovery* (New York, 1999).

McClendon, Muriel, *The Quiet Reformation: Magistrates and the Emergence of Protestantism in Tudor Norwich* (Stanford, CA, 1999).

McCoog, Thomas M., 'Construing martyrdom in the English Catholic Community, 1582–1602', in Ethan H. Shagan (ed.), *Catholics and the 'Protestant Nation': Religious Politics and Identity in Early Modern England* (Manchester, 2005), pp. 95–127.

McGrath, Patrick and Rowe, Joy, 'The imprisonment of Catholics for religion under Elizabeth I', *RH*, 20 (1991), 415–35.

McHardy, A. K., '*De heretico comburendo*, 1401', in Margaret Aston and Colin Richmond (eds), *Lollardy and the Gentry in the Later Middle Ages* (Stroud, 1997), pp. 112–26.

McIntosh, Marjorie K., *A Community Transformed: The Manor and Liberty of Havering, 1500–1620* (Cambridge, 1991).

McIntosh, Marjorie K., *Controlling Misbehaviour in England, 1370–1600* (Cambridge, 1998).

McLachlan, H. J., *Socinianism in Seventeenth-Century England* (Oxford, 1951).

McNiven, Peter, *Heresy and Politics in the Reign of Henry IV: The Burning of John Badby* (Woodbridge, 1987).

McSheffrey, Shannon, *Gender and Heresy: Women and Men in Lollard Communities 1420–1530* (Philadelphia, 1995).

Mendus, Susan (ed.), *Justifying Toleration: Conceptual and Historical Perspectives* (Cambridge, 1988).

Mendus, Susan and Edwards, David (eds), *On Toleration* (Oxford, 1987).

Miller, John, 'James II and toleration', in Eveline Cruickshanks (ed.), *By Force or by Default? The Revolution of 1688–9* (Edinburgh, 1989), pp. 8–27.

Miller, John, *Popery and Politics in England, 1660–1688* (Cambridge, 1973).

Miller, John, 'A suffering people': English Quakers and their neighbours', *P&P*, 188 (2005), 71–103.

Milton, Anthony, *Catholic and Reformed: The Roman and Protestant Churches in English Protestant Thought, 1600–1640* (Cambridge, 1995).

Milton, Anthony, 'A qualified intolerance: the limits and ambiguities of early Stuart anti-Catholicism', in Arthur F. Marotti (ed.), *Catholicism and Anti-Catholicism in Early Modern English Texts* (Basingstoke, 1999), pp. 85–115.

Monter, William, 'Heresy executions in Reformation Europe, 1520–1565', in Ole Peter Grell and Bob Scribner (eds), *Tolerance and Intolerance in the European Reformation* (Cambridge, 1996), pp. 48–64.

Moore, R. I., *The Formation of a Persecuting Society: Power and Deviance in Western Europe 950–1250* (Oxford, 1987).

Moore, Rosemary, *The Light in their Consciences: The Early Quakers in Britain 1646–1666* (University Park, PA, 2000).

Morrill, John, 'The Church in England, 1642–9', in John Morrill (ed.), *Reactions to the English Civil War 1642–1649* (London, 1982), pp. 89–114.

Morrill, John, *The Nature of the English Revolution* (Harlow, 1993).

Morrill, John, 'The religious context of the English Civil War', *TRHS*, 5th series, 34 (1984), 155–78.

Morrill, John (ed.), *Oliver Cromwell and the English Revolution* (Harlow, 1990).

Morton, A. L., *The World of the Ranters: Religious Radicalism in the English Revolution* (London, 1970).

Mullett, Michael, *Catholics in Britain and Ireland 1558–1829* (Basingstoke, 1998).

Mullett, Michael, 'From sect to denomination? Social developments in eighteenth-century English Quakerism', *Journal of Religious History*, 13 (1984), 168–91.

Murphy, Andrew R., *Conscience and Community: Revisiting Toleration and Religious Dissent in Early Modern Europe and America* (University Park, PA, 2001).

Neale, J. E., *Elizabeth I and her Parliaments*, 2 vols (London, 1953).

Nederman, Cary J., *Worlds of Difference: European Discourses of Toleration, c.1100–c.1550* (University Park, PA, 2000).

Nederman, Cary J. and Laursen, John Christian (eds), *Difference and Dissent: Theories of Toleration in Medieval and Early Modern Europe* (Lanham, MD, 1996).

Nenk, Beverley, 'Public worship, private devotion: the crypto-Jews of Reformation England', in David Gaimster and Roberta Gilchrist (eds), *The Archaeology of Reformation 1480–1580* (Leeds, 2003), pp. 204–20.

Nicholls, David, 'The theatre of martyrdom in the French Reformation', *P&P*, 121 (1988), 49–73.

Nirenberg, David, *Communities of Violence: Persecution of Minorities in the Middle Ages* (Princeton, 1996).

Norman, E. R., *Anti-Catholicism in Victorian England* (London, 1968).

Norwood, Frederick Abbott, *Strangers and Exiles: A History of Religious Refugees*, 2 vols (Nashville, 1969).

Nuttall, Geoffrey F., *Visible Saints: The Congregational Way 1640–1660* (Oxford, 1957).

Orr, D. Alan, *Treason and the State: Law, Politics and Ideology in the English Civil War* (Cambridge, 2002).

Pailin, David A., *Attitudes to Other Religions: Comparative Religion in Seventeenth- and Eighteenth-Century Britain* (Manchester, 1984).

Patterson, W. B., *King James VI and I and the Reunion of Christendom* (Cambridge, 1997).

Paz, D. G., *Popular Anti-Catholicism in Mid Victorian England* (Stanford, CA, 1992).

Peacey, Jason, 'The paranoid prelate: Archbishop Laud and the puritan plot', in Barry Coward and Julian Swann (eds), *Conspiracies and Conspiracy Theory in Early Modern Europe: From the Waldensians to the French Revolution* (Aldershot, 2004), pp. 113–34.

Peters, Kate, *Print Culture and the Early Quakers* (Cambridge, 2005).

Pettegree, Andrew, *Emden and the Dutch Revolt: Exile and the Development of Reformed Protestantism* (Oxford, 1992).

Pettegree, Andrew, *Foreign Protestant Communities in Sixteenth-Century London* (Oxford, 1986).

Pettegree, Andrew, *Marian Protestantism: Six Studies* (Aldershot, 1996).

Pettegree, Andrew, '"Thirty years on": progress towards integration among the immigrant population of Elizabethan London', in John Chartres and David Hey (eds), *English Rural Society, 1500–1800: Essays in Honour of Joan Thirsk* (Cambridge, 1990), pp. 297–312.

Pierce, Helen, 'Anti-episcopacy and graphic satire in England, 1640–1645', *HJ*, 47 (2004), 809–48.

Piqué, Nicholas and Waterlot, Ghislain (eds), *Tolérance et Réforme: Elements pour une généalogie du concept de tolérance* (Paris, 1999).

Plumb, Derek, 'A gathered church? Lollards and their society', in Margaret Spufford (ed.), *The World of Rural Dissenters 1520–1725* (Cambridge, 1995), pp. 132–63.

Polizzotto, Caroline, 'The campaign against *The Humble Proposals* of 1652', *JEH*, 38 (1987), 569–81.

Polizzotto, Caroline, 'Liberty of conscience and the Whitehall debates of 1648–9', *JEH*, 26 (1975), 69–82.

Popkin, Richard H., 'The deist challenge', in Ole Peter Grell, Jonathan I. Israel and Nicholas Tyacke (eds), *From Persecution to Toleration: The Glorious Revolution and Religion in England* (Oxford, 1991), pp. 195–215.

Porter, Roy, *Mind Forg'd Manacles: A History of Madness in England from the Restoration to the Regency* (London, 1987).

Price, F. D., 'The abuses of excommunication and the decline of ecclesiastical discipline under Queen Elizabeth', *EHR*, 57 (1942), 106–15.

Pritchard, Arnold, *Catholic Loyalism in Elizabethan England* (London, 1979).

Questier, Michael C., *Conversion, Politics and Religion in England 1580–1625* (Cambridge, 1996).

Questier, Michael C., 'Loyalty, religion and state power in early modern England: English Romanism and the Jacobean oath of allegiance', *HJ*, 40 (1997), 311–29.

Questier, Michael C., 'The politics of conformity and the accession of James I', *Historical Research*, 71 (1998), 14–30.

Questier, Michael C., 'Practical anti-papistry during the reign of Elizabeth I', *JBS*, 36 (1997), 371–96.

Racaut, Luc and Ryrie, Alec (eds), *Moderate Voices in the European Reformations* (Aldershot, 2005).

Ramsbottom, John D., 'Presbyterians and "partial conformity" in the Restoration Church of England', *JEH*, 43 (1992), 249–70.

Reay, Barry, 'The authorities and early Restoration Quakerism', *JEH*, 34 (1983), 69–84.

Reay, Barry, 'Popular hostility towards Quakers in mid-seventeenth-century England', *Social History*, 5 (1980), 387–407.

Reay, Barry, *The Quakers and the English Revolution* (London, 1985).

Rex, Richard, *Henry VIII and the English Reformation* (London, 1993).

Rex, Richard, *The Lollards* (Basingstoke, 2002).

Richards, Jeffrey, *Sex, Dissidence and Damnation: Minority Groups in the Middle Ages* (London, 1991).

Richardson, H. G., 'Heresy and the lay power under Richard II', *EHR*, 201 (1936), 1–28.

Roberts, Stephen, 'The Quakers in Evesham 1655–1660: a study in religion, politics and culture', *Midland History*, 16 (1991), 63–85.

Rogers, G. A. J., 'Locke and the latitude men: ignorance as a ground of toleration', in Richard Kroll, Richard Ashcraft and Perez Zagorin (eds), *Philosophy, Science and Religion in England 1640–1700* (Cambridge, 1992), pp. 230–52.

Rogers, Nicholas, *Crowds, Culture and Politics in Georgian Britain* (Oxford, 1998).

Roots, Ivan, *Commonwealth and Protectorate: The English Civil War and its Aftermath* (New York, 1966).

Rose, Craig, *England in the 1690s: Revolution, Religion and War* (Oxford, 1999).

Rose, Elliot, *Cases of Conscience: Alternatives Open to Recusants and Puritans under Elizabeth I and James I* (Cambridge, 1975).

Rose, R. B., 'The Priestley riots of 1791', *P&P*, 18 (1960), 68–88.

Roth, Cecil, *A History of the Jews in England* (Oxford, 1978 edn; first publ. 1941).

Rowlands, Marie B. (ed.), *Catholics of Parish and Town 1558–1778*, CRS Monograph Series 5 (London, 1999).

Rubin, Miri, *Gentile Tales: The Narrative Assault on Late Medieval Jews* (New Haven, 1999).

Rudé, George, 'The Gordon riots: a study of the rioters and their victims', *TRHS*, 5th series, 6 (1956), 93–114.

Russell, Conrad, 'Arguments for religious unity in England, 1530–1650', *JEH*, 18 (1967), 201–26.

Russell, Conrad, *The Causes of the English Civil War* (Oxford, 1990).

Russell, Conrad, *The Fall of the British Monarchies 1637–1642* (Oxford, 1991).

Russell, Conrad, *Parliaments and English Politics 1621–1629* (Oxford, 1979).

Ryrie, Alec, *The Gospel and Henry VIII: Evangelicals in the Early English Reformation* (Cambridge, 2003).

Sasche, William L., 'The mob and the Revolution of 1688', *JBS*, 4 (1964), 23–40.

Schilling, Heinz, 'Confessional Europe', in Thomas A. Brady, Heiko A. Oberman and James D. Tracy (eds), *Handbook of European History, 1400–1600*, 2 vols (Leiden, 1995), ii. 641–75.

Schochet, Gordon J., 'The Act of Toleration and the failure of comprehension: persecution, nonconformity and religious indifference', in Dale Hoak and Mordechai Feingold (eds), *The World of William and Mary: Anglo-Dutch Perspectives on the Revolution of 1688–1689* (Stanford, CA, 1996)., pp. 165–87.

Schochet, Gordon J., 'From persecution to "toleration"', in J. R. Jones (ed.), *Liberty Secured? Britain before and after 1688* (Stanford, CA, 1992), pp. 122–57.

Schochet, Gordon J., 'Samuel Parker, religious diversity, and the ideology of persecution', in Roger D. Lund (ed.), *The Margins of Orthodoxy: Heterodox Writing and Cultural Response, 1660–1750* (Cambridge, 1995), pp. 119–48.

Schwoerer, Lois (ed.), *The Revolution of 1688–1689* (Cambridge, 1992).

Scott, Jonathan, *England's Troubles: Seventeenth-Century English Political Stability in European Context* (Cambridge, 2000).

Seaver, Paul S., *Wallington's World: A Puritan Artisan in Seventeenth-Century London* (London, 1985).

Select bibliography of secondary sources

Seaward, Paul, *The Cavalier Parliament and the Reconstruction of the Old Regime, 1661–1667* (Cambridge, 1988).

Shagan, Ethan H., 'The English Inquisition: constitutional conflict and ecclesiastical law in the 1590s', *HJ*, 47 (2004), 541–65.

Shagan, Ethan H., *Popular Politics and the English Reformation* (Cambridge, 2003).

Shagan, Ethan H. (ed.), *Catholics and the 'Protestant Nation': Religious Politics and Identity in Early Modern England* (Manchester, 2005).

Shakespeare, Joy, 'Plague and punishment', in Peter Lake and Maria Dowling (eds), *Protestantism and the National Church in Sixteenth-Century England* (London, 1987), pp. 103–23.

Sharpe, J. A., '"Last dying speeches": religion, ideology and public execution in seventeenth-century England', *P&P*, 107 (1985), 144–67.

Sharpe, Kevin, *The Personal Rule of Charles I* (New Haven, 1992).

Sheils, W. J., 'Catholics and their neighbours in a rural community: Egton chapelry 1590–1780', *Northern History*, 34 (1998), 109–33.

Sheils, W. J., *The Puritans in the Diocese of Peterborough 1558–1610*, Northamptonshire Record Society 30 (Northampton, 1979).

Sheils, W. J. (ed.), *Persecution and Toleration*, SCH 21 (Oxford, 1984).

Shell, Alison, *Catholicism, Controversy and the English Literary Imagination, 1558–1660* (Cambridge, 1990).

Shoemaker, Robert B., *Prosecution and Punishment: Petty Crime and the Law in London and Rural Middlesex c. 1660–1725* (Cambridge, 1991).

Smith, Terence Stephen, 'The persecution of Staffordshire Roman Catholic recusants: 1625–1660', *JEH*, 30 (1979), 327–51.

Sommerville, Johann P., 'The "new art of lying": equivocation, mental reservation, and casuistry', in Edmund Leites (ed.), *Conscience and Casuistry in Early Modern Europe* (Cambridge and Paris, 1988), pp. 159–84.

Spaeth, Donald A., *The Church in an Age of Danger: Parsons and Parishioners, 1660–1740* (Cambridge, 2000).

Spaeth, Donald A., 'Common prayer? Popular observance of the Anglican liturgy in Restoration Wiltshire', in Susan Wright (ed.), *Parish, Church and People: Local Studies in Lay Religion 1350–1750* (London, 1988), pp. 125–51.

Spicer, Andrew, *The French-Speaking Reformed Community and their Church in Southampton 1567–c.1620*, Southampton Records Series 39 (Southampton, 1997).

Sprunger, Keith L., *Dutch Puritanism: A History of the English and Scottish Churches of the Netherlands in the Sixteenth and Seventeenth Centuries* (Leiden, 1982).

Spurr, John, 'The Church of England, comprehension and the toleration act of 1689', *EHR*, 104 (1989), 927–46.

Spurr, John, *English Puritanism 1603–1689* (Basingstoke, 1998).

Spurr, John, '"Latitudinarianism" and the Restoration Church', *HJ*, 31 (1988), 61–82.

Spurr, John, *The Restoration Church of England, 1646–1689* (New Haven, 1991).

Spurr, John, 'Schism and the Restoration Church', *JEH*, 41 (1990), 408–24.

Stachniewski, John, *The Persecutory Imagination: English Puritanism and the Literature of Religious Despair* (Oxford, 1991).

Stevenson, Bill, 'The social integration of post-Restoration dissenters, 1660–1725', in Margaret Spufford (ed.), *The World of Rural Dissenters 1520–1725* (Cambridge, 1995), pp. 360–87.

Susser, Bernard, *The Jews of South-West England* (Exeter, 1993).

Swanson, R. N., *Church and Society in Late Medieval England* (Oxford, 1989).

Thackray, I. Y., 'Zion undermined: the Protestant belief in a popish plot during the English Interregnum', *History Workshop*, 18 (1984), 28–52.

Thomas, Keith, 'Cases of conscience in seventeenth-century England', in John Morrill, Paul Slack and Daniel Woolf (eds), *Public Duty and Private Conscience in Seventeenth-Century England* (Oxford, 1993), pp. 29–56.

Thomas, Roger, 'Comprehension and indulgence', in Geoffrey F. Nuttall and Owen Chadwick (eds), *From Uniformity to Unity 1662–1962* (London, 1962), pp. 191–253.

Thomson, J. A. F., *The Later Lollards 1414–1520* (Oxford, 1965).

Todd, Margo, *The Culture of Protestantism in Early Modern Scotland* (New Haven, 2002).

Tolmie, Murray, *The Triumph of the Saints: The Separate Churches of London 1616–1649* (Cambridge, 1977).

Turchetti, Mario, 'Religious concord and political tolerance in sixteenth- and seventeenth-century France', *SCJ*, 22 (1991), 15–25.

Tutino, Stefania, 'Makynge recusancy death outrighte? Thomas Pound, Andrew Willet and the Catholic question in early Jacobean England', *RH*, 27 (2004), 31–50.

Tyacke, Nicholas, *Anti-Calvinists: The Rise of English Arminianism c. 1590–1640* (Oxford, 1987).

Tyacke, Nicholas, *The Fortunes of English Puritanism, 1603–1640*, Dr Williams's Library, 44th lecture (London, 1990).

Tyacke, Nicholas (ed.), *England's Long Reformation 1500–1800* (London, 1998).

Underdown, David, *A Freeborn People: Politics and the Nation in Seventeenth-Century England* (Oxford, 1996).

Underdown, David, *Revel, Riot and Rebellion: Popular Politics and Culture in England 1603–1660* (Oxford, 1985).

Ussher, R. G., *The Rise and Fall of the High Commission* (Oxford, 1913; repr. 1968, with preface by Philip Tyler).

Vallance, Edward, '"An holy and sacramental paction": federal theology and the solemn league and covenant in England', *EHR*, 116 (2001), 50–75.

Vallance, Edward, 'Oaths, casuistry and equivocation: Anglican responses to the Engagement Controversy', *HJ*, 44 (2001), 59–77.

Van Dülmen, Richard, *Theatre of Horror: Crime and Punishment in Early Modern Germany*, trans. Elisabeth Neu (Cambridge, 1990).

Vann, Richard T., *The Social Development of English Quakerism 1655–1755* (Cambridge, MA, 1969).

Select bibliography of secondary sources

Vigne, Randolph and Gibbs, Graham C. (eds), *The Strangers' Progress: Integration and Disintegration of the Huguenot and Walloon Refugee Community, 1567–1889: Essays in Memory of Irene Scouloudi*, Proceedings of the Huguenot Society of Great Britain and Ireland, 26 (2) (1995).

Vigne, Randolph and Littleton, Charles (eds), *From Strangers to Citizens: The Integration of Immigrant Communities in Britain, Ireland and Colonial America, 1550–1750* (Brighton and Portland, 2001).

Wabuda, Susan, 'Equivocation and recantation during the English Reformation: the "subtle shadows" of Dr Edward Crome', *JEH*, 44 (1993), 224–42.

Walker, F. X., 'The implementation of the Elizabethan statutes against recusants', unpubl. PhD thesis (University of London, 1961).

Walsh, John, 'Methodism and the mob in the eighteenth century', G. J. Cuming and D. Baker (eds), *Popular Belief and Practice*, SCH 8 (Cambridge, 1972), pp. 213–27.

Walsh, John, Haydon, Colin and Taylor, Stephen (eds), *The Church of England c.1689–c.1833* (Cambridge, 1993).

Walsham, Alexandra, *Church Papists: Catholicism, Conformity and Confessional Polemic in Early Modern England* (Woodbridge, 1993; 2nd edn 1999).

Walsham, Alexandra, '"The fatall vesper": providentialism and anti-popery in late Jacobean London', *P&P*, 144 (1994), 36–87.

Walsham, Alexandra, 'Ordeals of conscience: casuistry, conformity and confessional identity in post-Reformation England', in Harald Braun and Edward Vallance (eds), *Contexts of Conscience in Early Modern Europe 1500–1700* (Basingstoke, 2004), pp. 32–48, 191–6.

Walter, John, '"Abolishing superstition with sedition"? The politics of popular iconoclasm in England', *P&P*, 183 (2004), 79–123.

Walter, John, *Understanding Popular Violence in the English Revolution: The Colchester Plunderers* (Cambridge, 1999).

Watts, Michael R., *The Dissenters: From the Reformation to the French Revolution* (Oxford, 1978).

Waugh, Scott L. and Diehl, Peter D., *Christendom and its Discontents: Exclusion, Persecution, and Rebellion, 1000–1500* (Cambridge, 1996).

Webster, Tom, *Godly Clergy in Early Stuart England: The Caroline Puritan Movement, c.1620–1643* (Cambridge, 1997).

Whaley, Joachim, *Religious Toleration and Social Change in Hamburg 1529–1819* (Cambridge, 1985).

Whelan, Ruth and Baxter, Carol (eds), *Toleration and Religious Identity: The Edict of Nantes and its Implications in France, Britain and Ireland* (Dublin, 2003).

White, B. R., *The English Baptists of the Seventeenth Century* (London, 1983).

White, B. R., *The English Separatist Tradition from the Marian Martyrs to the Pilgrim Fathers* (Oxford, 1971).

White, Peter, *Predestination, Policy and Polemic: Conflict and Consensus in the English Church from the Reformation to the Civil War* (Cambridge, 1992).

Wiener, Carol Z., 'The beleaguered isle: a study of Elizabethan and early Jacobean anti-Catholicism', *P&P*, 51 (1971), 27–62.

Williams, J. Anthony, *Catholic Recusancy in Wiltshire 1660–1791*, CRS Monograph Series 1 (London, 1968).

Wilson, Bryan R. (ed.), *Patterns of Sectarianism: Organisation and Ideology in Social and Religious Movements* (London, 1967).

Wilson, Bryan, *Religious Sects: A Sociological Study* (London, 1970).

Wood, Diana (ed.), *Martyrs and Martyrologies*, SCH 30 (Oxford, 1993).

Worden, Blair, 'Toleration and the Cromwellian Protectorate', in W. J. Sheils (ed.), *Persecution and Toleration*, SCH 21 (Oxford, 1984), pp. 199–233.

Wright, Jonathan, 'Marian exiles and the legitimacy of flight from persecution', *JEH*, 52 (2001), 220–43.

Wright, Jonathan, 'Surviving the English Reformation: commonsense, conscience and circumstance', *Journal of Medieval and Early Modern Studies*, 29 (1999), 381–402.

Wright, Jonathan, 'The world's worst worm: conscience and conformity during the English Reformation', *SCJ*, 30 (1999), 113–33.

Wright, Stephen, 'The British Baptists and politics, 1603–49', unpubl. PhD dissertation (King's College, London, 2002).

Wykes, David L., 'Friends, Parliament and the Toleration Act', *JEH*, 45 (1994), 42–63.

Wykes, David L., 'Quaker schoolmasters, toleration and the law, 1689–1714', *Journal of Religious History*, 21 (1997), 178–92.

Wykes, David L., 'Religious dissent and the penal laws: an explanation of business success?', *History*, 75 (1990), 39–62.

Wykes, David L., '"To let the memory of these men dye is injurious to posterity": Edmund Calamy's "account" of the ejected ministers', in R. N. Swanson (ed.), *The Church Retrospective*, SCH 33 (Oxford, 1997), pp. 379–92.

Yardley, Bruce, 'George Villiers, second duke of Buckingham and the politics of toleration', *Huntington Library Quarterly*, 55 (1992), 317–37.

Yule, George, *The Independents in the English Civil War* (Cambridge, 1958).

Yule, George, *Puritans and Politics: The Religious Legislation of the Long Parliament* (Abingdon, 1981).

Yungblut, Laura Hunt, *Strangers Settled Here Amongst Us: Policies, Perceptions and the Presence of Aliens in Elizabethan England* (London, 1996).

Zagorin, Perez, *How the Idea of Religious Toleration Came to the West* (Princeton, 2003).

Zagorin, Perez, *Ways of Lying: Dissimulation, Persecution and Conformity in Early Modern Europe* (Cambridge, MA, 1990).

Zakai, Avihu, *Exile and Kingdom: History and Apocalypse in the Puritan Migration to America* (Cambridge, 1992).

Zakai, Avihu, 'Orthodoxy in England and New England: puritans and the issue of religious toleration, 1640–1650', *Proceedings of the American Philosophical Society*, 135 (1991), 401–41.

Zakai, Avihu, 'Religious toleration and its enemies: the Independent divines and the issue of toleration during the English Civil War', *Albion*, 21 (1989), 1–33.

Index

Note: 'n' after a page reference indicates the number of a note on that page.

Index

Index

deportation of religious dissenters 85, 103n
    see also exile
Devon 135, 137
Diefendorf, Barbara 139
Diehl, Peter 12
Dillon, Anne 174
Directory of Worship 18
dissenting Protestants (after 1662)
    integration with Anglicans 209–10, 275
    persecution of 19, 63, 84, 87–8, 128,
        139, 164, 172, 173, 197, 202, 203,
        250, 286, 309
    tolerance of 275
dissimulation *see* conformity, outward
divine right of kings 53–4
Dod, John 72
Dodwell, Henry 43
Donatists 3, 40, 89
Dorchester 112, 120
Dorset 114, 117, 145, 146, 273
Dort, Synod of (1618) 64
Dove, John
Dover 120
Drury, Robert 79
Dudley, Robert, Earl of Leicester 17
Durham, County 117, 283
Durkheim, Emile 106
Dury, John 245
Dutch Republic *see* United Provinces
Dutch Revolt 9, 25
Dworkin, Ronald 233

Eagles, George 77, 178
Earle, John 191, 203
education of dissenters, restrictions on 87
Edward VI, King 14
    as Josiah 44
    William Featherstone's claim to be
        (1555) 83
Edwards, Thomas
    Gangraena 27, 43, 122, 229, 284
Edwin, Sir Humphrey 193
Elizabeth, Princess, daughter of James I 15
Elizabeth I, Queen, 14, 15, 44, 45, 51, 59,
    179
    accession day of 118, 131, 179
    attempts to assassinate 121, 135
Elizabethan settlement 14, 17, 51, 252–3
Elmer, Peter 146
Elton, Geoffrey 89

Ely 144, 148
    diocese of 208
Emley, Richard 90
endogamy, tendencies towards 260, 303–9
enforcement of the law, difficulties and
        limitations of 90–1, 264, 270–2
Engagement (1650) 61, 199
Enlightenment 9
Episcopius, Simon 232
equivocation 47, 193–5, 198
Erasmus, Desiderius 6, 10, 109, 232, 237
Erastianism, rise of 49–53
Erastus, Thomas 50
Essex 55, 73, 77, 89, 114, 115, 117, 127, 131,
        132, 133, 138, 145, 167, 178, 184, 193,
        210, 259, 273, 275, 281
L'Estrange, Sir Roger 47, 49, 229
Etherington, John 71
Eusebius 27, 173
Evans, Arise 245
Evelyn, John 164
Evil May Day (1517) 132, 141
Exchequer 85
Exclusion Crisis 54, 120
excommunicates, duty to shun 128
excommunication 73–4
    loss of credibility as a sanction 74
execution of religious dissenters 42, 52, 53,
        56–7, 58–9, 75–9, 111–12, 162–3,
        167–9, 263
    counter-productive effects of 77, 169–
        70
    rejection of 58, 263–4
Exeter 77, 111, 273
exile 182–8
    dilemmas about legitimacy of 186–8

Familism and Familists *see* Family of Love
Family of Love 22, 27, 58, 61, 71, 81, 88, 89,
        90, 121, 122, 144, 148, 165, 250, 260,
        312–13
    dissimulation of 191–2, 194, 200, 201,
        202–3
    integration with the orthodox 208
fasting, as a punishment for heresy 70
Fawkes, Guy 15, 124, 317
Featley, Daniel 124–5
Fell, John, Bishop of Oxford 40
Fell, Thomas 271
Felsenstein, Frank 121, 316

354